Law's Dominion

Studies in Jewish History and Culture

Edited by

Giuseppe Veltri

VOLUME 60

The titles published in this series are listed at *brill.com/sjhc*

Law's Dominion

Jewish Community, Religion, and Family in Early Modern Metz

By

Jay R. Berkovitz

BRILL

LEIDEN | BOSTON

Cover Image: Metz in the 16th Century, in Braun, G. and Hogenberg, F. Beschreibung und Contrafactur der vornembster Stät der Welt. Cölln, 1574–1576. Vol. 2, no. 15, National Library of Israel.

Library of Congress Cataloging-in-Publication Data

Names: Berkovitz, Jay R., 1951– author.
Title: Law's dominion : Jewish community, religion, and family in early modern Metz / by Jay R. Berkovitz.
Description: Leiden ; Boston : Brill, [2020] | Series: Studies in Jewish history and culture, 1568–5004 ; volume 60
Identifiers: LCCN 2019037989 (print) | LCCN 2019037990 (ebook) | ISBN 9789004417397 (paperback) | ISBN 9789004417403 (ebook)
Subjects: LCSH: Jews—France—Metz—History—18th century. | Jews—France—Metz—Social life and customs. | Jews—Cultural assimilation—France—Metz. | Rabbinical courts—France—Metz—History—18th century. | Metz (France)—Ethnic relations.
Classification: LCC DS135.F85 M4726 2020 (print) | LCC DS135.F85 (ebook) | DDC 944/.3853004924009033—dc23
LC record available at https://lccn.loc.gov/2019037989
LC ebook record available at https://lccn.loc.gov/2019037990

Typeface for the Latin, Greek, and Cyrillic scripts: "Brill". See and download: brill.com/brill-typeface.

ISSN 1568-5004
ISBN 978-90-04-41739-7 (paperback)
ISBN 978-90-04-41740-3 (e-book)

This book is printed on acid-free paper and produced in a sustainable manner.

Contents

Preface

This book is the latest installment of an undertaking I began a quarter-century ago to reassess modes of cultural adaptation to the manifold challenges Jews encountered at the dawn of modernity. I could not have predicted then that this venture would require quite the scale of resources and effort that have been invested over these years. There were two main reasons for this. First, in the mid-1990s, the full scope of the primary sources directly bearing on this topic was either unknown or underappreciated, even by specialists. Second, when I initially turned my attention to this subject, the conceptual frame of the early modern period as a distinctive era had not yet attained its current status as an area of research that holds such great potential for historical study and interpretation. The present work seeks to explain how "the rule of law" served as the basic principle of Jewish social organization, as one of its core cultural values, and as the foundation for the relationship of the Jews to state and society. By "the rule of law" I have in mind the process of juridification, that is, the manner in which the institutionalization of law and judicial frameworks evolved in the early modern Jewish community. In the course of this development, more and more areas of communal life were subsumed under the authority of the law, as the community took greater notice of external legal and judicial systems. Whereas the important place of law in the social, cultural, and political transformation of Europe has become the subject of increasing scholarly interest, its role in shaping the social and political culture of the Jews, especially in the early modern world, is inadequately understood.

In choosing the title *Law's Dominion*, I intended to convey the law's vital role in circumscribing the cultural, religious, and political universe in which early modern Jews lived. Whether they were altogether compliant with the law—either civil or religious—is a question that pertains mainly to what was happening on the ground and reflects what this volume identifies as "judicial culture," that is, how courts render justice and enforce their judgments. "Legal culture," in contrast, refers to how individuals navigate the options they face when they seek to resolve their differences. Whether the focus is judicial culture or legal culture, we are less concerned with the question of compliance per se. Indeed, the failure to obey the law, whether in deliberate opposition to legal norms or as a result of laxity, by no means negates the role and function of the law as an all-encompassing framework that defined the duties and responsibilities imposed by the state, on the one hand, and those required of Jews as members of duly constituted and autonomous communities, on the other. But our focus is not limited to the fulfillment or nonfulfillment of obligations; it also addresses a larger set of questions relating to how the law was interpreted, contested, and enacted. In short, *Law's Dominion* tells the story of how this universe worked, especially how the Jews in the early modern world negotiated the competing obligations, expectations, and norms that stemmed from their complicated status as a self-governing minority in an absolutist state.

To this end, I have expanded the thematic focus of my two previous books and have extended several of their main methodological assumptions in new directions within a larger analytical framework than was possible in either of these earlier projects. *Rites and Passages* (2004) investigated changes in religious life, specifically the intricacies of ritual, to uncover underlying structures of thought and unstated social and behavioral norms in the century leading up to, and in the two generations following, the French Revolution. *Protocols of Justice* (2014), presented the surviving records of the rabbinic court of Metz, a city in the Moselle region of northeastern France, where a sizeable Jewish community had formed in the sixteenth century. Those court records, which date from the last decades of the ancien régime, were compiled in a Pinkas ("register"), property of the Archives of the YIVO Institute for Jewish Research in New York. During the two centuries since this rabbinic court met formally for the final time, on 1 July 1789, the Pinkas of the Metz Beit Din ("rabbinic court") had gone largely unnoticed by historians and legal scholars. The underlying assumption in *Protocols of Justice* was that careful investigation of these legal texts would yield a novel perspective on cultural adaptation. To that end, I concentrated on how the Beit Din functioned alongside the French civil courts and how expectations of legal conformity from the point of view of the state, affected the internal processes of adjudication and jurisprudence. The proceedings of the Beit Din not only contain astonishing evidence of procedural cooperation with the French judicial system; they also point to a conception of Jewish law that is conspicuous for its capacity to adapt to the challenging social and political environment of the late ancien régime.

When I first decided to research the proceedings of the Metz Beit Din, my hope was to advance the conversation begun by Ted Fram on how rabbinic court records could be useful to historians. Long before the appearance of Fram's book on rabbinic court diaries in eighteenth-century Frankfurt, *A Window on Their World*, and my own *Protocols of Justice*, I sensed that the historical importance of the Metz rabbinic court records would exceed our initial expectations. The community itself was renowned for its important part in the pre-revolutionary debate on citizenship and, before that, for the quality of its life and culture made famous earlier in the century by Glikl (bas Judah Leib) Hameln's renowned memoir. But owing to the dispersal of archival documents and the destruction of numerous community records especially during World

War II, the historical investigation of the Jewish community in early modern Metz, and in the northeastern provinces more generally, had not realized its full potential. Nor—mainly because of the technical difficulties they pose—had rabbinic court proceedings found their way onto the research agendas of Jewish historians.

My primary objective in publishing *Protocols of Justice* was to bring the large corpus of Metz court records to the attention of historians and legal scholars in an accessible format. In order not to delay the project longer than necessary, I chose to restrict my discussion of the judicial proceedings to major areas of litigation and jurisprudence painted with broad brushstrokes. These initial explorations of the Metz court proceedings dispelled the premise that, until the dawn of emancipation, the internal life of the Jewish community had experienced only limited exposure to the political and cultural forces at work in general society. Quite to the contrary, the Jews' legal integration into the deep structures of the larger society is richly documented throughout the deliberations of the rabbinic court. The evidence contained in the Metz Beit Din records told a story that varied sharply with the largely uncontested appraisal of the relationship between Jews and the surrounding society that dominates modern Jewish historiography. The use of court records to reassess basic assumptions about Jewish communal life and history was a critically important step—but only the first—in what I envisioned as a far more ambitious project. The bigger story, however, was beyond the purview of a book whose purpose was much more limited.

A proper reassessment of early modern communal life calls for efforts that extend well beyond the work published to date. *Law's Dominion* enlarges the conceptual framework employed in *Protocols of Justice*, expands its chronological arc, includes additional historical context and further elaboration on legal topics. The present volume supplements the relatively concise analyses of the judicial decisions in *Protocols of Justice* with in-depth investigations, intended to yield more concrete data on how practitioners of Jewish law, as well as its consumers, navigated the systems of Jewish and French law. *Law's Dominion* also broadens the range of sources beyond those consulted in the previous volume to shed light on the complicated role of law in the life of a community that faced significant internal and external challenges to its political, religious, and cultural identity.

Acknowledgments

From the time I began working intensively on the Metz community archival records, I have benefited from the wisdom and generosity of many people and institutions. I completed this book during a fellowship at the Israel Institute for Advanced Studies in 2018–2019. I am grateful to Professor Yitzhak Hen, IIAS Director, to Iris Avivi, Administrative Director, and to the entire IIAS staff for all that they did to make the year enjoyable and productive. I am also pleased to acknowledge the European Institutes for Advanced Study Fellowship Programme (EURIAS) for its generous support during my stay in Jerusalem at the IIAS.

I am especially appreciative of the members of the IIAS Research Group, "Rethinking Early Modern Jewish Legal Culture: New Sources, Methodologies and Paradigms," for the stimulating environment they created in our joint effort to advance the field of Jewish legal history. I trust that some of what I learned from our formal and informal conversations is evident in this book. Special thanks go to Ted Fram for reading an earlier draft of this book and for his helpful comments. I also wish to thank Debra Kaplan for her valuable comments on two early chapters, and the two anonymous readers who read *Law's Dominion* and offered useful advice.

The research for this book began roughly fifteen years ago. I acknowledge with thanks the National Endowment for the Humanities, which awarded me a year-long fellowship in 2011–2012. That year, I served as the Center for Jewish History's Inaugural NEH Senior Scholar. During my stay, I was able to work directly on the Metz Beit Din Pinkas manuscript, which is in the archival collection of the YIVO Institute for Jewish Research. I am grateful to Jonathan Brent, the Institute's Executive Director and to the entire YIVO staff for granting me access to the Metz manuscript and for all their assistance.

The following archives and libraries generously provided access to their resources: the Archives and Rare Book Room of the Jewish Theological Seminary of New York; the Special Collections of the Harvard Law Library; the staff of the Judaica Reading Room at the National and University Library, Jerusalem; the Central Archives of the History of the Jewish People, Jerusalem; and the Archives départementales de la Moselle. I appreciate the assistance given to me by each of these institutions.

None of these opportunities would have been feasible without the vigorous commitment to research and the generous support provided by the University of Massachusetts, Amherst. I am appreciative of its generous support for this project and for every research project I undertook during my career as a member of the faculty. I am particularly grateful for the subvention I received from the Graduate School's Research Council toward the publication of this volume.

Ben Frankel had primary responsibility for editing this volume. He was enormously helpful in improving the prose and clarifying the arguments advanced here. I wish to thank him and Ethelea Katzenell for their excellent editorial work. I am also grateful to Mary Van Steenbergh for her advice and assistance.

This is my second book with Brill Academic Publishers. I am grateful to Katie Chin and the Brill staff for all that they did to produce this volume.

I owe the greatest thanks to my wife Sharon, for her love, patience, partnership, and support. Our daughter Racheli and son-in-law Ephraim bring much joy to our lives, and for this we are very thankful.

Throughout her life, my mother, Lillian Berkovitz, has embodied the virtues of fortitude, resilience, and kindness, and I thank her for all that she has done for me and our family. I am also grateful to my brother Joel for his boundless devotion. My late mother-in-law, Goldie Levinson, a woman of intelligence and generosity, would have taken great pleasure in seeing the publication of this volume. It is in her memory that I dedicate this work.

Jerusalem, Israel
24 Sivan 5779
July 1, 2019

Abbreviations

A.D. Moselle	Archives départementales de la Moselle
Arch. JTSA	Archives of the Jewish Theological Seminary of America
BN	Bibliothèque Nationale
BT	Babylonian Talmud
CAHJP	Central Archives for the History of the Jewish People
HUCA	Hebrew Union College Annual
JMH	Journal of Modern History
JQR	Jewish Quarterly Review
JSS	Jewish Social Studies
JT	Jerusalem Talmud
M.	Mishnah
PKM	Pinkas Kahal of Metz
PMBD	Pinkas of the Metz Beit Din
REJ	Revue des études juives
Resp.	Responsa

Maps

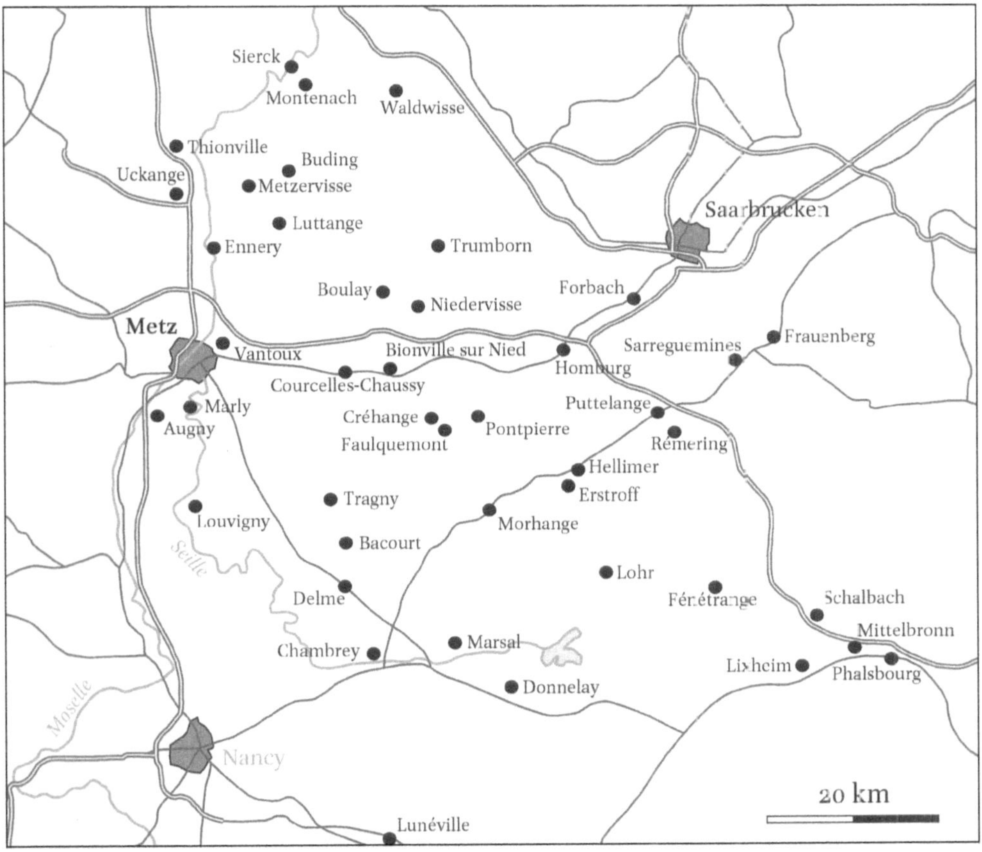

MAP 1 Department of Moselle

MAP 2 Europe in the 18th century

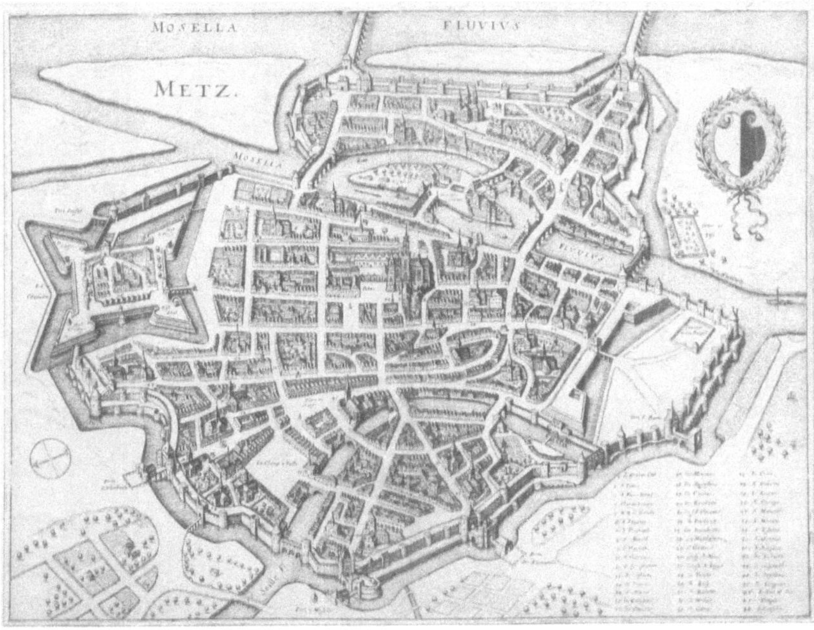

MAP 3 Metz, 1661. Matthaus Merian, artist

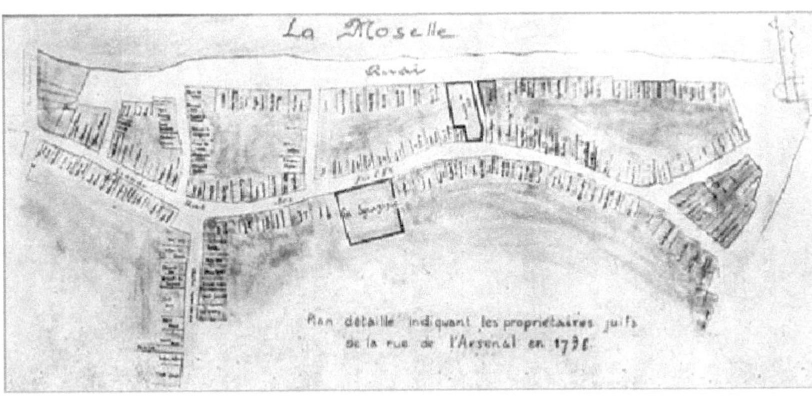

MAP 4 Jewish proprietors on rue de l'Arsenal (in Metz) in 1738

Introduction

The past two decades have witnessed a turn toward law and legal history that has begun to revolutionize the study of the Jewish past. Until recently, despite the prominence of law in the Jewish religious tradition, interest in legal history among early modernists was extremely limited. Medieval scholars have given more attention to legal history, though their work has placed emphasis primarily on legal theory and interpretation of the Talmud, codes, medieval commentaries, rabbinic responsa, and customary law. With few exceptions, historical analysis of medieval Jewish law has focused on its internal development. For early modern Jewish historians, the situation is much different. Beginning in the sixteenth century, hundreds of communal registers and compilations of legislation were produced and preserved by communities across Europe. Although these records are packed with legal material, the most important sources for the study of law and history are rabbinic court records. Nevertheless, interest in judicial decisions has been stymied by daunting technical obstacles that cannot be overcome without proficiency in Hebrew paleography and expertise in areas of Jewish civil and family law that are generally unfamiliar to historians. The recent interest in Jewish legal history reflects a newfound appreciation for law as a critically important component of social and intellectual history, drawing inspiration from the robust field of general legal history and its illustrious medieval and early modern traditions. The discovery and publication of hitherto unknown or overlooked legal texts has no doubt also stirred interest in the role of law as a crucial historical source.[1]

Heightened attention to rabbinic and lay court records over the past decade has added a new dimension to the study of Jewish law. In sharp contrast to legal codes that prescribe religious and social norms of behavior, and to rabbinic responsa that advance learned legal opinions often limited to theoretical and hypothetical concerns, court records are remarkably precise indicators of social and cultural trends. Judicial records provide a window onto the socio-economic conditions that prevailed in Jewish communities and convey a sense of the political pressures imposed by the state. They provide clear images not only of what prescribed law has to say about commercial and real property transactions, divorces, and inheritances, but also of how these areas of law

1 On Jewish legal history and its relationship to the social and economic history of the Jews, see Haym Soloveitchik, *Use of Responsa as Historical Source* (Jerusalem, 1990) [Hebrew]; Jay R. Berkovitz and Ephraim Kanarfogel, "Introduction [to Special Issue: New Perspectives on Jewish Legal History]," *Jewish History* 31 (2017): 1–6.

 | DOI:10.1163/9789004417403_002

were practiced and how life was lived. In contrast to the responsa literature, which generally reveals only a modest level of tension between law as codified law and law as practiced, court records mirror the day-to-day functioning of Jewish communities in virtually all areas of life. Variations in conditions from locale to locale underscore the importance of investigating such issues in their local contexts.

The methodological assumptions underlying the investigation of the legal sources treated in this volume are consistent with approaches that have evolved in the work of early modernists over the last quarter century. The goal is at once to uncover evidence of interaction between neighboring cultures while also taking account of the religious, social, and political constraints on the allure of such collaboration. Regrettably, the scholarship that dominates the study of Jewish law has not kept pace with advances in the field of early-modern Jewish history.[2] Seldom do efforts to explain legal creativity stray beyond the realm of abstract theory. In this regard, the assumptions of legal anthropology have proven especially useful, most of all its aversion to the idea that the law can be isolated from other disciplines. The anthropological approach seeks to embed the law in a larger context by casting a wider net on what is commonly considered legal. Nearly three decades ago, Thomas Kuehn stressed that legal anthropology contributed to our understanding of "the social processes and into the meanings of norms that cannot be obtained by concentrating on courts, legal professions, and the technical ... language of the law itself."[3] According to Sally Falk Moore, anthropology "inquires into the context of enforceable norms: social, political, economic, and intellectual. This includes, but goes further than, what Western governments and courts define as law. In anthropology, while the 'socio-legal' includes formal juridical institutions and their social surroundings, it also encompasses law-like activities and processing of establishing order in many social domains, formal and informal, official and unofficial, in our own society and in others."[4] Intended to offset the emphasis generally placed on the institutional aspects of judicial culture, legal anthropology "has increasingly taught historians to see legal

2 See the introduction to *Jewish Culture in Early Modern Europe: Essays in Honor of David B. Ruderman*, Richard I. Cohen, Natalie B. Dohrmann, Elchanan Reiner, and Adam Shear, eds. (Pittsburgh, 2014).

3 Thomas Kuehn, *Law, Family, and Women: Toward a Legal Anthropology of Renaissance Italy* (Chicago, 1991), 11. Also see John Jordan, "Rethinking Disputes and Settlements: How Historians Can Use Legal Anthropology," in *Cultures of Conflict: Resolution in Early Modern Europe*, ed. Stephen Cummins and Laura Kounine (Burlington, VT, 2016), 17–50.

4 Sally Falk Moore, "General Introduction: What is an Anthropological Approach to Law?" in *Law and Anthropology: A Reader*, ed. Sally Falk Moore (Oxford, 2005), 1.

texts, tribunals, and professionals as embedded in larger, more complex, contested social and cultural relationships."[5]

Law's Dominion charts the emergence and development of new conceptions of Jewish law in the early modern era by looking closely at the alternation between theory and practice. Central to this approach is what legal historians have referred to as "legal consciousness," defined as the "meanings of law circulating in social relations, ... a type of social practice reflecting and forming social structures."[6] Legal consciousness presumes that the social, economic, and cultural framework endows the law with a range of concrete meanings that are collectively constructed.

Three types of legal sources are at the heart of our investigation: rabbinic responsa; judicial rulings of rabbinic courts; and communal registers (*pinkasim*), which contain formal legislation and evidence of prevailing social norms. The rabbinic responsa consulted in this project are all published sources. The judicial rulings that serve as the basis for the analysis undertaken in this volume are recorded in the Pinkas of the Metz Beit Din, which is the property of the Archives of the YIVO Institute for Jewish Research in New York. Consisting of two leather-bound volumes, written in a semi-cursive Ashkenazic script and containing 1063 judicial cases, the entire Pinkas of the Metz rabbinic court was published five years ago by Brill Academic Publishers.[7] The most important new source employed in the present study is the Metz Pinkas Kahal (communal register) of Metz, which is the property of the Jewish Theological Seminary of New York. This bound manuscript dates from 1749 and to 1789.[8]

The Pinkas Kahal and the Pinkas Beit Din offer two distinctly different perspectives—two competing narratives—on the challenges of the eighteenth century. The Pinkas Kahal offers abundant evidence that communal leaders were anxious about the decline in the commitment of Metz Jews to the Jewish religious tradition. Rigorous efforts to reinforce religious observance, traditional sexual mores, and boundaries between the Kehillah and the surrounding society and its culture bear witness to a community struggling

5 Michael P. Breen, "Law, Society, and the State in Early Modern France," *JMH* 83 (June 2011): 355.

6 *The New Oxford Companion to Law* (Oxford, 2008), 695. See also Susan S. Sibley, "After Legal Consciousness," *Annual Review of Law and Social Science* 1 (2005): 323–68.

7 Pinkas Metz Beit Din, Record Group 128, Box 2, Collection of Rabbinical and Historical Manuscripts, YIVO Archives (hereafter, PMBD). Jay R. Berkovitz, *Protocols of Justice: The Pinkas of the Metz Rabbinic Court, 1771–1789*, 2 vols. (Leiden, 2014).

8 The Pinkas Kahal of Metz, Archives JTSA. Earlier Metz Kahal are at the CAHJP FMe 139; there are also fragments from the Pinkas Kahal dating from 1699 to 1702 that were published by David Kaufmann, ed. "Extraits de l'ancien livre de la communauté de Metz." *REJ* 19 (1889): 115–130.

to surmount the onslaught of modernity. The records of the Metz Beit Din, by contrast, tell a different story that varies substantially from traditional accounts of the relationship between Jews and the general society. According to the prevailing view, most Jews had limited exposure to broader social and cultural influences until the process of emancipation transformed the relationship between the Jews and the surrounding society. The rabbinic court proceedings offer detailed evidence that the Jews of Metz were far more engaged with the cultural and economic dimensions of the society around them than is generally assumed. Linguistic assimilation, compliance with bureaucratic requirements, and fluency in the material culture of northeastern France offer valuable indications of acculturation on the part of the Jews in Metz and in the *pays messin* (the province of Lorraine). Furthermore, the methods of adjudication and the conception of jurisprudence practiced by the Beit Din illustrate the broad scope of acculturation experienced by the urban—and, in many instances, even the rural—Jewish population. To draw attention to the wider legal context and to provide a basis for comparative legal analysis, I have consulted the French translation of Jewish civil law (*Recueil des lois, coûtumes et usages observés par les juifs de Metz*) that the Jewish community produced in 1743 at the urging of parliamentary and monarchical authorities and the general literature of customs books produced in the Moselle province. In sum, Metz judicial records attest to an astonishing level of engagement with French society and culture. The two narratives in the Kahal and Beit Din protocols evince the complex struggles facing a community at once absorbed by internal challenges and confident of its role in relation to the wider social reality.

The novelty of the method proposed here rests on the premise that responsa, communal registers, and judicial rulings, issued by rabbinic and lay courts ought to be approached as components of a single, though multifaceted, literary corpus. Although specific goals and means to their attainment varied widely, these three bodies of material were all products of interdependent constituencies, each with a sincere interest in seeing the law serve as an instrument for the realization of social and religious objectives. Parallel formulations in the Metz customs books are a valuable resource for understanding both the legal conventions practiced in the Jewish community and their relationship to general law. The interrelationship among these sources, and their intertextual links are essential for appreciating the intricate twists and turns of Jewish law in the modern era. No less important, they reveal the range of social concerns that are the backbone of historical analysis. These records provide a glimpse of communal life, of the public policy concerns that occupied local leaders, of the lives of individuals and families at various socio-economic levels as they endeavored to meet the economic challenges of a pre-industrial society. Not least of all, they reveal the struggles that Jews of all stripes faced as members of a minority population intent on preserving its collective identity amid a frequently hostile environment.[9]

With the records of the Metz Beit Din now available in a printed edition that has overcome the paleographic hurdles and eased many of the difficulties posed by the language and technical terminology found in legal sources of this type, the present volume seeks to explicate the judicial practices of the rabbinic court and its lay counterpart. A three-tiered approach takes account of (a) different types of cases brought before the lay and rabbinic courts, with attention to the relationship between legislation and judicial rulings; (b) the talmudic and halakhic background of cases brought before the rabbinic court; and (c) the interplay between the Beit Din and the French civil courts. While it is not possible at all times to track judicial rulings through each of these levels, since we do not have parallel texts in every instance, the overarching goal is to view the rabbinic court records within their wider contexts: the history of Jewish law, the local Jewish community, the wider society and culture with which the Jews interacted, and the French legal framework.

What emerges from these sources is a new narrative that has far-reaching implications for our understanding of central themes of pre-modern Jewish history: the nature and scope of Jewish communal autonomy; the relations between the Jews and the state; Jewish interaction with the surrounding society and culture; and the multifaceted nexus between acculturation and modernization. Focusing on prevailing norms, mechanisms of change, and emerging patterns of legal culture, *Law's Dominion* examines the practices of rabbinic and lay courts, jurisdictional negotiations between Jewish and non-Jewish courts, responsa, and communal bylaws, and seeks to understand how rabbinic and lay leaders struggled to meet the challenges to their authority. I have endeavored to address a series of important questions, large and small, more thoroughly than was possible in my earlier work. First, when considering their relationship to general law, how much weight ought we give to the legal, social, and political subordination of the Jews in pre-revolutionary France? Do the substantial parallels with French law, judicial consultations between rabbinic judges and French lawyers, and the influence of French law on the Beit Din's deliberations contradict what has been widely viewed as the wretched state in which the Jews found themselves prior to citizenship? Alternatively,

9 The renewed interest in communal records, actively promoted by the International Pinkassim Project and the National Library of Israel, is an important step in digitizing communal registers. The project is nonetheless at a very early stage. See http://web.nli.org.il/sites/NLI/English/collections/jewishcollection/pinkassim/Pages/default.aspx.

can the collaborative relationship with the French courts be construed as a bilateral relationship with the state and French law? How are we to understand the astonishing affinity of Jews to French culture, whether material, legal, or otherwise? Second, what more can rulings on issues such as succession, guardianship, and property tell us about the relationship of the Jewish community to the state? How much autonomy was there in the decades prior to the Revolution? What role was played by religion, that is, how much respect was given to religion in an emerging secular environment? Can conclusions about the respect and prerogatives that the state accorded Jewish litigants in Metz be applied to other western and central European communities?

Third, since the majority of the cases recorded in the Pinkas Beit Din reflect the interests of the middle and upper classes,[10] what can we learn about how ordinary Jews settled their disputes and, more generally, how they negotiated conflicts between their Jewish and French identities? To address these issues more fully, the present volume draws evidence from a wider range of cases, including those that touch on the interests of the poor. Overall, I have tried to strike a proper balance between these extremes, in order to portray the remarkable performance of the Metz rabbinic court and of the general Jewish population as accurately as possible.

Core legal texts pertaining to family offer entrée into a web of culture and relationships for which there is no other documentation. This is significant because the majority of cases that came before the Metz Beit Din were related, either directly or indirectly, to the family, particularly in the areas of inheritance, guardianship, marital property, and the participation of women in the judicial process. Rulings in these areas, and the legal mechanisms that evolved in response to changing social and economic conditions, contain images of women and family that are at variance with representations that emerge from prescriptive legal sources alone. Advances in the legal status of women were anchored in an expansive conception of Jewish law that was ably advanced by the rabbinic court.

---

10 See David Parker, "Sovereignty, Absolutism, and the Function of the Law in Seventeenth-Century France," *Past and Present* 122 (1989): 36–74. Parker argued that the royal administration "had become the property of the families, kin-groups and clienteles who had secured their positions within it" and that the state functioned primarily as "an arena for the regulation of conflicts inside the ruling class." Going a step further in *Class and State in Ancien Régime France: The Road to Modernity?* (London, 1996), 26–27, 180–81, 268, Parker recommended that more attention be given to the "day to day operation of the law and its general social and political functions," cited in Michael P. Breen, "Law, Society, and the State in Early Modern France," *JMH* 83 (June 2011): 353–54.

Two related arguments are at the heart of this book. The first is that Jewish communal autonomy in Metz was not only more thoroughgoing than is normally assumed but was largely undiminished by cooperation with state and municipal government. To be sure, tensions surfaced periodically when parliamentary authorities demanded compliance with French law at the expense of fidelity to Jewish law. However, any such stresses were generally eclipsed by the collaborative relationship between the Kehillah and state, on the one hand, and the collaborative relationship between the Beit Din and the French judicial system, on the other. Equally significant was the fact that the state authorized the Jewish community to regulate all areas of the life of its members, including conformity to religious standards, commercial dealings, marriage, divorce, inheritance, and criminal activity. Upholding the authority of Jewish communal government and institutions, including rabbinic jurisdiction in civil matters, was plainly in the interest of the state, first for reasons relating to the social and economic stability of the Jewish population, and second, on account of bureaucratic and political advantages that flowed from authorizing a loyal minority to govern itself without undue interference. In fact, the vitality of the community's judicial autonomy, and the scope of its overall authority, greatly exceeded the independence exercised by ecclesiastical courts and other corporate groups, such as French Protestants. While some Jews took their disputes to the French civil courts, the court of first instance was unfailingly the Beit Din. The decision to go to the French courts was, as a rule, motivated either by the conviction that the French judicial system was a legitimate venue for adjudicating particular legal issues or by the preference for a legal forum that had the teeth to enforce its rulings. On rare occasions, when a litigant was dissatisfied with the rabbinic court's decision and sought to overturn its judgment, the case could be taken to the Parlement (regional supreme court).

The second central argument of this book pertains to the role of religion in early modern European society. Many modern historians view religion as a body of beliefs and practices that were slowly eclipsed by the secularizing influence of modernization and were ultimately delegitimized by proponents of the European Enlightenment.[11] As originally conceived by sociologists more than forty years ago, the "secularization thesis" assumes that the more modern a society, the more secular it is. While the role of religion in some modern societies has diminished noticeably, critics such as José Casanova, Talal Asad, and Peter Berger reject the claim that this decline was inevitable or as far-reaching

11 See Kasper von Greyerz, *Religion and Culture in Early Modern Europe, 1500–1800* (Oxford, 2008).

as is widely assumed.[12] "As an analytical category," argues Jonathan Sheehan, "secularization plagues the efforts to connect the Enlightenment and religion." To overcome this, "we need to think not just about enlightenment, but also about its partner in the secularizing process, 'religion.'"[13] The view of the Enlightenment as the quintessence of modernity, or as the catalyst that set it in motion, has distorted the role of religion in the eighteenth century as a dominant force that governed the lives of most members of society. We would do well to examine, within the context of modernity, popular religiosity, resistance to change, cooperative ventures involving lay and rabbinic leaders, and how the meaning of religion has accommodated changing conditions.[14] Such inquiries accentuate the religious roots of modernity (as is apparent from their participation in the "secular aspects of the public sphere") and the acceptance of state authority in civil matters, as well as challenging the prevalent image of religion as dogmatic, uncompromising, and intolerant.[15]

In *Law's Dominion*, I explore the diverse ways religion continued to function throughout the eighteenth century as a basis for social cohesion and corporate identity. It was a cultural force that exerted a formative impact on the values Jews sought to realize and the boundaries that defined their relations with the state and society at large. Rituals embodied modes of thinking about historical origins, about interactions with the surrounding culture and society, and about the identification with particular cultural traditions. Through the lens of law in social context, this book delves into a world in which the classical traditions of Judaism were challenged by unprecedented social, economic, political, and intellectual upheaval. Public policy and judicial culture provide evidence that the Jewish social and legal heritage was interpreted anew at critical junctures during the seventeenth and eighteenth centuries. Yet in an era of dynamic social and political transformation, when challenges to religion as an authoritative source of moral values and social norms were on the rise, the conventions of Jewish communal life and time-honored religious traditions retained their staying power as respected sources of authority.

---

12 See José Casanova, *Public Religions in the Modern World* (Chicago, 1994); Talal Asad, *Formations of the Secular: Christianity, Islam, Modernity* (Stanford, 2003); Peter L. Berger, *The Desecularization of the World* (Washington, DC, 1999).

13 Jonathan Sheehan, "Enlightenment, Religion, and the Enigma of Secularization: A Review Essay," *American Historical Review* 108 (2003): 1071–72. Also see Simon Grote, "Religion and Enlightenment," *Journal of the History of Ideas* 75:1 (January 2014): 137–60.

14 See Jonathan Clark, *English Society, 1660–1832*, 2d ed. (Cambridge, 2000) and S. J. Barnett, *The Enlightenment and Religion. The Myths of Modernity* (Manchester, U.K., 2003).

15 David Sorkin, *The Religious Enlightenment: Protestants, Jews, and Catholics from London to Vienna* (Princeton, 2008), 1–3, 11–18, 21, 314.

The persistence of religion as a social and political force depended on the particular patterns of governance that controlled the spheres of public and private life. Lay control over public morality not only "proved more significant and came earlier than the ideas of the *philosophes* in giving dynamic impulse to the process of modernization," as Marc Raeff declared over forty years ago, but, paradoxically, it also accounts in great measure for the continuing role of religion as a seminal force in public affairs.[16] In the Jewish communities of Metz and elsewhere, a balance was struck between recourse to the Talmudic tradition and the demands of public policy.

Until Jewish leaders surrendered the privilege of communal autonomy in exchange for civic equality after the Revolution of 1789, religion remained the foremost—though certainly not the sole—source of law and legal norms upon which the governance of Jewish communities rested. The enduring role of religion in an era of social and political transformation is highly conspicuous in the legislation enacted by the lay leadership, as exemplified in the performance of philanthropy, the construction of communal memory, and the customary law that defined the established norms relating to marriage, guardianship, and inheritance. Evidence of the buoyancy of religion as a vital social, cultural, and political force is found in the patterns of lay governance and in the structures of everyday life. What distinguishes religion in the Jewish context was the coexistence of the ritual and civil components of communal life in a single framework, while each was acknowledged as a separate domain. The boundaries between them were most often respected, other times contested, and commonly blurred. The nearly exclusive preoccupation of the rabbinic court with the realm of civil law reveals the latter's ostensive detachment from the universe of ritual, though the civil and religious domains were never, and could not be, completely severed from one another. The interdependence of the two spheres is evident as well in both the lay-rabbinic cooperation and collaboration that characterized communal governance and in the culture of the rabbinic court.

Two major conclusions emerge from the arguments set forth in this book. First, Jewish autonomy was not the equivalent of a ghetto, either as a physical space in the case of Metz, or as a cultural mindset, as in most manifestations

16 Marc Raeff, "The Well-Ordered Police State and the Development of Modernity in Seventeenth- and Eighteenth-Century Europe: An Attempt at a Comparative Approach," *American Historical Review* 80 (1975): 1221–43. For a full elaboration of the idea of public law, first appearing in 1697, see Jean Domat, *Le droit public, suite des lois civiles dans leur ordre naturel*, vol. 3, *Oeuvres complètes, nouvelle edition revue corrigée*, Joseph Remy, ed. (Paris, 1829). On the evolution of the term *police*, see Daniel Gordon, *Citizens Without Sovereignty: Equality and Sociability in French Thought, 1670–1789* (Princeton, 1994), 18–24.

of self-government. At first blush, this may seem strange, since the rigorous demands of Jewish ritual—including Sabbath and festival observance, public prayer, religious education, care for the dead, and dietary laws—encouraged the formation of self-governing Jewish communities founded on the long-established ethos of separation. But evidence recorded in the protocols of the Beit Din reveals the remarkable degree to which the Jewish population was dependent on the surrounding society, not only for its economic well-being, but also for the innumerable services that it could not provide for itself. As consumers of French material culture, Metz Jews needed to be in close contact with the craftsmen and merchants who produced or imported housewares, building products, and fabrics, and with those who provided essential services. Intricate economic interaction with members of the general population included various collaborations with non-Jews, and the growing bureaucratic demands placed on all residents made it necessary for the Jews in Metz to become conversant with the general culture. Patterns of linguistic assimilation and fluency in the material culture of northeastern France were consistent with the rabbinic court's familiarity with established French civil procedures in areas such as the endorsement of bills of exchange, the execution of bearer documents, and the oversight of testaments, probate inventories, and guardianship. Compliance with the procedural requirements of the general courts went hand-in-hand with the development of a working relationship between the Jewish and French judiciaries. Overall, the patterns of acculturation outlined in *Law's Dominion* reinforced the foundation upon which Metz's shared legal culture rested.

Second, Jewish law displayed a remarkable capacity to be innovative and flexible. These qualities drew upon the vigorous interpretive traditions of the Jewish legal heritage and the Beit Din's adaptational approach, a product of its collaborative relationship with the community's lay administration and with the French justice system. Cooperation with the lay authority kept the court attuned to the community's policy concerns, while its relationship with the French courts opened the door to the adoption and adaptation of mechanisms from general jurisprudence. The Beit Din drew upon innovative instruments in Jewish law that it incorporated in its procedural toolkit to address changing socio-economic, cultural, and political conditions of the early modern period. This would occasionally require a reworking of medieval models of religious authority.

To explain how this was accomplished, *Law's Dominion* has added further evidence of the relationship between communal legislation, responsa, and judicial rulings, as well as observations concerning Jewish communities elsewhere that strengthen the comparative dimension of the present study. But more than simply adapting to the prevailing system of French law, rabbinic judges strongly acknowledged the interdependence of cases brought before the Jewish tribunal and the French civil court system. In fact, the detailed records of the Metz rabbinic court offer remarkable examples of how the doctrine of *dina d'malkhuta dina* ("the law of the kingdom is the law") was applied in practice. But even with this established principle of legal accommodation at its disposal, the Beit Din faced the unending dilemma of reconciling the competing demands of communal autonomy, on the one hand, and of the centralized governing institutions, on the other. While the demands made by municipal and royal authorities were mostly limited to the management of pluralism, it cannot be denied that efforts to coordinate the multiple expressions and frameworks of judicial culture in any territory inexorably functioned as a centralizing force. The navigation required of communal leaders accounts for the ability of the Jewish tradition, as understood by the various constituents, to encompass elements that would appear to be self-contradictory: autonomy and collaboration; lay and rabbinic authority; and tradition and innovation.

The portrait of the Jewish community in the pages that follow focuses on the function of law in internal communal affairs, its role in mediating between the Jews and government authorities, and its impact on the interaction of Jews with the larger world of French society and culture. This material is presented in three parts. Part One introduces the sources that are the focus of this study and traces the origins of the early modern Jewish community in Metz. Chapter one considers the challenges of using legal texts as an historical source and concludes with a discussion of what we know—or can reasonably surmise—about the production of the Pinkas of the Metz Beit Din. Chapter two offers a history of the establishment of the Metz community and an analysis of its religious, material, and economic culture.

Part Two explores the core issues concerning communal autonomy, governance, and authority. Chapter three examines the inner workings of the autonomous community, its modes of governance, and the legislation enacted to regulate electoral and administrative procedures; consumption; poverty and social welfare; juridical autonomy; and cultural boundaries between Jews and non-Jews. Chapter four centers on aspects of juridical autonomy, the methods of adjudication employed by lay and rabbinic tribunals, their legal authority, functions, and jurisprudential concerns. Emphasis is placed on the role of the rabbinic court as a communal agency, its relationship with the community leadership and legislation, and its role in shaping public policy. Chapter five places the Beit Din within the larger framework of legal traditions that evolved during the late Middle Ages and early modern period. The main argument is that the acculturation of Metz Jews and their integration in the legal and administrative bureaucracy of the region constituted the social foundation of the court's jurisprudence. Of central importance is the approach of the Beit Din to the challenges of multiple jurisdictions and conflict of laws, its familiarity with French law and judicial practice, the adaptational strategies it devised, and the broadening of the principle of *dina d'malkhuta dina*.

Part Three, which focuses on the family, illustrates where the dynamics of legal and judicial culture in Metz found concrete expression. Chapter six presents inheritance and guardianship as two case studies that illustrate the cultural history of the two institutions as they are portrayed in legal sources. Both inheritance and guardianship demanded extensive interaction with French authorities, particularly the courts, and therefore demanded navigation between the Jewish and French judicial systems. Chapter seven offers an extended examination of marriage in terms of its legal and economic dimensions; the role of women in commerce; and, most generally, the lives of women, the challenges they faced and evidence of their agency. Much of the analysis centers on property disputes, with special attention to the forces that altered the economic condition of women in the latter part of the eighteenth century. In the Conclusion and Epilogue the foregoing historical treatment of communal and juridical autonomy is considered in light of the surrender of civil jurisdiction, as required by the National Constituent Assembly, and the Napoleonic effort to ensure compliance with this demand.

Although this volume is concerned primarily with the early modern community of Metz, the story it seeks to tell is much larger. It may be natural to assume that because Metz was situated on the western periphery of Europe, far removed from the most celebrated events and intellectual movements of the seventeenth and eighteenth centuries, that its importance was negligible. Such a judgment would be an unfortunate error. Metz offers a fascinating case-study of the convergence of several distinct legal traditions—Roman law, canon law, customary law, and royal law—and, no less important, an example of the administrative challenges of managing a province that was, by many accounts, detached from the cultural and political center of France. However, the city of Metz and the *pays messin* were more firmly bound to the mainstream of French political and cultural life than is generally known, just as the Metz Jewish community maintained strong cultural ties to communities further to the north and to the east. But regardless of the size of a community or its location, Jewish communal life was shaped by disparate social, economic, cultural, and political forces that reveal that it is mistaken to judge the importance of any community by how well it "fits the mold."

Richly documented with valuable archival and printed sources, the Metz community struggled in much the same way as communities elsewhere to foster optimal conditions for the realization of social, cultural, and religious ideals in a setting shaped by the culture and politics of its time. By drawing upon the vast treasures that are embedded deeply in the minutes of the Metz Pinkas Kahal and the proceedings of the Beit Din, the present work seeks to shed light on communal structures, economic patterns, the dynamics of family life, and the role of law in the decades prior to the French Revolution. In these respects, the Jewish community of Metz offers a model and a medium to analyze Ashkenazic communities of the pre-emancipation era.

Finally, the principal argument presented in *Law's Dominion* is not that the autonomous regime in Metz should be taken as a model for other communities or that it was unique. Rather, I offer Metz as a case study of the challenges facing communities across Europe in the years before Jews attained citizenship. While local and regional conditions shaped the culture of each individual community in innumerable ways, collectively they contended with rather similar struggles. It is my hope that early modernists will find the material presented in these pages—particularly in the legislation enacted by a small Jewish community and the settlement of legal disputes in a small court that was highly conscious of the larger legal setting—of both interest and use. No less important, I trust that with its attention to methodological and substantive issues—positioned at the intersection of law and history—*Law's Dominion* will contribute to a broader consideration of the complex relationship between minorities and the general societies and cultures to which they belong.

PART 1

Foundations

CHAPTER 1

Jewish History through a Legal Lens

What does the pre-modern Jewish community offer students of law? What does the law offer students of pre-modern Jewish history? These two questions, which are at the heart of the present discussion, provide entrée into several longstanding debates concerning the relative authority of religious and lay leaders, the impact of state interference on Jewish juridical autonomy, and the degree to which Jewish law succeeded in adapting to changing social, economic, and political conditions. All told, they furnish a sense of the boundaries that separated the Jews as a minority population from the majority society, and they contribute as well to a greater understanding of the law's responsiveness to social, economic, religious, and political challenges. The early modern period was an era in which legal institutions, legal procedures, and the law itself pervaded all areas of life. David Parker has aptly referred to this wide-ranging phenomenon as "all-pervasive legalism' while David Bell has characterized France of the ancien régime as a "judicial society."[1] Modern historians appreciate the role of the law and the courts in shaping social norms and in developing state institutions in a general sense, but much less is known of the pervasive character of law in western Europe and its potential for deepening our understanding of the dynamics of social, cultural, and political change.

Jewish law and its relation to history has suffered a similar fate. Despite the centrality of law in Jewish culture and religion, little is known of the legal universe inhabited by Ashkenazic Jews of western and central Europe, or of the sources necessary for the study of Jewish legal history in the century and a half preceding the French Revolution. Whether it is law that influences society or society that shapes law are questions that continue to be of broad interest to theorists, but the basic assumption of the present work is that law and society are mutually constitutive, as understood by Michel de Certeau and Austin

1 See David Parker, *La Rochelle and the French Monarchy: Conflict and Order in Seventeenth-Century France* (London, 1980), 19; David A. Bell, "The 'Public Sphere,' the State and the World of the Law in Eighteenth-Century France," *French Historical Studies* 17:4 (1992): 933; Michael Breen, *Law, City, and King: Legal Culture, Municipal Politics and State Formation in Early Modern Dijon* (Rochester, 2007), introduction, 5ff; and idem, "Patronage, Politics, and the 'Rule of Law' in Early Modern France," *Proceedings of the Western Society for French History* 33 (2005): 95–113.

 | DOI:10.1163/9789004417403_003

Sarat, among others.[2] Our goal is to illustrate how law emerges from social interactions and political concerns, and is itself transformed in the process. In this chapter law is approached first as a source of social and cultural history. Law as entrée into history has become increasingly familiar territory for historians, though, quite rightly, they continue to ask what we can expect to gain from reading legal texts and what kind of narrative we anticipate writing based on these sources.[3] Since the historical data is encased in legal arguments and discourses, we are obliged to understand the legal context on its own terms and not simply as a means to extract social and cultural information. As will become apparent, the discrete disciplinary approaches of history and law intersect in several important ways.

Historians have long turned to legal sources for help in reconstructing the past. Indeed, the law is a vast arena that encompasses virtually every aspect of communal, family, social, economic, and religious life. In Jewish historical research, three types of legal sources have predominated: communal legislation, legal codes, and rabbinic responsa. Communal legislation offers the perspective of public law and policy; codes are a compendium of statutory laws that prescribe established norms of behavior; and rabbinic responsa offer a window into the minds of jurists actively engaged in legal decision making. To this list of standard legal sources, we add in the pages that follow a consideration of the Metz rabbinic court records, which are the single most important resource currently in print for understanding the conventions of judicial decision-making and the relationship between Jewish legal authorities and the state. Although many of the details set forth in the present discussion reflect the French context, there is much in this material that is pertinent to early modern western and central Europe generally. When mined historically, responsa literature, communal registers, and rabbinic court records can account for variations in legal decisions and interpretation, tensions between textual traditions and customary law, the influence of general law, and the impact of socio-economic forces. Regional variations in legal decisions and practices allow scholars to weigh the impact of varying social, economic, political, cultural, and religious forces.

The dire fate of French archival holdings, coupled with difficult challenges posed by rabbinic sources, severely complicate the study of Jewish

2 See Michel de Certeau, *The Practice of Everyday Life*, trans. Steven Rendall (Berkeley, 1984), and Austin Sarat, et al., *Crossing Boundaries: Traditions and Transformations in Law and Society Research* (Evanston, 1998), 1–17.

3 See Catherine Fisk and Robert Gordon, "'Law As …' Theory and Method in Legal History," *University of California Irvine Law Review* 1:3, 519–42.

legal history. Much of what has survived is widely scattered in archives in France, Israel and the United States, yielding a rather fragmented picture of Jewish life in the ancien régime. Even though many of the most important of the community's archival records were transported to North America after World War II and thus became accessible to a larger number of scholars, the material has attracted limited attention. The few exceptions included Zosa Szajkowski (whose publications were heavily indebted to the privileged access he gained by his theft of numerous files from French archival institutions) and Arthur Hertzberg, the author of *The French Enlightenment and the Jews*. Hertzberg's controversial indictment of Voltaire and other leading *philosophes* for laying the foundation for modern secular antisemitism was the book's central claim, but a large part of the study was devoted to detailed analysis of Jewish communal life and culture. Frances Malino, whose early work centered on Sephardic Jews in southern France, published a biography of Metz essayist and interpreter Zalkind Hourwitz, and studies focusing on challenges Jewish women posed to legal norms in eighteenth-century Metz. Few others in North American have ventured into this terrain.[4]

It is no surprise that a great deal more attention has been directed to these subjects in France. Gilbert Cahen and Samuel Kerner produced valuable contributions that built on earlier studies, such as those of Abraham Cahen and Roger Clément. Important studies published by Simon Schwarzfuchs, a native of Alsace who made his career in Israel, include the Metz *Memorbuch* and studies of communal bylaws, correspondence, and rabbinic contracts in pre-revolutionary Alsace and Lorraine. Much of the research on the pre-revolutionary period has concentrated narrowly on individual communities. Communal histories, often stirred by sentiments of local pride, became popular in the early twentieth century. This trend was reinforced after World War II, when a renewed concern for Jewish survival and continuity spawned efforts to preserve what had remained and to memorialize what was lost. The valuable

4 See Arthur Hertzberg, *The French Enlightenment and the Jews* (New York, 1968), and Zosa Szajkowski, *The Economic Status of the Jews in Alsace, Metz and Lorraine (1648–1789)* (New York, 1954), and idem, *The Jews in the French Revolutions of 1789, 1830, and 1848* (New York, 1970). For a critique of Hertzberg's view of the French Enlightenment, see Ronald Schechter, *Obstinate Hebrews: Representations of the Jews in France 1715–1815* (Berkeley, 2003), and idem, "The Jewish Question in Eighteenth-Century France," *Eighteenth-Century Studies* 32, no. 1 (1998): 84–91. On Szajkowski's exploits, see Lisa Leff, *The Archive Thief: The Man who Salvaged French Jewish History in the Wake of the Holocaust* (Oxford, 2015). Malino's publications on Metz include *A Jew in the French Revolution: The Life of Zalkind Hourwitz* (Oxford, 1996); idem, "Competition and Confrontation: the Jews and the Parlement of Metz," *Les Juifs devant l'histoire. Mélanges en l'honneur de Bernhard Blumenkranz* (Paris, 1985); idem, "Resistance et Rebellion à Metz au Dix-Huitième Siècle," *Juifs en France au 18e Siècle* (Paris, 1994).

studies of Moïse Ginsburger on scores of Alsatian communities exemplify these sentiments. In the last thirty years, larger, more systematic studies, such as those of Pierre-André Meyer and Françoise Job, examined the full range of social, economic, and political forces at work in the Jewish communities of Metz, Lunéville, and Nancy.[5]

In French historiography, the Revolution of 1789 has enjoyed privileged status as the virtually uncontested starting point of modern history, despite challenges advanced by historians in France, the United Kingdom, and the United States. Following prominent Marxist historian Georges Lefebvre, who viewed the Revolution as propelled by class interests, scholars such as Labrousse, Braudel, and Vovelle insisted that the Revolution had to be studied within the framework of long-term economic, religious, or cultural trends. A smaller group that included Soboul, Cobban, Palmer, Godechot, and Furet called for a radical reinterpretation of the event and its significance. Even so, for most historians the general assessment of the Revolution as the principal catalyst of modernity remains undiminished.[6] Among Jewish historians, too,

---

5 See Gilbert Cahen, "La Région Lorraine" in *Histoire des Juifs en France*, ed. Bernhard Blumenkranz (Toulouse, 1972); Samuel Kerner, "La vie quotidienne de la communauté juive de Metz au dix-huitième siécle (á partir du Pinkas inédit de cette communauté, 1749–1789)," (Thèse de Doctorat de 3e cycle, Paris, 1979); Abraham Cahen, "Le rabbinat de Metz pendant la période française, 1567–1871," *REJ* 7 (1884) 103–15, 204–26; 8 (1884) 225–74; 12 (1886) 283–97; 13 (1886) 105–26, and Roger Clément, *La Condition des Juifs de Metz dans l'Ancien Régime* (Paris, 1903). Schwarzfuch's most important studies devoted to the Jews in pre-revolutionary Alsace and Lorraine include *Le "Memorbuch" de Metz (vers 1575–1742)* (Metz, 1971), which he edited; idem, "Takkanot of the Jewish Community of Augny, Adjacent to Metz (1767)" [Hebrew], *Asufot* 8 (1994): 387–99; idem, "Three Documents from the Lives of the Jewish Communities in Alsace-Lorraine" [Hebrew], *Michael* 4 (1976): 9–31; idem, ed., *Le Registre de correspondence de la communauté juive de Lorraine. Copies des lettres des années 1783–1791* (Jerusalem, 2003); idem, "Regulations of the Nancy Community on the Eve of the French Revolution" [Hebrew], *Kobeẓ 'al Yad* 17 (2003): 289–46; idem, "La succession du Chaagat Arieh (1785–1786)," *REJ* 175:3–4 (2016): 309–65. On individual communities, see the valuable studies published by Moïse Ginsburger in *Revue des études juives* in the early twentieth century, and as separate monographs; Pierre-André Meyer, *La Communauté juive de Metz au XVIII siècle* (Nancy, 1993); Françoise Job, *Les Juifs de Lunéville aux XVIIIe et XIXe siècles* (Nancy, 1989); and idem, *Les Juifs de Nancy du XIIe au XXe siècle* (Nancy, 1991). On the state of the various Jewish community archives, see Zosa Szajkowski, *Franco-Judaica* (New York, 1962), xxiii.

6 Georges Lefebvre, *The Coming of the French Revolution* (Princeton, 1975), trans. R. R. Palmer. The list of historians who argued for *la long durée* approach include Ernest Labrousse, Fernand Braudel, Michel Vovelle, and members of the Annales School. Those who advanced revisionist interpretations of the Revolution included Albert Soboul, Alfred Cobban, Robert Palmer, Jacques Godechot, and François Furet, to name only most celebrated. For a review of these and other approaches, see Claude Langlois, "The French Revolution and 'Revisionism,'" *The History Teacher* 23:4 (August 1990): 395–404. Emblematic of the overarching trend is the

the focus on the political struggle for civic equality and the effects of the revolutionary upheaval in the nineteenth century has predominated, at the expense of sustained investigation of Jewish life in the pre-revolutionary era. This trend apparently has rested on the assumption that the cultural and religious traditions of the ancien régime were rendered obsolete by the powerful forces unleashed in 1789.[7]

The enduring impact of the Revolution has tended to blind modern historians to many of the most revealing aspects of French Jewish culture that include religious rites, liturgical traditions, and the rabbinic scholarship of the region. In its appraisal of pre-revolutionary cultural traditions, Franco-Jewish historiography has, to a remarkable degree, mirrored the perspective of those Jews who first bore the title *citoyens* and of the generations that followed. This growing detachment from the rich communal history of the Jews and their cultural universe confirms the observation attributed to Louis Althusser and to François Furet, that history began with the French Revolution—that, in Furet's words, "beginning in 1789, the obsession with origins, underlying the thread of all national history, came to be centered precisely on the Revolutionary break ... 1789 became the birth date, the year zero, of a new world founded on equality, the substitution of one birth date for another, in other words, the definition in time of a new national identity."[8]

For the next two centuries, generations of French Jews would recall the Revolution and the Constituent Assembly vote to admit their ancestors to citizenship as a momentous turning point, and they would view themselves as conclusive evidence of its transformative power. For enthusiasts of nearly every stripe, the Revolution was draped in the imagery of the Sinaitic revelation and was construed in messianic-redemptive terms. Revolutionary ideologues chose the Tablets of the Law to frame the Declaration of the Rights of Man and of the Citizen. This iconic image of the Decalogue adorned the French Revolution in a mantle of the sacred. For Jews, this was the beginning of an interpretive tradition that identified the ideals of Judaism with those of the Revolution. Memories of this historic transformation were rooted in an abiding sense of optimism that credited the Revolution with ending centuries of degradation, discrimination, and social exclusion. The idea of the Revolution as the starting point of history has been closely correlated to the disdain for the

---

title and contents of the volume edited by Ferenc Fehér, *The French Revolution and the Birth of Modernity* (Berkeley, 1990).

7 See François Furet, "Ancien Régime," in *A Critical Dictionary of the French Revolution*, ed. François Furet and Mona Ozouf (Cambridge, MA), 604.

8 François Furet, *Reinterpreting the French Revolution* (Cambridge, 1981), 2.

history of the pre-revolutionary era.[9] Historical research on the Jews of France has tended to take its cue in large measure from this thinking.[10]

Critical study of Jewish law, initiated by the early nineteenth century *Wissenschaft des Judentums* movement, concentrated on rabbinic literature, principally talmudic and midrashic sources. Medieval codes and commentaries began to receive greater attention in the twentieth century but remained largely ignored by historians. In the last six or seven decades, scholars have expanded their sources further to include rabbinic responsa literature. Two other sources, communal registers and the proceedings of rabbinic and lay courts, have been added more recently. Ideally, these three types of legal sources ought to be read together. To be sure, each was produced by a particular professional class (rabbinic jurists, lay officials, and rabbinic judges, respectively), embodied discrete functions, and signaled different levels of authority. But they all were the product of interdependent constituencies for which the law served as an instrument of social and religious objectives, though specific goals and means to attain them varied widely. It is equally apparent that none operated in complete isolation from the others. The interrelationship among these sources and their intertextual links offer a key to understanding the intricacies of Jewish law in the modern era, moving from theoretical concepts to practical rulings, and providing a window on the range of social concerns valued

9 See Patrice Higonnet, *Goodness Beyond Virtue: Jacobins during the French Revolution* (Cambridge, MA, 1998), 137–40.

10 See Renée Neher-Bernheim, "The Tables of the Law: One of the Symbols of the French Revolution," *Jewish Art* 16–17 (1990–91): 82–91, and Ronald Schechter, "The Holy Mountain and the French Revolution," *Historical Reflections* 40:2 (Summer 2014): 78–107. During the Bourbon Restoration, Joseph Salvador argued that Mosaic legal institutions were permeated with the principles of the Revolution. See Joseph Salvador, *Loi du Moïse* (Paris, 1822), and *Histoire des Institutions de Moïse et du peuple Hébreu*, 3 vols. (Paris, 1828). On Salvador, see Michael Graetz, *The Jews in Nineteenth Century France: From the French Revolution to the Alliance Israélite Universelle* (Stanford, CA, 1996), 163–93. The assertion of parallels between the Revolution and the Sinaitic revelation, and between the bestowal of civic emancipation and the exodus from Egypt, were, by the first quarter of the nineteenth century, a common theme in rabbinic sermons and artistic representations, much as was the claim that the Revolution was the fulfillment of the Judaic ideals of justice and progress. On the general trend to endow the Revolution with a messianic ideology, see Jacob Talmon, *Political Messianism: The Romantic Phase* (New York, 1960). For views of the Revolution as a messianic and revelatory event, see the remarks of Adolphe Crémieux, quoted in S. Posener, Adolphe Crémieux 2 vols. (Paris, 1943), 2:149, 220; Michael Marrus, *The Politics of Assimilation: A Study of the French Jewish Community at the Time of the Dreyfus Affair* (Oxford, 1971), 90–92, 106–107. For examples of early nineteenth-century works that stressed the centrality of emancipation, see Léon Halévy, *Résumé de l'histoire des Juifs modernes* (Paris, 1828) and Lion-Mayer Lambert, *Précis de l'histoire des hébreux depuis le patriarche Abraham jusqu'en 1840* (Metz, 1840).

by historians. Responsa, communal legislation, and court records together permit a close examination of the day-to-day activities of the Jewish community of Metz with respect to the family, commercial exchange, real estate transactions, and inheritance—and how these fields of law functioned in real life. These records offer a glimpse of communal life, of the public policy concerns that occupied leaders, of the lives of individuals and families of various socio-economic levels as they endeavored to meet the economic challenges of a pre-industrial society, and the struggles they faced as members of a minority population.

The nexus between legal ideas and their institutional expression illustrates how law is conceived as both a social and an intellectual enterprise, a distinction that is commonly drawn between external and internal legal history. External legal history is concerned with the history of law as embedded in its context, tracing social, economic, political, and cultural factors that have contributed to the development of a legal system and that elucidate the setting in which decision makers lived. Internal legal history, by contrast, is the history of law and legal rules. Its sources are codes, legal expositions, court records, and legislation; its practitioners in late medieval and early modern Europe were scholars trained in law, judges assigned the task of judicial decision making, and lay officials who bore increasing responsibility for drafting communal legislation.[11]

Taken together, external and internal legal history invite engagement with (a) the history of legal ideas; (b) the success or failure of attempts to institutionalize those ideas in societal structures; and (c) efforts to account for the development of law by considering the historical context. Two aspects of historical context require greater attention: historicist trends that are internal to the law; and the various ways that the law responds to social, economic, cultural, and political changes. The two offer a perspective on the emergence of novel legal mechanisms in response to new conditions. These trends are most pronounced when viewed within the continuum that links codificatory literature, rabbinic responsa, and judicial decisions.

Rabbinic Responsa Literature

Responsa literature is the richest and most reliable published resource for reconstructing the history of Jewish law. Structured as answers to queries

11 David Ibbetson, "What Is Legal History a History of?," in *Law and History*, ed. Andrew Lewis and Michael Lobban (Oxford, 2004), 33–40.

submitted by rabbinic peers or by judges to halakhic authorities (*posekim*), responsa address a wide range of ritual and civil concerns that touch on daily life. As a rule, responsa advance legal opinions based on classical sources. They typically list the interpretive steps that led a *posek* to his decision, and they include details of where a ruling stood in relation to earlier opinions.[12] They contain valuable details relating to the *Sitz im Leben* and to historical events. For example, much has been learned from responsa referring to the Ancona boycott, the impact of the Chmielnicki uprising of 1648–49 and the Thirty Years War, notwithstanding their questionable reliability and potential pitfalls as historical sources.[13] But even in those instances when rabbinic responsa appeared detached from daily affairs, they offer a valuable perspective on the history of the legal issues under discussion, especially when jurists endeavor to take account of the relevant talmudic and medieval halakhic sources. Particularly in the last half-century, responsa have gained wide recognition for the light they shed on patterns of communal leadership, the complexities of economic pursuits, the role of religion in daily life, and relations with neighboring gentile populations and ruling authorities.

With the publication of Jacob Katz's *Tradition and Crisis* and Haim Hillel Ben-Sasson's *Hagut ve-Hanhagah* sixty years ago, rabbinic responsa gained wide recognition as a valuable historical source for the study of late medieval and early modern Jewish history. The two works, composed by eminent Israeli scholars, drew heavily on this literature and from ethical-moral writings as well to reconstruct patterns of leadership and authority in Ashkenazic communities, to probe deep-seated social and religious tensions, and to examine the relations between Jews and the surrounding general society and culture. Over the past several decades, and especially with the establishment of the Bar-Ilan University Responsa Project in 1963, historians have gained easier access to rabbinic responsa and have employed these sources to measure, substantiate or disprove the impact of major historical events and trends. The spread of Sabbatianism, the reception of the Enlightenment, the decline of rabbinic authority, and the first stirrings of secularization are several of the major themes

12 Berachyahu Lifschitz, "The Legal Status of the Responsa Literature," in *Authority, Process and Method: Studies in Jewish Law*, ed. Ḥanina Ben-Menaḥem and Neil S. Hecht (Amsterdam, 1998), 59–100.

13 See, for example, Samuel de Medina, *Resp. Maharashdam* (Salonika, 1595), *Ḥoshen Mishpat*, nos. 54 and 59, and Gershon Ashkenazi, *Resp. 'Avodat ha-Gershuni* (Frankfurt, 1699), nos. 36 and 94. On the use of the de Medina responsa, along with others, see Marc Saperstein, "Martyrs, Merchants and Rabbis: Jewish Communal Conflict as Reflected in the Responsa on the Boycott of Ancona," *Jewish Social Studies* 43:3/4 (1981): 215–28.

in early modern Jewish history that have been studied profitably with the assistance of responsa.[14]

Through the study of responsa, the social and economic context of legal decision-making has come to be viewed as crucial to the development of Jewish law. While the "law on the books"—broadly defined as talmudic literature, commentaries, and novellae, in addition to medieval codes and commentaries—is a natural point of departure for examining the foundations of judicial rulings, responsa offer perspective on how the law was interpreted in light of real-life circumstances. Modern scholars recognize that responsa have an advantage over more standard sources of law insofar as they alone shed light on the adaptability of law to change. Typically, it is the inquiry posed by the questioner, rather than the response, that contains evidence of divergences of the law as practiced from prescribed law.

Rabbinic responsa offer valuable details of the judicial process that are unavailable from other sources. These include the collection of evidence and testimony, examination of witnesses, and administration of oaths. Some responsa reveal evidence of the underlying rationale of a halakhic decision. When *dayanim* turned to a *posek* with a query or for guidance concerning a case before a *beit din* or a *dayan*, responsa record details of the adjudication process that would otherwise be hidden from view. Such details are important for understanding the respective judicial roles of judges and jurists, and, more generally, the workings of the justice system in Jewish communities. Data unearthed both from communal records and from rabbinic responsa reveal disparities between early modern judges and jurists and their respective views of how judicial rulings are decided.[15] Nevertheless, though critically important

14 Jacob Katz, *Masoret u-Mashber: ha-Hevrah ha-Yehudit be-Motsa'ei Yemei ha-Beinayim* (Jerusalem, 1958). English edition: *Tradition and Crisis: Jewish Society at the End of the Middle Ages*, trans. Bernard D. Cooperman (New York, 1993); Haim Hillel Ben-Sasson, *Hagut ve-Hanhagah: Hashkefoteihem ha-Hevrati'ot shel Yehudei Polin be-Shilhei Yemei ha-Beinayim*, [*Thought and Leadership: The Social Views of Polish Jewry at the End of the Middle Ages*] (Jerusalem, 1959). For the debate between Katz and Ben-Sasson on responsa as historical sources, see Ben-Sasson, "Concepts and Reality in Jewish History at the End of the Middle Ages" [Hebrew], *Tarbiz* 29 (1960): 297–312; Katz, "On Halakha and Derush as Historical Sources" [Hebrew], *Tarbiz* 30 (1960): 62–68; and Ben-Sasson's rejoinder, 69–72. For additional examples of the use of responsa as an historical source, see Salo W. Baron, *The Jewish Community: Its History and Structure to the American Revolution*, 3 vols. (Philadelphia, 1942). Also see Soloveitchik, *The Use of Responsa as Historical Source*. On differences between responsa and court records in the realms of law and history, see Fram, *A Window on their World*, 68–86.

15 See Jay R. Berkovitz, "Competing Perspectives on Legal Decision-Making in Early Modern Ashkenaz." *Jewish History* 31:1–2 (2017): 149–71.

for the intellectual history of Jewish law, the legal rulings and interpretive strategies of the responsa are of limited value to historians insofar as they offer little consistent evidence of how the law was practiced.[16]

The number of printed volumes of responsa issued in Metz and Alsace in the eighteenth century, though relatively small, contains valuable information concerning local and regional legal issues. Until 1764, when the Hebrew press in Metz opened, works produced by heads of the rabbinic court or judges in Metz or in Alsace were printed in Germany. All told, the works published throughout the century and some that remained in manuscript until later include the following: Gershon Ashkenazi, *Resp. 'Avodat ha-Gershuni* (Frankfurt, 1699); Jacob Reischer, *Resp. Shevut Ya'akov*, pts. 1–3 (Halle, 1710), pt. 2 (Offenbach, 1719), and (Metz, 1789); Joseph Steinhardt, *Resp. Zikhron Yosef* (Fürth, 1773); Aryeh Leib Gûnzberg, *Resp. Sha'agat Aryeh* (Frankfurt-an-der-Oder, 1755); Gershon Koblenz, *Resp. Kiryat Ḥannah* (Metz, 1785); Joshua Heschel Lvov, *Resp. Penei Levanah* (Jerusalem, 2017); and Jacob Meyer, *Resp. Emet le-Yaakov* (Jerusalem, 2006). In addition, works composed in neighboring regions, such as Ya'ir Hayyim Bacharach's *Resp. Ḥavvot Ya'ir* (Frankfurt, 1699), include especially pertinent material for the legal history of the Jews in Metz and Alsace, as do the seven volumes of *novellae* published by Aaron Worms, titled *Me'orei Or* (Metz, 1790–1831).[17]

Communal Registers (Pinkasim)

Several types of community registers were produced in the early modern period. These include *pinkesei kahal* (communal registers), *pinkesei beit knesset*

16 On differences between responsa and court records in the realms of law and history, see Fram, *A Window on their World*, 68–86.

17 Two of the volumes of responsa listed here were only recently published. Jacob Meyer (1739–1830), rabbi in Rixheim, Niedernai, and of Strasbourg, left a large manuscript collection of responsa that was published by Machon Beit Aharon in 2006 under the title *Emet le-Yaakov*. Joshua Heschel Lvov (1693–1771), served as *dayan* in Metz for nine years (ca. 1714–1723) during Jacob Reischer's tenure as *av beit din*. Lvov's manuscript, *Penei Levanah*, was published by Machon Yerushalayim in 2017, ed. Ya'akov Yehoshua Buksbaum. Although Aaron Worms' *Me'orei Or* does not contain responsa, it contains valuable material concerning the religious life and practices of Metz Jews. His seven-volume opus was published under the following titles: *Me'orei Or*, vols. 1–3 (Metz, 1790–93); *Be'er-Sheva* (Metz, 1819); *'Od la-Mo'ed* (Metz, 1822); *Bin Nun* (Metz, 1827); *Ken Tahor* (Metz, 1831). On Worms, see Jay R. Berkovitz, "Authority and Innovation at the Threshold of Modernity: The *Me'orei Or* of Rabbi Aaron Worms of Metz," in *Me'ah She'arim: Studies in Medieval Jewish Spiritual Life in Memory of Isadore Twersky* (Jerusalem, 2001), 249–85.

(synagogue registers), *pinkasim* of various confraternities, *pinkesei ḥeshbonot* (account books), and *pinkasim* containing wills. No comparable registers have survived from the Middle Ages. The relatively small number of communal documents from the premodern period suggests that although communities maintained detailed tax records, it is unlikely that they kept more comprehensive records regularly or systematically, if at all. The earliest surviving *pinkasim*, from Germany and Italy, date from the early sixteenth century. Ashkenazic *pinkasim* likely were modeled after new administrative initiatives undertaken by early modern states. They contained communal bylaws (*takkanot*), detailed regulations concerning elections and tax assessment, election results, and rabbinic contracts. These registers were written in a language that combined Yiddish and Hebrew vocabulary, at times organized in accordance with Yiddish syntax and in other instances in keeping with Hebrew sentence structure.[18]

In the early modern era, autonomous communities enacted comprehensive legislation to administer the full range of religious and civil affairs.

18 For a detailed summary of the history of Ashkenazic *pinkasim*, see Stefan Litt, *Pinkas, Kahal, and the Mediene: The Records of Dutch Ashkenazi Communities in the Eighteenth Century as Historical Sources* (Leiden, 2008), 7–20. The largest number of eighteenth-century Metz *pinkasim* is held at the Jewish Theological Seminary of America in New York. These include the following: account book leaves, 1765, ms. 8343; Pinkas of synagogue in Metz, ms. 8475; ms. 3951; list of taxpayers, ms 8349; record book, daily expenses (1701), ms. 8349; taxes' roll of the Jews in the district of Metz (1785), ms. 8349; état de contribuables: list of taxpayers to the Jewish community of Metz (n.d.), ms. 8349; account book of taxation of kosher meat sold in Metz (1729, 1734), ms. 8349; Pinkas Kahal of Metz, ms. 8136, ms. 3704, and ms. 3789; tax records: nombre des chefs de familles des Juifs habitans de la ville de Metz, 18th century (1819), ms. 8349, ms. 9835; Metz account book, ms. 8137; Pinkas of the women's society, ms. 3953; Pinkas Tzava'ot (Wills), ms. 8855 and ms. 9835; account books for the collection of the Brancas tax (1753–1758 and 1772), ms. 8349; list of taxpayers, Pinkas Gaba'im of Metz (n.d.), ms. 8539. By comparison to Metz, the *pinkasim* of Moravia, of the Council of the Four Lands, and of Poznan, use Yiddish frequently, often almost interchangeably with Hebrew. The Frankfurt rabbinic court diary, like the Metz Pinkas Beit Din, was written mainly in Hebrew, but it contains far more Yiddish phraseology. See *Takkanot Medinat Mehrin* (*Constitutiones Congressus Generalis Judaeorum Moraviensium, 1650–1748*), ed. Israel Halpern (Jerusalem, 1952); *The Pinkas of the Va'ad Arba'ah Aratzot*, ed. Israel Halperin and Israel Bartal (Jerusalem, 1989); and *The Pinkas ha-Kesherim shel Kehilat Poznan*, ed. Dov Avron (Jerusalem, 1966). Prior to World War II twenty-three *pinkasim* were listed in the Landman inventory at the Metz community archives, but after the war they could not be located. Concerning the Metz communal register, which covers the years 1749–1789, see Schwarzfuchs, introduction to *Le Registre des délibérations*, 55. On Metz as a model for other communities, the *Conseil souverain* confirmed Rabbi Samuel Sanvil Weyl's authority in Haute-Alsace in 1719 by stating that the royal *lettres patentes* "conformed to the custom of Metz;" cited in Moïse Ginsburger, "Samuel Sanvil Weil: Rabbin de la Haute et Basse-Alsace (1711–1753)," *REJ* 96 (1933): 61.

Communal law, though drawing on talmudic and medieval Halakhah, developed more freely in the public and private law sectors. Public civil law governed the overall administration of each community, its elections, tax assessment and collection, and the relations of individuals to the governing authority. Private civil law concerned property, commercial transactions, family, and inheritance. Ritual law encompassed daily observances, regulations concerning Sabbath and holidays, dietary restrictions, prayer, and purification rites, and related as well to the main elements of family law, particularly marriage and divorce. The governance structure and institutional framework of the community provided a natural setting for the development of private and public law, whereas ritual law remained principally under the supervision and control of rabbis. *Posekim* issued legal rulings in all areas of Jewish law, and these were frequently published in collections of rabbinic responsa.

Seventeenth- and eighteenth-century communal registers make a compelling case for the authority of lay legislation. The robustness of lay legislation among Jews in western Europe was a resounding echo of the movement that James Whitman has called "customary-law constitutionalism." Its origins can be traced to the French state, though by the mid- to late seventeenth century its political roots were doubtless more broadly based. The legitimacy of lay governance was boosted by the upsurge of customary law in France and Germany. In the estimation of an increasing number of rabbinic authorities, lay authority was imperative to assist the community in carrying out the range of functions that its members entrusted to it. For some, lay sovereignty extended to the community's absolute right to regulate behavior, even when the legal methods employed were at odds with religious tradition. Communal legislation no longer drew its authority solely from the Jewish tradition but also from a set of broader assumptions concerning the importance of maintaining the common welfare and preserving the social order.

Lay and Rabbinic Court Records

Both in their own right and in rabbinic courts, communal norms commanded the weight of judicial authority in Metz. Indeed, late seventeenth century ideas evolved into a philosophy of Jewish law that became even more responsive to social, economic, and cultural shifts a century later. Records of the Metz rabbinic court reflect heightened economic collaboration with the non-Jewish population, a phenomenon consistent with the legal pluralism that prevailed in mid-eighteenth century France. In the rabbinic court, this legal pluralism found expression in the distinctly Jewish notion that divine law is fashioned through human ingenuity.

Rabbinic court records bridge the divide that commonly separates the disciplines of law and history. Accordingly, in recent years, early modern rabbinic courts have attracted increased attention. Although most court registers, such as those from Altona-Hamburg, Niedernai, Prague, and Siebież, exist in manuscript only, the Frankfurt rabbinic court diary recorded by Rabbi Hayyim Gundersheim and the proceedings of the Beit Din of Metz were published in 2012 and 2014 respectively. Scholars now have access to a more substantial corpus of judicial sources.[19] General historians, especially, recognize court records as a valuable source for understanding economic history and the dynamic role of law in society. As Anthony Grafton has suggested, "[t]he courtroom and the lawyer's study have turned out to be historical alembics where the methods of social and intellectual historians can be mingled in new forms, producing results of unsuspected richness."[20]

---

19 Exceptions to the general neglect of rabbinic court records include Mordechai Nadav, "Pinkas Beit ha-Din shel Kehillat Siebież, White Russia" [Hebrew], *Kiryat Sefer* 36 (1961): 410–16, 535–41; Edward Fram, *A Window on Their World: The Court Diaries of Rabbi Ḥayyim Gundersheim. Frankfurt am Main, 1773–1794* (Cincinnati, 2012), and Jay R. Berkovitz, *Protocols of Justice: The Pinkas of the Rabbinic Court of Metz, 1771–1789*, two vols. (Leiden, 2014).

20 See Anthony Grafton, "Introduction: Notes from Underground and on Cultural Transmission," in *The Transmission of Culture in Early Modern Europe*, ed. Anthony Grafton and Ann Blair (Philadelphia, 1990), 4. Outstanding research by scholars of medieval French, Italian, and Spanish Jewish history has provided very fine examples of the use to which court records may be put, but unfortunately these studies have failed to awaken more than passing interest in rabbinic courts of the early modern era. For recent historical treatment of courts and the use of court records in the writing of French history, see the following: David A. Bell, *Lawyers and Citizens: The Making of a Political Elite in Old Regime France* (New York, 1994); Breen, *Law, City, and King: Legal Culture, Municipal Politics, and State Formation in Early Modern Dijon*; Anthony Crubaugh, *Balancing the Scales of Justice: Local Courts and Rural Society in Southwestern France, 1750–1800* (University Park, PA, 2001); Suzanne Desan, *The Family on Trial in Revolutionary France* (Berkeley, 2004); Sylvie Perrier, *Des enfances protégées: La tutelle des mineurs en France (XVII*e*–XVIII*e *siècles)* (Saint-Denis, 1998); and Sarah C. Maza, *Private Lives and Public Affairs: The Causes Célèbres of Prerevolutionary France* (Berkeley and Los Angeles, 1993). For examples of work by Jewish historians who have made excellent use of court records, see Rebecca Winer, *Women, Wealth, and Power in Perpignan, c. 1250–1300* (Aldershot, U.K., 2006); Elka Klein, "Splitting Heirs: Patterns of Inheritance among Barcelona's Jews," *Jewish History* 16 (2002): 49–71; Rena Lauer, *Colonial Justice and the Jews of Venetian Crete* (Philadelphia, 2019); Jessica Marglin, *Across Legal Lines: Jews and Muslims in Modern Morocco* (New Haven, 2016); and Noa Shashar, "Agunot and the Men who Vanished in the Ashkenazi Realm, 1648–1850" [Hebrew] (Ph.D. diss., Hebrew Univ., 2012). Regarding the pattern of meetings

The Pinkas of the Metz Beit Din is the single largest collection of rabbinic court records currently in print. Two leather-bound volumes of 241 cream-color folio pages record 1063 judicial cases in approximately 400,000 words written in a semi-cursive Ashkenazic script. Hebrew is the predominant language, with no evidence whatsoever of Yiddish syntax. In this respect it differs from the Pinkas Kahal of Metz, which contains more Yiddish, albeit in a largely Hebrew text. Its highly compressed style, punctuated by numerous abbreviations and often unfamiliar subjects, its occasional illegibility, technical terminology, and frequent use of non-Hebrew vocabulary (mainly French, German, and Yiddish) all combine to pose daunting textual challenges.[21]

The Pinkas Beit Din preserves court deliberations beginning in July 1771. Earlier records were kept unsystematically.[22] The final recorded case is dated 7 Tammuz 5549, corresponding to 1 July 1789, just two weeks prior to the storming of the Bastille. An additional thirteen cases that can be documented at least through January 1790 attest to the institutional resilience of the Metz court amid the political turmoil that enveloped France in the summer of 1789 and the periodic anti-Jewish riots in Alsace and Lorraine in the autumn of that year.[23] Extensive evidence of Jewish acculturation and legal integration in the latter decades of the ancien régime provided by the Pinkas calls for reassessment of commonly held views, including the nature of Jewish communal autonomy in the pre-Revolutionary period and the attribution of Jewish assimilation wholly to the post-Revolutionary era.

---

of the rabbinic courts in Prague, we know that twelve judges served on the lower court, which convened each day between the afternoon and evening prayer services. Five judges sat on the higher court, which ruled on cases of matrimonial law and served as a court of appeals. For additional details, see Gutmann Klemperer, "The Rabbis of Prague: A History of the Rabbinate of Prague from the Death of Rabbi Loewe B. Bezalel (The High Rabbi Loewe) to the Present (1609–1879)," *Historia Judaica* 13 (1951): 76–77.

21 For details on the transcription process, see the preface to *Protocols of Justice*.

22 Several isolated cases that were heard by the Metz Beit Din prior to July 1771 are preserved in Archives départementales de la Moselle, Consistoire israélite 17J23 and 17J24. These include a case that came before the Beit Din of Rabbi Gershon Ashkenazi in 1690 (Cons. isr.17J23), and several cases that were heard by the Beit Din of Rabbi Shmuel Hilman in 1753, 1763, and 1764 (Cons. israélite. 17J24). Among the latter is a judgment concerning the status of three wills prepared by Froumette, widow of Eli Levi. See PKM, 15a. Cases that came before the Beit Din headed by Rabbi Aryeh Loeb Günzberg in 1769 and 1770 are also included in Cons. isr. 17J24, as are related materials, e.g. an argument written by Rabbi Mordechai Morhange (Merchingen) in 1788 concerning the modification of charitable bequests listed in the will prepared by his grandfather.

23 A dozen loose pages containing thirteen cases preserved together with the bound volumes of the Pinkas date from August 1789 to January See *Protocols of Justice*, Appendix 1. For a discussion of these riots, see below, chapter 2.

Records of the Metz Beit Din offer a basis for comparing its judicial activity with that of contemporary French courts. In the second half of the eighteenth century, French courts were not limited to adjudicating lawsuits and settling disputes concerning debts, inheritance, and property, which were in the category of *justice contentieuse* (contentious justice). There were matters related to *justice gracieuse* (noncontentious justice), which addressed important social needs, including marriage registration, guardians, probate inventories, and land transfers, like the affixing of the official seals. Cases in the former category were the most numerous in the civil justice archives. From all indications, cases involving indebtedness, especially in the eastern part of France, increased throughout the eighteenth century while the number of disputes relating to property or moral issues declined.[24] As in the French courts, the cases that were heard by the Metz Beit Din resolve themselves into the aforementioned types and further divide into several subdivisions. As a result of significant overlap, the percentages are unavoidably imprecise. Many cases encompassed multiple issues—usually a primary and a secondary subject, but sometimes more—so that the total exceeds one hundred percent. Litigation to recover loans and to salvage other outstanding monetary obligations accounts for the bulk of the cases brought before the court—roughly fifty-five percent. Commercial disputes, some of which involved the retrieval of debt, account for approximately twenty-five percent, and of the latter, roughly ten percent involved partnership disagreements. Approximately fifty percent of the cases in the Metz rabbinic court register are in some manner family-related; these include disputes concerning betrothals, dowries, marital property, inheritance, guardianship, and spousal rifts. Community-related issues constitute approximately five percent of the total. Intended as no more than a rough outline, the foregoing breakdown approximates the range of judicial activity encompassed in the Beit Din.

However, in one important respect the Metz Pinkas Beit Din differed from French court records. French courts occupied a more conspicuous role in public life and served a public function. They therefore took up high profile cases, since they were as concerned with moral lessons as with disposition of particular legal disputes. According to Roger Chartier, French courts of the second half of the eighteenth century were no longer "a viable site of power," but they remained influential in shaping the French collective imagination because they were so prominently associated by the public with moral depravity and wastefulness. Sara Maza has gone further by examining various *causes célèbres*

24 See Elise M. Dermineur, "The Civil Judicial System in France." *Frühneuzeit-Info* 23 (2012): 45–52, and Breen, "Law, Society, and the State in Early Modern France," 380.

in the latter decades of the ancien régime. She has shown how private affairs translated longstanding political divisions into personal and familial terms.[25] And since the French legal tradition placed great emphasis on the publication of landmark decisions as a tool to educate lawyers in jurisprudential methods, the public gained access as well to what transpired in the courtroom.[26]

By contrast, Beit Din rulings never saw the light of day. There is no evidence that the Metz rabbinic court records were at all known to the public—either Jewish or French—nor to any individuals outside the relatively small circle of jurists who may have consulted them. Owing to their dubious relationship to public history, rabbinic court records radiate a distinctly different image than do the French courts. The Pinkas Beit Din does not simply document case disposition but offers detailed presentations of arguments advanced by each of the litigants. It adjudicates mainly personal disputes relating to debt litigation, property disputes, contractual disagreements, inheritance conflicts, and its rulings are robust. Page after page, the Pinkas records the court's efforts to resolve cases either by determining which of the claims it heard was most persuasive or by crafting a settlement acceptable to both parties. Of particular importance is the fact that rabbinic court records preserve the voices of litigants, if only indirectly, alongside the judicial rulings. Rabbinic court records only rarely refer to celebrated historical events of the sort noted above. In fact, very few cases that came before the Metz Beit Din gained public notoriety of any kind outside the rabbinic court room. In rare cases, a case was appealed to a higher court, although this assessment could change once the civil court records are examined closely.[27]

Brimming with details of commercial transactions involving Jews and non-Jews, family law, inheritance, modes of jurisprudence, and recourse to civil courts, the Pinkas of the Beit Din offers historians a veritable embarrassment of riches.[28] To marshal this myriad of details requires an analytic framework

25 See Maza, *Private Lives and Public Affairs.*

26 See Roger Chartier, *The Cultural Origins of the French Revolution* (Durham and London, 1991), 179–80.

27 For an example of a case that was appealed to the Metz Parlement, see below, chapter 6, the discussion of 1786 judgment concerning the estate of Samuel Jonas Lévi.

28 See Samuel Kerner, "Les registres inédits des tribunaux rabbiniques de Metz (1771–1779) et de Niedernai (1755–1777)," *REJ* 138 (1979): 495–97. Sephardic communities in early modern Europe did not, as a rule, maintain separate courts dealing with civil cases. The first direct evidence when Bordeaux's rabbinic court started to function was in 1755 in the communal register. Questions concerning marriage, divorce, and certification of *shoḥatim* (ritual slaughterers) were typical of the cases brought before the Beit Din. As a rule, litigants submitted their complaints to communal leaders who would then decide whether a case deserved to be heard by the rabbinic court. Divorce cases were under the exclusive authority

capable of identifying wider patterns that can encompass the large array of disjointed and fragmented cases recorded in the protocol. The challenge is to extract something of historical value from the wealth of detail in these economic and domestic disputes. So, for example, what can be learned from seemingly mundane debtor/creditor cases should not be undervalued. More than simply collection cases, they tell us a great deal about what constituted social capital in the Metz community and what sorts of commercial conduct was respected or stigmatized.[29] In this respect Beit Din records differ from, and are more informative than, other near-contemporary documentary sources. In many instances this role has gone unnoticed when economic data are detached from the social and cultural context to which they belong, and there rabbinic court protocols may appear wanting. Moreover, Beit Din records appear to be deficient when compared to the memoir literature and personal letters that have survived from other communities or date from other times. Indeed, the contrast to the memoirs of the renowned Glikl Hameln, written more than a half-century earlier in the same Metz community, is rather striking. The valuable impressions of Jewish family and communal life that Glikl provided are nowhere to be found in the Pinkas, and the same could be said of her reflections on tensions between morality and piety, on the one hand, and commercial culture, on the other.[30] However, rabbinic court records have a different story to tell about, and often a unique perspective on, many of these very

of the Beit Din, whereas civil and criminal disputes were settled by arbitration before the *parnasim*. In the absence of governmental authorization to enforce their jurisdiction in civil affairs, Sephardic communities resorted to various forms of social pressure and moral suasion to maintain control over civil disputes, but their efforts were generally not successful. See Zvi Loker, "From Converso Congregation to Holy Community: The Shaping of the Jewish Community of Bordeaux during the 18th Century," [Hebrew] *Zion* 42 (1977): 56. See Simon Schwarzfuchs, ed., *Registre des délibérations de la Nation Juive Portugaise de Bordeaux* (1711–1787) (Paris, 1981). On the range of authority exercised by the Bordeaux Beit Din, see Zosa Szajkowski, "The Diaries of the Delegates of the Bordeaux Jews to the Malesherbes Commission (1788) and the National Assembly" [Hebrew], *Zion* 18 (1953): 40.

29 On the use of sources on credit and debt, see Philip T. Hoffman, *Growth in a Traditional Society: The French Countryside, 1450–1815* (Princeton, 1996), esp. 35–80; Philip T. Hoffman, Gilles Postel-Vinay and Jean-Laurent Rosenthal, "Private Credit Markets in Paris, 1690–1840," *The Journal of Economic History*, 52 (1992): 293–306. On credit and debt in the latter Middle Ages, see Daniel Lord Smail, *The Consumption of Justice: Emotions, Publicity, and Legal Culture in Marseille, 1264–1423* (Ithaca, NY, 2003). On several issues relating to theory, see Jay Smith, "No More Language Games: Words, Beliefs, and the Political Culture of Early Modern France," *American Historical Review* 102 (1997): 1413–44, and Clare Crowston, "Credit and the Metanarrative of Modernity," *French Historical Studies*, 34 (2011): 7–19.

30 Chava Turniansky, ed., *Memoirs of Glikl, 1691–1719* (Jerusalem, 2006).

same issues. In fact, without any comparable extant sources, such as diaries, memoirs, and letters, to offer insight into the private lives of Jews in the northeastern provinces of France, the importance of the Pinkas is immense.

As a rule, rabbinic court records offer a broader basis for reconstructing the various means of support and preponderant patterns of consumption—at least in the pre-revolutionary period—than any other available source. The economic data contained in the proceedings of the Metz Beit Din will doubtless prove invaluable in gauging the range and intensity of Jewish commercial activity in the pre-revolutionary era. But to fully exploit the rich sources contained in the Metz Pinkas, a range of analytical methods are needed to provide the context that is so often absent. In some instances, the tools of microhistory can be enlisted to fill in missing details from other sources or put cases together to get to the story that is not evident, especially where it may be possible to reconstruct the story behind the story by excavating personal tales and the cultural context of interpersonal relations.

It is apparent throughout the Beit Din protocols that details concerning the assumption of debt provide evidence of how individuals acquired daily necessities and endeavored to meet their obligations, especially at critical junctures in their lives. Equally important are the social connotations of credit and debt that were reflected in the esteem creditors gained through positive reputation, the honor that attached to debt repayment, or the stigma resulting from default. Universally indispensable across the social spectrum, credit and debt play a crucially important role in elaborating the human dimension of history.

Not normally associated with legal material but of particular value is what the Pinkas Beit Din has to tell us about the material culture of Metz Jewry and the human side of the law. Rabbinic court protocols contain vast resources with which one can gauge patterns of social, cultural, and material life in Metz and the surrounding countryside. Poignant images of individuals suffering poverty, and efforts to bring them relief, are recorded in communal sources of different types, as a case before the Beit Din in 1772 reveals about the difficult conditions of daily life and the policy questions they raised.[31] The Metz court records are also filled with resources for investigating the family, kinship, complexities of marriage, and women's roles. A profusion of details concerning the social and economic importance of betrothal agreements, dowries, marital property division, and inheritance arrangements represent a treasure trove of historical data. Particularly fascinating are cases that reveal the degree to which law, family, property, and business interests were tightly interwoven.

---

31 See PMBD, Vol. 1, pt. 1, no. 50, 15a. Cf. a case regarding the Hakhnassat Kallah Society, PMBD, Vol. 1, pt. 2, no. 58, 16b.

On occasion, the human story comes into view with unusual pathos, especially in cases of abandoned wives, young widows, and tales of deprivation. Several cases offer heartrending stories of women whose vulnerability was exposed by the death, illness, insolvency, or desertion of their husbands.[32]

Evidence of affluence and poverty may also be deduced from the size of the houses in which Jews lived, the dowries they gave their daughters, the size of their estates, and bequests to charitable projects. Equally instructive are the innumerable details concerning clothing, fabrics, jewelry, home furnishings, and the structural design of private dwellings. As Leora Auslander has observed, "it is in the everyday world that politics and the polity, economics and the economy, aesthetics and beauty, are concretized, experienced, and perhaps transformed—in short, lived."[33] Economic data contained in the Pinkas are most often embedded in the details of claims and counterclaims advanced by litigants or in the provisions set forth in marriage contracts, commercial and loan agreements, records of collateral held by creditors, probate inventories, lists of assets controlled by guardians, and partnership agreements.

Of particular note is the active participation of women in the judicial process and the Beit Din's recourse to assorted legal tools aiming to achieve desired goals. Legal mechanisms that came into play in response to evolving social and economic trends in the eighteenth century produced a measure of equality between husbands and wives that is apparent in numerous cases that came before the Beit Din. Accordingly, the picture that emerges from the court proceedings contrasts sharply with what has been construed on the basis of the prescriptive legal literature alone. This is clear, especially, from the importance attached to the work women performed beyond their domestic responsibilities. There is abundant evidence suggesting that wives borrowed and extended loans, occasionally without their husbands' authorization, to help support their families. The Beit Din records attest to the fact that they were entitled to possession of their assets and that patriarchal authority was not presumed to be inviolable. As borrowers and lenders, wives played an integral role in credit networks, ranging from formal *rentes* overseen by notaries to informal loans, pawning and barter. The rabbinic court recognized the autonomous loans of married women as binding for themselves and their husbands. To the extent that the ordinary lives of women in the early modern period have

32 See below, p. 344, for the cases of Miriam, a pregnant widow who came before the Beit Din claiming her *ketubah* and *tosefta*, and Rivka who had become destitute after her husband abandoned her and his family.

33 This quote appears in Leora Auslander, *Taste and Power: Furnishing Modern France* (Berkeley, 1996), 3.

suffered from a lack of attention, one trusts that the greater use of civil court records will go far in filling this gap in historical scholarship.[34]

While there is enormous value in the details of fashion, amusement, and cultural consumption, all of which signal the unremitting appeal of modern trends, this data must be historicized so that the voices and perspectives of those who were deeply absorbed in European culture, as well as the arguments advanced by their detractors, can be considered within a comparative analytical framework. Moreover, attention to structural issues and broader patterns of social change, and to gender as well, will enable scholars to assess how deviations in the eighteenth century compare to those of the medieval period and to corresponding patterns in contemporary Christian society. These steps are necessary to clarify to what degree social, cultural, and political forces shaped the local character of religious and secular pursuits. Efforts such as these will deepen our understanding of the complicated role of religion in modern society.[35] Seen in this light, sources pertaining to the humdrum of civil disputes certainly transcend what is conceived by many as narrowly "legal." To be sure, the limitations inherent in these records cannot be ignored, but owing to the dearth of sources pertaining to personal histories and family life in eighteenth-century Alsace and Lorraine, the Metz rabbinic court provides an unparalleled entrée into a world that has been largely hidden from sight.[36]

34 These findings are consistent with the work of Julie Hardwick, *Family Business: Litigation and the Political Economies of Daily Life in Early Modern France* (Oxford, 2009).

35 See the valuable discussion of how discourses of consumption have been entangled with the conceptualization of modernity in James Grehan, *Everyday Life and Consumer Culture in Eighteenth-Century Damascus* (Seattle, 2009).

36 Cf. Steven Wilf, "Law/Text/Past," *University of California Irvine Law Review* 543 (2011): 543–64. Several additional sources are crucial to the intricate history of Metz Jews. These include the French translation of Jewish civil law (*Recueil des lois, coûtumes et usages observés par les juifs de Metz*) produced by the Metz Jewish community at the urging of parliamentary and monarchical authorities; and the general literature of customs books, produced in Metz and the Moselle province, which are useful in establishing the wider legal context and in providing a valuable basis for comparative legal analysis. The customary law literature of Metz and the Moselle region is a valuable resource for understanding eighteenth-century customary law in relation to legal conventions practiced by the local Jewish population. The 1769 edition of the Metz *Coûtumes* is in the Special Collections of the Harvard Law School Library: *Coûtumes générales de la ville de Metz et pays-Messin: corrigées ensuite des résolutions des trois-etats de ladite ville, ès années 1616, 1617, & 1618. Nouvelle edition conforme à celle imprimée 1732* (Metz, 1769). For Jewish communal sources, see Pinkas Kahal of Metz (1749–1789), Arch. JTSA, and the Pinkas Ẓava'ot, Arch. JTSA, ms. 9835.

Law as a Cultural System

Within the larger corpus of Jewish legal literature, the standing of rabbinic court records is not clearly defined. They are unlike more standard legal sources that are either prescriptive (i.e., Codes) or are meant to address a newly presented question based on nuanced readings of earlier legal opinions. Beit Din records are unique in that they preserve the voices of the litigants, albeit at times imperfectly and unevenly, together with the rulings of the court.

To begin, we will address several threshold questions: (1) What authority did rabbinic court records have, and no less important, what authority did *batei din* have? (2) For whom were these records intended? (3) What prompted the decision to preserve the protocols of the Beit Din systematically, starting only in 1771 and not before? Scholars who have worked with court records provide some direction in answering these questions. In his detailed study of Neckarhausen, David Sabean advanced our understanding of the role of such records in preserving official memory. According to Sabean, there are three stages in this process: (a) recording the incident; (b) restaging the occurrence before the court in the presence of the various participants; and (c) its redaction to a standard 'case' by an official. Furthermore, Sabean found that many protocols were copied and sent to the city official or bailiff for further consideration, "and they were all examined in the periodic visitations. Each one, therefore, must also be considered as having been directed toward a higher audience, and even the form was affected by the relation."[37] It is highly unlikely that rabbinic courts were subject to lay review, though they appear to have followed communal legislation assiduously. Responsa literature, however, contains more explicit evidence of judicial review—albeit unofficial—conducted by *posekim* who looked over the procedural details and legalities of judgments issued by *dayanim* or rabbinic courts.[38]

Courts were an arena "where judges, lawyers, litigants, and communities came together to negotiate, contest, and use the law's symbolic and, at times, coercive authority." Justice was widely conceived as "a mode of social interaction between individuals, communities, and the state."[39] In the ancien régime, law served as a unifying force that produced, with varying degrees of success, a

---

37 David W. Sabean, in *Property, Production, and Family in Neckarhausen, 1700–1870*, 76–77.

38 For examples of review and criticism of rabbinic court decisions and judges, see Berkovitz, "Competing Perspectives on Legal Decision-Making," 165–70.

39 Hervé Piant, *Une justice ordinaire: justice civile et criminelle dans la prévôté royale de Vaucouleurs sous l'ancien régime* (Rennes, 2006). On the broader conceptual issues, see Lawrence Rosen, *Law as Culture: An Invitation* (Princeton, 2008).

shared culture and coherent community.[40] This was equally true in the Jewish court milieu. For the Jewish population of Metz and its environs, law would foster a concrete attachment to the society and culture from which they had been shunned. The unifying effect of law was even more pronounced, both on account of the autonomous powers it enjoyed and because the legislative authority and the judiciary were closely coordinated. Compared to the lower-level French civil courts (*bailliages*), the Beit Din was a highly accessible institution. It generally issued decisions without much delay, and the costs of litigation were modest.[41] In contrast to widespread dissatisfaction with the cumbersome, inefficient, and disordered court system of rural France,[42] contemporary sources do not record any criticism against judicial practices in the rabbinic court in Metz or elsewhere in Alsace and Lorraine. While silence alone is not proof, the number of cases—nearly sixty per year—recorded in the register of the Beit Din relative to the population of the community—somewhat less than 3,000—is a sign of confidence in its ability to render justice.

How this compared with the frequency that Jewish community members sought recourse in French civil courts will remain unknown until hard data drawn from the departmental archives of the Moselle have been systematically analyzed.[43] Even then, the evidence is not likely to be conclusive because in some instances litigants approached both the Jewish and the French legal systems, either simultaneously or sequentially.[44] Moreover, some cases that came before the Beit Din, as before any court, were never entered into the written record either because they were decided on the basis of oral pleading or the parties settled out of court. Additionally, the Beit Din's practice of

40 See Bell, *Lawyers and Citizens*, and Alexis de Tocqueville, *L'Ancien Regime et la Révolution* (Paris, 1967).

41 On the evasion of civil court expenses, see PMBD, Vol. 1, pt. 1, no. 4, 6a–7a; Vol. 2, no. 660, 146a; Vol. 2, appendix, case no. 30.

42 Criticism of the courts was widespread in the years leading up to the Revolution. Louis-Sebastien Mercier referred to them as "the mire and abominable chaos" in L.-S. Mercier, *Tableau de Paris*, 12 vols. (Amsterdam, 1788), 5: 338.

43 Even after the departmental archives are scoured, it will be difficult to determine whether the volume of litigation was increasing or decreasing as the century wore on, as there are quite a number of methodological hurdles to overcome. For two contrasting studies of the Parlement of Paris, see Colin Kaiser, "The Deflation in the Volume of Litigation in Paris in the Eighteenth Century and the Waning of the Old Judicial Order," *European Studies Review* 10 (1980): 309–36, and David Feutry, "The Historian's Mountain of Paper: The Parlement of Paris and the Analysis of Civil Suits in the Eighteenth Century," *French History* 26:3 (2012): 277–96.

44 See, for example, PMBD, Vol. 2, no. 274, 51b.

incorporating French judicial practices to dispute settlement may have discouraged litigants from taking their disagreements elsewhere.

To probe the cultural dimensions of law as closely as possible, the discussion that follows considers the legal norms as they were observed—or flouted—by litigants who brought their disputes to the Beit Din, as well as the judicial conduct of the Beit Din itself. A full appreciation of the interaction of Metz Jews with French law and judicial institutions will ultimately require an examination of archival sources that presently are beyond reach. The archives of the Metz Parlement are organized chronologically but not in a manner that permits research of specific topics or by the names of litigants.

Assessment of the legal discourse submerged deeply in the rabbinic court proceedings is complicated by their silence regarding the legal sources upon which they relied or the reasoning that informed their decisions.[45] As a rule, rabbinic courts did not make reference to talmudic traditions, medieval codes, responsa, or prior judicial decisions, much less define the underlying technical-legal issues or reveal the reasons behind their decisions (*ratio decidendi*). This approach stood in sharp contrast to methods employed by early modern French jurists who collected notable *arrêts* (judicial decisions) on questions of law and legal theory, and so contributed to the development of a system of French jurisprudence that laid the foundations for French political sovereignty. With monarchical and government support, and in the absence of relevant French customary law or royal edicts, written and printed notable *arrêts* attained the status of statutory law and were recognized as legal precedents. Their role in training lawyers in the interpretation of the law corresponded to a broad educational function reflected in the recognition they had achieved as "French jurisprudence."[46] In the view of sixteenth-century jurisconsult, Jean Papon, legal education "depended on access to precedent-setting French *arrêts*." To this end, Matthieu Pinault des Jaunaux published a collection of 500 judgments, issued between 1694 and 1714, that became a model for other such publications in France. He provided background information on each decision and commentary on the legal question before the court. The purpose of these publications was to minimize contradictions between judgments while also edifying lawyers regarding the court's jurisprudence. Known as "arrestography," this method emphasized the legal arguments of the parties

45 See Eliav Shochetman, "The Obligation to State Reasons for Legal Decisions in Jewish Law" [Hebrew], *Shenaton ha-Mishpat ha-Ivri* 6–7 (1979–80), 335–38.

46 Sarah Hanley, "The Jurisprudence of the Arrêts: Marital Union, Civil Society, and State Formation in France, 1550–1650." *Law and History Review* 21:1 (2003): 1–4, 10–11.

in order to discern the rational basis of the judgment. Others aimed to extract general principles from the interpretation of different legal sources.[47]

Why Jewish court records adopted a minimalist approach that eschewed the citation of earlier opinions or learned interpretation as in French judicial decisions is unclear. The choice may have rested on the assumption that these records would not be seen outside the narrow circle of jurists and communal officials in Metz. Perhaps the exceedingly modest mode of presentation enabled the court to speak unequivocally, and thus discourage either judicial appeal or accusations of judicial error. In addition, the failure to create a legal literature comparable to "arrestography" may be attributed, in part, to the diasporic conditions that shaped Jewish cultural production. Privileges granted to Jews and the nature of Jewish judicial institutions both varied widely. The absence of a centralized Jewish legal authority of any sort exacerbated the dispersion of legal scholars. Added to this was the cultural dimension: Learned Jewish law was practiced and published in extrajudicial sources, that is, in legal commentaries on major codes, such as Jacob ben Asher's *Arba'ah Turim* and the *Shulhan 'Aruk* produced by Joseph Caro and Moses Isserles, as well as in the voluminous rabbinic responsa literature.

All of these factors notwithstanding, the straightforward manner in which the protocols of rabbinic courts are presented should not be taken as evidence that their adjudicative process or interpretive underpinnings were uncomplicated. The immediate methodological challenge facing scholars is to identify, to the extent possible, the legal sources that presumably framed the issues that came before rabbinic courts and, then, to ascertain—even if only to infer—the rationales used in reaching judicial decisions. An equally difficult task is determining how talmudic law was implemented in the eighteenth century. Changing economic factors demanded reliance on new and, in some instances, unconventional legal strategies, and the unique position of Metz Jews in relation to French law made the challenges they faced even more acute.

Absent explicit pronouncements of the Metz Beit Din that might reveal the ideological, political, or legal underpinnings of its judicial reasoning and procedures, evidence of its modus operandi and legal thinking can be found in the warp and woof of litigation. Beit Din records are crucial for determining how those who turned to the Jewish judicial system related to the law and the

47 See Jean Papon, *Collection of Notable Arrêts* (1565), and Matthieu Pinault des Jaunaux, *Recueil d'arrêts notables du parlement de Tournay* (Valenciennes, 1702). On "arrestography," see *Interpretation of Law in the Age of Enlightenment: Form the Rule of the King to the Rule of Law*, ed. Morigiwa Yasutomo, Michael Stolleis, and Jean-Louis Halpérin (Dordrecht, 2011), 48–51. Also see W. Hamilton Bryson and Serge Dauchy, eds., *Ratio Decidendi: Guiding Principles of Judicial Decisions* (Berlin, 2006).

range of options that lay before them. Whatever the venue, "law provided the principal linguistic, cultural, and procedural framework through which individuals and corporations articulated, contested and resolved disputes over the allocation of resources, status, authority, and power."[48] The course of litigation furnishes telltale signs of acculturation and integration beyond the boundaries of the Jewish community. Beit Din cases reveal a high degree of interaction between the Jewish and French judiciaries. Routinely, the Pinkas provides numerous details of how litigants—and the Beit Din itself—navigated between the two legal systems. The growing complexity in the relationship of the Jews to state and society is reflected in questions of jurisdictional authority that the Beit Din encountered on an ongoing basis.

Scholars refer to this phenomenon as the tension between legal centralism and legal pluralism. Legal centralism is the idea that law is prescribed exclusively by the state, whereas legal pluralism refers to a multiplicity of legal orders and overlapping jurisdictions. 'Strong legal pluralism' refers to alternative legal orders that exist independent of the state's legitimizing mechanisms, while 'weak legal pluralism' refers to situations in which the state recognized the validity of different bodies of law for different groups in society.[49] Although the idea of the centralized state grew stronger in the course of the eighteenth century, few could envision the disappearance of rules enforced by diverse corporations. Those who accepted the notion of a 'weak' legal pluralism acknowledged the existence of multiple jurisdictions that remained subordinate to the supervision of the state. In fact, "most early modern Europeans would have agreed that a wide range of jurisdictions … could exercise legal authority with the approval of the ruler, who empowered and limited them." In the estimation of the state, legal pluralism was "a currency traded for a political or economic *quid pro quo*," and for various political and practical reasons kings extended and maintained jurisdictional rights and legal privileges.[50]

Comparable to the jurisdiction granted to seigneuries, merchant courts, and guilds, the authority of the Metz Beit Din was not considered a threat to the state's hegemony.[51] Juridical autonomy in Metz rested on the willingness

48 Michael P. Breen, "Patronage, Politics, and the 'Rule of Law' in Early Modern France," *Proceedings of the Western Society for French History* 33 (2005): 95–96.

49 John Griffiths first distinguished between 'strong' and 'weak' legal pluralism in "What is Legal Pluralism?" *Journal of Legal Pluralism and Unofficial Law*, 32:24 (1986): 5.

50 Richard J. Ross and Philip J. Stern, "Reconstructing Early Modern Notions of Legal Pluralism," in *Legal Pluralism and Empires, 1500–1850*, ed. Lauren Benton and Richard J. Ross (New York, 2013), 109 and 113–14.

51 Thus, one can marry according to Jewish ritual law, but the marriage only becomes legally valid upon the signing of a certificate issued by state authorities.

of Jewish jurists to modify their own legal orders and to draw on French civil regulations. In so doing, the rabbinic court recognized certain advantages of the competing legal order and, most important, displayed an ability to adapt to the centralized legal environment. In this respect, its approach reflected the view that "centralization ... was often not a top-down enterprise but rather an unintended consequence of localities drawing on central authority for their own particular purposes, which could at the same time further solidify jurisdictional diversity."[52]

For litigants who came before the Metz Beit Din, it was not simply a matter of choosing which legal order would best serve their needs. Substantial evidence indicates that the Beit Din succeeded in accommodating itself to the French legal system. In sharp contrast to Frankfurt, where the rabbinic court held fast to a conception of judicial exclusiveness, the Metz Beit Din did not insist on maintaining an utterly separate jurisdiction.[53] Its familiarity with the structure and principles of French law, as well as its cooperative relationship with royal and municipal judicial institutions, are unmistakable proof of the extensive interplay between the two legal systems. Indeed, the monarchy, jurists, and members of the judicial establishment all had an interest in fostering the integration of the Jews within the French judicial system while fully acknowledging the community's right to maintain its own jurisdictional authority.

The concept of legal pluralism becomes most valuable to historians when it moves beyond the topography of legal institutions and is understood as an index of the reciprocal relationship between law and society, or, as John Griffiths phrased it, when it is seen as "a concomitant of social pluralism."[54] While the proceedings of the Metz Beit Din provide clear evidence of the forces that fostered and sustained a unified community, they also attest to the fact that there was a shared culture that united members of distinct social groups, in this case Jews and Frenchmen. As the rabbinic court records reveal, the economic framework in which litigants functioned was more expansive than their own Jewish community. While religion and ethnicity remained the strongest forces in defining social affinities in northeastern France through the period under discussion, there also existed any number of social, economic, and political interests that Jews shared with their non-Jewish neighbors.

---

52 Ross and Stern, "Reconstructing Early Modern Notions of Legal Pluralism," 113.

53 See Fram, *A Window on Their World*, passim.

54 Griffiths, "What is Legal Pluralism," 38.

That litigants brought their disputes to legal institutions outside the Kehillah, in some instances with the blessings of the Beit Din and the communal leadership, suggests that Metz Jews were participating simultaneously in multiple social frameworks. Nevertheless, the extent to which these litigation patterns constituted a sense of belonging to a broader community should not be exaggerated. Shared religious, cultural, and historical roots, as well as social and legal disabilities, forged a distinctive Jewish identity that was separate from that of their surroundings. That said, there was greater attachment to general society than has been hitherto assumed. And although there were certainly instances when litigants played one legal system off against the other in order to achieve an optimal result, the notion had emerged in the civil legal sphere that a hierarchical relationship prevailed between the Beit Din and the French courts and that it was natural to go to the latter for certain kinds of cases.

Much of the discussion on legal pluralism over the past quarter-century has concentrated on the state and its readiness to accommodate alternative modes of legal ordering. Little discussion, however, has considered the capacity of enclave legal cultures, each from its own perspective, to accommodate the laws and hegemonic demands of the state.[55] The most immediate challenge facing the Kahal was whether, from the standpoint of Jewish law, the French civil courts had the legitimate right to exercise jurisdiction over the Jewish population. How did the Beit Din view French law and the French civil court system, known in rabbinic sources and communal records as *'arkha'ot shel goyim* (gentile courts)? The legal dictum *dina d'malkhuta dina* ("the law of the kingdom is the law"), attributed to the third-century Babylonian sage Samuel, presumably would bear directly on this question. But the scope of *dina d'malkhuta dina* continues to be the subject of substantial debate and its application has varied considerably in different periods and places.[56] Does the rule pertain only to matters between the king and his subjects, which would comprehend taxation, eminent domain, and punishment, or is it also valid in the realm of torts, lost property, and family law? Apart from divorce decrees, contracts drawn up in gentile courts or confirmed by the non-Jewish judicial system are considered valid. Underlying these issues was one of the most challenging dilemmas Jews face in the modern era: How was the Jewish community to comply with

55 For an example of a study that examines the conflict between religious and secular law from the perspective of ecclesiastical lawyers, see Richard Helmholz, "Conflicts Between Religious and Secular Law: Common Themes in the English Experience, 1250–1640," *Cardozo Law Review* 12 (1990): 707–28.

56 See Shmuel Shilo, *Dina d'Malkhuta Dina* (Jerusalem 1970).

the basic principle of *dina d'malkhuta* without abandoning the particular demands and constraints of the Jewish legal system?

While talmudic and medieval Jewish law strictly prohibited recourse to gentile courts,[57] several extenuating circumstances rendered this restrictive view more complicated than is commonly understood. Exceptions included, for example, the refusal of a litigant to appear before the Beit Din, the uncertainty concerning the power of the Beit Din to enforce its ruling, and the potentially unfavorable economic consequences arising from failure to seek resolution in the court with the highest jurisdiction.[58] No less important, the intricate financial entanglements with Christian borrowers and creditors invariably required efforts to settle disputes in multiple venues, sometimes simultaneously. When confronted with the challenge of competing jurisdictions, the Metz Beit Din had little choice but to exercise a very high degree of flexibility. Regrettably, its records tend not to distinguish among the various types of courts to which Jews brought their legal actions. In fact, the loaded term *'arkha'ot* was applied indiscriminately to French courts, and only rarely do Beit Din proceedings reveal the identity of the particular courts with which it interacted or to which Jewish litigants took their disputes.[59]

Whether legal centralism or legal pluralism dominated depends in large measure on how one defines the relationship of the autonomous Jewish community to the state in the final decades of the ancien régime. Selma Stern was among the first to advance the argument that the progressive intervention of the state in internal Jewish affairs was the main force responsible for the steady decline of the Kehillah, eventually paving the way for political emancipation. Jacob Katz adopted the Stern proposition, adding the claim that a compromised autonomy signified a weakening of rabbinic authority as well, which together generated cultural and intellectual modernization. While Katz based his view principally on conditions in Prussia and eastern Europe, it has been recently

57 Moses Maimonides, *Mishneh Torah*, Laws of Sanhedrin 26:7; Jacob b, Asher, Commentary to Sanhedrin, ch. 1, parag. 1 (Sanhedrin 23a); and Joseph Karo, *Shulḥan 'Arukh, Ḥoshen Mishpat*, §26. For a survey of the range of views held by late medieval and early modern *posekim*, see Azriel Hildesheimer, "Gentile Courts in Ashkenaz at the End of the Middle Ages," *Proceedings of the Tenth World Congress of Jewish Studies* (Jerusalem, 1990), 3:217–24.

58 On the economic ramifications of this issue, see PMBD, Vol. 2, no. 22, 5b.

59 When specific reference is made to a French court, it is most often to the Metz Parlement and less frequently to the Nancy Parlement and the *cours souveraine de Nancy* and the *bailliage* of Thionville. See, for example, PMBD, Vol. 1, pt. 1, no. 99, 33b; Vol. 1, pt. 2, no. 111, 28b; Vol. 2, no. 349, 65b; and Vol. 2, no. 254, 47b. On the wide range of courts and competing jurisdictions in France, see David Parker, "Sovereignty, Absolutism and the Function of the Law in Seventeenth-Century France," *Past and Present* 122 (1989): 36–74.

suggested that in France the state's centralizing mission was consistent with its subjugation of Alsatian Jewry and with the view of the French Enlightenment that corporate autonomy was incompatible with citizenship. Accordingly, with the advance of centralization, which set its sights on national unification and the aggregation of state power, Jewish communal autonomy was out of step with these wider political trends while the adherence to separate Jewish laws and customs had become—in the eyes of critics at least—emblematic of disquieting cultural dissonance.[60]

This view of centralism is problematic in several respects. To be sure, the state wished to assert its authority throughout France and looked askance at Jewish religious practices, but centralism as understood by the monarchy acknowledged the legitimacy of local customs and communal structures and took steps to maintain them. In the case of the Jews, political pressure to conform to the laws of the state was counterbalanced by an interest common to the Jewish community and French authorities. Jews could neither disregard the bureaucratic demands of government offices nor could they ignore the legal services provided by state or municipal authorities. Quite to the contrary, the state viewed the Metz Beit Din and its judicial rulings as compatible with the project of state-building that had intensified in the second half of the eighteenth century. Scattered throughout the deliberations recorded in the Pinkasim of the Kahal and of the Beit Din is evidence that the Kahal and the rabbinic court endeavored to delineate the boundaries of autonomy and to clarify the corporate identity of the Jews.

These efforts, specifically the accommodation of municipal and state law, were part of the larger goal of negotiating the relationship of Jews to the state. They found expression in two underlying judicial trends—to define legitimate recourse to the French civil courts and to define appropriate reliance on French law and what was of shared interest and jurisdiction. The phenomenon itself was not new, and in the case of Metz, the rabbinic court was compelled to adjust for royal and municipal laws. For its part, the absolutist state could hardly deny the legitimacy of customary law in provinces throughout the regime, especially in the areas of contracts, inheritance, and guardianship. This was a political strategy aimed at strengthening the central authority of the state, but not with the intention of erasing local customs.[61] On

60 See Selma Stern, *Die presussische Staat und die Juden* (Berlin, 1925), II/1, 123–149; Katz, *Tradition and Crisis*, 217–18; idem, *Out of the Ghetto: The Social Background of Jewish Emancipation, 1770–1870* (Cambridge, MA, 1973), esp. 31–33, and Shael Herman, "Review of *Protocols of Justice: The Pinkas of the Rabbinic Court of Metz*," in *The Review of Rabbinic Judaism* 19 (2016): 295–316.

61 See Csaba Varga, *Codification as a Socio-historical Phenomenon* (Budapest, 1991), 56–62.

this reading, the 1740 royal initiative to commission a compendium of Metz Jewry's laws and customs—the *Recueil des lois, coûtumes et usages observés par les juifs de Metz*—was not a scheme to encourage Jews to bring their disputes to royal courts and add revenue to the royal treasury. Although the *Recueil* was designed to serve as a reference tool for French judges when presiding over cases between Jewish litigants, it should be seen as a tactical effort to build on the pluralist paradigm.[62] In fact, two models of juridical autonomy prevailed in the second half of the eighteenth century. One stressed the jurisdictional preference in Jewish law to settle disputes in a Jewish court. A second model entailed adjudication in French courts, with the proviso that the judgment would be in accordance with Jewish law. The community was assured that producing the French compendium would not prejudice its authority to settle disputes in its own courts and that its judicial autonomy would remain unchanged.[63] The example of the *Recueil* suggests that state-building was not limited to the steady imposition of centralized law but should be regarded as the efficient management of diversity under state supervision. More broadly, early modern French jurists viewed the *ius civile* as comprising the Roman legal tradition, with accommodations for French provincial customs and royal legislation.[64]

---

62 See Nicolas-François Lançon, *Recueil des lois, coûtumes et usages observés par les juifs de Metz* (Metz, 1786). For a fuller discussion of the *Recueil*, see below, chapter 5.

63 *Lettres patentes*, 20 August 1742. The following is the original text: "Nous leurs avons réservé pour les contestations, qui naissent de Juifs à Juifs, la faculté de se pourvoir devant leurs Rabins, voulant aussi que les chefs de leurs communautés eussent la connoissance de leur police, religion, coutumes, cérémonies & impositions."

64 Out of the synthesis of French customs and Roman legal principles emerged a genuine French law that played a crucial role in the emergence of the modern state. In Metz *ius civile* was, effectively, "reformed Roman" law. On the law in Metz, see C.-J. Gabriel, *Observations détachées sur les coûtumes et les usages anciens et modernes du ressort du Parlement de Metz*. 2 vols. (Bouillon, 1787), and in the Lorraine province as a whole, see Albert Riston, *Analyse des coûtumes sous le ressort du parlement de Lorraine, adoptées au droit commun et aux lois particulières à cette province* (Nancy, 1782). Areas of Roman law were historically exempt from the *droit d'aubaine*, but in the eighteenth century it was extended to Provence and Languedoc in the south and to Metz in the east. This was part of the monarchy's efforts to extend its sovereignty by imposing uniform laws throughout the kingdom. See Peter Sahlins, *Unnaturally French: Foreign Citizens in the Old Regime and After* (Ithaca, 2004), 11–16. Upon royal initiative, the *coûtumes* of Metz were codified and in 1611 they were published for the first time, under Louis XIII. Two types of *coûtumes* were printed, one for the city of Metz and the other for the surrounding countryside. This compendium of Metz customs was published six additional times before the Revolution, the last time being in 1769. See *Coûtumes générales de la ville de Metz et pays-Messin: corrigées ensuite des résolutions des trois-etats de ladite ville, ès années 1616, 1617, & 1618. Nouvelle edition conforme à ...1732* (Metz, 1769).

In the last third of the eighteenth century, the judicial practices of the Metz Beit Din diverged from the general theory of self-containment and accommodationism that prevailed in Jewish communities throughout the Middle Ages. Historically, rabbinic courts were authorized to adjudicate internal disagreements involving Jewish litigants; disputes between Jews and non-Jews were commonly remitted to the general courts, if the parties so chose. Aggressive action from about mid-century against women who sought recourse in French civil courts from adverse Beit Din rulings regarding marital property settlements imply ongoing community efforts to preserve the illusion of a self-contained system.

With the opening of the rabbinic court register in 1771, however, we encounter a Beit Din that was attentive, as were lay communal leaders, to the complex relationship that implicated the Jews, the state, and society in an intricate web. Guided by the combination of pragmatism and shifting cultural affinities, the Beit Din adapted to a world of multiple jurisdictions of comparable validity.[65] By the 1770s and 1780s the Metz Beit Din could no longer sustain the myth of a Jewish legal system wholly independent of the state's civil system. Signs of this development were evident as early as 1720 when the communal leadership narrowed the definition of litigation that would violate the ban on recourse to non-Jewish courts.[66] Nevertheless, even two decades later, the presiding justice of the Beit Din, Rabbi Jonathan Eibeschütz, objected fiercely to the liberal stance that, in his view, overstepped traditional boundaries.[67]

Although at mid-century rabbinic and lay leaders disagreed on the optimal or even acceptable degree of collaboration with the French courts, it had become evident to all that the economic and political realities of the day precluded detachment from the larger judicial environment. By the 1770s, a more collaborative relationship between the Metz Beit Din and the French civil courts had evolved. This rapport, however, did not unfold in a linear fashion, nor does it correlate directly with the advance of secularization and cultural modernization that typified economic elites. As in the medieval period, the

65 This is not to suggest that the Metz Beit Din would have recognized either a divorce given in civil court or a state ruling requiring Jews to desecrate the Sabbath. In general, from the standpoint of Halakhah, ritual obligations and restrictions were understood to be beyond the scope of *dina d'malkhuta* and therefore impervious to state interference. Marriage and divorce were singled out as areas shielded from state regulation. See BT Gittin 9b.

66 See the fragments of the Pinkas Kahal of Metz, dating from 1720, in Central Archives of the History of the Jewish People, FMe 139. It is stated there that certain types of notes can be litigated in non-Jewish courts because the fact that the debtor owes the creditor a certain sum is not a matter of dispute. See below, chapters 3, 4, and 5.

67 See Eibeschütz, *Urim ve-tumim*, on *Ḥoshen Mishpat* §26 and below, chapter 2.

degree of interaction between Jewish and general law was a product of social and economic forces that shaped behavior within Jewish communities and even within family life. To the extent permitted by the Metz records, the present effort to explain the inner workings of the Beit Din aims to uncover the culture of the public sphere, or spheres, as understood by Jews living at once in two worlds, Jewish and general. As I hope will become apparent, the legal realm offered a framework from which new rules of engagement between the Jewish minority and the surrounding society and culture steadily emerged.

The Production of the Metz Pinkas Beit Din

Precious little is known about the production of the Metz Beit Din records. We cannot state with certainty under whose direction these records were produced, for whom they were intended, or toward what end they were preserved in written form. Nevertheless, there was nothing novel or uncommon about providing litigants with written copies of court rulings. Such documentation was intended to confirm an admission of debt, the withdrawal of a claim, the exoneration of an individual from unsupported accusations, or the severance of a widow from her husband's estate, to name only several of the more common types of validation provided by the Beit Din.[68] In some instances, the court was asked to issue a *ma'aseh beit din* (a formal judgment) to certify that it had resolved a particular matter.[69] The litigant's purpose could be exculpation from an unfounded accusation, confirmation of ownership over property, or establishing the legality of a commercial transaction. Written rulings of this sort were frequently produced as evidence in cases that continued over the course of months or even years.[70] On occasion the Beit Din expressed its intention to preserve a written version of its rulings with the following formula:

68 See, for example, PMBD, Vol. 2, no. 260, 49a; Vol. 2, no. 324, 61a. In the case of separation (*silluk*), see PMBD, Vol. 2, no. 289, 53a. Concerning exculpation from unfounded accusations, see, PMBD, Vol. 1, pt. 2, no. 3, 2b; PMBD, Vol. 1, pt. 2, no. 18, 5a; Vol. 1, pt. 1, no. 58, 17b; Vol. 2, no. 495, 100a.

69 The legal standing of a *ma'aseh beit din* is attested in the talmudic statement, in BT Bava Meẓia 17b, that "every *ma'aseh beit din* is the virtual equivalent of a document placed in the hand [of the claimant]." For the use of the term when referencing previous rulings, see PMBD, Vol. 2, no. 16, 3b, and no. 333, 62b.

70 See, for example, PMBD, Vol. 1, pt. 1, no. 2, 5a. On a case of contested ownership, see PMBD, Vol. 2, no. 498, 100b. In Vol. 2, no. 216, 40b, regarding a paternity accusation that was determined to be unsubstantiated, the Beit Din stated "therefore, this [*ma'aseh beit din*] will be in his hand to cover eyes [that is, as a mode of deception] to show to all that the aforementioned slander is a lie and there is no substance to it."

"And now this avowal (*hoda'ah*) is placed in written form by us, the Beit Din, for [the purpose of] preservation."[71] Akin to this, in 1765, the Pinkas Kahal made it obligatory for each communal official who attended a meeting of the Kahal to record his view in writing and not merely state it orally.[72]

Although the communal register does not contain an explicit directive concerning the formal preservation of judicial records, by the mid-1760s the Kahal required the *av beit din* and the rabbinic court to document individual legal decisions. Regulations issued in 1766, just prior to the appointment of Rabbi Gûnzberg, set forth detailed rules instructing the *av beit din* to keep "a special list of each ruling, both those he decided on his own and those decided with other judges. Litigants were not obligated to pay the *dayanim* until after the ruling was put in writing." Non-compliance with the requirement to give litigants the written ruling prior to the redemption of debts was a punishable offense.[73] Repeating a *takkanah* that was enacted in 1720, article 109 of the 1769 Takkanot stated that "every ruling of the Beit Din must be written and signed, in other words, initialed by the full Beit Din, before the ruling is pronounced in the presence of the litigants." It was stipulated, further, that "it is prohibited for either of the litigants to pay the other even a *perutah* (the proverbial peppercorn), until they have seen the written and signed judgment. And if the Beit Din fails to produce the written ruling in advance, the litigants must deposit court expenses with the presiding syndic (*parnas ha-ḥodesh*), and then the syndic will be obligated to enforce compliance with this article."[74]

From this communal statute it can be surmised that only in the last third of the eighteenth century did the nexus between the recording of a judgment in writing and its validation as law become standard procedure. In the Parlement

71 For the formula expressing the intent to preserve a written version of a judicial ruling, see, for example, PMBD, Vol. 1, pt. 1, no. 68, 21b. The Hebrew original was as follows: מעתה ניתן הודאה זו לכתוב מאתנו ב"ד למשמרת.

72 PKM 58a. On record-keeping, see Alexandra Walsham, "The Social History of the Archive: Record-Keeping in Early Modern Europe," *Past & Present* 230, Issue supplement 11 (November 2016): 9–48.

73 PKM, 65a. See Simon Schwarzfuchs, "The Rabbinic Contract of the Sha'agat Aryeh in Metz," *Moriah* 15 (1986): 86, parag. 13.

74 See art. 5 of the 1720 Takkanot, a fragment of the Pinkas Kahal, in CAHJP, FMe 139, and Art. 109 of the 1769 Takkanot, in PKM, 82b. The following is the 1769 formulation:

כל פסק בית דין מוז דער פס׳ כתוב וחתום שהיינו גפאראפֿט זיין מכל הבית דין קודם דר פסק איז גזאגט ווירט לפני הבעלי דינים ואסור לשנ בעלי דינים אפילו פרוטה אחת פסק געלט צלין עד לאחר שיראו הפסק כתוב וחתום איזט כנ"ל. ובאב הבית דין דען פסק ניט שריבן וגם גפאראפֿט האבין מקודם כנ"ל זולן הבעלי דינים הפסק מעות משליש זיין ביד הפה"ח ואז מוטל על הפה"ח כפיה צו טוין לקיים ארטיקל הלז.

The 1769 Takkanot have been recently published in *Jüdische Gemeindestatuten aus dem aschkenasischen Kulturraum, 1650–1850*, ed. Stefan Litt (Göttingen, 2013).

of Paris, the procedure was more explicitly articulated in several steps. At the initial hearing the clerk took notes, which he then conveyed to the registry (*greffe*) for copying onto parchment and delivery to the attorneys. Once filed, these minutes were compiled and recopied into a parchment register by a special clerk. This last step was essential because it constituted the court's decision as a source of law. Finally, only after all fees were paid at the *greffe* was the ruling entered into the register and executed.[75] Whether a similar procedure was followed in Metz is unclear, but it is plausible to so surmise.

What accounts for the decision to embark on the systematic recording of the Beit Din's rulings remains a matter of speculation. It is widely assumed that a prime determinant was increased government interest in internal Jewish affairs, but the fact that the court proceedings were recorded in Hebrew makes this explanation largely unconvincing. Nor does the decision appear to have been related to the nation-wide judicial reform undertaken by Louis XV through his chancellor, René de Maupeou, in 1771.[76] That similar compilations of rabbinic court rulings elsewhere, including German communities, date from roughly these same years raises further doubts about the role of local (that is, French) forces in prompting this unprecedented development.[77] Andreas Gotzmann has proposed that the decision to chronicle the judicial records of the rabbinical court of Hamburg-Altona-Wandsbek was prompted by the order that courts transfer a percentage of their fees and the fines they imposed to government authorities. But were this simply a matter of recording court fees and fines, the massive detail contained in the Beit Din protocols would have been unnecessary. Nor does the progressive involvement of the state in marital

75 Feutry, "The Historian's Mountain of Paper," 279–80, 289.

76 Louis XV viewed the refusal of magistrates to register royal edicts as an act of contempt and therefore attempted to centralize political control over the judiciary by abolishing the *parlements* and by substituting new upper courts that had no influence over policy. The new judicial system eliminated the sale of magistracies and made judges salaried officials; in 1774, Louis XVI restored the old *parlements*. See Isser Woloch, *The New Regime: Transformations of the French Civic Order, 1789–1820s* (New York, 1994), 299–300. No evidence of new orders concerning judicial record keeping is noted in John A. Carey, *Judicial Reform in France before the Revolution of 1789* (Cambridge, MA, 1981), and no other works on seigneurial tribunals mention a change in record keeping that was introduced as a result of a royal ordinance. One may note, however, that a royal edict calling for the creation of *de conservateurs des hypothèques sur les immeubles réels et fictifs* was enacted in June 1771. See Édit no. 1014, in François-André Isambert, *Recueil général des anciennes lois françaises, depuis l'an 420 jusqu'à la révolution de 1789* (Paris, 1821–1833), 22: 530–37.

77 For parallel developments in early nineteenth-century Italy, see J. P. Filippini, "La comunitá israelitica di Livorno durante il periodo napoleonico," *Rivista italiana di studi napoleonici*, XIX (1982), 23–113, where records of civil judgments were summarized and preserved in large numbers in places like Livorno.

property and inheritance disputes provide a satisfactory explanation. In civil cases the general practice was to seal these judicial files or destroy them after a settlement had been reached to prevent reopening of the case and the attendant renewal of domestic acrimony.[78]

Each of the foregoing efforts to account for judicial record keeping is rooted in the state's presumptive interest to control internal Jewish affairs. There may be a more plausible explanation. *Pinkesei kahal*, the registers maintained from the seventeenth century, attest to the value the Jewish community attached to record keeping. Once the rabbinic court in Metz became a permanent communal institution empowered to exercise judicial authority to the exclusion of private or ad hoc courts—which occurred only after the mid-eighteenth century—it too commenced formally documenting its proceedings.[79] The systematic compilation of rabbinic court cases in the 1770s presumably started not long after the Beit Din began to function as an official agency of the Kahal and was consistent with the expectation of communal institutions to maintain detailed records.

Seigneurial records, by comparison, normally contained a listing of litigants, the source of dispute, and the action taken that day. While in some instances a lengthy dossier containing *mémoires procès-verbaux*, and *jugements* may have been appended to a case, these were rare occurrences that nonetheless required written procedure. Peasants frequently complained that written procedures were overly expensive. Cases for which there was no dossier were either appealed to a higher court (hence materials would be filed in a *bailliage* court or in the Parlement), discarded altogether, or resolved through arbitration before a notary. In such disputes it seems that a lawsuit was only the initial stage in effort to resolve differences between the parties. Initiating legal action was frequently a party's maneuver to prove the seriousness of its intent. Ultimately, however, the suit would be settled via arbitration, which was a faster and less expensive solution.[80] In some instances Jewish litigants first brought their disputes to the civil courts and subsequently went to the rabbinic court for arbitration, and no doubt vice versa. In a case of alleged malfeasance by guardians who managed the estates of minors, the Beit Din stated in no uncertain terms that the arbitration ruling issued by the French court would be implemented "with full force, as if it were enacted before the

78 See Andreas Gotzmann, "At Home in Many Worlds? Thoughts about New Concepts in Jewish Legal History," *Jahrbuch des Simon-Dubnow Instituts* 2 (2003): 413–36, esp. 423–24, and Stefan Ehrenpreis, "Legal Spaces for Jews as Subjects of the Holy Roman Empire," *Jahrbuch des Simon-Dubnow-Instituts* 2 (2003): 478–79.

79 See Berkovitz, "Competing Perspectives on Legal Decision Making," and below, chapter 4.

80 See Crubaugh, *Balancing the Scales of Justice*.

Beit Din."[81] The rabbinic court, for its part, proceeded to set forth in detail how the funds would be paid out.

The protocols of the Metz Beit Din were detailed summaries of judicial proceedings—not direct transcriptions of courtroom arguments—produced by court scribes. So it was, as well, in the Parlement of Paris. Details of judicial deliberations reported in written form amounted to less than a complete reproduction of the minutes of the cases heard by the court.[82] Recording of verbatim testimony was rare. In those instances in which direct statements appear in the Metz rabbinic court register, the language employed was usually the local Yiddish vernacular, though in a few instances the testimony was recorded in Hebrew.[83] The objective was, it seems, to document the court's decisions in a manner that could be consulted when needed at a later time. This system would doubtless enable the Metz communal leadership, as well as judges on the bench, to control the expanding details of litigation. On bureaucratic grounds alone the preservation of written records of earlier court decisions proved indispensable to settle disputes that had been heard on numerous earlier occasions.[84] In fact, by keeping such records the Beit Din maintained vital documentation of recourse to the French courts, especially important in those instances when the interplay between the two legal systems was a crucial factor either in the Beit Din's immediate ruling or in ongoing litigation.[85] Finally, it is not unlikely that the decision to keep formal records signified a new chapter in the emergence of the Beit Din as an official institution.[86]

---

81 See, for example, PMBD, Vol. 1, pt. 2, no. 49, 14b, where litigants affirmed that what was stated in the French translation of the arbitration was in accord with the law of the land and would be upheld to the fullest extent of the law. Concerning the implementation of the arbitration settlement with "full force," see PMBD, Vol. 1, pt. 1, no. 110, 37a.

82 Feutry, "The Historian's Mountain of Paper," 287–88.

83 For several examples of direct testimony in Yiddish, see the following cases: PMBD, Vol. 2, no. 428, 82a, and no. 515, 104b–105a. For examples of testimony recorded in Hebrew, see PMBD, Vol. 2, no. 199, 38a, and Vol. 2, no. 311, 57b–58a.

84 See, for example, PMBD, Vol. 1, pt. 2, no. 51, 15b, where the case involved a disparity between two court judgments.

85 In one case, the Beit Din asserted emphatically that its decision, once recorded, was final, implying that it could not be overturned by a ruling issued by another court, including the French courts. See PMBD, Vol. 1, pt. 1, no. 4, 6b. For additional evidence of the importance attached to documentation of the interplay with the French judicial system, see the listing of *arrêts, sentences*, and *traités* issued by various French courts and officials that was recorded in the Pinkas Kahal, ms. 3704.

86 By this I am not referring to the transition from orality to written records. Many cases heard by the Beit Din had already been recorded in writing earlier in the century and

Although it is difficult to identify the precise role scribes played in determining the content, form, and language of the cases they recorded, here is what we can deduce about their function. First, the recurring statement of scribes that the court issued its decision "after the litigants argued at length," suggests that the final version of the Pinkas was an abbreviated text that had undergone editing. In several instances, there are statements at the end of a case that the judgment was copied from a pre-existing document. Such postscripts included the formula "copied letter by letter" (*hu'atak ot be'ot*), followed by one of the following phrases: *guf peturim* (a document certifying receipts); *guf ha-pesak beit din* (a document containing the judgment of the Beit Din); *guf hoda'ah* (a document of admission of a debt); or *guf ma'aseh beit din* (a document certifying an act of the Beit Din). Second, the term used to denote approval by the judges or by the *parnas* is *geparapht*, which is derived from the French *parapher*, here in the form of a Yiddish past participle, *geparapht*, sometimes rendered as *gebarapht*, which is equivalent to *paraphiert*. The literal meaning of *parapher* is "to initial" and in the Beit Din records denoted approval or confirmation.[87] In each of these instances, a certificate entered into evidence or a document certifying receipts, admission of a debt, a judgment of the Beit Din, or an act of the Beit Din, were approved either by the chief justice (*av beit din*), the judges, or in some instances the presiding syndic (*parnas ha-ḥodesh*). Third, variations in handwriting, in addition to the assorted signatures affixed at the ends of collations of cases, reveal that several different court stenographers—probably six altogether—were commissioned to record the judicial proceedings during the eighteen years chronicled in the Pinkas.[88] The largest number of entries appears to be in the hand of a single scribe, Juspa Katz, whose name is recorded in seven cases that span fifteen

especially after mid-century; some are conserved in the Archives départementales de la Moselle, Consistoire israélite 17J24. Although the work of Michael Clanchy concerns the medieval period, it is nonetheless useful for thinking about the role of written records in the history of early modern legal institutions. See Michael T. Clanchy, *From Memory to Written Record: England 1066–1307*, 3rd ed. (Chichester, 2013), esp. 274–80. On textualization and Jewish legal culture in the medieval period, see Talya Fishman, *Becoming the People of the Talmud: Oral Torah as Written Tradition in Medieval Jewish Cultures* (Philadelphia, 2011), passim. On the related issue of recording notes, see Ann Blair, "Note Taking as an Art of Transmission," *Critical Inquiry* 31 (2004): 85–107, and idem, "The Rise of Note-Taking in Early Modern Europe," *Intellectual History Review* 20 (2010): 303–16.

87 See PMBD, Vol. 1, pt. 2, nos. 4 and 5, 2b; no. 22, 6b; no. 77, 20b; no. 82, 21b; nos. 85–86, 23a. For several examples, see PMBD, Vol. 1, pt. 2, no. 87, 23b and no. 128, 32b.

88 See, for example, PMBD, Vol. 1, pt. 1, no. 35, 13a.

years.[89] Finally, the types of scribal errors one encounters in the Pinkas manuscript, including the occasional transposition and omission of letters and, less frequently, the omission of a word, suggest that scribes were copying from some earlier version of the text, possibly in the form of notes that had been prepared in advance. Overall, the stylized prose used in recording the proceedings—punctuated throughout by the inclusion of biblical phrases and technical expressions drawn from talmudic and halakhic literature—suggests that the text of the Pinkas was the product of meticulous preparation by erudite scholars of rabbinic law and well-trained scribes.

Paradoxically, the methodical character of the recorded proceedings is borne out by occasional irregularity in the sequencing of cases in the Pinkas. The failure to maintain strict chronological order suggests that, aside from complications pertaining to the final settlement of certain disputes, the preparation of the case summaries for inclusion in the court register was neither instantaneous nor hurried.[90] In fact, abundant evidence indicating that the text underwent a final editorial stage, at which time the scribe entered corrections and added words and phrases in the margins, confirms that production of the Pinkas was quite a deliberate undertaking. The absence of source citations and the dearth of rhetorical stratagems or legal argumentation in the Beit Din ruling might suggest, at first blush, that these case summaries were intended primarily for notational purposes. But the care exhibited in creating what is, overall, a clearly written corpus characterized by classical rabbinic erudition and unmistakable signs of painstaking editorial revision, suggests that this may have been intended as a reference work that could be consulted by rabbinic court judges or communal leaders. The graceful Hebrew prose throughout most of the manuscript bears this out and may be taken as the clearest proof that the Metz protocols were meant to be preserved and consulted.[91] In fact, it seems that the decision to maintain these court records

---

89 Katz is referred to as *sofer sta"m d'B"D* (court scribe trained in the writing of Torah scrolls, *mezuzot*, and *tefillin*). The first mention is in PMBD, Vol. 1, pt. 1, no. 35, 13a, and the last time is in Vol. 2, no. 612, 132a.

90 The lack of chronological order can be seen clearly in the opening pages of the Pinkas and in numerous other instances. See PMBD, Vol. 1, pt. 1, nos. 1–3, 5a–6a; Vol. 1, pt. 2, nos. 50–74, 89–100; Vol. 2, nos. 537–540, 631–633.

91 For example, the terms of a guardianship arrangement that came before the Beit Din in 1771 was renegotiated nine years later, as recorded in PMBD, Vol. 2, no. 241, 44b. when the orphans of Michael Barschingen had come of age. The preservation of the original case (PMBD, Vol. 1, pt. 2, no. 8) undoubtedly facilitated the work of the court.

in an official manner was intended to serve as a faithful record of communal memory. Although these records were never published, nor is there any indication that publication was intended in the future, by engaging in this impressive undertaking of meticulous record keeping the Beit Din eschewed the propensity for administrative concealment that typified many judicial institutions of the day. The parallels between the production of the Beit Din records and the printed trial briefs of French law courts is not intended to imply equivalence between the two systems but nonetheless suggest that, like the civil records, the Metz Pinkas was created with a view to exerting a public impact beyond the confines of the court's four walls.[92]

92 The relative clarity of the handwriting of communal scribes and the overall appearance of the text may be appreciated by comparing it to the often-illegible minute book of the Niederenheim community, 1781–1783; see Arch. JTSA microfilm no. 8133. Even so, the quality of the summaries in the Pinkas Metz Beit Din and the care with which the manuscript was copied are occasionally uneven. See, for example, PMBD, Vol. 2, nos. 615–625, 133a–135a, where there are numerous scribal errors. For an extensive discussion of the printing of *mémoires judiciaires* and its historical significance, see Maza, *Private Lives and Public Affairs*, 19–67, 112–30.

CHAPTER 2

The Foundations of the Metz Kehillah

For roughly two centuries, historians have employed phrases such as "tradition and crisis," "ghetto and emancipation," and "out of the ghetto" as the scaffolding to chart the trajectory of Jewish modernization. But precisely when this transformation began and what its most salient features were remain contentious issues. Some trace the beginnings of Jewish modernization to the cultural and social impact of the Renaissance and Reformation, to the intellectual advances of science and philosophy in the sixteenth and seventeenth centuries, or to the structural changes that transformed the early modern European society and economy. Those who hold modernization to be a belated phenomenon typically cite the European Enlightenment, the French Revolution, or secularization as the key agents of change; others situate modernity in a host of internal cultural and religious developments that indirectly echoed external forces. These widely divergent interpretations of when Jews first "entered" the modern world attest to fundamental disagreements on the nature of modernization itself.[1]

But these disparate views rest on one ostensibly unshakable assumption: that until their fateful encounter with the surrounding society, whenever and wherever this transpired, Ashkenazic Jews remained culturally distinct from and only rarely engaged with the world beyond the ghetto. This assumption is reinforced by the argument that many Jews who anticipated the dawn of a new era, who were involved in the struggle for civic equality, or who reflected on it with hindsight, conceived of modernization as a redemptive act that promised to redress the miseries and privations of the medieval Jewish condition. Invariably, these indignities were understood to reflect the separation and estrangement of Jews from the dominant social and cultural framework to which most of the general population belonged. Ultimately, according to this perspective, the erosive impact of modernity may first be discerned only upon the demise of communal autonomy. Until then, the Kehillah continued to be a bastion of traditional social and religious ideals and served as the framework

1 On the range of views advanced by leading historians of the twentieth century, see Michael A. Meyer, "Where Does the Modern Period in Jewish History Begin?" *Judaism* 24 (1975): 329–38, and for an analysis of research trends that have emerged during the past thirty years, see David Ruderman, *Early Modern Jewry: A New Cultural History* (Princeton, 2010). Ruderman's work is the first to attempt a comprehensive portrait of European Jewry that is based predominantly on facets of Jewish culture and experience.

 | DOI:10.1163/9789004417403_004

for their realization in daily life. As long as the Kehillah remained intact, the perils of modernity presumably could be kept at bay.[2]

This characterization of the autonomous community as the last bulwark against the onslaught of modernity rests on several assumptions that require reconsideration. First, the prevailing assessment of autonomy is based on a somewhat static conception of the ancien régime that is at odds with considerable evidence of dynamic social and cultural change, abundant complexity regarding religious praxis and authority, and evolving patterns of communal leadership in the century preceding the Revolution. Second, the ascendancy of the urban laity in Metz, manifested in the extensive regulation of religious, social, and moral behavior, is routinely taken as evidence of the progressive decline of rabbinic authority. The gradual consolidation of rabbinic duties, the widening differentiation in the functions of rabbi and communal leader, and the growing independence of the rabbinate from commercial dealings, point to a redefinition of the role of the rabbis and their relationship to the governing body. This was a transformation that reflected a reworking of the medieval model of religious authority, especially as it related to public policy. Third, tradition and modernity are regularly essentialized, which has led to a view of each in binary terms. Recent research has clarified that neither was as absolute as previous generations of historians imagined, or as David Ruderman has suggested, the danger of "the false dichotomy between tradition and modernity" is "the implied teleology of a supposed progression from one to the other."[3]

A fourth premise that underlies the standard depiction of the traditional community in its final stages is that acculturation—a minority's affinity to, or appropriation of, the beliefs and behaviors of the dominant culture—is the measure of modernization. Nearly sixty years ago, Azriel Shoḥet argued that laxity in ritual observance, sexual immorality, adoption of the mores of the surrounding culture, and the preoccupation with material comfort at the turn of the eighteenth century paved the way for even more major changes that would unfold almost a century later. Jacob Katz denied that violations of

2 Katz, *Tradition and Crisis*, 183–236. On modernization as a redemptive act, see the discussion of the paradigm "Paradise, Paradise Lost, Paradise Regained," in Schechter, *Obstinate Hebrews*, chap. 3. For examples of scholarship that conceived of Jewish modernization in France mainly as a product of the Revolution, see Phyllis Cohen Albert, *The Modernization of French Jewry: Consistory and Community in the Nineteenth Century* (Hanover, NH, 1977), and Paula Hyman, *The Emancipation of the Jews of Alsace: Acculturation and Tradition in the Nineteenth Century* (New Haven, 1991).

3 David B. Ruderman, "Looking Backward and Forward: Rethinking Modernity in the Light of Early Modernity," in Jonathan Karp and Adam Sutcliffe, eds., *The Cambridge History of Judaism*, Vol. 7: The Early Modern World, 1500–1815 (Cambridge, 2018), 1107.

religious and social norms were historically significant unless consciously justified by a new value system inspired by external sources and made possible by the collapse of communal structures. Shoḥet and Katz did not disagree that behavior patterns that became prevalent in the eighteenth century were indicators of modernizing trends. Rather, the key difference between them was the weight they attached to the forces that motivated the departure from traditional norms. Shoḥet and Katz were oddly in agreement that the allegiance to tradition or, conversely, the embrace of modernity, could be gauged either by what Jews did or thought they were doing when they participated in general culture. Simply put, the progressive laicization of communities across Europe should not be confused with secularization and its professed antagonism for religion.[4]

Katz's approach to modernization remains dominant among Jewish historians despite evidence of greater interaction with general society than had been known when mid-twentieth historians produced their findings. His training in sociology and his interest in ideological movements were the pillars of a distinctive method of historical analysis that emphasized intellectual and structural changes. Seeking to understand the origins and ideology of Jewish assimilation, he concentrated on the writings of practitioners of the Haskalah (Jewish Enlightenment movement), their assessment of tradition, and the programs they proposed to implement in the Jewish community. But by giving priority to the struggle between modernizers and traditionalists, his analysis of assimilation ultimately diverted attention from other sectors of the Jewish community that interacted with society at large, and from the practices of ordinary folk, particularly those who displayed religious conservatism and popular piety. Although Katz firmly rejected the triumphalist claim that pre-modern Judaism evinced intellectual stagnation and an antiquated rabbinic culture, he tended to view Jewish life in the last third of the eighteenth century largely through the lens of the *maskilim* (practitioners of Haskalah).[5]

4 See Azriel Shoḥet, *'Im Hilufe Tekufot* (The Beginnings of the Haskalah in Germany) (Jerusalem, 1960), and Jacob Katz, *Out of the Ghetto: The Social Background of Jewish Emancipation, 1770–1870* (Cambridge, MA, 1973), 34–36. For a recent examination of the abandonment of religious norms, the denial of beliefs, and growing indifference to religious authority in early modern Europe, see Shmuel Feiner, *The Origins of Jewish Secularization in Eighteenth-Century Europe* (Philadelphia, 2010). It is nonetheless doubtful that the category "secular" is adequate to describe the complexities of modern Jewish identity.

5 See David N. Myers, "Rebel in Frankfurt: The Scholarly Origins of Jacob Katz" in *The Pride of Jacob: Essays on Jacob Katz and His Work*, ed. Jay M. Harris (Cambridge, MA, 2002), 9–27. Cf. Sheehan, "Enlightenment, Religion, and the Enigma of Secularization." Frances Malino has credited proponents of the French Haskalah with having formulated a distinct ideology of emancipation that reflected local political and cultural conditions during the revolutionary

The present study approaches these issues from a different vantage point. It rests on the assumption that acculturation was broadly characteristic of the Jewish historical experience and was by no means limited to the seventeenth and eighteenth centuries alone. Less certain, however, are the circumstances in which this process unfolded, and the degree communal leaders viewed it as a threat to the social and religious status quo. While there is abundant historical evidence to suggest that acculturation will proceed even in the absence of conditions that are conducive to cultural exchange, certain structural elements within society create conditions that commonly account for cultural interaction between Jews and non-Jews. A more reliable indicator of modernity is "integration," a phenomenon that is taken here to signify participation by members of a minority in the mainstream activities of the larger society (though it does not refer to the more advanced process of social assimilation that is characteristic of Jewish life in the World War II era).[6] Historians have consistently assumed that except for highly unusual circumstances, such as prevailed in medieval Spain or Renaissance Italy, integration was virtually inconceivable in the absence of civic equality. The abundant evidence of integration and cultural adaptation gives the lie to this assumption.

Signs of integration and cultural adaptation among Jews in Metz were far more extensive than previously recognized. Metz communal records, the proceedings of the rabbinic court, and French legal sources all attest to Jewish involvement in the deep structures of the general society. Minorities were naturally drawn to services supplied by French agencies and to institutions of the ancien régime to meet their everyday needs. This powerful attraction was in tension with the prevailing social, economic, religious, and political conditions in France that disqualified the Jews as members of the French nation. In keeping with the regulations enacted by the monarchy, Metz Jews were required to reside in *le quartier juif* and were subject to humiliating disabilities that included obligations to wear the Jewish badge, listen to the monthly sermon in a church, and bear exceptionally burdensome taxes. As a group, they were set

---

years. In making the case for distinctiveness, she disputes the overriding importance that historians have traditionally assigned to the Berlin Haskalah. See Frances Malino, "Jewish Enlightenment in Berlin and Paris," in Michael Brenner, Vicki Caron and Uri R. Kaufmann, eds., *Jewish Emancipation Reconsidered: The French and German Models* (Tubingen, 2003). In the same volume, Dominique Bourel expressed reservations about the intellectual and cultural vitality of France, considering the absence of serious public debate about Jewish emancipation. While there is much that is correct in the claims of both Malino and Bourel, the weight they attach to Haskalah's role as the prime measure of Jewish political culture and intellectual vitality is overstated relative to more robust Metz rabbinic culture.

6 On early modern patterns of acculturation in Rome and its broader implications, see Kenneth Stow, *Theater of Acculturation: The Roman Ghetto in the Sixteenth Century* (Seattle, 2001).

apart from the surrounding society, characterized as no less than *un peuple isolé* by the Catholic *Almanach des Trois Evêchés* (in 1788).[7] What is striking about the history of Metz Jewry is the degree to which it remained impervious to the disabilities they suffered in the realms of taxation, economic restrictions, mobility, and residence.

Return to France and Establishment of the Metz Community

Settlement patterns in the sixteenth and seventeenth centuries highlight the unevenness that characterized attitudes toward the Jews in the early modern era. Territorial annexation was the most immediate factor accounting for the growth of the Jewish population in France. Equally significant was the economic utility of the Jews, which called for a reconsideration of medieval policies. During the rule of Louis XI, nearly a century after the Jews were expelled for the final time from France in 1394, foreigners were encouraged to settle in Bordeaux and Bayonne. Incentives for their immigration and resettlement included substantial commercial privileges and exemption from the *droit d'aubaine*, the law that entitled the monarchy to seize the estate of a deceased foreigner. The newcomers included *conversos* who had left the Iberian Peninsula to escape the Inquisition—referred to as *nouveaux Chrétiens in* the *lettres patentes* that Henri II issued in 1550. In the next two centuries, as many came to identify openly as Jews, their numbers grew to approximately 5,000. These members of the Portuguese Nation, as they preferred to be known, resided in six localities in southwest France: Bordeaux, Bayonne, Biaritz, Saint-Jean-de-Luz, Bidache, and Peyrehorade. In the papal province of Comtat Venaissin, further to the southeast, there were additionally 2,500 Jews who resided in four *carrières* ("streets, districts"): Avignon, Carpentras, Cavaillon and Isle-sur-Sorgue. France did not formally annex these lands until 1791.

The return of Jews to France evoked spirited disagreement in various sectors of French society. Privileges permitting Jews qua *nouveaux Chrétiens* to remain in Bordeaux and pursue their livelihood depended on the often-conflicting interests of the monarchy, the Bordeaux Parlement, and the local merchant guilds. To stimulate the economy, the kings extended protection to the Portuguese merchants and permitted them to settle in ports and other

7 Anon., "Communauté des Juifs," *Almanach des Trois Evêches pour l'année 1788* (Metz, 1788), 213.

towns of the southwest and to engage freely in commerce. Cardinal Richelieu's efforts to halt proceedings against *conversos* charged with Judaizing epitomize the importance the crown attached to the new policy.[8] On other occasions, however, the monarchy reversed itself, as in 1615, when Louis XIII demanded that all Jews, converted or not, leave France. This edict was issued in deference to local Bordelaise merchants who objected to competition from the newcomers. Consistently supportive of the Portuguese population, the local Parlement contested the royal edict and prevented its ratification.

Later in the century, the devastating economic downturn that followed the revocation of the Edict of Nantes (1685) induced a more favorable policy toward the Jews. In 1723, Louis XV issued *lettres patentes* that for the first time formally recognized the *nouveaux Chrétiens* as the Jews they were.[9] Henceforth, members of the Portuguese Nation were permitted to purchase and lease land. By mid-century, the Jews of Bordeaux had become conspicuous in banking, grain trade and chocolate making, maritime trade, and shipbuilding. In Bayonne, Jews imported wool and gold and were active in the silk and wine trade. Vigorous resistance to Jewish membership in the guilds prevailed most everywhere in France, except in Bordeaux and to a lesser extent in Bayonne, where Jews were excluded from the chocolate makers' guild.[10]

Jewish life in southern France was shaped by political forces and economic conditions that were distinctive to the region. In Bordeaux and in the rural localities of Bidache, Pehrehorade and Labastide-Clairence, residential Jewish areas were concentrated in a few streets, but no separate Jewish quarter was established. Bayonne did not permit Jews to reside in the city at all; they therefore all lived in Saint-Esprit on the right bank of the Adour River. Whether the Jews were legally subject to the *droit d'aubaine* was debated throughout the eighteenth century, and even in Bordeaux repeated efforts to apply this law to the Jewish population ceased only by order of the local Parlement in 1758. In the Papal States Jews lived in crowded, dilapidated hovels, were subjected to harsh taxation, and were also required to wear yellow hats. Accusations of ritual murder still had credibility, as in the case of a Jew from Boulay who was burned to death in 1670 for the alleged murder of a Christian child.[11] For

8 See Jonathan Israel, *European Jewry in the Age of Mercantilism* (New York, 1985), 116–18.

9 See Hertzberg, *The French Enlightenment and the Jews* (New York, 1968), 78–112; Frances Malino, *The Sephardic Jews of Bordeaux: Assimilation and Emancipation in Revolutionary and Napoleonic France* (Tuscaloosa, 1978), 1–22.

10 Gérard Nahon, "From New Christians to the Portuguese Jewish Nation in France," Haim Beinart, ed., *Moreshet Sepharad: The Sephardic Legacy*, 2 vols. (Jerusalem, 1992), 2:336–64.

11 Zosa Szajkowski, "The Jewish Status in Eighteenth-Century France and the 'Droit d'Aubaine,'" *Historia Judaica* 19 (1957): 147–61; idem, *The Economic Status of the Jews in*

Christian theologians, the wretched condition of the Jews furnished proof of divine rejection. To curb their harmful influence, many communities in the northeast and southwest required Jews to regularly attend church sermons. But, in all likelihood, far-reaching regulations that severely prohibited social and economic contact between Christians and Jews in Avignon and Comtat Venaissin, such as those that were enacted in 1725 by the Holy See, were honored only in the breach.[12] Owing to the special circumstances of their settlement, there were no explicit laws limiting contact with Christians in Bordeaux and Bayonne, nor were there restrictions on economic activities that were at all comparable to the limitations imposed in Alsace and Lorraine.

Conditions in the northeast were quite different. As the territories of Alsace and Lorraine came under French dominion in the sixteenth and seventeenth centuries, the Jewish population grew steadily. Like numerous other Jewish communities in France, the Metz Kehillah was reestablished in the sixteenth century, nearly two centuries after the expulsion of 1365. Although there were signs of a continued Jewish presence in the city as late as 1500, Jews no longer had formal permission to reside in Metz after they were expelled. Following the conquest of Metz in 1552, Jews from Germany and Poland were permitted to settle in the Moselle to provide credit to local residents and to the military garrison. The ordinance of 1567 formalized their status and introduced several provisions regulating admission, taxes, residence, and lending practices. In 1595, three years after Metz, Toul, and Verdun—les Trois-Évêchés (the Three Bishoprics)—came under French control, Henri IV issued privileges guaranteeing the public practice of Judaism in Metz and nearby villages.

Beginning in 1603, the small Jewish population constituted an official community clustered in the Saint Ferroy quarter along the Rimport, where it erected a synagogue in 1619 and established various communal agencies and an elected council consisting of six *parnasim* (syndics), three of whom were rabbis. Upon the reunification of Metz with the newly annexed episcopal territory and with the establishment of the Parlement of Metz in 1633, followed by the founding of the *bailliage* eight years later, Metz was slowly integrated into the administrative and justice systems of the French monarchy and

---

Alsace, Metz, and Lorraine, 28–71; Hertzberg, *French Enlightenment and the Jews*, 34, 54–63; 249–65.

12 Pierre-André Meyer, *La Communauté juive de Metz au XVIIIe siècle* (Nancy, 1993); Szajkowski, "Population Problems of Marranos and Sephardim," *Proceedings of the American Academy of Jewish Research* 27 (1958): 83–103; S. Posener, "The Social Life of the Jewish Communities in France in the Eighteenth Century," *Jewish Social Studies* 7 (1945): 271–326.

emerged as the provincial capital.[13] At the time, there were nearly four hundred Jews in Metz of a total population of roughly 20,000, as reported by the president of the Parlement de Metz.[14] The *lettres patentes* of 1632 were reaffirmed in 1657 and in 1687 by an *arrêt de conseil*. Jewish juridical autonomy, though upheld by the Metz Parlement, came at a high price. The nearly three thousand members of the Jewish community at the end of the ancien régime paid an annual *droit d'habitation, protection, et tolerance* of 20,000 livres to the duc de Brancas.

By dint of the city's strategic position at the time of the Thirty Years War, and owing to the growth in its political prominence during the last third of the seventeenth century, the fortunes of Metz improved greatly. Located along the Moselle and Seille rivers, Metz became an important commercial center, especially for textiles. Its economic vitality, enhanced by the presence of the military garrison it hosted and the rich natural resources in the surrounding agricultural region, encouraged substantial immigration.[15] During the one hundred-fifty years prior to the Revolution, Metz emerged as a major center of Jewish life in Europe and the westernmost outpost of Yiddish-speaking Ashkenazic Jewry in the early modern era (see map 1). Jews continued to settle in Metz and in other towns and villages in the Moselle, which was the most densely populated region of the northeast. These included, among others, Augny, Bionville, Boulay, Bouzonville, Courcelles-Chaussy, Delme, Ennery, Forbach, Frémestroff, Louvigny, Marsal, Metzervisse, Morhange, Phalsbourg,

---

13 See Moïse Ginsburger, "Les Juifs de Metz sous l'ancien régime," *REJ* 50 (1905): 112–14; Georges Weill, "Recherches sur la démographie des juifs d'Alsace du XVIe au XVIIIe siècle," *REJ* 130 (1971): 53–55; Zosa Szajkowski, "Demographic Aspects of Jewish Emancipation in France during the French Revolution," *Historia Judaica Judaica* 21 (1959): 7–36; Jean-Bernard Lang and Claude Rosenfeld, *Histoire des Juifs en Moselle* (Metz, 2001), 45–50. On the involvement of the monarchy in the French takeover of Metz, including the local tensions that erupted with respect to the division of jurisdictional authority, see Patricia Behre Miskimin, *One King, One Law, Three Faiths. Religion and the Rise of Absolutism in Seventeenth-Century Metz* (Westport, CT, 2002), 16–40. On the history of the Metz Parlement, see the useful but dated work of Emmanuel Michel, *Histoire du Parlement de Metz* (Paris, 1845).

14 Reported on 12 October 1635, in Gilbert Roos, *Relations entre le Gouvernement Royal et les Juifs du Nord-Est de la France au XVIIe siècle* (Paris, 2000), 30. For additional population data, see Jean Rigault, "La population de Metz au XVIIe siècle," *Annales de l'Est* 3 (1951): 307–16.

15 For background on the "Frenchification" of the province of Lorraine and on Metz especially, see Charles T. Lipp, *Noble Strategies in an Early Modern Small State: The Mahuet of Lorraine* (Rochester, NY, 2011), esp. 89–113.

Puttlelange, Sarreguemines, Sarrelouis, Sierck, Thionville, Uckange, and Vantoux (see map 2).[16]

A large percentage of the Jewish population was involved directly or indirectly in army provisioning. Horses, forage and fodder for livestock, grain, and loans to soldiers were the leading commodities supplied by Jewish purveyors. Army purveying led to other commercial undertakings in the civilian sector, often under royal protection, and collaboration between Jewish purveyors and the military, which had extended to Alsace during the Thirty Years War, contributed to the steady growth of Jewish settlement along the Upper and Lower Rhine Valley in the ensuing decades.[17] By the end of the century, leading advisors to Louis XIV had steered the king away from parochial Christian interests that had, to this point, dominated royal policy. The results were visible throughout the northeast of France. By 1679, while the Christian population increased slightly, the number of Jews had doubled.[18]

Population growth strengthened the economic position of Metz Jews but also took its toll. Heightened tensions between Jews and their Christian neighbors were already in evidence in the first half of the seventeenth century. Local opposition to the Parlement's registration of the *lettres patentes* in 1633 was enflamed by concerns over economic competition voiced by various tradesmen, especially cloth merchants and the butchers' guild. Despite their incontestable economic utility, Jews in the Moselle region found themselves positioned precariously between competing royal and local policy interests.[19] Colbert in particular was confident that the economic benefit that Jews provided to the state far outweighed the grievances of local merchants. Reporting on regional conditions in 1697, royal Intendant Jacques Etienne Turgot lauded the impressive achievements of Metz's Jewish merchants. They constituted "a kind of republic and neutral nation" that enabled them to travel with ease and transport merchandise across national boundaries. Turgot noted local complaints concerning their unfair advantage in procuring merchandise more swiftly than their competitors and their ability to sell at lower prices. As the number of Jews grew and their commercial success became more apparent some local authorities advocated curtailment of continued Jewish settlement in the region. However, the Jews' crucial role in supplying the army with food

16 See Meyer, *La communauté juive de Metz au XVIII*^e^ *siècle*, and Lang and Rosenfeld, *Histoire des Juifs en Moselle*, 50–84.

17 See Meyer, *La Communauté juive de* Metz, 93–103.

18 Roos, *Relations entre le Gouvernement Royal et les Juifs*, 127–29.

19 Miskimin, *One King, One Law*, 54.

and horses assured them the special privileges granted by the crown.[20] On 9 July 1718, Louis XV issued *lettres patentes* that confirmed their privileges, and these were registered in the Metz Parlement on 3 September 1718, with some modifications.[21] By 1784 there were nearly 20,000 Jews in Alsace and 5,000 in the duchy of Lorraine. Smaller communities formed in Paris, Lyons, Marseilles, and Nîmes, though most regions of France, and many large cities such as Strasbourg, excluded Jews entirely.[22]

Relative prosperity attained by successful financiers, merchants, and army purveyors is apparent from regulations enacted by communal leaders to control consumption in the 1690s and throughout much of the eighteenth century. With the expansion of commercial opportunities, partnerships of various sizes engaged in the purchase and sale of livestock while individuals and small groups were involved as brokers of wax, gems, and other commodities. The largest commercial enterprises, especially in the horse and grain trade, were operated by consortiums of as many as ten parties, among them non-Jewish financiers and traders. Large-scale commerce, especially involving government contracts, required travel to Paris, and in such cases standard restrictions on intercity mobility were relaxed. Small enterprises, such as cheese production, were conducted in private homes.[23] The size of dowries, the scope of

20 Charles W. Cole, *Colbert and a Century of French Mercantilism* (New York, 1939). See Hertzberg, *French Enlightenment and the Jews*, 20–21.

21 Michel, *Histoire du Parlement de Metz*, 515.

22 Hertzberg, *French Enlightenment and the Jews*, 19–28; Weill, "Recherches sur la démographie des juifs d'Alsace," 53–55; Zosa Szajkowski, "Demographic Aspects of Jewish Emancipation in France during the French Revolution," *Historia Judaica* 21 (1959): 7–36; Marianne Calmann, *The Carrière of Carpentras* (Oxford, 1984); and Sahlins, *Unnaturally French*.

23 See Miskimin, *One King, One Law*, 47–65. For additional sources on Jewish life in the seventeenth century, see Gilbert Roos, *Relations entre le gouvernement royal et les juifs du nord-est de la France au XVIIe siècle* (Paris, 2000). Also see Anchel, *Les juifs de France*, 169–93; and Hertzberg, *French Enlightenment and the Jews*, 125–26, 213. For sources in the Beit Din records on commercial enterprise, see the following: Horse trade: PMBD, Vol. 1, pt. 2, no. 51, 15a; sheep trade: Vol. 2, no. 355, 67a; cows: Vol. 1, pt. 2, no. 184, 42b–43a; Vol. 2, no. 89, 17b; Vol. 1, pt. 2, no. 29, 9b; Vol. 2, no. 536, 109b. Forage: Vol. 1, pt. 1, no. 64, 19b–20a; Vol. 1, pt. 1, no. 144, 46a; Vol. 1, pt. 2, no. 50, 15a (partnership for forage, straw, and oats); Vol. 2, no. 25, 6b; Vol. 2, no. 435, 83b; Vol. 2, no. 511, 103b; Vol. 2, no. 633, 137b–138a. Wax: Vol. 2, no. 110, 22a; Vol. 2, no. 303, 55b. Brokerage: Vol. 1, pt. 1, no. 46, 15a. Gems: Vol. 2, no. 596, 128a. Cheese: Vol. 1, pt. 2, no. 123, 30b; in Vol. 2, no. 249, 46b, the sale of cheese beneath a shop prompted the storeowner to complain that the pungent smell was harming his business; he asked the Beit Din for a restraining order on the cheese maker. The Beit Din ruled in favor of the plaintiff. However, a similar complaint a year later, recorded in PKM, 121a, yielded an opposite ruling by the Kahal. It decided that the benefit to the community precluded objections to the foul odor of the cheese.

commercial transactions, inheritance bequests, charitable gifts, and valuables listed in probate inventories offer additional evidence of affluence, though such prosperity was limited to the upper echelon of the Jewish population.

For its part, the Kahal generously supported the Metz yeshivah and its full-time students, and the community was able to attract many of the most illustrious Talmudists in Europe who accepted the offer to serve the prestigious community as *av beit din*. Under these circumstances, numerous children of wealthy families from communities across the German border applied for the *ḥezkat ʿironit* (residence permit) when they became engaged to marry the son or daughter of a Metz resident. The costs of procuring the *ḥezkat ʿironit*, in addition to taxes on dowries and on inheritance and, if necessary, the indemnification of the payment of the exit tax were steep. These taxes, which ranged from one percent of a new couple's dowry to eight percent of a resident's property, were over and above the usual communal, local, and royal taxes.[24] Since these financial burdens were beyond the reach of most immigrants, only the affluent could afford to settle in Metz, which was doubtless consistent with the community's interest in attracting prosperous newcomers. Moreover, the high costs surely outpaced income levels, so that the gap between rich and poor became much wider over the course of the eighteenth century.

The large westward migration exerted pressure on communities in Germanic lands, France, England, and Holland to meet the needs of refugees who escaped the ravages of persecution and the concomitant economic crisis. Political changes in the West went hand in hand with the rise of new centers of economic opportunity. Among the new arrivals were large numbers of poor, homeless Jews, known in Jewish communities as *Betteljuden* or *Schnorrjuden* (beggar Jews). In light of increasing geographic dispersal and communal segregation, begging became an acute problem in European society in the early modern era. How to relieve the condition of beggars was a divisive issue, especially in light of the growing anti-alien bias fomented by the increased immigration of foreigners.[25] Pressures posed by immigration exacerbated the precarious economic circumstances in which Jews were living in the eighteenth century.

Conditions in southern France were no better. Owing to the severe economic plight of Jewish immigrants and *conversos* who sought a new beginning, the

---

24 See PKM, 36a, 37a, 66a–67a, and 74a. Also see the 1769 Takkanot, Art. 48, fol. 79a, for restrictions on individuals who settled without the permission of the Kahal. For a discussion of several wider legal ramifications of the *ḥezkat ʿironit*, see Ya'ir Ḥayyim Bacharach, *Resp. Ḥavvot Ya'ir* (Frankfurt, 1699), no. 80.

25 See Moses Shulvass, *From East to West* (Detroit, 1971), passim, and S. Posener, "The Social Life of the Jewish Communities in France in the 18th Century," *JSS* 7 (1945): 221–23.

Jewish communities of Bordeaux, Bayonne, and Avignon displayed uneasiness about supporting the poor. In the case of Bordeaux, in the early seventeenth century this attitude manifested itself in firm resistance to the settlement of any additional Jews and with half of all families dependent on charity, the community leadership felt compelled to expel residents, both Sephardic and non-Sephardic families, some of whom had lived in the community for twenty years. In 1648, ninety-three poor Sephardic families were expelled from Bordeaux, Bayonne, Dax, and Bidache. In 1735, the Bordeaux Kehillah decided that only the Sephardic poor were eligible to receive charity, and in 1744 it undertook to expel Ashkenazic and Italian Jews while prohibiting the Sephardic poor from trading in used goods. Nearly two decades later, a large number of Sephardim were again expelled from Bordeaux, as were poor immigrant *conversos*. In Saint Esprit and Avignon, communal leaders followed a similar policy of expelling vagabonds to reduce competition in trade while also limiting the number of poor entitled to receive charity.[26]

Troubles in the Lorraine region, reflected in diminishing revenues and decreasing salaries in the second half of the eighteenth century, may explain the Jewish population decline in Metz from 3,000 in 1714 to just over 2,000 in 1789, at a time when the general population of the city was increasing. The Pinkas Kahal contains substantial evidence of financial difficulties that had begun to plague the community, including complaints that communal revenues did not keep pace with expenses (1772). Insufficient cash reserves, compounded by heavy taxes and duties, made it impossible for the community to meet its charitable commitments. As a result, it became necessary to limit the number of foreign students admitted to the Metz yeshivah (1780), and the *av beit din* approved a request that funds collected for the *yishuv* in Eretz Israel be used for local needs instead (1782). There was a steady decline in the number granted the right of domicile in the community. In the years 1759–1769, twenty-four foreigners were naturalized, and in the next two decades there was a total of thirteen.

Takkanot recorded in the Pinkas Kahal in 1780 and devoted to residential permits—though never formally enacted—expressly record that economic strains on the community were of increasing concern: "The times are more and more troubling, and it is necessary to erect ramparts to improve the condition

26 Zosa Szajkowski, "Sephardim, Ashkenazim and Avignonese Jews," in *Jews in the French Revolutions of 1789, 1830 and 1848* (New York, 1970), 254–57. In 1760 Avignonese leaders enacted *takkanot* that gave them the right to expel vagabonds. On attitudes toward *foreign Jews in Bordeaux and on sick care in the community, see Le Registre des délibérations de la Nation Juive Portugaise de Bordeaux*, parags. 173, 182, 382–83, and 417.

of our holy community."[27] In Alsace conditions were no better. From 1775 Strasbourg saw its river trade decline in favor of that of Mayence, resulting in a lower volume of sales to merchants in many Rhenish towns.[28] All this was aggravated by the influx of immigrants from Poland, most of whom were poor, including many young men who arrived in Metz and were sapping communal resources. The number of rabbis and their students exceeded the number of available positions, forcing many to migrate to Germany and to Switzerland.[29] Correspondingly, a reduction in aid to the itinerant poor signaled the progressive pauperization of Jews who resided permanently in Metz.[30]

Throughout the ancien régime, the vast majority of Jews in the northeastern provinces was limited by imperial decree to money lending, trading in old clothes, and cattle dealing. They were subjected to humiliating legal disabilities such as the infamous *péage corporel* (body tax), and in some areas they were obliged to wear yellow hats. The *arrêts* issued by the Metz Parlement in 1703, 1707, and 1708 required Jews to wear the yellow hat in the city, on pain of a fine of three *livres* and a charity payment of six *livres*; the seven elected officials of the community were exempt from this obligation, however.[31] Heavy taxes, including the notorious Brancas tax, which was intended as a protection duty, impelled the Metz community to borrow large sums from Christian lenders, so that by the end of the ancien régime the community's total debt was nearly a half-million livres. Although the community counted numerous

27 C. E. Labrousse, *Esquisse de mouvemnent des prix et des revenues en France au XVIIIe siècle* 2 vols. (Paris, 1933), 1:88, 304; 2:468, 598, 602; *Histoire écononomique et sociale de la France*, 2:399. For a full description and for a translation of the text of the *takkanot* see Kerner, *La vie*, 75–78, 184 bis, and appendix, xxii–xxxvi. Also see Anchel, *Les Juifs de France*, 165–67.

28 Franklin Ford, *Strasbourg in Transition, 1648–1789* (Cambridge, MA, 1958), 142–57.

29 On the deterioration of the financial condition of the Jews in northeastern France, see Szajkowski, *Jews in the French Revolutions*, 204–205.

30 See Claudia Ulbrich, *Shulamit and Margarete: Power, Gender, and Religion in a Rural Society in Eighteenth-Century Europe* (Boston, 2004), 174; Hertzberg, *French Enlightenment and the Jews*, 129–32; and Szajkowski, *Economic Status of the Jews in Alsace, Metz and Lorraine*, 67–90. Hertzberg viewed a 1782 rabbinic decision permitting the use of the charity box intended for Eretz Israel to support formerly affluent families who had become impoverished as clear evidence of increasing privation. On the establishment of charitable foundations by three of the wealthiest Jews of the region, including Cerf Berr, Moïse Blien, and David Terquem, see Moïse Ginsburger, "Une fondation de Cerf Berr," *REJ* 76 (1923): 47–57, and Jay R. Berkovitz, "Jewish Philanthropy in Early Modern and Modern Europe: Theory and Practice in Historical Perspective," in *Toward a Renewed Ethic of Jewish Philanthropy*, ed. Yossi Prager (New York, 2010), 108–10.

31 Emmanuel Michel, *Histoire du Parlement de Metz* (Paris, 1845), 513–14.

wealthy merchants and financiers among its members, the majority of Jews of the Moselle showed signs of economic vulnerability.[32]

Modest improvement in the legal standing and treatment of Metz Jews may be discerned in the second half of the eighteenth century. The distinguishing clothing demanded of them was a formless hat, a small, dark coat, and white sleeves.[33] By 1760, they were no longer expected to attend church sermons, and the *droit d'aubaine*, which empowered the government to seize the estate of a deceased foreigner, was no longer applied to them.[34] In 1769 the Parlement of Metz found several Frenchmen guilty of theft from a Jewish home in Mittelbronn, and they were put to death. The ruling, which rested exclusively on the testimony of Jews, was viewed as a landmark case. Several years later, in 1775, Pierre-Louis Lacretelle pleaded before the Parlement of Nancy on behalf of two Jews who requested certificates as merchants in Thionville. He argued that the Jews were not *aubaines* but *régnicoles*, entitling them to the economic privileges enjoyed by other citizens. Although the petition failed, it anticipated the Jewish emancipation discourse of the 1780s.[35] Jewish financiers and merchants took their non-Jewish debtors and clients to court when they defaulted on their payments. In fact, most cases involving Jewish lenders were lawsuits initiated by Jews against their gentile debtors. Legal recourse against delinquent debtors and traders was essential to the viability of moneylending and commerce, and Jewish lenders felt reasonably assured that their claims would receive a fair hearing.[36]

32 See Zosa Szajkowski, *Autonomy and Communal Jewish Debts during the French Revolution of 1789* (New York, 1959), 33. Much less frequently, they were subject to physical danger, as the 1670 ritual murder accusation and execution of Raphaël Lévy in the village of Boulay attests. See Pierre Birnbaum, *A Tale of Ritual Murder in the Age of Louis XIV: The Trial of Raphaël Lévy*, trans. Arthur Goldhammer (Stanford, CA, 2012).

33 Michel, *Histoire du Parlement de Metz*, 514.

34 On the *droit d'aubaine*, see Sahlins, *Unnaturally French*.

35 See the efforts of one author to discredit the Mittelbronn ruling in the court of public opinion: Charles-Marguerite Mercier Dupaty, *Justification de sept hommes condamnés par le Parlement de Metz en 1769, sur les seules dépositions de juifs plaignans* (Paris, 1787). Also see Pierre-Louis Lacretelle, *Plaidoyer pour deux Juifs de Metz contre l'Hotel de Ville et le corps des marchands de Thionville* (Brussels, 1785). On the *droit d'aubaine*, see Zosa Szjajkowski, *Jews and the French Revolutions of 1789, 1830, and 1848* (New York, 1970), 220–31. On Lacretelle's determined efforts on behalf of Jewish merchants, see Schechter, *Obstinate Hebrews*, 77–79; more generally, see Bell, *Lawyers and Citizens*, 164–67, 175–80.

36 Szajkowski asserted that no cases of Jews found guilty of practicing usury (illegally), based on reports by historians Roger Clément, *La Condition des Juifs de Metz dans l'Ancien Régime* and Robert Anchel, *Les juifs de France*. See Szajkowski, *Jews and the French Revolutions*, 178–82. However, the Metz Kahal was aware of a problem in this regard and

The realm of law, then, both in the theoretical sense and as practiced in French courts, was an arena that had become comparatively free of the more pronounced injustices and ignominies that Jews experienced in other areas of life. With certain qualifications the term "legal integration" may be a more apt description of this process, at least as it comes into view in the proceedings of the Metz rabbinic court. Legal integration refers to the Jews' acknowledgment of prevailing systems of law and justice and their compliance with administrative, bureaucratic, and legal requirements imposed by the state. Where full acquiescence was either impossible or undesirable, the rabbinic court and the communal leadership navigated a course that met the demands of local and state law while remaining faithful to Jewish legal norms. To be sure, navigating plural jurisdictions was a vital, time-honored strategy practiced by autonomous Jewish communities in the Middle Ages, though the degree of interaction between the Jewish and general legal systems varied from one locality to another. In eighteenth-century Metz, where the institutions of French law were pervasive and imposing, the Beit Din displayed considerable familiarity with state and local institutions and, when necessary, went to substantial lengths to gain knowledge of the intricacies of French law. That said, the boundaries drawn by the Metz community would need to define the acceptable modes of accommodation to French law and legal institutions. The copious signs of acculturation discussed below reflect the process of legal integration that was underway.[37]

Echoing enlightened absolutist policies in central Europe, the French monarchy had its own plan for the Jews. In 1784 Louis XVI issued two new pieces of legislation that abolished the body tax and granted Alsatian Jews freedom to engage in commerce and trades. Yet, several months later restrictions were imposed on the growth of the Jewish population and on its involvement in moneylending. In fact, in the late 1770s, rising tensions relating to the role of Jews in the regional economy had already become apparent. In 1777–1778, thousands of forged receipts were circulated in Alsace in order to defraud Jewish lenders of their rightful payments. Although the Sovereign Council of Alsace confirmed that the debts owed to Jewish lenders were still outstanding, and notwithstanding the fact that those responsible for the forgeries were convicted and brought to justice, there was great popular support for François Hell,

in 1786 exhorted community members who were engaging in what it described as exploitative lending practices to French youth. See PKM, 133b–134b.

37 For a similar phenomenon in Hamburg, see David H. Horowitz, "Fractures and Fissures in Jewish Communal Autonomy in Hamburg, 1710–1782," (Ph.D. diss., Columbia University, 2010), 132–41.

who masterminded the scheme, and for the pamphlet he published to justify his allegations.[38] Despite the widely recognized need for credit, the Jews' preponderance in moneylending continued to be viewed, especially in the rural countryside, as a sign of avarice and as a symbol of the religious enmity that divided Jews and Christians. To their critics, the Jews embodied a corporate particularism that was incompatible with the values of citizenship. These sorts of sentiments were expressed even by those who favored improvement in the Jews' legal status. Thus, in the prize-winning essay he submitted to the Metz Royal Academy of Sciences in 1785, Abbé Henri Grégoire conceded that the Jews were degenerate and depraved but insisted that despite these disabilities they could be regenerated morally and physically. His criticism was not lost on French *maskilim* who challenged his anti-Jewish prejudices.[39]

Escalating political turmoil during the months leading to the French Revolution took a heavy toll on the Jews in Alsace and Lorraine. Beginning in March, riots exposed Jews and their property to extreme danger, and new restrictions were imposed on their mobility within the region. The Metz Parlement issued an *arrêt* prohibiting poor wayfarers (vagabonds) from visiting the community on the Passover holiday. Whether the *arrêt* was intended for the city only or would be enforced in the surrounding communities as well was a question of immediate concern to leaders of Medinat Lothringen (the province of Lorraine) and for which they sought clarification. On 18 March, the Lorraine leaders informed the Metz Kahal that if the law were to be implemented widely, then the Lorraine communities would need to prepare a sufficient amount of *matzah* to accommodate the "legions of visitors" likely to flood the province.[40] A letter sent five days later, on 23 March, referred to the situation as follows: "[O]ne day is more difficult than the next with respect to the evil of the nations." It is clear that the order, which had come from the

38 On the false receipts affair, see Schechter, *Obstinate Hebrews*, 67–73.

39 Roger Clément, *La condition des juifs de Metz sous l'ancien régime* (Paris, 1903), 129–34. See Mona Ozouf, "Regeneration," in François Furet and Mona Ozouf, *A Critical Dictionary of the French Revolution* (Cambridge, MA, 1989), trans. Arthur Goldhammer, 779–90. On Grégoire's role in shaping the revolutionary ethos, see Alyssa Goldstein Sepinwall, *The Abbé Grégoire and the French Revolution: The Making of Modern Universalism* (Berkeley, 2005). For evidence of oppositions to Grégoire's views, see idem, "Strategic Friendships: Jewish Intellectuals, the Abbé Grégoire, and the French Revolution," in Ross Brann and Adam Sutcliffe, *Renewing the Past, Reconfiguring Jewish Culture: From Al-Andalus to the Haskalah* (Philadelphia, 2004), 189–212.

40 *Le Registre de correspondence de la communauté juive de Lorraine. Copies des lettres des années 1783–1791*, recueilli et presenté avec une introduction et des notes par Simon Schwarzfuchs (Jerusalem, 2003), no. 166 (18 March 1789), 126–27.

grand prévôt of the *maréchaussée* (the police), was issued in relation to vagabonds only and not to the "respectable poor" or to needy Torah scholars.[41]

Just days later, describing riots that occurred in Nancy, Lorraine leaders commended the army for the protection it provided to Jews and also warned the Jewish population to behave with caution:

> The rioters broke through walls, doors and brick, and all windows and doors were shattered, so that the dwellings were temporarily unlivable. Were it not for the great officers who sent large brigades to watch over us with estimable protection, there would be no surviving this [onslaught]. Now things are quiet. Great is the need to treat the non-Jews honestly [*temimut*] and to avoid anything God forbid that is a desecration of the Divine Name [*ḥillul ha-Shem*].[42]

Praising the military for restoring quiet to Jewish homes and the synagogue in Nancy, Lorraine communal leaders wrote a week later and asked the Metz Kahal to furnish them with a *copie collationnée*, an official copy, of all the privileges that the Metz community had with respect to their cemetery.

> That is to say, we already have *lettres patentes* from the king that were registered with the *Greffe de Parlement*. But we need to get a *copie* from the *Commandant en chef de la Province*, [confirming] the validity of his order, when there is time, to serve as a protection against the masses, so that if they plot to destroy, to revolt and transgress, they will be shamed and frightened by our lord's order and the order of the guards. And since we know that you have in your bags various writings and letters from every commandant, from Maréchal de Belleisle to Maréchal de Broglie, etc., send us the *copie* that was confirmed by the notary, because the hour requires this.[43]

Communal leaders displayed faith that the rule of law would protect them from widespread violence, and though in retrospect this might have been

---

41 That the order had come from the head of the police is evident from the Metz Kahal's answer to the previous letter. See *Le Registre de correspondence de la communauté juive de Lorraine*, no. 168 (23 March 1789), 128. On the "respectable poor," see Chapter 3, below.

42 Ibid., no. 169 (27 March 1789), 128–29.

43 Ibid., no. 170 (1 April 1789), 129–30. Maréchal de Belleisle, father and son, were dukes who governed the city from 1737 to 1761. Maréchal de Broglie was the commander of the region when the letter was sent; he would be appointed secretary of defense the following July.

naïve, it remained a source of hope even during the tumultuous and ominous spring of 1789.

Prior to the Revolution, then, widespread unrest in the Alsatian countryside, fueled by powerful anti-Jewish sentiment, contributed to feelings of insecurity, anxiety, and terror in Jewish communities. The foregoing accounts add important details to the impressions of Zosa Szajkowski in his studies of the riots in Alsace and Metz that erupted during the summer of 1789 and continued in the ensuing autumn months. The following year the police provided protection at the Metz synagogue after the Jewish community and members of the municipal council expressed fear that violence could erupt there once again. Similar concerns registered in 1792 were no doubt reinforced by reports that Jewish homes in eighteen communities were ransacked and innumerable sacred Hebrew books and manuscripts were destroyed, as depicted vividly by a resident of Issenheim, among others.[44] According to Szajkowski, the Jews were not singled out for their money lending practices but were victims of the anxiety felt by Alsatian farmers who expected to assume ownership of lands worked by Jews. He concluded that economic self-interest outweighed anti-Jewish sentiment as the main cause of violence against Jews.[45] Szajkowski's assessment of the origins and significance of the riots fails, however, to explain the vehemence of the furor directed specifically at Jews. It is conceivable that the antipathy generated by religious difference, economic anxiety, ideological opposition, or social unrest could remain at once vehement and non-violent. However, the social structure and economic conditions that prevailed in the rural countryside, and the particular role of religion in the local culture, may account for how the village population could be easily whipped into a frenzy. At times this could lead to uncontrollable aggression. For these reasons, it is apparent that the Jewish leadership's faith in the rule of law as protection against mass violence waned in the months following the Revolution.

The characterization of Metz Jews as *un peuple isolé* by the *Almanach des Trois Evêchés* on the eve of the Revolution was less a description of the local

44 See the testimony of Gavriel Wahl, quoted in Zosa Szajkowski, "Riots Against Jews in Metz in 1792" [Hebrew], *Zion* 22 (1957): 76.

45 Zosa Szajkowski, "Anti-Jewish Riots during the Revolutions of 1789, 1830, and 1848," *Zion* 20 (1955): 82–89. According to Szajkowski, the Jews sought to destroy written evidence of the debts they owed or of the fact that they were not the owners of these lands. They recognized that without documents they could not collect money owed to them and they therefore demanded a legal remedy enabling them to collect even though their names were missing from the documents. The *comité legislative* of the National Assembly opposed this step out of concern that lenders would demand more than they were owed. In Szajkowski's view, the destruction of documents and the refusal of lawmakers to enable Jews to collect what was owed to them contributed to the deterioration in their status.

Jewish population and more a sign of Christian uneasiness about the Jewish purchase of homes beyond their own neighborhood. Such concerns almost certainly prompted the journal to stress the ostensive isolation of the Jews to provoke opposition to expansion of their residential area. Religious bias likely predisposed the Catholic publication to overstatement in its description of the local Jewish population and its separation from the social mainstream. Based on many of the sources now available, it appears unlikely that the legal restrictions on the Jews' livelihood and mobility were applied as rigorously and consistently as the language of the *Almanach* implied. While evidence of the strained relationship between Metz Jews and the surrounding society can neither be denied nor dismissed, conditions on the ground were far more complex. Participation in the life of the surrounding society frequently contradicted official arrangements and policies *vis-à-vis* Metz Jewry.

Ritual and Identity

The massive relocation of European Jewish populations in the sixteenth and seventeenth centuries, and the wide-ranging social disruptions that ensued, left an indelible impression on the signs and symbols of religious ritual. Metz, and more generally the northeastern provinces of France, were no exception. On the one hand, time-honored patterns of religious culture ruptured, and on the other, the challenges of displacement and loss sparked efforts both to preserve old rituals and to adopt new practices. The revolution in printing revitalized diverse traditions that would have otherwise remained inaccessible and unknown. Tensions resulting from population movements were complicated by the pronounced cultural and political chasm separating eastern and western European Jewries and found expression in the competition between German Jewry and Polish Jewry for recognition as the standard-bearer of the Ashkenazic tradition.

In France, prayer books, like customs books, contributed to the consolidation of religious practice and to the entrenchment of local identity. The popular character of these compilations is evident in their frequent recourse to midrashic imagery, parables, and rabbinic folklore.[46] Ritual customs shed

46 See Elizabeth Eisenstein, *The Printing Press as an Agent of Change*, 2 vols. (Cambridge, MA, 1979), 1:71–73; Elhanan Reiner, "The Ashkenazic Elite at the Beginning of the Modern Era: Manuscript versus Printed Book," *Polin* 10 (1997): 85–98, and Menachem Elon, *Jewish Law: History, Sources, Principles*, 4 vols., trans. from Hebrew by Bernard Auerbach and Melvin J. Sykes (Philadelphia, 1994), 3:1138–48. Also see Jay R. Berkovitz, "Jewish Law

light on recondite structures of thought and behavior, and on the nature of the identification of communities in northeastern France with the western Ashkenazic heritage. They offer a window on the collective transformation of early modern Jewry.[47]

Until the end of the ancien régime, the area from Metz in the west to Prague in the east was a unified cultural entity in which the traditions of western Ashkenaz, as distinct from those of Poland-Lithuania, remained dominant.[48] A close examination of ritual observance reveals that the cultural history of the Jews in Alsace-Lorraine oscillated between two competing expressions. Local traditions tended to dominate in rural Alsatian communities, whereas in Metz a pan-Ashkenazic ethos enjoyed greater prominence. Rituals of remembrance evinced the allure of Ashkenazic culture in the broadest sense, though typically with a local variation. Nevertheless, the integration of broader patterns of Ashkenazic culture into the local consciousness was a source of continuing tension, as reflected in controversies over liturgy and religious customs.

Rituals offer entrée to a perception shared by Jews and their non-Jewish neighbors of the world as an ominous place threatened both physically and spiritually by demons. In the face of uncertainty, rituals offered protection from the frightening powers of evil spirits while also lending a semblance of order to life. Rituals served a variety of social and cultural functions as well. They were a means to forging bonds among individuals, especially as community members joined together in marking life passages, and enabled individuals to satisfy their need for public recognition. By bringing ordinary people and elites together, ritual celebrations fostered a strong collective identity. Finally, they provided a framework for the re-enactment of the great stories and the central messages of the Jewish tradition. Ritualized remembering fashioned the collective consciousness of the Jewish people and forged its religious ideals, emphasizing belief in divine providence, the power of prayer, the efficacy of repentance, the chosenness of Israel, and the primacy of ethical behavior. Festivals and fasts marking historical deliverance and destruction provided a

and Ritual in Early Modern Germany," in Dean P. Bell and Stephen G. Burnett, eds., *Jews, Judaism and the Reformation in Sixteenth-Century Germany* (Boston, 2006), 499–502.

47 See Arnold Van Gennep, *Manuel de folklore français contemporain* (Paris, 1943); Catherine Bell, *Ritual Theory, Ritual Practice* (New York, 1992); Victor Turner, *The Anthropology of Performance* (New Yok 1988); and S. Moore and B. Myeroff, "Secular Rituals: Forms and Meaning," *Secular Ritual* (Amsterdam 1977).

48 Census records and marriage contracts offer detailed evidence of the shared religious culture that united Jewish communities on either side of the Rhine. See Simon Schwarzfuchs, "Alsace and Southern Germany: The Creation of a Border," in Brenner, Caron and Kaufmann, eds. *Jewish Emancipation Reconsidered*, 5–17.

historical lens for understanding contemporary developments. Rituals were formative elements in the traditional view of the world.[49]

Popular religious culture was rarely detached completely from literary sources. As a rule, manifestations of folk religion in late medieval and early modern Europe emerged alongside the normative system of Halakhah. Initially transmitted orally, many ritual practices developed in response to the stresses and strains of daily life. In due course, numerous protective rites and folkways coalesced with biblical, midrashic, and talmudic sources. Frequently, the result was an amalgam of elite and popular religion, characterized not so much by internal dichotomy but by functional accord.[50] Childbirth is a case in point. The multiple risks of pregnancy and birth made bearing children terrifying experiences for most women. Ten percent of women died from childbirth-related causes in France during the ancien régime and approximately twenty-five percent of newborns did not survive the first year; more than forty percent of children did not reach the age of five.[51] According to popular belief, evil spirits lurked about mother and baby; the use of incantations and amulets, especially against Lilith, aimed to protect mother and baby. Emblematic of customs observed in the Alsace and Lorraine regions was the practice of wearing amulets of mineral and vegetable origin, the placing of a piece of iron in the delivery room as an anti-demonic device, the display of an article of the husband's clothing, and the tying of amulets made of snakeskin to the childbed. To gain instruction in the preparation of amulets, including one for childbirth, men (and women) could typically consult *Sefer Raziel*, a popular manual first published in Amsterdam in 1701 and reprinted nearly forty times thereafter. The book's popularity was doubtless enhanced by its traditional rabbinic style and air of authenticity, drawing as it did upon *Heikhalot* and *Merkabah* mysticism, the literature of *Hasidei Ashkenaz*, and the mystical doctrines of pre-Lurianic Kabbalah.[52] The wider availability of printed texts gave impetus to the merger

49 See Nissan Rubin, *The Joy of Life: Rites of Betrothal and Marriage in the Talmud and Midrash* [Hebrew] (Tel Aviv, 2004), 23–24. Also see Milton Singer, *When a Great Tradition Modernizes* (New York, 1972) and Richard Schechner, *Performance Theory* (New York 1988). The connection between remembering and repentance is a dominant theme of Rosh Hashanah, which is known in the rabbinic tradition by the name "Yom Ha-Zikkaron," the Day of Remembrance. Although the act of remembering refers to divine memory, humans endeavor through prayer to evoke divine memory.

50 See Peter Brown, *The Cult of the Saints* (Chicago, 1981).

51 François Lebrun, *La vie conjugale sous l'ancien régime* (Paris, 1975), 139–42.

52 See Herman Pollack, *Jewish Folkways in Germanic Lands (1648–1806)* (Cambridge, MA, 1971), 16–17; Freddy Raphaël, "Rites de naissance et medecine populaire dans le judaïsme rural d'Alsace," *Revue de la société d'ethnographie française* 1 (1971): 83–94. For antecedents, see Elisheva Baumgarten, *Mothers and Children: Jewish Family Life in Medieval*

of popular and elite religion and may well be taken as a mark of modernity, so far as the process lent legitimacy to non-rabbinic ritual practices.

Prayer books compiled in eighteenth-century Metz contain compelling evidence of the fusion of elite and popular religious trends. In fact, liturgical collections actively shaped and sustained the traditional worldview of the Jews of Alsace-Lorraine. A vital agent of culture, the printed prayer book offered considerable guidance for attaining ritual literacy and the deepening of religious belief, as illustrated by its important role in the dissemination of kabbalistic customs and lore.[53] Metz *siddurim* typically included entire sections of the kabbalistic *Tikkunei Shabbat* and selections from the regimen vitae (*hanhagot*) literature detailing *minhagim* ascribed to Rabbi Isaac Luria.[54] In these texts, worshippers were urged to perform a range of Lurianic practices, including ritual immersion before the onset of the Sabbath and the study of the weekly Torah portion along with the corresponding sections of the Book of the Zohar.[55] Zoharic passages were adduced to reinforce commonly accepted obligations, such as wearing special clothing on the Sabbath and lighting the Sabbath candles, and thereby endow these with added spiritual meaning. Instructions for neutralizing the harmful effects of husks of evil (*kelipot*) were included for those desiring to worship with the proper intention on the Sabbath; worshippers were also urged to focus on welcoming the *Shekhinah* (Divine Presence) when reciting the last stanza of the *Lekha Dodi* hymn with the approach of the Sabbath. Similarly, at the departure of the Sabbath, individuals were advised to read the entire Torah portion of the coming week, "because by so doing one beckons the abundance (*shefa*) of the approaching Sabbath."[56]

Europe (Princeton, 2004), esp. chs. 1 and 3. On *Sefer Raziel*, see Mordecai Margaliot, *Sefer Ha-Razim* (Jerusalem, 1966), and Joseph Dan, *Torat Ha-Sod shel Hasidei Ashkenaz* (Jerusalem, 1968).

53 See Zeev Gries, *The Book as an Agent of Culture, 1700–1900* (Tel Aviv, 2002).

54 *Tikkunei Shabbat*, a popular collection of Sabbath laws and *piyyutim*, was printed in the early seventeenth century. Though attributed to Isaac Luria (1534–1572), it was likely the work of Abraham Berukhim (ca. 1515–ca. 1593). On its numerous printings, see Haim Liberman, *Ohel Raḥel* (Brooklyn, 1980–84). *Tikkunei Shabbat* contains passages from the Zohar to be recited prior to each of the three Sabbath meals, and the order of Havdalah. Later editions, including the one appearing in eighteenth-century Metz prayer books, includes laws and customs for the eve of the Sabbath. See the reference to Lurianic practice in *Tefilah ke-Minhag Ashkenaz u-Folin* (Metz, 1765), 48b, and in "Seder ha-Ma'amadot," 4b.

55 The Zohar, a mystical commentary on the Torah attributed by tradition to Rabbi Simon bar Yohai, is identified by scholars as a product of thirteenth-century Castille.

56 *Seder Tefilah ke-Minhag Ashkenaz* (1765), pt. 2, 1a–2a, 12b, 18a, 20b, and 66b.

Lurianic rites and customs proliferated in eighteenth-century Alsace and Lorraine, as attested by a wide array of evidence. Towards the beginning of the century, a group assembled in Metz for midnight vigils in accordance with Lurianic custom to engage in ecstatic prayer, study, and mourn the destruction of Jerusalem.[57] Later in the century, a prayer composed in honor of Louis XVI and Marie Antoinette confirms the penetration of Lurianic images and concepts into the formal synagogue ritual. The prayer includes seven short petitions requesting that God recall the merit of the patriarchs, prophets, and kings of Israel, and concludes with familiar Lurianic imagery: "And in the merit of the holy names … and their vowels, words, letters, and meanings, will [God] protect us and destroy all of the thorns that encircle the supernal *Shoshanah* [the Divine Presence]." The rabbi of Sierentz formally approved the inclusion of the prayer in the daily synagogue service, presumably with community consent.[58] In addition, assorted *teḥinnes* ("supplicatory prayers") composed specially for life-cycle events, such as men whose wives were in labor, were reproduced in Metz prayer books, as were instructions for the performance of the widely practiced *tashlikh* and *kapparot* penitential ceremonies. Included as well were *teḥinnes* to be recited by women when they performed the three women's mitzvot—the ritual taking of *ḥallah* (dough taken from bread), the separation of wives from their husbands during menstruation, and the lighting of Sabbath candles. The inclusion of these ceremonies in later editions—despite the determined opposition of the community's leading halakhic authority and chief rabbi, Rabbi Aaron Worms (1754–1836)—suggests that *siddurim* were produced without the involvement or approval of rabbinic authorities and confirms the disjuncture between popular and elite religion.[59]

In addition to the role ritual played in negotiating the challenges and uncertainties facing individuals, it offered a means for Jews to relate collectively to their historical origins, to define their relationship to the surrounding society and culture, and to affirm their affinity to particular cultural traditions. The last of these functions was the most contested. Serving as a vital repository

57 See Gershon Koblenz, *Resp. Kiryat Hannah* (Metz, 1789), no. 2.

58 The prayer, printed in Basel, does not include a date. The original text is in the National and University Library, Jerusalem, L 58. I thank Paul Fenton for his assistance with this text.

59 On *teḥinnes* for pregnant women, see ibid., pt. 4, 39b–40a; on *tashlikh* and *kapparot*, see ibid., pt. 2, 125b. The *tashlikh* ceremony was included in the *Maḥzor shel Rosh Hashanah ke-Minhag Ashkenaz* (Metz, 1817), pt. 1, 125b, though there is no mention of the *kapparot* rite in the *Maḥzor shel Yom Kippur* (Metz, 1817). On the literature of *teḥinnes*, see Chava Weissler, *Voices of the Matriarchs: Listening to the Prayers of Early Modern Jewish Women* (Boston, 1998).

of memories specific to a community—or region—ritual practices were naturally a source of both communal pride and strife, especially at the onset of the early modern period.[60] Shaped as Jewish collective identity was by the experiences of expulsion, migration, and the rebuilding of new communities, in the west an even greater premium was placed on exactitude in performance of religious customs. Precisely because ritual practices, as distinct from laws, were a vital means of continuity with past generations, their role in the local culture was passionately contested by rabbis and laypersons alike. From the sixteenth century, debates about the authenticity of such rituals also turned on the question of the centrality of textual traditions.[61]

Liturgical rites observed in Metz confirm that members of the Jewish community viewed themselves as part of the broader heritage of western Ashkenaz and as adherents of a vibrant local tradition. Two major collections of prayers published in Metz in 1765 and 1768 contain the standard elements of the western Ashkenazic liturgy, such as *Ma'arivim*, i.e., poetic embellishments inserted in the evening prayers for festivals.[62] Distinctive rites observed in Frankfurt and Poland were also incorporated in the Metz prayer books. This practice signaled the wider social and cultural implications of liturgical compendia. Titles of two Metz prayer books, the *Seder Tefilah ke-Minhag Ashkenaz* (The Order of Prayers According to the Ashkenazic Rite, 1765) and the *Maḥzor ke-Minhag Ashkenaz u-Folin* (Prayers According to the Ashkenazic and Polish Rite, 1768), indicate that they embraced the broader Ashkenazic tradition that extended beyond Metz, eastward to Poland. Variances between eastern and western rites were also included regularly, as is apparent in the Metz Yom Kippur *Maḥzor*. For example, only the first half of the alphabetically arranged *piyyut* (liturgical poem) *Ya'aleh* was recited in the west, whereas in Poland the custom was to recite the *piyyut* in its entirety. Similarly the order of *Shome'a Tefilah 'Adekha* recited in Metz conformed to the western tradition. Conversely, certain *piyyutim* that were commonly recited in Poland, were not included in the Metz editions.[63]

The unusual format of the Metz volumes evinced the sociocultural variegation and geographical mobility characteristic of large communities, and

60 See Van Gennep, *Manuel de folklore français contemporain*. Also see Robert Muchembled, *Popular Culture and Elite Culture in France, 1400–1750*, trans. Lydia Cochrane (Baton Rouge, 1985) and Edward Muir, *Ritual in Early Modern Europe*, 2nd ed. (Cambridge, 2005), 21–61.

61 See Berkovitz, "Jewish Law and Ritual in Early Modern Germany," and idem, "Crisis and Authority in Early Modern Ashkenaz," *Jewish History* 26:1–2 (2012): 179–99.

62 See Daniel Goldschmidt, *Mahzor le-Yamim Nora'im*, 2 vols. (Jerusalem, 1970), 1: xxxi–il.

63 For evidence that *Imru l'Elohim* and *Ma'aseh Elohenu* were not included in the Metz order of prayers, see *Maḥzor ke-Minhag Ashkenaz u-Folin* (Metz, 1768), 7b–8a, 93b.

doubtless gained a decided market advantage over *siddurim* and *maḥzorim* that customarily incorporated only one or two variant rites.[64] Moreover, the inclusion of liturgical variants was designed to meet the needs of a local population whose ranks reflected fluidity of movement between France and Germany, augmented by immigrants from points further east. In an era characterized by substantial population movement, liturgical variants functioned as markers of identity in heterogeneous communities. At the same time, the self-image of communities in Alsace-Lorraine as culturally undifferentiated from their counterparts to the east corresponded to the perception of the northeastern provinces that prevailed in mainstream France and was reinforced by economic policies promoted by the monarchy. Until the collapse of the ancien régime, rigorous customs restrictions all but set apart the northeastern territories from the interior of France, though trade with foreign countries was subject to more limited regulation.[65]

Given its implications for collective identity, the decision of which liturgical rite a community would observe was occasionally the subject of intense debate. Factors bearing on the question could include the tradition established when the community was founded, the arrival of immigrants who observed different practices, or the personal preference and political influence of the community's rabbinic authority. The fact that the community of Ribeauvillé, for example, was willing to adopt the *rituel* of Frankfurt following the arrival of its newly elected rabbi, Süssel Moïse Enosch, in the mid-eighteenth century, suggests that local traditions were not sufficiently entrenched to forestall innovation, or more simply, that there was a predisposition to German customs. By contrast, faced with a similar situation in 1766, the community leadership of Metz firmly rejected an attempt by Rabbi Aryeh Loeb Günzberg to substitute a custom that contravened local convention. Not long after he arrived in Metz, the independent-minded Günzberg became embroiled in controversy. On the first day of *Shavu'ot* (The Feast of Weeks) he took exception to the long-standing practice of reciting the hymn *Akdamut* following the first verse of the Scriptural reading. In accord with the opinion of many rabbinic authorities that the insertion was an unwarranted interruption, he preferred that the hymn be recited before the Torah reading. Günzberg sought to apply a more

---

64 For distinctive elements of Metz local practice, see *Maḥzor shel Rosh ha-Shanah ke-Minhag Ashkenaz* (Metz, 1817), 28b where the order of verses in the Musaf prayer differed from the recitation elsewhere. For additional details on Metz synagogue customs, see Berkovitz, *Rites and Passages*, 59–85, and for an illustration of the impact of distinctive liturgical traditions on the value and marketability of prayer books, see PMBD, Vol. 1, pt. 1, no. 122, 40b.

65 John Lough, *An Introduction to 18th Century France* (London, 1960), 70.

rigorous halakhic standard, but the strong-willed communal leadership stood firmly against its newly appointed rabbi in defense of local tradition. Insulted by this rebuff, the rabbi refused to ever preach in that synagogue again.[66]

In its response to Rabbi Günzberg, the Metz leadership stubbornly upheld the supremacy of local tradition, which corresponded to the prominence of custom steadfastly preserved in the *siddurim* of Alsace and Metz. The earliest edition of *Seliḥot mi-kol ha-Shanah ke-Minhag Elsass* (Penitential Prayers for the Entire Year According to the Alsatian Rite), published in 1691, reveals that the Alsatian rite originated as *minhag Colmar* and was observed by Rabbi David Sulzburg, head of the rabbinic court and the yeshivah in Breisach.[67] Aside from this single collection of penitential prayers, however, no other compendium of Alsatian liturgical traditions survives and there are no indications that a distinct rite was preserved. In Metz, where no distinct order of *seliḥot* is extant,[68] local customs were nonetheless interspersed throughout the series of *siddurim* and *mahzorim* published by the local printing house. Copious notations indicated where the Metz customs diverged from the Frankfurt, Ashkenazic, Polish, or Amsterdam rite,[69] and detailed instructions guided the worshipper in the proper order of the *piyyutim*,[70] the correct manner of recitation (e.g., where to begin or if a *piyyut* was to be recited responsively), and the replacement of commonly recited *piyyutim* with preferred variants.[71]

In addition, the *siddurim* refer to several practices that were unique to Metz. In the case of belated news of a parent's death received on the intermediate days of a festival, the custom in Metz was to wait to the end of the festival before rending one's garment. This practice diverged from the

---

66 On the rite adopted in Ribeauvillé, see *Archives israélites de France* 5 (1844): 542–47. Concerning the Günzberg incident, see Cahen, "Le rabbinat de Metz pendant la période française," *REJ* 12 (1886): 294–95. For a defense of the Metz custom, see Koblenz, *Resp. Kiryat Hannah*, no. 7. Cf. Worms, *Od la-Mo'ed*, 13a.

67 *Seliḥot mi-kol ha-Shanah ke-Minhag Elsass* (Frankfort am Main, 1691). The volume was republished in 1725, and numerous times thereafter, including an edition by Wolf Heidenheim (Roedelheim, 1838). On the 1691 edition, see Sarah Frankel, "Concerning Two Lost Books That Were Found" [Hebrew], *Alei Sefer* 10 (1982): 141, and Hayyim Schmeltzer, note in *Kiryat Sefer* 59 (1984): 646.

68 The Metz *seliḥot* volume was entitled *Seliḥot ke-Minhag Ashkenazim*.

69 For specific synagogue customs performed in Metz, see *Seder Tefilah ke-Minhag Ashkenaz* (Metz, 1765): concerning the order of *Taḥanun*, see 35a–b; regarding the recitation of *Birkhat Kohanim* on a festival that falls on the Sabbath, see 48b. For Metz variants to the standard order of scriptural verses in the *Musaf* of Rosh Hashanah and Yom Kippur according to most Ashkenazic communities, see *Maḥzor ke-Minhag Ashkenaz u-Folin* (1768), pt. 1, 28b; for other examples of similar variances, see 14a, 42a, and 43a.

70 *Maḥzor* (1768), 5b–6a, 81a, 90a, 159b–160a, 169a, 174a.

71 Ibid., 65a–b, 93b; *Maḥzor le-Fesach, Shavu'ot, ve-Sukkot* (Metz, 1769), pt. 2, 49, and 126b.

prevailing Ashkenazic *minhag* to perform the ritual on the intermediate days for parents but not for other family members. In Poland, by contrast, it was customary to rend garments for any relative who had died.[72] In a number of areas of Jewish law, Aaron Worms cited local traditions preserved in the writings of his father, Rabbi Abraham Aberlé Worms and his mentors, Rabbi Isaac Netter of Bouxwiller and Rabbi Leib Gugenheim, evidently in the hope that one day they would be restored to active practice.[73]

Local rites of remembrance also draw attention to the complexity inherent in Metz Jewry's collective identity. A memorial prayer composed by Rabbi Moses Cohen Narol (d. 1659), a refugee from Poland appointed head of the Metz rabbinic court in 1649, epitomizes an extraordinary effort to embrace the memory of the tens of thousands of Polish Jews murdered in the Chmielnicki uprising (1648–1649). The adoption of the prayer by the Metz Kehillah reveals the sense of intercommunal unity that pervaded Jewish consciousness. The author, employing the metaphor of a single organism, affirmed at the end of his elegy that "[all] communities are united as one person." Perhaps more remarkable than Narol's initiative is that the Metz community continued to recite the prayer twice a year for at least two centuries. Moreover, by choosing to remember the victims of the 1648–49 massacres on the Sabbaths preceding Shavu'ot and Tisha b'Av (Ninth of Av)—the same Sabbaths when it was customary throughout Ashkenaz to recall the memory of the Crusader martyrs—the Metz community conflated the two catastrophes into a single rite of remembrance. This was a highly unique effort to integrate episodes that were part of the broader patterns of European Jewish history into the local culture and consciousness.[74]

---

72 *Maḥzor le-Fesach, Shavu'ot, ve-Sukkot* (Metz, 1769), pt. 2, 53b; for the opposing view, see Isserles, Glosses to *Shulḥan 'Arukh* (Cracow, 1571), *Oraḥ Ḥayyim* §547:6; Abraham Gombiner, *Magen Avraham* (Dyhernfurth, 1692), *Oraḥ Ḥayyim* §547:3. Aaron Worms noted that in his day many were not accustomed to rend their garments on *ḥol ha-mo'ed*, even for a parent. See *Od la-Mo'ed*, 138a. On an unusual custom concerning *eruv ḥaẓerot* before the Passover holiday, see *Maḥzor le-Fesach, Shavu'ot, ve-Sukkot*, pt. 2, 100a.

73 See, for example, *'Od la-Mo'ed* 26b, 29a and *Ken Tahor* 111a.

74 Moses Cohen Narol, a student of Rabbi Joel Sirkes, was the author of *Birkhat Tov* (Venice, 1713), a collection of homilies on the Pentateuch. Narol's elegy for Polish Jewry, titled *Baqashah*, was first published in Amsterdam (1699), and subsequently in Metz (1764 and 1777) and Lunéville (1806). In these three instances, it was printed in a handbook that included the *piyyut* "Geroni Nihar," which was recited in Metz on the "four fasts," and occasional prayers recited during the period between Rosh Hashanah and the end of Sukkot. For the reference to the *Bakashah* in the Metz liturgy, see *Seder Tefilah ke-Minhag Ashkenaz* (1765), 79b. For a listing of prayers composed in memory of the Chmielnicki martyrs, see Simon Bernfeld, *Sefer ha-Dema'ot*, 3 vols. (Berlin, 1926), 3:160–84, and

More specific to local history was the fast that Metz Jews observed on 25 Tevet to commemorate the anniversary of the burning of Raphaël Lévy, falsely accused of ritual murder in 1669.[75] The trope linking past suffering with contemporary deaths and persecution continued into the nineteenth century. In the *Yizkorbuch* (memorial book) of the Haguenau community recorded the names of victims of the Damascus blood libel alongside the list of earlier martyrs, beginning with the era of the Crusades.[76] By viewing victims of past and present persecutions as part of a single continuum, this pattern of memorialization accentuated the medieval roots of Franco-Jewish culture.[77]

Before the Revolution the cultural history of Alsace-Lorraine was informed by a struggle between two competing claims, one regional and the other local. The assertion that the eastern provinces of France belonged to the larger cultural universe of Ashkenaz competed with the contention that there was an indigenous, centuries-old Alsatian Jewish culture. Regional identity, which was associated with Ashkenaz in the broadest sense, tended to be homogenous, whereas local identities reflected greater diversity and a measure of pluralism. Questions concerning Jewish cultural identity in France were related to a long-standing debate over the authentic character of Ashkenaz. Was Ashkenazic culture limited to the religious customs that developed in the Rhineland in the eleventh through the fifteenth centuries, or was it receptive to influences from other traditions? With the emergence of Poland-Lithuania as the unrivaled center of Jewish life in the fifteenth and sixteenth centuries, the center of gravity shifted eastward, away from France, Germany, and the Hapsburg Empire. Efforts to codify Jewish law in the sixteenth century brought the issue to a head, especially as reflected in the glosses added by Rabbi Moses Isserles to the *Shulḥan 'Arukh*. Which ritual and legal traditions would reign supreme—those of the west, that is, of classical Ashkenaz, or those of the east as interpreted by

---

Michael Handel, *Gezerot Taḥ ve-Tat* (Jerusalem, 1950), ch. 3. Of all the communities beyond Poland, only Metz and Venice recited elegies that were composed locally.

75 Patricia Behre, "Raphael Levy: 'A Criminal in the Mouths of the People,'" *Religion* 23 (1993): 19–44. Also see Natalie Zemon Davis, *Women on the Margins: Three Seventeenth-Century Lives* (Cambridge, MA, 1995), 17.

76 "Yizkorbuch of Haguenau," cited in Paula Hyman, *The Emancipation of the Jews of Alsace* (New Haven, 1991), 71–72.

77 The fast of the twentieth of Sivan, which marked the massacre of the Jews of Blois in 1171, was a parallel ritual tradition. See David Wachtel, "The Ritual and Liturgical Commemoration of Two Medieval Persecutions" (M.A. Thesis, Columbia University, 1995), and Jacob J. Schacter, "Remembering the Temple: Commemoration and Catastrophe in Ashlenazic Culture," in *The Temple of Jerusalem: From Moses to the Messiah*, ed. Steven Fine (New York, 2011), 275–302.

Polish rabbinic authorities—remained a highly contested issue well into the nineteenth century.

In his major opus, *Me'orei Or*, Rabbi Aaron Worms argued that the Isserles rulings had assigned undue weight to Polish *minhagim* and woefully insufficient attention to classical Ashkenazic sources. Accordingly, the Metz scholar maintained, the customs Isserles recommended diverged from well-established usages observed in communities west of Prague. With this assault on Isserles's preeminence, Worms boldly reclaimed the western tradition to which Alsace-Lorraine (and Germany) had strong historic ties. His efforts to rescue the classical Ashkenazic liturgy were built upon a clear preference for the legacy of Rabbi Jacob Moellin (Maharil) of Mainz (ca. 1360–1427).[78] Worms sought to reconstitute an authentic Ashkenazi ritual that was independent of eastern influences and aligned with the burgeoning interest in classical traditions that was emblematic of the Enlightenment and Romanticism.

Material Culture

Sources on material consumption offer important perspective on acculturation and class formation in the seventeenth and eighteenth centuries. An impressive variety of fabrics, clothing, jewelry and valuable gems, which are listed in collateral and probate inventories, offer evidence of the affinity of Metz Jews with French culture.[79] Fabrics include *drap d'or* (cloth woven with gold)

78 Attitudes toward the Isserles glosses ranged from strident criticism to praise. See Moshe Rosman, "The Image of Poland as a Center of Torah Learning after the 1648 Persecutions," *Zion* 51 (1986): 440. Also see Eric Zimmer, "Reactions of German Jewry to Influences of the Center in Poland in the Early Seventeenth Century" [Hebrew], *Sinai* 102 (1988): 226–40, and Benjamin S. Hamburger, "The Historical Foundations of Minhag Ashkenaz," in *Minhagim of Worms according to Juspe Shamash*, 101–105, I. M. Peles, ed. For the harshest critique, see Hayyim ben Bezalel Friedberg, *Viku'ah Mayyim Hayyim* (Amsterdam, 1712), introduction. On Worms's preference for Maharil over Isserles, see *Be'er Sheva* (Metz, 1819), 14b; 31b–32a; cf. *Od la-Mo'ed*, 32b, 51a, and 109a.

79 Probate inventories, which list assets and material possessions drawn up by government officials in the process of settling the estate of the deceased, are valuable historical sources. Like lists of collateral taken on loans and detailed records of expenditures on behalf of orphans, these inventories afford a glimpse into the accumulation and consumption of material goods and offer great potential for investigating acculturation. For an example of a Metz probate list, see PMBD, Vol. 1, pt. 2, 43b, no. 185; for a list of collateral, see PMBD, Vol. 1, pt. 1, 16b, no. 54, and for a list of expenditures made by guardians, see PMBD, Vol. 1, pt. 2, 8a–9a, no. 29. The vast literature on probate inventories includes the following instructive studies: John Bedell, "Archeology and Probate Inventories in the Study of Eighteenth Century Life," *Journal of Interdisciplinary History*

and *drap d'argent* (cloth woven with silver); *drap d'Elbeuf* (fabric produced in Elbeuf, a town in Normandy specializing in weaving wool); *drap de Sicile* (a silk fabric produced in Sicily); *gros de Tours* (a thick, ribbed silk produced in Tours); *parterre* (light silk damask); *tamis* (a plain-woven fabric of wool); *tapette* (carpet); *treillis* (coarse French canvas); *dauphine cannelée* (fluted cotton or woolen cloth); and *damasquiné* (fine grade linen).[80] Clothing cut from fine fabrics included a *roquelaure* (a knee-length cloak lined with colored silk and often trimmed); men's waistcoats; *sargenes* (a coat made from linen, wool and silk); woman's satin *camisole*; and various ornamented skirts. Various styles of jewelry also appearing in the Beit Din records included *colliers* (necklaces) ornamented with pearls and other stones; *breloques* (charm bracelets); earrings decorated with four stones, known as *boucles de nuit*; a pocket watch with a polished case and a barleycorn *guilloché* back; rings made of a pair of *diamant de roses; camée* (sculpted) jewelry and engraved silver and gold; and *strass* (rhinestones) and other precious gems. Dinnerware, commonly listed in inventories of various types, included *faïence* (earthenware); silver wine goblets; *serviettes* made of fine cloth; a *saladier*; and cookware such as a *casserole*. One request for an appraisal of several items held as collateral on a loan included a decorative silver decanter in the form of a ship—a popular table adornment among the affluent.[81]

Restrictions on lavish clothing and jewelry, imposed by the Kahal within the framework of sumptuary laws, offer a valuable list of apparel and personal effects favored by Metz Jews. The first set of Metz regulations were issued in August 1690.[82] The last decade of the seventeenth century was an era of

31 (2000): 223–25; and Philip Benedict, "Bibliothèques protestantes et catholiques à Metz au XVIIe siecle," *Annales: Economies, Sociétés, Civilisations* 40 (1985): 343–70. Cf. David Horowitz, "Domestic Interiors of Two Viennese Jewish Elites Probate Court in Vienna," *Early Modern Workshop: Resources in Jewish History*, 2005, http://www.earlymodern.org/workshops/2005/horowitz/text01/intro.php?tid=54.

80 See PMBD, Vol. 1, pt. 2, no. 122, 30b; no. 224, 50a; no. 255, 54b; Vol. 2, no. 66, 12a; no. 170, 34a; no. 270, 50b. See Alain Becchia, *La draperie d'Elbeuf, des origines à 1870* (Rouen, 2000); Louis Harmuth, *Dictionary of Textiles* (New York, 1915), passim; and William M. Reddy, "The Structure of a Cultural Crisis: Thinking about Cloth in France Before and After the Revolution," in *The Social Life of Things: Commodities in Cultural Perspective*, ed. Arjun Appadurai (Cambridge, 1986), 261–84. Cf. Grehan, *Everyday Life and Consumer Culture in Eighteenth-Century Damascus*.

81 See PMBD, Vol. 2, no. 565, 118a; no. 318, 60a; Vol. 1, pt. 1, no. 91, 31a; Vol. 2, no. 423, 80b; no. 318, 60b; no. 20, 4b; no. 461, 90a; no. 102b; no. 361, 67b; no. 172, 34b; Vol. 1, pt. 2, no. 121, 30a; Vol. 1, pt. 1, nos. 5–6, 7b; Vol. 2, no. 68, 17b. On the role of material objects as exchange items, see Fontaine, *L'Economie morale*.

82 Cahen, "Règlements somptuaires," 79–80. Art. 1 refers to exemptions on the number of rings that could be worn by women on certain occasions, such as the woman who

expanding commercial activity for the Jewish community, marked by a wider distribution of wealth and the greater availability of imported fabrics. Much of the focus of the 1690s legislation was on regulating extravagance in the clothing and jewelry worn by women. Clothing was routinely designed with silver, gold, or pearls, and new fashions were adopted without concern for the prohibition against imitating gentile customs (*ḥukkot ha-goyim*). The 1692 Takkanot issued stringent restrictions prohibiting any man, woman, or child from bringing veils, bonnets, coat borders or any other part of their dress to non-Jewish tailors, but it appears that this restriction was ignored.

Details concerning hairstyle and fashion that were included in the regulations, as well as the resistance these laws encountered, confirm a heightened fascination with the surrounding culture.[83] The 1690 law proscribed all coiffures in imitation of the styles of gentile women, except for girls under the age of eleven, who were permitted to wear coiffures *en cheveux*. Additional restrictions banned girls and boys from wearing ostrich feathers or fur in their hats. *Peignoirs* were prohibited to all women, including girls over the age of eleven, and pleated coats were forbidden to all. Glikl Hameln had noted this in her memoir: "When I first came here [in 1700], Metz was a very beautiful, pious community and the *parnasim* were all worthy men who verily adorned the council room. In those days not a man who sat in the council room wore a *perruque* [wig], and no one heard of a man going out of the *Judengasse* to bring a case before a gentile tribunal."[84] By enacting sumptuary laws in 1690, Metz leaders may have been expressing concern precisely for some of the changes that struck Glikl as odd. Restrictions on fashion were applied in a selective manner, and young men and women were permitted to attend the Metz *bal*, if invited, provided that their dress conformed to communal regulations. Social intermingling with non-Jews was presumably not unusual, nor was it a source

---

accompanies the bride to the synagogue on the morning of the wedding and on the first Sabbath after the wedding until the exit from the synagogue. Also see exemptions for brocades used for religious ceremonies, in Art. 14, and for exceptions, see Art. 18. On the dress restrictions for those attending the ball, see Art. 32. On restrictions at the *Rhinport*, see Art. 7. Concerning music restrictions, see Art. 19.

83 Resistance to the legislation may be discerned from the text of the 1691 regulation. Noting the spread of "calumnies and slander" against members of the special commission charged with the enforcement of these laws, the commission of twelve issued a warning that the 1690 law must be obeyed. Stern warnings and threats of penalties and fines signaled the growing rift between the leadership and the masses on this issue. For other examples of cultural borrowings, see below.

84 *The Memoirs of Glikl*, ed. and trans. Chava Turniansky (Jerusalem, 2006), 578–579. See Natalie Zemon Davis, *Women on the Margins: Three Seventeenth-Century Lives* (Cambridge, Mass., 1995), 5–62.

of undue anxiety for communal leaders, provided that outside the ghetto Jews remained clearly identifiable by their appearance.[85] Furthermore, the absence of explicit warnings against imitating non-Jewish customs or fashion in the first years of the legislation suggests that such trends had become both commonplace and, in all likelihood, impervious to communal regulation.

The 1694 sumptuary law announced that all women over fifteen years of age, presumably irrespective of marital status, would be required to wear a coat and veil when attending synagogue.[86] According to the 1697 law, married women were prohibited from appearing in the synagogue without a veil. Married women were required to wear *manteaux* (topcoats) in the synagogue, irrespective of the time or day, but a new bride received a special dispensation to enter the synagogue without a *manteau* for the first month following her wedding. Eighty years later, the requirement of wearing a topcoat would be applied more rigorously to men: any head of household found promenading in the *quartier juif* without a *manteau* would be disqualified from serving as an elector in the community council.[87] Concerning restrictions on wigs, rings, or jewelry intended specifically for youth, the Metz regulations were curiously silent.[88] The 1769 Takkanot imposed restrictions on strolling in public while wearing *mantelettes* of muslin, of transparent light fabric, of thick linen (*toile*

85 1690 Takkanot, Art. 28, 32, repeated in the 1697 Takkanot, Art. 20. Based on the evidence in Italy, Bonfil has argued that sumptuary laws did not aim to prevent the intermingling of Jews and non-Jews but represented an attempt to dissuade Jews from adopting gentile fashion because these were defined as negative. See *Jewish Life in Renaissance Italy*, 104–11.

86 1690 Takkanot, Art. 22; 1694 law, prologue.

87 PKM, 80a, 1769 Takkanot, Art. 64. The *mantel* was part of the normal attire of Jewish men in Germanic lands. It had no sleeves, was thrown on the shoulders as a cape, while worn over the coat. A separate *mantel* known as a *schülmantel*, also known in Hebrew as a *sarbal*, was reserved for the Sabbath. In one instance in 1768, a Metz householder violated the prohibition against conducting commercial transactions with unmarried merchants and with men during the first three years of marriage; as a punishment, he could not participate in any religious activity in the two synagogues, including prayer, nor to wear the *schülmantel*. For a French translation of the 1769 Takkanot, see Samuel Kerner, "Le règlement de la communauté de Metz de 1769," *Annales de l'Est* 24 (1972): 210–53. Generally, the prohibition against wearing the *schülmantel* was a penalty applied by the Kahal for certain commercial violations. This penalty carried a measure of public humiliation. See ibid., 205–206. For details on the *mantel*, see Pollack, *Jewish Folkways*, 89–92, and 263–64, n. 50. This regulation was relaxed on Christian holidays, and exceptions were made for physicians, cattle and horse dealers, and men who had reached the age of seventy.

88 According to Pollack, *Jewish Folkways*, 258, n. 19, the silence of the Metz ordinances was uncommon, but two of his references do not bear this out. See *Takkanot Moravia*, no. 297, p. 99, and Aryeh Leib Feinstein, "Nitei Ne'emanim," *Ha-Asif* 6 (1893): 171. According to Glikl, , "burghers and engaged couples among the non-Jews seldom or never wore jewels. Instead it was the fashion to wear gold chains." See *Memoirs of Glikl*, 130–31.

mat), or of silk. Less expensive materials identified in the *takkanah* were *toile peinte, perse* or other fabrics not of silk, transparent fabric, or *en toile*. The fact that *mantelettes* woven of less costly fabrics could be worn anywhere, while on the Jewish street it was permissible to wear *mantelettes* composed of more expensive materials, including muslin and silk, suggests that leaders were still concerned about the potential ill-effects of conspicuous consumption.[89]

In a similar vein, the numerous disputes brought before the Beit Din that pertained to building construction and repairs, water damage, and privacy concerns bring to light otherwise hidden aspects of everyday life in the eighteenth century.[90] In a case that concerned the management of public space, residents of a building were fined by the civil court for failing to keep the rear of the property free of litter; the court instructed them to hire a gardener to keep the property clean in accordance with the requirements of the law. A dispute regarding the relocation of an outhouse, specifically concerning the claim that the work was not performed correctly, was brought to the *police-court* and was subsequently resolved to the satisfaction of the residents via an appeal to the Parlement de Metz.[91] In a similar case, the placement of an outhouse adjacent to a separation wall between two properties became a contested matter; in this instance it was the Beit Din that was asked to settle the question of the potential physical harm that might result.[92] Disputes pertaining to construction, plumbing, and shared space reveal that it was extremely common for Jews to hire non-Jewish workers and to seek the opinion of non-Jewish experts regarding an entire range of building issues. Such patterns reveal the natural dependence of Jewish residents in Metz, and perhaps to a less significant degree in the countryside, on the general French population to help meet its ordinary, everyday needs.

Numerous references to luxurious fabrics, ornate clothing, housewares, and precious stones reveal a strong attraction to contemporary styles. Jewish merchants who imported fine fabrics to Metz from various producers in northern and central France were responsible, at least in part, for the sophisticated taste in the Jewish community, as were pawnbrokers who accumulated and sometimes sold silver and gold tableware received in pledges. These examples confirm that even prior to the Revolution, cultural influences transcended social barriers, and this appears to have been true for a larger segment of the

---

89 1769 Takkanot, Arts. 14–16, 5. See Baron, *Jewish Community*, 2: 301–307; 3:200–203, nn. 13–19; Pollack, *Jewish Folkways*, 86–91.

90 See, for example, PMBD, Vol. 1, pt. 2, no. 149, 36b.

91 PMBD, Vol. 2, no. 246, 45b.

92 PMBD, Vol. 1, pt. 2, no. 228, 51a.

Jewish population than is commonly assumed.[93] The allure of fine fabrics, clothing, dinnerware, and jewelry is recorded in extraordinary detail throughout the Pinkas Beit Din and somewhat less so in the Pinkas Kahal. In the aggregate, the unfailing fascination with luxury assists in sketching the portrait of an acculturated minority—undeniably the elite among them, but not limited to that segment alone—that inhabited virtually the same world as their French neighbors. Culinary utensils, fabrics, and jewelry were part of a culture that Metz Jews shared with members of the society at large in the last decades of the ancien régime. Evidence of social and economic interaction between Jewish and gentile tradesmen confirms the emergence of chronic social friction, but also suggests that the Jewish community in late seventeenth-century Metz was hardly insular.[94]

These trends are not surprising. Evidence of acculturation in Metz echoed comparable tendencies among Jews across the continent. Communities, whatever their size, were never self-sufficient. As elsewhere, the Jews in Metz were restricted in their employment and trade, and their capacity to produce goods and services was extremely limited. They purchased items they required in order to meet their everyday needs, much as their non-Jewish neighbors did. Were the shared experiences of Jews and Frenchmen in late eighteenth-century Metz any more pronounced than the relations between Jews and gentiles in other localities? To be sure, the attractiveness of French style and its pervasiveness within urban settings cannot be discounted. But more significantly, evidence of cultural affinity interspersed throughout the pages of the community's *pinkasim* confirm the validity of signs of social integration experienced by members of the Metz Kehillah. As consumers of French material culture, Metz Jews needed to be in close contact with the craftsmen who produced housewares, building products, and fabrics, and with those who provided essential services. These patterns of acculturation, in whatever form they assumed, buttressed the foundation upon which Metz's shared legal culture rested.

93 Hertzberg, *French Enlightenment and the Jews*, 126–30, 370.

94 See Patricia Behre Miskimin, "Jews and Christians in the Marketplace: The Politics of Kosher Meat in Metz," *Journal of Economic History* 26 (1997): 147–55. French legislation requiring Jews to wear a yellow hat dated from earlier in the seventeenth century, but in 1657 it was modified to no longer apply to the *av beit din* and the seven syndics; for other community members the requirement would subsequently apply only in the city streets. Between 1708 and 1715 the community tried, unsuccessfully, to persuade the government to repeal this legislation; however, by mid-century, the custom had disappeared entirely. See Gilbert Cahen, "La Région lorraine," in Bernhard Blumenkranz, ed., *Histoire des Juifs en France* (Paris, 1972), 114.

Economic Integration

In the economic realm, one encounters equally impressive signs of engagement with French civil society. In the last decade of the seventeenth century, Jewish lenders provided large-scale financing and Jewish merchants supplied horses, grain, tents, and other provisions for soldiers in the Metz garrison and beyond. Signs of significant economic expansion in the region, and of rapid urban growth as well, were evident by the beginning of the eighteenth century.[95] Metz Jews frequently availed themselves of various legal instruments that were commonly employed in French society, the most important of which were formal contracts. In one instance, following the death of the wealthy army purveyor Moïse Blien, his daughters and sons-in-law had drawn up a civil contract that obligated them to provide their mother, Malka, with a stipend of 3,000 livres per year, in exchange for her *ketubah*. The Beit Din was asked to rule on the scope of the obligation that was established in the civil contract and its bearing on matters of Jewish marital law.[96] Such enquiries, one may assume, were rather routine.

Jews also made regular use of financial instruments commonly employed in the local and regional economies. Among the most prominent of these was the *constitution de rente*, also known as *rentes constituées*.[97] Neither the phrase *constitution de rente* or *rentes constituées* appears as such in the Metz court register; they appear only separately, as either *rente* or *constitution*. *Rentes* were annuities that were purchased with no expectation of repayment of the

95 See Philip Benedict, ed., *Cities and Social Change in Early Modern France* (London, 1989), 29–32.

96 PMBD, Vol. 1, pt. 1, no. 65, 21a.

97 For a full exposition on *constitution de rente*, written in the period under discussion, see Robert-Joseph Pothier, *Traité du contrat de constitution de rente* (Paris, 1763). Pothier (1699–1772), a highly influential French jurist, published widely on contract law. On *rentes constituées* in the Metz customary law, see *Coûtumes générales de la ville de Metz et pays-Messin* (1769), Titre XIV, Art. 13, 485–86; Art. 19, 493–98. The terms *rentes* and *constitution* never appear together in the Pinkas. *Rente* by itself appears ten times, once as *rente viagère*. For the latter, see PMBD, Vol. 1, pt. 2, no. 78, 20b. The term *constitution*, which appears thirty-four times in the Pinkas, is usually connected to a house or to land; in some instances, it is used in conjunction with *le fonds perdus*. To regain some portion of their investment, *rentiers* sought out buyers in secondary markets. See John H. Munro, "The Medieval Origins of the Financial Revolution: Usury, Rentes, and Negotiability," *The International History Review* 25 (2003): 505–62. For the broader context of eighteenth-century French economic history, see Hoffman, *Growth in a Traditional Society*, Hoffman, et al., "Private Credit Markets in Paris," 293–96 For a discussion of the use of *rentes* by Jews and by their gentile creditors, see Szajkowski, *Economic Status of the Jews in Alsace, Metz and Lorraine*, 83–86.

principal. They offered the buyer a steady annual income stream either for the duration of one's life or in perpetuity. The Hebrew phrase "*sekhirut ha-bayit*" is roughly equivalent to the term *rentes*. A *rente* was an annuity paid out over the life of the annuitant in exchange for an immediate payment or series of payments. Also known as *rente viagère*, a life annuity was either purchased or was used as security for a loan. Since it expired upon the death of the annuitant, this type of annuity was more frequently referred to in the proceedings of the Beit Din as *fonds perdus*—literally "lost funds"—that did not pass to heirs.[98] With this financial instrument, in whichever form, a creditor or investor provided money to the debtor in exchange for rent payments, although no formal loan was transacted.

A related instrument that appears frequently in the rabbinic court proceedings was a *constitution*. This was a vehicle that normally referred to a mortgage on a house or land. In one case, a house that was part of an estate was mortgaged for a 200 livres *constitution*, and this amount was paid out as an annuity to another party. In this respect, a *constitution* functioned as a secured debt and as an annuity for the creditor. It typically paid the same five percent return as on a conventional loan—as, for example, in the case of a *contrat constitution* executed by a man and his wife for 165 livres, calling for a payment of eight livres to be paid out annually. The sums were often much higher, as in the case of a father who transferred ownership of his house to his son and received an annuity of 1,200 livres. Regarding another house, a *constitution* payment of 1,000 livres per year was owed to the creditor as a life annuity, as established by agreement. In a case in which a man had fallen behind on the payments he owed according to the terms of his *contrat constitution*, the land in his possession was sold, subsequently yielding an annuity for his widow.[99] The reason that Jews traded in annuities, despite having been so heavily engaged in moneylending, was related to certain advantages of one sort of loan over another. Conventional loans, though calculated at a per annum rate of interest and capable of being rolled over, were generally intended for the short term and were used primarily for commercial exchange. *Constitutions* and *rentes*, though not as popular, served a different role as a vehicle for long-term

98 The expression *fonds perdus* appears dozens of times in the Beit Din register. See, for example, PMBD, Vol. 1, pt. 1, no. 65, 21a, concerning a disputed *contrat à fonds perdus*. In this case the daughters and sons-in-law of Malka Blien, widow of the wealthy army supplier and tax-farmer Moïse Blien, promised to pay her a life annuity in exchange for jewelry and precious stones. The expression also appears in PKM, 55a.

99 See PMBD, Vol. 1, pt. 2, no. 141, 34b; Vol. 1, pt. 2, no. 18, 43a; Vol. 2, no. 161, 32a; Vol. 2, no. 189, 53b; no. 573, 120b.

credit and investment. In fact, owing to economic exigencies, Jews not only sold annuities but also purchased them as a way of obtaining long-term credit themselves.[100]

Along with the prominence of these and other financial instruments throughout the pages of the court register, numerous cases reveal extensive business relations between Jews and non-Jews. Such dealings included merchandising, army provisioning, and financing. Wheat, horses, and clothing were the most popular commodities supplied by Jewish merchants. The larger purveyors extended credit to Jewish and gentile borrowers, discounted notes, and purchased bills that had come due. As one would expect, the scale of these business ventures varied considerably, depending on their geographical range, the amount of credit available, and the number of sub-purveyors involved at the local level. Overall, the percentage of army purveyors in Alsace has been estimated at up to a third of the male adult Jewish population, a ratio that we may assume was roughly the same, if not higher, in the Metz region.[101] Along with providing supplies and loans to soldiers in military garrisons, several Jewish partnerships and consortia were involved in purchasing uniforms from military regiments or from the royal treasury, presumably to be resold in secondary markets; one telling example was the procurement of uniforms from the *infanterie du régiment royal de Bavière*.[102] From army purveying it was natural for some merchants to offer their wares to the civilian population, as was the case in horse and grain trade,[103] but large-scale merchandising was conducted mainly in relation to the military. A probate inventory detailing the property left by Rabbi David Hertzfeld in 1776 lists among those who owed money to the deceased seven heads of military regiments: Orléans, Poitou, La Couronne, Royal Roussillon, Touraine, Auvergne, and Navarre. Although the

100 Cf. Kessler, *A Revolution in Commerce*, 58. On the purchase of *rentes* from non-Jewish creditors, see Szajkowski, *Economic Status of the Jews in Alsace, Metz and Lorraine*, 79–83, 87–91.

101 See Michael Graetz, "Jewish Economic Activity between War and Peace: The Rise and Fall of Jewish Army Suppliers" [Hebrew], *Zion* 56 (1991): 255–73. On the importance of the military to the local and regional economy, see David M. Hopkin, *Soldier and Peasant in French Popular Culture 1766–1870* (Rochester, NY, 2003), and Emile G. Leonard, *L'Armée et ses problèmes au XVIIIe siècle* (Paris, 1958).

102 See PMBD, Vol. 1, pt. 2, no. 177, 41a; no. 181, 42a; Vol. 2, no. 141, 28a; no. 206, 39a; no. 560, 116b–117a. For references to agreements between Jews and the monarchy to provide supplies for the army, generally known as *traités*, see PMBD, Vol. 1, pt. 1, no. 64, 20b and Vol. 2, no. 582, 123a. A reference to a *traité* in Vol. 2, no. 411, 78b–79a does not make clear with whom the agreement was made.

103 Anchel, *Les juifs de France*, 169–93; Hertzberg, *French Enlightenment and the Jews*, 125–26, 213.

total amount still owed was modest—approximately 12,000 livres—the lending network had a long reach. Similarly, a debt of approximately 2,500 livres was owed to Mordechai Ḥalfon and Jacob Morhange, who, as partners, held a bill of exchange from the captain of Salis-Grisons, a Swiss regiment, and another from the captain's wife. Each bill of exchange was executed in Longwy, a village in the Moselle, located approximately sixty-five kilometers southeast of Metz. The success of such ventures no doubt demanded determined efforts to earn and maintain the trust of this specialized clientele. Complications resulting from such joint enterprises frequently caused disputes among the Jewish partners requiring adjudication by the Beit Din.[104]

With the expansion of Jewish trade in the eighteenth century, rivalries with local merchants almost certainly escalated, as has been previously demonstrated in the historical literature.[105] However, in some instances commercial dealings of one sort or another involved intricate partnerships with non-Jews that were predicated on collaborative ventures of various types.[106] Whether the unavoidable complexities of provisioning were worked out agreeably or became embroiled in litigation, these business dealings rested on principles of economic interdependence and jointly valued commercial activity between Jews and non-Jews. In pre-Revolutionary France, business partnerships were "a microcosm of civil society" to the extent that they embodied sociability and depended on the consent of all participants. As understood by

104 See PMBD, Vol. 1, pt. 2, no. 124, 31a–31b. It seems improbable that Rabbi Hertzfeld, who was the director of the Metz community *beit midrash* (study hall), would have had the time to devote to an extensive lending operation with clients at considerable distances. Although there is currently no evidence other than the information cited in the Pinkas, one wonders whether the wife of Rabbi Hertzfeld assisted her husband in some managerial capacity. The bills of exchange owed by the captain of the Swiss regiment and his wife are noted in PMBD, Vol. 2, no. 583, 123a–123b, and no. 637, 139a. Concerning a debt owed by the captain of another Swiss regiment, Castellas, see PMBD, Vol. 2, no. 64, 12a.

105 Szajkowski, *The Economic Status of the Jews in Alsace, Metz and Lorraine*, 63–67.

106 For a case that richly details business transactions involving Jews and non-Jews, and includes technical language pertaining to commerce, see PMBD, Vol. 1, pt. 1, no. 59, 17b. Also see: PMBD, Vol. 1, pt. 1, no. 63, 19a; Vol. 1, pt. 2, no. 49, 14a; Vol. 1, pt. 2, no. 67, 18b; Vol. 2, no. 194, 28b; no. 203, 38b; no. 292, 54a; no. 350, 66a; no. 593, 127a; and no. 633, 138a. For an example of a dispute between Jewish partners that resulted from joint ventures involving non-Jews and subsequently required adjudication by the Beit Din, see, "Mémoire pour le Comte de Leuenhaupt … contre Moyse Blien," 29 January 1762, cited in Zosa Szajkowski, *Franco-Judaica: An Analytical Bibliography Pertaining to the Jews in France, 1500–1788* (New York, 1962), 64, no. 659. Also see ibid., no. 177, concerning the storage of merchandise in the home of a gentile outside the Jewish quarter.

seventeenth-century jurist Jean Domat, a partnership was no less than "a liaison, which is a type of brotherhood."[107]

It was not unusual for a dispute between Jewish litigants to hinge on the purchase of a financial instrument that they as partners had secured from gentile clients. In one instance, after purchasing *rentes* from the Marquis des Essarts in Paris, two Jewish partners subsequently sold them, in the presence of a notary, to two gentile clients on behalf of a third partner. The ensuing dispute among the Jewish partners was not unusual in terms of its complexity. It involved a demand for payment from the third partner who was owed money by one of the other partners; his payment would be contingent on the issuance of a warrant by the civil court guaranteeing the promissory note that he held in hand. In this case, the Beit Din succeeded in working out a compromise agreement.[108]

Commercial entanglements involving Jews and non-Jews required complex maneuvering to navigate through what was, frequently, a legal maze. In one case, heirs to an estate urgently needed to block a land sale that would have depleted funds owed to the estate, and they therefore submitted a formal remonstrance at the *conservateur des hypothèques* (land registry).[109] In a case concerning a debt owed to the heirs of Aaron Steinbiedersdorf by a Christian, the heirs were required not only to submit papers to the court at Morhange as evidence of their claim but also to be represented legally by their guardian, Berman Alsace. To receive compensation for lost income while undertaking this assignment and the travel it involved, Alsace required authorization from the Beit Din. The rabbinic court was also asked to provide a copy of its approbation regarding the amount of the old debt for inclusion in a letter from an *avocat*.[110] Efforts of this sort, which were not unusual at all, presumed a detailed understanding of the legal system and the bureaucratic demands it made on members of the general population.

Evidence of Jewish-gentile economic interdependence, ranging from routine business dealings to occasional collaborations, challenges the stereotypic image of the Jews as alien to the society around them. It is nonetheless unclear how to interpret the fragmented data that has survived. In one instance it is noted that a partnership consisting of Jews and non-Jews met and concluded an agreement in a tavern, a public space of unquestioned social and economic significance by most accounts, suggesting that such meetings may not have

107 On partnerships in Paris, cf. Kessler, *A Revolution in Commerce*, 157–58.

108 PMBD, Vol. 2, no. 447, 86a. Here the Hebrew expression for *rentes* is *demei sekhirut karka'ot*.

109 PMBD, Vol. 2, no. 581, 122b.

110 PMBD, Vol. 1, pt. 2, no. 120, 30a.

been so unusual.[111] On the other hand, the fact that some partnerships involving Jews and non-Jews were formed on the basis of a *traité* means that such arrangements may have been somewhat out of the ordinary. Zosa Szajkowski assembled extensive data on Jews who acted as intermediaries for gentile creditors, and as transferees as well, and though this cannot be taken to imply sociability in the sense that Domat may have envisioned partnerships, the social, economic, and legal significance of such relationships must not be underestimated. In some instances, Jewish creditors used the names of gentiles as *prête-noms* (figureheads) when extending loans, and in other circumstances they lent their own names to gentile creditors.[112] One should nonetheless exercise caution before discarding the alien image of the Jews entirely. To assume that a socio-economic version of the "neutral society" to which Jacob Katz referred in *Tradition and Crisis* had emerged in northeastern France at any time before the end of the ancien régime would be an exaggeration. In either case, the written agreement that accompanied these various transactions created a durable bond between the parties to the contract.[113] In fact, it may be assumed that the proliferation of early modern legal procedures came to define the limits of human behavior and formalized notions of responsibility toward members of other groups and cultures.

These and other examples of collaboration were doubtless more common among the upper strata of Jewish communities in western and central Europe. Indeed, litigants who came before the Metz Beit Din stemmed disproportionately from the communal and rabbinic elite and their families. Nevertheless, the processes described in this chapter suggest that the unmistakable imprint left by the surrounding culture on Jewish life was not limited to the elite alone but extended to the broader urban Jewish population. This is reflected in the assimilation of French language and linguistic patterns into everyday affairs, the familiarity with general legal concepts and technical terminology, the affinity with French material culture, and the complexities that were attendant on economic interaction between Jews and non-Jews.

111 See PMBD, Vol. 2, no. 593, 127a. For a recent discussion of the social and economic role of taverns in the early modern period, see Robert Liberles, *Jews Welcome Coffee: Tradition and Innovation in Early Modern Germany* (Waltham, 2012), 6–14 and passim.

112 Szajkowski, *Jews and the French Revolutions of 1789, 1830, and 1848*, 166–80. For a case in which gentiles and Jews served as figureheads, see PMBD, Vol. 1, pt. 2, no. 21c, 47b.

113 See Kessler, *Revolution in Commerce*, 162–63.

PART 2

Community, Governance, Authority

CHAPTER 3

Communal Autonomy and Governance

The evidence amassed in the Metz communal and rabbinic court registers compels a reappraisal of Jewish life in the pre-revolutionary era. Together, these sources delineate the three-way relationship among the Jews, the state, and society at large that contrasts sharply with the account adopted by modern Jewish historiography. It is commonly assumed that after the mid-eighteenth century Jewish communal autonomy was no longer compatible with absolutism. Simon Dubnow, Selma Stern, Salo W. Baron, and Jacob Katz, to name several leading figures, each argued that the absolutist state steadily rescinded the autonomy it had granted to the Kahal and to rabbinic courts. This change, they maintain, stemmed from a political shift that transformed central and western European régimes. The emergent centralized state, with rigorous regulatory tools at its disposal, was unwilling to tolerate the Church's failure or refusal to conform to its laws. Jewish autonomy was treated in a manner that resembled the treatment of the Church and other corporate entities. By these accounts, government interference in the internal affairs of the Jewish community reduced communal and rabbinic courts to voluntary arbitration panels while dispute settlement in civil courts of the realm was broadly encouraged.[1]

Details of the legislation issued by the Metz Kehillah, when considered alongside the proceedings of the Beit Din, call for us to revisit the conventional understanding of the relationship between the Jewish community and the state. Recent research on Jewish communities in central Europe confirms that it was not state interference alone that set limitations on communal autonomy. Coincident with governmental action, individual members of the community appealed to the state to curtail the authority of the Kahal and limit the scope of rabbinic jurisdiction. The work of Verena Kasper-Marienberg stands out in this regard. Internal Jewish disputes in Frankfurt were frequently brought to local non-Jewish courts and even to the Imperial Aulic

---

1 Selma Stern, *Die preussische Staat und die Juden* (Berlin, 1925), II/1, 123–149; Katz, *Tradition and Crisis*, 217–18; Salo W. Baron, "New Approaches to Jewish Emancipation," *Diogenes* 29 (1960): 57–58; Chimen Abramsky, "The Crisis of Authority within European Jewry in the Eighteenth Century," in *Studies in Jewish Intellectual and Religious History*, ed. Siegfried Stein and Raphael Loewe (Tuscaloosa, 1979), 13–28. Kenneth Stow has traced this development to the sixteenth century. See "Jewish Pre-Emancipation: *Ius Commune*, the Roman *Comunità*, and Marriage in the Early Modern Papal State," in *Festschrift in Honor of Robert Bonfil*, ed. Elisheva Baumgarten, et al. (Jerusalem, 2010), 79–102.

 | DOI:10.1163/97890044 7403_005

Council, often at the behest of members of the Jewish community.[2] David Horowitz has found similar evidence regarding the triple community of Altona-Hamburg-Wandsbek. The Hamburg Senate archives and the civil court records reveal continuous recourse to non-Jewish courts and frequent challenges to communal and rabbinic authority. Jewish communal sources evidence internal discord between residents who defended the community's disciplinary regimen and those who challenged communal and rabbinic authority. Increasing social and economic integration of Jews in Hamburg, their espousal of a "new rhetoric of civic belonging," and the growing refusal of Jews to appear when summoned before the Beit Din offer evidence of eroding community discipline. Although the entanglement with state sovereignty was a powerful factor in this transformation, it was the internal opposition to the jurisdiction of the Jewish community that was primarily responsible for the erosion of autonomy. In Horowitz's estimation, these internal forces were more powerful than the impact of the centralizing state.[3]

Conditions in Metz suggest a rather different dynamic that reflected the particularities of the French political landscape, though there was a larger transformation at work across central Europe that yielded some similar results and comparable rhetoric. Christian Wilhelm Dohm, approached by Moses Mendelssohn in 1781 to provide a statement of defense following a wave of incitement against Jewish communities in Alsace, published a memorandum that same year under the title *Über die bürgerliche Verbesserung der Juden* (*On the Civil Improvement of the Jews*). Dohm argued that the continued jurisdiction over legal disputes in accordance with Jewish law and the exercise of religious controls such as the *ḥerem* were not incompatible with the bestowal of civic equality by the state. Mendelssohn, like Dohm, objected strongly to the view of orientalist scholar Johann David Michaelis, that so long as Jews observed their laws, they would be unable to participate in civil society. However, Mendelssohn regarded the exercise of rabbinic controls to be an affront to the

2 See Verena Kasper-Marienberg, *"Vor Euer Kayserlichen Mayestät Justiz-Thron": Die Frankfurter jüdische Gemeinde am Reichshofrat in josephinischer Zeit* (1765–1790) (Innsbruck, 2012), esp. 50–52, 132–45. For a similar conclusion, see Monika Preuß, *'sie könnten klagen, wo sie wollen': Möglichkeiten und Grenzen rabbinischen Richtens in der frühen Neuzeit* (Göttingen, 2014), 127–31. For adjudication in lower courts, also see Sabine Ullmann, "Die jüdische Minderheit vor dörflichen Niedergerichten in der Frühen Neuzeit," *Geschichte und Gesellschaft* 35 (2009): 534–60.

3 David Horowitz, "Fractures and Fissures in Jewish Communal Autonomy in Hamburg, 1710–1782," (Ph.D. diss., Columbia University, 2010), 3–8, 20–21, 151–61.

principles of the Enlightenment.[4] Dohm's vision corresponded more closely to conditions in France.

The autonomy enjoyed by the Jewish community of Metz was more robust and comprehensive than is generally assumed, and there are few signs of state interference in communal affairs or judicial matters. To be sure, tensions surfaced periodically when governmental demands for compliance with French law threatened the autonomy of the Kehillah, but these occurrences were less common than is usually assumed.[5] From the resettlement of Jews in Metz and in other regions of France in the sixteenth century, the state became the Jewish community's political guarantor. It empowered the Jewish communal leadership to regulate behavior in accordance with norms recorded in its bylaws. To achieve social, economic, and political stability, the state was committed to upholding the authority of the Jewish communal leadership and its institutions, including rabbinic jurisdiction in civil matters. Moreover, freeing a loyal minority from undue interference conferred manifest bureaucratic advantages on the state. Each of these considerations was consistent with the royal administration's longstanding acknowledgment of local customary law as an essential dimension of the legal culture that prevailed through the end of the ancien régime.

An additional factor, the growth of constitutionalism in early modern western and central Europe, further shaped the character of Jewish communal governance.[6] Social and political measures, introduced in order to advance the organization and regulation of communal life, were recorded in quasi-constitutional documents—*pinkesei kahal*—starting in the sixteenth century.[7] Modern constitutionalism, which stood in opposition to absolutism,

4 Alexander Altmann, "The Philosophical Roots of Moses Mendelssohn's Plea for Emancipation," *Jewish Social Studies* 36:3–4 (July–October, 1974): 191–202; idem, *Moses Mendelssohn: A Biographical Essay* (Philadelphia, 1973), 465 and passim; Shmuel Feiner, *Moses Mendelssohn: Philosopher of the Enlightenment*, trans. from Hebrew by Anthony Berris (New Haven, 2010), 135–36, 149–51.

5 See PKM, 131a for an example of a call made by the Metz Kahal to representatives of communities in the Moselle in the summer of 1785 to discuss ways to show support for residents of Barschingen, who were facing legal challenges from governmental authorities and were incurring significant legal expenses.

6 On the emergence of early modern constitutionalism, see James Q. Whitman, *The Legacy of Roman Law in the German Romantic Era: Historical Vision and Legal Change* (Princeton, NJ, 1990), 41–45, 61–73, 84–86. For additional sources on the history of the Jewish community, see Baron, *The Jewish Community*. passim.

7 See Litt, *Protokollbuch und Statuten aus Jüdische Gemeindestatuten*. On the medieval foundations of constitutionalism, see Janelle Greenberg and Michael J. Sechler, "Constitutionalism Ancient and Early Modern: The Contributions of Roman Law, Canon Law, and English Common Law," *Cardozo Law Review* 34 (2013): 1021–47.

was the foundation of limited government through checks and balances and the separation of powers.[8] In communities that were founded on constitutionalism, there appears to have been a greater tendency to coordinate with the surrounding legal system at either the municipal or the state level. Judicial cooperation, as will become apparent, did not undermine Jewish communal autonomy.

When compared to the authority exercised by French ecclesiastical courts and other corporate bodies, Jewish judicial autonomy—its independence and range of authority—stands out conspicuously. While collaboration between the spiritual and temporal powers aimed to protect religious orthodoxy and the social order in early modern France, the division between the religious and secular areas of responsibility was more clearly defined in the general society than in the Jewish community. Nor did this division bear any resemblance to the relationship between rabbinic courts and the state. The concern of the Church, as set forth in royal legislation issued in 1695, related to all that "involved the sacraments, monastic vows, divine worship, ecclesiastical discipline, and other purely spiritual matters," whereas the monarchy assumed responsibility for citizens and their welfare in the broadest sense.[9] Over the course of the next seventy years, the Crown acceded to the arguments advanced by parlementaires concerning the supremacy of the secular authority in religious affairs. As the external discipline of the Church steadily fell under the jurisdiction of the state, lay encroachment on the authority of the ecclesiastical courts proceeded apace.[10] By striking contrast, there is little evidence of anticlericalism in the state's policy on Jewish autonomy. Lay and rabbinic courts of Metz were permitted to function without noticeable interference by government authorities.

With very limited exceptions, the Metz Beit Din was consistently the court of first instance. Deviation from this general rule was for the most part motivated by either a preference for a forum capable of enforcing its ruling or by the desire to appeal the judgment to a higher authority that could reverse the lower court's decision. The opposing positions of the community and of individuals may be understood as the divergent interests of producers and consumers

8 See Neil Walker, "Constitutionalism and the Incompleteness of Democracy: An Iterative Relationship," *Rechtsfilosofie & Rechtstheorie* 39 (2010): 206–33.

9 Jeffrey Merrick, "Conscience and Citizenship in Eighteenth-Century France," *Eighteenth-Century Studies*, Vol. 21, No. 1 (Autumn, 1987): 49–50.

10 See John McManners, *Church and Society in Eighteenth Century France*, 2 vols. (Oxford, 1998), 1:156–57, 192–98; Merrick, "Conscience and Citizenship," 48–58. For a discussion of earlier efforts to limit the jurisdiction of ecclesiastical courts, see Helmholz, "Conflicts Between Religious and Secular Law."

of justice. Growing numbers of consumers had become aware of the options available in the general judicial system and in some instances acted in the interest of achieving their goals. It is widely assumed that when individuals took their disputes to the civil courts, invariably the intent was to achieve a more favorable judgment than they believed possible in the rabbinic court. It is also assumed that such recourse transgressed—whether consciously or unconsciously—the jurisdictional boundaries of rabbinic or communal autonomy. Before these assumptions can be proven or refuted, more data are needed concerning the frequency of recourse to non-Jewish courts and whether these were indeed acts of defiance of communal or rabbinic authority.

Metz offers a model that is sharply at variance with the pattern presumed dominant in early modern Europe. The Metz communal registers and rabbinic court records alter the way we understand the nature and scope of Jewish communal autonomy, the relationship between the Jews and the state, and the complex interaction with the surrounding society and culture. This chapter and the next are devoted to investigating how the autonomous community functioned, with special attention to its legislative efforts, the role of the judiciary, and the construction of religious and social norms.

• • •

Jewish life in early modern France was organized, as elsewhere, within the self-governing communal structure, the Kehillah. Each community prescribed norms of social and religious conduct that were recorded in the Pinkas Kahal and, once formally enacted as legislation, assumed the status of by-laws (*takkanot*). The latter, too, were recorded in the Pinkas and, in some instances, were published separately. Their purpose was to maintain social and economic equilibrium, to preserve correct relations with government authorities and the neighboring gentile population, to prevent the deterioration of religious and moral values, and to promote social welfare. Toward these ends, communal legislation delineated the obligations of residence and regulated immigration; set forth the charitable obligations incumbent on community members; determined procedures for the appointment of communal officials and functionaries; and imposed taxes. Additionally, it defined moral and religious standards in the public sphere, in areas that included sexuality, marriage, divorce, and inheritance; enacted guidelines for the resolution of legal disputes and rules for the prevention of criminal activity; and approved measures that regulated material consumption and commercial transactions.

Alongside characteristics that were shared throughout Europe, communal governance evinced regional variations concerning integration within the general society, the degree of autonomy granted by the state, and local cultural traditions. In the southwestern communities, where the aristocratic tradition of the Iberian Peninsula was much in evidence, authority was concentrated in a small group of wealthy merchants and bankers. But the autocratic regime of the Nation also was a consequence of the specific circumstances surrounding the establishment of these communities. Since most of the earliest immigrant families were poor, the wealthier among them paid taxes on their behalf and emerged as the Nation's legal representatives. Dissident members of the community fiercely opposed the autocratic style of the affluent members of the community and demanded representation in the leadership body, but the king upheld the authority of the more established leaders. Similar disputes in Saint-Esprit-lès-Bayonne disrupted communal affairs for much of the century, but the royal authority supported the official administration of the Nation there as well.[11]

Throughout Alsace and Lorraine, the social and political underpinnings of communal autonomy corresponded to the general pattern of self-government practiced in Ashkenazic communities of central and eastern Europe. Reconfirmed by the state periodically over the course of the seventeenth and eighteenth centuries, the right to self-government "in religion and in their inner concerns" referred primarily to jurisdiction in the civil and ritual spheres.[12] The authority vested in Jewish legal institutions depended on the power of the state, and were it not for the government's interest in enforcing compliance with Jewish law, Jewish communal leaders would have had little power at all.[13] As in other localities, the Metz Kehillah was granted the right to collect taxes, regulate behavior, oversee social welfare, and settle legal disputes according to its interpretation of talmudic law. Jewish self-government enjoyed the support of European rulers because its role in the collection of taxes and as a reliable framework for social control was widely acknowledged, as it had been for centuries. These institutions and the frame of mind of the communal leadership were based on models inherited from medieval Jewish communities and adapted to prevailing socio-economic and political conditions in the early modern period.[14]

---

11 *Le Registre des délibérations de la Nation Juive Portugaise de Bordeaux*, 9–13, and no. 279; Zosa Szajkowski, "Conflicts within the Eighteenth-Century Sephardic Communities of France," *Hebrew Union College Annual* 31 (1960): 167–80.

12 See Cahen, "Le rabbinat de Metz pendant la période française," *REJ* 7 (1883): 103–107, 215–16; *REJ* 8 (1884): 257–58. The 1595 text appeared on 106–107.

13 See Katz, *Tradition and Crisis*, 77.

14 On the range of judicial and legislative powers of *tovei ha'ir*—also known as *benei ha'ir* or *anshei ha'ir*—see Tosefta Bava Metiza 11:23ff; BT Bava Batra 7b–8a; Megilah 26a, and

Communal legislation aimed to maintain internal equilibrium in the face of dynamic social and cultural change, a widening gap between rich and poor, acute generational tensions, the erosion of sexual mores, the blurring of class distinctions, and challenges to traditional religious observance. The following discussion considers communal legislation issued in several areas: electoral and administrative procedures; consumption and social status; poverty and social welfare; juridical autonomy; and religious and moral conduct.

Electoral and Administrative Procedures

Electoral and administrative procedures in Alsace, Lorraine, and Metz rested on a broader foundation than in the southern communities, though eligibility requirements for communal office in Metz in particular became increasingly exclusionary over the course of the century.[15] In the second half of the eighteenth century, it had become evident to leaders in Alsace that the challenges facing their communities demanded a centralized approach. A regional meeting was held in 1763 in Niedernai, where statutes governing the appointment of deputies for Lower-Alsace were issued in preparation for a meeting in Bischeim. Similar meetings were held in Strasbourg in 1776 and 1777 and in Rosheim in 1777. The official agenda for these assemblies included a new initiative to assist the poor; tax assessment; unauthorized marriages; taxes on dowries; and men and women dancing together. The protocols of these meetings were signed by Cerf-Berr, Aron Meyer of Mutzig, and Lehmann Netter of Rosheim, each of whom possessed the title *préposé général de la Nation Juive*. Provincial assemblies met in 1777, 1780, and 1783 and enacted *takkanot* that addressed matters of common interest to the forty-two communities of the Upper and Lower Rhine represented at the assembly. It was determined that the decisions passed at these meetings would be binding upon all the communities within the province.[16]

Maimonides, *Mishneh Torah*, Laws of Neighbors, chs. 5–6. On the role of *migdar milta* ("to stem the tide of immorality") as the impetus for enacting medieval communal decisions, see Irving A. Agus, *Rabbi Meir of Rothenburg: His Life and His Works as Sources for the Religious, Legal, and Social History of the Jews of Germany in the Thirteenth Century* (Philadelphia, 1947). Also see Samuel Morell, "The Constitutional Limits of Communal Government in Rabbinic Law," *JSS* 33 (1971): 87–107.

15 See Abraham Cahen, "Règlements somptuaires de la communauté juive de Metz à la fin du XVIIe siècle," *Annuaire de la Société des études juives* 1 (1881): 77–129.

16 See Isidore Loeb, *Extrait du protocole de la nation de l'assemblée du 21 Iyyar 5537*: 178–79 and 193–98; Weill, "Rabbins et Parnasim dans l'Alsace du XVIIIe siècle," 102–104; Richard

These decisions reaffirmed seigneurial authority in external affairs and introduced uniform statutes that governed the internal life of communities throughout Alsace in the following areas: the election of local *parnasim*; the relative authority of local and regional *parnasim*; internal policing; civil jurisdiction; rabbinic authority; taxation; higher talmudic education; record keeping; religious and social controls; social welfare; and inheritance. *Takkanot* that ordered the hierarchy of regional and local communal *parnasim* were recognized as royal law in the 1784 *lettres patentes*. Local *parnasim* were responsible for internal matters such as the appointment of synagogue officiants; synagogue administration; tax collection; and maintaining order.[17] A typical Alsatian community was administered by an elected council, headed by a rabbi, that exercised a range of punitive powers including fines, public declaration of wrongdoings, withholding of religious honors, and the communal ban (*ḥerem*). Since communities in Alsace were small, syndics were elected by the entire Jewish population of male taxpayers. The passage of legislation by the assemblies did not become policy, nor could new resolutions be enforced, until they were confirmed by the territorial assemblies of the *seigneuries*. Nor were elections considered lawful without confirmation by the provincial organization and the royal Intendant.

Roughly half the communities in Upper and Lower Alsace were headed by a *parnas*. At the end of the seventeenth century there was one *parnas* per community in the bishopric of Strasbourg, whether a community consisted of one or several villages. In Brisach the duties of the three elected *parnasim* were limited to managing the budget and carrying out rabbinic decisions. In Saverne the *parnasim* were named by the episcopal authority and in Haguenau they purchased their charges, which were subsequently confirmed by the Intendant and Magistrat. Elie Schwab, rabbi of the Prefecture, sought to control the appointment of local *parnasim* in his jurisdiction by opposing several of the nominations and, on one occasion, attempted to secure the election of a family relative.[18] As a rule, the local *parnasim* were either named by the *seigneur* (as in Strasbourg), elected (as in Neuf-Brisach or in Haguenau), or chosen by the rabbi. Those appointed by the *seigneur* presumably acted as representatives of the feudal authority, though like those who were elected, they undoubtedly

---

Cohen, introduction to Heb. ed. of Grégoire, *Essai sur la régénération* (Jerusalem, 1989), 14–15; and Berkovitz, *Rites and Passages*, 53–58.

17 Articles 21–23, 1784 *lettres patentes*, cited in Loeb, *Extrait du protocole de la nation;* id., "Les Juifs à Strasbourg depuis 1349 jusqu'à la Révolution," *Annuaire de la société des études juives* 2 (1883): 101–102.

18 On Schwab's efforts to control the election of *parnasim* in 1724 and 1738, see Moïse Ginsburger, "Elie Schwab, rabbin de Haguenau (1721–1747)," *REJ* 44 (1902): 116.

performed a similar range of communal functions, from policing to forming lists for taxation.[19]

Communal governance in Alsace was distinguished by the active participation of rabbis alongside *parnasim* in the governing body. The Alsatian rabbinate enjoyed considerable authority in local community and regional affairs; in Lorraine the *av beit din* was authorized to enforce his own judgments or those of another court, and to "publicize, prohibit, fine, and pronounce the *ḥerem*."[20] This contrasted sharply with Sephardic communities in the south, where rabbis were excluded from the governing body and were subordinated to the syndics in every area beyond the narrowly defined ritual sphere. According to the Bayonne communal statutes of 1752, the rabbi was not to take part in the communal affairs of the Nation and was restricted to purely ritual functions, such as officiant, inspector, and teacher.[21] For most of the ancien régime, the Alsatian rabbinate enjoyed substantial authority in local community affairs, and until the beginning of the eighteenth century numerous rabbis were included within the ranks of communal leadership in Metz as well, though this would lessen with time.[22] In Alsace the rabbinate struggled vigorously throughout the eighteenth century to maintain its authority in communal affairs. In 1741, Rabbi Samuel Weyl of Upper Alsace sought government approval for changes in the election and appointment of communal officials, and he also called for government participation in supervising these procedures. Pursuant

19 Weill, "Rabbins et Parnassim," 102–103.

20 For failure to answer a summons, the Metz Beit Din ordered the seizure of property, as exemplified by an inheritance dispute in which one of the heirs delayed coming to the court in respond to his brother-in-law's claims. See PMBD, Vol. 1, pt. 2, no. 2, 2a–b. For a case of a fine imposed for causing humiliation, see PMBD, Vol. 1, pt. 2, no. 58, 16b.

21 On disparate trends in Bordeaux and Bayonne with respect to the role of rabbis in the governing body, see Berkovitz, *Rites and Passages*, 21–23. For limitations imposed on rabbinic freedom, see *Le Registre des deliberations de la Nation Juive Portugaise de Bordeaux*, nos. 85, 121, and 437; on the teaching duties of the rabbi, see no. 62. Cf. Hertzberg, *French Enlightenment*, 245. The responsa published by Rabbi Raphael Meldola, *av beit din* of Bayonne, reveal that an effort had been made in the 1730s to exercise greater rabbinic authority in communal affairs, but this proved ultimately unsuccessful. See Raphael Meldola, *Resp. Mayyim Rabbim* (Amsterdam, 1737), pt. 2, nos. 62–65. For limits on the rabbi's authority to Bayonne, see Art. 33 of the 1753 *règlement*, and Gérard Nahon, *Les "Nations" juives portugaises du sud-ouest de la France (1684–1791)* (Paris, 1981), Arts. 33 and 196.

22 For Alsace, see the extract from the "Protocol of the Medinah," 28 May 1777, Arts. 2, 3, and 14, published in *Blätter für jüdische Geschichte und Litteratur* 2 (1901): 18–22; 28–29, and paraphrased in French by Loeb, *Extrait du protocole de la nation de l'assembiée du 21 Iyyar 5537*; Loeb "Les Juifs de Strasbourg," 181–98. Of the sixty-eight *parnasim* mentioned in the Metz *Memorbuch*, forty-one used the title "rabbi," as well. For examples, see viii, and notice nos. 57, 76, 673, 839, and 861.

to his plan, local *parnasim* were elected democratically and installed by the rabbis and the regional *parnasim*. Royal authorities approved Weyl's initiative, and it had the force of law in Upper Alsace, the lands of Klinglin, the abbey of Murbach, the county of Ribeaupierre, the county of la Noblesse-Immédiate, and the bishopric of Strasbourg. Centralization reinforced rabbinic authority in local affairs and strengthened the common interests of the grand rabbinate, the regional leadership, and governmental authorities. The rabbi alone was authorized "to judge, to teach religion, to contract marriages, to pronounce divorces," and he was also obliged to oversee "the conduct of all the Jews in the entire Haute-Alsace." Rabbinic duties typically concerned most areas of family and community law, including marriage and divorce, hearing witnesses, certifying ritual slaughterers, guardianship, and the conferral of rabbinic titles.[23]

In Metz, rabbis and rabbinic institutions were frequently consulted on policy questions and legislation, though lay officials dominated the communal administration since the late seventeenth century. A description of electoral and administrative procedures in a fragment dating from 1699 to 1702 records that taxpayers of the community elected a college of forty members, and a body of eleven members from among the forty was assigned the task of naming the members of the administrative council for a term of three years. That council was composed of twelve members, consisting of five *parnasim* and seven *tovim* (assistants). In 1702, the number of *parnasim* was reduced to nine and, thereafter, no more than four *parnasim* and five *tovim* were appointed at one time. Communal legislation was entrusted exclusively to the college of forty; it alone was authorized to enact new statutes while a special commission of nine members was charged with overseeing the legislative process. Initially, a committee responsible for redacting the statutes was composed of twelve persons, and an executive commission of nine members was responsible for completing the redaction process. A committee of five ensured the implementation of statutes and oversaw community fiscal accounts.[24] In the late 1750s and early 1760s, the pages of the Metz communal register were filled with vigorous discussion of new legislation, including detailed exchanges concerning the collection of charity and the functions of *parnasim*.[25]

---

23 Georges Weill, "Rabbins et Parnassim dans l'Alsace du XVIIIe siècle," in *Les Juifs dans l'histoire de France*, ed. Myriam Yardeni (Leiden, 1980), 101–103, and see the discussion of the contract of Rabbi Isaac Aaron of Phalsbourg in Simon Schwarzfuchs, *Du Juif à l'israélite. Histoire d'un mutation* (Paris, 1989), 45–46.

24 David Kaufmann, "Extraits de l'ancien livre de la communauté de Metz," REJ 19 (1889): 116.

25 PKM, 25a–b, 27a–b, 30a–31b; 35b.

The two colleges had full powers to execute their decisions, and the Kahal was required to lend its formal endorsement.[26] By the mid-eighteenth century, the electoral college had been enlarged from 40 to 99 members, consisting of 33 individuals each from the lower, middle, and upper classes of the community. The college chose 21 electors—seven from each order—who, in turn, chose the *parnasim*. Eligibility for the office of *parnas*, according to the 1752 Takkanot, included holding a residence permit having been married at least thirty years (twenty-two for holders of a rabbinic degree); a net worth of at least 5,000 crowns; and previous service as an administrator of the charity fund. As the electoral base grew, more rigorous demands were made of those seeking public office. In 1764, for example, the net worth requirement was set at 20,000 crowns, so that only the wealthiest members of the community would be able to assume positions of leadership. Rabbis would have been unable to meet these requirements unless they engaged primarily in business.[27]

Rabbinic endorsement of lay communal leaders' standards of social order and public responsibility in Metz came in the form of an important volume of responsa, *Ḥavvot Ya'ir*, authored by Rabbi Ya'ir Ḥayyim Bacharach (1638–1702). Bacharach, one of the leading *posekim* of early modern Ashkenaz, served briefly as rabbi in Koblenz before taking up residence in Worms, where he devoted himself to rabbinic scholarship and assumed a position as *dayan* in the community. He was also in Metz for a short stay following the invasion of Worms by the French army in 1689. His halakhic rulings, published in 1699, were among the most influential of their day and throughout the eighteenth-century. His authority in the areas of ritual and civil law was much admired throughout Europe, and especially in Metz and Alsace, where his responsa were cited regularly by leading halakhic authorities. Most of all, he articulated in the clearest terms the legal and philosophical underpinnings of lay-rabbinic cooperation as understood in eighteenth-century Metz and in other western European communities. In a departure from the limited authority accorded to communal leaders by leading *posekim* in the seventeenth century, Bacharach fully acknowledged the legitimacy of lay governance in those areas of public life beyond the administration of communal affairs, such as tax assessment

26 Kaufmann, "Extraits de l'ancien livre de la communauté de Metz." Also see the prologue to the Metz sumptuary regulations of 1690 [5450], in Abraham Cahen, "Règlements somptuaires de la communauté juive de Metz à la fin du XVIIe siècle," *Annuaire de la Société des études juives* 1 (1881): 86 and 97, n. 2.

27 See PKM, 30a–b for the subdivision of the Metz community into three classes, as defined by the valuation of assets. Regarding eligibility requirements for the office of *parnas* in 1764, see PKM, 58a.

and collection, administration of fines and punishments, and property and commercial transactions.[28]

According to Bacharach, the authority of communal legislation rested primarily on the elected status and representative capacity of communal leaders "who enjoy the public trust" and strive for "the preservation of the collective body."[29] Formulated within a halakhic context, Bacharach's approach bore resemblance to contemporary political theory and jurisprudence found in the writings of Jean Bodin, Johan Gottlieb Justi, Johann Jakob Moser, and Samuel Pufendorf.[30] Bacharach adamantly denied the right of any individual to disobey the law, to the extent that the law reflected the will of the majority of the community. Communal sovereignty embodied the Kahal's authority to enact and to amend legislation as it saw fit, including measures aimed at protecting religious values. In support of a community's right to regulate behavior in areas beyond the bounds of Jewish law and custom, Bachrach invoked a talmudic passage (BT Sanhedrin 46a) that authorized a *beit din* to impose corporal punishment even in instances not sanctioned by the Torah.[31] Accordingly,

---

28 Bacharach, *Resp. Ḥavvot Ya'ir*, nos. 57 and 81. Bacharach's approach is relevant not only to the discussion of the theoretical underpinnings of communal government and related concerns regarding rabbinic authority. His influence in areas such as the recitation of the mourners' *kaddish* by women, discussed for the first time in *Resp. Ḥavvot Ya'ir*, no. 222, in matters relating to commercial practices (no. 45), and a daughter's inheritance (no. 63) resonated among *posekim* throughout Europe. For examples of citations of Bacharach in northeastern France, see Reischer, *Resp. Shevut Ya'akov*, pt. 1, no. 102 and Joseph Steinhardt, *Resp. Zikhron Yosef* (Fürth, 1773), *Even ha-'Ezer*, no. 5; for a contrary understanding of Bacharach's position, see Gershon Koblenz, *Resp. Kiryat Ḥannah* (Metz, 1785), no. 35. For citations of Bacharach on a host of other subjects, see Joshua Heschel Lvov, *Resp. Penei Levanah* (Jerusalem, 2017), nos. 5, 10, 28, 42, 82, 102, and 105; *Resp. Kiryat Ḥannah*, nos. 4–5, 7, and 45; Aaron Worms, *Be'er Sheva* (Metz, 1819), 46a.

29 *Resp. Havvot Ya'ir*, no. 81. The expression used in reference to a sphere outside the authority of Halakhah is דלא שייכא בדין ודת של תורה כלל; concerning the overall purpose of the sumptuary laws, he wrote: שהתקנות התם הם לתכלית קיום הקיבוץ. Cf. Pinkas Kahal, 34b, where regulations concerning the distribution of charitable gifts were defended as contributing to "the good of the community" (*le-tovat ha-kehillah*).

30 See Jean Bodin, *On Sovereignty: Four Chapters from the Six Books of the Commonwealth*, trans. and ed. Julian H. Franklin (Cambridge, 1992). For parallels to German jurists, see Mack Walker, "Rights and Functions: The Social Categories of Eighteenth-Century Jurists and Commercialists," *Journal of Modern History* 50 (1978): 234–51.

31 See *Resp. Havvot Ya'ir*, no. 57. See Fram, *Ideals Face Reality*, 46, and also see Katz's comment in *Tradition and Crisis*, 296, n. 20—that although Bacharach derived the authority of lay officials to issue legislation from the fact that they were elected by the majority, he attributed this position to Rabbi Eliezer b. Joel ha-Levi (Ravya) and his school. Nevertheless, as Katz pointed out, Bacharach's claim regarding lay authority went much further than Ravya's justification of the right of the community to impose its will on the individual.

laws governing consumption were under the legitimate jurisdiction of the lay leadership because they concerned a halakhically neutral sphere, but their ultimate justification, he asserted, rested on their having functioned as a barrier to public immorality. In his view, the Kahal was empowered to act according to its own understanding, without concern for consistency with Jewish law. He acknowledged the legitimacy of laws founded on principles of equity and justice, arguing that it was unnecessary to confer sacral force upon communal law.[32]

Even so, in Bacharach's view, it was imperative that halakhic authorities assist the Kahal in carrying out the range of functions with which it was entrusted by community members. He displayed a determination to strengthen the foundations of communal authority, even when this meant curtailing liberties that were halakhically permissible or radically expanding the boundaries of communal authority.[33] He maintained that the assent of a major rabbinic authority (*adam ḥashuv*) was not necessary to ratify communal legislation, stating emphatically that the community need not "listen to one who unearths the origins of laws" provided they "approximate Torah law … in accordance with their perception and judgment … [nor] do they need to explain their reasoning, as long as they direct their heart to heaven."[34] Responsibility to the collective was an autonomous value requiring vigilant oversight, even at the expense of full compliance with the halakhic system. The community

32 *Resp. Havvot Ya'ir*, no. 57. Bacharach classified questions concerning food consumption, clothing and matchmaking as extra-halakhic and therefore under the legitimate jurisdiction of the lay leadership. Regrettably, Bacharach did not expound in detail on his understanding of equity and justice. On halakhic *lacunae*, see Gerald Blidstein, "Halakhah and Democracy," *Tradition* 32 (1997): 14–15.

33 Out of concern for potential harm to the public reputation of the Kahal as the supreme governing body, Bacharach limited an individual's right to request a second deferral of payment of a communal fine, even though this was allowable under Halakhah. Similarly, in a case involving several individuals who refused to share the expense of a public service (hiring an expert to sound the *shofar*), he ruled that they could be justifiably barred from deriving benefit from that service. He argued that the exclusion was based on the principle of *tikkun ʿolam* (the collective good) and should not be viewed as a violation of the talmudic principle of *zeh nehene ve-zeh lo ḥaser* ("this one benefits and the other does not suffer loss"). For examples of rulings that privileged communal duties over halakhic obligations out of concern that the latter might well encourage noncompliance with public responsibility, see *Resp. Ḥavvot Ya'ir*, nos. 127 and 186. For similar use of the phrase *tikkun ʿolam*, see nos. 45, 84, 137, 147, and 154.

34 See *Resp. Havvot Ya'ir*, nos. 57 and 81. Cf. Joel Sirkes, *Resp. Bayit Ḥadash* (New), (Koretz, 1785), no. 43; idem, *Bayit Ḥadash, Tur Ḥoshen Mishpat* 2. *Shulhan ʿArukh, Ḥoshen Mishpat* §231. See Elon, *Jewish Law*, 2: 752–757. Cf. Moses Maimonides, Hilkhot Mekhirah 14:11, where the *ḥakham ḥashuv* (important sage) is identified with the political activity embodied in the phrase *letaqen ma'aseh ha-medinah* ("to institute matters of state").

had the authority to proceed however it deemed appropriate, which could include ordering further investigations and imposition of oaths.[35] Bacharach averred that although communal leaders were not obliged to account for their actions from the standpoint of Jewish law, they must remain committed to the fundamental standards of natural law, much as Rabbi Moses Isserles (ca. 1520–1572), head of the yeshivah in Crakow and leading *posek* of Ashkenazic Jewry, had stipulated. In contrast to Rabbi Joel Sirkes (1561–1640), *av beit din* of Cracow and one of the foremost Talmudic scholars and halakhists of Poland in the following generation, Bacharach confirmed the sovereignty of the lay communal leadership in no uncertain terms.[36]

Although the rabbis of Metz acknowledged the authority of the *parnasim*, none articulated quite so positive an approach to communal authority as Bacharach. During the first half of the eighteenth century in particular, rabbinic leaders were concerned that communal legislation had encroached on areas that were the exclusive purview of Halakhah. The partnership model of lay and rabbinic leaders, as envisioned by Bacharach, was frustrated by a degree of jockeying for position. The terms of the contract offered to Rabbi Abraham Broda in 1708 stipulated that the head of the Metz rabbinic court was required to lend his formal assent to communal legislation intended to curb immorality and was barred from issuing the *ḥerem* without communal authorization. Broda's successor, Rabbi Jacob Reischer, who ended his career in Metz in 1733, objected in principle to legislation enacted by "unlettered *parnasim*" when it spurned rabbinic opinion, and especially when a regulation targeted an issue beyond the curtailment of immoral behavior (*le-migdar milta*). His concern for the lack of qualifications displayed by *parnasim* in his own day was based on a talmudic model requiring the position of *parnas ha-tzibbur* (public leader) to be filled by a recognized halakhic expert.[37] Though an outspoken critic of *parnasim* "who are not worthy of leadership," and despite his complaints that "their silence surpasses their speech when they rule on matters of law before the rabbis," Reischer acknowledged both their authority to enact laws and their superior standing in the community. He explained further that "it is already known that with respect to communal consent (*haskamat ha-kahal*) we follow the intent of those who enacted the *takkanot* and not the [apparent] meaning of the language [of the *takkanah*] ..." In matters of personal property, he

---

35 *Resp. Havvot Ya'ir*, no. 57.

36 See Joel Sirkes, *Resp. Bayit Ḥadash* (New), (Koretz, 1785), no. 43, especially his comments on BT Bava Batra 9a. For additional examples and discussion, see Jay R. Berkovitz, "Crisis and Authority in Early Modern Ashkenaz," *Jewish History* 26 (2012): 190–94.

37 See BT Gittin 60a and BT Ta'anit 10b.

expressly recognized the judicial authority of lay courts and the jurisdiction of lay judges.[38]

After mid-century, Metz communal law formally declared the functions of *dayan* and syndic incompatible—a decision that effectively excluded rabbis from holding official positions in the communal government.[39] In Alsace, a decided preference to hire natives of the region invariably led to commercial entanglements, corruption at the highest levels of communal leadership, and the sullying of rabbinic prestige. In Metz, in the aftermath of a dispute over rabbinic succession in 1625, eligibility for the position of *av bet din* was restricted to individuals with no local family ties. Once that matter was resolved, the decision was taken to limit the position of *av beit din* to foreign rabbis in order to protect against special interests, and that the nomination would require the king's formal approval.[40] A body of approximately fifty electors drawn from various sectors of the population, most heavily from the ranks of community officials and the wealthy, nominated the Metz *av beit din*. The electors included: six communal leaders, either syndics or members of the administrative council; the 18–20 members of the rabbinic tribunal, that is, all those who were eligible to be chosen as the *assesseurs* of the grand rabbi; and thirty men selected by lottery from each of the three economic classes of the community. Only during the rabbinic tenure of Ukraine native Rabbi Moses Cohen Narol was the new appointment policy formalized: the duties of the grand rabbi were consolidated, and the *lettres patentes* of 1657 required that the choice be submitted to the approbation of the king.[41]

---

38 Jacob Reischer, *Resp. Shevut Ya'akov*, pt. 1, nos. 1, 11, and 87; pt. 2 (Offenbach, 1711), no. 143 and pt. 1, no. 137. Cf. Ẓevi Ashkenazi, *Resp. Hakham Ẓevi* (Amsterdam, 1712), no. 131, where communal legislation is endorsed as the "equivalent of a *takkanah* of the Great Court for all of Israel, to the degree that anyone who swears that he will not abide by the *takkanat ha-kahal* is likened to one who swore that he would nullify a Torah command." Cf. idem, *Resp. Ḥakham Ẓevi, Likutei Teshuvot*, no. 116.

39 See PKM, 40b, where one rabbi is reported to have recused himself from becoming appointed *parnas* because he hoped to become a *dayan* in the future.

40 For examples of the earliest *takkanot* prohibiting the appointment of an *av beit din* with kin in the local community, see Israel Schepansky, *The Takkanot of Israel*, 4 vols. (Jerusalem, 1992), 4:408–409. On their spread to central and western Europe, see Azriel Shohet, *'Im Ḥilufe Tequfot* [*The Beginnings of the Haskalah in Germany*] [Hebrew] (Jerusalem, 1961), 93–94. In Metz, the regulation concerning the ineligibility of rabbis with kin (*pesulei 'edut*) in the community to be considered for the position of *av beit din* was recorded several times in the Pinkas Kahal. See, for example, PKM, 63b (1756).

41 See Narol's description of King Louis XIV's visit to the Metz synagogue, published by Zecharias Frankel, "Eine historische Notiz," *Monatsschrift für Geschichte und Wissenschaft des Judentums* 21 (1872): 44–47. Also see Shlomo Eidelberg, "The Jews of Worms During the French Conquest (1688–1697)," *Proceedings of the American Academy of Jewish Research*

Once the new policy was implemented, the Metz community was able to attract many of the most distinguished rabbinic personalities in Europe to the position of *av beit din*. The list included Gershon Ashkenazi, Abraham Broda, Jacob Reischer, Jacob Joshua Falk, Jonathan Eibeschütz, Samuel Hilman, and Aryeh Loeb Günzberg.[42] Lower-level rabbinic positions, however, were filled by local rabbis. Various charitable foundations provided employment for scholarly relatives of the founders. One leading patron of Jewish education, Moïse Blien, arranged for his son-in-law, Rabbi Isaac Netter of Bouxwiller, to acquire a residence permit (*ḥezkat ʿironit*), to subsequently head the local *kloiz* (a privately supported academy), and to receive a communal tax exemption.[43] Other positions, including rabbinic directors of the publicly-funded *beit midrash* (study hall) and assistant communal rabbis, were consistently filled by members of the local community.[44] In the duchy of Lorraine, there was one regional rabbinate, based near Nancy. From 1737, when the office of grand rabbi was created, until the end of the century, there were only three rabbis—Nehemiah Reischer, Jacob Perle, and Jacob Schweich—who had filled that position. A convocation of *parnasim* and community representatives, totaling thirty, elected the rabbi of Lorraine. Other rabbinic functionaries served in the rural countryside, thus forming a sub-rabbinate. The grand rabbinate of Lorraine was itself subordinate to the authority of the Metz rabbinate and, in some instances, the Metz Beit Din was called upon to adjudicate more difficult matters.[45]

In Metz, rich merchants and financiers were in firm control of communal governance during the century and a half prior to the French Revolution.

---

60 (1994): 91–93. See Cahen, "Le Rabbinat de Metz," *REJ* 7 (1883): 103–16; *REJ* 8 (1884): 255–74; *REJ* 12 (1886): 283–97; *REJ* 13 (1886): 105–14; and Moïse Ginsburger, "Les Juifs de Metz sous l'ancien régime," *REJ* 50 (1905): 112–28.

42 See Cahen, "Le Rabbinat de Metz," REJ 7 (1883): 220–23, and Moses Shulvass, *From East to West* (Detroit, 1971), 42. Rabbi Narol was succeeded by Rabbi Jonas Teoumim Fraenkel (1659–69), who also came to France to escape the Chmielnicki massacres. For details on the appointment of Rabbi Eibeschütz, see his correspondence with the Metz communal leadership in Raphael Blum, ed., "Trois lettres autographes de feu Rabbi Jonathan Eibenschutz," *Univers israélite* 9 (1853): 27–32. Rabbi Hilman's contract was reprinted in *Blätter für jüdische Geschichte und Litteratur* (1900): 39–40, and Rabbi Günzberg's contract was published and annotated in Simon Schwarzfuchs, "The Rabbinic Contract of the Sha'agat Aryeh in Metz," *Moriah* 15 (1986): 81–90.

43 PKM, 14b and 39a–b; also see Kerner, *La vie*, 174–75, and idem, "Un registre messin du XVIIIe siècle," *Archives juives* 7 (1970–71): 43.

44 See Samuel Kerner, "Salaries et salaires dans la communauté de Metz au XVIIIe siècle, d'aprés un ancien registre messin," *Archives juives* 8 (1971–72): 34.

45 See the rabbinic contract of Nehemiah Reischer, published in Schwarzfuchs, "Three Documents," 11–12.

Although they outstripped the authority of the rabbinate in communal affairs, there is little if any suggestion of conflict between the lay and religious leadership nor are there indications that lay leaders endeavored to assume control of the judiciary.[46] In fact, there is ample evidence in both the Pinkas Kahal and the Pinkas Beit Din that rabbis and lay communal leaders worked cooperatively.[47] Decades before the French Revolution, governing bodies of the Jewish community were in the throes of transformation, as evident in efforts to redefine the relationship of the rabbinate and lay authority. These included the progressive consolidation of rabbinical duties, the differentiation in the roles of rabbi and communal leader, and the growing independence of the rabbinate from commercial involvement. While such developments were affected by a host of variables that include the urban-rural divide, regional economic factors, and the degree of openness to external cultural influences, rabbis in Metz were central to most areas of governance. In an era of dynamic social and cultural change, the goal of the Metz sumptuary legislation was to maintain internal equilibrium threatened by a widening gap between rich and poor, acute generational tensions, the erosion of sexual mores, and the blurring of class distinctions.

Consumption and Social Status

Restrictions on the display of extravagant attire and the size and expense of religious celebrations was a commonplace in Jewish communities across the continent. Early modern legislation shared with medieval sumptuary law a commitment to the wider societal struggle to limit excessive consumption, motivated by the goal of instilling the religious virtue of modesty or the concern that ostentation would arouse resentment among the neighboring gentile population.[48] But early modern sumptuary laws were subsumed within broad controls aiming to regulate Jewish religious and social behavior. Prompted

46 Such developments are consistent with the theory that, after 1650, the struggle to suppress deviant behavior passed from ecclesiastical to lay powers. See Peter Burke, *Popular Culture and Elite Culture* (London, 1978), 208–41.

47 See Georges Weill, "Rabbins et Parnassim dans l'Alsace du XVIIIe siècle," in Myriam Yardeni, ed., *Les Juifs dans l'histoire de France* (Leiden, 1980), 96–109.

48 The origins of Jewish sumptuary regulations can be traced to twelfth-century Ashkenaz and, by the fifteenth century, these laws became very common; in Renaissance Italy alone over eighty sets of sumptuary laws were enacted. In Eastern Europe, the earliest known sumptuary laws were included in the Cracow *takkenot* of 1595. See Louis Finkelstein, *Jewish Self-Government* (New York, 1925), 228, 281–95, 373–75; Baron, *Jewish Community*, 2:301–307; 3:200–203; Pollack, *Jewish Folkways in Germanic Lands*, 86–91; and Cecil Roth,

by the far-reaching demographic and socio-economic changes of the period, they responded to three distinguishing features of modernity: urbanization, changes in class structure, and evolving notions of gender. The increasing density of social life in the city demanded strategies enabling urban dwellers to identify strangers and to reinforce hierarchical divisions in society. One concern was that the use of luxury items by members of the lower social strata threatened to blur identifying markers of social rank. Consumption, it was argued, ought to correspond to rank, not means.[49] With the transition from agrarianism to market economies, characterized by international commerce, manufacturing, and free enterprise, the status quo was threatened, particularly as communities became ever more receptive to cultural influences from the outside. In an era of wider distribution of wealth, and with the appearance of a younger generation made affluent by new economic opportunities, communal ordinances sought to exclude from the communal power structure a younger generation whose wealth derived from an expanding mercantile economy.[50]

Regulations enacted by the Metz Kahal in the late seventeenth century exemplify these wider trends. Although these restrictions resembled provisions of the royal declaration pronounced at Saint-Germain earlier in the century (1633), the immediate context for the Metz sumptuary legislation enacted in 1690–97 was the severe economic downturn resulting from France's involvement in the War of the Grand Alliance. The objectives envisioned by communal leaders were far more ambitious than what would normally be expected at a time of austerity. While seventeenth- and eighteenth-century sumptuary laws appear at first blush to be little more than a restatement of medieval controls on extravagance, they were, in fact, part of the expanding regulation of public behavior in the early modern absolutist state.[51]

Foremost among the unspoken goals of the Metz sumptuary laws was the enhancement of the prestige of the community's elite members. The laws issued in the 1690s exempted communal leaders, their wives, sons, and unmarried daughters, from most of the restrictions on jewelry and clothing that were imposed on community residents. Later in the eighteenth century, in 1769, bolder measures were instituted, including directives concerning synagogue protocol and the distribution of honors. Regulations that differentiated visibly

"Sumptuary Laws of the Community of Carpentras," *Jewish Quarterly Review* 18 (1927–28): 357–83.

49 Alan Hunt, *Governance of the Consuming Passions: A History of Sumptuary Law* (New York, 1996), esp. 4–11, 108–41.

50 See Roche, *France in the Enlightenment*, 110–11, and idem, *The Culture of Clothing: Dress and Fashion in the ancien régime* (Cambridge, 1996), trans. Jean Birrell, 27–29, 49–66.

51 See Raeff, "The Well-Ordered Police State."

between the superior status of older, married men, and the inferior status of younger, unmarried men were added where none had existed before. The new emphases of the 1769 Takkanot were consistent with earlier legislative efforts to stabilize prevailing hierarchies, an objective that far outweighed the moral concerns that were generally set aside in the case of wealthy members of the community. Clearly, it was not extravagance per se that was regarded as offensive, but the untoward display of ostentation that posed a threat both to Jewish-gentile relations and to the internal social order.[52] Metz communal leaders imposed rigorous restrictions on consumption to reinforce social divisions—whether based on age, gender, wealth, or occupation.

Growing anxiety about the youth of the community and its insubordination was the impulse for a wide range of legislative measures.[53] Elementary education became compulsory in 1690, reflecting an effort to extend communal authority over institutions that had been, to this point, either independent or semi-independent. Detailed legislation regulated the hours of instruction, the duties of teachers, and their salaries. All fathers were to provide their children through the age of fourteen with tutors, on pain of forfeiture of the right to reside in the community. Children of the poor were to be taught at the community's expense and assistance was promised to those who requested support. In addition, the Metz laws required young men between the ages of fourteen and eighteen to study at least one hour per day. The communal interest in ensuring the success of the educational legislation is evident in the overall conception of the school, the testing procedures, and especially the penalties for noncompliance. These penalties, including the forfeiture of a son's right of residence and the subjection to monetary fines, show that the provisions of the compulsory schooling program were interwoven with issues of social standing, personal status, and legal rights.[54]

---

52 On the relaxation of restrictions for the elite, see the 1690 Takkanot, Art. 30, and the 1697 Takkanot, Art. 25. On synagogue honors, see the 1769 Takkanot, Arts. 20, 25–26, and 29.

53 For measures aiming to address the instability of youth, see 1769 Takkanot, Arts. 5–6, 20, 26, 29, 51, 80, and 95. Cf. Elliott Horowitz, "A Jewish Youth Confraternity in Seventeenth-Century Italy," *Italia* 5 (1985): 36–97. For additional sources, see idem, "Les Mondes des jeunes juifs en Europe," in *Histoire des jeunes en Occident*, eds. G. Levi and J.-C. Schmitt (Paris, 1996), 1:114–16, and Pollack, *Jewish Folkways*, 74–75.

54 For a French translation of the *takkanah* that made elementary education compulsory, see Abraham Cahen, "Enseignement obligatoire édicté par la communauté israélite de Metz," *Revue des etudes juives* 2 (1881): 303–305. For similar problems in Bordeaux, see *Le Registre des délibérations de la Nation Juive Portugaise de Bordeaux (1711–1787)*, ed. Simon Schwarzfuchs (Paris, 1981), nos. 273 and 280. For Bayonne, cf. Nahon, *Les Nations juives portugaises du sud-ouest de la France*, document LXXV, 240–44.

Takkanot enacted in 1769 were far more comprehensive than earlier legislative measures concerning youth. Following the establishment of a central elementary school in 1751,[55] reports of truancy and fears of heightened idleness and crime prompted stricter requirements of study in preparation for the *bar mitzvah* ceremony.[56] The 1769 regulations reveal still greater concerns about adolescents, the disturbances they reportedly caused, and the ongoing struggle to prevent sexual immorality among unmarried men and women. Regarding the latter, paternity suits and extra-marital pregnancies were routinely recorded in the communal register and in the rabbinic court protocols.[57] Detailed enactments that restricted the movement of boys and girls, including valets and servants, on the Sabbath and festivals, point to a serious concern not voiced in the 1690s. The new legislation prohibited young people from visiting the neighboring quarter, much less venturing beyond the gate of the city. Unmarried men and women were forbidden from promenading on the Rhinport, even if they were accompanied by a parent. Also new to the mid-eighteenth century were regulations prohibiting the smoking of tobacco at the wharf, both for householders and youths, evidently for fear that this borrowed custom might penetrate the community proper.[58] Women and girls were not permitted to stroll arm-in-arm on the Jewish street, on the Rhinport, or any other place, at any time. As a meeting place for youth, the Rhinport offered an outlet for those seeking freedom from communal controls. With travelers and wares from afar arriving regularly, the port was a natural linkage and outlet to the wider world, and the dangers it posed were evident to the communal leadership.[59]

55 See "Acte de fondation d'un collège hébraïque à Metz, 1751," *Archives juives* 7 (1970–71): 45–50.

56 PKM, 76b, 1769 Takkanot, Article 10.

57 See PKM, 101a. For wider trends, see Daniel Roche, *The Culture of Clothing: Dress and Fashion in the Ancien Régime* (Cambridge, MA, 1996), trans. Jean Birrell, and Hunt, *Governance of the Consuming Passions*. See Frances Malino, "Competition and Confrontation: The Jews and the Parlement of Metz," in *Les Juifs au regards de l'histoire: Mélanges en l'honneur de Bernhard Blumenkranz*, G. Dahan, ed. (Paris, 1985), 327–41.

58 PKM, 76b, 1769 Takkanot, Arts. 3, 5.

59 Ibid. The prohibition against groups of women walking together in the street, except to fulfill a religious obligation, was included in the Forlì *takkanot* of 1418, in Finkelstein, *Jewish Self-Government*, 285–86. No more than three women, two maidens, or large groups of men were permitted to walk together through the streets. Cf. M. Y. Berdischevsky, "In Their Mothers' Womb," in *Kitvei Micha Yosef Bin-Gurion* (Tel Aviv, 1965), 1:102: "A generation went and a generation came and a new generation arose in Israel, a generation that began to walk on the Sabbath at the borders of the city."

Increased emphasis on marriage as a marker of social status was consistent with the foregoing concerns, especially after the mid-eighteenth century. In 1768 the Kahal warned that those who sell food and drink, including coffee, may not serve an unmarried man or woman, whether residents of Metz or visitors, and will be fined for violating the regulation. The concern was that this "causes young people to become accustomed to human pleasures." Restrictions on hiring unmarried men or those married less than three years included uncompromising constraints on lending them money. The punishment for violating this regulation was the denial of the right to attend the community synagogues and to wear the *schulmantel*.[60] Included in the 1769 Takkanot were several articles that stressed a sharp distinction between the standing of the unmarried and the married, and between younger and more established couples.[61] In the commercial realm as well, the *takkanot* distinguished carefully between boys, bachelors, younger married and older married men. Boys younger than fifteen years were prohibited from engaging in commerce; if a boy violated this restriction before reaching the age of thirteen, he would be prevented from reading the Torah publicly on the occasion of his *bar mitzvah*, and any subsequent failure to respect this law would be subject to a fine. An unmarried man was expected to yield to a householder (presumably a married man) if the two were selling their wares at the same house.[62] Furthermore, the 1769 Takkanot upheld earlier legislation (of 1723) that prohibited commercial dealings with either unmarried men or householders in their first two years of marriage.[63] In this way the community endeavored to protect the standing of householders against competition posed by individuals not yet established in the community. Any unmarried man conducting commerce in Metz, in the province of Lorraine, or in any region of France, was required to pay to the inspectors ten percent of his profits.[64] Furthermore, no unmarried man, whether or not in possession of the right of domicile, could gain authorization to slaughter animals unless he maintained a business association (as a butcher) with a householder. The lone exceptions to this rule were orphans,

60 PKM, 69a–69b.

61 For details on eligibility requirements, see Hertzberg, *French Enlightenment and the Jews*, 234–35. See PKM, 77b, 1769 Takkanot, Arts. 20, 25–26, 29.

62 PKM, 79a, 1769 Takkanot, Arts. 46, 51.

63 PKM, 80b, 1769 Takkanot, Art. 80. Exemptions were granted to orphans and bachelors with the permission of their fathers. For parallels, see Gershon Hundert, "Jewish Children and Childhood in Early Modern East Central Europe," in *The Jewish Family: Metaphor and Memory*, David Kraemer, ed. (New York, 1989), 89.

64 PKM, 81b, 1769 Takkanot, Art. 95.

who were authorized to perform ritual slaughtering while still unmarried.[65] All in all, the phrasing of these and other restrictions suggests that the foregoing goals were rarely achieved and that the community ultimately sought to control rather than wholly undermine the dealings of younger, less established residents. Although the motivation for these regulations was clearly economic, they evince no less a commitment to preserving the social hierarchies of age and marital status.

Poverty and Social Welfare

Anxiety about public disorder, which included social unrest, disease, and economic instability, was a powerful motive underlying communal efforts to alleviate poverty.[66] Closely related to the continuing transformation in the governance and organization of early modern communities, the regulation of philanthropy was shaped by carefully articulated public policy considerations. It also mirrored deepening social divisions in the Jewish community. Arrangements to care for the poor and to oversee philanthropic efforts were as diverse as the Jewish communities that put them into practice. Apart from the *Schutzgeld* ("protection money"), most communities exempted the poor from state taxation and other communal contributions. Some communities, such as Ancona, authorized an unlimited number of poor guests at celebrations, while the Lithuanian Council in 1667 demanded the inclusion of a minimum of two poor persons among every ten guests. Lending societies offering loans at low or no interest were established in numerous communities. The care provided to the sick was a regular feature of charity, as was the support given to their families. *Bikkur ḥolim* societies were formed to visit the sick, and many communities maintained hospitals—originally established as hospices for strangers—that were known by the term *hekdesh*, once reserved for consecrated sacrificial offerings at the ancient Temple in Jerusalem.[67] Communities assumed responsibility for the appointment of guardians to oversee the legal affairs of orphans and manage their finances. From 1648, some communities, such as the Spanish-Portuguese community in Amsterdam, created special asylums for orphans that were modeled after non-Jewish establishments.

65 PKM, 83b, Art. 120.

66 In late sixteenth-century England, for example, poor relief came to be closely linked to public works projects, such as the repair of bridges, highways, and churches. More generally, see Brian Pullan, *Poverty and Charity: Europe, Italy, Venice, 1400–1700* (Aldershot, U.K., 1994). For concerns expressed in Metz regarding economic difficulties, see PKM, 65b.

67 On the Metz *hekdesh*, see Kerner, "La Vie quotidienne," 112–23, 149–68.

Funds were raised to dower poor brides, as in the case of the Lithuanian Council in 1623, and support was earmarked for beggars and vagabonds.[68]

Jewish communal legislation exemplified the growing disapproval of idleness and vagrancy in early modern European society. In Treviso some residents insisted on requiring the poor themselves to remove the billet (entitling them to food and lodging) from the community chest in order to humiliate them and discourage them from returning a second time to their hosts.[69] In the Florence ghetto, communal leaders designed an elaborate system of charitable contributions to prevent begging, evidently in compliance with governmental efforts to control the size and stability of the Jewish population. The state required the community to report all foreign Jews who remained without permission for more than three days. Householders were not permitted to receive foreign Jews into their homes without permission of the Nove Conservatori del Dominio, and communal leaders had the authority to expel Jews from the ghetto with the approval of state authorities.[70] *Takkanot* issued by the Cracow community in 1595 prohibited the poor, upon pain of imprisonment, from soliciting contributions from door to door or while sitting in the street. They were given a weekly distribution by the community *shamash* (beadle). In 1623 the Lithuanian Council limited the stay of beggars to twenty-four hours, and several years later it added the requirement that communities along the Polish border immediately deport beggars at the Council's expense. The community of Posen enacted a *takkanah* in 1672 that prohibited all begging by outsiders and denied them transportation out of the city. In 1736 the community of Eisenstadt blocked communal support to beggars who were not considered upright (*hagunim*). Although individual payment of funds to the poor was not regulated, charitable contributions imposed by the community could be disbursed only by communal officials who adhered to policy directives.[71] As a rule,

68 Baron, *Jewish Community*, 2:323–33.

69 Judah Mintz, *Resp. Mahari Mintz* (Venice, 1552), no. 7. Other sources point to a similar sentiment. Comparing the practice of *tzedakah* in Brody, Rabbi Ezekiel Landau condemned the evasion of charitable obligations in Prague: "Many rich men turn back the poor despite his possession of a *plet*. The poor man is sent here and there, while the supervisors have no power to enforce their will." See *Derushei ha-Zelaḥ* 9a, 26d, cited in Baron, *Jewish Community*, 3:209, n. 35, and in general, 3:323–33.

70 Stefanie Siegmund, *The Medici State and the Ghetto of Florence: The Construction of an Early Modern Jewish Community* (Stanford, 2006), 87 ff.

71 See Elliott Horowitz, "'Let the Poor Be Members of Your Household': Charity, Poor and Social Control in European Jewish Communities Between the Middle Ages and the Beginning of the Modern Era," in *Religion and Economy: Connections and Interactions*, ed. Menahem Ben-Sasson (Jerusalem, 1995), 210, 226–31; and Baron, *Jewish Community*, 2:321–25.

communal norms and halakhic rulings differentiated between hospitality, which was intended for the rich and honorable, and *tzedakah*, which was to be limited to the poor.[72]

Leaders of Jewish communities throughout Alsace convened in the 1760s and 1770s to hammer out a unified policy to overcome the enormous difficulties posed by poverty. In the Lower Rhine this involved drawing up a comprehensive list of the poor to facilitate distribution of aid, organizing contributions for the *maḥatzit ha-shekel* (half shekel sent annually to Jerusalem), and levying a new tax on dowries.[73] Despite widespread poverty, Alsatian communities raised money for the creation of a central *beit midrash* (study house) for the entire province. Community leaders in Upper and Lower Alsace placed a priority on the creation of institutions where young men would be able to study without interruption or distraction. Half the funding was provided by fines, two-ninths from the tithe on dowries, and the balance from voluntary contributions. These efforts were in addition to the continuing solicitation of funds to support the regional yeshivot of Sierentz and Ettendorf. The two academies were designated as beneficiaries of a tax of one-half of one percent on every inheritance, and ten percent from each dowry was to be paid either to the Ettendorf yeshivah if the groom was a native of Upper Alsace, or to the Sierentz yeshivah if he hailed from Lower Alsace. Those honored as *sandak*[74] at a circumcision were required to contribute to the central *beit midrash* if they were in the possession of at least 600 guldens. To ensure that these obligations were carried out in accordance with the regional *takkanot, mohalim* were instructed to provide the *gabba'im* with lists of persons who performed these functions.[75]

The Metz communal register and the protocols of the rabbinic court offer detailed evidence of concerted efforts to relieve the hardships of poverty. As an urban center, Metz was beset by the pressing need to accommodate the increasing number of beggars that sought communal support.[76] One of the earliest

72 See *Sefer Minhagei Maharil*, no. 60. The tendency of Moses Isserles to rule leniently on questions concerning dietary laws when honor was owed to guests, and Ḥayyim ben Beẓalel's contention that such leniencies were unwarranted, since most guests were not deserving of honor nor were hosts generally happy about their presence, represent opposite extremes in the halakhic approaches to hospitality.

73 See Loeb, "Les Juifs de Strasbourg," 178–79 and 193–98.

74 The person who holds the baby on his knees during the circumcision ceremony, sometimes translated as "godfather."

75 Loeb, "Les Juifs de Strasbourg," 178–79 and 193–98, and "Protocol of the Medinah" (28 May 1777), Arts. 3, 12, 14, 15, 23, 27–29, 34.

76 See Brian Pullan, "Charity and Poor Relief: The Early Modern Period," *Encyclopedia of European Social History* (New York, 2001), vol. 3, 447–452.

innovations was to supply itinerant poor with billets (*pletten* in Yiddish) that afforded poor travelers meals and lodging in the community. Evidence of the practice has been traced to fifteenth-century Treviso, where it was approved by Rabbi Judah Mintz (Padua, d. 1506) because it enabled the poor to receive hospitality without being shamed. In Metz every householder was required by communal law to acquire *pletten*, inscribe his name on each one, and deposit a certain number in the community chest in proportion to one's wealth. Poor travelers would then draw tickets to secure meals and lodging, at no cost, offered at the homes of community members.[77] To qualify for support, eligible poor registered with the communal authorities.[78]

The 1769 Takkanot reveal rigorous efforts to manage various forms of charitable giving required of residents and, in general, to reinforce public confidence in its administration of public aid. Article 33 stated that the *gabbai* would ensure that the list of names of the poor, and their number, would be managed carefully. Article 34, which imposed limits on the number of invited guests at the *Wachnacht* (Eve of Circumcision) celebration, excluded the poor from the stipulated limit. Article 76 stated unconditionally that any bequest set forth in a will, including gifts to charity, were valid, even if they drew on debts or on pledges of non-Jews. According to Article 91, the duty to purchase *pletten* was equivalent to the obligation to pay communal taxes.[79] Article 123 warned individuals who solicited assistance without authorization that this was an offense that was punishable by a fine.[80]

Growing poverty in Metz is evident from several communal regulations that were issued in the following decade. In 1772, the community initiated a more structured program to meet the needs of numerous itinerant poor who sought public support. Concerned that "the economic condition of the community is worsening each day, with transients arriving from near and far," the Kahal enacted a regulation it coordinated with the municipal authorities. Entry into the city was authorized solely through the Chambière gate, where guards

77 See PMBD, Vol. 2, no. 148, 29a. See *Resp. Mahari Mintz*, no. 7 and Baron, *Jewish Community*, 2:322. In Alsace, young couples were granted an exemption from the obligation of purchasing *pletten* during the first year of marriage. See Loeb, "Les Juifs à Strasbourg," 185, Art. 11. Concerning restrictions on giving *pletten* to youth, see PKM, 37a (discussed below).

78 See PKM, 34b.

79 See PKM, 81a, Art. 91 of the 1769 Takkanot, and PMBD, Vol. 1, pt. 1, no. 20, 10b; Vol. 2, no. 7, 2a; no. 71, 13a; and no. 148, 29a.

80 See Judah Mintz, *Resp. Mahari Mintz*, originally published in Venice in 1553, ed. Asher Siev (New York, 1995), no. 7. On conditions in Alsace, see Loeb, "Les Juifs à Strasbourg," 185, Art. 11.

admitted visitors on Tuesdays and Fridays only. The plan projected that on the various Jewish holydays two hundred visitors would be admitted and would receive *pletten*. However, certain restrictions applied. Young men and women above the age of fifteen were denied entry and were not eligible to receive aid, and several other factors, including place of residence and distance travelled, determined whether visitors would be included among the two hundred permitted to enter.[81] A few years later, in 1777, the Pinkas Kahal reported that community members were falling behind in meeting their tax obligations and that the imposition of various fines and punishments had failed to remedy the situation. Clearly, as the report stated, the lower and middle classes were incapable of paying their share of the tax burden. On account of the worsening economic situation, the Kahal decided to take the unprecedented step of accepting partial tax payments in monthly installments. In 1778 the cost of *pletten* was reduced for householders unable to afford them.[82]

Related to the policy on begging was the larger question of controlling immigration to the Metz Kehillah—a central item on the community's social welfare agenda. Many individuals sought a residence permit (*ḥezkat ʿironit*) to join family members or conduct business locally. Economic growth, which enhanced the desirability of Metz as a place of residence, attracted children of wealthy families who applied for the *ḥezkat ʿironit* when they became engaged to marry a Metz resident.[83] By any measure, the costs were substantial and often outpaced income levels. As the gap between rich and poor became even wider, only the well-off could afford to settle in Metz. Efforts to attract individuals or families to share the heavy tax burden had become a matter of communal policy, which explains, in part, the complaint in 1780 by a Metz *parnas* about the growing number of beggars and the subsequent reduction in aid to poor wayfarers.[84] The Kahal devised elaborate formulas regarding the costs of procuring residence rights and paying the exit tax and the tax on dowries and on inheritance. These taxes, which ranged from one to eight percent were over and above assorted communal, local, and royal taxes.

Economic advances and urban growth in the eighteenth century widened the social and economic gap between rich and poor.[85] Rabbinic courts were

81 PKM, 92a.

82 PKM, 106b–107a. The use of *pletten* met with some resistance among individuals who believed that the assessment of their assets was too high. See PMBD, Vol. 1, pt. 1, no. 20, 10b and Vol. 2, no. 71, 13a.

83 See PKM, 36a, 37a, 66a–67a, 74a.

84 Ulbrich, *Shulamit and Margarete*, 174; Hertzberg, *French Enlightenment and the Jews*, 125; PKM, 110b, 120a, 122a, 122b.

85 *Cities and Social Change in Early Modern France*, ed. Benedict, 29–32.

frequently occupied with cases of litigants who had defaulted on loans and became impoverished. The effects of poverty and economic strain are discernable not only in the limited range of residential options available to young persons seeking to marry. They also exacerbated the circumstances in which women were regularly trapped. As elsewhere, women in Metz were particularly vulnerable to economic volatility. Ironically, the role of women in the expanding economy of the eighteenth century exposed them to financial risks and pressures of a new sort. In localities where women were engaged in commercial activities, it was possible to hold them liable for debts of their spouses. By virtue of access to her husband's property, irrespective of her employment status, the burden of proof fell upon a wife to demonstrate her separate ownership of property that would not be reachable to satisfy a husband's debts. In the modern period, as women more regularly engaged in gainful employment, there was a growing acknowledgment that they were able to amass property of their own.[86]

Given the economic difficulties that burdened numerous families, the Beit Din was approached with requests that it authorize emergency assistance measures. Individual efforts and communal measures on behalf of poor brides were extremely common. The Hakhnassat Kallah confraternity was a well-established charity and a favorite of testamentary bequests. Nevertheless, funding was not adequate to meet the needs of the community. In 1775, a new regulation was passed—that no unmarried woman was eligible to receive communal aid until she worked in the Metz community for two years.[87] For this reason, it was not uncommon for women to assume positions as domestic servants to establish themselves in the community and to earn the money needed for a dowry.[88]

In some instances, the Beit Din was approached by fathers who were unable to provide the dowry they had promised according to the terms of the engagement agreement.[89] When individuals desperately needed funds and asked the Beit Din to order relatives to contribute, the Beit Din would normally rely on

86 See Anchel, *Les Juifs de France*, 154–56, on the population decline in Metz in the last decades of the eighteenth century. See BT Bava Batra 52b, and Katz's analysis in "The Married Woman," 115–16. Cf. Clare Crowston, "Family Affair: Wives Credit, Consumption, and the Law in Old Regime France," in *Family, Gender, and Law in Early Modern France*, Suzanne Desan and Jeffrey Merrick, eds. (University Park, PA, 2009), 62–100.

87 PKM, 100b.

88 See chapter 6, below.

89 See, for example, PMBD, Vol. 1, pt. 1, p. 14b; Vol. 1, pt. 2, no. 10, 3b and no. 222, 50a; Vol. 2, no. 120, 21b and 24b–25a.

the principle *kofin ʿal ha-tzedakah* (enforcing charity), by which the court was authorized to demand payment of charitable contributions from relatives. In one instance, Rabbi Aaron Ennery had promised an excessively large dowry for his not-so-young daughter, and now, with the approach of the wedding, the union was in jeopardy. He asked the Beit Din to impose a payment schedule on his relatives. The Beit Din ruled that relatives could not ignore the plea and calculated the obligation of family members based on the degree of kinship and financial worth. Some two dozen relatives were assessed a total of 273 livres so that the wedding could proceed. In another case, Aaron Steinbiedersdorff, an octogenarian in dire financial straits, asked the Beit Din to assess several of his relatives for support. The Beit Din demanded that, for a period of three months, two of his relatives contribute 10 sous each per week and a third relative 5 sous per week. Each was permitted to deduct these contributions from their *ma'aser* contribution. As for Aaron's son Jacob, whom the father accused of willful neglect, the Beit Din authorized the *parnas* in Steinbiedersdorff to exercise all modes of coercion against him, if the accuracy of the accusation could be confirmed.[90]

When a will provided for charitable gifts, family members might ask the Beit Din to reassign earmarked funds to assist heirs who had experienced unforeseen economic reversals. For example, in 1780 Itzig Hess of Metzervisse argued that since the order to distribute funds from the trust established by his father-in-law could not have anticipated the future needs of his offspring, it stood to reason that had the testator known that his daughter would find herself in dire economic straits, he would have bestowed all of the proceeds on her. The Beit Din reported that a judgment issued two years earlier referred to assistance that had been allocated for several years for the creation of a dowry for each of his granddaughters (daughters of his other daughter Perlche). Of the 135 livres that was distributed annually, only half that amount remained, and of that, 22 livres was given each year to the poor of the city. The Beit Din allocated half of the remaining 45 livres to Itzig, with the balance to be reserved for the other relatives. Each one's entitlement would be based on the closeness of their relationship to the testator, as established in the court's ruling. If no closer relative could be identified, Itzig would be permitted to take the full 45 livres.[91]

90 PMBD, Vol. 1, pt. 2, no. 4, 13b. Cf. PMBD, Vol. 2, no. 363, 68a; Vol. 2, no. 467, 93a; Vol. 2, no. 503, 102a. For the Steinbiedersdorf case, see PMBD, Vol. 2, no. 90, 18a.

91 See PMBD, Vol. 2, no. 223, 41b.

Juridical Autonomy and Recourse to Non-Jewish Courts

Recourse to non-Jewish courts was portrayed in the Pinkas Kahal and in rabbinic writings as a major threat to communal authority and to the integrity of the Jewish legal system. Individuals who took their disputes to gentile courts—the *'arkha'ot shel goyim*—were consistently denounced by medieval and early modern rabbinic authorities as having betrayed the Torah. According to the dominant rabbinic interpretation of Exodus 21:1, *Ve-eleh ha-mishpatim asher tasim lifneihem* ("These are the laws that you shall place *before them*" [italics inserted]), the term *lifneihem* was understood to refer exclusively to Jewish judges. The severity of the prohibition was underscored by the fact that it remained in force even when both parties agreed to resolve their differences outside the community. Moreover, Rashi's interpretation, based on *Midrash Tanḥuma*, declared that the prohibition was binding even in instances when the law that was applied in the gentile court was identical to Jewish law.[92]

Throughout the Middle Ages, halakhic authorities followed this view consistently, asserting that no distinction was to be made based on the nature of the legal system administered in gentile courts. In the view of Moses Maimonides, the Beit Din was obliged to impose the *ḥerem* on any individual who took his dispute to gentile courts. The *Shulḥan 'Arukh* was unequivocal in its insistence on the exclusivity of Jewish jurisdiction: "It is forbidden to litigate before non-Jewish judges or in their courts, even if they rule in accordance with Jewish law, *and even if both litigants have agreed to litigate before them*" [italics inserted]. Nevertheless, the historical record confirms that under certain circumstances Jews in Ashkenaz took their disputes to non-Jewish courts, though this was not nearly as common a practice as in territories controlled by Muslims.[93] In

92 See the view of Rabbi Tarfon in BT Gittin 88b, and the commentary of Rashi on Exodus 21:1. According to *Midrash Tanḥuma*, Mishpatim 3, recourse to gentile courts was no less than a profanation of the name of God because the act implied inadequacy on the part of Jewish law.

93 See Moses Maimonides, *Mishneh Torah*, Laws of Sanhedrin 26:6–7, and Solomon Duran, *Resp. Ḥut ha-Meshulash* (Amsterdam, 1874), pt. 3, no. 6. On the steadfastness of the prohibition even when the parties to a dispute agreed on adjudicating in a gentile court, see *Shulḥan 'Arukh, Ḥoshen Mishpat* §26:1. Concerning Muslim courts, see S. D. Goitein, "The Interplay of Jewish and Islamic Laws," in *Jewish Law and Legal History in the Modern World*, in the *Jewish Law Annual*, Supplement 2, ed. Bernard Jackson (Leiden, 1980), 61–77; Gideon Libson, "Legal Autonomy and the Recourse to Muslim Courts by Protected People According to Muslim Sources during the Geonic Period" [Hebrew], in *The Intertwined Worlds of Islam: Essays in Memory of Hava Lazarus-Yafeh*, ed. Nahem Ilan (Jerusalem, 2002), 334–92, and idem, "Concerning the Prohibition of Recourse to Non-Jewish Courts and the Imposition of Communal Bans" [Hebrew], in *Halakhah and Justice: Menachem*

early modern Ashkenaz, despite the shrill rhetoric that characterized rabbinic opposition to litigation in gentile courts, adjudication outside the Jewish community could not be prevented. Yet, such recourse to non-Jewish courts typically occurred when a party was appealing a rabbinic court ruling, and even these instances were with the consent of both parties and only after they received the express authorization of the rabbis.[94]

In fact, the issues were more complex than meets the eye. Despite fierce opposition in the Talmudic and halakhic tradition, communal leaders, both lay and rabbinic, reserved the right to decide in which circumstances such recourse was permitted and when it was not.[95] For example, when a defendant had refused to participate in the rabbinic court proceeding to which he was summoned, the plaintiff would be authorized to seek relief in a non-Jewish court. Justified as an effort to "rescue funds," as Maimonides characterized it, recourse to the non-Jewish court was traditionally viewed as a last resort.[96] Rabbi Eibeschütz made no secret of his strong opposition to two *takkanot* issued by the community. He objected strenuously to a provision authorizing

---

Elon Memorial Volume, eds. Arye Edrei, et al. (Jerusalem, 2018), 265–303; Joseph Hacker, "Jewish Autonomy in the Ottoman Empire: Its Scope" [Hebrew], in *Transition and Change in Modern Jewish History*, ed. Shmuel Almog, et al. (Jerusalem, 1987), 349–88; Uriel I. Simonsohn, *A Common Justice: The Legal Allegiances of Christians and Jews under Early Islam* (Philadelphia, 2011); Amnon Cohen, *Yehudei Yerushalayim ba-me'ah ha-shesh-'esreh le-fi te'udot Turkiyot shel beit ha-din ha-shara'i* (Jerusalem, 1976); idem, *Jewish Life under Islam: Jerusalem in the Sixteenth Century* (Cambridge, MA, 1984); and idem, *A World Within: Jewish Life as Reflected in Muslim Court Documents from the Sijil of Jerusalem (16th Century)*, 2 vols. (Philadelphia, 1994). On Jews in nineteenth-century Moroccan courts, including an extensive review of the historiography on the subject, see Marglin, *Across Legal Lines*.

94 See Hildesheimer, "Gentile Courts in Ashkenaz at the End of the Middle Ages," and Katz, *Tradition and Crisis*, 83. Permission to appeal to non-Jewish courts had been advanced several centuries earlier by Isaac ben Moses of Vienna, who affirmed the validity of their judgments. See Ḥayyim ben Isaac, *Pisqei Or Zarua*, pt. 3, *Pisqei Bava Qama*, Laws of Non-Jewish Courts 3 (Brooklyn, 1996). On the Metz prohibition to going to gentile courts and the instances when this was considered permissible, see the 1769 Takkanot, Arts. 65–68.

95 Katz, *Tradition and Crisis*, 97. Focusing on communities further to the east, Moshe Rosman has identified four categories of conflicts where Jews turned to non-Jewish authorities to serve as the arbiter: supracommunal conflicts; intra-communal disputes; conflicts between the Kahal and individuals; quarrels between individuals. See Moshe Rosman, "The Role of Non-Jewish Authorities in Resolving Conflicts within Jewish Communities in the Early Modern Period," *Jewish Political Studies Review* 12.3–4 (Fall 2000): 53–65. Metz sources do not contain evidence of comparable trends.

96 See Maimonides, *Mishneh Torah*, Laws of Sanhedrin 26:7 and *Shulḥan 'Arukh, Ḥoshen Mishpat* §26:2.

members of the community to sue in the general courts when both parties were in agreement.[97] He also railed against a *takkanah* that authorized recourse to the civil courts to recover funds represented by bills of exchange (*ḥilluf ketav*).[98]

> I observed in the holy community of Metz, and so it is in the other Ashkenazic communities, that communal *takkanot* concerning bills of exchange (*ḥillufei ketav*) offer litigants the option to seek judgment in the non-Jewish courts. Who permitted this to them? For though the assumption is that since the community [leaders] allowed it, it is as if all inhabitants of the city agreed and accepted it upon themselves, even if everyone is satisfied, it is prohibited to give honor to idolatry … and even if we say that the law concerning bills of exchange is [one of the] laws of the kingdom that is peculiar to the commercial laws in every state and is not included among the laws of the state that the king enacted, then it is acceptable for a Jewish court to rule according to the law of the king, because the king enacted it and so the litigants agreed when they initially wrote the bill of exchange, that it will have full validity of royal law, but none of this permits them to litigate in the *ʻarkhaʼot*—a matter they have no right to do. Is the law of the king preferable to the law of the King of the world that is the law of the holy Torah? And although they are litigating in such matters, it is prohibited to litigate "before them" and I am therefore disturbed by this matter, but since there is no power to nullify it because they have become habituated to this *takkanah* and unwilling to listen, and so whosoever has the ability to nullify it shall receive a reward from the Lord of Justice.[99]

---

97 Cf. Libson, "Concerning the Prohibition of Recourse to Non-Jewish Courts."

98 A *ḥilluf ketav*, the Hebrew equivalent of a bill of exchange, was given as payment. Such bills of exchange were generally transferable, as were promissory notes.

99 See Jonathan Eibeschütz, *Yaʻarot Devash*, pt. 1, 35a [Elul, 5545], and pt. 2, 17a, and idem, *Urim ve-Tumim, Ḥoshen Mishpat* (Altona, 1763), §26.

> והתבוננתי כמו שראיתי כאן ק״ק מיץ, וכן הוא בשאר קהלות אשכנז, אשר תקנות הקהל בענין ח״כ [חילוף כתב] שיש רשות לבע״ד [לבעלי דין] לדון אצל המשפט ערכאות, מי התיר להם זה, דאף דאמינא דהואיל ותקנו הקהל הוי כאלו הסכימו כל בני עיר וקבלו עליהם, הא אפילו כולם מרוצים אסור להתייקר שם עבודה אלילים... ואפילו נימא דדינא ח״כ הם דיני דמלכותא דבר פרטי לתקנות המו״מ במדינה, ואינו בכלל שארי נימוסי ומשפטי טיב מדינה שחקק עליהם המלך, דזהו ניחא שיש לב״ד של ישראל לפסוק כחק המלך ההוא, כי כן יסד המלך וכן קבלו הבע״ד בכתבם תחילה הח״כ שיהיה לו כל תוקף חק המלך, אבל אין כל זה מועיל שיהיו הם מורשים לדון בערכאות, דבר שאינו ברשותם, וכי עדיף חק המלך מחקו של מלכו של עולם שהוא דין תורה הקדושה, ומ״מ אעפ״י שהם דנים בכך אסור לדון לפניהם. לכן רע עלי המעשה, אפס אין כח לבטלו כי נשרשו בתקנה זו מבלי שומע, ומי שיהיה כחו יפה יבטלו ויקבל שכר מאלקי המשפט.

On Eibeschütz, see S. Posener, "The Social Life of Jewish Communities in France in the Eighteenth Century," *Jewish Social Studies* 7 (1945): 215–17.

Clearly frustrated, Eibeschütz conceded that he was powerless to abolish the practice because it had become firmly established through the *takkanah*.

The *takkanah* that troubled Eibeschütz appears to have dated from 1720. It declared that any member of the community who brought a dispute to the local municipal court (*ʿarkhaʾot ʿironit*) would be subject to the *ḥerem*, "with the exception [of one who sought to recover] a *ḥilluf ketav* or *billet à ordre* (promissory note) for which it was permissible to sue in the *ʿarkhaʾot*."[100] Article 68 of the 1769 Takkanot was even more permissive. It stated that, while the prohibition against suing a fellow Jew in the general court was very grave, this did not apply when the matter in dispute was money lent for merchandise, a *ketav yad*,[101] a *ketav yad au porteur*,[102] an *ordre*,[103] or a *ḥilluf ketav* contract.[104] Lacking the power to enforce its judgments, the Kahal authorized plaintiffs to use the authority of the state to recover funds that would otherwise be lost. The Kahal, with the approval of the *av beit din*, evidently understood the recovery of funds corresponding to each of the foregoing instruments as a non-adversarial proceeding, because the document in each case constituted legal proof of the claim. Accordingly, since the claim itself was not disputed, the legal action in court was no more than a bureaucratic procedure. Metz communal legislation thus made clear the conditions under which litigants could legitimately seek legal remedy in the French courts. Authorization to bring a defendant to the non-Jewish court, either when he refused to appear before the Beit Din or when he physically threatened a plaintiff, was a matter of general agreement among medieval *posekim* and was codified in the *Shulḥan ʿArukh*.[105] Early

---

100 CAHJP, FMe 139. In this fragment of the Pinkas Kahal, it is stated that certain types of notes can be litigated in non-Jewish courts because the fact that the debtor owes the creditor a certain sum is not a matter of dispute. Here is the relevant passage:

ומכש״כ שיהי׳ אסור לשום אדם מקהלתינו ליקח איזה קומיסיאהן מן איזה אדם שיהי׳ ומאיזה מקום שיהי׳ לירד עם ב״י [בן ישראל] חבירו בערכאות בעונם בחרם כנ״ל חוץ ח״ך או בילי״ע אורד״ר יהי׳ מותר לתבוע בערכאו׳.

101 A *ketav yad* is a written promise to pay. Though signed by the debtor, it was unattested and, therefore, it did not constitute a lien.

102 Lit. "to the bearer," referring here to a promissory note "payable to the bearer."

103 Words in a draft that directs a person to pay money or deliver goods to another individual.

104 PKM, 80a, Art. 68:

אסור לכל מי אשר בשם ישראל יכונה הן פה בקהלתינו הקדושה יע״א. או ממדינתינו לתבוע שום ב״י בערכאות בדא״ה הן בשבילו או בשבילו ב״י אחר מקהלתינו או ממדינתינו או ממדינה אחרת. חוץ על תביעת ממון סחורו׳. כ״י. כ״י אפורטער. או אורדר. ח״ק קונטרא אינם בכלל. גם אסור במש״כ שלא לעשו׳ שום סומאסיאון או אסינאסיאהן להגאון אב״ד נר״ו או לה״ה הקהל י״ץ או לה״ה הגובי׳ ובעלי השגחו׳ י״ץ.

The 1769 Takkanot have been recently published in *Jüdische Gemeindestatuten aus dem aschkenasischen Kulturraum*, 353–95.

105 *Shulhan ʿArukh, Hoshen Mishpat*, §28.

modern *takkanot* expanded the terms of this license by permitting recourse to non-Jewish courts when the two sides agreed on the venue or when there was documentation verifying what was owed, so that the case could no longer be considered adversarial. Under such circumstances, recourse to civil courts did not fall under the prohibition of *'arkha'ot shel goyim*.

The Beit Din was naturally obligated to uphold lay communal legislation, and its judgments were consistent with this policy.[106] That litigation in the French civil courts had become a routine practice is not in doubt. The key issues related to questions concerning the types of cases that were brought by Jews to the French civil courts, how such recourse was understood by the lay and rabbinic leadership, and in what ways this phenomenon affected cases that came before the Beit Din. Answers to such questions will deepen our understanding of the dynamic of integration that became increasingly prevalent in the late ancien régime.

---

106 See PKM, 80a, Art. 71. See Eibeschütz's discussion of *membrany* (bearer notes) in *Urim ve-Tumim, Shulhan Arukh, Ḥoshen Mishpat*, §104. This was known in French as *au porteur*, "to the bearer," as in the following:

> והנה דעת קצת חכמים לדבר בממרני שיכול ליתן אותו לכל המוציאו וכן נהוג בק״ק מיץ בכתב שקורין בלשון אשכנז אפארטעהר רוצים לומר דבזה לכו״ע גובין לפי שטרא דהרי יוכל ליתנם זה לזה וזה לזה. ולא הבנתי אטו ברשיעי עסקינן שקרנים הלא נשאל פיהם בב״ד מי הוא המלוה ועל כרחם יודו שמזה הם וחזר הדבר לאיש אחד ומהכ״ת יגבה יותר הא בממרני וכתב הנ״ל אין שעבוד כלל רק הלואה משוי שעבוד ולכן אין בזה פקפוק.
>
> והנה הרב בעל שבות יעקב יצא לידון בדבר חדש בחלף כתב הואיל ונזכר בתוכו כפי נימוס החלף כתב א״כ קיבל על עצמו חוק החלף כתב וחוק המלך בחלף כתב לפרוע לפי חלף כתב, ודבריו צ״ע דא״כ יחלוקו לפי ממון כדעת ר״ח כי כך יסד הנימוס בחלף כתב ובטלת ד״ת, ולכן דבריו צ״ע כי זו לא שמענו. ובאמת לדידי צ״ע במטלטלין לפי דהעליתי לעיל בסעיף א׳ דליכא בהו כלל שעבוד בשום אופן, א״כ בנפרעים מן מטלטלין למה לא יחלוקו כדעת ר״ח לפי ממון, דהא בזה לא שייך טעמא של הרי״ף דשעבודו של זה במנה חל כמו שעבודו של זה במאתים, דהרי״ף אמרו בקרקע דחל שעבודו אבל במטלטלין דלא חל שעבודו כלל ואין בהם קדימה כלל רק מתורת פריעת בעל חוב מצוה וכופין אותו אפילו מגלימא דעל כתפיה א״כ עליו המצוה לפרוע, וכי כך המצוה אם חייב לזה מנה ולזה מאתיים ויש לו מאתיים זהובים שיפרע לזה הכל ולזה רק מאה, הלא זה אין מאומד הדעת כלל הלא מצוה לחלק לפי ערך הלואה ושעבודו לא חל כלל. ודוחק דגוף משתעבד ובגוף נאמר דחל שעבודא על מאה כמו על מאתיים, ולאחר מיתה האידנא דתקנו גאונים י״ל דעשאוהו כשל תורה כאילו השעבוד חל עליו, וצ״ע כי לא מצינו בזה למחברים והכל כתבו דשעבודא חל אנכסי ולא מיירי כלל משעבוד הגוף, וצ״ע.

Commercial practice established that a *membrana* could be presented for payment even after it was transferred from person to person, without endorsement and without the agreement of the original lender. While *membrany* offered clear advantages to merchants, their status was problematic in the view of many *posekim* because they failed to meet certain procedural requirements demanded by talmudic law. While indebtedness according to the formal Halakhah applied to a specific individual and could not be transferred, *posekim* were willing to sanction the use of *membrany* as an acceptable means of collecting funds if communal leaders had so determined its suitability. Their reasoning was based on several considerations, including allowances made for the benefit of the marketplace (*takkanat ha-shuk*) and *dina d'malkhuta dina*. See Fram, *Ideals Face Reality*, 116–43.

Policing Religious and Cultural Boundaries

Maintaining religious commitment and cultural distinctiveness of their coreligionalists in northeastern France was a major concern of Jewish communal leaders throughout the eighteenth century. Metz and the Alsatian countryside represented distinct socio-economic and political universes where the challenges of modernization were experienced differently. In Alsace, what was perceived as excessive exposure to French village culture troubled communal leaders, whereas Metz leaders were distressed by signs of erosion in religious observance and moral conduct.

At a series of Alsatian regional assemblies that were held in the mid-1770s through the early 1780s, communal leaders addressed a host of widespread problems ranging from poverty and fiscal matters to concerns about the harmful influences of village life. The thirty-six resolutions adopted by the 1777 Niedernai assembly—the best documented of the regional meetings—related principally to religious discipline and practice. Twenty-eight deputies were assigned the task of examining the proposed statutes and submitted their conclusions to the regional *parnasim* and to the grand rabbis for their approval, though the *takkanot* did not have the force of law until they were confirmed by seigneurial or royal authorities.[107] In some instances, rabbis assumed leading roles in regional planning and administration. Rabbi Wolf Reichshofer, for example, headed the body of *parnasim* in the Hanau County, convened assemblies at his home, and had the authority to take action against any individual who did not obey the assembly's decisions. Consistently, the *takkanot* of Alsace aimed to reinforce rabbinic authority and ritual observance. The Niedernai assembly justified its legislative measures by asserting that they came under the rubric of *le-migdar milta* (to stem the tide of immorality). On this basis young men and women were prohibited from promenading together on Sabbaths and festivals, either within or beyond the city, and were restricted in passing from one community to another, unless it was to perform a religiously ordained act.[108]

Assorted *charivari* borrowed from the surrounding village culture were a main target of the Alsatian legislation. According to one such custom, young men would purchase on behalf of a bridegroom, prior to his wedding, the honor of binding the Torah scroll during the synagogue service in exchange for *portal*—likely a quarter measure of wine—so they could eat and drink

---

107 See J. Weil, "Contribution à l'histoire des communautés alsaciennes au 18ème siècle," *REJ* 81 (1925): 169–71.

108 See "Protocol of the Medinah," Art. 23.

together.[109] This custom, a variation on the widely-practiced *charivari*, had been modified to accord with Jewish religious practice. The custom of going to greet the bridegroom or bride on a horse was likewise prohibited, and the practice was punishable by a large fine. Historically, *charivari* functioned both as a mode of social control, expressing public opposition toward those who violated time-honored customs and, paradoxically, as a protest against the prevailing social order. Jewish communal leaders in Alsace strenuously condemned such rites for their rowdiness and vulgarity, viewing them as a reflection of non-Jewish influence and a sign of youthful rebellion against authority. The *charivari*, therefore, was declared "absolutely null and void," with the amount of a fine to be levied by the grand rabbi. Even so, the *charivari* remained part of village life in western and central Europe well into the nineteenth century.[110]

Efforts to suppress dancing between men and women offer further evidence of anxiety concerning youth and sexuality. Such restrictions, though not unprecedented, were relatively rare before the sixteenth century. They echoed medieval Christian assertions that dancing was immoral and in poor taste.[111] Rabbinic objections were based on the concern that dancing violated established standards of modesty and could lead to infringement of Sabbath and festival restrictions. Rabbi Joseph Steinhardt of Niedernai reserved his strongest language for mixed dancing on the grounds that it was likely to arouse immoral desires and lead to sexual impropriety. His own strenuous efforts to prevent dancing in Niedernai (ca. 1755) echoed the opposition mounted by leaders in his own community and in Metz. He was distressed by the youth in his community who had taken exception to rabbinic interference and informed against him to the government that had authorized their dance. Steinhardt succeeded in persuading the governor to permit the matter to remain under

109 The practice was characterized as *minhag asher lo tov* (an unseemly practice). It is likely that *portal* referred to a quarter measure of wine, Viertel. See Eric Zimmer, "Marriage Customs in Worms," *Sinai* 86 (1980): 23, and *The Minhagim of Worms*, pt. 2, p. 3, n. 14.

110 See "Protocol of the Medinah," Art. 27. This custom appears to have been a variation on the well-known *charivari* practiced in late medieval France and elsewhere. The *charivari* aimed to disrupt the first week of marriage, especially when there was a gross disparity in age between husband and wife. See Natalie Z. Davis, "The Reasons of Misrule: Youth Groups and Charivaris in Sixteenth-Century France," *Past and Present* 50 (1971): 41–75. For a specific example of the demand that all newlyweds furnish *vin donné* as a tribute to the community, see Robert Muchembled, *Popular Culture and Elite Culture in France, 1400–1750* (Flammarion, 1978), trans. by Lydia Cochrane (Baton Rouge, 1985), 96. On similar marital customs in Padua and elsewhere, see Horowitz, "Les Mondes des jeunes," 118–19.

111 See Marianne Ruel, "Les Chrétiens et la danse dans l'Europe du nord-ouest, XVIe–XVIIIe siècles," *Historiens et Géographes* 84 (1984): 171, 180.

rabbinic control, though in at least one other community governing authorities forced the rabbi to rescind the *ḥerem*.[112]

Concerned with the rowdiness that typically accompanied dancing, the Rosheim assembly in 1777 ruled that it would be permissible to dance only at weddings and at the *Shabbes Schenkwein* (the Sabbath following the wedding).[113] At Niedernai the assembly issued a *takkanah* voicing anxiety about the intermingling of unmarried men and women, and about the general disorder it could cause. The assembly warned that this prohibition would be announced in all the synagogues of the region in the name of the grand rabbis and of the regional *parnasim*, and failure to comply was punishable by a large fine. Furthermore, no man, married or unmarried, was permitted to dance with a married woman, even at a wedding.[114] Alongside the overriding concern of these communal regulations—preventing the intrusion of non-Jewish customs into the Jewish community—were efforts to distinguish between acceptable and unacceptable circumstances for dancing.[115] The *takkanah* stopped short of prohibiting unmarried men and women from dancing with one another or of preventing husbands from dancing with their wives. Typically, communities limited dancing between the sexes to religious celebrations, aiming in this way to keep it under control.[116]

Steps to combat the deleterious effects of rural culture were intertwined with the active promotion of religious authority. The 1777 provincial *takkanot* confirm this point. Article 1 declared that noncompliance was tantamount to a violation of "the law of our holy Torah, which has been transmitted to the august rabbis, *parnasim* and *manhigim*, and to the *shtadlanim* of the *Medinah*."[117] Rabbis were enlisted as conveners of local elections, and fines aiming to uphold

112 Joseph Steinhardt, *Resp. Zikhron Yosef* (Fürth, 1773), no. 17.

113 The Rosheim protocol was published and translated by Loeb into German and French, in "Les Juifs de Strasbourg," 178–79 and 193–98. Cf. the *arrêté* of the community council of Rosheim, Art. 3, in *Extrait du protocole de la nation de l'assemblée du 21 Iyyar 5537*, 193–94. The phrase *Shabbes Schenkwein* originated with the custom of honoring the bridegroom on the Sabbath preceding his wedding with wine sent to his home. See *The Minhagim of Worms*, pt. 1, 40, n. 27; 46, n. 18; pt. 2; 46, n. 1; and 253.

114 See "Protocol of the Medinah," Art. 28.

115 For a similar appraisal of the *takkanah* issued for Venice and Padua in 1507, see Reuven Bonfil, "Aspects of the Social and Spiritual Life of the Jews in the Venetian Territories at the Beginning of the Sixteenth Century" [Hebrew], *Zion* 41 (1976): 84.

116 For a fuller treatment of the historical significance of dancing and its relationship to popular culture, see Zvi Friedhaber, "Religious Dancing in Marriages Conducted as Meritorious Deeds" [Hebrew], in *Folklore Research Center Studies* 3 (Jerusalem, 1972), 165–87. For related sources, see Pollack, *Jewish Folkways*, 39, and Reischer, *Resp. Shevut Ya'akov*, pt. 1, no. 103.

117 "Protocol of the Medinah," Art. 1. Compare *Resp. Rashi*, Elfenbein ed., no. 247.

the authority of the *parnasim* could not be imposed without the approval of the *av beit din*. Likewise, the power to impose the *ḥerem* against an individual who committed a religious infraction was contingent on the authorization of the rabbinic court. In addition to bolstering the position of *av beit din* as a central communal figure, the Alsatian *takkanot* protected the exclusive authority of the rabbis in religious affairs. No individual was permitted to issue rulings in matters of ritual law without the authorization of the *av beit* din in the local community or region, and only the rabbi appointed in a particular locale could be approached with halakhic queries. Once a rabbi was consulted on a halakhic question, the questioner was prohibited from turning to a second rabbi on the same matter. Any person who violated this regulation would be fined and his house and utensils would be declared unkosher. Local *parnasim* were warned against authorizing any individual to conduct a wedding without written permission either from the *av beit din* or, when the position of *av beit din* was vacant, from the *dayan* of the community. In general, the Alsatian legislation endeavored to put a stop to practices that violated established religious norms. Others focused on reinforcing the exclusive authority of the rabbinic court to settle differences among Jewish litigants. Even communal leaders themselves were subject to efforts to shore up tradition, as all were urged to attend synagogue mornings and evenings.[118]

Detailed regulations issued by Alsatian leaders indicate the growing anxiety around religious commitments, but their main purpose was to prescribe normative practice in Alsace.[119] Efforts to promote standards of religious conduct, especially in relation to the behavior of unmarried men and women, cannot be taken as proof of a religious decline but as a response to behavior that in any era was not at all unusual. Rather, the ebb and flow of religious commitment was met by the firm resolve to revitalize the moral and religious foundations of Judaism. This was typified by the decision to create a central *beit midrash* for the entire province; efforts to fund the regional *yeshivot* of Sierentz and Ettendorf also continued unabated. Although there already were numerous *yeshivot* and *batei midrash* that offered opportunities for intensive study, community leaders of Upper and Lower Alsace believed that it was necessary to

118 "Protocol of the Medinah," Arts. 3–4, 9, 13, 17.

119 Weill, "Rabbins et Parnasim dans l'Alsace du XVIIIe siècle," 103–104, and J. Weil, "Contribution à l'histoire des communautés alsaciennes au 18ème siècle," *Revue des études juives* 81 (1925): 169–71. On the provincial organizations, see the "Extract from the Protocol of the Medinah," 28 May 1777, published in *Blätter fur jüdische Geschichte und Litteratur* 2 (1901): 18–22; 28–29.

establish institutions where study could continue without interruption for up to three years.[120]

Despite similar patterns of communal organization, Jewish life in Metz was distinguished from that of Alsace in several respects. Communal leaders in Alsace and Metz shared a deep-seated anxiety about the challenges that threatened to undermine the social and religious status quo, however, the *takkanot* enacted in Alsace differed in their assessment of the most serious problems facing the Jewish community. Ordinances approved by the Alsatian provincial assemblies in the decade prior to the Revolution reflected a legislative agenda that was more narrowly focused than in Metz. While communal leaders in both Alsace and Metz shared a deep-seated anxiety about threats to the social and religious status quo, the *takkanot* enacted in Alsace reveal greater apprehension about external cultural influences. In Metz, communal legislation reflected concern that standards of religious observance were eroding. These differences can be explained by the fact that the two regions epitomized the urban and rural settings, respectively.

Alsace and Metz exemplified two distinct frameworks in which the encounter between tradition and modernity varied substantially. They also prefigured the two divergent social contexts—rural and urban—that determined how Ashkenazic Jews would interpret the diverse implications of Emancipation in the nineteenth century. In Metz, the main objective of communal legislation was emblematic of the growing regulation of public behavior in the early modern period. Unlike medieval sumptuary law, which was motivated by the fear that ostentation might arouse resentment among the neighboring gentile population, early modern regulations came in response to new challenges posed by the increasing density of urban life and the accompanying social transformation. The Metz *takkanot* reinforced social divisions based on age, gender, and wealth, and sought to maintain internal equilibrium in the face of acute generational tensions, the erosion of sexual mores, and the blurring of class distinctions.

In the second half of the eighteenth century, Metz communal leaders concluded that conditions warranted renewed efforts to halt the erosion of moral conduct. As compared with *takkanot* issued in the late seventeenth century, the 1769 regulations were especially rigorous, mirroring the anxiety that Metz leaders felt regarding the dereliction of youth, the decline in sexual morality, and the blurring of social status. Games of leisure and chance were also prohibited by the 1769 Takkanot, which specifically targeted wagering on billiards

120 Ibid., Arts. 3, 12, 14, 15, 23, 27–9, and 34.

or cards. Any person found playing these games in the city, quarter, or prison without the authorization of the Kahal—even at a distance of five hours travel beyond the gate of the city—would lose the right to participate in religious activities in the two community synagogues for a period of three years, even if this meant foregoing a family *fête*. Attendance at the *Comédie* was also listed among the prohibited acts for which the perpetrator would be subjected to *ḥerem*, fine, and public denunciation.[121]

Concerns about the violation of sexual norms were hardly new. The aggressive approach taken by Rabbi Eibeschütz before mid-century left an unmistakable imprint on communal legislation. Disturbed by reports of sexual contact before marriage, Eibeschütz had pledged in 1744 to insert a clause in the betrothal contract requiring couples to refrain from physical contact until after their wedding. It appears unlikely that he was successful, but anxiety about the sexual mores of young men and women prompted the Kahal nearly a quarter century later, in 1769, to take action against sexual intimacy between men and women engaged to be married. Among engaged Huguenot couples, premarital intercourse after the religious engagement ceremony, known as *fiançailles*, was a common practice, such that Protestant leaders sought to suspend the religious ceremony. The practice of cohabitation between formal betrothal and wedding declined by the late seventeenth century, but premarital conceptions still accounted for ten percent of first births in the eighteenth century. In the Jewish community, the phenomenon continued to be of concern, so that the 1769 Takkanot, in contrast to the silence of earlier legislation, prohibited betrothed couples from being in each other's company at night, even in the presence of a guardian.[122]

In a similar vein, communal leaders adopted an Eibeschütz ruling issued in 1746, requiring women to arrange their cemetery visitations a day or two before Rosh Hashanah and Yom Kippur, since the morning before these festivals was normally reserved for men. Nearly a quarter century later, in 1769, the Metz Kahal introduced a new provision that aimed to reduce social interaction between men and women by designating separate days for their annual cemetery

121 PKM, 79a, 1769 *règlement*, Art. 44.

122 On Eibeschütz's intent to insert of the clause in the betrothal contact, see *Ya'arot Devash*, pt. 1, 62. For warnings against *yiḥud* (being alone with opposite sex), see PKM, 79a, 1769 Takkanot, Art. 43 and again in 1777, in PKM, 101a. Regarding engaged couples, the *takkanot* also stated that the beadle should not issue invitations to the *shpinholz* until after the couple had been punished. On *fiançailles*, see Guy Cabourdin and Georges Viard, *Lexique historique de la France d'Ancien Régime* (Paris, 1978), 136. On the decline of cohabitation following the *fiançailles*, see Robin Briggs, *Early Modern France, 1560–1715* (Oxford, 1998), 190.

visits.[123] These sources reflect concerns about the involvement of women in public ritual, the interaction of men and women at liminal moments, and the disorderly conduct of public rites.[124] By adopting a particularly stringent position that prohibited women from attending funerals entirely, the Metz *takkanah* went several steps beyond Eibeschütz's outspoken criticism of sexual libertarianism.[125]

Fear of utter moral collapse prompted the enactment of measures not only intended to reduce exposure to sexual temptations but also to crack down on violators of sexual norms. Beginning in the 1760s, repeated references to perpetrators of sexual impropriety fill the pages of the Pinkas Kahal. Fulminations against unchaperoned meetings of men and women, pregnancies of unmarried women, and reports of adulterous affairs, were accompanied by threats of unyielding punishment. These included the *ḥerem*, denial of the right to pray in either of the community's two synagogues, a monetary fine, and retraction of the *ḥezkat ʿironit*. In some instances, the Kahal required the offender to undergo public humiliation. Female domestic servants who became pregnant were presumed to be promiscuous and were to be led through the street in daylight, in full public view.[126] Men charged with licentious or immoral behavior were required to confess aloud before the Kahal in the synagogue. Stringent measures such as heavy fines and the public disclosure of improprieties were now judged necessary, if only to act as a deterrent to other members of the community.[127]

---

123 1769 Takkanot, Art. 62. Exceptions included women who lived in the home of the deceased, two women from the burial society, and two from the Shrouds Society. For Eibeschütz's concerns about men and women at the cemetery, see *Ya'arot Devash*, pt. 1, 262. Other communities in central Europe, such as Triesch (1687) and Prague (1692) had recorded similar measures. See Jacob R. Marcus, "The Triesch *Hebra Kaddisha*, 1687–1828," *Hebrew Union College Annual* 19 (1945–46): 180, and the Prague *takkanah* of 1692, Art. 25 in *Jüdische Centralblatt* 8 (1889): 51–52. Cf. Joseph Juspa Hahn of Nördlingen, *Yosif Omez* (Frankfurt am Main, 1723), 327 on avoiding frivolity in the cemetery.

124 See Joseph Karo, *Beit Yosef, Yoreh Deah* (Venice, 1551), 359, for the zoharic custom to prevent women from going to the cemetery. For an attempt to neutralize the halakhic significance of the zoharic passage, cf. Aaron Worms, *'Od la-Mo'ed* (Metz, 1822), 140a. See Yedidia Dinari, "The Profanation of the Holy by the Menstruant Woman and the 'Takanot of Ezra,'" [Hebrew] *Te'uda* 3 (1983): 35–36, where it is proposed that the prohibition derives from the Lurianic conception of impurity. On the perception of women as a source of disorder in need of discipline, see James Farr, *Authority and Sexuality in Early Modern Europe* (New York, 1995), 19–31.

125 Eibeschütz regularly railed against sexual immodesty, excessive frivolity, and inappropriate physical contact; see *Ya'arot Devash*, pt. 1, 19, 37, 42, 61–2, 231, and 240. Cf. "Protocol of the Medinah," 28 May 1777, 18–22; 28–29; paraphrased in French by Loeb, "Extrait du protocole de la nation de l'assemblée du 21 Iyyar 5537," 181–91, Arts. 23, 27–28.

126 PKM, 78b, 1769 Takkanot, Art. 42; 94b.

127 See Eibeschutz, *Ya'arot Devash*, 1:37, 62, 217, 231, 262, and PKM, 48b, 51b' 67a, 69a, 74a, 101a.

The foregoing initiatives signal a considerable degree of cooperation between the lay and rabbinic authorities at mid-century. But they also reveal Eibeschütz's acknowledgment a decade earlier that ultimate authority was vested in the lay leadership, as is apparent from his comment concerning the legitimacy of a *takkanah* enacted by the Metz Kahal on the jurisdiction of *dayanim*: "This is indisputable, because it is a *takkanah* of a city and [members of] the Kahal accepted it upon themselves. And in such matters, the townspeople may enact *takkanot*."[128] Though a consistently vocal critic of ordinances enacted by the lay leadership, Eibeschutz was bound by the constitutional framework of the community he served.

Notwithstanding the wealth of documentary sources, it is difficult to judge community leaders' success in ensuring strict conformity to communal norms. Reports that sexual permissiveness had become more widespread, that exposure to popular culture had gained in popularity, and that recourse to the French civil courts had become more common offer evidence that is helpful in assessing social and religious trends. The fact that such behavior is referenced repeatedly in the Pinkas Kahal, was targeted continually by communal legislation, and was addressed in the proceedings of the Beit Din, reinforces the reliability of these reports. Communal legislation enacted in the late seventeenth century and throughout much of the eighteenth century was intended to frustrate the persistence and proliferation of aberrant behavior. Tough measures were intended as a deterrent against individuals who flouted traditional norms and communal laws.

Whether the adoption of the mores of the surrounding culture—as noted routinely in the Metz communal register and in the records of the rabbinic court—were tantamount to the rejection of traditional norms is equally debatable. The repeated condemnation of luxury and extravagance, first in the sumptuary laws of 1690–97 and subsequently in the 1769 Takkanot suggests that these trends were on the rise. They were met by the harsh criticism voiced by Eibeschütz during his tenure as *av beit din* in the 1740s. His sermons were filled with discontent with the adoption of the fashion and modes of conduct that prevailed among the general population. He had little patience for men who grew long hair, shaved their beards, drank coffee, and attended the theater, and he ridiculed "men and boys [who] wear fine clothing, curl their hair, wear 'gentile wigs' and look into the mirror to make certain that everything is in right, that none of the hair on their head is visible." Likewise, he derided those who chose to conceal the ritual fringes that were normally worn openly, and those who wore "tiny phylacteries hidden under their wigs." Time

128 See Eibeschutz, *Urim ve-Tumim, Ḥoshen Mishpat* §5:3; idem, *Ya'arot Devash*, 1:37, 62, 217, 231, 262.

spent learning French, arithmetic, and dance was condemned as a frivolous distraction from Torah study.[129] In the hope of elevating the general moral climate, Eibeschütz urged Metz residents to engage in the daily study of moralistic works to fortify their resistance to sexual temptations. In his own teaching routine he instituted the study of *Shenei Luḥot ha-Berit* (*Two Tablets of the Law*), a seventeenth-century pietistic-mystical work composed by Rabbi Isaiah Horowitz in Frankfurt.[130] Echoing Eibeschütz's biting criticism of contemporary mores, one Alsatian rabbi, Naftali Hirtz Halevi Schone explained the widespread failure to pray with proper intention as a result of the preoccupation with "unimportant matters, on commercial affairs."[131] The simplest solution, in the estimation of these rabbinic observers, was to retreat from worldly enticements.

The responses of Jewish communal officials in the two major centers of Jewish life in northeastern France reflected widely divergent perspectives on how to act on the myriad challenges of the day. In Alsace, communal leaders vested the rabbinate with ultimate authority in internal affairs while strenuously supporting rabbinic efforts to bolster the population's commitment to traditional behavior and values.[132] The penetration of cultural influences from surrounding villages, and the indirect effects of economic modernization, resulted in very modest social and religious changes there as well, but these could hardly be characterized as modernization.

In Metz, communal legislation addressed the dynamic changes of the early modern period, particularly the evolving urban reality created by the new mercantile culture and the exposure to modern trends. Communal controls that drew directly and indirectly on principles of Jewish law may appear to have challenged the rabbinate's authority as the supreme interpreters of Halakhah

---

129 For his condemnation of excessive materialism, see *Ya'arot Devash*, pt. 1, 22–23; against gentile fashions and wigs, see pt. 1, 40, pt. 2, 2–3, 22; on the preoccupation with luxury, see 127; on the preference for secular pursuits, see pt. 1, 35–6.

130 On the importance of moral literature to bolster the moral fiber of the community, and on Eibeschütz's own efforts to institute its study, including sections of the *Shenei Luḥot Ha-Brit* on a regular basis, see *Ya'arot Devash*, pt. 1, 225–26.

131 Naftali Hirtz Schone, "Responsa, novellae, sermons," Institute for Microfilmed Hebrew Manuscripts, ms. 12875, 50. The following is the original quotation:

ועתה בדור הזה הוא דור פרוץ בעו"ה ולא די שאינן מכוונים בתפלתם כראוי מפלפלין גם אחרי׳בדברים בטלים בעסקי מו"מ ואלה ברכב ואלה בסוסים ואין אנחנו בשם ה׳ אלקים נזכיר, וזה הוא רע לשמים ומקטלין עשר ספירות כמבואר בספר המפואר לר"ש מלכו הנ"ו.

Citing Solomon Molcho, *Sefer ha-Mefoar: Be'urim be-Sodot ha-Torah* (Amsterdam, 1709), Schone wrote that the behavior he found appalling was a cosmic menace that threatened to destroy the ten *sefirot*.

132 Berkovitz, *Rites and Passages*, 35–85.

and public morality. But in regulating moral and religious behavior, communal legislation was not bound by Jewish law and, in fact, made use of non-halakhic approaches. Nevertheless, there is no evidence that the empowerment of the laity came at the expense of rabbinic authority. Communal structures remained in place, religious institutions were supported firmly, and rabbinic and lay leaders continued to cooperate until the end of the ancien régime. References in the Pinkas Kahal to the participation of local halakhic authorities in matters of communal administration and decision-making confirm this phenomenon.[133] Election ballots were opened only in the presence of the *av beit din* and community clerks, and the *av beit din* administered the oath of office to elected officials. When a pertinent legal question arose concerning a public policy matter, it was the chief rabbi, or the Beit Din, that provided the authoritative ruling.[134]

When new *takkanot* were drafted and confirmed, they were read publicly in the two community synagogues. In advance of the public reading of the 1769 Takkanot, the proclamation delivered in the synagogue emphasized that a primary goal of the new legislation was to uphold the three pillars of the Jewish tradition—"the pillars of Torah, worship, and charity." The oath administered to *parnasim* and lower level officials contained phrasing borrowed from the Jewish religious tradition, such as the pledge to lead the community "for the sake of heaven" and "to serve this people in holy service as was done long ago by experts in the Torah."[135] In the final analysis, lay and rabbinic authorities found common cause in their struggle to meet the challenges facing their coreligionists in northeastern France while defusing the sort of tensions that afflicted communal government elsewhere.

The legislative agenda in eighteenth-century Metz attests to significant social, cultural, and religious changes that stood in contrast to those in the predominantly rural economy and the high level of acculturation attained by the Sephardic population in southern France.[136] With the emergence of the public

---

133 PKM, 135b. Cf. Amalia Kessler, *A Revolution in Commerce: The Parisian Merchant Court and the Rise of Commercial Society in Eighteenth-Century France* (New Haven, 2007), 74–78, for a parallel discussion of merchant courts that called upon local parish priests to assist in arbitrating merchant disputes. This was a remarkable phenomenon, and likely somewhat uncommon, given the anticlerical sentiment in French urban centers, whereas in Jewish communities, in France at least, such cooperation was not exceptional.

134 PKM, 43a, 43b, 90a, 90b, and 135b.

135 PKM, 45b, 47b, 48a, 76a, 121a, and 133b.

136 Laws governing social and religious behavior in the communities of Bordeaux and Bayonne—whether in relation to youth, social hierarchies, or the decline in religious standards—were a rarity, evidently because the idea of a restricted role for religion in everyday life, like the tendency to downplay overt elements of social distinctiveness, were

welfare as a value independent of halakhic constraints or of religious justification, the Metz initiatives signify a first stage of the modernization of French Jews that unfolded nearly a century before the Revolution. These efforts to consciously mold society on the basis of public policy concerns were rooted in the belief that tougher standards of order were necessary to counterbalance the potentially disintegrative trends that posed new challenges in the second half of the eighteenth century. The reinforcement of religious observance, traditional sexual mores, and social hierarchies bear witness to a community struggling to maintain its cultural distinctiveness precisely at a time when its members had begun to integrate in French society.

The Kehillah's wall of defense was not insurmountable. According to several leading historians, pleasure-seeking had become more defiant and unburdened by guilt in the eighteenth century. This characterization, and the numerous depictions of deviation from religious norms, are likewise based on evidence supplied by rabbinic detractors and can rarely be considered impartial. They overwhelmingly reflect the perceptions of the rabbinic class, their concerns about laxity in religious observance, and their hypersensitivity to minor infractions, but they do not constitute reliable evidence in their own right. Nor does the rhetoric of rabbinic exhortation, especially in the absence of other sources, offer a sound basis for determining the motivations and intentions of transgressors.

Details of fashion, amusement, and cultural consumption offer invaluable evidence of the powerful appeal of modern trends. However, this material must be examined in its proper historical context so that the voices and perspectives of those who were deeply absorbed in European culture, as well as the arguments advanced by their detractors, can be considered within a comparative analytical framework. Attention to structural issues and broader patterns of social change will enable scholars to assess how deviations in the seventeenth and eighteenth century compared to those of the medieval period and to corresponding patterns in contemporary Christian society. These

an outgrowth of the *converso* experience. The high degree of acculturation achieved by the Sephardic population, as expressed especially in dress and language, was enough to render such laws pointless. In Bordeaux, restrictions on jewelry and embroidered fabrics were issued for a short time, but no comparable measures were enacted in Bayonne; see Henri Léon, *Histoire des Juifs de Bayonne* (Paris, 1893), 387. However, Léon's report of an unsuccessful attempt by Rabbi Raphael Meldola to introduce sumptuary legislation in Bayonne was based on a misreading of Meldola, *Resp. Mayyim Rabbim* (Amsterdam, 1737), no. 64. His mistake was repeated in Hertzberg, *French Enlightenment and the Jews*, 241, and in my own *Rites and Passages*, 41 and 252, n. 20. It appears that Meldola was not referring to Bayonne but to Belgrade; I am grateful to Joseph Prager for bringing this correction to my attention.

steps are necessary to clarify the degree to which social, cultural, and political forces shaped the local character of religious and secular pursuits. Regardless of the conclusions drawn, the conflation of acculturation, secularization, and the erosion of tradition threatens to distort the role of religion in early modern culture.

The example of Metz suggests that even advanced acculturation was possible within a traditional religious framework, and that the equation of modernization with secularization is based on a faulty assumption concerning the nature of Jewish culture and community in the ancien régime.[137] As will be demonstrated below, a powerful ethos of engagement with the cultural and economic dimensions of the society arose from an unlikely source—the rabbinic court of Metz and the legal traditions of Judaism. Clear indications of acculturation—especially legal acculturation—is manifest in the protocols of the Metz Beit Din and its judicial conduct.

137 See Shmuel Feiner, *Origins of Jewish Secularization in Eighteenth-Century Europe*, trans. by Chaya Naor (Philadelphia, 2010). Focusing on the behavioral aspects of secularization, Feiner traces the roots of Jewish secularization to the beginning of the eighteenth century, much as Azriel Shoḥet argued in *ʿIm Hilufe Tequfot*. Feiner's most important contribution is the detailed illustration of secularizing trends, as reflected in the attraction of European culture and amusements, the emergence of the city in the eighteenth century as a cultural center to which the broader public had access, and the growing tension in urban communities between members of the modernizing elite and their rabbinic critics.

CHAPTER 4

Lay and Rabbinic Judicial Authority

Of all the privileges extended to Jews over the course of their history, the authority to adjudicate civil disputes ranked among the most highly valued and the most vigorously defended. At various times, whether under Roman, Christian, or Muslim rule, communities enjoyed the right to establish courts, to appoint their own judges, and to enact and enforce legislation, though the means of enforcement varied widely. Disputes relating to civil and criminal law, inheritance, guardianship, marriage, divorce, and communal obligations were adjudicated in several different types of tribunals: ad hoc rabbinic courts assembled at the initiative of a local rabbi or when litigants each chose a judge, joined by a nonaligned third judge; communal tribunals, comprised of lay officers, that customarily heard cases of a public nature; and established rabbinic courts usually consisting of three trained rabbinic experts who adjudicated based on talmudic law as interpreted in their day. At times, two or more of these bodies operated side by side.

Whichever institutional pattern prevailed, only the courts that operated with communal approval were regarded as an acceptable forum for settling civil disputes between Jews. In most circumstances, rabbinic authorities viewed recourse to gentile courts as a religious offense, a betrayal of the Talmudic tradition. Recourse to civil courts—a more common occurrence than has generally been assumed—was consistently proscribed by communal legislation as a flagrant violation of community discipline. Historically, Jewish courts were the primary venue where competing lay and rabbinic interpretations of Jewish law, on the one hand, and the interaction between Jewish law and general law, on the other, were negotiated. In this respect, the courts offer entrée to the most salient features of Jewish communal life during the past two millennia.[1]

With the firm support of the monarchy and, to a lesser extent, of the local authorities, Jewish communities exercised jurisdiction in both civil and religious affairs. Under the terms set forth in the royal privileges, they enjoyed the right to establish courts and to appoint judges. The judicial autonomy conferred

1 On medieval rabbinic courts, see Simḥa Assaf, *Batei ha-din ve-sidreihem aḥar ḥatimat ha-Talmud* [*Jewish Courts and their Procedures after the Talmudic Period*] (Jerusalem, 1923–24); Katz, *Tradition and Crisis*, 80–87; and Ephraim Kanarfogel, *The Intellectual History and Rabbinic Culture of Medieval Ashkenaz* (Detroit, 2012), 38–84.

 | DOI:10.1163/9789004417403_006

on the Metz Jewish community contrasted sharply with the predominant trend in France with respect to the ecclesiastical courts. The scope of authority exercised by these courts was circumscribed within strict boundaries set by the Crown and secular magistrates. Not only offenses of public order were within the sole jurisdiction of lay judges, but even distinctly sectarian matters such as blasphemy, sacrilege, and the performance of marriages outside a priest's own parish. Clerics' immunity from lay courts was limited solely to civil cases in which the cleric was a defendant, when two clerics were in litigation against each other, or when the matter did not pertain to property, commerce, or wages. But disputes concerning the election and dismissal of functionaries involved with order and upkeep of the church, wills, gifts to the church, the rental of pews, altercations in church, and maintenance of registers, were under the authority of the civil courts. Secular courts had jurisdiction even in matrimonial cases, "when the final fact of marriage was disputed, where promises had been broken, abductions were alleged, where dowries and inheritances were concerned." *Séparation de corps et d'habitation* was handled in secular courts, though it was possible to go to ecclesiastical court just as well, since canon law considered adultery by either party grounds for separation. Ecclesiastical courts, however, did not have the power to impose temporal penalties. In rare circumstances, a criminal act would come under the joint jurisdiction of lay and ecclesiastical authorities. In those cases when the penalty imposed on clerics was severe, such as excommunication, imprisonment in a monastery, or withdrawal of ministerial functions or benefice, the secular and ecclesiastical courts were expected to handle the case jointly.[2]

Lay encroachment on the authority of the ecclesiastical courts was most conspicuous where the boundaries between ecclesiastical and secular jurisdiction were unclear. Parlements asserted that the civil consequences of vows were contingent on genuine consent, and this was to be determined by lay inquiry alone. When disciplined by bishops, parish priests were permitted to use *appel comme d'abus* (appeal for abuse of jurisdiction) to go before Parlements.[3]

2 See McManners, *Church and Society in Eighteenth Century France*, 1:192–98. Sacraments and burial of dead were affairs of clergy, though secular authorities were watchful in case of public insult, as were vows, and were thus exclusively matters of the ecclesiastical court. According to Jeffrey Merrick, magistrates "routinely undermined ecclesiastical jurisdiction" by using "the *appel comme d'abus*, which allowed for appeals to royal courts in religious cases involving alleged abuses of clerical authority." See Merrick, "Conscience and Citizenship in Eighteenth-Century France," 52. On the larger context of religious culture, see Timothy Tackett, *Religion, Revolution and Regional Cultures in Eighteenth-Century France (The Ecclesiastical Oath of 1791)* (Princeton, 1986), 127–58.

3 McManners, *Church and Society in Eighteenth Century France*, 1:156–57.

Central to the dispute between the Church and the magistracy was the controversial papal bull *Unigenitus* (1713), issued by Clement XI, which reaffirmed prior condemnations of Jansenism. *Unigenitus* was promulgated at the request of Louis XIV, who aimed to quash the Jansenist faction. The object of papal concern was the Jansenist commentary on the New Testament by French theologian Pasquier Quesnel. His 101 propositions included the claim that conscience justified defiance of Church decrees.[4] The debate in France intensified in 1730 upon Louis XV's ratification of the *Unigenitus*, which unleashed vigorous protest by the magistrates and parlementaires. They warned that concerns over unjust excommunication threatened the political order by discouraging the "loyalty and obedience" owed to the king. Moreover, since it was agreed that matters related to external discipline of the Church were under secular jurisdiction, they argued that the King was obligated to shield his subjects from abuses of clerical authority such as denial of burial rights.

Two additional arguments strengthened the case for lay authority: parlementaires insisted that the clergy was accountable to the king even in matters related to the spiritual domain; they further asserted that withholding sacraments from Jansenists was indistinguishable from unjust excommunication. Tensions between the Crown and the Parlements escalated in 1731 when the Royal Council issued an *arrêt* asserting that the King alone was empowered to delegate the authority of ecclesiastical courts. Cases that fell between spiritual and temporal jurisdictions were henceforth placed under the exclusive authority of the monarch, not his judges, and he would continue to exclude the Parlements.[5] By seeking to resolve questions of nonconformity raised by the wide-ranging *Unigenitus* debate, the King and his magistrates not only succeeded in asserting the independence of lay jurisdiction but also laid the foundation for the eventual disengagement of citizenship from the profession of Catholicity.[6]

European historians have long characterized the foregoing political battle as a struggle between two adversaries—the spiritual and temporal powers—that shared little common ground. According to this view, lay hegemony attained a firm institutional footing by purportedly extending its influence in areas formerly under the authority of the Catholic Church. Dependent as this view is on the largely discredited secularization thesis, its underlying assumptions

4 Pasquier Quesnel, *Nouveau Testament en français avec des réflexions morales* (Paris, 1692).

5 McManners, *Church and Society in Eighteenth Century France*, 2: 477.

6 Merrick, "Conscience and Citizenship in Eighteenth-Century France," 48–58. Also see Peter Sahlins, "Fictions of a Catholic France: The Naturalization of Foreigners, 1685–1787," *Representations* 47 (Summer, 1994): 85–110.

no longer enjoy universal acceptance. Neither are its wider implications valid for the study of Jewish history, though they continue to inform Jewish historiographical approaches to modernity in France and elsewhere. Undue emphasis on anticlerical dimensions of modernization, lay-rabbinic tensions, and the influence of the Haskalah has obscured the importance of religion as the basis for social cohesion and corporate identity in the Jewish community. This emphasis also has hindered recognition of efforts by the lay and rabbinical sectors to reach accommodation in matters of communal governance and public policy.[7]

State authorization to adjudicate civil and religious disputes was the linchpin of Jewish judicial autonomy in Metz. Nevertheless, throughout much of the century preceding the French Revolution, the authority of the Jewish community to judge civil disputes was challenged repeatedly from within and without.[8] In the late seventeenth century, rabbinic courts were the locus of tensions between religious and lay leadership—much as they had been in Poland, Lithuania, and Moravia decades earlier. The exclusive jurisdiction of these tribunals in civil matters was challenged regularly by individuals who threatened to take their disputes to the general courts. In one instance, in 1693, a Jewish resident of Metz approached the French authorities with a request to conduct his legal battles in the royal courts. Concerned by what it viewed as a threat to its authority, the Metz Kehillah responded aggressively by sending a delegation to Paris and, with the support of the Metz Parlement, ultimately prevailed.[9] In 1706, the Kahal sought confirmation from the Parlement that cases involving Jewish litigants were not to be tried in the *Cour de Parlement* but only in rabbinic tribunals. Several years later, in 1709, an irate resident of the Metz community who was disgruntled over a decision issued by the Beit Din, threatened to take his inheritance dispute to the Metz civil court. Rabbi Abraham Broda, then the presiding justice of the Beit Din, responded by pronouncing the *ḥerem* against him, at which point the threat to bring a civil suit

7 Jonathan Clark rejected the assumption that the Enlightenment was generally hostile to religion, arguing that "eighteenth-century religion ... [was] at the very heart of English intellectual life in the period of the Enlightenment." See Jonathan Clark, *English Society, 1660–1832*, 2d ed. (Cambridge, 2000), 28. Also see S. J. Barnett, *The Enlightenment and Religion. The Myths of Modernity* (Manchester, U.K., 2003), and Simon Grote, "Religion and Enlightenment," *Journal of the History of Ideas* 75:1 (January 2014): 137–60.

8 For examples of challenges to the civil jurisdiction of the rabbis, see Cahen, "Le rabbinat de Metz pendant la période française," *REJ* 8 (1884): 257–58, 262–66; Malino, "Competition and Confrontation," 327–32.

9 Cahen, "Le rabbinat de Metz pendant la période française," *REJ* 7 (1883): 103–107, 215–16; *REJ* 8 (1884): 257–88, 262–66. Also see Kerner, "La Vie quotidienne," 224–34; Hertzberg, *French Enlightenment and the Jews*, 239–42; and Clément, *La condition des juifs de Metz*, 91–92.

against the community was withdrawn. The standoff occurred amid allegations of the local judiciary that, by judging civil disputes, Jewish courts were seeking "to establish ... a sovereign and despotic authority that disrupts the order of the kingdom," thus placing the Jewish nation in opposition to the absolutist state. A year later, the Metz Kahal issued a sharply worded *takkanah* warning that any individual who approached the non-Jewish courts to settle a dispute would be subject to "all of the curses and oaths written in the Torah ... and there will be no cure for this." The *takkanah* stated further that any person who violated this ordinance would not be included in the Sabbath prayers pronounced on behalf of community members and would be publicly disgraced.[10]

The Metz community's troubles regarding civil jurisdiction were entangled in the political struggle between the Parlements and the French monarchy. Jurisdictional authority was perhaps the most conspicuous issue that highlighted these historically complex relations. The French monarchy consistently supported the authority of the Kahal and the Beit Din as the most effective means of regulating conduct in the Jewish community. In 1715, shortly after ascending the throne, Louis XV issued new *lettres patentes* that firmly upheld the authority of rabbis and communal leaders to judge in civil cases.[11] The royal edict was a clear reaffirmation of the Metz Jewish community and its privileges and reflected a larger effort to acknowledge local and provincial autonomy. It was accompanied by the restoration of the right of preregistration remonstrance to the twelve provincial Parlements—a right that had been abolished in 1673. The Parlements were superior courts of appeal that heard cases involving larger sums and capital crimes. Charged with the registration of royal *ordonnances* and edicts, they had the authority to control customary laws in each province. To this end they often supplanted local courts that had existed prior to the imposition of royal control. In Germany, by comparison, the powers of the rabbinic court were curtailed much more aggressively than in France, as the provisions of the New Jewry Legislation at Hamburg in 1710 and the Prussian General Jewry Code of 1730 demonstrate.[12]

---

10 A.D. Moselle 17J23 Jur 15e, cited in Jordan Katz, "To Judge and to Be Judged: Jewish Communal Autonomy in Metz and the Struggle for Sovereignty in Eighteenth-Century France." *JQR* 104:3 (2014): 443–46. The complaint, which was made by the *Procureur du Roi*, is cited and translated by Katz, ibid., 445–46. For the original document, *Plainte du Procureur du Roi contre l'établissement d'un tribunal juive à Metz et réponse du rabbin à ce sujet*, 22 October 1709, see CAHJP FMe 260.

11 On tensions between the Parlement and the Metz community, see Katz, "'To Judge and to Be Judged,'" 457–60. On the struggle over the *Lettres patentes, 31 décembre 1715*, see Arch. JTSA, microfilm no. 8347.

12 See *German-Jewish History in Modern Times*, 1:253–54. By the 1770s evidence of rabbinic acquiescence to compromises on the autonomy of Jewish law had become more

As the centralization process advanced steadily in the first half of the eighteenth century, the provincial Parlements were resistant to the monarchy's vision and were regarded increasingly as a threat to royal authority. The reign of Louis XV was, to the end, a period of rising tensions between state-sponsored institutions promoting centralization, on the one hand, and local authorities pressing for the recognition of local governance and the expansion of local traditions, on the other.[13] As early as 1634 the Parlement reserved the right to hear cases between Jews that did not involve matters of "religion or internal police." For the next century and a half, the rabbis asserted their authority as final arbiters in matters between Jews and in certain instances exercised the power to excommunicate those who appealed to the royal courts. As a rule, the Metz community found an ally in the king, who instinctively recoiled at parlementaire claims, whereas the Parlement tended to be unsympathetic and even hostile to juridical autonomy.[14] In 1734 the Parlement decided to limit the civil jurisdiction of the Beit Din to cases in which the parties agreed voluntarily to submit to arbitration; it also curtailed the pronouncement of the *ḥerem* and the right to impose disciplinary measures.[15]

An initiative undertaken jointly by the monarchy and the Parlement shortly before mid-century elicited acute anxiety among Jewish leaders concerned that it would chip away at the community's judicial autonomy. Royal authorities approached the Metz Kehillah with the demand that it furnish an abridged translation of the *Ḥoshen Mishpat* (civil law) and *Even ha-'Ezer* (family law) sections of the *Shulḥan 'Arukh* so that cases between Jew and Jew could be properly adjudicated by French judges on the basis of Jewish law.[16]

---

apparent, as some rabbis were resigned to the narrowing of judicial prerogatives. Rabbi Ezekiel Landau of Prague, for example, approved the transfer of bankruptcy proceedings to a secular court on the grounds of *dina d'malkhuta dina*. See Landau, *Derushei Ha-Zelah*, fol. 32c, cited in Jacob Katz, *Tradition and Crisis*, 346, n. 9. For additional sources on the autonomy debate, see Frances Malino, "Attitudes Toward Jewish Communal Autonomy in Prerevolutionary France," in *Essays in Modern Jewish History: A Tribute to Ben Halpern*, Frances Malino and Phyllis Cohen Albert, eds. (East Brunswick, NJ, 1982), 95–117; Szajkowski, "Jewish Autonomy Debated and Attacked"; and Alexander Altmann, *Moses Mendelssohn: A Biographical Study* (Philadelphia, 1973), 470–74.

13 See James Collins, *The State in Early Modern France* (Cambridge, 1995), 77–156.

14 See Clément, *Condition des Juifs*, 67–76, and Katz, "'To Judge and to Be Judged,'" 447–49.

15 Agreement by both litigating parties was originally a requirement of Roman law. See, for example, *Codex Justinianeus* I, 9, 7–8, discussed in Jean Juster, *Les juifs dans l'Empire Romain* 2 vols. (Paris, 1914), 2: 101–106.

16 *Recueil des lois, coutumes et usages observés par les juifs de Metz*, m.s. 11 March 1743, in AN H 1641. The work was deposited with the Metz Parlement in 1743 and was eventually published in Metz in 1786. According to Frances Malino, this demand originated with the Metz Parlement in August 1740. On the genesis of the translation, see BN, *Lettres patentes*

On 20 August 1742, royal authorities issued the formal call via *lettres patentes*, which were registered in the Parlement ten days later. The monarchy offered reassurance that "[w]e have reserved to them for disputes, which arise between Jews and Jews, the right of recourse to their Rabbis, while also desiring that the leaders of their communities should have knowledge of their [own] police, religion, customs, ceremonies, and impositions."[17] Nicolas-François Lançon, a respected French legal scholar and *conseiller au Parlement*, completed work on the *Recueil des lois, coûtumes et usages observés par les juifs de Metz* in 1743.[18] His introduction to the compendium indicates that from the standpoint of the French authorities, the translation project accorded with the underpinnings of Jewish legal autonomy. As stated in the *lettres patentes*, the initiative to compile Jewish civil law in a French compendium would not prejudice the right of Jews to resort to rabbinic authority and their right (*faculté*) to settle their disputes in their own courts would remain unaffected.[19] In principle at least, the community's juridical authority was reconfirmed.

The demand for a French translation of Jewish laws and customs was consistent with the broader effort of royal authorities to record the customs of hundreds of communities throughout France. It was also prompted by the conviction that Metz Jews were likely to resort to French civil courts in larger numbers, if only to appeal, and that irrespective of the court in which Jewish litigants chose to settle their disputes, "they must be judged according to their own laws and customs."[20] The state made it clear that it was willing to tolerate the Jews' legal diversity and juridical autonomy, provided these could be managed under its central authority. Lançon produced an extract of the work, which he deposited with the *greffe de la Cour* in 1743, shortly after it was completed.[21] The French abridgement of Jewish law was the first of several

du roi, 20 août 1742 and A.D. Moselle 17J23 Jur 45. On the French translation and its historical background, see Katz, "'To Judge and to Be Judged," and Shael Herman, "Tout Fait Maison: A Law Code Crafted by the Eighteenth Century Jewry of Metz," *Review of Rabbinic Judaism* 21:1 (2018): 1–56.

17 *Lettres patentes*, 20 August 1742: "Nous leurs avons réservé pour les contestations, qui naissent de Juifs à Juifs, la faculté de se pourvoir devant leurs Rabins, voulant aussi que les chefs de leurs communautés eussent la connoissance de leur police, religion, coutumes, cérémonies & impositions."

18 Nicolas-François Lançon, *Recueil des lois, coûtumes et usages observés par les juifs de Metz* (Metz, 1786). For Eibeschütz's objections to litigation in gentile courts, see his *Urim ve-Tumim, Ḥoshen Mishpat* (Altona, 1763), §26. On the genesis of the translation, see BN, Lettres patentes du roi, 20 août 1742 and A.D. Moselle 17J23 Jur 45. For the historical background and context, see Katz, "'To Judge and to Be Judged.'"

19 *Lettres patentes*, 20 August 1742.

20 Lançon, preface to *Recueil des lois, coûtumes et usages observés par les juifs de Metz*.

21 See Emmanuel Michel, *Histoire du Parlement de Metz* (Paris, 1845), 515–16. The extract

compendia demanded of central European Jewish communities. Some decades later, for example, the Prussian government ordered Rabbi Hirsch Levin to prepare a German compendium of Jewish law, *Die Ritualgesetze der Juden*, that would serve as a legal reference for German judges ruling on disputes concerning inheritance, wills, guardianship, marriage, and property.[22] Despite his concern regarding the intended use of the compendium and notwithstanding his disapproval of Kehillah legislation permitting limited recourse to French courts, Rabbi Eibeschütz cooperated in producing the French translation presumably because of the growing tendency to resort to the general courts and the substantial pressure placed on him.[23]

Historians have overwhelmingly portrayed the second half of the eighteenth century as the period when Jewish communal autonomy declined steadily until its ultimate demise. Some historians take Eibeschütz's departure for Altona-Hamburg at mid-century as the critical point at which rabbinic authority began to weaken irreversibly. They argue that in the absence of Eibeschütz's determined efforts to defend juridical autonomy, it became much more difficult to withstand secularizing trends and mounting government pressure.[24] It is also widely assumed that over the course of the early modern period—particularly in the second half of the eighteenth century—the standing of rabbinic courts, their role in communal life, and their power to enforce their judicial decisions steadily deteriorated. Recourse to French civil courts was presumed to be not only symptomatic of this trend, but also a major factor that accelerated the erosion of autonomy.

Lending strength to this argument is the indisputable fact that rabbinic hegemony had become the object of escalating derision in public discussions of

---

was deposited at the Parlement on 11 March 1743. The work was published in 1786. On the impact of the *Recueil*, see below, chapter 5.

22 *Die Ritualgesetze der Juden* (Berlin 1778), the compendium of Jewish law produced for Prussian Jewry, was prepared with the assistance of Moses Mendelssohn. This work that rested on the *Judenordnung* of 1750 but envisioned further narrowing of rabbinic jurisdiction; rulings would be issued without consulting the Jewish courts, as the *Judenordnung* had stipulated. Issues concerning property were to be adjudicated in Prussian courts, based on Jewish law. See Michael Brenner, S. Jersch-Wenzel, and Michael Meyer, eds., *German-Jewish History in Modern Times*, 4 vols. (New York, 1996–1998), 3: 254; David Sorkin, *Moses Mendelssohn and the Religious Enlightenment* (Berkeley, 1996), 104–107; and Gil Graff, *Separation of Church and State: Dina de-Malkhuta Dina in Jewish Law* (Tuscaloosa, 1985), 32–33.

23 A comparative study of the various compendia of Jewish law that were produced in the eighteenth century is an important scholarly desideratum.

24 Salomon Posener considered Eibeschütz the last Metz rabbi to impose his authority on the leadership of the community. In his view, rabbinic authority in communal matters weakened from approximately the 1760s. See S. Posener, "The Social Life of Jewish Communities in France in the Eighteenth Century," *JSS* 7 (1945): 215–17.

Jewish emancipation. Rabbinic jurisdiction in the civil realm, critics claimed, evidenced Judaism's conflation of the religious and political spheres, and was taken as proof of the failure of Jews to observe the laws that united French citizens. Communal autonomy was portrayed as a major obstacle to full participation in French society, and once the Revolution vanquished the ancien régime, the National Assembly turned its attention to Jewish juridical authority in areas that had come under the jurisdiction of the state. Ultimately, the conferral of civic equality upon the Jews of Alsace and Lorraine in September 1791 was conditioned on their agreement to surrender this privilege. In a matter of months after the French Revolution, rabbinic courts no longer convened to hear civil cases—at least not formally—which brought the era of communal autonomy officially to a close.[25] The argument concerning the decline of Jewish autonomy is accurate only in the context of public discussions of the Jews' eligibility as citizens—in the decade prior to the Revolution and in its aftermath. But the assessment of internal tensions between lay and rabbinic authorities is less persuasive, as it is based on incomplete evidence and, in some instances, on the interpretation of the historical evidence that is unsustainable.

In 1781, following new privileges granted by the King, the Kahal announced in the two synagogues of the community that Jews had to bring their disputes to the *av beit din*, or before the Kahal, as stated in the royal privileges.[26]

> [But] anyone who brings a suit against his fellow is obligated to summon the defendant before *dinei Israel* [Jewish law], and [if] one summons his fellow to the *arkha'ot* prior to appearing before the Beit Din, the Kahal must demand of the *arkha'ot* officials that they send the litigants to *dinei Israel* on the basis of the aforesaid privileges, and aside from the fact that the plaintiff in the *arkha'ot* must reimburse the Kahal's expenses, he will

25 Scholarship devoted to critical perspectives on rabbinic adjudication and communal autonomy in eighteenth-century Germany has centered, to a great degree, on the views of Moses Mendelssohn and proponents of the Haskalah movement. See Altmann, *Moses Mendelssohn: A Biographical Study* 470–74; David Sorkin, *Moses Mendelssohn and the Religious Enlightenment* (Berkeley, 1996), 104–107; and more recently, Daniel B. Schwartz, *The First Modern Jew: Spinoza and the History of an Image* (Princeton, 2012), esp. 35–52. On the range of views toward autonomy in France, see Frances Malino, "Zalkind Hourwitz, Juif Polonais," *Dix Huitième Siècle* 13 (1981), 79–89; idem, *A Jew in the French Revolution: The Life of Zalkind Hourwitz* (Malden, MA, 1996); idem, "Attitudes toward Jewish Communal Autonomy in Prerevolutionary France," in *Essays in Modern Jewish History: A Tribute to Ben Halpern*, ed. Frances Malino and Phyllis Cohen Albert (East Brunswick, NJ, 1982), 95–117; and Zosa Szajkowski, "Jewish Autonomy Debated and Attacked during the French Revolution," *Historia Judaica* 20 (1958): 31–46.

26 See Schechter, *Obstinate Hebrews*, 29.

> pay an additional fine imposed on him by the Kahal. This does not include litigation pertaining to bills of exchange, promissory notes, or contracts. The matter will be upheld according to the *tikkunei kahal.* Ratified in the meeting room of the Kahal ... 24 Sivan 5541.[27]

With the monarchy on its side, the Kahal acted confidently to secure its judicial authority through legislation and the range of punishments imposed on anyone who dared settle a dispute outside the community. Even so, tensions between the Kahal and Parlement surfaced when several cases involving women, inheritance, and marital property were taken on appeal to the higher court. Efforts to settle legal affairs outside the Jewish community appeared to breach the jurisdiction of the Kahal and the Beit Din while challenging the conventions of Jewish law and custom.[28] But by and large, such cases tended to fall either within the guidelines of communal legislation that permitted certain types of recourse to gentile courts or were specially authorized by the Beit Din. Appeals were either motivated by the need for a legal forum capable of enforcing its rulings or submitted to a higher court following on dissatisfaction with a rabbinic or communal court ruling. All told, disputes brought to the French courts, whether to lower tribunals or to the Parlement, were relatively rare.

The evidence that the state actively disrupted the routine functioning of the autonomous Jewish community and undermined its authority structure may be reliable for eastern Europe but is less convincing in the west. With few exceptions, the absolutist state in central and western Europe respected the leadership hierarchy of Jewish communities and defended their prerogative to govern based on their law of choice. It is nonetheless important to note that there was no forum where the Beit Din or the Kahal could challenge the usurpation of its jurisdiction comparable to that of clerical deputies who assembled in the Estates Général to protest the secular magistrates' abuses of power.[29] Whether the argument concerning the hardiness of autonomy in Metz can be applied to other communities in western and central Europe will ultimately depend on the findings of historians of these areas.

---

27 PKM, 24 Sivan 5541 (page number illegible).

28 See Cahen, "Le rabbinat de Metz pendant la période française," *REJ* 7 (1883): 103–7, 215–16; *REJ* 8 (1884): 257–58; Frances Malino, "Resistance and Rebellion: The Jews in Eighteenth Century France," *Jewish Historical Studies* 30 (1989): 55–70; and Katz, "'To Judge and to Be Judged,'" 450–54. Also see the case of Samuel Jonas Lévi, discussed below, chapter 6.

29 See Joseph Bergin, *The Politics of Religion in Early Modern France* (New Haven, 2014), 75, 80–85, 142–44, 302–304, and idem, *Church, Society, and Religious Change in France, 1550–1730* (New Haven, 2009).

Lay and Rabbinic Tribunals

Options for settling differences varied according to community and region. As a rule, in larger communities there were two main legal forums for settling disputes: the community court and the rabbinic court. In community courts, which could be traced to antiquity, lay officials judged civil disputes and matters of public concern based on principles of equity and common sense.[30] The "courts of Syria," a talmudic precedent for lay judicial authority, was adduced by Rabbi Jacob Reischer, Metz *av beit din*, in his responsum on lay judges. Such courts ruled according to reasoned judgment (*omed ha-da'at*), statutes (*ḥukkim*), and customs (*nimusim*). Their judicial authority was based on the approval of the population that appointed them, even in accordance with general law.[31] Although Reischer was disturbed by the appointment of *dayanim* who failed to meet the professional qualifications set forth in Jewish law, he endorsed the creation of a lay court alongside the rabbinic court much as non-rabbinic courts had been established in Germany, Poland-Lithuania, and Italy to settle commercial disputes. In his view, lay judges could act as mediators, rather than as judges armed with statutes: "The principle ... is that where they [members of the community] accepted upon themselves the authority of one, or two, or even three who are not learned in the law, their judgements are [nonetheless] valid."[32] Reischer specifically acknowledged the jurisdiction of non-ordained judges in cases involving personal property and damages. While his ruling may have been intended to dissuade residents from settling their disputes in gentile courts, it was no doubt taken to affirm the authority of the Kahal to hear certain types of cases and to issue legal rulings independently.[33]

---

30 On early modern lay courts, see Elon, *Jewish Law*, 1:27–28, 31–32; Katz, *Tradition and Crisis*, 80–82, 297 nn. 25–26, 298 nn. 30–31.

31 On "courts of Syria," see BT Sanhedrin 23a and the comments of Menaḥem ha-Me'iri, *Beit ha-Beḥirah*, ibid., and Nissim Gerondi, novellae to Sanhedrin 23a. Solomon b. Aderet, *Resp. Rashba*, pt. 2, no. 290:

> The experts in a town can force litigants to appear before them, but if there are those who are not experts, they can be appointed according to the will of the townspeople, provided this is for the sake of heaven. If they were accepted by the townspeople, then it is permitted, and no one of them can disqualify them. This is 'courts of Syria.'

See Elon, *Jewish Law*, 1:24–26, esp. n. 80; 132–33, esp. n. 174.

32 Reischer, *Resp. Shevut Ya'akov*, pt. 1, no. 137. The original Hebrew text is as follows: כלל יוצא מדברינו היכא דקבלו עלייהו יחיד או שני הדיוטת או אפי׳ תלתא דלא גמירי כלל דיניהם דין.

33 See Reischer, *Resp. Shevut Ya'akov*, pt. 2, no. 143. For sources pertaining to authority of lay judges, see ibid., pt. 1, no. 137; Solomon ben Aderet, *Resp. Rashba*, 2: 290, where justification for a lay tribunal was linked to an effort to discourage residents of a town from going to non-Jewish courts; Moses Isserles, *Shulḥan 'Arukh, Ḥoshen Mishpat* §8:1 and §22:1; idem, *Resp. Rema*, no. 33; and Solomon Luria, *Resp. Maharshal*, no. 93. On early modern

Legal disputes in the Metz Kehillah were adjudicated either by the executive body of the community, the Kahal, which served in a judicial capacity, in addition to performing its administrative and legislative functions, or by the Metz Beit Din. No details regarding the identity of the judges who sat on the Kahal court have been preserved.[34] Public policy issues were the principal focus of the Kahal court, though commercial and family disputes occasionally came to its attention. As a rule, the questions it addressed concerned either the constitutionality of, or infractions against, community bylaws. Most common to come before the Kahal were cases pertaining to residence permits, community employees, election procedures, and taxation, as well as disputes concerning testamentary charity when the community was named a beneficiary.[35] In one instance, the widow of Rabbi Isaac Netter of Bouxwiller hired an attorney who argued that she was entitled to continue receiving a tax exemption and food allowance until such time as her husband's replacement as head of the *beit midrash* was appointed.[36] In a case regarding several women who were appointed as aides in the *hekdesh* (hospice) to care for the sick, the court ruled that they and their husbands were eligible for communal tax immunity. Confronted with the issue of whether the appointment of a non-Jewish nurse to work in the *hekdesh* was in accord with communal law, the Kahal ruled that the selection would stand, though from this point forward the governing council alone would exercise authority in deciding who would fill the position.[37]

In language and style, litigation recorded in the communal register was virtually indistinguishable from cases entered in the Beit Din protocols. The presentation of arguments and judgments in the two registers were nearly

lay courts, see Elon, *Jewish Law*, 1:27–28, 31–32, and Katz, *Tradition and Crisis*, 80–82, 297 nn. 25–26, and 298 nn. 30–31. On the ascription of the status of a *beit din* to *tovei ha'ir*, dating from the tenth century, see Ron S. Kleinman, "Conflict of Interest of Public Officials in Jewish Law: Prohibition, Scope and Limitations," *Jewish Law Association Studies* 10 (2000): 93–116.

34 In Article 25 of the 1769 Takkanot, the Kahal is referred to as a court. See PKM, 45a.

35 Concerning the compensation owed to *shamashim* (assistants) to ritual slaughterers, see PKM, 76b. On payment for *hezkat 'ironit* by someone living outside of Metz, see 74a; regarding a request for a communal tax reduction, see PKM, 87b; on the tax owed on the dowry of a woman whose husband lived in the province of Lothringen (Lorraine) but she did not, see PKM, 95a. For a case concerning testamentary charity, see PKM, 15a, and for similar cases, see 15b, 16a–17a, and 86a.

36 PKM, 66a and 85a. Içik Pussweiler was the rabbi of the *beit midrash* established with a substantial gift by his father-in-law, Moïse Blien. Blien had stipulated that his son-in-law be appointed and that the Kahal exempt him from taxes and imposts. Pussweiler later requested a dispensation on taxes he owed on the Blien estate, and the Kahal found in his favor.

37 PKM, 36b, and 85a.

identical, and it was not uncommon for parties to be represented by an attorney. In fact, a regulation recorded in the Pinkas Kahal stated that if an individual was embroiled in a dispute with a member of the Kahal, the Kahal was obligated to appoint a lawyer to represent him. Occasionally, an attorney who was a regular *dayan* on the Beit Din, represented a litigant in a case concerning a residence permit.[38] Decisions of the Kahal, whether the product of its judicial function or its more general executive capacity, were referred to as a *ma'aseh ha-kahal*, a formulation parallel to the phrase *ma'aseh beit din* commonly used in the rabbinic court register. The term *pesak*, normally reserved for a formal court of law, was also employed by the Kahal when referring to the lay court's judicial decisions. Lay judges who served on the Kahal court were occasionally designated as *shoftim*, a term we may assume was chosen intentionally, so as not to be confused with *dayanim* who sat on the rabbinic court.[39] However, the fact that cases before the Kahal, more often than not, concerned public law underscores the jurisdictional boundaries that distinguished the two judicial bodies and the mutual recognition they each enjoyed.

More commonly, disputes were brought before the local rabbi and were subsequently presented to a *posek*, a *dayan*, or a *beit din* (either rabbinic or lay) for resolution. The type of *beit din* to which litigants turned could range from a standing court to an ad hoc tribunal created by the two parties by the method known as *zabla*, an acronym for *zeh borer lo eḥad* (each chooses one judge). These alternatives were not in fact a matter of choice, since the size of the community, its location, the prevailing legal traditions determined which of the options was most apposite. The records of the Frankfurt and Metz rabbinic courts reveal concern that litigants might go to the general courts if they were displeased with the court's ruling. Frankfurt communal leaders warned that litigants who failed to obey the court's ruling would pay a fine to the community and to the non-Jewish authorities. In Metz, litigants were required to sign an agreement that they would "affirm and abide by" (*le'asher u-lekayyem*) the decision of the court.[40]

---

38 PKM, 57b, Art. 7 and 74a.

39 See PKM, 2a, 34a, 45a, 85a, 86a–86b, and 87b where several cases came before the Kahal in its capacity as a judicial body. For the use of the phrase *ma'aseh ha-kahal*, see PKM, 14b, 24b, 33a, 34a, 39b; for the phrase *torat pesak* (legal decision), for example, see 33a; for *pesak ha-kahal*, see 56b. For use of the term *shoftim* in reference to lay judges, see PKM, 51a, 51b, and 75a.

40 See Fram, *Window on Their World*, 121 n. 51, and Berkovitz, *Protocols of Justice*, Vol. 1, pt. 1, no. 74, 24b, and Vol. 2, no. 571, 119b–120a. Owing to the disjuncture between prescriptive and historical sources, the subject is in need of a new, systematic, and comparative treatment. For now, see Hildesheimer, "Gentile Courts in Ashkenaz at the End of the Middle Ages" and Fram, *Window on Their World*, 50–62.

The Beit Din owed its prominence to its origins in antiquity and to the vast body of talmudic law it interpreted. It was only in the early modern period, however, that rabbinic courts were formally established as communal institutions. While the vast evidence of rabbinic courts assembled by Ephraim Kanarfogel for medieval Ashkenaz cannot be denied, the difference is that rabbinic courts in the early modern period enjoyed greater institutional distinction.[41] In the medieval period there were no formal documents that established rabbinic courts in Sephardic or Ashkenazic communities, whereas the early modern rabbinic courts, having ranged from impermanent to permanent institutions, enjoyed a more official status that was mandated by the lay communal leadership. In an era when Jewish communities and a wide range of communal agencies were duly constituted by the laws of the state and, in accordance with legislation, recorded in public registers, rabbinic courts were authorized, possibly for the first time, to adjudicate the full range of civil disputes, including cases involving commercial transactions, in addition to matters of family law. Judicial authority in civil and family disputes was the hallmark of communal autonomy.

Seventeenth- and eighteenth-century records suggest that, with some important exceptions, fixed rabbinic courts were unknown in central and western European communities until the second half of the eighteenth century. The expulsion of the Jews from most of western Europe in the late Middle Ages had destroyed Jewish communities or left them in disarray. Despite major rebuilding programs that accompanied resettlement efforts in the west, early modern rabbinic courts were slow to regain the institutional standing they enjoyed centuries earlier. Larger and more established communities in eastern Europe offer greater evidence of institutional stability. Communal records east of Prague attest to the ubiquity of *dayanim* who were formally appointed to the office by the community.[42] Communal *pinkasim* referred to them by the titles *dayanei ha-kehillah* (communal judges) or *dayanim kevu'im* (fixed judges).

Conditions in free imperial cities, ecclesiastical territories, and Habsburg possessions were different, however. In 1603, a synod convened at the autumn

---

41 See Kanarfogel, *The Intellectual History and Rabbinic Culture of Medieval Ashkenaz*, 38–84. On rabbinic courts in fifteenth-century central Europe, see Yedidya Dinari, *The Rabbis of Germany and Austria at the close of the Middle Ages* [Hebrew] (Jerusalem, 1984), 119–44.

42 In contrast to the situation in the west, communities and law courts continued to function despite the collapse of Poland after 1656. It is interesting to note that *zablas* evidently functioned in areas where there were firmly established courts, though this may have been primarily for purposes of arbitration or in temporary situations, as suggested by the formation of a *zabla* described in *Pinkas Va'ad Arba Aratzot*, ed. Israel Halpern (Jerusalem, 1945; 2nd ed., ed. Israel Bartal, Jerusalem, 1989/90), no. 21 (Spring 1595).

trade fair in Frankfurt am Main called for the establishment of five regional rabbinic courts, each with appellate authority, in Frankfurt, Worms, Friedberg, Fulda, and Günzburg.[43] The creation of regional courts was part of a larger effort to form territorial rabbinates and to appoint district judges (*dayanei ha-medinah*); regional panels were intended for litigants who wished to appeal arbitration rulings in their local communities.[44] In Prussia, the Jewry Laws of 1722–1723, 1730, and 1750 restricted rabbinic jurisdiction to ceremonial and ritual affairs, and as a result, Jewish courts became forums for arbitration to which litigants could turn voluntarily. If litigants were dissatisfied with the decision of the arbitrators, they could seek binding justice in the civil courts.[45] Pronouncements admonishing community members not to bring disputes to non-Jewish courts were among the resolutions passed by rabbinic and lay assemblies to buttress autonomous jurisdiction. Evidence of increased litigation in non-Jewish courts, combined with new restrictions imposed by the state on the scope of rabbinic authority, is widely taken as evidence that central European rabbinical authority had weakened in the eighteenth century.[46]

Referring to his experience as a judge on the Prague Beit Din and as *av beit din* in Anspach, Worms, and Metz, Rabbi Jacob Reischer reported that *zabla* courts were the favored forum in most disputes because they met the standard of judicial probity. His account of conditions in Metz attests to the fact that the community did not appoint fixed judges but settled disputes by forming semi-ad hoc *batei din*. That the *av beit din* routinely served as the third judge is an indication that a communal appointment as "chief justice of the court" was no proof that there was a standing *beit din*:

---

43 Mordechai Breuer, "The Early Modern Period," in *German-Jewish History in Modern Times*, ed. Michael Meyer (New York, 1996), 1:88.

44 Ibid., 1:203–204. See also Eric Zimmer, *Jewish Synods in Germany during the Late Middle Ages, 1286–1603* (New York, 1978), 71, 96–99.

45 See Alan Mittelman, "Continuity and Change in the Constitutional Experience of German Jewry," *Jewish Political Studies Review* 13, nos. 3–4 (Fall 2001): 71–105.

46 Breuer, "Early Modern Period," 1:253–54. For divergent models of rabbinic appointment and succession in rural and urban areas in northeastern France, see Jay R. Berkovitz, *Rites and Passages: The Beginnings of Modern Jewish Culture in France, 1650–1860* (Philadelphia, 2004), ch. 1. Metz sources suggest that the equation of Jewish litigation in non-Jewish courts with rabbinic decline, or that it was inspired by insubordination against authority, may be an overstatement. For views that challenge the claim that recourse to gentile courts was a symptom of the decline of Jewish communal and rabbinic authority, see Fram, *A Window on their World*, 54–62; Verena Kasper-Marienberg, "From Enlightenment to Emancipation," *The Cambridge Companion to Judaism and Law*, ed. Christine Hayes (Cambridge, 2017), 196–203; and Monika Preuß, *'sie könnten klagen, wo sie wollen.' Möglichkeiten und Grenzen rabbinischen Richtens in der frühen Neuzeit* (Göttingen, 2014), 7–12, 127–31.

> In many communities, even though they had permanent judges, there were numerous cases in which the parties compromised and agreed to litigate in *zabla* proceedings. Indeed, even in those communities that had permanent courts, there were special cases, normally, highly significant ones, in which *zabla* arbitration was the preferred option so that true justice would be achieved.... In our town, there is no fixed court, and we use the *zabla* method, which is the custom of the pious men of former days, and is in accordance with talmudic practice.... *Zabla* is also to be recommended in our days since the town elders often appoint their relatives and acquaintances as permanent judges even though they are neither honest nor worthy.[47]

On practical grounds, Reischer argued, the advantages of the ad hoc court system outweighed the merits of the permanent Beit Din.

Reischer balked at efforts in Metz to create a fixed court, though he could not deny that they had the authority to do so. He maintained that *zabla* courts were a well-established custom (*minhag vatikin*) in full accord with talmudic tradition (based on BT Sanhedrin 23a) and that permanent courts were at variance with the historically more authentic practice. But most of all, he argued that *zabla* courts were preferable on judicial grounds. In his estimation, there was no assurance that a fixed court would be more effective in resolving disputes, particularly when cronyism invariably led to the appointment of unqualified and unacceptable judges. Accordingly, Reischer favored *zabla* courts because, at the very least, the selection of a *dayan* by each litigant would ultimately balance out the other and the result would be acceptable to both parties.[48] The principal difference between a *zabla* court and a community-established institution was a matter of jurisdiction: the former derived its authority from the consent of the litigants (*kiblu 'alayhu*), while the community-established court enjoyed the right to summon anyone subject to its jurisdiction and to compel appearances by means of various penalties at their disposal. For these reasons, maintained Reischer, it was customary to seek a compromise via a *zabla* court when a large sum was in dispute, even in communities where there were fixed judges. He concluded that since the *zabla* format rested on solid judicial and legal foundation (*shurat ha-din veha-halakhah*), the practice should not

---

47 Reischer, *Resp. Shevut Ya'akov*, pt. 2, no. 143.

48 Ibid. Some attributed the *zabla*'s advantage to the balance of views it naturally fostered or to the fact that each of the judges selected by the litigants acted on behalf of the party that chose him, effectively serving as an attorney. See *Encyclopedia Talmudit*, s.v. "Zabla," vol. 11, 685–86, nn. 20–21.

be changed.[49] The east-west disparity in the institutional patterns of rabbinic courts is an indisputably important component of the vastly different histories of communal life in eastern and western Europe. But this would change.

The Metz Beit Din was established as a standing communal court in the mid- or late-1760s, though we do not have precise information regarding the circumstances surrounding its founding. Rabbi Eibeschütz reported during his tenure as *av beit din* that it was not uncommon for litigants to approach a *dayan* to rule on their dispute. By so doing they accepted the judge's judicial authority instead of going to a local court. He cited a regulation issued by the Kahal stating that, in any case involving less than twenty-five Reichsthaler, the *av beit din* was authorized to handle it himself, to avoid unnecessary court costs. The Kahal repeated this prerogative two decades later. Eibeschütz added that, when a case was not straightforward, he would judge it himself only in consultation with the Beit Din, so that "each [of the members of the court] will shoulder a portion of the beam." While it is impossible to establish, on the basis of Eibeschütz's statement alone, whether the Beit Din he mentioned was a standing court or an ad hoc tribunal, references to *zabla* courts in the communal register in 1762 are proof that the permanent Beit Din had not yet been instituted, since it is clear that the two types of courts did not coexist. Until the establishment of the Beit Din as the exclusive rabbinic court of Metz, we may assume that a high degree of judicial discretion was exercised.[50]

---

49 Reischer, *Resp. Shevut Ya'akov*, pt. 1, no. 137. According to Reischer, *dayanim* who were chosen but were not learned (*gemiri*) were still eligible to judge. Also see Bacharach, *Resp. Havvot Ya'ir*, no. 147. Reischer followed the ruling of Moses Isserles, *Shulḥan 'Arukh, Ḥoshen Mishpat* §3:1, that the authority of unqualified judges was contingent on their formal acceptance by the litigants. According to Isserles, "if there are fixed judges in the city, a litigant cannot say 'I will not take my case before them but instead before a *zeh borer* [*zabla*], and so is the custom in our city."' On the disqualification of a *dayan* serving on a *zabla* court because he was a relative, close friend, or enemy, see *Ḥoshen Mishpat* §22.1; Joseph Colon, *Resp. Maharik*, Shoresh 16; and Bacharach, *Resp. Havvot Ya'ir*, no. 2.

50 Eibeschutz, *Urim*, no. 3, "Laws of Judges," in *Shulhan 'Arukh, Ḥoshen Mishpat* §3:3. The following is the original Hebrew text:

אעפ״י וכו׳ מצות חכמים שיושיב עמו אחרים. ואם באו לפניו לדון בסתם בלי כפיה, הוה כאלו קבלוהו עליו ומותר לדון יחידי, כן דעת בעל שארית יוסף (סימן יז) והב״ח (סעיף ט), וכן העיד הט״ז בשם זקינו הגאון שנהג כן דלא כמהרש״ל בתשובה (סימן לה), וראיה שלהם מירושלמי (סנהדרין פ״א ה״א) דמבואר דרבי אבהו היה דן יחידי, ושאלו הא תנן אל תהי וכו׳, והשיב כיון שמעצמן באים הוי כאילו קבלוני, ע״ש. והש״ך (סק״י) צידד כיון דסתם קבלה הוא לדון דין תורה, ואם כן אינו מועיל קבלת ב״ד בסתם לדון יחידי אם לא שאומר בפירוש איני יכול לדון לכם דין תורה, או שהדין דין פשוט למאוד, ודבריו נכונים. ופה ק״ק מיץ תקנת קהל מה שהוא פחות מכ״ה ר״ט שאב״ד ידון לבד, שלא להרבות שכר דיינים, וזהו לדעתי אין בו פקפוק כיון דהוא תקנות עיר וקבלו קהל על עצמם, וכהאי גוונא רשאים בני העיר לתקן, מ״מ כל שאין הדבר פשוט כביעתא בכותחא אני נזהר לדונו יחידי כי אם בצירוף ב״ד כי היכי דלימטיה שיבא מכשורא (סנהדרין ז ב), וה׳ יצילנו משגיאות.

Nearly from its inception, the Metz Kehillah succeeded in attracting renowned rabbinic scholars to serve as chief justice of the rabbinic court and head of the community's talmudic academy (yeshivah). The arrival of Rabbi Aryeh Loeb Günzberg coincided with a new chapter in the history of the Metz Beit Din. Günzberg (1695–1785), the mainstay of the Metz Beit Din during the period documented in the Pinkas, was best known as a renowned Talmudist and author of the celebrated *Sha'agat Aryeh* (*The Roar of the Lion*), which he had published in 1755. Prior to his arrival in Metz, Günzberg served as rabbi in Pinsk, as head of the yeshivah in Minsk, and as rabbi of Volozhin between 1750 and 1755. He remained in Poland-Lithuania until 1764, except for brief periods in Frankfurt and Berlin. He was appointed *Av Beit Din* in 1765 at the age of seventy and was actively engaged as head of the court until shortly before his death twenty years later. While in Metz he published *Turei Even*, a work of *novellae* on three talmudic tractates: *Rosh Hashanah*, *Ḥagigah*, and *Megillah* (1781).

Correlating the jurisprudence of the Beit Din headed by Günzberg with the prodigious legal scholarship he published is an exceedingly difficult challenge; both *Sha'agat Aryeh* and *Turei Even* are works of classical talmudic learning that focus on broad conceptual analysis rather than on the sort of practical issues that occupied the Beit Din. Günzberg's leadership as chief justice of the rabbinic court is a dimension of his professional persona that is not discernible in his published work and is at variance with the semblance of detachment from quotidian matters that is dominant in his writings. The Pinkas of the Metz rabbinic court confirms that the Aristotelian distinction between theoretical and practical disciplines was fully appreciated by the distinguished jurist. With Günzberg at its helm, the Metz Beit Din enjoyed a reputation as one of the foremost rabbinic courts of its day.[51]

For the later communal regulation (in 1766) authorizing the *av beit din* to judge a case on his own, see PKM, 65a. For a reference to *zabla*, see PKM 45b. Art. 27.

51 *Sha'agat Aryeh* (Frankfurt-an-der-Oder, 1755). *Turei Even* (Metz, 1781) contained glosses to several tractates of the Talmud (*Rosh ha-Shanah*, *Ḥagigah*, and *Megillah*) and miscellaneous *novellae*. His posthumously published works include *Resp. Sha'agat Aryeh ha-Ḥadashot* (Vilna, 1874); *Gevurot Ari* (Vilna, 1862, 1907) consisted of *novellae* on *Ta'anit*, *Yoma*, and *Makkot*. Several of his responsa are also found in the compendium on the divorce of Cleve. Further research will undoubtedly reveal more fully whether the distinction between the theoretical writings published by Günzberg and the practical rulings of the court he headed was apparent or real. The Metz court register offers modest biographical detail concerning Rabbi Günzberg and his family, referring to his final illness and following his death when several inheritance issues were in dispute. See PMBD, Vol. 1, pt. 2, no. 87, 23a–b; Vol. 2, no. 513, 104a; no. 515, 104b; no. 531, 108b; and no. 585, 124a. On the

Once the Metz Beit Din came into its own as a public institution, it operated in full compliance with communal legislation and with the confidence of the lay governing body. Its establishment as a fixed communal court yielded several important results. First, the formation of a permanent court fostered a robust judicial culture. In the records of the Metz and Frankfurt rabbinic courts there is evidence of reliable traditions of jurisprudence that stemmed from the standardization of judicial procedures and the evolution of a modus vivendi with the communal leadership on the one hand and the French justice system on the other. The Beit Din was bound procedurally by communal law and was expected as well to comply with the laws of the state and of the city. Consequently, the Beit Din not only held consultations with French lawyers, but on occasion it awaited a judgment from a French court before issuing its own ruling. Second, the process of institutionalization was reinforced by a body of communal legislation that defined in which circumstances litigants were to bring their disputes to French courts and when they were not. The Metz Beit Din was able to rule confidently on the sensitive issue of when to authorize recourse to the non-Jewish courts and when to incorporate general law in its deliberations. It would not be an exaggeration to say that the Beit Din of Metz represents the model *par excellence* of a strong communal court that was highly effective in deterring recourse to non-Jewish courts in the eighteenth century—more successfully it would seem than courts elsewhere. Third, it appears that the belated establishment of permanent rabbinic courts after mid-century accounts for the production of official court registers that date from the 1770s, though in this regard one cannot discount the growing importance attached to record-keeping in the eighteenth-century.

Owing to its firm institutional standing and the prominence of its chief justice, the Metz Beit Din developed the authority to rule with noticeable self-assurance. However, this did not prevent the court from soliciting advice of *posekim* or expert French legal counsel, as mentioned above. To ensure the proficiency of the court, the functions of *dayanim* were professionalized and the scope of their authority widened. *Dayanim* who were appointed to the Beit Din assumed the role of representatives of the community at large, which lent a public character to the court's deliberations in whatever area of law was involved.[52] All told, the Metz Beit Din rendered judgments that enjoyed the

---

dispute surrounding his inheritance, see Simon Schwarzfuchs, "La succession du Chaagat Arieh (1785–1786)," *REJ* 175:3–4 (2016): 309–65.

52 See, for example, PMBD, Vol. 2, no. 538, 110a–110b, for a judgment that sought to ensure that the liability of guardians and their wives would stand up according to both Jewish law and French law. See also examples in cases in which the Metz Beit Din authorized litigants to seek justice in the French civil courts, in ibid., Vol. 1, pt. 1, no. 77.

respect of both communal leaders and halakhic authorities while in full compliance with French law. This was true in all areas of law, whether litigation concerned succession, the protection of minors, the disposition of marital property, or the range of commercial and financial disputes that typically came to court.

Operating alongside the court of the Kahal, the Beit Din was the primary communal forum to which litigants brought their legal disputes. Each case was heard by three judges: the *av beit din* together with two adjunct rabbis. In accordance with standard procedure in Jewish law, three judges heard each case; in most every instance, until Günzberg's illness and death in 1785, the tribunal consisted of the *av beit din* together with two associate *dayanim*. In the course of the eighteen years that are chronicled in the Pinkas, fifteen rabbinic judges rotated on the Beit Din alongside the chief justice. Of these sixteen judges, four sat on the bench for the entire period and several others performed their duties for most of those years.[53] As an institution, the Beit Din was empowered by the Kahal to judge civil disputes that arose among Jewish residents of Metz and the *pays messin* (the surrounding countryside of the Moselle). It was not unusual for the court to hear cases involving litigants who came from beyond the greater Metz region; most wished to resolve commercial disputes and some approached the Beit Din with a request for a permit to take up residence in Metz.

Among the disciplinary measures employed by the courts were fines, the confiscation of property, and the *ḥerem* (communal ban). There is no record, however, of corporal punishment in the Beit Din proceedings during the years 1771–1789. Two types of communal ban predominated: the *ḥerem* (major ban) and the *niddui* (minor ban). The *ḥerem* was a form of social ostracism that occasioned full exclusion from religious and communal life, and the annulment of religious privileges, including Jewish burial, permission to marry,

53 For a listing of the sixteen judges who sat on the Beit Din, see Berkovitz, *Protocols of Justice*, Hebrew volume, Appendix 2. Serving for the entire period were Aaron Ennery (Unrich); Joseph (Yozel) Morhange (Merchingen); Mordechai Levi; and Aberle Picard. Most of the judges were not known outside of Metz, apart from David Disbeck (1715–1794) and Aaron Worms (1754–1836). Disbeck, the author of *Pardes David* (Solzbach, 1786), was a *dayan* in Fürth before assuming a position in Metz as *resh metivta* and *dayan* (1778–1784/5); he subsequently served as *av beit din* in Baiersdorf and in Beirut. Worms, the author of the seven-volume *Me'orei Or* (Metz, 1789–1831), would later serve as a delegate to the Assembly of Jewish Notables and the Paris Sanhedrin; toward the end of his life, he was appointed consistorial grand rabbi of Metz. See Jay R. Berkovitz, "Authority and Innovation at the Threshold of Modernity: The *Me'orei Or* of Rabbi Aaron Worms of Metz," *Me'ah She'arim: Studies in Medieval Jewish Spiritual Life in Memory of Isadore Twersky* (Jerusalem, 2001), 249–85.

and more routine social interaction, while the *niddui* entailed the revocation of the privilege of holding public office, leading prayer services, being called to the Torah, and attending various celebrations. As the primary communal forum where legal disputes were adjudicated, the Metz Beit Din typically met two or three times a week and considered roughly sixty cases per year. These are strong indications of the stability and continuity that characterized the court's work during nearly two decades of service to the community. Equally impressive is the geographical reach of the Metz Beit Din. Litigants came from near and far—from Augny located just eight kilometers southwest of Metz and as far as Frankfurt, which was a distance of 260 kilometers. To accommodate individuals who were unable to travel to Metz from distant communities in the Moselle, the rabbinic court occasionally made special arrangements. Thus, in a case involving the settlement of a widow's claims on the estate of her husband in Metzervisse, to reduce expenses, the local *ḥazan* (synagogue official) was deputized by the Beit Din to administer the widow's oath (*shevu'at ha-ketubah*), in the presence of one witness.[54] Altogether, more than one hundred villages throughout the Moselle countryside and beyond are mentioned in the court proceedings.[55] These distances reveal much about the far-flung commercial and financial dealings of Metz residents, the attraction of Metz as an urban center in relation to neighboring rural areas, and the growing centralization of authority in the Moselle region and in the province of Lorraine.[56]

In Metz, as in other communities, royal and municipal authorities defined the scope of the jurisdiction exercised by the Beit Din. The Beit Din was empowered by the state to enforce its judicial rulings, but within the limits the state placed on the use of force. The use of physical force was not, as a rule, authorized, and severe criminal offences were turned over to the civil authorities.[57] Offenders who committed serious wrongdoings such as fraud,

---

54 PMBD, Vol. 1, pt. 1, no. 76, 26b.

55 See Appendix 4 in *Protocols of Justice*, Vol. 2, 1012–16.

56 Traversing even short distances was difficult and time-consuming. From Thionville to Metz—a distance of thirty kilometers—could take up to six hours by foot. Travel between towns in the eighteenth century was normally via the *diligence*—the stagecoach—which was drawn by either four or six horses and traveled at an average speed of six kilometers per hour. A more comfortable means of travel was the *post chaise*, a carriage designed for two passengers that was introduced in France in the early eighteenth century. For a description of travel in France after the turn of the nineteenth century, see Henry Redhead Yorke, *Letters from France, in 1802*, 2 vols. (London, 1804), 1:20–29. Cf. Michael North, *Material Delight and the Joy of Living: Cultural Consumption in the Age of Enlightenment in Germany* (Burlington, VT, 2008), 27–44.

57 See Katz, *Tradition and Crisis*, 76–77, 86–87. For a fine for humiliating someone, see PMBD, Vol. 1, pt. 2, no. 58, 16b.

slander, or violations of sexual morality, were punished with penalties ranging from fines to the *ḥerem*. In order to accomplish its mission, the Beit Din relied on a range of non-violent measures, including religious and moral exhortation, social pressure, monetary fines, and legal impairments that were meant to induce compliance with its judgments. Limitations on the use of force undoubtedly account for the judicial restraint regularly evidenced by the Metz Beit Din. Consistent with this tendency was a propensity by litigants to resolve their disputes through negotiated compromise rather than by seeking a judgment in accordance with the strict law. Accordingly, parties frequently bound themselves by formal agreement to accept the settlement proposed by the court, as indicated, for example, by the phrase *bererat ha-ẓedadim* ("arbitration agreement of the parties").[58] Other measures employed by the Beit Din, such as establishing the amount of compensation for individuals responsible for supervising the investments of an estate, whether formal guardians or financial advisers, were a type of indirect enforcement that was no less effective.[59]

On certain occasions, the court found it necessary to caution recalcitrant litigants that failure to respond to a summons carried severe legal consequences. In the case of Gershon Coblence, who refused to appear before the Beit Din to settle a dispute with Yozel Cahen, the Beit Din threatened to serve him with a contempt of court order (*pekudat ḥerem*) and to employ unspecified "other forms of coercion." How effective these threats could have been without the backing of the state is questionable, and this likely explains why Gershon remained adamant in his "rebellion and refusal, holding up the words of the rabbis to ridicule." Given no alternative, Yozel sought authorization from the Beit Din to bring his claim to the French court. The Beit Din informed Gershon that it had approved the transfer of the case to the civil court, and following his response that he did not object, the rabbinic court handed over control of the written documentation, in French, to Yozel so that he might sue in the civil court.[60] In a similar case, the Beit Din warned a litigant that by refusing to appear in court, he forfeited his right to take an oath denying the claim, either in relation to their father's estate or to the partnership between his father and brother. Moreover, he and his attorney would lose the right to challenge the note of indebtedness for which his brother sought payment and surrender

58 For examples of arbitration, see PMBD, Vol. 2, no. 620, 134a; no. 660, 146a. The expression *bererat ha-ẓedadim* appears in PMBD, Vol. 1, pt. 2, no. 49, 14a. The Metz Takkanot fixed the text of arbitration agreements and granted lay leaders the right to judge certain cases on their own. See PMBD, Vol. 1, pt. 2, no. 134, 33b. Cf. Ferrand, "Arbitration in Early-Modern France."

59 See, for example, PMBD, Vol. 1, pt. 1, no. 92, 31a.

60 PMBD, Vol. 2, no. 60, 11b.

the right to contest any other claims prior to execution of the note.[61] Warnings that spelled out the legal repercussions that would inevitably follow from non-compliance with the court's directives, though certainly not effective in every instance, doubtless had a deterrent effect that generally kept matters in line with the community's goals.

Fundamental to the question of enforcement was the presumption shared by both the Kahal and the Beit Din that the authority of the rabbinic court extended to the entire range of social and economic activity in which Metz Jews were engaged. The authority of the Beit Din may be subdivided as follows: (a) its authority in its own right; (b) its authority relative to the Kahal qua judiciary;[62] and (c) its authority relative to French law and the civil courts. In a dispute that centered on commercial practices, the Beit Din made it clear that it alone was the arbiter of legal norms. So, for example, it rejected the argument advanced by one defendant that since the purchase he had initiated did not require immediate cash payment, he could take up to a half year to pay "as is customary among merchants." Rejecting the defendant's argument, the Beit Din stated that "legally, his only term [of payment] is the term [set by] the Beit Din, which is thirty days from today, in accordance with the claim advanced by the plaintiff."[63] In a dispute concerning a walkway joining two residences, the building's owner, Feivush Katz, was instructed by the Beit Din to hire experts to determine the cause of rotting beams and sodden stones that were beginning to crack. The Beit Din subsequently ruled that Katz was responsible for repairing the walkway and for removing the materials that posed a danger to others.[64] When outstanding debts remained unpaid, the Beit Din stated emphatically that it would take action to compel delinquent borrowers to pay what they owed.

Although the precise nature of the action threatened by the Beit Din was ordinarily not spelled out, the coercive power to which it referred was not of its own making but originated with the Kahal. Warnings of *kefi'ot u-negishot* ("compulsions and legal actions"), the phrase employed regularly in the Metz communal and court registers, were intended to reinforce legislative

---

61 PMBD, Vol. 2, 12b, no. 69.

62 In the Register of the Council of Lithuania (*Pinkas ha-Medinah, o Pinkas Va'ad ha-Kehillot ha-Rashi'ot bi-Medinat Lita, 1625–1761*) ed. Simon Dubnow (Berlin, 1925), no. 364 (Va'ad 5399 = 1638/9), it is stated that "communal leaders will adjudicate disputes concerning arendas, customs, fines and punishments, and communal *dayanim* will adjudicate monetary disputes. Communal leaders are not to stick their head in civil disputes and *dayanim* are not to stick their head in matters that do not concern them."

63 See PMBD, Vol. 2, no. 204, 38b.

64 PMBD, Vol. 1, pt. 2, no. 101, 26b.

enactments and court rulings. According to the guidelines set forth by the Kahal in 1766, the *av beit din* was authorized to impose a fine of six livres unilaterally, though if he acted together with Beit Din a fine as high as six Reichsthaler could be imposed. Only with the authorization of the Kahal was the *av beit din* permitted to impose a fine above that amount. But irrespective of the amount of the fine, the *av beit din* could neither impose a fine nor take any related action without the authorization of the Kahal.[65]

In addition to the threat of fines, the Beit Din warned guardians to meet their financial responsibilities as set forth in its judicial decision or face legal action either in the community or beyond.

> And now our decision is issued, sanctioned by all the coercive measures at its disposal, that the guardians will uphold all that we, the Beit Din, have decided regarding the expenses of the guardians. And if they refuse to uphold [this], then, aside from the coercive measures that will be imposed on them, here and in Pfalzburg, permission is granted to the relatives of the orphans to take any action within their power against the *apotroposim* to uphold all that we the Beit Din has ruled concerning the expenses of the *apotroposim*.[66]

The powers of coercion that are mentioned frequently in the Pinkas Kahal and in the Pinkas Beit Din were more than rhetorical devices.[67] The rabbinic contract issued to Rabbi Günzberg in 1766 granted him the authority to impose *kefi'ot u-negishot* on those who refused to appear before the Beit Din or to comply with its judgment. Moreover, the contract stipulated that if he failed to exercise his powers of coercion, the *av beit din* would be subject to a fine imposed the Kahal. These coercive measures were spelled out in the 1769 Takkanot, especially in Articles 68 and 71. The *takkanot* provided that the *ḥerem* would be issued as often as necessary, together with stiff fines and other severe punishments.[68]

The Pinkas Beit Din provides details concerning measures of enforcement available to the rabbinic court. When Leima Orshil ignored Beit Din warnings to redeem pledges valued at 1,200 livres, he was declared liable for the difference

65 See PKM, 64b, and in Schwarzfuchs, "The Rabbinic Contract of the Sha'agat Aryeh in Metz," 84, parag. 5. Also see PKM, 14b.

66 PMBD, Vol. 1, pt. 1, no. 36, 13b. Also see Vol. 1, pt. 1, no. 74, 25a; Vol. 1, pt. 2, no. 49, 14a; Vol. 1, pt. 2, no. 154, 38a.

67 For an example of rhetoric, see PKM, 45b–46a.

68 See Schwarzfuchs, "The Rabbinic Contract of the Sha'agat Aryeh in Metz," parag. 16. The contract stipulated that the *ḥerem* was not included among the various *kefi'ot u-negishot*.

between the valuation of the collateral items and the amount he owed. He was also declared responsible for the costs of the *ma'aseh beit din* and the appraisal performed by experts. The Beit Din announced that when thirty days had elapsed following its official warning, each pledge would immediately revert to its owner and Orshil would become accountable for each debt.[69] In another case concerning an unpaid debt related to a longstanding dispute over water damage to the walkway between two homes, the Beit Din stated that "with regard to the debt owed to him [one of the parties], let justice be done between them; that is, coercion by the Beit Din [shall be employed to recover] what he is owed."[70] Hundreds of rulings of this sort were predicated on the assumption that residents of the broader Metz Jewish community—both in the city and in the countryside—overwhelmingly respected the judgment of the Beit Din, pursued justice in the rabbinic court, and yielded to its jurisdiction. To ascertain the degree to which this assumption is correct will require both quantitative data that is currently unavailable and additional clarification how the Jews of late eighteenth-century Metz understood the "pursuit of justice."

Lacking authorization to exercise physical coercion, the Beit Din's leverage was limited to the imposition of certain social and economic disabilities or to warnings of detrimental legal consequences of contempt for the court's will. Moreover, the court could presume that community pressure, when added to its own powers of moral suasion, were sufficient in most cases to discourage defiance of its authority. Ultimately, its authority was rooted in the fact that individuals depended on the community and its leaders for their physical security, livelihood, social needs, and religious observance. Where these intricate interrelationships were either attenuated or became, for some reason, superfluous, the authority of the Kahal and of the Beit Din declined. In one instance, the expression "*she-eino taḥat ha-rabbanut*" ("who is not under the rabbinate") was used to identify an individual who was beyond the authority of the community and of the Beit Din such that the enforcement of the court's ruling was rendered impossible.[71] But for most residents of the community, the authority of the Kahal and of the Beit Din remained unchanged until the end of the ancien régime.

The fact that many disputes were settled through negotiated compromise rather than by imposing Torah law (*din Torah*) may indicate that the Beit Din found itself in a competitive environment where its exclusive jurisdiction was regularly challenged. The Beit Din could at times insist that its judgment

69 PMBD, Vol. 1, pt. 2, no. 81, 21b.
70 PMBD, Vol. 1, pt. 2, no. 101, 26b.
71 PMBD, Vol. 1, pt. 2, no. 225, 50a.

was unassailable; in one instance it stated emphatically that one could not appeal a *ma'aseh beit din* crafted under these circumstances.[72] In some instances, litigants approached the Beit Din as a court of arbitration, a role it carried out through one or more of the following: the crafting of a formal arbitration agreement (*ketav pesher*, *shetar pesher*, or *pesharah*); the enactment of a *kinyan sudar* (lifting a handkerchief to signify the undertaking of a commitment); and the gesture of a *teki'at kaf* (a handshake to seal an agreement).[73] In those instances when the Beit Din functioned as a court of arbitration, it was able to exercise greater judicial freedom, either because the rules of evidence were not as strictly applied or because it was willing to consider extralegal factors of equity more seriously.

Hundreds of cases in the Pinkas involved arbitration, either initiated by the parties themselves or encouraged by the Beit Din. In such cases, litigants were required to affirm in advance, through an act of *kinyan* (an act that formalizes a contractual obligation), their readiness to abide by the court's ruling.[74] A settlement could be imposed by the Beit Din, as in a case of a marital rift stemming from the (second) wife's objection to the behavior of the husband's sister and daughter, or the Beit Din might craft a negotiated settlement, as it sometimes did in the best interests of orphans.[75] In other instances, the Beit Din prevailed upon the parties to accept its recommendation for a settlement. After examining the value of the estate and related documents, the courts stated, simply, that "we persuaded the two sides to compromise."[76]

72 See, for example, PMBD, Vol. 2, no. 310, 57b. The declaration of the Beit Din was consistent with BT Bava Meẓia 17b, though the intent of the Metz Beit Din in this case appears perhaps more unqualified than in the general talmudic usage.

73 See Jérôme Ferrand, "Arbitration in Early-Modern France (16th–18th cent.)," *Legal History Review* 77 (2009): 103–55. In Jewish law, see Asher Gulak, *Yesodei ha-Mishpat ha-Ivri: Seder Dinei Mamonot be-Yisrael al pi Meqorot ha-Talmud veha-Posekim*, 2 vols. (Berlin, 1922), 1:30. The expression *pesher karov le-din* (i.e., a compromise that approximates law) appears once in the Pinkas, in PMBD, Vol. 2, no. 23, 6b. On the introduction of *takkanot* that established rules for the imposition of the law of arbitration, see Robert Bonfil, *Rabbis and Jewish Communities in Renaissance Italy* (Oxford, 1990), trans. from Hebrew by Jonathan Chipman, 220–35. The *takkanot* fixed the text of arbitration agreements and granted lay leaders the right to judge certain cases on their own. Cf. PMBD, Vol. 1, pt. 2, no. 134, 33b, where the Beit Din ruled that the compromise agreement could not be appealed because it had been executed through a formal *kinyan* by the parties to the dispute.

74 See the following examples: PMBD, Vol. 2, 120a, no. 571; Vol. 2, no. 620, 134a; and no. 660, 146a. For the use of the expression *bererat ha-ẓedadim*, which can be translated as "the arbitration agreement of the parties," see PMBD, Vol. 1, pt. 2, no. 49, 14a. Cf. Fram, *A Window on their World*, 62.

75 PMBD, Vol. 1, pt. 2, no. 50, 14b, and PMBD, Vol. 1, pt. 2, no. 51, 15a.

76 PMBD, Vol. 1, pt. 1, no. 14, 9a.

Sources of Law

Rabbinic courts made every effort to rule in accordance with the talmudic and halakhic tradition, but as community institutions they were required to remain in full compliance with communal by-laws (*takkanot ha-kahal*). This hierarchy of laws, and the expanded scope of communal legislation governing consumption, sexual immorality, and the insubordination of youth, certainly empowered the laity, but there is little or no evidence of lay encroachment on rabbinic authority or of the more pronounced expressions of lay-rabbinic tensions noted elsewhere. In Poland, tensions centered on rabbinic appointments, the use of the *ḥerem* against recalcitrant individuals, and communal legislation. At issue was whether the lay leadership could act independently of halakhic oversight. A major rift erupted in the seventeenth century when leaders of the Council of the Four Lands routinely enacted *takkanot* or imposed the *ḥerem* without gaining the express approval of halakhic authorities, a tendency that was strongly contested by Rabbi Joel Sirkes, the foremost rabbinic figure of the day.[77] In Metz, a powerful urban laity legislated standards of moral and religious behavior that were dictated by a staunch concern for social order that drew explicitly on the rhetoric of religious tradition.[78]

The Beit Din rulings drew on several bodies of Jewish and general law.[79] The sources of Jewish law included talmudic principles, Halakhah as codified and interpreted by medieval and early modern *posekim*, and communal legislation. General law consisted of royal legislation, municipal ordinances, parliamentary decisions, and local customs. Traditional Jewish law, based on the Talmud and medieval and early modern codes, is the legal foundation upon which the Beit Din rested. However, with one exception, no texts of the Jewish legal tradition are ever referenced by name in the rabbinic court proceedings; even oblique references to the views of *posekim* or to rabbinic responsa are extremely rare. Nevertheless, the occasional use of a talmudic phrase or of a halakhic argument that presumably guided judges in their decisions offers unmistakable clues as to the sources upon which the Beit Din relied. In a handful

---

77 See Joel Sirkes, *Resp. Bayit Hadash* (Additional), (Korzec, 1785), no. 43. On trends in Poland, see Adam Teller, "The Laicization of Early Modern Jewish Society: The Development of the Polish Communal Rabbinate in the 16th Century," in *Schöpferische Momente des europäischen Judentums in der frühen Neuzeit*, ed. Michael Graetz, 333–49 (Heidelberg, 2000); Fram, *Ideals Face Reality*; and Dean Bell, *Jews in the Early Modern World* (Lanham, 2008), 102–104, 131.

78 Prologue to 1769 Takkanot, in PKM, 76a.

79 On the various sources of French law, which cumulatively came to be known as the *ius commune*, see below, chapter 5.

of cases the Beit Din indicated that its primary objective was general compliance with Torah law, to which it referred as *dat ve-din torateinu ha-kedoshah*.[80] While the precise role of Torah law in the deliberations of the Beit Din cannot be pinpointed, the phrase certainly offers a strong sense of the court's legal and religious orientation.

Lay communal legislation enjoyed the weight of unchallenged authority in the Beit Din deliberations. Referenced in court proceedings by such phrases as *pesak ha-kahal, tikkun ha-kahal, taknon ha-kahal*; and *pekudat ha-kahal*,[81] communal law had bearing on virtually all areas adjudicated by the Beit Din, including contracts, guardianship, inheritance, the division of marital property, partnerships, and support for the poor. In one instance, the Beit Din adduced a bylaw, cited as a *tikkun ha-kahal*, stating that a verbal declaration (*dibbur be-ʿalma*) within the context of a partnership agreement was legally binding.[82] Local customs (*minhagim*) were frequently written into the communal legislation but could just as well remain unwritten, even when the legislation referred to the precise wording employed in contracts. For example, on the basis of local tradition, the phrase *lah u-leyoẓ'ei ḥalaẓeha davka* ("for her and for her descendants only") was incorporated in the text of the *shetar haẓi ḥelek zakhar* promissory note that enabled fathers to allocate one-half of a male portion of the estate to daughters. The Beit Din emphasized that the inserted phrase, indicating the testator's intent to assign assets directly to a daughter and her children, was unassailable because of the acknowledged dependability of the Kahal's community scribe (*safra d'mata*; comparable to the village clerk, or *Dorfschreiber*). Relying similarly on local custom, the Beit Din ruled in an inheritance case that a silver key chain was not deemed a form of

80 For the sole citation of a responsum in the Metz register, Jacob Poppers, *Resp. Shav Ya'akov* (Frankfurt, 1742), see PMBD, Vol. 2, no. 657, 145b, On the general tendency of rabbinic courts not to cite sources, see Eliav Shochetman, "The Obligation to State Reasons for Legal Decisions in Jewish Law," [Hebrew] *Shenaton ha-Mishpat ha-Ivri* 6–7 (1979–80): 335–38. For examples of reliance on talmudic sources, especially with respect to guardianship, see PMBD, Vol. 1, pt. 1, no. 4, 6b; no. 11, 8b; no. 18, 10a; PMBD, Vol. 1, pt. 2, no. 10, 4a; no. 26, 7b; and PMBD, Vol. 2, no. 301, 55a; no. 469, 93b; no. 652, 143b. Overall, there are two general references to the opinion of *posekim* in the Pinkas: Vol. 2, no. 409, 78a–b and no. 462, 91a. For a reference to an unspecified responsum, see Vol. 2, no. 443, 85a. For references to *dat ve-din torateinu ha-kedoshah*, see PMBD, Vol. 1, pt. 1, no. 15, 11a; PMBD, Vol. 1, pt. 2, no. 84, 22b, and no. 136, 33b. For examples of calls for greater latitude than what Jewish law would customarily offer, see PMBD, Vol. 2, no. 440, 84b and no. 632, 137a.

81 For references to communal legislation, see PMBD, Vol. 1, pt. 1, no. 4, 6b; no. 41, 14a; no. 115, 39a; no. 134, 43b; Vol. 1, pt. 2, no. 20, 5b; Vol. 2, no. 182, 36a; 52b, no. 280 no. 335, 63b.

82 PMBD, Vol. 2, no. 270, 50b.

jewelry, and therefore a widow was not automatically entitled to it when her settlement was finalized.[83]

It was not uncommon for the Beit Din to take account of widely observed customs that it considered implied conditions of contracts. For example, on the question of whether the lessors or lessees of a haystack were responsible for insuring that the structure would support the weight of the grain and for cleaning the road leading to the cowshed, the Beit Din ruled that liability would be in accord with prevailing custom as determined by Jewish or non-Jewish experts. Likewise, regarding responsibility for cleaning the street outside a residential building, the court adopted the local custom—in this instance, that residents on the ground floor were normally held accountable. Usages that enjoyed the status of local custom (*minhag ha-medinah*) or common trade practices (*minhag soḥarim*) could, in certain instances, override statutory legislation.[84] The priority assigned to common practices surely rested on the legal principle *minhag mevatel halakhah* ("custom nullifies law"), as stated in the Jerusalem Talmud, though the Beit Din never articulated this reasoning explicitly.[85] Business relationships were governed by the presumed understanding of the parties at the time of a contract's execution. In civil contracts, Halakhah became secondary to verbal stipulations or even unspoken assumptions that reflected broadly accepted understandings. In certain circumstances, such practices were formalized in communal laws enacted by the Kahal.[86]

The doctrine *dina d'malkhuta dina* ("the law of the kingdom is the law") also served as the basis for establishing the conventions that governed such

83 PMBD, Vol. 1, pt. 2, nos. 85 and 86, 22b–23a. The Beit Din reasoned that if the key chain was commonly considered jewelry, it would be recognized as hers; but if it was generally treated as a functional chain, then it would be included in the estate to which the heirs were rightfully entitled. On court scribes, see Simḥa Asaf, *Batei ha-din ve-sidreihem aḥarei ḥatimat ha-Talmud* (Jerusalem, 1924), 99–106. On the "established custom here in Metz" that the person depositing a dowry deducts a third for *ma'aser*, see PMBD, Vol. 1, pt. 2, no. 212, 48a.

84 See PMBD, Vol. 2, no. 25, 6b, and Vol. 2, no. 416, 80a. For examples of the Beit Din's reliance on, or reference to, *minhag ha-medinah*, see PMBD, Vol. 2, no. 346, 65a and no. 620, 134a.

85 See JT Bava Meẓia 7:1 and Yevamot 12:1. In JT Bava Meẓia 7:1 it is stated that the work schedule is determined by local custom, despite the Torah's definition of a day as extending from sunrise to sunset. Attributed to third-century Rav Hoshaya, the principle that custom annuls the law was extended to civil and commercial law. Cf. Moses Isserles, *Shulḥan 'Arukh, Ḥoshen Mishpat* §369:11 and 73:14. For a more complete treatment of the impact of local custom on Jewish law, see chapters 3–5, below.

86 On the Beit Din's inquiry into Jewish merchants' practices in order to determine liability for damages, see PMBD, Vol. 2, no. 133, 27a. On *minhag ha-medinah*, see Vol. 2, no. 620, 134a.

agreements. It is noteworthy that the Beit Din was reluctant to issue a ruling when there was uncertainty about the relationship of such customs to formal law. In a case of an immigrant rabbi, Jacob Frisani, who had received a government permit to reside in Mittelbronn, the Beit Din was unable to judge whether he was bound by all of the obligations incumbent on residents—to share fully in the responsibility to supply *pletten* (tickets for food and lodging) to the poor and, upon his arrival in the community, to deliver the advance payment (*me'ot hakdamah*) to the Kahal.[87] The Beit Din therefore instructed Frisani's attorney to seek clarification from a French legal expert concerning the status of an individual whose residence permit (*ḥezkat ha-yishuv*) was issued by the government and not by the community itself.[88] As in so many other instances, there is no further evidence indicating how the Beit Din ultimately ruled.

The absence of overt challenges to the authority of the Beit Din, at least as reflected in the court register, contrasts sharply with the portrayal of rabbinic authority that has emerged in other sources and communities. Frances Malino found several inheritance cases concerning women who challenged Jewish juridical autonomy in the Metz Parlement and by so doing left a mark on the politics of autonomy in the ensuing decades.[89] Jewish autonomy, as portrayed in the Metz communal register and rabbinic court records, also contrasts with the picture that emerges in Altona-Hamburg-Wandsbek, as noted earlier. Internal opposition to the jurisdiction of the Jewish community was responsible for the weakening of autonomy, while communal controls that were meant to restrain community members within the boundaries of Jewish law and custom ultimately proved to be ineffective.[90] This is not to deny that the situation in Metz was viewed with alarm. For example, Article 17 of the 1769 Takkanot required the *ḥazan* (synagogue official) and the *av beit din* to remind the congregants that those who violated the precepts of the Torah or who did not obey teachers would not be included in the special prayer recited on festivals on behalf of

87 The practice in most communities in western and central Europe was to supply the itinerant poor with billets, known in Yiddish as *pletten*; see below.

88 See PMBD, Vol. 2, no. 119, 24b.

89 See Malino, "Competition and Confrontation," 327–41. For a discussion of parallel conditions in Germany, see David Sorkin, *The Transformation of German Jewry, 1780–1840* (New York, 1987), 49–50. Sorkin asserts that state encroachment on communal autonomy stripped rabbis of their civil jurisdiction, and as a result, Jews turned to non-Jewish courts. In Sorkin's words, "the absolutist states' political interference and mercantilist economics impinged on the Jewish community at the moment in which its religious leadership was least able to respond with intellectual self-assurance and confidence in having the support of its constituents." Conditions in the Metz diverged considerably from this model.

90 Horowitz, "Fractures and Fissures in Jewish Communal Autonomy in Hamburg."

the entire community.[91] The syndics of Metz, for their part, were unwilling to yield on the issues of communal authority and rabbinic jurisdiction. Inclusion in the 1769 Takkanot of a stern warning against bringing a fellow Jew before the French courts—exceptions to the rule notwithstanding—was a clear attempt to maintain juridical autonomy by maximizing social pressure. As in previous decades, the Monarchy and the Parlement were divided in their policy; the king remained the main patron of Jewish autonomy and the Parlement its sharpest detractor. Several years later, the king reconfirmed rabbinic jurisdiction in civil affairs, but the Parlement subsequently limited that authority to instances in which Jews chose of their own accord to submit to Jewish courts.[92] Once again, in 1784, rabbinic jurisdiction was reconfirmed by Louis XVI, only to be subsequently limited by the Parlement to those cases in which Jews voluntarily submitted to the authority of the Beit Din.[93] On the eve of the Revolution, the authority of the Metz rabbinate continued to be deeply rooted in the consent of its community members.

So glaring is the absence of blatant challenges to the authority of the Beit Din, at least as reflected in the records that have been preserved, that the omission could well have been deliberate, in which case the Pinkas Beit Din might be viewed as a political document.[94] Before we can consider jurisdictional questions that would involve the French civil courts at various levels, the balance of this chapter will address the legal foundations of the Beit Din, with particular attention to the sources of law upon which it relied, its functions and authority, and the judicial procedures it employed.

Judicial Procedure

Neither the operating procedures at work in the Beit Din, nor the principles that governed the application of ancient Jewish law in a modern framework, are ever set forth explicitly in the Metz proceedings. As in other judicial

91 PKM, 77b, Art. 17 of the 1769 Takkanot.

92 For details, see Hertzberg, *French Enlightenment and the Jews*, 241–43.

93 See Hertzberg, *French Enlightenment and the Jews*, 237–44. On the warning in the 1769 Takkanot, see Art. 68 in PKM, 79b, published in French in Kerner, "Le règlement de la communauté juive de Metz de 1769," 229–30.

94 On church-state relations in the eighteenth century, see McManners, *Church and Society in Eighteenth-Century France*, 23–25, 157, 196–97, and 361. For the possible application of the community court and integrationist models to pre-revolutionary efforts to sort out jurisdiction over religious affairs, see Adam S. Hofri-Winogradow. "A Plurality of Discontent: Legal Pluralism, Religious Adjudication and the State," *Journal of Law and Religion* 26.1 (2010): 57–89.

systems, the rabbinic court was occupied with conflicting arguments reviewing evidence, and conducting further investigations to clarify the facts of various pending cases. The final decision, or the determination by the court as to which steps were to be taken next, was a critical part of the judicial process.

In more than a third of the cases that were brought to the Metz Beit Din, litigants were represented by their own attorneys. This is likely to have been a commonplace in rabbinic courts in other communities as well. The scope of legal representation in rabbinic courts had expanded considerably in the sixteenth to the eighteenth centuries. Initially, attorneys were authorized to act on behalf of the claimant alone, as set forth in the *Shulḥan 'Arukh*. By the eighteenth century, legal representation of defendants had become a widely accepted phenomenon in rabbinic courts. In contrast to the practice in French civil courts, however, attorneys in the Beit Din were not professional lawyers but were most often off-duty judges or, in certain instances, elected officials or leading community figures. When the documentary or physical evidence in a case was inconclusive and the ruling was expected to hinge exclusively on the testimony of the litigants, the Beit Din could require them to appear without legal representation.[95]

The costs of litigation in the *parlements*, sovereign courts, and royal tribunals were relatively high and the judicial process tended to be protracted, which could cause complications. The substantial costs borne by Jews in the French civil courts increased markedly by the extra expense of paying interpreters and court officers, especially when it was necessary to persuade an interpreter or *avocat* to respond without delay to the argument of an opponent. Often, the

95 *Shulḥan 'Arukh, Ḥoshen Mishpat* §122–129. On the history of legal representation in Jewish law, see Nahum Rakover, *The Jewish Law of Agency in Legal Proceedings* [Hebrew] (Jerusalem, 1972), and Aaron Kirschenbaum, "Representation in Litigation in Jewish Law," *Diné Israel* 6 (1978): xxv–xli. Despite its growing acceptance, legal representation encountered strong opposition in some quarters. See, for example, the critical comments of Bacharach, *Resp. Ḥavvot Ya'ir*, no. 124. For an instance when the Beit Din was unwilling to permit legal representation, see PMBD, Vol. 2, no. 450, 87a. The main difference between a representative and a lawyer concerns the question of responsibility for creating the argument. Is a representative primarily an agent of the litigant or the person someone who crafts and argues the case? In Frankfurt, the latter is more commonly found, whereas in Metz it is mainly the former. In the Metz Beit Din, women frequently represented by an agent who was not necessarily acting in the role of "lawyer." The term *ma'amad* was used in Metz to signify "in the presence of," often in conjunction with the term *morsha* ("representative"). This last term appears about 400 times in the Metz Pinkas, or in roughly 100 cases, whereas in Frankfurt it was more common. The greater prevalence of legal representation in Frankfurt could well mean that litigants in Metz were less affluent than in Frankfurt. It is possible, though still a matter of speculation, that women in Metz felt greater confidence to speak on their own behalf in the Beit Din.

weight of these expenses could delay the collection of debts owed to the estate and occasionally placed these potential assets at risk, as one inheritance dispute reveals.[96] The burden that these costs placed on litigants threatened certain arrangements that had been worked out in the community, especially to the benefit of orphans, and in such cases the Beit Din might propose a solution that could alleviate the pressure.[97]

Costs in the Beit Din were much lower and the court was capable of rendering a decision reasonably swiftly. Likewise, lower courts tended to be less expensive and were, as a rule, more efficient.[98] Even so, there were occasions when the Beit Din required parties to post security sufficient to cover the costs of taking the case and executing a judgment.[99] Litigants commonly attempted to recover civil court costs by including these in the claims brought before the Beit Din; in addition to offering indications of the heavy expenses in the French system, such claims provide evidence of the multiple forums to which Metz Jews brought their disputes. It is no surprise that the avoidance of litigation costs in French civil courts prompted litigants in some instances to work toward a compromise.[100]

As in most judicial systems, the resolution of disputes ultimately depended on the availability of apposite evidence that would enable the Beit Din to render a decision favoring one party or the other. This was true of contracts, purchase and sale of land, loans and debts, business partnerships, accusations of mismanagement of estates, inheritance, and conflicts between husbands and wives. In many cases, if not most, the evidence was circumstantial and inconclusive, particularly when the case involved an unsubstantiated claim that was denied by the defendant. In such instances, several options were available to the Beit Din. The most widely used method to resolve a dispute was imposing an oath on the defendant, and in certain circumstances on the plaintiff. It could be administered in several different forms, depending on the type of case before the Beit Din. Various categories of oaths were employed, as necessary, to address the peculiarities of certain types of transactions: the guardianship

96 See PMBD, Vol. 1, pt. 2, no. 49, 14a; Vol. 2, no. 22, 5a. For an example of the use of funds to ensure prompt action by a court official, see PMBD, Vol. 2, no. 599, 128b.

97 See, for example, PMBD, Vol. 2, no. 462, 90b.

98 For an example of a case that came before the Metz Beit Din on dividing the costs of a judgment in the French civil court, see PMBD, Vol. 1, pt. 1, no. 102, 35a. Cf. Breen, *Law, City, and King*, 379.

99 PMBD, Vol. 1, pt. 1, no. 9, 8a.

100 See, for example, PMBD, Vol. 1, pt. 1, no. 4, 7a; Vol. 1, pt. 2, no. 74, 19b; Vol. 1, pt. 2, no. 199, 46a; and Vol. 2, no. 511, 103b. On the economic attractiveness of compromise, see PMBD, Vol. 2, no. 22, 5a–b.

oath, the commercial oath, the partnership oath, and the *shevu'at ha-ketubah* (marriage contract oath).[101]

Several scenarios were routinely followed in the Beit Din proceedings, each based on talmudic models. If the defendant admitted to part of the claim and denied the balance (known in the Talmud as *modeh be-mikstat*), he would have to undergo what was termed a "biblical oath."[102] This oath—comparable to the medieval *serment purgatoire* ("purgatory oath") that was recognized by the common law—would acquit the accused of the balance after he paid what he acknowledged owing; if he refused to swear he would be obligated to pay the claim in full.[103] Although the *serment purgatoire* fell into disuse by the end of the twelfth century, the Jewish form of the oath continued to be administered in rabbinic courts throughout the middle ages and early modern era.

In another scenario, if the court denied a claim, even if based on evidence that was not entirely satisfactory—for example, the testimony of one witness—the defendant need not take the oath. When the claimant had no proof to rebut a general denial, the defendant would be acquitted under biblical law. However, in accord with rabbinic law he would be required to swear an informal oath—a post-Mishnaic oath known as the *shevu'at heseit.* Though according to biblical law the defendant was exempt from taking an oath, rabbinic law imposed the *shevu'at heseit* on the presumption that no plaintiff would knowingly make an entirely groundless claim.[104] Additionally, it was ordained that a defendant had the option of reversing the *shevu'at heseit* by insisting that the plaintiff undergo an oath in his stead, in order to collect his claim. If the claim was uncertain (*ta'anat safek*), the defendant would be acquitted upon

---

101 Several other types of oaths were also administered in the Beit Din, such as *shevu'at shomrim,* which required the defendant to swear a *shevuah d'oraita* that he was not negligent regarding care for the object. See BT Bava Metzia 5b, and in PMBD, Vol. 1, pt. 2, no. 45, 13a.

102 See BT Bava Qama 106b–107a and Ketubot 18a.

103 See R. C. van Caenegem, *Legal History: A European Perspective* (London, 1991), 93–111.

104 In the view of Rashi, BT Bava Meẓia 5a, s.v. *heseit,* means "imposition" (based on 1 Samuel 26:19). According to talmudic sources and medieval codes, the *heseit* oath would either induce the defendant to admit his debt rather than swear falsely, or would establish his credibility if he were to take the oath. See BT Shevu'ot 40b; Maimonides, *Mishneh Torah,* Laws of Plaintiff and Defendant 1:3; and *Shulḥan 'Arukh, Ḥoshen Mishpat* §87. There was greater leniency regarding *shevu'at heseit* given that litigants were not required to hold a Torah scroll while taking the biblical oath (Shevu'ot 38b). It is interesting that the *shevu'at heseit,* instituted in the time of the *amora'im,* was based on the presumption that "a man will not take legal action unless there is legitimacy to his claim." (BT Shevu'ot 40b). Although it is presumed that defendants would ordinarily not be so brazen as to deny a legitimate claim in the presence of their creditors (BT Bava Meẓia 3a), this argument is ultimately set aside on the basis of the possibility that a debtor might fully deny a claim in order to evade the creditor temporarily.

his denial of the claim, without an oath; if the claim were certain (*ta'anat vaddai*), then the defendant would be required to take the informal oath and then would be acquitted.[105]

The oath required of litigants was a decisory oath that determined the outcome of the litigation. If the litigant who was asked to take the oath proceeded to do so, he was judged to have won the lawsuit, whereas if he refused, he forfeited. What were the religious and social underpinnings of a system that relied so heavily on oaths? The system rested on the assumption that litigants would prefer to pay their debts rather than suffer the severe religious penalty for violating the prohibition against giving false testimony. Equally powerful, perhaps, were the social consequences for an individual discovered to have sworn falsely. The penalties were harsh enough to give pause to those who might have contemplated perjury. In cases of widows who were required to undergo the *shevu'at ketubah*, a reluctance to take the oath was quite common—either out of fear of having inadvertently removed an item from the estate or, more likely, on account of the humiliation and distrust that were implicit in the oath.[106] In the civil-law courts, by contrast, a litigant could be asked to take the oath only when the party who bore the burden of proof was unable to meet a standard that consisted of certified written evidence (such as a notarized document) or a combination of lesser proofs, such as an un-notarized document and the testimony rendered by a witness. Ultimately, it was for the judge to decide which party would be required to take the oath, based on which of the litigants was believed to have pertinent information and on the social standing of the parties.

Written evidence was not required by the Beit Din, however; it routinely conducted investigations into the backgrounds of the litigants, the testimony of witnesses and family members, and statements of the litigants. If these efforts yielded inadequate results, the Beit Din would then resort to an oath. In paternity cases, if the evidence was inadequate to determine if the defendant

105 On *hippukh ha-shevuah* ("reversal of an oath"), see BT Shevu'ot 41a, which raises the question whether the reversal of an oath is limited to rabbinic oaths or may be applied to biblical oaths as well, and *Shulḥan 'Arukh, Ḥoshen Mishpat* §87:11. Also see PMBD, Vol. 1, pt. 1, no. 129, 42b; Vol. 1, pt. 2, no. 229, 51a; Vol. 2, no. 139, 27b; Vol. 2, no. 593, 127a. On *ta'anat vadai and ta'anat safek*, see Maimonides, *Mishneh Torah*, Laws of Oaths 11: 5, 7, 9, 16, and 20.

106 See, for example, PMBD, Vol. 1, pt. 2, no. 183, 42a, and Vol. 2, no. 463, 91b. In such cases it was not uncommon for a widow to willingly forgo a claim concerning certain items to which she was entitled in order to avoid taking the oath. See, especially, the case of Reitzcha, widow of Zalman of Vantoux, in PMBD, Vol. 2, no. 154, 30b; also see Vol. 2, no. 31, 57b–58a. On the reluctance of widows to take the *shevu'at ketubah* in the tannaitic period, see BT Gittin 35a. Also see Samuel Halevi Segel, *Naḥalat Shiv'ah* (1667) (Jerusalem, 2006), no. 18.

was responsible or the object of slander, the Beit Din typically would ask the defendant to take an oath affirming that he was not liable, which would absolve him of responsibility. As a rule, an oath would not be administered in paternity suits unless the Beit Din had discovered the defendant to have an untarnished record with respect to sexual behavior. In a case where a husband accused his wife of theft, she was required to swear that she had removed nothing of her husband's property, and by so doing she was exonerated.[107]

Several procedural details were designed to increase the power that oath-taking exerted over the litigant and to enhance its reliability as an instrument to uncover the truth. One was a talmudic ritual requiring the individual to hold a sacred object (*nekitat ḥefeẓ*), which included either a Torah scroll or a printed volume of the Pentateuch, or to swear while the ark in the synagogue was opened. Although the *nekitat ḥeifeẓ* ceremony was originally envisioned only in cases of biblical oaths (*shevu'ot d'oraita*), the ritual was extended to certain rabbinic oaths (*shevu'ot d'rabbanan*) as well. Whichever the case, the ritual aimed to enhance the solemnity of the oath and its juridical effect.[108] In other circumstances the Beit Din required that the claimant be present when the oath was administered to the defendant.[109] Third, a debtor could be required to declare upon pain of the *ḥerem* that he lacked the funds to fulfill an obligation or that he had not demanded that an oath was taken needlessly. In certain circumstances a *kabbalat ḥerem* was required of an individual who refused to pay a debt he allegedly owed. The *kabbalat ḥerem* functioned much like an oath, though it appears that the violation of the *kabbalat ḥerem* was less severe than a conventional oath. By undertaking the *ḥerem*, a party affirmed his innocence and thereby invalidated the claim advanced by the opposing party.[110]

When a ruling required the subdivision of property or the rotation of living spaces at certain intervals, the Beit Din administered a lottery (*goral*) as the most impartial method of settlement.[111] As in the case of oaths, the parties to the dispute would normally be present at the time of the lottery and personally involved in accepting it as a method of dispute resolution in order for it to

107 For an analysis of parallel issues, see Amalia Kessler, "Enforcing Virtue: Social Norms and Self-Interest in an Eighteenth-Century Merchant Court," *Law and History Review* (Spring 2004): 71–118. Concerning cases that ended with an oath, see below, chapter 7. For the case of a wife accused of theft, see PMBD, Vol. 2, no. 295, 54b. On the thoroughness of the Beit Din's investigations, see PMBD, Vol. 2, no. 221, 41b, and nos. 428–429, 81b.

108 See BT Shevu'ot 38b and BT Gittin 35a.

109 See PMBD, Vol. 2, no. 526, 107b. See Dov Frimer, "The Role of the Lawyer in Jewish Law," *Journal of Law and Religion* 1 (1983): 299–300.

110 On *kabbalat ḥerem*, see *Shulḥan 'Arukh, Ḥoshen Mishpat* §92:11. See PMBD, Vol. 1, pt. 1, no. 52, 16a, and no. 102, 26b; Vol. 2, no. 334, 63a, and no. 541, 111b.

111 The lottery was used frequently. See, for example, PMBD, Vol. 1, pt. 1, no. 3, 5a.

have validity. This is referred to in one instance as *kiyyum ha-goral* (execution of the lottery).[112]

Functions of the Beit Din

As a communal institution, the Metz Beit Din filled four principal functions. First and foremost, it was a judicial body that was the primary, though not the exclusive, public venue for the resolution of disputes among residents of the greater Metz community. Litigants regularly came from the towns and villages of the Moselle countryside as well, and in some instances from more distant localities when business dealings brought them into contact with Moselle residents. Second, the Beit Din performed a wide range of bureaucratic functions comparable to those performed in the French lower courts. These included the confirmation of legal documents and contracts, determining eligibility to receive charitable gifts, the execution of wills, the settlement of inheritance disputes, and the appointment and supervision of guardians. Third, the Beit Din was called upon to interpret communal legislation and its application in matters of social control and supervision that included taxes, charity obligations, residence permits, and consumption.[113] Fourth, the Beit Din maintained a record of judicial rulings.[114] Although this range of functions resembled the judicial, legislative, and executive tasks typically performed by early modern French courts, the Beit Din acted more as an arm of the Kahal executive and coordinated itself more closely with the general policy guidelines set forth by the community's governing body. Furthermore, the centralized authority of the Kahal was more pronounced than that of the state, albeit on a much smaller scale, so that the independence of the rabbinic court was more narrowly circumscribed.[115] In the summary of a particularly thorny paternity case, the Beit Din stated that its ruling was consistent with its obligation "to uphold the bylaws of the community." But since the evidence to establish who was at fault was inconclusive, the court decided to impose the *ḥerem* on both the young woman and the young man. Reflecting on its charge as a public institution and its social responsibility, the Beit Din stated that the purpose of the

---

112 See PMBD, Vol. 1, pt. 2, no. 41, 12b.

113 On *pesak ha-kahal*, see PMBD, Vol. 1, pt. 1, no. 134, 43b, concerning a case of orphans; also see Vol. 1, pt. 2, no. 49, 14a–14b.

114 See. for example, PMBD, Vol. 1, pt. 2, no. 82, 21b; Vol. 2, no. 402, 75b; Vol. 1, pt. 2, no. 110, 28a.

115 Cf. Collins, *The State in Early Modern France*, 15, and William Beik, *Absolutism and Society in Seventeenth-Century France: State Power and Provincial Aristocracy in Languedoc* (Cambridge, U.K., 1985), 226.

law was to guard against promiscuous trends.[116] Though conscious of its own subordinate status to the Kahal and to communal law, the Beit Din managed to exercise more than a modicum of autonomy.

Jurisdiction in civil cases encompassed both adversarial litigation, mediation, and ordinary bureaucratic procedures. The Beit Din heard cases concerning debt collection, disputed partnership agreements, inheritance quarrels, division of marital property, breached marital agreements, slander, paternity claims, and guardianship. At times the court was asked to establish whether there were grounds for a civil suit initiated by a plaintiff; occasionally, it encountered cases of legal and economic complexity, as, for example when the disposition of an estate involved disbanding a large partnership.[117] More frequently, the Beit Din had to determine the legality of various financial and commercial transactions. It responded to requests to validate contracts (*shetarot*) of various types, as in the case of gift contracts, and to confirm wills that had been produced by French civil authorities.[118] In such instances, the court would conduct an investigation to gather evidence and information. For example, the Beit Din was asked to review the *shetarot* prepared by Mordechai Terquem to facilitate the transfer of property to his granddaughters following his death.[119] In another case, it addressed the legal implications of endorsement to third parties.[120] When ruling on such matters, the Beit Din frequently sought the opinion of French legal experts, both to remain in compliance with French law and because commercial and economic convention demanded conformity in the broadest sense. On other occasions, the Beit Din consulted professionals to assess the value of a contested object or conferred with experts to ascertain the technical accuracy of claims presented by litigants.[121] As in the case of merchant courts, the Beit Din understood one of its primary functions to be mediation—reconciling parties to a compromise (*pesher*) they had approved—and its efforts to encourage a settlement followed procedure that was standard in Metz.[122]

116 PMBD, Vol. 2, no. 450, 87a–b.

117 PMBD, Vol. 2, no. 9, 2a.

118 PMBD, Vol. 2, no. 149, 29a.

119 PMBD, Vol. 2, no. 18, 4a.

120 PMBD, Vol. 1, pt. 1, no. 67, 21b. In this instance, the Beit Din instructed litigants to ask two *avocats* whether Loeb would place himself at risk by providing the endorsement himself. If the *avocats* indicated that there was no risk, he would be obligated to provide his endorsement with security, and the other party would give his. But the claimants were not authorized to force him to give his endorsement.

121 See, for example, PMBD, Vol. 1, pt. 2, no. 121, 49b.

122 On merchant courts, see BT Bava Meẓia 83a and *Shulḥan ʿArukh, Ḥoshen Mishpat* §331:1, and the discussion in Elon, *Jewish Law: History, Sources, Principles*, vol. 2, 880–87. For an

The purview of authority vested in the Metz Beit Din extended to a host of bureaucratic functions it was expected to perform in the ordinary course. These included the valuation of objects held as collateral for loans, preparation of inventories of various types (probate, debts, and partnership), appointment of guardians,[123] and division of property in estates. Among its administrative duties were various tasks that included certifying debts; documenting admission of indebtedness made before the Beit Din; and providing licenses that authorized the leasing of property to recover a delinquent debt, as in a case when the property was only partly owned by the creditor.[124] According to community *takkanot*, every ruling of the Beit Din had to be written and signed by the *dayanim* before the judgment could be pronounced in the presence of the litigants and prior to being enforced.[125] Moreover, litigants were to be provided with a written copy of the judgment, which served as documentary proof of a debt owed by one party to another; the withdrawal of a monetary demand or a claim of liability, especially with respect to the accountability of guardians and their heirs in the handling of the estate of orphans (fatherless children);[126] the separation of a widow from her husband's estate;[127] the certification of trustworthiness (*ḥezkat kashrut*) to invalidate unfounded accusations and acts of defamation against women by their husbands;[128] and the exculpation of individuals accused of paternity or promiscuity when the evidence was deemed

example of an effort by the Beit Din to encourage the two sides to compromise, see PMBD, Vol. 1, pt. 1, no. 14, 9a. The term *pesher* can also mean, simply, an agreement by both sides to abide by the decision of the court. See, for example, PMBD, Vol. 1, pt. 2, no. 111, 28b.

123 See the use of the phrase *avuhon d'yatmei* in the rabbinic contract of Nehemiah Reischer, Art. 5, published in Simon Schwarzfuchs, "Three Documents from the Lives of the Jewish Communities in Alsace-Lorraine" [Hebrew]. *Michael* 4 (1976): 9–12. In Metz, the situation was more complicated. The Beit Din did not enjoy sole authority to appoint guardians but shared this function with the civil authorities. See PMBD, Vol. 1, pt. 2, no. 84, 22a–b. Who had the authority to appoint guardians, and what were the legal implications, was not a new question. See the gloss of Isserles, *Shulḥan 'Arukh, Ḥoshen Mishpat*, §290:17, where he added that an *apotropos* who was appointed by the gentile court must provide a (written) record of the transactions in the account of orphans because, according to Rivash (no. 324), this was the procedure according to the laws of gentiles.

124 PMBD, Vol. 2, no. 456, 89b; Vol. 1, pt. 2, no. 162, 39b; Vol. 1, pt. 2, no. 166, 40a; Vol. 1, pt. 2, no. 173, 41a,; Vol. 2, no. 551, 113b; Vol. 2, no. 592, 127a; Vol. 2, no. 382, 71a.

125 The first written evidence of this requirement appeared in the 1720 Takkanot, Art. 5, CAHJP, FMe 139, and in subsequent enactments, such as the 1769 Takkanot, Art. 109, in PKM, 82b.

126 See, for example, PMBD, Vol. 2, no. 260, 49a; Vol. 2, no. 324, 61a.

127 See, for example, PMBD, Vol. 2, no. 283, 53a.

128 See below, chapter 7.

to be wanting.[129] Litigants frequently asked the court to formalize such judgments as a *ma'aseh beit din*, that is, a judgment that attested to the validity of a particular transaction and that could be adduced as concrete substantiation or legal confirmation in instances of contested property. These *actes juridiques* were especially important in cases that might be subject to ongoing litigation before the Beit Din in the future.[130]

In addition to the responsibility it assumed for resolving varied complaints and civil disputes, the Beit Din was engaged alongside the Kahal in wider efforts to regulate public behavior and maintain order. As a constituent agency of the community, the rabbinic court itself was not authorized to set policy; however, it was regularly expected to address legal issues that were pertinent to larger policy questions and in this regard its rulings were clearly useful to the communal leadership. This is especially apparent in its handling of cases of sexual impropriety and in the supervision and regulation of the indigent population locally and in the surrounding countryside. Informed on one occasion that a woman who was engaged to be married had become pregnant, the Beit Din summoned her and her fiancé to ascertain whether he was the father. If the couple intended to marry, the court needed to ensure compliance with the talmudic law that prohibited a man from marrying a woman who either was pregnant by another man or was nursing another man's child until the child is twenty-four months old.[131] At the purely judicial level, the Beit Din was periodically approached with technical-legal questions relating to residence rights and restrictions. For example, concerning an agreement by the Kahal to reduce the *Abzug* owed by Hendele Reise, the Beit Din was asked whether, in light of her and her husband's impoverishment, her brother would be permitted to advance her the sum she owed the Kahal.[132] The court ruled that this

129 See, for example, PMBD, Vol. 1, pt. 2, no. 3, 2b; no. 18, 5a; no. 58, 16b; Vol. 2, no. 495, 100a. On the formula used to express the Beit Din's intention to preserve a written version of its ruling, see, for example, PMBD, Vol. 1, pt. 1, no. 68, 21b.

130 PMBD, Vol. 1, pt. 1, no. 2, 5a. For a case of a request for a *ma'aseh beit din* to confirm property ownership, see PMBD, Vol. 2, no. 497, 100b.

131 PMBD, Vol. 1, pt. 2, no. 205, 47a. See below, chapter 7.

132 The *Abzug*, which had its origins in the feudal Germanic customs and seigneurial practices, required individuals who changed residence to leave to the town and the city that they abandoned a portion of their goods. In early modern France and Germany, the *Abzug* was formalized as a tax that was imposed on any resident of the city or region who had decided to leave, or on an inheritance transferred to a person who was not a resident of the city or region. Taxes, which ranged from one to eight percent, were over and above various communal, local, and royal tax obligations. For an early mention of the Abzug, see René Choppin, *Oeuvres*, 5 vols. (Paris, 1662), 2:118. For references in the Metz communal register, see the PKM, 24b.

arrangement was permissible but stipulated that the funds she received would be for her expenses alone and could not be accessed by her husband. At the same time, the court confirmed the validity of the abatement in the amount she owed annually to the Kahal.[133]

Historically, rabbinic courts assumed the role of protector of orphans, widows, and the poor, and the Beit Din of Metz was no exception. Medieval rabbinic courts looked after the welfare of the disadvantaged and defended their rights, particularly when individuals were unable to navigate the judicial system on their own. The phrase *avuhon d'yatmei* ("father, or patron, of orphans"), commonly used in reference either to *batei din* or to the *av beit din*, epitomized a degree of assertiveness on behalf of orphans—and others in need—that greatly exceeded the range of functions ordinarily performed by courts of law.[134] Likewise, the expression *ta'aninan le-yatmei*—"we [the Beit Din] argue on behalf of orphans"—exemplified the supervisory and paternal function of the rabbinic court as it was understood in medieval communities and later interpreted in Metz.[135] To be sure, efforts such as these reflected a strong commitment to the welfare and interests of the disadvantaged.

Supervision of guardianship demanded perhaps more of the Beit Din's attention than most other functions. The court was responsible for the selection of guardians in consultation with family members and for coordinating the official appointment with the civil court. It was involved in defining the duties of guardians and for imposing legal constraints on them. Accordingly, the court oversaw guardians' collection of outstanding debts and facilitated their contacts with translators and *avocats* in preparation for court appearances when the estate required legal representation. It also administered the legal relationship between guardians appointed to jointly manage the estate of minors. Accordingly, it restricted the ability of one guardian to bring lawsuits and grant discharges, compromises, and time extensions to debtors without the consent of the other guardian. Nor was any guardian authorized to sell property of an orphan without the consent of the other guardian(s) and of the Beit Din. The

133 PMBD, Vol. 1, pt. 1, no. 115, 39a. For the continuation of the case, see PMBD, Vol. 2, no. 199, 38a.

134 See BT Gittin 37a and Bava Qama 37a. For the use of the phrase in reference to the Metz Beit Din, see, for example, PMBD, Vol. 1, pt. 2, no. 184, 42b; Vol. 2, no. 31, 7b; no. 323, 61a; no. 446, 85b; no. 587, 125a.

135 See, for example, PMBD, Vol. 1, pt. 1, no. 103, 35a, where the role of the Beit Din followed the comments of Samuel ben Me'ir (Rashbam) on BT Bava Batra 52a, based on BT Gittin 48b. According to this view, the rabbinic court must make the case for anyone unfamiliar with his own assets, especially orphans, because a person is generally unaware of the (real) property owned by his father.

rabbinic court also stipulated how and where the guardian could hold funds belonging to orphans.[136]

In concrete terms, the Beit Din displayed substantial flexibility and considerable skill in negotiating compromises and exacting concessions from family members, business partners, guardians, and creditors to ensure that orphans and widows would meet their minimal needs and attain the maximum advantage to which they were entitled in any transaction. In one case the Beit Din succeeded in persuading creditors to nullify their lien on property held by orphans, and in a dispute concerning the division of an estate, one party made its agreement to a compromise contingent on the Beit Din's assurance that the arrangement was satisfactory from the standpoint of the young daughter whose entitlement to the estate had been in question.[137] Such cases highlight the confidence the Beit Din managed to gain in the community. When widows and orphans competed for the assets held in the estate of their deceased husband and father, it was not uncommon for the Beit Din to work vigorously to attain a settlement that was equitable to each side. This is evident in the Beit Din's handling of a disagreement between Tzivla, widow of Feivish Levi, and her two daughters. On the basis of her *ketubah*, Tzivla was entitled to all the assets in her husband's estate. The rabbinic court prevailed upon her to surrender a symbolic sum of money to the girls, and in exchange, it offered to exempt the mother from the widow's oath, provided the amount she was willing to concede was acceptable to the daughters. Once the court gained the assent of the mother, it proceeded to structure a detailed plan for the girls' maintenance that would remain in effect until they were each married.[138]

---

136 PMBD, Vol. 1, pt. 2, no. 84, 22a–b. The Pinkas stated here that the *apotroposim* over minors had to be appointed in the *arkha'ot*, and until that was done, it was prohibited to handle anything in the estate of the deceased, even preparation of the *inventaire* was impossible without the appointment of an *apotropos*.

באשר שכל זמן שלא נתמנה אפטרופס בערכאו׳ על יתומים קטנים יד כל אדם אסורת להתעסק שום דבר בעזבון המנו׳ הנ״ל ואפילו לעשות אינוואנטער אי אפשר לעשות מבלי התמנות אפטרופס.

Compare PMBD, Vol. 1, pt. 1, no. 77, 27a. Cf. *Coûtumes générales de la ville de Metz* (1769), Titre IX.

137 See PMBD, Vol. 1, pt. 2, no. 62, 17b, and Vol. 2, no. 9, 2a; no. 22, 5a. For a detailed account of the Beit Din's efforts on behalf of a recently orphaned young girl, Toybe, see PMBD, Vol. 1, pt. 1, no. 74, 24b–26b. The court labored to achieve a consensus among family members by persuading the girl's mother to agree to serve as *mère tutrice* together with her son-in-law as *curateur*. This was envisioned by the court as the best way to collect debts owed to the estate. In addition, after coming to terms with the older brothers, the Beit Din was able to arrange for Toybe to receive a substantial share of the estate.

138 See PMBD, Vol. 1, pt. 2, no. 183, 42a–42b. Also see Vol. 1, pt. 2, no. 21, 6a, and for an additional example, see Vol. 2, no. 229, 42b.

Concerning a dispute over the suitability of the living space occupied by an orphan together with his uncle, the Beit Din paid a visit to investigate whether the physical conditions in the home met the required standard. It also hired a nurse to provide a medical perspective, and two additional nurses to corroborate the opinion of the first. After taking these steps the Beit Din was persuaded that the orphan was not mistreated and there were no grounds for legal action against the guardians.[139] In its efforts to protect the assets of a young girl under guardianship, the Beit Din considered two options. One solution advanced by Metz communal leaders required each of the guardians' wives to subordinate the lien on her husband's assets arising under the couple's *ketubah* to ensure that, if necessary, the ward would have a priority claim against the guardians' estates without concern that these would be depleted should their wives be recognized as first creditors. The second option entailed signing a contract that would indemnify the orphan from financial loss. Since the Beit Din itself was not certain which option was preferable, it advised the parties to consult a French lawyer. That opinion, stated the Beit Din, would be binding.[140] In a case concerning a complicated partnership dispute that was expected to have an adverse effect on the children of the deceased partner, the Beit Din assertively ruled in the interests of the orphans.[141] Similarly, the Beit Din refused to accept the general accounting produced by the *apotroposim* but instead demanded a detailed account in order to know precisely how successfully the guardians had handled the property to the benefit of the orphans.[142]

Efforts such as these reflected a strong commitment to the welfare of the disadvantaged.[143] To this end, the court exploited the natural reluctance of widows to undergo the oath (*shevu'at ketubah*) certifying that she had removed nothing from her husband's estate and did not receive any payment while he was alive. In one instance, sensing a widow's discomfort with the procedure, the Beit Din recommended her exemption in exchange for her agreement to maintain her two daughters, at her own expense, with food and lodging until

139 PMBD, Vol. 2, no. 328, 61b–62a. PMBD, Vol. 2, no. 538, 110a–b, and Vol. 1, pt. 2, no. 36, 11b. For additional sources, see PMBD, Vol. 1, pt. 2, no. 51 15b; Vol. 1, pt. 2, no. 136, 33b.

140 PMBD, Vol. 2, 110a–b, no. 538, and Vol. 1, pt. 2, 11b, no. 36. It seems to have been an established tradition in the Metz Kehillah—but evidently not required—to demand joint liability of guardians and their wives, and this echoed a provision of Metz customary law. According to *Coûtumes générales de la ville de Metz*, Titre IX, Art. 11, 294–95, the property of guardians was mortgaged *solidairement* in order to protect the property of orphans. For an example of a case where this was not required by the Beit Din, see PMBD, Vol. 2, no. 310, 57a.

141 PMBD, Vol. 1, pt. 2, no. 51, 15b.

142 PMBD, Vol. 1, pt. 2, no. 136, 33b.

143 See PMBD, Vol. 1, pt. 2, no. 62, 17b, and Vol. 2, no. 9, 2a; no. 22, 5a.

they each were married, and to provide to each a quarter of her house as a dowry. In a similar instance, the Beit Din was able to grant the exemption from the oath in exchange for a cash payment to each of the daughters.[144]

In certain special circumstances, the Beit Din undertook extraordinary legal measures and interventions on behalf of individuals in need. In one instance, the court authorized a widow to sell two synagogue seats and to collect the full value of her *ketubah*, even though a lien had been placed on the husband's estate—now the property of the orphans—since a portion thereof had been earmarked as a charitable bequest. Selling the seats enabled the widow to remove the lien on her *ketubah* and *tosefta*,[145] in accordance with both Jewish and general law. In another case of a woman abandoned by her husband shortly before their daughter's wedding, the Beit Din permitted her to sell the synagogue seats her husband owned and to transfer a seat he owned in the women's section of the synagogue to the Kahal in order to meet the dowry commitment and to pay the community taxes owed by the husband. To provide additional support for the dowry, the court authorized the transfer of a portion of the funds that had been earmarked in her grandfather's will to pay the tuition of ten students.[146] In several cases pertaining to men who approached the Kahal with urgent requests for funds to help them provide the dowries they had promised in their daughters' engagement agreements, the Beit Din was instructed to apportion the financial burden among the fathers' relatives.[147]

Although the Kahal directed the Beit Din to implement this policy, the court felt obliged to confirm the legality of using coercion to collect charity, particularly in light of certain ambiguities in the talmudic tradition and as understood by medieval interpreters of Halakhah. It ruled that coercion was justified when the targeted contributors were related to the father and when the purpose was to avert the humiliation that the bride would undoubtedly suffer from the delay or cancellation of her wedding. In response to the petition made by Rabbi Aaron Ennery, the Beit Din specified the amount each of the nearly two dozen relatives was obligated to contribute, presumably based on the communal tax assessment. The Beit Din stated: "We have found that the law is with him [the

144 PMBD, Vol. 1, pt. 2, no. 183, 42a, and pt. 2, no. 21, 6a. For an additional example, see Vol. 2, no. 229, 42b.

145 The *tosefta*, also known as *tosefet ketubah*, was an amount supplemented to the standard *ketubah* by the groom to match the amount of the dowry.

146 See PMBD, Vol. 1, pt. 2, no. 251, 54a, and Vol. 1, pt. 2, nos. 146–147, 36a.

147 See, for example, PMBD, Vol. 1, pt. 1, no. 42, 14b; Vol. 1, pt. 2, no. 47, 13b; Vol. 2, no. 106, 21b; and no. 120, 24b–25a. Also see the register of Metz wills, Arch. JTSA, ms. 9835. Cf. Hardwick, *Family Business*, 24–36.

father], that relatives are [to be] coerced to give charity, especially for a matter as important as providing a dowry for a poor bride, so that she will not suffer embarrassment." Justification for coercion in this case rested on the premise that the inability of the bride's father to meet his obligation would be the cause of her mortification. The plight of poor brides who received distributions from the Hakhnassat Kallah society was another matter however, and relatives of indigent brides were not subjected to coercive measures.[148] All told, the Pinkas is filled with scores of examples illustrating the Beit Din's energetic efforts urging compromise and generosity to benefit those whose weaknesses had been exposed or had become vulnerable to life's vicissitudes.[149]

As an advocate for the needy, the Beit Din assumed responsibility for managing the legal issues related to charitable giving. It regulated the delivery of philanthropic services that were strained by the large number of beggars[150] and oversaw the relief that confraternities provided to the poor, particularly when complications internal either to the organization's administration or to its ethos demanded the court's expertise. In one instance two arbitrators from the Hakhnassat Kallah Society approached the Beit Din concerning a member who threatened to resign over a policy dispute and forcefully remove the society's minute-book from its meeting room in protest. The Beit Din ruled that, in accordance with the confraternity's bylaws, the irate member was required to pay a fine if his resignation was final, but it absolved him of responsibility for a second fine for his act of defiance.[151] In nearly a dozen cases, the Beit Din handled inquiries concerning the practice of supplying the itinerant poor with *pletten* (billets), that provided poor travelers meals and lodging in the community. Questions ranged from the basis upon which the *pletten* obligations were allocated to each resident to how to sanction individuals who refused to share

148 PMBD, Vol. 1, pt. 2, no. 47, 13b. Cf. Halperin, ed., *Takkanot Medinat Mehrin* (Jerusalem, 1952), 56, no. 174, where the demand on relatives was formulated somewhat differently. On the use of legal coercion to collect charity, see the discussion of pertinent halakhic sources in Berkovitz, "Jewish Philanthropy in Early Modern and Modern Europe," 96–97. Wilma Pugh argues that bequests to poor relatives or to servants ought to be understood as the fulfillment of a personal obligation rather than as anonymous charity. Cf. W. J. Pugh, "Catholics, Protestants and Testamentary Charity in Seventeenth-Century Lyon and Nîmes," *French Historical Studies* 9 (1980): 479–504.

149 In response to a request by Aaron of Steinbiedersdorf, an octogenarian in need of financial assistance, the Beit Din assessed three relatives the weekly sum of ten sous each, which they could deduct from their *ma'aser* contribution, if they so desired. See PMBD, Vol. 2, 18a, no. 90. See PMBD, Vol. 1, pt. 1, no. 95, 32a; Vol. 1, pt. 2, no. 14, 4b; pt. 2, no. 51, 15b; Vol. 2, no. 503, 101b–102a.

150 See PMBD, Vol. 2, 29a no. 148.

151 See PMBD, Vol. 1, pt. 2, 16b, no. 58.

the responsibility. In at least one case the Beit Din considered the obligation of heirs to fulfill their father's unredeemed *pletten* obligations. The Beit Din ruled that the requirement to purchase *pletten* was a condition of residence and was equivalent to the obligation to pay communal taxes.[152] Resistance to the obligations associated with poor relief invariably surfaced among those who believed that assessments of wealth were too high. Cases of discontent with the *pletten* system, resulting in a refusal to share the burden, tended to occur more frequently in the surrounding villages—as in the cases of Louvigny, Lichtingen, and Augny—where the economy was more modest than in urban areas such as Metz proper.[153]

Policy differences on how to address the problem of poverty surfaced on occasion. In 1772 several members of a philanthropic confraternity that provided clothing to poor school children threatened to resign unless the organization agreed to use a more reliable method to identify suitable recipients of assistance. Beyond addressing the legal question of whether funds collected for one charitable purpose could be transferred to another, the case summary offers a graphic depiction of poverty in Metz. Some of the poor, it was reported, did not even have sufficient clothing to cover themselves.[154] Rabbinic court records also indicate how unusually heavy tax burdens or financial ruin resulting from economic reversals left some community members living in extremely modest circumstances. In fact, the experiences of some litigants correspond to Glikl Hameln's accounts of the spectacular rise of certain merchants and the catastrophic collapse of others. Even hints of moral and religious tension are occasionally evident in the dry legal arguments recorded by the Beit Din.

The important role of the rabbinic court in clarifying the legal parameters of social welfare was consistent with its standing as the community's supreme judicial body. Accordingly, the Beit Din was regularly approached with requests to settle disputes between the Kahal, either as plaintiff or defendant, and individual community members. On several occasions, the Kahal submitted an issue for consideration by the Beit Din to verify that an action it wanted to take was legally justified. For example, the Kahal approached the Beit Din to determine if it could sell the books it held as collateral on a loan it had extended several years earlier (that was now past due) to Moïse May, owner of the

---

152 See PKM, 81a, Art. 91 of 1769 Takkanot, and PMBD, Vol 1, pt. 1, no. 20, 10b; Vol. 2 no. 7, 2a; no. 71, 13a; and no. 148, 29a.

153 See PMBD, Vol. 1, pt. 1, no. 20, 10b, and Vol. 2, no. 71, 13a. For additional sources on charitable giving, see PMBD, Vol. 1, pt. 2, no. 191, 45a; PMBD, Vol. 1, pt. 1, no. 50, 15b, and Vol. 1, pt. 2, no. 6, 3a; PMBD, Vol. 2, no. 228, 42b.

154 See PMBD, Vol. 1, pt. 1, no. 50, 15a. Cf. a case regarding the Hakhnassat Kallah Society, PMBD, Vol. 1, pt. 2, no. 58, 16b.

Metz Hebrew press, in order to help the proprietor weather a financial crisis.[155] Some cases were contract disputes. In one instance, the Kahal sued a member of the community, Eisik Schweich, for increasing the height of a separation wall between the courtyard of his home and the courtyard outside the new women's section of the synagogue; the Kahal claimed that the wall exceeded the height stipulated in the original purchase agreement. The Beit Din ruled in favor of the Kahal and that Schweich bring the wall into compliance with the terms in the contract.[156] Similarly, a case concerning the purchase of a house previously owned by the Kahal came before the Beit Din. The Kahal sued for violation of a condition in the purchase and sale agreement stipulating that neither the buyer nor his heirs would ever maintain a horse stable or cowshed on the premises. Again the Beit Din ruled in favor of the Kahal.[157]

Regardless of which party prevailed, when the Beit Din was approached on such matters, at least in those cases in which the Kahal subjected itself to the authority of the rabbinic court, it was cast in the role of arbiter of communal norms. The Beit Din assumed this important public function even in disputes between private parties where the Kahal itself was not directly implicated. For example, when a young woman became pregnant before her wedding, the father of the bride threatened to impound the funds that the groom's father deposited with a third party, The Kahal was uncertain how to proceed and turned the case over to the Beit Din. The rabbinic court reviewed the evidence, studied a responsum produced by the rabbi of Niedernai, and considered several procedural irregularities before ruling that the groom could acquit himself by taking an oath that would entitle him to the reimbursement of the disputed funds.[158] Similarly, the Beit Din's role as the community's highest judicial body was in evidence when it was asked to judge several disputes between neighbors to determine whether a resident was liable for violations of privacy law.[159] Not infrequently, the range of issues treated in various types of litigation drew

---

155 PMBD, Vol. 1, pt. 1, no. 122, 40b. May was unable to overcome his financial difficulties and was forced to leave Metz for Germany. Several years later, in 1775, his son-in-law, Goudchaux Spire Levy, reopened the press. See Guillaume Ferdinand Teissier, *Essai philologique sur les commencemens de la typographie à Metz* (Metz, 1828), and Noé Gruss, "L'imprimérie hébraïque en France (XVIe–XIXe siecles)," *REJ* 125 (1966): 77–91.

156 PMBD, Vol. 2, no. 189, 36b.

157 PMBD, Vol. 2, no. 89, 17b. For cases where the Beit Din ruled against the Kahal, see below.

158 PMBD, Vol. 2, no. 443, 85a. The oath in question was akin to the *serment purgatoire*; see above, and Van Caenegem, *Legal History: A European Perspective*, 93–111.

159 See, for example, PMBD, Vol. 1, pt. 2, no. 167, 40a. On the general issue of privacy within the framework of Jewish law, see Nahum Rakover, "Privacy: Injury Caused by Unwanted Observation," *Jewish Law Association Studies* 14 (2004): 221–34.

attention to the larger question of the relationship of the Beit Din to the community leadership and communal legislation.[160]

Efforts to regulate communal norms were closely related to the role the Beit Din assumed in deciding questions of public policy, including the legality of certain constitutional issues. On occasion, the rabbinic court was asked to rule on the eligibility of individuals to serve as *parnasim* (syndics). In one instance, the guardians of the orphans of Seligmann Wittersheim asked the court to judge the suitability of *parnasim* to sit in judgment on matters pertaining to them. Citing a Metz *takkanah* that disqualified judges either based on their familial relationship to the litigants or on account of personal antagonism to them, the guardians argued that the *parnasim* were ineligible because of a conflict of interest. The Kahal responded that the *takkanah* applied only in situations where *parnasim* were approached by litigants and asked to judge in matters involving individuals. When a case pertained to the Kahal itself, so it was argued, it was impractical to disqualify *parnasim* and to select community members who might lack the requisite expertise in communal law and customs. Upon careful review of the *takkanah*, the Beit Din rejected the argument advanced by the Kahal. It ruled that either family relations or personal antipathy were indeed grounds for disqualification under any circumstances, and that the *parnasim* in question were therefore ineligible to sit in judgment of the two guardians.[161] In the view of the Beit Din, then, the Kahal in its judicial capacity was required without exception to abide by the rules and conventions of a rabbinic court.

Disagreements between the Kahal and individuals over communal policy were also brought before the Beit Din. In one instance, the Kahal was rebuffed when it sought legal support for its position regarding attendance at a synagogue established in the home of the late financier, David Terquem. Creation of the small synagogue had been authorized by the *av beit din* and recorded in the Pinkas Kahal. So that attendance at the main synagogue would not be adversely affected, the number of worshippers was limited to sixteen householders, in addition to a cantor and a beadle. At issue was the question of who

160 For examples of cases that went from the Kahal to the Beit Din, see PKM, 55a and PMBD, Vol. 1, pt. 1, no. 115, 39a.

161 The *takkanah* was recorded in PKM, 88b. For the case that came before the court, see PMBD, Vol. 2, 78b, no. 410. For an election query brought to the Beit Din by the Kahal in 1774 on the eligibility of two men whose wives were cousins, see PKM, 99a. For a discussion of the legal issues concerning the disqualification of communal officials on account of conflict of interests—whether familial, personal, or economic—and its derivation from the ineligibility of judges for similar reasons, see Kleinman, "Conflict of Interest of Public Officials in Jewish Law."

would decide which worshippers could attend the Terquem synagogue. The Kahal claimed it had that authority, whereas Terquem's son argued that his father had reserved the right to select the worshippers himself and that this remained a prerogative of the family. In the end, the Beit Din ruled that the Kahal did not enjoy the right to choose the worshippers and further, that no worshipper could be excluded for lack of a residential permit.[162] In a case pertaining to a testamentary gift, the Kahal asked the Beit Din to rule on its right to exercise control of the funds, in accord with its own judgment, against the wishes of the heirs. The Beit Din confirmed that the Kahal had the authority to alter the use of the gift so long as the goal was consistent with, if not identical to, the will of the testator.[163]

On occasion, the Beit Din served as the legal forum where accusations of malfeasance or negligence could be leveled against the Kahal. In a dispute over the fulfillment of the terms of a trust set forth in the will of Moise Blien, the testator's son-in-law, Seligmann Wittersheim accused the Kahal of failing to maintain on an annual basis, as agreed, three poor Alsatian students who had been selected to study in the *beit midrash* created by Blien. After investigating the historical record, the Beit Din rejected Wittersheim's demand for payment of 1,500 livres—the amount allegedly not disbursed by the Kahal for student support during the fifteen years since the trust was established. The evidence showed that the Kahal had acquitted itself properly in discharging its obligation and was therefore exonerated of any fiduciary responsibility. At times questions arose concerning the performance of individual *parnasim*. When two *parnasim* in Vallières-Les Bordes were suspected of mismanaging the debts and expenses associated with the estate of a deceased community member, it was the Beit Din that proceeded to remedy the problem. After issuing repeated warnings to the suspect *parnasim*, it appointed a *dayan* to supervise the handling of the estate and to reestablish trust among the heirs and beneficiaries of the will.[164]

In certain circumstances, a judicial ruling of the Beit Din could serve as the basis for a policy reassessment by the Kahal. A Metz resident died while traveling in the countryside of Lorraine, and in a departure from standard practice in the province, members of the community nearest to where the death occurred refused to assume the cost of burial and interment, and then shipped

162 PMBD, Vol. 2, no. 13, 3a.

163 PMBD, Vol. 1, pt. 2, no. 20, 5b. The case concerned the Grumbach estate, which is discussed below, chapter 6.

164 PMBD, Vol. 2, no. 92, 18b1. Concerning the *parnasim* in Vallières-Les Bordes, see PMBD, Vol. 2, no. 368, and no. 371, 69a.

the corpse to Metz for burial. After burying the deceased locally, the Metz Kahal turned to the Beit Din, seeking guidance on how to respond in similar circumstances in the future. The Beit Din ruled that the residents of Lorraine were obliged to bury whoever died in the province, whether a resident or a wayfarer, in their own cemetery and to absorb all related expenses. This obligation was understood to be in conformity with the talmudic dictum stating that a deserted corpse (*met mitzvah*) should be buried in the place where he has died. The Beit Din commented further that if, after its ruling was made public through its conveyance to the rabbi of Nancy, members of Lorraine communities continued to send corpses to Metz and remained unwilling to defray the costs of the burial plot and other accompanying expenses, the Kahal had the right to return those corpses to communities from whence they came. In its advisory capacity, the Beit Din guided community leaders in setting policy for far-flung communities.[165]

Disputes that were directed to the Metz Beit Din by communities in outlying towns and villages confirm the expansive authority of the rabbinic court and the pivotal role it played in the Moselle countryside. In one instance, the Beit Din upheld the right of a resident of Louvigny, which was twenty-two kilometers south of Metz, to block the community's plan to increase taxes to assist the poor and to meet other communal needs so long as a new valuation was not performed. Likewise, it sustained the objection of longstanding members of three communities located several kilometers from Metz—Vantoux, Vallières-Les Bordes, and Mey—to make additional contributions to the building fund of a new synagogue if they were the owners of seats purchased earlier. Furthermore, the court called attention to the payment schedule, set out in detail in each of the respective community *pinkasim*, that was intended to ensure the fulfillment of the obligations required of all community members. Any resident who failed to meet these obligations and other commitments related to synagogue honors was to be disciplined with coercive measures imposed by the *parnasim* and *gaba'im*, including the denial of eligibility to be called to the Torah so long as an obligation remained unpaid. The Beit Din also offered detailed directives concerning the building plan, which included

165 PMBD, Vol. 2, no. 301, 55a. On the status of the *met mitzvah* and the priority assigned to it in Jewish law, see BT Sanhedrin 47b. For background to this ruling, see René Weiner, "L'ancien cimetière juif de Nancy," *Bulletin mensuel de la société d'archéologie lorraine et du Musée historique lorrain* (1912): 84–87. No authorization for the establishment of a Jewish cemetery in the environs of Nancy was granted before Louis XVI issued *lettres patentes* to this effect in November 1787. Until then, options for Jewish burial in the Lorraine were quite limited. On conflicts between the Metz Kehillah and the outlying communities in the province, including Nancy, see Szajkowski, *Jews and the French Revolutions*, 673–78.

the construction of a room where the Kahal would eventually meet. The community assembly room was to be built in the garden on the south side of the synagogue, and until it was erected, the *parnasim* were under orders to plant vegetables on that parcel of land.[166]

Vested with wide-ranging judicial powers, the Beit Din exercised an abiding influence on the self-governing communal structure. Its efforts reinforced the jurisdiction of the Kahal in matters of public law—in Metz and throughout the Moselle. Likewise, the Kahal provided the Beit Din with institutional support and a measure of independence that accounts for the substantial authority it enjoyed among members of the community. Both the Kahal and the Beit Din, while profiting from advancing centralization in France and in western Europe, exemplify the perspective articulated by James Boyd White concerning the crucial role of the law in shaping the contours of communal life: "Law is the central art by which culture and community [are] established, maintained, and transformed."[167] Rooted in the law—both at the level of policy and judicial practice—the all-encompassing efforts to regulate communal life continued steadfastly until the very end of the ancien régime—virtually undeterred by the fact that Metz Jews had become embedded in the surrounding social, cultural, and political landscape.

---

166 See PMBD, Vol. 1, pt. 1, no. 20, 10b. PMBD, Vol. 2, no. 631, 137a.

167 See Simon Schwarzfuchs, "Takkanot of the Jewish Community of Augny, Adjacent to Metz (1767)" [Hebrew], *Asufot* 8 (1994): 387–98. On centralization in Alsace and Lorraine in the 1770s, see Berkovitz, *Rites and Passages*, 53–54. For the quotation by James Boyd White, see his *Heracles' Bow: Essays on the Rhetoric and the Poetics of Law* (London, 1985), 28.

CHAPTER 5

Navigating the Challenges of Multiple Jurisdictions

In the course of the eighteenth century, Jewish residents of Metz and of the *pays messin* had come to share the most basic assumptions and general habits of mind that prevailed in the larger society in which they lived.[1] This was true in a broad, cultural sense for legal professionals and legal consumers alike. As the case of the Jews singularly demonstrate, legal sources can be uniquely helpful in determining the degree of a group's participation in the deep structures of the general society. Notwithstanding the resistance commonly shown to individuals regarded as alien to the majority culture,[2] the Jews, as any minority, were dependent on the larger economy for their livelihood. They met their everyday needs by either purchasing or relying on routine services provided by bureaucrats, professionals, and craftsmen. Through interactions of this sort, however limited in scope, Jews formed an incontestable attachment to general society that was manifested in occasional recourse to the local justice system and in elements of the larger legal culture that Jews absorbed. This was a natural consequence of the diasporic condition wherever Jews resided, though it varied widely in accordance with local forces.

Communal autonomy conferred substantial latitude on Jews and other self-governing bodies to manage their own judicial affairs free of excessive government interference, provided they remained within the general legal boundaries defined by the monarchy. This tacit agreement mediated the natural tension between fulfillment of Jewish ritual and civil law, on the one hand, and compliance with the law of the land, on the other. How rabbinic courts handled the challenges posed by multiple legal frameworks depended on a host of social and political factors that were peculiar to each region or city in which Jews lived. The Metz Beit Din, like the Metz Kahal, learned to navigate between the systems of Jewish and French civil law.

The French legal culture in which the Jewish community existed was shaped by the convergence of four distinct streams of medieval law. These included Roman law, as contained in Justinian's Corpus Juris Civilis and amended by

1 Habits of mind, or habitus, which "orients actions and inclinations," is created by an interplay between social structures and individual choice. See Pierre Bourdieu, *Distinction: A Social Critique of the Judgement of Taste* (London, 1984).

2 For a similar perspective with respect to ecclesiastical lawyers in medieval England, see Richard Helmholz "Conflicts between Religious and Secular Law: Common Themes in the English Experience, 1250–1640," *Cardozo Law Review* 12 (1990): 707–28.

 DOI:10.1163/9789004417403_007

glossators and commentators in the Italian universities; customary (local) law; canon law; and merchant law. Together, three of these rivulets (excluding canon law) came to be known as the *ius commune*. Not to be confused with the common law of England, the *ius commune* in France, Spain, and other European states shared a common core of legal principles, especially its partiality for codification.

The legal map of France was divided into two regions—north and south of the Loire—along a line extending from Geneva to La Rochelle. The South, *le pays de droit écrit*, was governed by Roman law that was accepted as the customary law; the North, *le pays de coûtumes*, representing about two-thirds of the kingdom, was governed by local and provincial customs.[3] Historically, ecclesiastical law had governed marriage and family matters, inheritance, and religious life. Property disputes and criminal matters were largely under the jurisdiction of the secular courts. But the jurisdictional boundaries separating ecclesiastical and civil courts were not always so clearly defined, especially in marital and inheritance disputes involving property. Complicating this not-so-neat division of the realms of religious and civil law was the fact that France was, in the words of Julie Hardwick, "an overlapping multi-layered patchwork of jurisdictions and law codes where local regulations existed alongside national ones."[4] Widely contending hegemonic claims in a single polity were made by judicial bodies representing the interests of royal and municipal authorities, civil and ecclesiastical legal traditions, corporate groups, and written and customary law. Jurisdictional clashes were frequent and hard fought.[5]

Early modern jurists sought to synthesize customary laws through jurisprudence and royal legislation. Beginning in the late Middle Ages and over the next several centuries, custom was gradually transformed into customary law through the process of redaction and reform. In 1453 Charles VII issued a decree calling for an official compilation of the customs of the kingdom. In roughly the same period, the *parlements* in the South adopted Roman law

3 It has been argued that the competence and respectability of lawyers were promoted by the revival of Roman law. See William J. Bouwsma, "Lawyers and Early Modern Culture," *American Historical Review* 78:2 (April 1973): 310, where it is maintained that the conservatism of lawyers enabled them to act as agents of change.

4 The quote is from Julie Hardwick, *The Practice of Patriarchy: Gender and the Politics of Household Authority* (University Park, PA, 1998), 51. Cf. Hardwick, *Family Business*, 61. On the history of jurisdictional conflicts, also see Parker, "Sovereignty, Absolutism and the Function of the Law in Seventeenth-Century France," 36–74.

5 See Harold Berman, *Law and Revolution, The Formation of the Western Legal Tradition* (Cambridge, 1985), 10, where it suggested that the pluralism of Western law could exacerbate political and economic conflicts while also serving to resolve them.

in preference to customary rules, whereas in the North the *parlements* tended to assimilate local customs.

The consolidation of local customs assured their preservation, but the intended political goal was to advance the supremacy of enacted law. As customs became *ius scriptum*, the emergence of customary law was a vital stage in the transition to legal unification. The binding force of custom derived from the king's legislative authority, which was the decisive factor in the development of law. During Louis XV's reign, the orientation toward local customs and autonomy was decidedly more positive than under his great grandfather, Louis XIV, though royal law took precedence whenever customary law was silent. The codification of customs through their replacement with statutory laws enacted by a central authority was a significant step in overcoming regional divisions.[6] Nevertheless, it was in the interest of the monarchy to preserve customary laws because local self-governance was a strategic asset in the royal administration. The absolutist state could hardly deny the legitimacy of customary law throughout the regime, especially in the areas of contracts, inheritance, and guardianship. This was a political strategy aimed at strengthening the central authority of the state, but not with the intention of vitiating local customs.[7]

By the end of the following century, jurisprudence, which contained both customary and Roman elements, had emerged as a legitimate source of law. Most compendia of customs were not compiled until the sixteenth century, when a total of sixty general customals and three hundred special customals were assembled. These were often revised in light of Roman law. Upon their official compilation in a written corpus, lawyers extracted general principles of French law that became known as the Common Customary Law of France. Supplementing the customary laws were royal ordinances that became important in the sixteenth and seventeenth centuries. From this point forward, each province in France would have its own legal code, making it unnecessary to prove the legitimacy of customs.[8]

The French viewed the *ius civile* as consisting primarily of the Roman legal tradition, with accommodations made for French provincial customs and royal legislation. Emphasis was placed on judicial decisions rather than on legislative action. The synthesis of French customs and Roman legal principles

6 See Collins, *The State in Early Modern France*, 146–56; Zoë A. Schneider, *The King's Bench: Bailiwick Magistrates and Local Governance in Normandy, 1670–1740* (Rochester, NY, 2008), 18; and Varga, *Codification as a Socio-historical Phenomenon*, 56–62.

7 See Csaba Varga, *Codification as a Socio-historical Phenomenon* (Budapest, 1991), 56–62.

8 See Kenneth Pennington, *The Prince and the Law, 1200–1600: Sovereignty and Rights in the Western Legal Tradition* (Berkeley and Los Angeles, 1993), 92–105, and Mousnier, *Les institutions de la France*, 1:78–82.

produced a genuine French law that played a crucial role in the emergence of the modern state.[9] Metz, previously part of the Holy Roman Empire, came under the influence of Roman law. According to Barthélemy-Joseph Bretonnier (1656–1727), *avocat* in Lyon, Roman law was recognized as the common law in official legal texts in several localities in northern France, including Burgundy, Franché-Comité, Metz, Toul, Cerdun, and Thionville.[10] Case law also bore the clear imprint of efforts to impose "French" civil law. In Metz *ius civile* was, in effect, "reformed Roman" law.[11] In 1569 Charles IX had granted *lettres patentes* for the codification of the customs of Metz, but it was not until 1613, under Louis XIII, that the *Coûtumes* were first published. Two types of *coûtumes* were printed—one for the city of Metz and the *pays messin* (the neighboring countryside), and the other for the *bailliage* and bishopric of Metz. The compendium of Metz *Coûtumes* was published six additional times prior to the Revolution, in the years 1616–1618, 1730, 1732, and 1769. The *Coûtumes générales de l'Eveché de Metz*, which was comprised largely of canon law, was printed in

---

9 On the judicial impact of Roman law, see David Parker, *Class and State in Ancien Régime France: The Road to Modernity?* (New York, 1996), 8–22. On custom and law, see Donald R. Kelley, "'Second Nature': The Idea of Custom in European Law, Society, and Culture," in Anthony Grafton and Ann Blair, eds., *The Transmission of Culture in Early Modern Europe* (Philadelphia, 1990), 131–72. On the efforts of early modern jurists to unify the law through jurisprudence and royal legislation, see Sarah Hanley, "The Jurisprudence of the Arrêts: Marital Union, Civil Society, and State Formation in France, 1550–1650," *Law and History Review* 21:1 (2003): 1–40, and Marie Seong-Hak Kim, "Civil Law and Civil War: Michel de L'Hôpital and the Ideals of Legal Unification in Sixteenth-Century France," *Law and History Review* 28:3 (2010): 791–826.

10 Bretonnier's views were recorded in M. Claude Henrys, *Oeuvres avec les observations sur les changemens de la jurisprudence depuis la mort de l'auteur ...* par Barthélemy-Joseph Bretonnier (Paris, 1718). See *Continental Legal History Series*, 11 vols. (Boston, 1912–1928), 1:208; Peter Arend Jan van de Berg, *The Politics of European Codification: A History of the Unification of Law in France, Prussia, the Austrian Monarchy and the Netherlands* (Groningen, 2007), 125–80, esp. 143–45; and William Carey Morey, *Outlines of Roman Law, Comprising its Historical Growth and General Principles* (New York, 1914), 196.

11 On the law in Metz, see C.-J. Gabriel, *Observations détachées sur les coûtumes et les usages anciens et modernes du ressort du Parlement de Metz*. 2 vols. (Bouillon, 1787), and in the Lorraine province as a whole, see Albert Riston, *Analyse des coûtumes sous le ressort du parlement de Lorraine, adoptées au droit commun et aux lois particulières à cette province* (Nancy, 1782). For an illustration of how the division between Roman and customary law played out in relation to monarchical law, see the discussion of the *droit d'aubaine* in Sahlins, *Unnaturally French*, 5–55. Areas of Roman law were historically exempt from the *droit d'aubaine*, but in the eighteenth century it was extended to Provence and Languedoc in the south and to Metz in the east. This was part of the monarchy's efforts to extend its sovereignty by imposing uniform laws throughout the kingdom.

1772, though it had been prepared some decades earlier.[12] These collections of customary law and learned commentary were intended as handbooks that would be used by judges and jurisconsultants of the province. It is of no small significance that the same person, Nicolas-Louis Dilange (1666–1743), advisor to the Parlement de Metz, was responsible for producing the compendia of customs of both the city and the bishopric. This does not suggest that the dividing line between state and ecclesiastical law was at all blurred, but it is fair to say that the two systems co-existed and enjoyed comparable legal standing.

Reflecting this broader development, the notable *arrêts* and royal edicts that regulated marital affairs constituted what Sarah Hanley has identified as the "French Marital Law Compact." In this area, then, the accommodation of French customs and Roman legal principles was crucial in the emergence of the modern state. The French state viewed marriage as a legal contract related to the public good and, accordingly, French law as practiced in the civil courts governed in marital property disputes.[13] But cases were not limited to the choice of governing law. Jurisdictional conflicts between municipal authorities and the royal courts, the *bailliages*, arose routinely in cases ranging from commercial transactions and the appointment of guardians to the affixing of seals on estates of the deceased and the preparation of post-mortem inventories. It was not uncommon for such rivalries to result in litigation between institutions. In one instance, in Dijon in the mid-seventeenth century,

12 The 1613 edition of the Metz *Coûtumes* was reproduced three times in the years immediately following its initial appearance, with corrections and revisions, under the title *Les Coûtumes générales de la ville de Metz et pays-Messin: corrigées ensuite des résolutions des trois-etats de ladite ville, ès années 1616, 1617, & 1618*. The 1730 edition, as its subtitle indicates, was "enriched with a commentary" produced by Nicolas-Louis Dilange. The 1732 edition, like the printing in 1769, was virtually unchanged, except for a slightly modified format and new pagination. Cf. *Coûtumes générales de l'Eveché de Metz, commentées par M. Dilange* (La Haye, 1772). This edition also included *Les Coûtumes municipales des villes et chatellenies de Remberviller, Baccarat et Moyen*, which was accompanied by commentaries that Dilange added. See Jean Caswell and Ivan Sipkov, *The Coutumes of France in the Library of Congress: An Annotated Bibliography* (Clark, NJ, 2006), 55–56.

13 See Hanley, "The Jurisprudence of the Arrêts," 8 and 14, n. 10, where it is emphasized that the shift from Roman paternal consent to parental consent corresponded to French inheritance practice that was unknown in Roman law. Hanley attributed this to the convergence of a French nationalist spirit and legal humanism among jurists who aspired to a synthesis of Roman law and French customary law. For examples of the conjunction of these distinct legal traditions, which were frequently presented side by side, see *Coûtumes générales de la ville de Metz et pays-Messin* (Metz, 1769), passim.

a compromise agreement was reached and subsequently ratified by the Parlement of Burgundy to establish shared jurisdictional authority.[14]

In such a complex legal environment, the Jewish community of Metz could scarcely escape state scrutiny. In 1742 the monarchy and the Metz Parlement demanded of the Kahal an abridged translation of Jewish civil law and family law to assist French judges in adjudicating cases between Jewish litigants based on Jewish law. Nicolas-François Lançon, jurist and *conseiller au Parlement*, completed work on the *Recueil des lois, coûtumes et usages observés par les juifs de Metz* in 1743.[15] His introduction to the compendium confirms that from the standpoint of French authorities, the project accorded with the underpinnings of Jewish legal autonomy. As pledged in the *lettres patentes*, the French compendium would compromise the right of Jews to seek relief in Jewish courts: "We have reserved them for disputes, which arise between Jews and Jews, the right of recourse to their Rabbis, while also desiring that the leaders of their communities should have knowledge of their [own] police, religion, customs, ceremonies, and impositions."[16] The demand to produce the *Recueil* was consistent with broader efforts of royal authorities to record the customs of hundreds of communities throughout France. Whether it was also a response to the growing number of appeals from Jewish court decisions that were being prosecuted in French courts is uncertain. But in whatever forum Jewish litigants chose, the *lettres patentes* envisioned that "they must be judged according to their own laws and customs."[17] By so doing, the state both

---

14 See Breen, "Patronage, Politics, and the 'Rule of Law' in Early Modern France," 106–12, where competing jurisdictional claims in Dijon are analyzed.

15 *Recueil des lois, coutumes et usages observés par les juifs de Metz*, m.s. 11 March 1743, in AN H 1641. The work was deposited with the Metz Parlement in 1743; it was later published by Lançon in 1786. For the historical background and context, see Katz, "'To Judge and to Be Judged," and Shael Herman, "Tout Fait Maison." For Eibeschütz's objections to litigation in gentile courts, see his *Urim ve-Tumim*, *Ḥoshen Mishpat* (Altona, 1763), §26. see Katz, "'To Judge and to Be Judged.'"

16 *Lettres patentes*, August 20, 1742: "Nous leurs avons réservé pour les contestations, qui naissent de Juifs à Juifs, la faculté de se pourvoir devant leurs Rabins, voulant aussi que les chefs de leurs communautés eussent la connoissance de leur police, religion, coutumes, cérémonies & impositions."

17 Lançon, preface to *Recueil des lois, coûtumes et usages observés par les juifs de Metz*. On parallel developments in Prussia, see Graff, *Separation of Church and State: Dina de-Malkhuta Dina in Jewish Law*, 32–33; and Sorkin, *Moses Mendelssohn and the Religious Enlightenment*, 104–107. Cf. Moses Mendelssohn, *Die Ritualgesetze der Juden* (Berlin, 1778), a work that rested on the *Judenordnung* of 1750 but envisioned further diminution in rabbinic jurisdiction; rulings would be issued without consulting the Jewish courts, as the *Judenordnung* had stipulated. Issues concerning property were to be adjudicated in Prussian courts based on Jewish law.

accepted Metz Jewry's legal diversity and juridical autonomy and asserted its central authority.[18]

Jewish communal leaders and the Metz Parlement manifested widely divergent reactions in the years immediately following the completion of the translation, Initially, Metz syndics expressed concern that judging Jewish civil cases in the French courts would erode community discipline and impair its ability to collect taxes. The Parlement's response—that the *Recueil* signaled the determination to realize the loftier goal of Jews' integration as full members of the state—anticipated the debate surrounding Jewish citizenship in the revolutionary era. For their part, Metz communal leaders countered that the privilege of juridical autonomy that it had historically enjoyed was the same privilege granted in other Christian countries and, further, that the implied distinction between the authority of civil law and ritual law was unsound. To expect the Jews to surrender their jurisdiction in civil matters would be no less than to deny them freedom to practice their religion.[19] This debate eventually gave way to a new reality. In the quarter-century before its formal publication in 1786, the manuscript version of the *Recueil* became known to jurists both in France and beyond,[20] and during this period the compendium rose in stature in the eyes of both the Parlement and Jewish communal leaders. It was used by the Parlement when Jewish litigants desired to be judged under Jewish law, and leaders of the Metz Kehillah asserted its authoritative status as an independent source of Jewish law. Litigants utilized the translation when arguing a case in the Parlement and acknowledged its benefit in defending Jewish customs against claims that they were inconsistent with the laws of the regime. Even if the *Recueil* did not ultimately play quite the role envisioned by either the monarchy or the Parlement, the prospect of Jewish integration within the larger legal framework was on the horizon.[21]

The commissioning of the *Recueil des lois, coûtumes et usages observés par les juifs de Metz* reveals an important dimension of autonomy. Although designed as a reference tool for French judges presiding over cases between Jewish litigants, the compendium should more properly be seen as a tactical effort to

18 See Emmanuel Michel, *Histoire du Parlement de Metz* (Paris, 1845), 515–16. The extract was deposited at the Parlement on 11 March 1743. The work was published in 1786. On the impact of the *Recueil*, see below, chapter 5.

19 For an analysis of the Jewish and French responses to the *Recueil*, based on unpublished archival sources, see Katz, "'To Judge and to Be Judged,'" 456–60.

20 See, for example, Johann Friedrich Fischer, *Commentatio de statu et jurisdictione Judaeorum, secundum leges Romanas, Germanicas, Alsaticas* (Bauer, 1763), 107.

21 Katz, "'To Judge and to Be Judged,'" 464–67.

build on the pluralist paradigm.[22] Two models of juridical autonomy prevailed in the second half of the eighteenth century. One stressed Jewish law's preference that its community members settle disputes in a Jewish court. A second model—preferred by many French jurists and doubtless by some members of the Jewish community as well—entailed adjudication in French courts, with the proviso that the judgment would accord with Jewish law. The assurance in the *lettres patentes* that the *Recueil* would not infringe on the right of Jews to settle their disputes in their own courts was consistent with Jewish legal autonomy as understood by Metz communal leaders.[23] The example of the *Recueil* suggests that state-building was not limited to the imposition of centralized law but aspired to the efficient management of diversity under state supervision.[24] Paradoxically, legal integration—both in theory and fact—is evident in the proceedings of the Beit Din itself.

It would be unwarranted to construe the Beit Din's compliance with the rules of the larger legal universe as little more than capitulation to external pressure. The coexistence of diverse legal jurisdictions was part of a broader cultural matrix that was characteristic of other urban centers. The rabbinic court operated within this world of overlapping legal jurisdictions, and its jurisprudential methods were influenced accordingly. For these reasons, the records of the Metz Beit Din are an extraordinary resource for investigating

22 See Lançon, *Recueil des lois, coûtumes et usages observés par les juifs de Metz*.

23 *Lettres patentes*, 20 August 1742. The following is the original text: "Nous leurs avons réservé pour les contestations, qui naissent de Juifs à Juifs, la faculté de se pourvoir devant leurs Rabins, voulant aussi que les chefs de leurs communautés eussent la connoissance de leur police, religion, coutumes, cérémonies & impositions."

24 Out of the synthesis of French customs and Roman legal principles emerged a genuine French law that played a crucial role in the emergence of the modern state. In Metz *ius civile* was, effectively, "reformed Roman" law. On the law in Metz, see C.-J. Gabriel, *Observations détachées sur les coûtumes et les usages anciens et modernes du ressort du Parlement de Metz*. 2 vols. (Bouillon, 1787), and in the Lorraine province as a whole, see Riston, *Analyse des coûtumes sous le ressort du parlement de Lorraine*. Areas of Roman law were historically exempt from the *droit d'aubaine*, but in the eighteenth century it was extended to Provence and Languedoc in the south and to Metz in the east. This was part of the monarchy's efforts to extend its sovereignty by imposing uniform laws throughout the kingdom. See Sahlins, *Unnaturally French: Foreign Citizens in the Old Regime*, 11–16. Upon royal initiative, the *coûtumes* of Metz were codified and in 1611 they were published for the first time, under Louis XIII. Two types of *coûtumes* were printed, one for the city of Metz and the other for the surrounding countryside. This compendium of Metz customs was published six additional times before the Revolution, the last time being in 1769. See *Coûtumes générales de la ville de Metz et pays-Messin: corrigées ensuite des résolutions des trois-etats de ladite ville, ès années 1616, 1617, & 1618. Nouvelle edition conforme à ... 17[illegible]2* (Metz, 1769).

the interplay between law, society, and culture. To appreciate how the Beit Din negotiated the challenges it faced, it is first necessary to consider the nature of the relationship of Jews to the surrounding society, culture and institutions in Metz and the Moselle region. It becomes evident from the records of the rabbinic court that the judicial behavior of the Beit Din, while faithful to the principles of classical Jewish jurisprudence, developed in response to shifting cultural norms that were gaining a firm footing among members of the Metz Jewish community. Evolving patterns of acculturation can be discerned in dress, language, material culture, and assimilation to the legal framework of the Metz region.

The argument advanced here—that the Jews of Metz were in the throes of integration within the city's larger legal framework—contravenes the conventional view that owing to their political incapacity, legal inequality, and economic restrictions, Jews were consigned to the margins of French society in the pre-revolutionary years. To be sure, Metz Jews were required to reside in *le quartier juif* and were subject to degrading obligations to wear the Jewish badge, listen to the monthly sermon in a church, and bear exceptionally burdensome taxes. But it is not clear that the legal restrictions on their livelihood and mobility were applied as rigorously and consistently as some sources imply.[25] Moreover, the judicial realm came to represent for many Jews an arena somewhat removed from the more pronounced injustices and ignominies they experienced in other areas of life.[26] The term "legal integration" is a more apt description of this process, at least as it comes into view in the proceedings of the Metz rabbinic court. As used here, legal integration acknowledges the prevailing systems of law and justice through compliance with administrative, bureaucratic, and legal obligations imposed by the state. The boundaries drawn by the Metz community defined the acceptable modes of accommodation to French law and legal institutions. Where full acquiescence was either impossible or undesirable, the rabbinic court and the communal leadership navigated a course that accommodated the demands of local and state law while remaining faithful to Jewish legal norms.

---

25 Anon., "Communauté des Juifs," *Almanach des Trois Evêches pour l'année 1788* (Metz, 1788), 213.

26 For two cases, one heard by the Metz Parlement in 1769 and the other by the Nancy Parlement in 1775, that offer evidence of a positive turn in the attitude toward Jews in the courts, see Charles-Marguerite Mercier Dupaty, *Justification de sept hommes condamnés par le Parlement de Metz en 1769, sur les seules dépositions de juifs plaignans* (Paris, 1787), and Pierre-Louis Lacretelle, *Plaidoyer pour deux Juifs de Metz contre l'Hotel de Ville et le corps des marchands de Thionville* (Brussels, 1785). Also see Sahlins, *Unnaturalty French*, 15–55, and Szjajkowski, *Jews and the French Revolutions*, 220–31.

In eighteenth-century Metz, where the institutions of French law were pervasive and imposing, the Beit Din displayed considerable familiarity with state and local institutions and went to great lengths to become acquainted with the intricacies of French law. Copious signs of acculturation reflect the process of legal integration that had become more pronounced in the second half of the century. Evidence of legal acculturation and integration, reflecting the adoption of French behavioral patterns and cultural values, may be divided into four categories: (1) language; (2) production of bi-lingual documents; (3) patterns of litigation in the Beit Din; (4) the judicial behavior of the Beit Din in relation to the French civil courts and French law.

Although the protocols of the Beit Din are highly stylized texts produced by professional scribes under the guidance of the judiciary itself, the language and images conveyed in the Metz rabbinic court records offer strong indications of how litigants themselves viewed the law and the range of options that lay before them. The profound influence of French culture—both legal and non-legal—on Jewish life was partly due to the impact of the centralized administrative bureaucracy famously portrayed by Tocqueville and no doubt was also a product of France's powerful cultural allure.[27]

Language

The conspicuous imprint of French culture is evident from the extensive assimilation of French terminology pertaining to material culture, commercial transactions, and judicial procedure. The linguistic evidence found in the Pinkas Kahal and the Beit Din is a matter of particular significance, since it is reasonably certain that French was not spoken on a daily basis among the Jews of the northeast region of France—not in Metz, nor in the villages in the Moselle, nor in the entire rural countryside of Alsace and Lorraine. There is little doubt that the proceedings recorded in the Beit Din—including arguments, testimonies, and deliberations—were conducted in the western Yiddish dialect spoken by the Jews of the Moselle and throughout the northeast region. Much less frequently, French terms appear in the Pinkas Kahal. Examples include אפורטער (*au porteur*), to the bearer; דעקלאראסיאון (*déclaration*); פוהן פערדי (*fonds perdus*), lost funds; פיע דע ראי (*pied de roi*), the king's foot; אורדעננץ (*ordonnance*); קלעקטר (*collector*); ראפורטער (*rapporteur*).[28] On numerous

27 Alexis de Tocqueville, *L'Ancien Regime et la Révolution* (Paris, 1967).

28 The following references appear in the Pinkas Kahal: *au porteur*, PKM, 52a; *déclaration*, PKM, 118a; *fonds perdus*, PKM, 55a; *pied de roi*, PKM 96a; *ordonnance*, PKM, 100a; *collecteur*, PKM, 105a; *rapporteur*, PKM, 131a.

occasions Yiddish phrases or statements of several sentences were recorded as the verbatim testimony of one or more of the litigants; less frequently, such testimony was rendered by the court scribe in Hebrew, though it is presumed that such passages were paraphrased in the course of the transcription of the proceedings.[29]

Despite the concern voiced by sympathetic observers such as Abbé Henri Grégoire that the language barrier posed an insurmountable obstacle to social integration and civic emancipation, Metz Jews were far more integrated linguistically within the larger society than, for example, their coreligionists elsewhere in the northeastern provinces.[30] A substantial percentage of the vocabulary borrowed from the French attests to the Beit Din's familiarity with the framework of French jurisprudence and the basic mechanics of French law. A partial list of terms referring to civil courts and their personnel, judicial procedures, legal documentation, and deliberations includes פארלעמאן (*parlement*); פרעזעדאָי (*présidiaux*), royal courts; באליאַש (*bailliage*), a royal court headed by a ליעטענאן שענראל (*lieutenant général*); גרעף (*greffe*) and ג־עפיע (*greffier*), registry of court records and court clerk; סעלע (*scellé*), official seal of the court; פראטעקאהל (*protocole*); אווקאט (*avocat*), lawyer; פראקרער דעֶראָי (*procureur du roi*), royal solicitor; אסינגאסיאהן (*assignation*), summons or subpoena; פורסוויט (*poursuite*), a legal proceeding; סאנטאנס (*sentence*), a judgment; אפעֶל (*appel*), appeal; דאסיע (*dossier*); פיעס שיסטיפיקאטיף; (*pièce justificatif*), a supporting document; קופיע (*copie*); and גראס (grosse), a copy of a document prepared by a notary in accordance with instructions of the court. Technical legal terminology is abundantly represented in the following: פרעֶטנאָם (*prête-nom*), a nominee or figurehead in a financial transaction; דיקלעראסיאן דעֶביעֶן (*déclaration des biens*); קלאהטור (*clôture*), closure of a will; קודסעֶל (*codicil*), a supplement to a will; סאלידערמאן (*solidairement*), joint liability; סוברעקאסיאן (*subrogation*), substitution of a claim against one person for a claim against another; אוואנס (*avance*), advance on a

29 For examples of Yiddish testimony, see PMBD, Vol. 2, no. 389, 71b; no. 394, 72b; no. 515, 104b–105a. For direct testimony recorded in Hebrew, see PMBD, Vol. 1, pt. 2, no. 29, 9b; Vol. 2, no. 511, 103b. Despite the overall fidelity to Hebrew scribal conventions throughout the Pinkas, there are several instances when the court scribe appears to have been "thinking in Yiddish." The term *ba'al ḥov*, which generally signifies "creditor" in Hebrew, is used on several rare occasions as "debtor"—its meaning in Yiddish. See, for example, PMBD, Vol. 1, pt. 1, no. 143, 46a; Vol. 1, pt. 2, no. 26, 7b; Vol. 2, no. 455, 89a; and no. 505, 102b. For both meanings—as creditor and debtor—in the same source, see Lvov, *Resp. Penei Levanah*, no. 36.

30 Henri Grégoire, *Essai sur la régénération physique, morale et politique des Juifs* (Metz, 1789), 28–29, and the discussion in Sepinwall, *The Abbé Grégoire and the French Revolution*, 133, and idem, "Les Paradoxes de la régénération révolutionnaire: le cas de l'abbé Grégoire," *Annales historiques de la Révolution française* 321 (1998): 69–90. Also see the PKM, 79b–80b, 1769 Takkanot, esp. arts. 57–78.

loan; סיניפיקאסיאהן (*signification*), notification of a judicial act; דעפֿאָ (*défaut*), judgment by default; וואקאסיאהן (*vacation*), fee paid to court clerk; דעמאשאינטרע (*dommage-intérêt*), a suit for monetary damages; and קונט שודיסיער (*compte judiciaire*), an account of expenses ordered by the court in the course of settling a dispute.[31] The foregoing vocabulary reveals a close working knowledge of the French judicial system and procedures.

Among the fiscal terms that pervade the Metz Bet Din proceedings, one encounters the following: אקסעפטאסיאהן (*acceptation*), an order or draft that a person has accepted; דעפוזיטער (*dépositaire*), bailee; דעֶשעֶרש (*décharge*), discharge; מיינלעווע (*main-levée*), release of mortgage; פָּארטיפֶעל (*portefeuille*), portfolio; פרישער (*priseur*), appraiser; קונסיטיסיאהן (*constitution*), an annuity that was either purchased or served as a security against which money was borrowed; ראנט וויאשער (*rente viagère*), life annuity; קונפיסקאסיאהן (*confiscation*), a seizure that was purchased as a right from the government; פרעסקריט (*préscrit*), a lapsed cheque; and רעסי (*récut*), receipt. Vocabulary pertaining as well to commercial exchange include אנדאסעמן (*endossement*), endorsement; אנטרמאָיעמאַן (*atermoiement*), deferment of payment of loan; אגט דעוואָיאש (*acte de voyage*), transport of merchandise; and לעֶטר דעֶ וואָיטור (*lettre de voiture*), bill of lading. Terms referring to the livestock trade, an important area of Jewish commercial involvement in the Moselle, included פוראש (*fourrage*), fodder for livestock and פֿאָה גרעניעֶ (*grenier à foin*), a haystack.[32]

In numerous other instances, a French term or phrase was transliterated and used instead of the comparable Hebrew term employed in traditional sources. This tendency can be observed in the terms referring to various types of contracts, official documents, civil court procedures, and legal terminology of a technical nature. One recurrent example is the term אינוואנטער

31 The following are references in the Pinkas Beit Din to selected terms in the list: *bailliage*, Vol. 1, pt. 2, no. 49, 14a; *présidiaux*, Vol. 2, no. 631, 137a; *lieutenant général*, Vol. 2, no. 254, 47b; *greffier*, Vol. 1, pt. 1, no. 136, 44a; *scellé*, Vol. 2, no. 554, 115a; *procureur du roi*, Vol. 2, no. 587, 125a; *assignation*, Vol. 2, no. 143, 28a; *poursuite*, Vol. 1, pt. 1, no. 55, 17a; *pièce justificatif*, Vol. 2, no. 506, 102b; *grosse*, Vol. 2, no. 50, 10a; *prête-nom*, Vol. 1, pt. 2, no. 37, 12a; *déclaration des biens*, Vol. 1, pt. 2, no. 111, 28b; *clôture*, Vol. 1, pt. 1, no. 49, 14a; *codicil*, Vol. 1, pt. 2, no. 54, 16a; *solidairement*, Vol. 1, pt. 1, no. 130, 43a; *subrogation*, Vol. 1, pt. 1, no. 4, 7a; *signification*, Vol. 1, pt. 2, no. 120, 30a; *dommage-intérêt*, Vol. 2, no. 319, 60b; *compte judiciaire*, Vol. 2, no. 310, 57b.

32 The following are references in the Pinkas Beit Din to several of the terms listed above: *au porteur*, Vol. 1, pt. 1, no. 74, 25a; *acceptation*, Vol. 2, no. 23, 6a,; *dépositaire*, Vol. 2, no. 633, 138a; *main-levée*, Vol. 2, no. 168, 33b; *portefeuille*, Vol. 2, no. 23, 6b; *priseur*, Vol. 1, pt. 2, no. 183, 42a; *atermoiement*, Vol. 1, pt. 1, no. 14, 9a; *acte de voyage*, Vol. 2, no. 277, 52a; endossement, Vol. 1, pt. 1, no. 58, 17b; *lettre de voiture*, Vol. 2, no. 91, 18a; *fourrage*, Vol. 1, pt. 1, no. 64, 20a; and *grenier à foin*, Vol. 2, no. 25, 6b.

(*inventaire*), which is employed hundreds of times instead of חשבון (*ḥeshbon*), the term that commonly appears in halakhic literature. For example, in its discussion of the appointment of guardians, the *Shulḥan 'Arukh* used the expression *ḥeshbon ha-metaltelim veha-karka'ot veha-ḥovot* (list of movable and immovable property and debts) to refer to the inventory of the real property and debts left by the deceased.[33] Another example of the same phenomenon is the use of the term *malle*, which is the French equivalent of the more frequently employed Hebrew *argaz* (strongbox). The frequent use of, and even preference for, French terms for bills of exchange, endorsement, and joint liability reflects both an intimate knowledge of the fundamentals of finance and commercial transactions as practiced both locally and abroad as well as the natural tendency for foreign vocabulary to become incorporated into conventional usage. The same holds true for the phrase פאר בענֶפּיס באינוואנטר, *par bénéfice d'inventaire*, which pertains to inheritance, and קונסרוואטר דעס היפאטיק, *conservateur des hypothèques*, which refers to a land registrar. Unlike the terms *inventaire* and *malle*, neither of these technical phrases was glossed in the text of the Pinkas, which implies that they were readily known to the Jewish population at large.[34]

Equally instructive are those instances in which Hebrew terms or phrases are followed directly by the corresponding French idiom.[35] For example, referring to a man who had been appointed משגיח (guardian of orphans) in the French civil court, the text added שקורין קאראטער, "who is called *curateur*." Similarly, following the Hebrew פטורים, the text states שקורין דעשארש, "that is called *décharge*." Several lines after this, the expression תנאי החזרה is glossed by the addition of the transliterated phrase שאַרש דעראפארטע, corresponding to *charge de répartir* (delayed payment).[36] Likewise, the phrase כתיבה ומסירה is glossed as טראנספורט (*transport*),[37] בכתב is rendered as פאר עקרי (*par écrit*),[38] and חדר is glossed as סאל אמאנשע (*salle à manger*).[39] When presenting the term עקול the texts add שקורין סעזי, "which is called seizure," a reference to the seizure of assets initiated in the

33 See *Shulḥan 'Arukh, Ḥoshen Mishpat* §290:3. While the substitution of a foreign word for a well-established Hebrew term is certainly not unknown in halakhic literature, the phenomenon demands attention as to its implications for cultural adaptation. On the wider use of the transliterated word *inventaire*, for example, see Bacharach, *Resp. Ḥavvot Ya'ir*, no. 58. On the use of the term *malle*, see PMBD, Vol. 1, pt. 1, no. 12, 9a.

34 The phrase *par bénéfice d'inventaire* appears in PMBD, Vol. 1, pt. 2, no. 54, 16a; *conservateur des hypothèques*, Vol. 2, no. 581, 122b.

35 This was by no means unique to Metz. See, for example, Ezekiel Landau, *Resp. Noda b'Yehudah*, passim.

36 PMBD, Vol. 1, pt. 2, no. 38, 12a.

37 PMBD, Vol. 2, no. 346, 65a. "Transport" denotes an assignment of a note or credit.

38 PMBD, Vol. 2, no. 599, 128b.

39 PMBD, Vol. 2, no. 566, 118b.

civil courts.[40] In each of the foregoing instances, glossing was intended solely for the purpose of explaining the Hebrew by providing a French translation. From these examples and numerous others, we may surmise that in technical matters there was, rather remarkably, greater familiarity with the French terminology than with the Hebrew.[41]

While the aforementioned examples do not alone constitute sufficiently convincing proof of acculturation, they are nonetheless representative of a precise technical vocabulary that was presumably employed by Jews in Metz to meet the demands that commerce and governmental bureaucracy imposed on all residents.[42] Overall, the foreign vocabulary in the Pinkas consists of approximately 400 lexical items from French and 50 from German, in addition to roughly 150 in Yiddish. When combined with indicators from other quarters, the linguistic evidence—particularly the French usage—is both impressive and compelling.

---

40 PMBD, Vol. 2, no. 627, 136a.

41 The transliteration of hundreds of French terms into Hebrew also suggests that Metz Jews knew an oral patois though they were familiar with standard written French to a lesser degree. Aside from several exceptions, the Hebrew rendition of French terms was governed purely by phonetics while no visible importance was attached to orthography. The Hebrew spelling of the French *renonciation* (רענוסאסיאה), for example, omits the second 'n'; the word *acte* appears as אגט, where a 'g' replaces the 'c'; and the final letter of French words, when silent, is routinely omitted, as in קונטרא (*contrat*), אסיסטאן (*assistant*), אנדאסמאן (*endossement*), and רעשימאן (*régiment*). For אסיסטאן (*assistant*), see Vol. 1, pt. 2, no. 49, 14a; for אנדאסמאן (*endossement*), see vol. 1, pt. 1, no. 58, 17b; and for רעשימאן (*régiment*), see Vol. 1, pt. 2, no. 123, 31a. In these cases, it is apparent that the Hebrew spelling consistently reflected what Jews were likely to have heard in oral discourse rather than what they read (or did not read). But there are two instances where the final letter ('t') in the French spelling often appeared in the Hebrew transliteration: אדוואקאט (*avocat*) and פארלימענט (*parlement*). See, for example, PMBD, Vol. 1, pt. 1, no. 65, 21a. and Vol. 2, no. 3, 1b; טראנספורט (*transport*), Vol. 1, pt. 2, no. 48, 13b. Frequently, the Hebrew appears as אדוואקאט (*advocat*), with the letter 'd,' which was likely influenced by the Yiddish pronunciation. For the spelling of פארלימענט, with the final 't', see PMBD, Vol. 1, pt. 2, no. 54, 16a; no. 66, 18a; no. 130, 33a; no. 137, 33b; Vol. 2, no. 246, 45b. Cf. the transliteration of *préscrit* as פרעסקריט, Vol. 2, no. 268, 50b. We also encounter numerous examples of רעגימענט, which appears with the final 't'; see Vol. 1, pt. 1, no. 64, 19b. From these exceptional cases we can speculate that Metz Jews had gained special familiarity with this word after having seen it numerous times in written form, quite possibly in public advertisements or signs.

42 For comparable questions concerning the significance of parallel legal terminology, cf. Gideon Libson, *Jewish and Islamic Law: A Comparative Study of Custom during the Geonic Period* (Cambridge, MA, 2003), 14.

Production of Bi-lingual Documents

In areas requiring specific compliance with French law, and occasionally in matters of individual discretion as well, numerous types of documents were translated from Hebrew and formally produced in French so they could be filed with the appropriate government office. A royal decree issued by Louis XIV on 11 January 1701 obligated Jews to deposit with a notary an official French summary of the *ketubah*, known as a *contrat de mariage*, within fifteen days after the wedding.[43] These civil marriage contracts contained the provisions set forth in the *ketubah*, in abbreviated form and translated into French, signifying that its terms were valid in the French civil courts.[44]

Likewise, certain types of wills and codicils were rendered in French.[45] As a rule, there were two different types of wills: charitable testaments and more conventional wills that were filed in the Metz Parlement.[46] Wills that called for the creation of a charitable trust to be administered by the community were generally produced in Hebrew by the *ne'emanei kehillah* (Jewish notaries), whereas wills that contained directives for the division of assets among heirs were prepared by French notaries and deposited with the civil court.[47] Probate inventories required by government authorities were also recorded by notaries, as were lists of outstanding debts owed to the deceased or owed by the estate. Special stipulations such as the indemnification of a widow against future claims were also executed in the presence of a notary.[48] In cases involving guardianship, the Beit Din required a formal translation of the discharge document into French.[49] Likewise, transport documents intended for the

43 The purpose of this requirement, according to Zosa Szajkowski, was to protect Christian creditors against default by Jewish debtors, in case the property changed hands; see his "Alsatian Jewish Inventories in the Hebrew Union College Library," *Studies in Bibliography and Booklore* 4:2 (1959): 96–97. Also see Gildas Bernard, *Les familles juives en France* (Paris, Archives Nationales, 1990). On the conception of civil marriage in early modern France, see Hardwick, *The Practice of Patriarchy*, 51–55.

44 See, for example, PMBD, Vol. 1, pt. 1, no. 10, 8b; no. 76, 26b; no. 142, 46a; Vol. 2, no. 59, 11a; no. 81, 15a.

45 See, for example, PMBD, Vol. 2, no. 107, 21b.

46 On Reizele Alsace's will that was in French, see PBDM, Vol. 1, pt. 2, no. 54, 16a. For Reizele Spire's Hebrew will, see Arch. JTSA, ms. 9835.

47 See, for example, PMBD, Vol. 2, no. 23, 6a, where mention is made of three wills, the first produced "when he was healthy ... the second when he was on his death-bed ... and the third in French in the *'arkha'ot*." Also see Vol. 2, no. 107, 21b. For the will of Abraham Jacob, of the village of Steinbiedersdorf, which was translated into French, see Ulbrich, *Shulamit and Margarete*, 283.

48 See PMBD, Vol. 2, no. 310, 57a–b; also see no. 313, 58b.

49 See, for example, PMBD, Vol. 1, pt. 2, no. 25, 7b, and Vol. 1, pt. 2, no. 37, 12a.

conveyance of funds and merchandise were produced in French translation.[50] Significantly, translations of documents into French from Hebrew and Yiddish, including receipts, arbitration agreements, and notes of indebtedness, indicate that even internal transactions required documentation that could be read by French court officials.[51]

Although the foregoing examples suggest that French literacy was more prevalent among Metz Jews than has been generally assumed, there is little doubt that facility in French was far less extensive in the countryside than among the urban elite. Even fifty years after the Revolution there were still Jews in the small towns and villages of Alsace and Lorraine who could not speak French.[52] Beit Din records suggest that although the scribes assigned to record case summaries were familiar with a wide range of technical French vocabulary pertaining to judicial procedure and financial instruments, their fluency in French may have been limited primarily to oral proficiency. In addition to the ubiquity of technical legal terminology in the Beit Din records, frequent references to popular French vocabulary are also present. Social and economic conditions in Metz demanded greater competence, and even fluency, in French than elsewhere in the northeast.

Patterns of Litigation in the Beit Din

Valuable evidence of legal acculturation on the part of the Jews in Metz and their coreligionists in the *pays messin* may be discerned as well in various patterns of litigation and, more regularly, in the humdrum of administrative tasks that are recorded in Beit Din proceedings. Observance of social and legal norms was evident in the behavior of litigants seeking to settle disputes concerning business partnerships and commercial transactions, torts, inheritance, guardianship, and payment of debts. The intricacies of commerce demanded technical competence of Jewish judges in numerous areas, especially in the

---

50 See PMBD, Vol. 1, pt. 1, no. 61, 18b; Vol. 1, pt. 2, no. 55, 16a; Vol. 1, pt. 2, no. 176, 41a.

51 See, for example, PMBD, Vol. 1, pt. 2, no. 37, 12a; Vol. 1, pt. 2, no. 49, 14a; and Vol. 1, pt. 2, no. 130, 33a.

52 Paula Hyman, "The Social Contexts of Assimilation: Village Jews and City Jews in Alsace," in *Assimilation and Community: The Jews in Nineteenth-Century Europe*, eds. Jonathan Frankel and Steven Zipperstein (Cambridge, 1992), 114–20. Aaron Worms, a native of Geislautern who studied in the Metz yeshivah and later served as a *dayan* on the Beit Din, and delegate to the Napoleonic Sanhedrin, reported that he was denied the position of Metz consistorial grand rabbi for most of his career because he was not able to speak French. See Aaron Worms, *Bin Nun* (Metz, 1827), 186a, cited in Jay Berkovitz, "Patterns of Rabbinic Succession in Modern France," *Jewish History* 13 (1999): 80.

endorsement of bills of exchange and the execution of bearer documents that would conform to the procedural requirements of the general courts.

Knowledge of the legalities of commercial transactions and local customs was an important aspect of the acculturation process. A case involving a merchant from Metz who had business dealings in several villages in the Lorraine illustrates just this point. Seligmann Charleville sent his assistant to Courcelles-Chaussy to collect on a promissory note owed by a gentile client and to prepare a transport document that denoted the assignment of a note in Seligmann's name. However, the assistant made several errors that revealed his inexperience with the procedures normally followed in the execution of loan documents, his ignorance of civil court procedures, and his negligence in paying customs taxes. The Beit Din rejected the assistant's argument that he was unaware that French legal requirements differed for notes of a higher value; it therefore held him responsible for the error and instructed him to reproduce the necessary documents. However, the Beit Din did accept the claim that he was unacquainted with the commune of Frouard requirement to pay the customs duty before hitching a horse at an inn, since the practice was not uniformly observed throughout Lorraine.[53] This concession notwithstanding, anyone involved in business and commercial trade was expected to be familiar with French court protocols and commercial practices, and it therefore represented a standard to which individuals could be held legally accountable.

Evolving patterns of judicial activity in the eighteenth century made recourse to French tribunals for several purposes neither exceptional nor a breach of Jewish communal norms. Demands for debt repayment—whether as settlement of outstanding loans or unpaid merchandise—were not deemed to violate the prohibition of *arkha'ot shel goyim* if they were supported by documentary evidence. Widows or abandoned wives commonly demanded payment of their *ketubah* and *tosefta* in the civil courts because the marriage contract, once translated into French and notarized, was a legally recognized agreement that was registered with government authorities. By the last third of the eighteenth century, efforts to settle marital property disputes in the civil court were within the range of normative conduct, and in most cases such actions were presumed to be authorized by the Beit Din or the Kahal. This pattern was undoubtedly related as well to the limited enforcement options available to Jewish communal authorities, but the rationale for going to French

53 PMBD, Vol. 2, no. 346, 65a. The case evokes Voltaire's famous witticism concerning the fragmented nature of the pre-Revolution legal system: "When you travel in this kingdom, you change legal systems as often as you change horses." Voltaire, *Oeuvres* VII (1838), Dialogues, 5.

courts rested on the legal force of the contract per se. Such action had become a fairly widespread phenomenon in northeastern France and in territories of the Holy Roman Empire.

Disincentives to taking action in French courts included not only higher costs but also the concern that a civil suit could be harmful to one's professional reputation. In one case a respected merchant alleged that he had been publicly shamed by being sued in a civil court and threatened to seek redress in the civil court if he could not secure compensation under Jewish law. Rejecting his claim, the Beit Din issued an injunction (*ḥerem*) that banned further action, either in the civil court in order to obtain *dommages-intérêts* (compensation for public humiliation) or in the Beit Din where one could seek an award for *boshet* (shame) as understood in Jewish law.[54] What can be gleaned from this dispute and from a case involving a *melamed* (tutor) in Niedervisse who sued his employer in civil court for failure to pay his wages, is that in the eyes of the Beit Din legal efforts by defendants seeking to recover civil court costs were unjustified.[55] Although in some instances the Beit Din imposed fines on those who initiated legal action in the civil courts, these tended to be quite modest. By the mid-1770s, recourse to the civil courts was an undeniable fact that the Beit Din could oppose only with symbolic gestures.

Contracts and related documents were ordinarily prepared with the assistance of French notarial and legal services. Record keeping was viewed universally as an essential function within the pervasive bureaucratic culture of late eighteenth-century France, and governmental officials were considered the most reliable to perform these duties. Accordingly, it was not uncommon to deposit official documents with a notary, even when a particular matter was completely internal to the Jewish community. For example, Hirtz Halphen, guardian of the estate of Mordechai Terquem, deposited official documents relating to bequests designated for the testator's granddaughters with a French notary and not with each individual heir.[56] Probate inventories could only be prepared with civil court authorization.[57] Most details concerning the guardianship of orphans, including the initial appointment, preparation of the inventory of the estate (by a notary), and sale of movable items belonging to the estate (by the sheriff) were under the purview of French governmental officials. In a case where guardians were charged with withholding documentation

54 On the heavy costs of litigation in the French courts, see PMBD, Vol. 1, pt. 2, no. 49, 14a; on the ban on efforts to obtain compensation after having been sued in a French court, see PMBD, Vol. 2, no. 319, 60b.

55 See PMBD, Vol. 1, pt. 1, no. 106, 36b.

56 PMBD, Vol. 2, no. 18, 4a.

57 PMBD, Vol. 2, no. 591, 126b, and no. 594, 127b.

concerning their duties to and liability for the minors under their tutelage, the guardians argued before the Beit Din that the documentation was with the office of the civil court clerk, was easily accessible, and offered proof of the funds they had been holding and how it had come into their hands. Not surprisingly, the Beit Din readily accepted this argument.[58]

Efforts to circumvent restrictions on the entitlement of widows to the estate of their deceased husbands reveal familiarity with French legal norms. Special arrangements that enabled testators to allocate assets to their spouses more equitably than was permitted by Jewish law were not uncommon. Sometimes testators drew up two wills, one in Hebrew and the other in French. Abraham Hess of Metzervisse drafted a will according to the formal requirements of Jewish law that did not recognize a wife as her husband's heir, and a second document, prepared in the presence of a notary, containing instructions to gift his entire estate to his wife, Froumette. Other cases illustrate similar efforts to circumvent the strict application of Jewish law regarding the testamentary rights of surviving spouses.[59] The forgoing examples reveal a rather steadfast confidence in French notarial services and the legal system.

In quite a few cases, litigants sought the opinion of French legal experts when the question was of jurisdictional interest to both Jewish and French law. On some occasions, litigants hired French lawyers when they needed legal representation in routine commercial transactions or property transfers.[60] There were also instances when litigants contacted *avocats* whose opinion or advice they believed would strengthen their cases, especially when they sought to protect their assets in the face of multiple contingencies.[61] In one case, amidst a dispute concerning the will left by Reizele Alsace (d. 14 March 1773), widow of Berman Spire, the named natural heirs and beneficiaries contested the distribution of the assets and approached a French attorney, Pierre-Louis Roederer, with a request to clarify their legal rights. His opinion, produced formally as a legal consultation, reveals the skill exhibited by the parties to the dispute in navigating the French judicial system.[62] Likewise, in a dispute concerning

58 PMBD, Vol. 2, no. 633, 137b.

59 See PMBD, Vol. 2, no. 38, 8b, and no. 311, 57b–58a. In the first of these cases, the testator bequeathed to his wife one-third of all his movable property. In its decision, the Beit Din ruled that the transaction would be delayed for one year to ensure that all other terms of the will were fulfilled. In the case of Froumette, widow of Seligmann Wittersheim, no condition was imposed by the Beit Din on the transfer of funds. See PMBD, Vol. 2, no. 317, 60a.

60 See, for example, PMBD, Vol. 1, pt. 2, no. 242, 52b–53a.

61 See, for example, PMBD, Vol. 2, no. 629, 136a.

62 See PMBD, Vol. 1, pt. 2, no. 54, 16a. For the consultation that was solicited by the heirs and beneficiaries named in the will, see Berkovitz, *Protocols of Justice*, Hebrew volume,

the transfer of funds to a woman engaged to be married, the executor of her grandfather's will sought the opinion of three *avocats* in order to protect the estate from claims that might be made by other daughters of the deceased or their heirs. The question was whether the transfer had to be made immediately or whether the executor had the option to delay. Unwilling to take any chances, the couple to be married consulted three other *avocats* of their own choosing. As in numerous other cases, each party sought legal counsel outside of the rabbinic court, even though the matter at hand had all the markings of an internal dispute.[63] But, in fact, how one defines "internal" is not at all simple, since all transactions in the period under examination, whether "external" or "internal," were guided by broader financial and commercial conventions. No legal question could any longer be viewed as impervious to wider considerations.

Judicial Behavior of the Metz Beit Din

The entrenchment of law within society and its institutions is crucial for understanding the jurisprudence of the rabbinic court of Metz. Two caveats follow from this premise. First, since law is "so deeply embedded in the particularities of each culture," as Lawrence Rosen has argued, "carving it out as a separate domain and only later making note of its cultural connections distorts the nature of both law and culture."[64] Second, law is not only a top-down, centralized phenomenon produced by governing elites under the auspices of

Appendix 3. For the Hebrew translation of the French text, dated 30 August 1773, see the A.D. Moselle, Consistoire israélite 17J24. It is not known whether the French original is still extant. The fact that the document was translated into Hebrew, presumably to facilitate its review by the judges in the Beit Din, suggests that members of the rabbinic court may not have been fully at ease in reading French. Roederer produced his opinion in this case during the period when the Metz Parlement was suppressed, following the closing of the Parlement of Paris during the Maupeou Reform of 1771. Roederer eventually gained an appointment to the Metz Parlement where he was seated in 1780; he subsequently emerged as a champion of Jewish emancipation. See Kenneth Margerison, "P.-L. Roderer: The Industrialist as Revolutionary Author(s)," *Eighteenth-Century Studies*, Vol. 2, no. 4 (Summer, 1978): 473–88.

63 See PMBD, Vol. 2, no. 629, 136a. In some instances, the Beit Din refused to resolve a dispute out of concern that its ruling might contravene French civil law. This could also manifest itself in an unwillingness to rule, as when the Beit Din authorized a son-in-law to approach the French court to collect a debt owed by his father-in-law and his share of the inheritance.

64 Lawrence Rosen, *Law as Culture: An Invitation* (Princeton, 2006), xii. Clifford Geertz has argued that law is basic to how members of a society view themselves and their relationships to one another, "in a word, constructive; in another, constitutive; in a

bureaucratic institutions, but is also a decentralized process that, coming from below, embodies the norms practiced by the rank and file. Accordingly, law as applied in the courts is invariably shaped by the practices and perspectives of the broader community in which they operate.[65] While the protocols of the Beit Din were, to be sure, highly stylized texts produced at the instruction of the court itself, it is also apparent that the language and images conveyed in these records evince the culture of the consumers of law as conspicuously as the culture of jurists. The Metz proceedings shed light on how litigants viewed the law and the range of options available to them. Hardly impervious to the influence of economic, cultural, and political factors in the surrounding society, the Metz Beit Din was responsive to changes that profoundly shaped the lives of community members.

The Metz Parlement, as we have seen, endeavored to limit the community's jurisdiction to cases where the parties agreed voluntarily to submit to arbitration, and failing that, it also tried to curtail the right to impose disciplinary measures.[66] On the other hand, notwithstanding intermittent challenges to the jurisdiction of communal and rabbinic courts by individuals who appealed their disputes in French courts, the monarchy firmly upheld the authority of rabbis and communal leaders throughout most of the eighteenth century to judge civil cases. The view of the monarchy presented here is consistent with revisionist scholarship on Absolutism that has offered a more nuanced understanding of the workings of the seventeenth- and early eighteenth-century monarchy. As William Beik argued, "the dominant paradigm shifted from a centralizing, modernizing monarch to a king maintaining and defending a traditional society." In his view, the "social collaboration" model of absolutism portrays monarchs as exercising their power "by collaborating with socially powerful elites—at court, in Paris and in the provinces. Government was characterized by compromise, negotiation, and sharing of resources in a manner which maintained and supported hierarchical differences."[67] As Michael

---

third, formational." See Clifford Geertz, *Local Knowledge: Further Essays in Interpretive Anthropology* (London, 1983), 167–244, esp. 218.

65 See Julia Eckert, "From Subjects to Citizens: Legalism from Below and the Homogenisation of the Legal Sphere," *Journal of Legal Pluralism* 53–54 (2006): 45–75.

66 For examples of challenges to the civil jurisdiction of the rabbis, see Cahen, "Le rabbinat de Metz pendant la période française," *REJ* 7 (1883): 103–107, 215–16; *REJ* 8 (1884): 257–58; REJ 8 (1884): 257–58, 262–66.

67 See William Beik, "The Absolutism of Louis XIV as Social Collaboration," *Past and Present* 188 (August 2005): 195, and idem, *Absolutism and Society in Seventeenth-Century France: State Power and Provincial Aristocracy in Languedoc* (Cambridge, 2011). For a valuable review of revisionist scholarship on eighteenth-century absolutism, see Breen, "Law, Society, and the State in Early Modern France," 346–86.

Breen has shown, current scholarship has challenged the emphasis formerly placed on the centralizing state and its propensity to discipline insubordinate populaces; instead historians now favor courts "that promoted state formation from below."[68]

Judicial practices of the Metz Beit Din mirror this model of government collaboration and challenge the dominant historiographical assessment of medieval and early modern Jewish autonomy. The conventional appraisal closely resembled the self-image of the Kehillah as self-reliant and self-contained in the face of state and society that were presumed to be adversarial and hostile. In such circumstances, there was a compelling logic to maintaining exclusive authority over civil cases. So while rabbinic courts were never the exclusive forum for the adjudication of civil disputes, communities in early modern Ashkenaz—and rabbinic leaders in particular—struggled persistently to sustain the myth of judicial exclusivity.

The Metz Beit Din signified a dramatic turnabout from the paradigm that typified Jewish conceptions of self-government and adjudication in the preceding decades. In the last third of the eighteenth century, the Jewish communal leadership of Metz became more attentive to the complex relationship that drew the Jews, the state, and French society together. As evidence earlier in the century reveals, this relationship was hardly unprecedented, but it is only after mid-century that signs of the paradigm shift are apparent. The Beit Din proved itself responsive to practical demands and to shifting cultural affinities by adapting to a world of multiple jurisdictions. Implicit in the rabbinic court's adaptational approach was the acknowledgement that the Jewish population was heavily dependent on the surrounding society not only for its economic welfare but also for the innumerable services that it could not provide for itself. Moreover, intricate economic interaction with members of the general population and the growing bureaucratic demands placed on all residents fostered a growing working relationship between the Jewish and French judiciaries. By the 1770s, as the rabbinic court protocols made abundantly clear, the illusion of a Jewish judicial system that existed entirely outside the state's civil system could no longer be sustained.

Two competing paradigms in the eighteenth century—legal centralism and legal pluralism—offer a framework for understanding this shift. Legal centralism embodied the idea that law was the exclusive domain of the state and the foremost instrument of state bureaucracy; it demanded that foreign systems subordinate themselves to its authority. Legal pluralism, by contrast,

68 Breen, "Law, Society, and the State in Early Modern France," 380.

acknowledged the validity of multiple legal orders and jurisdictions. The translation of Jewish civil and family law into French contained elements of both pluralism and centralism; it was pluralist to the extent that it recognized the right of Jews to be judged by their own laws, and it was centralist in that it envisioned the ideal legal forum as state-sponsored.

With the persistent encouragement of the state and its institutions, law functioned as a homogenizing force among diverse sectors of French society in the second half of the eighteenth century. The far-reaching effects of legal centralism were evident in the Metz Kehillah, where a powerful impulse was felt among communal leaders, and especially within the Beit Din, to work cooperatively with the French legal system. Although there are neither signs of coercive pressure exerted by the monarchy or municipal authorities, nor overt indications of capitulation by the Metz Kahal, the need to coordinate seems to have been felt most keenly in areas involving property, monetary exchange and contractual agreements.

Once established as a permanent court, the Metz Beit Din came to be viewed as one among many judicial institutions in the region, and the legitimacy of the Jewish community's jurisdictional authority was implicitly confirmed alongside that of royal and provincial institutions. The Beit Din adopted the idea of shared laws and institutions, acknowledging the interdependence of the Jewish and civil court systems by virtue of binding French court rulings, cases of Metz community members pending in French courts or disposition of cases implicating non-Jewish parties. Under these circumstances, a collaborative relationship between the Jewish and French courts—a mosaic of interlocking pieces—emerged.[69] This shift was doubtless driven by interests shared by the Jewish community and French authorities. Jewish leaders understood that it was not practicable for members of their communities to ignore the bureaucratic demands and legal services of the state. The state, for its part, viewed the Metz Beit Din and its adjudication of civil cases as consistent with the project of French state-building that had intensified in the second half of the eighteenth century.[70]

In fact, it appears that the cooperative relationship between the French civil courts and the Metz Beit Din resulted in part from the implicit recognition

69 See, for example, PMBD, Vol. 1, pt. 1, no. 77, 27a, and Vol. 2, no. 256, 47b and no. 345, 64b. For a discussion of legal pluralism and centralism in a medieval setting, cf. Simonsohn, *A Common Justice*, 11–31, 61–95, 116–33, 203–12, 286–300.

70 See, for example, 27 Tamuz 5523 [1763] entry in PKM [page number illegible], which notes the impending visit of the *Conseillier du Parlement* to the Jewish street in Metz to see how the community was handling mischief-makers—clear evidence of government interest in the policing efforts of the Kahal.

of the rabbinic court as one among many institutions in the French judicial system. France was divided into thirty-six *généralités*, each governed by a royal intendant; civil and criminal cases were heard at *bailliages* or *présidiaux*—two local royal tribunals. The *parlements*, the highest-ranking courts in France, exercised judicial and legislative powers. Thirteen such sovereign courts were in major population centers, including the Metz Parlement, which was established in 1633. The overlapping and often competing jurisdictions of these and other courts call attention to the fact that there was no single legal structure in France nor was there a unified system of taxation.[71] In addition, in the last third of the eighteenth century there appears to have been a realignment of the three main forces that had bearing on rabbinic jurisdiction in civil affairs: the Monarchy, the Parlement, and the Beit Din. Earlier in the century, the Parlement labored to curtail rabbinic jurisdiction, and in response the Monarchy often stepped in to reaffirm rabbinic authority in civil affairs. In the 1770s, however, the Parlement and the Beit Din appear to have entered a new relationship built on the collaborative model.[72]

Jews in Metz, as elsewhere, enjoyed the freedom to live according to Jewish law, but this was more than a privilege. In all legal matters documented in the *Recueil* and others, Jews had no alternative to Jewish customary law, including inheritance law. With only the limited exceptions noted, this rule went unchallenged. Nevertheless, Jewish and French jurists generally agreed that Jewish inheritance law had to comply with the *procedural* guidelines of French law. While, so far as I am aware, there are no cases in which Metz governmental authorities interceded to force compliance with French inheritance customs, Jewish individuals were free to contest any aspect of the inheritance protocol when they believed the distribution failed to conform to French civil procedure. The Beit Din, for its part, had the dual task of faithfully interpreting and applying the law in accord with Jewish tradition while also assuring procedural compliance with prevailing Metz customs or royal laws. This pertained to the way wills were drawn up (technical language; translation into French) or that property transactions on which inheritance cases often turned had to accord with French contract law. For these reasons, the Beit Din regularly consulted

---

71 On the jurisdiction of *bailliage* courts, see Roland Mousnier, *Les institutions de la France sous la monarchie absolue, 1598–1789*, 2 vols. (Chicago, 1979–1984), 2:255–74.

72 The idea of a realignment of the Monarchy, the Parlement, and the Beit Din was proposed by Frances Malino in response to a paper I delivered at a meeting of the Association for Jewish Studies in 2010. Whether the collaborative attitude of the Beit Din toward the Metz Parlement was borne out as well in the Parlement's dealings with the Beit Din will be determined only after the Moselle departmental archives have been systematically studied.

French lawyers for clarification. These were all emblematic of how the Beit Din navigated between the two systems.

The protocols of the Metz Beit Din invite an entirely different set of questions: How did jurists within the rabbinic court system respond to challenges to Jewish law posed by non-Jewish legal systems? Is there any evidence that judicial procedure in the Beit Din, or the interpretation of the law itself, was influenced by French law or by the possibility of recourse to French civil courts?[73] How did the phenomenon of legal pluralism influence the methods of adjudication and jurisprudence employed in the Metz rabbinic court?

While legal pluralism emerged during the past quarter-century as an important analytical tool among legal historians, relatively little is known of the concrete methods that Jewish courts employed to navigate multiple legal orders.[74] The protocols of the Metz Beit Din contain evidence of legal pluralism that is apparent in its impact on the court's methods of adjudication, the adoption and adaptation of legal perspectives and mechanisms from French jurisprudence, the concrete influence on procedure, and in substantive areas of law such as commerce, lending, inheritance, and marital property. This development was related to increasing social mobility in France that stemmed in part from the transition to capitalism in the second half of the eighteenth century. Legal pluralism did not reduce either the tendency to adopt or the need to implement generally accepted judicial practices, nor the demand for compliance, especially among minorities. In the specific case of the Jews, compliance fostered a firm attachment to state and society through the internalization of legal and administrative norms, particularly as these related to commerce, torts, guardianship, and inheritance.[75] The familiarity with French

73 Jacob Katz, *Exclusiveness and Tolerance: Studies in Jewish-Gentile Relations in Medieval and Modern Times* (Cambridge, MA, 1961), 52. See also Asaf, *Batei ha-din ve-sidreihem*, 11–24. For examples of the influence that recourse to gentile courts brought to bear on Jewish law and jurisprudence under medieval Islam, see Libson, *Jewish and Islamic Law*, 45 and 111. Libson points to the leniency of geonic *takkanot* concerning the "rebellious wife," particularly her ability to obtain a divorce without delay and without forfeiting her *ketubah*, as having been enacted as a strategic ploy aiming to preclude recourse to Islamic courts.

74 Recent publications by Jewish historians have nonetheless begun to raise the profile of legal pluralism considerably. Simonsohn's work on medieval Islamic society and Jessica Marglin's research on nineteenth-century Morocco have each advanced our understanding of the role of legal pluralism in the general courts to which Jews took their cases and have shed light on the challenges posed by the conflict of laws. See Simonsohn, *A Common Justice* and Marglin, *Across Legal Lines*.

75 See Susan S. Silbey, "Legal Culture and Cultures of Legality," in *Handbook of Cultural Sociology*, ed. John R. Hall, Laura Grindstaff, and Ming-cheng Lo (London, 2010), 470–79.

law is evident in the routinization of civil procedures in the Beit Din and in its navigation of overlapping jurisdictions as defined by the Jewish and French justice systems.

This process could not proceed without consideration of its implications for the integrity of the Jewish legal system, especially the degree of reconciliation with talmudic law. The application of talmudic law to conditions in eighteenth-century Metz demanded familiarity with royal legislation and local ordinances. This would require the reinterpretation of talmudic law, especially as understood in medieval codes and commentaries, and its application to novel conditions. Conceptually, the growing influence of legal centralism was not an unprecedented hurdle for Jewish law. The principle of *dina d'malkhuta dina* ("the law of the kingdom is the law") was well established within Jewish legal culture. Beginning the third century, the question of where to draw the line concerning the scope of *dina d'malkhuta dina*—whether it was limited to taxation, eminent domain, and punishment, or extended as well to the realm of torts, lost property, and family law—had been an important practical issue for rabbinic courts. It served as a source for accommodationism, though there is wide disagreement on its scope and application. Can there be compliance with the laws of the land without abandoning the obligations and constraints of the Jewish legal system? This question had direct bearing on how Jews would succeed in complying with the laws of the land without abandoning the particular demands imposed by the Jewish legal tradition.[76]

Methods of adjudication practiced in the Metz Beit Din reveal unavoidable tensions between its role as guardian of autonomy and its efforts to navigate the political challenges imposed by competing jurisdictions. These

76 There is general agreement that *dina d'malkhuta dina* applies to civil law (*mamona*) but not to ritual law (*issura*), though the principle can have indirect implications in the ritual sphere. For examples, see Aaron Rakefet-Rothkoff, "Dina D'Malkhuta Dina—The Law of the Land in Halakhic Perspective," *Tradition* 13 (Fall, 1973): 11–13. Concerning its application in judicial matters, R. Solomon ben Aderet ruled that *dina d'malkhuta dina* pertains "only to matters of state and not to other matters ordinarily dealt with by the courts," cited in Joseph Caro, *Beit Yosef, Hoshen Mishpat* §26:6. R. Moses Isserles ruled that a *beit din* must uphold a civil law enacted by the state even when it contradicts the Halakhah if such a law is for the betterment of society (*le-takkanat benei ha-medinah*). See Rema, *Hoshen Mishpat* §369:11, and the opposing view of R. Shabbetai Cohen, *Siftei Cohen, Hoshen Mishpat* §73:39. See Aaron Kirschenbaum and Jon Trafimow, "The Sovereign Power of the State: A Proposed Theory of Accommodation in Jewish Law," *Cardozo Law Review* 12 (1990): 925–40; Shilo, *Dina d'Malkhuta Dina,* passim; and critical comments on Shilo's opus by Jacob J. Schacter, "Dina de-Malkhuta Dina—A Review," *Diné Israel* 8 (1977): 78–95. For examples of how *dina d'malkhuta dina* was applied in the Metz Beit Din, see Jay R. Berkovitz, "Acculturation and Integration in Eighteenth-Century Metz," *Jewish History* 24:3–4 (2010): 271–94.

strains remained beneath the surface and only rarely, if ever, found expression in the rhetoric of the court proceedings. Although the rabbinic court surely viewed itself as having remained faithful to the talmudic and halakhic tradition, broader social, economic and juridical forces in the eighteenth century demanded greater flexibility than rabbinic courts exhibited elsewhere. While judicial coordination may well have relied on any of several approaches available in Jewish legal theory, there is no explicit indication of how the *av beit din* or his fellow judges viewed such matters. The overwhelming evidence is that the Beit Din was not solely responding to political pressures but was sincerely concerned with addressing the needs of its constituents.[77]

Given the prevailing political constraints and exigencies of the second half of the eighteenth century, the state could hardly deny the validity of legal pluralism. Accordingly, it confirmed the legitimacy of the Jewish community's jurisdictional authority—in both theoretical and practical terms—alongside the jurisdiction of royal and provincial bodies. The Beit Din was certainly aware of the contingent nature of the relationship between Jewish law and general law. Tensions between its role as arbiter of Jewish law and as agent of the Kahal are no less apparent. In its capacity as a communal institution, the Metz Beit Din was expected to comply with communal bylaws (*takkanot ha-kahal*), even when the latter were not fully in accord with talmudic law. The priority attached to communal legislation signaled the preeminence of the Kahal leadership, and as the scope of laws that regulated consumption, social relations between men and women, and the behavior of youth expanded, the impact of lay empowerment became ever more apparent. As indicated earlier, a powerful urban laity in Metz legislated standards of moral and religious behavior that were inspired by an abiding concern for social order. That the authority of the Metz laws rested principally on secular arguments, though frequently reinforced by the rhetoric of religious tradition, confirms that navigation of competing jurisdictions was a multi-faceted project beset by internal as well as external challenges.

Precisely because the boundaries between the two legal systems were not as rigidly demarcated as is commonly assumed, communal leaders found it necessary to define when recourse to the civil courts was justified and when it was not. To be sure, medieval and early modern codes had spelled out guidelines indicating how to proceed when adjudication within the Jewish judicial system was either impossible, unenforceable, or would not yield a just resolution of a dispute. Changing social and economic parameters contributed to a growing tendency to settle disputes in the general courts, though recourse to

77 See Rosen, *Law and Culture*, xii.

French courts remained—at least on the books—a contentious act in violation of the sovereignty of the Jewish community and a betrayal of Jewish law.[78] But on the ground, things were much different. Where guardians appointed to manage the estate of orphans had refused to pay a physician for medical services he had provided, the Beit Din granted the claimant authorization to sue in the civil courts.[79] Likewise, the Beit Din authorized an individual to sue in the civil court for what he was owed in inventory and escrow funds.[80] In other instances, the Beit Din refused emphatically to approve recourse to the civil courts. Even though recourse to gentile courts for purposes of litigation was strictly prohibited, Talmudic law recognized the validity of contracts produced by notaries and confirmed in gentile courts. Built into the system was the acknowledgement that special circumstances would occasionally require reliance on non-Jewish tribunals, particularly when one of the parties refused to appear before the Beit Din.

Evidence drawn from the 1769 communal legislation suggests that the relationship to gentile courts had developed much beyond what was envisioned by medieval halakhists. Jewish property transfers were commonly transacted in the French courts while only those transactions that placed the rights of other Metz Jews at risk were regulated by the Kahal. If an individual who owed money to another Jew sold a house in the French court, no Jew was permitted to purchase that house, apart from the creditors to whom the money was owed.[81] In addition, halakhic authorities permitted recourse to gentile courts when a legal matter concerned maintenance of public order, land purchase, or taxation. By displaying a neutral and, at times, positive orientation toward the French judicial system, the Metz Beit Din appears to have abandoned a longstanding adversarial tradition *vis-à-vis* the much deprecated *'arkha'ot shel goyim*. In the latter years of the ancien régime, the rabbinic court adopted an understanding of general law qua civil custom that was taken into consideration when matters of Jewish law were adjudicated. By the last third of the eighteenth century, French civil procedures

78 See Tur, *Ḥoshen Mishpat* §26.

79 PMBD, Vol. 1, pt. 1, no. 103, 35a.

80 See PMBD, Vol. 1, pt. 1, no. 37, 13b, where authorization to sue in the civil court was granted, but only after a week. Similarly, in Vol. 1, pt. 1, no. 77, 27a, the Beit Din authorized Ḥayyim Püttlingen to sue in the civil court for money he was owed. For a similar authorization, see PMBD, Vol. 1, pt. 1, no. 106, 36b.

81 See 1769 Takkanot, Art. 65, in PKM, 80a. For additional evidence of how the Kahal as a legislative body navigated between the French and Jewish judicial systems, see 1769 Takkanot, Art. 66.

were incorporated in the Beit Din and had gained currency among members of the Jewish community. The Beit Din's familiarity with the basic structure and principles of French law, as well as its cooperative relationship with royal and municipal judicial institutions, are unmistakable proof of the considerable interplay between the two legal systems. By accommodating itself to the French legal system, the Beit Din acknowledged a more limited form of judicial autonomy, perhaps, as did the Kahal. In fact, since the conferral of autonomy was not viewed as a threat to the state's hegemony, the jurisdiction that the Metz Beit Din enjoyed may be viewed as a weak form of legal pluralism. Thus, while one could marry according to Jewish ritual law, it was the certificate issued by the secular authorities that formally validated the marriage.[82]

In the course of the struggle to uphold its authority, the Beit Din demonstrated a willingness to adjust its own legal orders and even, in certain instances, to incorporate elements of French civil law when considering a dispute. At the procedural level especially, the rabbinic court recognized certain advantages of the competing legal order and displayed the capacity to adapt to the centralized legal environment. To be sure, the question of external influence is fraught with difficult and often insurmountable complexities. Can one take the innumerable instances of borrowings of terms from French jurisprudence as proof of influence on the Beit Din? At issue is the difficulty in identifying sources of legal norms and traditions. Arguably the most reliable ways to demonstrate "influence" is to uncover mutual contacts and encounters between jurists of the two systems. In the rabbinic court proceedings evidence of consultations with French lawyers is not uncommon, though it is unlikely that there were direct contacts between Jewish and French judges. It is also improbable that *dayanim* on the Beit Din read French legal tracts. Yet by necessity, however it was accomplished, Jewish jurists gained familiarity with French law and legal procedure and took that law into account, particularly when disputes involved the two (or more) legal systems.

For its part, without surrendering its own authority, the Beit Din regularly acknowledged the interdependence of cases brought before the rabbinic judges and those taken to the French civil court system.[83] On numerous occasions the Beit Din made clear that it would need to await the judgment of the

82 On weak and strong pluralism, see Griffiths, "What is Legal Pluralism?" *Journal of Legal Pluralism and Unofficial Law* 24 (1986): 1–55.

83 See, for example, PMBD, Vol. 1, pt. 1, no. 77, 27a. See, also, PMBD, Vol. 2, no. 256, 47b and no. 345, 64b for references by the Beit Din to cases that had been settled in the *bailliage*.

French court before it could issue its own ruling. In a case concerning the division of living space, the Beit Din declared that its decision was valid "so long as the gentile courts do not object."[84] It is striking that the Beit Din was hampered by contingencies of this sort even in matters that were presumably of minimal interest to the authorities. In such cases, the pendulum had swung more in the direction of legal centralism than pluralism, at least as far as the rabbinic court's understanding was concerned.[85]

The collaborative spirit evinced by the Beit Din cannot be fully appreciated without noting the jurisdictional boundaries that the Kehillah leadership drew or that evolved at the grassroots level over the course of the eighteenth century. Three points stand out. First, evidence of cooperation with the French judicial system, or signs of influence on the internal workings of the rabbinic court were limited strictly to civil concerns. Ritual matters generally did not come before the Metz Beit Din unless they were related directly or indirectly to a civil dispute. Based on a well-established talmudic tradition that was strongly endorsed by medieval halakhic authorities, ritual was shielded—in principle, if not in practice—from external influence or interference.[86] Second, compliance with French law and judicial practice tended to be a pragmatic response to disputes brought to the Beit Din and should not be viewed as having an underlying ideological motivation. Third, there are no explicit examples of the Beit Din authorizing a dispute to be taken to the French courts unless all other avenues had been exhausted. But it is significant that the Beit Din was willing to hear, routinely and without prejudice, cases that involved prior recourse to those courts.

These developments typified a broader trend in France concerning the competing prerogatives of clerical and civil authorities. But in sharp contrast to the ecclesiastical courts, the Metz Beit Din enjoyed substantial independence from state interference and control. Where there was evidence of procedural irregularities in ecclesiastical courts—whether in cases concerning contractual

---

84 PMBD, Vol. 1, pt. 1, no. 3, 6a.

85 See Julia Eckert, "From Subject to Citizen: Legalisation from Below and the Homogenisation of the Legal Sphere," *Journal of Legal Pluralism* 53–54 (2006): 45–75.

86 For two exceptional examples of disputes concerning ritual, see PMBD, Vol. 1, pt. 2, no. 53, 15b, and Vol. 2, no. 42, 9a. In the first case, several individuals attempted to remove a cantor from his position in the synagogue serving the communities of LaGrange and Manom (Manhofffen) on the strength of two accusations: that the cantor was a Sabbath violator and that he had struck a guest. In the second case, a husband claimed that his wife failed to maintain Jewish dietary laws in the home. Also see PMBD, Vol. 2, no. 71, 13a–b, concerning a suit against a resident of Lichtigen for his failure to share responsibility for *pletten*, the communal *etrog*, providing support for guests in the adjacent villages, and the writing of a *sefer Torah*.

matters, offenses against the public order, or the civil consequences of strictly religious affairs—municipal and royal courts firmly imposed their jurisdiction and exercised the right to overturn the decisions. Moreover, the powers of ecclesiastical courts were limited to canonical penalties.[87] However, the state granted the Beit Din greater latitude to resolve internal differences based on Jewish legal traditions related primarily to civil matters. Still, neither the Kehillah nor the Beit Din was able to ignore pressures to coordinate with and adapt to general law. Adaptation was a highly complex phenomenon that posed dilemmas for any minority committed to maintaining its cultural distinctiveness while acknowledging the need to be part of the larger social, cultural and economic matrix.

As an institution serving a minority population, the Metz Beit Din was alert to the importance of adjusting to the changing social and economic environment, especially in areas such as inheritance, purchase and sale, and contracts. The Metz rabbinic court exemplified those minority systems that incorporated procedural details from the majority. Moreover, legal systems belonging to different cultures frequently respond in similar ways to the same reality. The adaptability of the Metz rabbinic court was reinforced by a tendency within French officialdom to view the Beit Din, despite its autonomous standing, as part of the general French judicial system. Concomitantly, French legal terms were assimilated by the Beit Din and applied to certain internal procedures that corresponded to bureaucratic actions and to judicial processes observed in the general courts. For example, in a case in which a defendant refused on five occasions to respond to an order issued by the Beit Din to come to court, the plaintiff executed a *sommation*, an official summons to appear before the Beit Din.[88] In cases involving the purchase and sale of real property, Jewish litigants adhered to widely-established procedures while the Beit Din was the forum where numerous claims based on French law were advanced and settled, though many went to the French courts as well. In one instance, a litigant in the Beit Din demanded that each side split the cost of the *contrôle*, the document registering the verification of payment.[89] The use of terms such as *sommation* and *contrôle* is consistent with the suggestion that the Beit Din had become, for all intents and purposes, adjunct to the French judicial system.

---

87 See McManners, *Church and Society in Eighteenth-Century France*, 1:23–25, 157, 196–97, 361. For the possible application of the community court and integrationist models to pre-revolutionary efforts to sort out jurisdiction over religious affairs, see Adam S. Hofri-Winogradow. "A Plurality of Discontent: Legal Pluralism, Religious Adjudication and the State" *Journal of Law and Religion* 26.1 (2010): 57–89.

88 PMBD, Vol. 2, no. 612, 132a.

89 PMBD, Vol. 1, pt. 1, no. 136, 44a.

In some cases, the dominant legal system served as a catalyst to awaken legal norms or procedures that had been in a latent state until then.[90]

Three procedural trends in the Metz Beit Din reflected a clear acknowledgment of legal pluralism, which it could scarcely deny, and a more cautious acceptance of legal centralism, which doubtless stemmed from pragmatic considerations: (1) The pervasiveness of French law in specific areas such as the appointment of guardians, the division of marital property, and inheritance promoted cooperation with the French civil courts and authorities. (2) The Beit Din's close acquaintance with documents and procedures of the French legal system, together with the universal acceptance of notarization to certify civil transactions, contributed to a broadly conceived approach to law. This included the Beit Din's recognition of civil contracts and the weight it attached to such documents in the course of its deliberations. (3) Aware of the limits of its authority, the Beit Din was willing to rein in its own judicial powers while conceding the validity and even the advantage of French civil procedures. In this competitive environment, the Metz community came to expect of its rabbinic court judicial procedures that compared favorably to those practiced in the French courts. The Beit Din's adoption of several parallel legal devices, while confirming the influence of the dominant culture, was an oblique form of cultural resistance that may have induced litigants to settle their differences within the Jewish legal framework.

The Acquaintance with French Law and Judicial Procedure

The Beit Din's cooperation with the French civil courts was evident in most areas of law. In the realm of debt collection, for example, the Beit Din acknowledged that an agreement in the civil court established binding rules for extending additional time to repay debts.[91] Even though such a ruling was hardly necessary from a legal standpoint, the action of the rabbinic court represented a formal ratification of the arbiters' decision, lending it greater standing in the Jewish community. Equally revealing is the convergence between the two legal systems in areas involving property transfer. For example, the disposition of marital property assumed a uniquely civil character with the jurisdictional move from ecclesiastical courts to civil courts. For Jews this first found expression in the royal decree of 1701, which required them to

90 For a useful discussion of comparable methodological concerns in relation to the influence of Islamic law on Jewish law, see Libson, *Jewish and Islamic Law*, 2–15.

91 See PMBD, Vol. 1, pt. 2, no. 33, 10b.

deposit a French translation of their marriage contracts with royal notaries.[92] Of particular significance is the recognition of Jewish marriage as a civil act that entitled, if not encouraged, redress of property grievances in the civil courts. Similarly, owing to the abiding interest of the crown in the post-mortem transfer of property, probate inventories were executed without exception in the French civil courts.[93] These were routine matters that characteristically entailed the cooperation of the rabbinic court.

Evidence of this sort reveals the court's keen awareness that Jews in Metz and its environs inhabited two distinct legal universes—Jewish and French—and that the Jewish judicial system was inexorably interconnected with French law and judicial procedure. This is illustrated, in part, by repeated and respectful references to judgments issued by the *bailliage* court on cases brought by Jewish litigants who subsequently came before the rabbinic court or who still had cases pending in the French civil courts.[94] The terminology appearing in the proceedings of the rabbinic court in reference to French civil court rulings and procedural regulations—*dinei ʿarkhaʾot, mishpat ʿarkhaʾot*, and *nimusei ʿarkhaʾot*—are devoid of the pejorative overtones associated with term *ʿarkhaʾot shel ʿovdei ʿavodah zarah* (courts of idolaters), for example—that commonly appear in rabbinic writings of the period.[95] Even more striking, there was a strong acknowledgment of the interrelationship of the cases brought before the Beit Din and those brought in the French civil court system.[96] In several instances, the Beit Din decided to await a ruling in the French civil court before issuing its own decision. In a case of alleged malfeasance on the part of guardians responsible for managing the estate of minors, three French arbiters were asked to broker a settlement "for the benefit of the orphans." The Beit Din expressed full support for this step and stated emphatically that the

92 On changes in French law, see Hanley, "The Jurisprudence of the Arrêts," 8 and 14, n. 10. According to Zosa Szajkowski, this requirement was meant to protect Christian creditors against default by Jewish debtors, in case the property changed hands; see his "Alsatian Jewish Inventories in the Hebrew Union College Library," *Studies in Bibliography and Booklore* 4:2 (1959): 96–97. Also see Jean Fleury, *Contrats de mariage juifs en Moselle avant 1792* (Metz 1989), and André Aaron Fraenckel, *Mémoire juive en Alsace. Contrats de Mariage au XVIII*[e] *siècle* (Strasbourg, 1998), xiii.

93 See, for example, PMBD, Vol. 1, pt. 1, no. 10, 8b.

94 See, for example, PMBD, Vol. 1, pt. 2, no. 49, 14a; Vol. 2, no. 554, 47b; and no. 354, 64b, for references to cases that had been settled in the *bailliage*.

95 See, for example, PMBD, Vol. 1, pt. 2, no. 37, 12a; no. 92, 24b; no. 218, 49b; Vol. 2, no. 310, 57b; no. 363, 68a; no. 467, 92b.

96 See, for example, PMBD, Vol. 1, pt. 1, no. 77, 27a.

arbitration ruling would be implemented "with full force, as if it were enacted before the Beit Din."[97]

Some of the actions recorded in the Pinkas reveal the imprint of broader societal trends on the legal culture of Metz Jews and what they may have expected of the Beit Din. These included the appointment of women as guardians, the weight attached to wills as instruments the validity of which could be upheld independently of halakhic statutes, and the acknowledgement of joint or community property in marriage. Although there is undisputed halakhic precedent for each of these developments, social convention and legal conservatism frequently stood in opposition to them. The Beit Din's authorization of these departures from traditional practice suggests the apparent influence of cultural shifts that were likely to have originated in the surrounding French milieu. Internal changes and external influences were without doubt interrelated. It is therefore likely that the impact of broader legal trends and cultural influences in early modern France had a bearing on the way Jewish law was adjudicated by the Beit Din and is apparent in the penetration of French legal norms into the Metz Jewish community.

Additionally, it should be borne in mind that interaction between the Beit Din and the French judicial system was a human encounter. It entailed the fostering of relationships—sometimes in a one-time meeting and on other occasions in repeated interactions with a cohort of bureaucratic officials, at varying levels, that included notaries, translators, *greffiers*, scribes, sheriffs, and *avocats*. Whether these relationships promoted a collaborative spirit is impossible to state with certainty, though it seems likely that it left its imprint on the Beit Din's approach to French law.[98]

The administration of talmudic law in eighteenth-century Metz demanded familiarity with royal legislation, local ordinances, and various types of documentation required by the French judicial system.[99] Expertise in dealing with officers of the civil courts was necessary as well. These skills were widely in evidence, as for example in cases involving compliance with the commercial law

97 See PMBD, Vol. 1, pt. 1, no. 110, 37a.

98 The evidence from Metz appears to be consistent with the portrayal of the progressive independence of local judicial officers from royal control in the seventeenth and eighteenth centuries. For a discussion of spheres of personal power created by the judicial and administrative authority of *bailliage* and seigneurial judges, see Schneider, *The King's Bench*.

99 For example, in a case concerning the appointment of a guardian, the Beit Din stated that "it is known to all that in the civil court it is impossible to do anything large or small, whether to prepare an inventory or to occupy oneself with the estate without the appointment of a guardian and *curateur* where an orphan is involved." See PMBD, Vol. 1, pt. 2, no. 99, 25a; Vol. 2, no. 252, 47a; and Vol. 2, no. 632, 137a.

and in disputes concerning marriage, divorce, and inheritance. The acquaintance of the Beit Din with many of the particulars of French law and court procedures was consistent with a growing perception of the Jewish judiciary and Jewish law as having become conjoined with, if not incorporated into, the general judicial system of France.

For the Jews' part, the advantages of the integrative model were not immediately apparent, and indeed the dangers to their judicial autonomy troubled Rabbi Eibeschütz and the community's lay leaders. But a generation later there appears to have been greater receptivity to the idea. A public demonstration of this harmonious spirit was the special *fête* the Metz Jewish community sponsored to mark the reinstatement of the Parlement in 1775. The significance of the occasion was captured in, if not projected by, the application of the verse from Isaiah 1:26: "He will restore your judges and magistrates as before and afterward your city shall be called the city of justice, a faithful city."[100] Although the political importance of participation in the civic celebration cannot be ignored, there is no reason to assume that the Jewish community was insincere in its identification with the official return of the seat of justice to Metz. Close examination of the legal discourse that is embedded in the Beit Din records conveys a fuller appreciation of the dynamics of interaction with French society and culture. In example after example one encounters compliance with administrative and bureaucratic standards imposed by local and state law, but with no signs of annoyance or discontent.

Sweeping social, economic, and political forces in the second half of the eighteenth century fostered a general familiarity with French law among members of the Metz Jewish community. As a practical matter, the demands of daily life called for even greater knowledge of the particulars of the French legal system. Familiarity with the French judicial system and with French law in general is reflected in the Beit Din's acquaintance with legal terminology, as noted earlier, with legal concepts, and with legislation that were pertinent to cases under its review. Its compliance with French law demanded attentiveness to various regulations imposed by local authorities and courts, in several cases concerning guidelines for maintaining latrines.[101] In another instance, the Beit Din stated that French law was the basis for the method it employed in determining priority in the collection of a debt: "Precedence with respect

---

100 Noted in Simon Schama, *Citizens: A Chronicle of the French Revolution* (New York, 1989), 110–11. The Hebrew text of Isaiah 1:26 is as follows: "ואשיבה שפטיך כבראשנה ויעציך כבתחלה אחרי כן יקרא לך עיר הצדק קריה נאמנה".

101 See PMBD, Vol. 1, pt. 1, no. 3, 6a; no. 144, 46a; Vol. 1, pt. 2, nos. 227–228, 51a; no. 167, 40a; Vol. 2, no. 246, 45b; no. 479, 95b; no. 624, 134b.

to the remaining creditors follows the law practiced in the general courts."[102] Regularly confronted with the demands of competing jurisdictions and conflicting legal systems, the Metz Beit Din met the challenges of legal pluralism by adapting to the system of law that prevailed in the city of Metz and within the greater Moselle region. This was evident in cases involving inheritance, marital property, debt repayment, commercial transactions and partnerships. It is clear that neither the Jewish population of Metz nor its rabbinic court were in a position to mount any significant resistance to the powerful trend of either legal pluralism or centralism—first, because the guiding principle of *dina d'malkhuta dina* was accommodationist by nature and its goal was to minimize legal discord, and, second, because the infrastructural power of the state, with its emphasis on the central role of administrative bureaucracy, reinforced the advantage and importance of coordinating various institutions under a unified French legal system.[103]

Numerous cases brought before the Beit Din posed dilemmas from the standpoint of judicial authority. Litigants who brought their disputes to the rabbinic court were undoubtedly aware of the complexities involved in navigating between the jurisdictional sway of the Jewish and French legal systems respectively. There are quite a few complex cases where the roles of the two judiciaries and of Jewish and French law more generally, were intricately interwoven. In a case involving a mutual decision to break off a marital engagement, for example, a young man and woman came before the Beit Din in order to formally nullify their prior agreement and to renounce any future monetary claims against each other. (The engagement was being terminated because the young man was named by a pregnant woman as the father of her child, an accusation he vehemently denied.) It is noteworthy that the parties renounced the agreement to marry "in accordance with Torah law and in accordance with the civil law ... in whichever court it will be, whether by Jewish law or by the laws of the nations." This formulation was customarily employed when parties to a dispute wished to release each other from prior debts or agreements regardless of the forum in which such differences might be adjudicated. Each party agreed that the annulment of previous understandings and commitments would be enforceable in either of the two systems of law. According to the terms of the release, they were each free to marry another person of their choosing. The two sets of parents were also present for the declaration

102 PMBD, Vol. 1, pt. 2, no. 32, 10b: דין קדימה לשאר ב"ח כדין ערכאות. Cf. PMBD, Vol. 1, pt. 1, no. 4, 7a, concerning a lien placed on a portion of sold property.

103 See Michael Mann, "The Autonomous Power of the State: Its Origins, Mechanisms and Results," *Archives européennes de sociologie* 25 (1984): 185–213.

pronounced before the Beit Din, and they likewise agreed to withdraw any remaining claims against each other. As crafted by the Beit Din, the renunciation agreement extended full legal protection to each side in case the other party decided to advance a formal appeal against the agreement.[104]

Navigating the Two Systems

A formulaic expression that appears routinely in the Metz communal and court records—"whether according to the Law of Israel or the Law of the Nations" (*bein be-dinei Yisrael u-vedinei ummot ha-ʿolam*)—had come to signify the two legal worlds in which the Jews of Metz lived. A common phrase in rabbinic responsa as well, it does not itself denote a legal principle, as does *dina d'malkhuta dina*. It is a statement indicating that a legal action or ruling met, or was intended to meet, the standards of both Jewish and general law. But this meaning had evolved substantially from its usage in the Middle Ages to the early modern period. Most often the phrase referred to the range of jurisdiction options that were available when a dispute involved a Jew and a gentile.[105] It also served as a rhetorical phrase denoting that any forum—Jewish or non-Jewish—was acceptable when one of the litigants was unwilling to come to the Beit Din. In such circumstances, however, Rabbi Solomon Luria cautioned that this must not be taken as license for recourse to gentile courts, and if a lender proceeded to sue the borrower according to the laws of nations, "we object, and if he does not comply, we impose the ban on him."[106] What was, in the estimation of Rabbi Joseph Colon, little more than a scribal convention that was not meant to be taken literally, came to represent, by the late seventeenth

104 PMBD, Vol. 1, pt. 2, no. 218, 49b; see, also, Vol. 2, no. 247, 45b. For the phrase בין בד"י בין בא"ה, and slight variants, see BT Gittin 44a. The phrase is found as well in several early modern responsa such as Joseph Colon, *Resp. Maharik*, no. 10. According to R. Solomon Luria, *Yam shel Shelomo*, Bava Kama 8:65, the formula, when inserted in a contract, was the equivalent of gaining prior authorization from the Beit Din to litigate in the gentile court should this become necessary. See the following additional examples: PMBD, Vol. 1, pt. 2, no. 32, 10a and 10b; Vol. 1, pt. 2, no. 49, 14b; no. 128, 32b; Vol. 2, no. 310, 57b; no. 397, 73a.

105 See, for example, Isaiah Di Trani ha-Zaken, BT Bava Kama 113a, s.v. *le-havri'aḥ*.

106 *Yam shel Shlomo*, BT Bava Kama ch. 8. The following is the original quote:
כיוצא בזה דנתי כבר על מה שנהגו לכתוב בשטרות בין בדיני ישראל בין בדיני אומות. ואמרתי חלילה וחס שיהיה רשות למלוה לתבוע אותו בדיני האומות. אפילו שניהם עומדים בפנינו, ואמר לוה למלוה, שיתבענו בדיני האומות אם ירצה. מחינן ליה שלא יתבענו, ואי לא ציית משמתינן. והא דכתבינן בין בדיני האומות. יש לפרשו שלא לעקר דברי תורה, כגון אי גברא אלימא הוא, ואין כח ביד בתי דיני ישראל, אז יש לו רשות להביא אותו בדיני האומות, שלא יפסיד ממונו ע"כ.

century, the authorization to adjudicate in a gentile court or in accordance with gentile law.[107]

Evidence of modest change in the general understanding of the phrase can be discerned in the seventeenth century. In *Sefer Naḥalat Shiv'ah* by Samuel Halevi Segel, the use of the formula underscored that a *ketubah* obligation could not be legitimately subverted in any circumstance, whether in a Jewish or non-Jewish court.[108] While it is unclear that this was any more than a rhetorical device intended to underscore the severity of the obligations, the phrase was used more boldly in an exemplar of a loan note published by Segel that granted the bearer the right to seek payment in any court, Jewish or gentile, without the authorization of any rabbi, communal leader, or sovereign.[109] Even so, repeating Colon's contingency, Segel cautioned that the initial effort must be to adjudicate according to Jewish law, and only failing that, would a lawsuit in a non-Jewish court be permitted. In the late seventeenth century, Rabbi Gershon Ashkenazi understood the phrase as absolving an individual of legal liability, whether according to Jewish or non-Jewish law.[110]

By the time it appeared in the Pinkas Kahal and the Pinkas Beit Din between the mid- and late-eighteenth century, the phrase "whether according to the Law of Israel or the Law of the Nations" had shifted from the restrictive rhetoric of the Middle Ages to a more precise usage referring to positive acts performed in compliance with both Jewish and French law. The phrase was commonly used in several contexts: (a) It conveyed the Beit Din's compliance with Metz customary law regarding the appointment of guardians, the assignment of duties, and the requirement to appoint two types of guardians.[111] It

---

107 *Resp. Maharik*, no. 187, apparently in accordance with his father's opinion.
דאף על גב שנוהגין הסופרי׳ לכתוב בשטרות בין בדיני ישראל בין בדיני אומות העולם לא דרשינן לשון הדיוט לומר שיוכל לתובעו בדיני אומות העולם משום דעבירה היא ואפילו דין שהאומות דנין אותו כדין ישראל ההולך לפני דייני אומות העולם עובדי ע״ז מחלל ש״ש ומייקר שם ע״ז הלכך צריך לתובעו בדיני ישראל עכ״ל.

108 Segel, *Sefer Naḥalat Shiv'ah*, "Shetarot," nos. 16 and 25.

109 Segel, *Sefer Naḥalat Shiv'ah*, "Shetarot," no. 28:
מעתה ומעכשיו בקנין סודר ובתקיעת כף ובחומר הנ״ל מחייבים ומשעבדים אנחנו את עצמינו נגד בל המביא כנ״ל בכל תורת חיוב ושיעבוד ובכל אופני החיוב והשיעבוד שבכל אופן היותר מועיל ככל תקנות חז״ל. שבאם נעבור ולא נפרע לכל המביא כנ״ל את כל סך הנ״ל לזמן הנ״ל וכנ״ל שהכח ורשות תונה לו מעכשיו לכוף ולנגוש אותנו על הוצאותינו כסדרן או שלא כסדרן ובכל מיני כפיות ונגישות בעולם, הן שנינו יחד או אחד מאתנו איזה מאתנו שירצה, והיאך שירצה כל המביא כנ״ל, לפני כל בית ין שיחפוץ, בדיני ישראל ובדיני אומות העולם, בלי רשות שום רב מנהיג ומושל שבעולם.

110 *Resp. 'Avodat Ha-Gershuni*, no. 70. Cf. no. 83, where Ashkenazi declared that the guaranto ('*arev*) could not exempt himself, either in a gentile court or in Jewish law. The followin is the original Hebrew: שלא יהיה היזק וגרם היזק בין בד״י ובין בדא״ה מכל מה שהפה וכו׳.
Also see Bacharach, *Resp. Ḥavvot Ya'ir*, no. 137.

111 PMBD, Vol. 2, nos. 259–260, 48b–49a.

referred to rules concerning the discharge of guardians according to both legal systems in order to avoid future appeals or claims[112] and it was intended to indemnify guardians against the prospect of suit by orphans in French courts. It further signified that the liability imposed on guardians was "in accordance with the law of Israel and of the nations."[113] (b) It indicated that the preparation of a probate inventory was in conformity with French law.[114] (c) It affirmed that the annulment of a marital engagement was irreversible in both Jewish and general courts.[115] And (d) it protected an agreement concerning property placed in trust from future challenges in French courts.[116] In each of the forgoing instances, the phrase "according to the Law of Israel or the Law of the Nations" signaled the Beit Din's acknowledgement that members of the Jewish community lived in two worlds and struggled to abide by two systems of law. Overall, "according to the Law of Israel or the Law of the Nations" applied to a wider range of circumstances and related more directly to judicial matters than *dina d'malkhuta dina*. But both evinced the political *savoir faire* required of the Kahal when cases related to French law came before the rabbinic court.[117]

Efforts to resolve the dilemmas posed by competing jurisdictions are most immediately apparent in the Beit Din's treatment of French civil contracts. The basic logic of its approach rested on the talmudic law (BT Gittin 10b–11a) that recognized the validity of documents formally executed in the general courts. It was not until the thirteenth century, however, that such agreements were accorded full legitimacy by medieval halakhists. In his glosses to the *Shulḥan 'Arukh*, Moses Isserles affirmed the legality of notes signed by gentiles and produced in gentile courts when these concerned the purchase and sale of property and the collection of debts. In the Metz Beit Din, cases involving overlapping jurisdictions often turned on the legal status of civil contracts as understood in Jewish law. In a case that came before the Beit Din in the summer of 1777, a woman presented a civil contract stating that the property of her deceased father had been mortgaged to her in the amount of 2,446 livres.

112 PMBD, Vol. 2, no. 308, 56a–56b.

113 PMBD, Vol. 1, pt. 2, no. 249, 53b.

והאפטרופסי׳ יכניסו את עצמם בד״י ובדא״ה בכל אחריו׳ שבעולם רק אם הב״ד והקרובי׳ מרוצי׳ שהארגז יהי׳ ברשו׳ האפטרופסי׳ אזי מרוצים בהתמנו׳ אפטרופסי׳ ובתנאי שהב״ד והקרובי׳ יקצבו להם דמי כשכורתם כראוי לכל שנה עבור טרחתם. ואם יקצבו הב״ד והקרובי׳ דמי משכורתם שיוכשר בעיני משגיחם אזי יכניסו בהתמנו׳ האפטרופסי׳ כפי שיצא מפי ב״ד.

Also see PMBD, Vol. 2, no. 310, 57a–57b.

114 PMBD, Vol. 1, pt. 2, no. 184, 42b–43a.

115 PMBD, Vol. 2, no. 1, 1a.

116 PMBD, Vol. 2, no. 403, 76a–76b.

117 For an example of an estate inventory was prepared by both a notary and *ne'emanei hakehillah* (Jewish notaries), see PMBD, Vol. 1, pt. 2, no. 49, 13b.

On that basis, she requested that the Beit Din prevent her brother from selling their father's property and from leasing it to any other person(s) for a period of three years. Her argument rested on the claim that by having become part owner of her father's house, she had the status of an abutter, and as such she enjoyed the right of refusal in certain circumstances. She also requested authorization to seize rental money that was owed to her brother and to collect on her debt after satisfaction of the first creditors. The Beit Din decided in her favor in each matter. It ordered the repossession of the house and ruled that the brother was prohibited from leasing the property without his sister's consent since she had the first right to collect all of the rent that had accrued since their father's death. This was a bold ruling that rested squarely on the undisputed weight that the rabbinic court assigned to the civil contract. As a rule, the Beit Din was adamant about enforcing civil contracts.[118]

In another case that hinged on the weight accorded to civil contracts by the Beit Din, the interplay between Jewish and French civil law emerges with even greater clarity. In spring 1778, the Beit Din heard a dispute between a mother and son, each armed with a civil contract to authenticate their respective claims. Michael Picard of Donnelay approached the Beit Din, together with his uncle Loeb Picard. He maintained that pursuant to a notarized bill of sale dated 14 November 1752, Loeb had purchased the house from his brother

118 For the main sources concerning contracts produced in non-Jewish courts, see BT Gittin 10b–11a and 19b; Isserles, *Shulḥan 'Arukh, Ḥoshen Mishpat* §68 and §253:32. For limitations on the application of gentile law out of concern that this would lead ultimately to the nullification of Jewish law, see Isserles, *Shulḥan 'Arukh, Ḥoshen Mishpat* §369:11. For an extensive discussion of the legal issues, see Shilo, *Dina de-Malkhuta Dina*, 312–402. The reason for the objection to adjudication in gentile courts is disputed. The *Shulḥan 'Arukh, Ḥoshen Mishpat* §22:3 states that if the litigants accepted a gentile judge to preside over their case, such acceptance is meaningless, even if the acceptance were via a *kinyan*. However, the Mordechai is then quoted that after the fact, the decision is binding. Viewing the two statements as contradictory, the Shach distinguished between acceptance of the court, which is not valid, and the acceptance of a particular judge, which is valid. Accordingly, in his view, it is permissible to arrange for a gentile to arbitrate for Jews. Rashi, in Gittin 23b, disqualified *gittin* and *kiddushin* based on the general principle that the signature of a gentile who has no standing in the halakhic process of *gittin* is of no legal value. In the opinion of Moses Nahmanides, the disqualification was based on the failure to adhere to the rules of Halakhah. Maimonides, taking a narrower position, validated שטרי ראיה only. See Maimonides, *Mishneh Torah*, Laws of Lender and Borrower 27:1. Cf. PMBD, Vol. 1, pt. 1, no. 4, 7a, where priority concerning the creditors was determined in accordance with *dina d'malkhuta dina*. Also see PMBD, Vol. 2, no. 14, 3a. On the enforcement of civil contracts, see PMBD, Vol. 1, pt. 1, no. 59, 17b. Also see the extended discussion in David Malkiel, "Jews and Wills in Renaissance Italy: A Case Study in the Jewish-Cultural Encounter," *Italia* 12 (1996): 7–69.

Abraham (Michael's father) and thereafter permitted his nephew to live in the house rent free. In opposition, Michael's mother Miriam, now the wife of Hirtz Donnelay, presented to the Beit Din a civil contract—her *contrat de mariage* of 14 January 1751—between her and her first husband, Abraham, indicating that she had deposited her dowry of 1,200 livres with him at the time they were married. She argued that since she possessed no assets of her own at the time of her divorce from her first husband, the rights conferred by her *ketubah*, as recorded in the civil marriage contract, entitled her to take possession of the house. In its summary the Beit Din stated that

> once we heard the words of Miriam and saw the engrossed[119] contract attesting to the fact that she deposited 1,200 livres with her first husband, that is, prior to the contracted sale of the house to Loeb, we ruled that she is obligated to take an oath, the *shevu'at ketubah*, as required by Jewish law, and following this, to arrange an appraisal of the house. Assuming the house is valued at no more than the amount of her dowry, it will be transferred to her possession in lieu of her *ketubah*.[120]

This case is instructive, not only because it attests to the recognition accorded by the Beit Din to the validity of the civil contracts held by either party to the dispute. It is also made clear that once the Beit Din ruled that the civil marriage contract had legal priority over the bill of sale, the next step was to invoke traditional Jewish law—the administration of the oath required of a divorcée or widow—before she could be awarded the value of her *ketubah* or the transfer of any property.[121]

In the spirit of procedural cooperation that characterized many of its efforts, the Beit Din saw to it that contractual agreements and documentation were recognized in French courts. In one instance, after crafting an arbitration agreement concerning the division of disputed estate assets, the Beit Din stated, as it often did, that neither party could deny the validity of the compromise that each had duly accepted as binding. The court then declared that

119 A copy of a legal document prepared by a notary and copied legibly onto parchment paper at the instruction of the court.

120 PMBD, Vol. 2, no. 50, 10a. In compliance with talmudic law (BT Gittin 34b), the Beit Din regularly imposed the *ketubah* oath on widows in order to verify that they did not dispose of any property from the estate of her husband and did not receive any payment from her husband while he was alive.

121 For an example of a case where the Beit Din expressed agreement with the bride's attorney that efforts ought to be made by the brother of her fiancé to arrange for a contract in the civil court so that half of the house will belong to her. PMBD, Vol. 1, pt. 1, no. 138, 44b.

"what is written in the translation [of the agreement] executed today complies with the law of the land and shall be upheld to the fullest extent of the law."[122] This example, which we may assume was repeated in other instances, reflects a consciousness of parallel systems of justice—Jewish and French—that entailed technical skill coupled with diligent efforts to ensure coordination between the two.

The Impact of French Law on Rabbinic Jurisprudence

In addition to affirming the court's familiarity with French law, the records of the Beit Din contain clear signs of its having taken that law into consideration in its own deliberations. This was not an unprecedented phenomenon nor limited to the Beit Din. Bylaws recorded in the Pinkas Kahal of Metz refer to a special dispensation permitting *parnasim* to remove official papers of the Kahal from the community meeting room (*ḥadar ha-kahal*) to show to French legal experts and translators.[123] In certain aspects of civil procedure, for example, Rabbi Yeḥiel ben Asher's *Arba'ah Turim* followed Spanish civil law.[124] Excluding occasions when litigants exercised their discretion to seek legal advice outside the community, there are indications that the Metz Beit Din occasionally instructed parties to a dispute to consult French *avocats* to clarify details of French law.

In several cases the Beit Din itself initiated consultations with legal experts, most often in order to avoid running afoul of French law and judicial norms. Precisely what motivated these consultations is deceptively simple. In seventeenth- and eighteenth-century France, consultation had become a well-established facet of legal culture. It was a service provided by lawyers, known as *avocats consultants*, who did not plead cases but offered professional counsel outside the courtroom. Hervé Leuwers's study of lawyers traces the growth in the honor and independence of *avocats* in the seventeenth and eighteenth centuries, initially under Louis XIV, when a series of royal ordinances and judicial *arrêts de règlement* enhanced their public standing and legal

122 PMBD, Vol. 1, pt. 2, no. 49, 14b. The following is the original citation:
ומה שכתוב בטראדאקסיאהן שנעשה כהיום הן מצד דינא דמלכות' יקוים בכל תוקף ועוז.

123 PKM, 18a, art. 20.

124 On this tendency, see Ephraim E. Urbach, "Methods of Codification: The Tur of R. Yaacov ben Asher" [Hebrew], *Proceedings of the American Academy of Jewish Research* (1980): 1–14; and Yehuda Galinsky, "The Four Turim and the Halakhic Literature of Fourteenth-Century Spain: Historical, Literary, and Halakhic Aspects" (Ph.D. diss., Bar-Ilan University, 1999).

competence.[125] Their professed impartiality and their reputation for dedication to the public welfare fostered a bond of trust with clients and judges alike. In a wider sense, their ability to disseminate their ideas in print as *consultations, mémoires judiciaries*, or *factums* enabled them to become an influential voice of public opinion.[126] It is significant to note that, at least on the basis of the explication of a ruling offered in one case, the Beit Din was apparently able to read legal opinions produced by French *avocats*.[127]

By turning to *avocats* for legal assistance, the Metz Beit Din revealed its dependence on detailed knowledge of French law and judicial practice. French *avocats* were regularly engaged to clarify the law when disputes between Jews implicated non-Jews as well. In a case that involved Berman Alsace, who owed money to the estate of Abraham Steinbiedersdorf, and a Frenchman named Brougham, who was in debt to Alsace, Alsace brought a suit against Brougham in the *cours souveraine de Nancy*. In the first instance the Steinbiederdorf estate sued Alsace in the Beit Din to secure payment of debt. Then Alsace sued Brougham in Nancy court to recover funds from his debtor. The Nancy court found in favor of Alsace and issued an *arrêt* permitting him to confiscate and sell lands that had belonged to Brougham when the loan was first contracted. That Alsace required a judgment from a French court in order to seize and then sell land owned by Brougham to satisfy his debt to the Steinbiedersdorf estate illustrates not only the complicated nature of Jewish-gentile financial dealings, but also reveals how Jews depended on the general judicial system to attain justice. In this case one of the non-Jewish creditors employed a French legal mechanism known as a *lettre de paréatis* to shift jurisdictions to the detriment of the estate of Abraham. According to French law, a judgment could not be executed outside of the jurisdiction of the judge who had pronounced it unless there was a formal declaration transferring enforceability of a judicial decision from one jurisdiction to another. Such *lettres de paréatis*, which were delivered by the Keeper of the Great Seal, by the Chancellors of the Parliaments, or with

125 See Hervé Leuwers, *L'invention du barreau français, 1660–1830: la construction nationale d'un groupe professionnel* (Paris, 2006).

126 See Bell, *Lawyers and Citizens: The Making of a Political Elite in Old Regime France*; idem, "Barristers, Politics and the Failure of Civil Society in Old Regime France," in *Lawyers and the Rise of Western Political Liberalism: Europe and North America from the Eighteenth to Twentieth Centuries*, ed. Terence Charles Halliday and Lucient Karpik (Oxford, 1997), 25–36; and Maza, *Private Lives and Public Affairs*, 112–130.

127 See PMBD, Vol. 1, pt. 2, no. 242, 53a. The assumption that the judges on the Beit Din were fully at ease with French legal documents may not be accurate in every instance. See Appendix 3 for the legal consultation provided by Pierre-Louis Roederer, translated from French into Hebrew, presumably to facilitate its review by the Beit Din, in Archives départementales de la *Moselle*, Consistoire israélite 17J24.

the permission of the local judge, were familiar to the Beit Din and figured in the strategy employed by litigants.[128]

Uncertainty about sharing civil court costs was another issue that surfaced from time to time before the Beit Din. In one case, three litigants approached the Beit Din seeking a judgment on the apportionment of legal expenses incurred in the recovery of unpaid debts that the Chevalier de Boucq had owed to each of them. The question before the Beit Din was whether the court fees were to be shared equally or divided proportionately according to the size of the debt. Two of the litigants argued against the third that they had all agreed to divide the expenses proportionately. The Beit Din ruled that they must consult an *avocat* to determine how such matters were handled in the courts of Lorraine.[129] This case exemplifies a complexity with which Metz Jews were repeatedly confronted when a financial transaction involving a gentile merchant or client required legal action in the general courts. In such cases, though the dispute before the Beit Din was an internal one, the fact that the case would ultimately be decided in the general court prompted the Beit Din to seek the advice of French legal counsel. When a widow sought authorization to deduct certain expenditures from her husband's estate in order to ensure that her *ketubah* and *tosefta* settlement would be sufficient to meet her needs, the Beit Din ordered her to present documentation of her expenses to an *avocat* who would then determine whether in French law these were excluded when creditors sought restitution.[130] Here, too, because the dispute involved creditors who were not Jewish, the Beit Din found it necessary to ensure compliance with general legal practice.

Even when a case involved Jews only and no legal action was pending in the French courts, French *avocats* were occasionally invited to provide their expert opinion. In a dispute concerning the terms of a contract to pay the communal tax on behalf of a family member, the Beit Din recommended that the parties consult French legal experts though the issue implicated only Jewish law and communal affairs.[131] In some instances the Beit Din endeavored to

---

128 See PMBD, Vol. 1, pt. 2, no. 111, 28b, and Vol. 2, no. 505, 102b.

יהי׳ עי״כ שיסתעף והוצאו׳ ההיזק וכל במשפט עומד להיו׳ פריאטיס עפ״י הנ״ל ר״א להזמין בערכאו׳
ותבע הכל מכיסו לשלם הנ״ל ר״א מחויב.

On the term paréatis, see Jean Brisaud, *The History of French Private Law* (Boston, 1912), 599.

129 Also see PMBD, Vol. 1, pt. 1, no. 102, 35a, where the Beit Din called for sharing civil court costs. Cf. PMBD, Vol. 1, pt. 2, no. 157, 38b. On sharing the legal costs of an appeal, see PMBD, Vol. 2, no. 246, 45b.

130 PMBD. Vol. 1, pt. 1, no. 119, 40a.

131 PMBD. Vol. 1, pt. 1, no. 65, 21a.

sidestep a dispute out of concern that its ruling might contravene French civil law. In spring 1783 Zalman Cahen lodged a complaint with the Beit Din against Feivelman, a physician serving the community. Cahen had purchased the right to payment of *rentes* previously held by Isserle Lissa. Feivelman had blocked the transfer and secured a seizure of the *rentes* in satisfaction of unpaid medical bills that he claimed against Lissa. Cahen sought removal of the seizure, claiming that his purchase pre-dated imposition of the seizure. In response, Feivelman's attorney claimed that civil law accorded his client, a physician, privileged status and, hence, priority over other creditors and, moreover, that the treatments were administered before the transfer of the *rentes*. In turn, Cahen's attorney maintained that even if Feivelman were to prevail, the physician would have to affirm the details of his treatments and that his claim should be limited to the fee schedule set by the civil courts.[132]

To deal with these claims and counterclaims, the Beit Din instructed the parties to seek the opinion of *avocats* concerning the law of the land (*dina d'malkhuta*) on the following questions: (a) Does a physician have priority over other creditors?[133] (b) Is a physician's word customarily presumed to be reliable, and in this case was Feivelman's testimony concerning the date of treatment credible? Seemingly in disregard of a general trend in Jewish law that privileged physicians over other creditors, the Beit Din determined that the opinion of the *avocats* would be binding on the two parties on the basis of *dina d'malkhuta*. And if Feivelman's credibility were undisputed, the Beit Din speculated, perhaps he would not need to take an oath to affirm the facts of the case as he presented them. In effect, by being unwilling to proceed further without clarification from legal experts and by not wishing to clash with French law, the Beit Din effectively ceded its authority to the civil courts. It concluded that the opinion of the *avocats* would be binding on the two parties, in accordance with the law of the land.

In a similar case—a dispute between Feivelman and the family of the late Jacob Steinbiedersdorf over a claim of unpaid medical bills—the Beit Din based its ruling on the standard of "trustworthiness" as understood in French law. Also at issue was whether trustworthiness (Heb. *ne'emanut*) is presumed even in the absence of an oath. Once again, the Beit Din urged the parties to consult French *avocats* for clarification. It is striking that the rabbinic court

---

132 PMBD, Vol. 2, no. 445, 85b.

133 On the priority enjoyed by physicians among creditors, see *Pitḥei Teshuvah*, *Shulḥan 'Arukh, Even ha-'Ezer* §102. For regulations concerning the payment owed to physicians for home visits at night, see "A Takkanah of the Community of Metz," excerpted in "Pirchei ha-rimonim, me'asef le-kol ha-maḥanot," n.d., in YIVO Archives, RG 223, Part II, Folder 146, item 18.

was willing to accede to non-Jewish legal standards in a case that involved Jewish litigants exclusively, especially when there are clear halakhic guidelines as to the measure of trustworthiness, and especially insofar as *dina d'malkhuta dina* did not generally apply in such cases.[134]

Also evident from the solicitation of French legal opinion is the Beit Din's acknowledgment of the limits of its authority. This is apparent from its readiness to circumscribe its own judicial powers and prerogatives while recognizing the validity—and in some instances even the advantage—of French civil procedures. On occasions when the legality of certain types of endorsements was uncertain, the Beit Din urged litigants to seek the opinion of experts in French law. In one instance, the Beit Din indicated that whether it would demand that an endorsement be made without surety depended on the legal risks attendant to the endorsement of a bill of exchange obtained from a third party. The Beit Din admitted candidly that the advice provided by the *avocats* would guide it in its ruling on the halakhic status of the endorsement, the requirement to provide security, and the ultimate satisfaction of a debt.[135] A dispute concerning a debt owed to Ḥayyim Püttlingen by his deceased father-in-law similarly bewildered the Beit Din. Ḥayyim's brother-in-law, Berman Alsace, who was the executor of the estate, insisted that there was a legal hindrance to the removal of funds, and Ḥayyim challenged that interpretation. Unable to come to a decision on its own, the Beit Din authorized Ḥayyim to approach the French civil court in order to collect the debt and his share of the inheritance. Effectively, the Beit Din looked to the civil court to decide whether Ḥayyim's debt could be satisfied while the question of the estate remained unresolved.[136] Similarly, in a case concerning the right acquired by Jews to act as horse-trading agents, the Beit Din inquired whether it was customary for horse dealers to pay mediation fees on merchandise sold to Jews.[137] Seeking clarification on a procedural aspect of French commercial law in another case, the Beit Din instructed litigants to inquire of two *avocats* whether the wording of a transport document, that assigned a note or a credit, would be enforceable in the civil courts. The

134 PMBD, Vol. 2, no. 445, 85b and PMBD, Vol. 1, pt. 1, no. 103, 35a. In this case, the Beit Din differentiated between the part of the case it would handle itself and the part that required the advice of *avocats*. See Vol. 2, 37a, no. 193. On limits concerning the application of *dina d'malkhuta dina* when each of the disputing parties is Jewish, see Isserles, *Shulḥan 'Arukh, Ḥoshen Mishpat* §26. For indications of latitude in the application of the principle *dina d'malkhuta dina*, see Shabbetai ha-Cohen, *Siftei Cohen, Hoshen Mishpat* §73:39.

135 PMBD, Vol. 1, pt. 1, no. 67, 21b. On the role of *avocats*, see PMBD, Vol. 1, pt. 2, no. 157, 38b.

136 PMBD, Vol. 1, pt. 1, no. 78, 27a.

137 See PMBD, Vol. 1, pt. 1, 15a, no. 46.

Beit Din stipulated that if they answered in the negative, then the transaction would be considered null and void.[138]

Respect for the legal procedures of the civil court system was a consistent theme in the Beit Din rulings, as illustrated by a dispute between Iẓig Friedberg's widow and David Terquem, a wealthy *gabbai* (trustee) of the Metz Kehillah. Seeking to recover money the deceased owed him, Terquem formally seized the outstanding debts owed to the estate. Iẓig's widow argued that she had first priority in the collection of the debts, based on rights guaranteed by her *ketubah*, which predated Terquem's claim. Since he was a later creditor, she demanded that he remove the seizure. Terquem, for his part, insisted that, despite being a later creditor, he had priority because his seizure of moveable property and loan notes was recognized in Jewish law as set forth in BT Ketubot 90a, as explicated by the Tosafot, and as codified in *Ḥoshen Mishpat* §104:3. (One may presume that Terquem could not have known this legal subtlety unless he had received legal advice from an expert in Jewish law.) Nevertheless, the Beit Din declared that it would follow the ruling of the French civil court, reasoning that if the French court were to recognize Terquem as a first creditor, then he would be obliged to cede half the collected funds to Iẓig's widow; if the widow were given priority by the French court, then the Beit Din would authorize her to collect all the debts and she would not be obligated to give Terquem anything.[139] Ultimately, then, the Beit Din's ruling depended on the decision of the civil court; the civil court would determine who had priority, and the rabbinic court would make its ruling contingent on that. Here, however, there was only the appearance of shared authority. The judgment of the Beit Din artfully melded talmudic and French law into a single ruling, but this was done only after it had received word of the French civil court decision. Since the Beit Din was hardly able to challenge French law, it accommodated itself to this reality as best it could.

Coordination with French law was necessary to ensure that the extent of liability assumed by guardians was sufficient to protect the minors under their tutelage. On occasion, the Beit Din called for a consultation with an *avocat* to determine whether the assumption of joint and several liability by the wives of the guardians was functionally equivalent to a legal *contrat*.[140] If the

---

138 PMBD, Vol. 1, pt. 2, no. 48, 13b.

139 PMBD, Vol. 1, pt. 1, no. 19, 10b.

140 The Beit Din used the talmudic phrase *'arevut kablanut*, a higher level of responsibility than is normally assumed by a guarantor. See BT Bava Batra 173b–174a, and *Shulḥan Arukh, Ḥoshen Mishpat* §129:18. As a rule, a creditor must approach the debtor/borrower first in order to recover a debt, but when the guarantor is an *'arev kablan*, the creditor may approach him first. See Gulak, *Yesodei ha-Mishpat ha-Ivri*, 2:93–94.

avocat's answer was in the affirmative, the Beit Din averred, the wives would be expected to assume full liability with their husbands automatically, but if the *avocat* stated that a formal *contrat* was necessary in order to impose responsibility on the parties, then the guardians and their wives would be obligated to draw up a contract accordingly.[141] Whichever method was adopted, the Beit Din's basic assumption was the same: guardians were responsible for the assets with which they were entrusted, and their liability ought to extend to their wives, although this was not imposed consistently.[142] In a case involving a father who was appointed guardian over his daughter in the civil court, he was instructed by the Beit Din to obtain an *avis*—a formal legal opinion—from *avocats* concerning his daughter's entitlement to the estate.[143]

The Beit Din would often turn to *avocats* for procedural advice when it wished to avoid legal missteps that might lead to an appeal of the Beit Din's decision in the French courts.[144] However, the court did not follow the advice of French legal experts in every instance. In one case, a resident of Metz, Yukav (Jacob) Sarrelouis, wanted to purchase the house in which he was living, as he could no longer remain as a tenant and there were no other homes available to rent. He closed the deal with the seller's attorney after agreeing on the price and a payment schedule. Subsequently, another interested party, Akiva, offered the seller a higher price, ignoring Yukav's admonition that by so doing Akiva would be in violation of the Jewish law of unfair competition (*hasagat gevul*). Akiva's attorney argued that Yukav's purchase of the house was of no legal consequence because the seller was not present at the transaction and, furthermore, because no written contract establishing the purchase was executed at the time. Akiva's acquisition of the property, by contrast, was executed through a conventional bill of sale produced by the seller himself. In this case, the Beit Din ruled in favor of Yukav, arguing that he had the morally superior position, even though the oral agreement between Yukav and the seller's attorney was not sufficient for the acquisition of property according to Jewish law, and despite the fact that Akiva held a valid bill of sale. While conceding that the agreement reached by Akiva and the seller was binding under French law, and that this entitled him to acquire the house, the Beit Din based its ruling

141 PMBD, Vol. 2, 110a–b, no. 538.

142 See below, chapter 6, for a fuller discussion.

143 PMBD, Vol. 2, 5a, no. 22. The father was advised by the *avocats* to bring his arguments to the civil court in order to avoid the risk of liability. See below, chapter 7, for a more complete discussion of the case.

144 PMBD, Vol. 1, pt. 2, 35a, no. 144.

on moral considerations expressed within the Jewish legal tradition and proceeded to nullify Akiva's transaction.[145]

In some instances, the Metz Beit Din conceded not only the validity but even the advantage of French civil procedures. It recognized that the attainment of redress would occasionally be served as well, and possibly better, through recourse to the French civil courts. This was certainly true with respect to the enforcement of rabbinic court rulings. In cases in which the defendant refused to appear in the Beit Din, the court issued a *shetar seruv*—a document indicating that the defendant had refused to participate in the rabbinic court proceedings and authorizing the plaintiff to seek relief in a non-Jewish court. Justified as an effort to "rescue funds," as Maimonides characterized it, recourse to the non-Jewish court was traditionally viewed as a last resort.[146] The Metz Beit Din took a different position that echoed legislation enacted by the Kahal earlier in the eighteenth century. Rabbi Jonathan Eibeschütz, it will be recalled, strongly opposed Metz communal legislation that permitted recourse to the civil courts when a creditor held documentary proof of the amount he was owed. That *takkanah*, which had been recorded two decades earlier, stated that any community member who brought a dispute to the local non-Jewish court would be subject to the *ḥerem*, "with the exception of a *ḥilluf ketav* (bill of exchange) or *billet à ordre* (promissory note) [for which] it was permissible to sue in the *ʿarkhaʾot*."[147]

The exclusion from the prohibition of *arkhaʾot shel goyim* rested on the assumption that each of the foregoing instruments furnished legal proof of the claim and did not require an adversarial proceeding to recover the funds that were owed. Understood as no more than a procedural matter, the claim could be settled in the civil court and did not violate the ban on recourse to gentile courts. Although the foregoing legislative effort to narrow the prohibition of *arkhaʾot shel goyim* had a halakhic pedigree that can be traced to the seventeenth century, the formulation in the Metz *takkanot* no doubt drew support

145 PMBD, Vol. 1, pt. 2, 52b–53a. On the prohibition of *hasagat gevul*, see BT Bava Batra 21b and *Shulḥan ʿArukh, Ḥoshen Mishpat* §156. The argument employed by the Beit Din in defense of Yukav's position was the talmudic principle *ʿani ha-mehapekh be-ḥararah* (in BT Kiddushin 59a).

146 See Maimonides, *Mishneh Torah*, Laws of Sanhedrin 26:7 and *Shulḥan ʿArukh, Ḥoshen Mishpat* §26:2.

147 See above, chapter 3. The original source of the *takkanah* is CAHJP, FMe 139. In this fragment of the Pinkas Kahal it is stated that certain types of notes can be litigated in non-Jewish courts because the fact that the debtor owes the creditor a certain sum is not a matter of dispute. Article 68 of the 1769 *takkanot* went a step further by excluding disputes concerning money lent for merchandise or any loan for which there was uncontested documentary evidence. See PKM, 80a, 1769 Takkanot, Art. 68.

as well from an established principle in French law that the document in such cases constituted legal proof of a claim. One could not proceed with a distraint—a seizure to procure satisfaction of a debt—unless there was some documentary right, either a (written) judgment or a notarial deed. A creditor under a notarial deed had the right to act directly against the debtor through a distraint, whereas a creditor with a deed under a private seal could obtain execution only after securing a judgment of conviction.[148]

Limited in its ability to enforce its judgments, the Kahal authorized plaintiffs to use the power of the state to recover funds that would otherwise be lost. The Beit Din was naturally obligated to uphold the communal legislation, and its rulings were consistent with this policy.[149] According to French law, when an heir realized that the debts of the deceased exceeded the value of the estate, he or she could formally disclaim the succession. By refusing to receive any undetermined good that belonged to the deceased, they were released from all the debts owed by the estate. To be discharged from such obligations, the heirs were required to sign an act of renunciation, and the shares that were repudiated were then transferred to the remaining legatees. For its part, the Beit Din fully recognized the validity of the act of renunciation that was performed in the civil court. Thus, when there were insufficient assets to satisfy the heavy debt owed by the estate of the deceased, as in a case in 1785, the Beit Din affirmed the action taken by Hirtz Lévi in the civil court to renounce his inheritance. Several years later, on 1 July 1789, at the last session of the Beit Din recorded in the Pinkas, David Sansone, facing a similar predicament, relinquished his share in his father's estate by a civil act of renunciation (*renonciation par acte*). By so doing, ruled the Beit Din, he effectively surrendered on his own behalf and on behalf of his heirs, the rights of inheritance as set forth in Torah law.[150] Alternatively, an heir could invoke the instrument

148 Jean Brisaud, *History of French Private Law*, 597–98.

149 Also see Pinkas Kahal of Metz, art. 71. Also see Eibeschutz's comment in *Urim ve-Tumim Ḥoshen Mishpat* §104.

150 See Henry Dyson, *French Property and Inheritance Law: Principles and Practice* (New York 2003), 309–11. The Levi and Sansone cases were recorded in PMBD, Vol. 2, no. 540, 111a and no. 660, 146a. Cf. PMBD, Vol. 1, pt. 2, no. 49, 14a. On the renunciation of inheritance in Jewish law, known as *silluk* or *meḥilah*, see Maimonides, *Mishneh Torah*, Laws of Marriage 12:9 and 23:5–7 and Laws of Inheritance 6:8; Shmuel ben Me'ir (Rashbam) and Tosafot to BT Bava Batra 124a, s.v. *ve-'im*. According to *Shulḥan 'Arukh, Ḥoshen Mishpat* §107:17, if heirs inherit nothing from the deceased, they are not obligated to pay his debts. As a rule, heirs are liable for debts provided they do not exceed the value of the assets held by the deceased at the time of distribution. Contingent assets (ראויים), in contrast to debts, are excluded from this calculation.

in Roman law, *par bénéfice d'inventaire*, whereby he or she could accept the succession and receive the benefit of inventory since this would limit the liability for a parent's debt to no more than the actual value of the estate.[151]

Even so, there were instances in which the Beit Din imposed conditions that modified the application of French civil law in the Jewish community. The institution of guardianship furnishes such an example. Although guardians were appointed in the French court, the Beit Din stipulated in one case that Jewish guardians were not to hold the funds belonging to the estate of orphans under their tutelage, as was the general practice, but were required to place the assets and important papers in a specially designated strongbox. Furthermore, in the view of the Beit Din, a Jew could not be appointed a guardian unless the choice was acceptable to the relatives, even if he or she had been so designated by the testator. In general, although guardianship was an institution governed by French law, the Beit Din carefully managed its administrative details and legal nuances while remaining highly attentive to the well-being of the children, the concerns of families, and the broader interests of the Jewish community.

Despite the success of the Beit Din in navigating between the two legal systems, some signs of tension did surface on occasion, though these are generally concealed in the Pinkas. In the course of handling the large estate left by Seligmann Wittersheim, the Beit Din offered rare advice about the appointment of *apotroposim* and the difficulties they sometimes encountered:

> And since the entire contents of this estate will be in the hands of the *apotroposim*, it is not enough that dependable men are chosen, but they must also be trustworthy, because it is impossible to report the exact nature of the estate reliably without giving an account of the true nature of the debts owed to the government authorities. On account of their honor it was necessary to conceal a handbreadth in the *inventaire* without revealing their name, and only the amount of the debt was recorded, and on the back of the promissory note and bill of exchange the notary affixed his stamp, which is called *paraphe*.[152] And with persons like this, one must proceed slowly. Also with regard to the remaining debts one needs to be highly attentive. Sometimes [these are] in the villages, and sometimes they [require] an extension to rescue a portion of the debt so that there will not be a judicial appeal. It is good to settle and in such matters it is impossible to find *apotroposim* with all the aforesaid virtues

151 See PMBD, Vol. 1, pt. 2, no. 54, 16a. Get more info from Hebrew volume.

152 This is the French term "paraphe," which meant to proof or approve.

> and qualities, dependable and trustworthy, knowledgeable, and capable of gaging with the scale of his intellect how and what to do for the benefit of the estate owners.[153]

These observations reveal challenges facing a minority population that were seldom made explicit. The Beit Din acknowledged the difficulties facing the Jewish community in managing its affairs without becoming suffocated by bureaucratic and legal pressures exerted by the state. Circumstances demanded much sensitivity, discretion, and political savvy.

The relationship between the Metz Beit Din and the French civil courts was shaped by complex social, cultural, political, and legal forces. Indeed, the Beit Din's collaborative interaction with French legal officials and institutions confirms the integration of the rabbinic court within the legal structure of the state while also pointing to the shared concerns of the two systems. French jurists designed a system of jurisprudence that inimitably contributed to the rising prestige of civil law and to greater uniformity in legal matters. Especially important in this development was the modern state, which exerted its authority through two forms of influence—despotic power and infrastructural power, as Michael Mann has demonstrated. Referring to the state's capacity to implement political decisions throughout the realm, infrastructural power developed vigorously in the eighteenth century and was ultimately more influential than the reliance on sheer force. The infrastructure of the modern state was manifest in its bureaucracy, which embodied its capacity for organization and its ability to enforce its decisions. And owing to increased literacy of the populace, the standardization of coinage, weights and measures, and the enhancement of communication and transportation, the state succeeded in penetrating civil society. In the eighteenth century the infrastructural powers of the state were strengthened through the courts. Wider jurisdiction extended

153 PMBD, Vol. 2, no. 313, 58b:

ובאשר שכל ונוכחת של עזבון כזה יהי׳ מונח ביד האפטרופסי׳ לא די שראוי לבחור באנשים בטוחים כי אף צריכי׳ להיות אנשים נאמני׳ כי אי אפשר למסור מהות עזבון כזה מבלי נתינו׳ נאמנות מצד מהות החובו׳ שיש בהן נגד שררו׳. אשר מצד כבודם הי׳ צריך לכסות טפח באינוואנעטר מבלי לגלות ולפרש את שמם ולא נרשם שם רק הסכום של החוב וע״ג הכ״י והח״כ עשה הנאטער את ציון שלו שקורין פאראַף. ועם אישי׳ כאלה צריך לילך לאט עמהם. גם בענין שאר חובו׳ צריך התבוננות רב. לפעמים בכפרי׳ ולפעמי׳ בהרחבת זמן. גם לפעמים כדי להציל מקצת החוב או כדי שלא יתעורר משפט. טוב הוא לפשר ולענייני׳ כאלה הוא מן הנמנע למצא אפטרופסי׳ בכל המעלות ומדו׳ כנ״ל בטוחי׳ ונאמני׳ ובעלי מדע להיו׳ שוקל בפלס השכל איך ומה לעשות לטובת בעלי העזבון.

the long tentacles of the state's imposing bureaucracy and assured its legitimacy through the medium of law.[154]

In France more than elsewhere, legal pluralism was a social, cultural, and political reality that could not be evaded. It was not "the dying remnant of something once more vital," as some have imagined, but "an essential feature of the social organization of politics."[155] The accommodation to French law rested on the unmistakable acknowledgement by the Metz Kahal and Beit Din of the institutional and juridical power of the French absolutist state. No less important, the realm of law offered a framework from which new rules of engagement with the surrounding society and culture could emerge.

154 See Mann, "The Autonomous Power of the State," 185–213.

155 Ross and Stern, "Reconstructing Early Modern Notions of Legal Pluralism," 112.

PART 3

Family Affairs

CHAPTER 6

Guardianship and Inheritance: Managing Family Estates

As an institution, the family encompasses perhaps the widest range of subjects pertaining to daily life: individual and household consumption, maintenance of residential property, patterns of work, spousal relations, sexual behavior, parental strategies to marry off children, and inheritance. Historically, family has served as the foremost framework for defining personal identity, socializing and educating children, providing a livelihood for its members, offering mutual support to members of its network kin, and promoting religious values, while shaping lives from birth to death. In the broadest sense, then, as it is represented in legal sources that have survived from the seventeenth and eighteenth centuries, the family offers a panoramic view of life in Metz and the surrounding countryside. The main foci of this and the next chapter seek to illumine the relationship of the family to community and state as reflected in communal records.

Guardianship

The evolution of guardianship as practiced in Metz sheds light on family support systems, kin networks, and the complexities of communal autonomy in the early modern era. Guardianship was a venerable institution that assumed several forms, but the most common was the public duty to appoint guardians charged with protecting the interests of minors. This type of guardianship was regulated by governmental authorities and required substantial coordination between Jewish and general law. Owing to the state's special interest in the welfare of children, government regulation of the appointment of guardians was comprehensive, as was its supervision of the numerous obligations and financial responsibilities they assumed. Extant legal sources—both Jewish and general—illustrate how a well-established institution that was practiced in Jewish communities since antiquity assumed a unique character due to the interaction of local, state, and Jewish legal systems. This was hardly the case in all localities where Jews resided. The *takkanot* of Cracow (1595) severely excoriated those who sought to appoint an *apotropos* (the talmudic term for guardian) under the auspices of the non-Jewish authorities. Relying on earlier *takkanot* from the town of Tyszowce, the community vowed to fight such

 | DOI:10.1163/9789004417403_008

efforts vigorously.[1] As the Metz material confirms, communal approaches to guardianship were firmly grounded in, and shaped by, the social, legal, and political framework in which Jews lived. It was inconceivable to sidestep cooperation with governmental and judicial authorities, and by the mid-eighteenth century the Kehillah had fully internalized this ethos.[2]

Appointment as a guardian was considered an enviable position by enterprising individuals who believed that they could benefit from controlling a sizeable estate. Guardians sometimes found themselves managing so much wealth that they could profit handsomely from the investment and leveraging of the assets under their control. But regulations governing estate management were complex, and if the assets were limited, it could be difficult to turn a profit. Seventeenth- and eighteenth-century French legal treatises contained lengthy sections detailing the circumstances that would exempt an individual from assuming a position, such as advanced age, suggesting that guardianship was not viewed as an attractive position in every instance.

According to Metz customary law, guardians could not claim a formal salary from their wards. However, Beit Din proceedings record numerous cases of compensation (*sekhar tirḥatam*) allocated to *apotroposim* for their efforts, and wards were obligated to pay their part. The amount, referred to as *demei maskurto* (salary), depended at times on the Beit Din and other times on the family.[3] In one case, guardians were promised a salary for the first year only because of the anticipated effort necessary to collect outstanding debts. This award required special authorization by relatives and confirmation by the Beit Din,[4] though in most instances the guardian was the surviving parent—as a rule the father. In cases where wards sued their guardians for fraud, the guardians were frequently relatives (uncles, cousins) or remarried mothers. Compensation was usually the percentage above five percent that the guardians were able to earn on their investments, though the percentage

1 Meir Balaban, *History of the Jews in Krakow*, 2 vols. (1931, 1936), vol. 1, 330.

2 The appointment of *apotroposim* could also be a matter of some discretion. At the time of the impending remarriage of Froumette, widow of Seligmann Wittersheim, the Beit Din oversaw the appointment of two new guardians who were to supervise the affairs of the two minor sons of Seligmann. Substantial debt was still owed to the estate, including funds owed by Seligmann's former business partners that were not to be distributed to the children, evidently by agreement, until a significant amount of time had elapsed. See PMBD, Vol. 2, no. 313, 58b.

3 For an example of the latter, see PMBD, Vol. 1, pt. 2, no. 84, 22a. On *demei maskurto*, see Vol. 1, pt. 2, no. 249, 53b. For an example illustrating the Beit Din's role in determining the amount of payment, se PMBD, Vol. 2, no. 213, 40a. For an example of reliance on the judgment of relatives, see PMBD, Vol. 1, pt. 2, no. 36, 11b.

4 PMBD, Vol. 1, pt. 2, no. 99, 26a.

varied considerably.[5] Guardians appointed to manage the estate of Seligmann Wittersheim received a set amount of compensation that by any standard was substantial because in this case debt collection required considerable negotiation. They each were paid 900 livres per year for the first three years, and 600 livres per year thereafter.[6]

The Beit Din assumed oversight over most aspects of guardianship, though the chief justice was warned that no *apotropos* could be appointed without the formal approval of the Kahal. If any *dayan* initiated the process on his own, the Kahal would nullify the appointment and he would be suspended from serving on the Beit Din for six months.[7] The following tasks fell to the Beit Din: selecting guardians in consultation with members of the family; coordinating their official appointment with the civil court; defining the duties of and legal constraints on guardians; overseeing the collection of outstanding debts owed to the estate; and facilitating contacts with translators and *avocats* in preparation for civil court appearances when the needs of the estate required legal representation. The rabbinic court also administered the legal relationship between pairs of guardians appointed jointly to manage the estate of minors. It imposed restrictions on the ability of one guardian to bring lawsuits and grant discharges, compromises, and time extensions to debtors without the consent of the other guardian. It ascertained that no property belonging to minors was sold by either guardian without the consent of the other guardian(s) and of the Beit Din. The rabbinic court also stipulated how and where the guardian could hold funds belonging to minors.[8]

---

5 See PMBD, Vol. 2, no. 177, 35a. According to the will of Nota Bing, compensation for the *apotroposim* was set as the amount earned in excess of eight percent. However, the Beit Din expressed concern that at this percentage it would be difficult to invest the funds in the estate successfully; therefore, it instructed the *apotroposim* to give the ward only five percent. See PMBD, Vol. 2, no. 464, 91b–92a.

6 See PMBD, Vol. 2, no. 313, 59a. For additional examples, see PMBD, Vol. 1, pt. 2, no. 66, 18a; no. 99, 25b; no. 249, 53b; Vol. 2, no. 100, 20a; no. 258, 58b; no. 440, 84b. For an extensive list of efforts made on behalf of the orphans of Leib Chambri in May 1771, including details of compensation given to the *apotropos*, Leib Delme, see PMBD, Vol. 1, pt. 1, no. 99, 33a–b.

7 PKM 108b, December 1778.

8 PMBD, Vol. 1, pt. 2, no. 84, 22a–b. The Pinkas stated that by law guardians over minors were appointed in the French civil court, and until this step was completed, nothing in the estate of the deceased could be touched nor was the preparation of the *inventaire* permitted. The following is the original Hebrew formulation:

באשר שכל זמן שלא נתמנה אפטרופס בערכאו׳ על יתומים קטנים יד כל אדם אסורת להתעסק שום דבר
בעזבון המנו׳ הנ״ל ואפילו לעשות אינוואנטער אי אפשר לעשות מבלי התמנות אפטרופס.

Cf. PMBD, Vol. 1, pt. 1, 27a, no. 77, and *Coûtumes générales de la ville de Metz*, Titre IX. Concerning compensation for *apotroposim* and their expenses, see PMBD, Vol. 1, pt. 2, no. 99, 25b.

Metz *Coûtumes* followed Roman law closely. Roman law distinguished between two types of guardians: the *tutela* (*tuteur* in French) was responsible for the care and protection of the child; and the *cura* (*curateur*) oversaw the child's property and represented the child in court until s/he reached the age of twenty-five. Three types of *tutela* were recognized in Roman law: (1) *testamentaria*—the guardian named in the parent's will; (2) *legitima*—next of kin; and (3) *dativa*—a guardian appointed by the magistrate. According to Roman law, a guardian was obligated to attend to the interests of the ward as he would his own and was held liable for damages if he overstepped his authority or misappropriated the ward's property. Guardians were therefore required to provide sureties or pledges. When there were several guardians, they were jointly and severally liable, that is, each was considered responsible for the entire amount pledged. Individuals who proposed an incompetent or dishonest guardian to the magistrate, or even attested to their suitability, bore responsibility for harm to the estate.[9]

Courts in medieval France convened the relatives of the child to take part in the process of designating a tutor. This practice, known as a *conseil de famille*, exemplifies how Roman law was adapted to customary usage.[10] The Jewish community's accommodation to the French rules of guardianship is apparent in the Beit Din's painstaking compliance with the delicate blend of customary and Roman law. This included the convening of family members to designate a *tuteur*—a practice observed in the Metz Kehillah as in Christian communities. Proceedings of the Beit Din reported regularly that the "relatives also expressed their opinion" or that, in one case, it had deemed a certain individual an inappropriate choice as a guardian, but nonetheless deferred to the opinion of the family.[11] It was not uncommon for the rabbinic court to declare "[w]e the Beit Din therefore assembled relatives of the deceased on the father's side and mother's side to guide us in the proper way concerning *apotroposim*."[12] By all accounts, the Beit Din approached the matter with the utmost seriousness to avoid, to the extent possible, the appointment of guardians who would place the future of the ward at risk. In one instance it demanded of a prospective *apotropos* to bring written evidence of his investment experience and

9 This description is based on Rudolf Sohm, *The Institutes of Roman Law, 1841–1917* (Oxford, 1892), trans. from 4th ed. by James Crawford Ledlie (Oxford, 1892), 395–407.

10 Cf. Richard H. Helmholz, "Roman Law of Guardianship in England, 1300–1600," *Tulane Law Review* 52 (1978): 223–57.

11 See PMBD, Vol. 2, no. 100, 20a; Vol. 2, no. 252, 47a. It was not unusual for the Beit Din to state that the family was best suited to determine who was best suited for an appointment. See the reference to *asefat kerovim* (family gathering) in PMBD, Vol. 2, no. 177, 35a.

12 PMBD, Vol. 1, pt. 2, no. 84, 21b.

required him to provide assurance to the court that he was capable of increasing the value of the funds entrusted to him.[13]

On the appointment of guardians, the Metz *ius civile* comprised elements of both Roman law and customary law.[14] French courts were inclined to set aside the preference in Roman law for the *tutor legitimus* and instead appointed the *tutor dativus*, upon the advice of the family. Roman law preferred the family member, the *tutor legitimus*, to the *tutor dativus* for that reason. Where no guardian was named in the will, the courts made the appointment themselves, though they tended to do so in a way that was compatible with the family's wishes.[15]

The proliferation of Roman law resulted in the gradual disappearance of the concept of joint parental authority that had evolved in the Middle Ages. *Patria potestas*—the absolute power of the father—was cited increasingly, though not the authority conferred upon mothers over their children. According to Roman law, women were only appointed guardians if they renounced remarriage at the death of the children's father; otherwise, they forfeited the right of guardianship over their own children. While this was true according to French usage as well, the customary law did not limit guardianship to males. In customary law regions, the two categories of women who were authorized to become guardians were the mother and the paternal grandmother, but only over their own children or grandchildren. In some cities, such as Toulouse, that procedure was automatic for mothers (*tutelle légitime*). As stated in the 1769 edition of the *Coûtumes générales de la ville de Metz et pays-Messin*, guardians named in the husband's will were preferred over the mother, but she could just as well be named *tutrice* by her husband; she would remain her children's legal guardian as long as she did not remarry. In this matter, given that Metz was governed primarily by customary law, the nomination of a guardian had no legal force unless it was confirmed by a judge, but the judge would only make a ruling after the children's relatives had convened and their opinions had been polled.[16]

13 PMBD, Vol. 1, pt. 1, no. 92, 31a.

14 In Roman law, mothers were automatically granted the status of guardians, whereas in customary law, the appointment needed to be confirmed by a judge. On the complexity of regulations and practices concerning guardianship, see Grace E. Coolidge, *Guardianship, Gender, and the Nobility in Early Modern Spain* (Burlington, Vt., 2011); Giulia Calvi, "Reconstructing the Family: Widowhood and Remarriage in Tuscany in the Early Modern Period," in *Marriage in Italy, 1300–1650*, ed. Trevor Dean and K. J. P. Lowe (Cambridge, 1998); and Julius Kirshner, "Introduction," *Jewish History* 16 (2002): 1–14.

15 Helmholz, "Roman Law of Guardianship in England."

16 Detailed rules and regulations concerning guardianship were recorded in the *Coûtumes générales de la ville de Metz et pays-Messin*, Titre IX, Arts. 1–17, 278–99. For earlier legal

It is precisely on this point that traditional Jewish legal practice diverged from normative judicial procedure in the Metz civil courts. In the 1770s, rabbinic courts were still ill-disposed to appoint any woman—including a natural mother—to the position of guardian. This disinclination was consistent with the concern, as formulated by Rashi and elaborated by medieval *posekim* such as Rabbi Solomon ben Aderet (Rashba), that women were not capable of managing the finances of an estate.[17] In the Middle Ages women were nonetheless appointed guardians if they were known to have the requisite financial expertise. In the seventeenth century, Rabbi Joel Sirkes more formally asserted that when a woman had business experience and acumen, even exceeding the capacity of men as providers, a rabbinic court could appoint her without hesitation.[18] Even so, although women were legally eligible to serve as guardians if appointed by the testator himself, rabbinic courts were reluctant to make such appointments on their own. Fully alert to the advantage available to them under French law, Jewish women occasionally approached the civil courts in order to be named guardians of their children. They thus played a decisive role as mediators between the two judicial systems.[19] In a case that came before the Beit Din in 1771, the widow of Jacob Coblence had approached the French civil court and was appointed guardian of her children "according to their laws"

---

traditions, and on differences between Roman law and customary law, see Jean Domat, *The Civil Law in its Natural Order* (1689), vol. 1, parags. 1377–78. On the effects of remarriage on guardianship issues, see Sylvie Perrier, *Des enfances protégées: la tutelle des mineurs en France* (*XVII*^e^–*XVIII*^e^*siècles*) (Saint-Denis, 1998), 57–70. Cf. Thomas Kuehn, "'*Cum Consensu Mundualdi*': Legal Guardianship of Women in Quattrocento Florence," *Viator* 13 (1982): 309–33; C. Klapisch-Zuber, *Women, Family and Ritual in Renaissance Italy* (Chicago, 1985); and Helmholz, "Roman Law of Guardianship in England."

17 See BT Gittin 52a, and Rashi, s.v. "*nashim*"; *Shulḥan 'Arukh*, *Ḥoshen Mishpat* §290:2, and Solomon ben Aderet, *Resp. Rashba*, 3:428. On the general subject of guardianship in Jewish law, see Ya'akov K. Reinitz, "The Guardian of Orphans in Jewish Law: His Responsibilities, Methods of Supervision and Control over Him," (Ph.D. diss., Hebrew University, 1984), and idem, "The Appointment of Women as Guardians" [Hebrew], *Bar-Ilan Law Studies* 4 (1986): 167–203. On the range of views advanced by medieval and modern halakhic authorities, see Yeḥiel S. Kaplan, "The Power of Interpretation: Religious Scholars Elevate the State of Female Guardian in Jewish Law," *Cardozo Journal of Law and Gender* 14 (2008): 533–47.

18 For detailed evidence of Jewish widows who were appointed as guardians in the medieval period, see Winer, *Women, Wealth, and Community in Perpignan*, 47–75, 107–32. For exceptions to the general rule, see Simḥa Assaf, "The Appointment of Women as Guardians" [Hebrew], *Ha-Mishpat Ha-Ivri* 2 (1926): 75–81. For Sirkes' view, contra Rashi, see *Bayit Ḥadash, Arba'ah Turim, Ḥoshen Mishpat* §290:

"ולכאורה משמע מפירוש רש"י היכא דידוע דאשה זו נותנת ונושאת בטוב והיא בעלת מחיה כמו שנמצא לפעמים אף יותר מאיש יכולין להעמיד אותה אפילו לכתחלה דאינה דומה לעבדים וקטנים."

19 Some successful women became *apotropsot*. See PMBD, Vol. 2, no. 285, 53a.

(*be-nimuseihem*), a clear reference to the Metz *Coûtumes*.[20] Following her civil appointment, the Beit Din recognized her status *ex post facto*, though there is no evidence that this was the preference of the deceased. In this case and in cases involving disputes over marital property, the relationship of the Beit Din to the French civil courts comes into view rather clearly. The handling of the case and the recommendation as to how to execute the discharge of the guardians in conjunction with the court-appointed *curateur* signal the emergence of a cooperative relationship between the two judicial systems.[21]

Initially, the Beit Din bemoaned the trend to appoint women guardians, but could do little to halt it. New social and political conditions that had compromised its judicial powers at mid-century were, in the latter third of the eighteenth century, certainly still influential. Throughout the protocols of the Beit Din, as we have seen, French legal and cultural norms were ubiquitous. Moreover, owing to heightened interaction with general society, it was no longer possible to prevent members from taking cases outside the community nor was it politically prudent to malign those who did so.[22] In 1772, in the absence of any acceptable alternative, the Beit Din proceeded to appoint Esther, widow of Zalman of La Grange, as *mère tutrice* over her young daughter, while her son-in-law was named *curateur* for her three older sons. In this case, as in other such cases, Esther agreed to assume the position of guardian on condition that family members and the Beit Din supported her appointment. The titles *mère tutrice* and *curateur* indicate clearly that the Beit Din had acted

20 PMBD, Vol. 1, pt. 1, no. 5, 7a–7b. For similar use of the term *be-nimuseihem*, see PKM, 15a. On the practice of appointing women as guardians in France, see Christopher Corley, "Gender, Kin, and Guardianship in Early Modern Burgundy," in *Family, Gender, and Law in Early Modern France*, ed. Suzanne Desan and Jeffrey Merrick (University Park, PA, 2009), 183–222. Use of the term *be-nimuseihem* in medieval and modern responsa may indicate some familiarity of halakhic authorities with general law and, possibly, interest on their part in technical discrepancies between the two systems. See, for example, Solomon Duran, *Resp. Tashbeẓ*, 3:301 (Amsterdam, 1743); Jacob Moellin, *Resp. Maharil ha-Ḥadashot* (Jerusalem, 1977), no. 143; Gershon Ashkenazi, *Resp. 'Avodat ha-Gershuni* (Frankfurt, 1699), no. 102; and Reischer, *Resp. Shevut Ya'akov*, pt. 2, no. 176.

21 For additional discussion of cases concerning guardianship that came before the Metz Beit Din, see Jay R. Berkovitz, "Civil Law and Justice in the Rabbinic Tribunals of Eighteenth Century Metz," *Iggud: Selected Essays in Jewish Studies* (Jerusalem, 2008), 87–99.

22 Until the records of the French civil courts are researched thoroughly, we have no way of determining how many Jews exercised this option. It is also uncertain whether litigants first sought arbitration in the rabbinic courts and then proceeded to civil courts, or vice versa. The precise role of socio-economic status in such decisions is still undetermined.

in compliance with the bureaucratic conventions and legal procedures of the Metz judicial system.[23]

Advances of this sort did not occur smoothly or consistently, however. In 1773 the Beit Din appointed Matha, widow of David Terquem, *apotropos* over her children at the instruction of her late husband and following confirmation by a male relative. This, stated the Beit Din, was "the proper and honest course," even though it conceded that it was not customary to appoint a woman as an *apotropos*. It based its ruling on its own sense of justice, on the provision in the will to appoint two overseers with her, and on the authority of the testator himself to appoint a woman as guardian.[24] Of greater legal consequence, Matha was appointed *mère tutrice* by the French civil court and assumed responsibility for securing all that her children were entitled to receive from their father's estate, based on inheritance law, his will, and the *shetar ḥaẓi ḥelek zakhar*.[25] By contrast, in a case heard in 1774, the deceased had left instructions for his widow and his brother to assume the duties of guardianship, but the Beit Din was unwilling to go forward with the appointment. It averred that since, according to Jewish practice, a woman was generally not appointed *apotropos*, and because the brother was unable to assume this role, it would designate a rabbi to collect the debts still owed to the estate.[26] It is of no minor significance that despite unambiguous instructions from the husband, the Beit Din refused to appoint a woman as guardian because no male relative was prepared to join her in assuming this responsibility. In the following year, however, the policy of the Beit Din showed clearer signs of flexibility, and by the mid-1770s the appointment of Jewish women as guardians had become more of a commonplace in the Metz civil courts.

A decade later, the Beit Din and the civil court appointed Alicha Alsace as a guardian, along with her brother Berman, over Alicha's children. Significantly, however, there is no indication that her husband had left instructions for

---

23 See PMBD, Vol. 1, pt. 1, no. 74, 24b–26a. The title *tuteur* or *mère tutrice* acknowledged the guardian's status under French law as an official figure charged with representing the minors under the age of fourteen for boys and twelve for girls; the title *curateur* denoted a person charged with responsibility for representing young adults under the age of twenty five. For the continuation of the case, see PMBD, Vol. 1, pt. 2, no. 99, 25b. On the distinct role of the *curateur*, see Perrier, *Des enfances protégées*, 208–213.

24 PMBD, Vol. 1, pt. 2, no. 99, 25b.

25 A *shetar ḥaẓi ḥelek zakhar* was a promissory note that enabled fathers to allocate one-half of a male portion of the estate to daughters See PMBD, Vol. 1, pt. 2, no. 49, 14a, and no. 99, 25b; also see Vol. 1, pt 1, no. 104, 35b. The case of Matha, widow of David Terquem, was also brought before the French civil court. See Archives départementales de la Moselle, B 1558–1559.

26 See PMBD, Vol. 1, pt. 1, no. 137, 44a-b.

his wife to serve as guardian,[27] nor was there any such evidence in the case of the widow Sherele, who was proposed as guardian over her children at about the same time.[28] In other instances we see that brothers of the deceased came to an agreement that their sister-in-law was the best choice as guardian for her children. The Beit Din concurred by subsequently appointing the widow as guardian over the estate while appointing one of the brothers as *curateur*. This trend continued, and within the next several years the appointment of women as guardians over their children's estates was not only unexceptional but was even advocated by the Beit Din when it believed that the situation warranted it.[29]

Concerning the duties required of guardians, the Beit Din's understanding of these requirements echoed those of Roman law, as the charge to Isaac Cohen in 1780 stipulated:

> We have therefore issued a judgment that Isaac will manage the aforesaid estate for the benefit of the orphans to the fullest extent possible. He will oversee as appropriate the sale of movable property and is responsible for reaching a settlement with the creditors, to their [the orphans'] benefit. Similarly, he is responsible for letting the house to one who is well-suited in his eyes, for the benefit of the orphans. And following the sale of the movables, he shall present to the Beit Din the list of proceeds from the sale of the movables and from the entire contents of the estate.[30]

---

27 See PMBD, Vol. 1, pt. 1, no. 77, 27a; no. 104, 35b; no. 116, 39b; Vol. 1, pt. 2, no. 31, 9b; no. 48, 13b; no. 127, 32a; no. 154, 38a; Vol. 2, no. 129, 26a; no. 446, 85b; no. 506, 102b; no. 632, 137a–b.

28 See PMBD, Vol. 2, no. 109, 22a.

29 See PMBD, Vol. 2, no. 651, 143a. Cf. PMBD, Vol. 1, pt. 1, no. 77, 27a; no. 137, 44a; Vol. 2, no. 254, 47b. Cf. Nicole Pellegrin and Colette H. Winn, eds. *Veufs, veuves et veuvage dans la France d'Ancien Regime* (Paris, 2003), 44: "The matrimonial system in regions governed by customary law is much more protective of the widow and her interests than the system in the southern regions.... In that part of the realm under customary law, the wife takes back her property, but above all she has the right to one half of the furnishings and (marital) acquests as community property." For an example of efforts taken by the Beit Din to persuade a mother to become the guardian of her daughter, together with her son-in-law, see PMBD, Vol. 2, no. 452, 88a. On tensions between law and custom, and on the success of numerous women in becoming guardians, see Corley, "Gender, Kin, and Guardianship."

30 PMBD, Vol. 2, no. 252, 47a. The following is the original text:
לזאת יצא מאתנו בתורת פס״ד שכ״ה אייזק הנ״ל יתעסק בעזבון הנ״ל לטובת היתומים עד שידו מגעת. ולהיו׳ עומד על גבו להשגיח כראוי במכירת המטלטלי׳ ולפשר עם ב״ח לטובתם. וכמו כן להשכיר הבית לכי שיוכשר בעינו לטובת היתומים ולאחר המכירת מטלטלין יציע לפני ב״ד הרשימה מה שעלה הדמי מכירה של המטלטלין ומכל ונוכחת מה שימצא בעזבונה.

The importance attached to the welfare of children, which is repeated twice in the foregoing passage, was a crucial concern in the adjudication of guardianship cases and was apparent in other areas as well, such as the settlement of commercial disagreements when these had bearing on children. The court's interest in settling disputes for the benefit of the orphans was consistent with growing concern over child welfare in eighteenth-century France and doubtless was a factor accounting for the heightened attention of the Beit Din to guardianship cases.[31]

On the appointment of *apotroposim*, the Beit Din offered the following procedural guidance when it was necessary to replace a recently deceased guardian:

> Following the death of Feivish Sofer ... the Beit Din stated that an *apotropos* must be appointed in the *arkha'ot* because in the *arkha'ot* it is impossible to appoint one *apotropos* himself if there is not a *curateur* with him. Therefore, the Beit Din recommends convening a meeting of relatives to determine their opinion, with the approval of the Beit Din, as to who is fitting in their eyes to be appointed *apotropos*, according to the laws of Israel, and *curateur* according to the laws of the nations, in place of Feivish. And the heirs of Feivish argued that they should be discharged of any liability, according to the laws of Israel and according to the laws of the nations, that their ancestor may have incurred from the foregoing guardianship.[32]

The heirs' petition to be absolved of responsibility for harm done during the previous guardian administration indicates that liability was not limited to guardians alone. After polling four relatives of the orphans, the Beit Din received a recommendation to appoint Gavriel Brisach. Following this, the rabbinic court stipulated:

> ... that, in the Beit Din, he will be called *apotropos*, and in the *arkha'ot*, *curateur* of all the assets of the orphans of Baruch, according to what is listed in the inventory of all that is owned by the orphans to this day, and that Yozel Levi will present in the Beit Din. Concerning all of this, Yozel and Gavriel will be on equal footing with respect to the assets of the orphans, with no advantage of one over the other, nor may they act in

31 See Gerber, *Bastards: Politics, Family, and Law in Early Modern France*, 169–74.

32 PMBD, Vol. 2, no. 259, 48b.

> either a small matter or a large one without the other's knowledge. Only in the *arkha'ot* will Yozel be known as *tuteur* and Gavriel as *curateur*.[33]

The Beit Din noted that the differentiation between *tuteur* and *curateur* was pertinent only to the French courts, which were insistent on maintaining the formal distinction between the two.[34] There the entire legal framework was governed by local customs, as the Beit Din conceded: "It is evident to all that, in the *arkha'ot*, it is impossible to do anything, large or small, whether the preparation of the *inventaire* or anything related to the management of the estate without [first] appointing an *apotropos* and a *curateur* when a young orphan [is concerned]."[35] Though never set forth in formal legislation, the duties of *apotroposim* can be established on the basis of rabbinic court rulings. The *mashgiḥim* were required to handle the legal affairs of the estate, including engaging the *meliẓim* (translators) and *avocats* when it was necessary to go to civil court. Although they did not regularly receive wages for their efforts, in accordance with Metz customary law, they were eligible to receive modest compensation, termed *sekhar tirḥatam*, during the first year or more when exceptional efforts to collect outstanding debts owed to the estate of the deceased were often required. If travel beyond the immediate area was necessary, the *apotroposim* were obliged to go and would receive reimbursement for their expenses.[36]

Liability for violating the rules governing guardianship was well established in both Roman law and Metz customary law. According to Roman law, guardians who failed to discharge their duties faithfully were to be removed during the period of guardianship and the court could assert a claim on behalf of the child. Roman law required that the guardian deposit funds or furnish personal guarantors to secure his trustworthy performance before assuming his position. In some instances, however, no assurance was required, either when *tutores testamentarii* were appointed, or when a *tutor legitimus* was found to be "an honest person." The assurance could also be waived when guardians took a formal oath. Some French historians have suggested that the simplification of the practice of guardianship was a compromise with, or an enrichment by, customary practice.[37]

33 Ibid.

34 See PMBD, Vol. 2, nos. 258 and 260, 48b–49a.

35 PMBD, Vol. 2, no. 632, 137a.

36 PMBD, Vol. 1, pt. 2, no. 99, 25b.

37 On the assumption of joint and several liability contracted by tutors, even if not expressly stipulated, see Robert Joseph Pothier, *Treatise on Law of Obligations and Contracts*, vol. 1, parags. 266–267.

French and Jewish law held guardians to different standards of liability. According to the *Coûtumes générales de la ville de Metz de 1730* Titre IX, Article 11, *tuteurs* were required to provide full assurance and were jointly liable (*hypotéquez solidairement*) against negligence or malfeasance. Accordingly, from the day they assumed their duties, a lien was placed on their assets. The Beit Din acknowledged that "all the liability [of *apotroposim*] derives from the fact that they were appointed in the *arkha'ot*," which indicates that their liability did not stem from Jewish law. Neither the *Shulḥan 'Arukh* nor the *Recueil des lois, coûtumes et usages observés par les juifs de Metz* required guardians to assume liability for losses resulting from unwise investments of the property of the estate. According to *Shulḥan 'Arukh, Ḥoshen Mishpat* §290:5, when an *apotropos* appointed by the Beit Din was suspected of consuming the assets of wards under his tutelage, he was to be dismissed and another appointed in his place. However, if the *apotropos* had been appointed by the father in his testament (known as *testimentaire*), he would not be dismissed, because it was considered conceivable that he was consuming property that was his own. But, in this case as well, if witnesses testified that he was squandering the assets of the orphans, he would be dismissed. Rabbi Moses Isserles added that if an *apotropos* lent money belonging to minors without proper authorization, the Beit Din was to recover the money from the borrower and return it to the orphans. Rabbi Joshua Falk (1555–1614), author of *Sefer Me'irat Enayim*, commented that if the Beit Din was unable to extract the money from the borrower, then the *apotropos* was considered to have acted criminally because he neglected to secure suitable protection for the loan.[38]

Because there was no clear precedent in Jewish law for imposing liability on guardians, the Metz Beit Din could do little more than encourage guardians to assume liability if assets of the estate were depleted due to their negligence. In so doing, the court aligned the norms of guardianship observed in the Jewish community with Metz customary law. When demanded by relatives of the orphan, the Beit Din required the assumption of joint liability of guardians

38 Joshua Falk, *Sefer Me'irat Einayim, Hoshen Mishpat* 290:5, subparag. 13. In a case that came before Ezekiel Landau, in *Resp. Noda be'Yehuda*, pt. 2, *Ḥoshen Mishpat*, no. 34, he explained that the *apotropos* lent the orphan's funds via a note (*shetar ḥov*) without taking a pledge because he was certain about the reliability of the borrower. Although this was contrary to accepted practice, the *apotropos* was not considered liable because it was assumed that the Beit Din had instructed him to do as he saw fit. But, if the Beit Din did not so instruct the *apotropos*, then he certainly had no right to lend without a pledge and he would be obligated to make restitution from his own assets. In the opinion of Moses Nahmanides, by contrast, an *apotropos* was exempt from *peshi'ah*, a criminal act. See *Ḥiddushei Ramban*, Gittin 52b, s.v. *halakhah*."

according to the requirements of Jewish law and of the French courts. Thus, in a case involving the appointment of two *apotroposim* for the children of Matha Ganz, widow of David Terquem, the will stated that the *apotroposim* will accept liability according to Jewish law and the law of nations, "as much liability as there is in the world."[39]

Since the assumption of liability by the wives of guardians was unknown either in the Metz *Coûtumes* or in Jewish law, the Kahal found itself in uncharted territory. The legal force that underlay the liability of guardians' wives rested on two security instruments that were adapted to the French legal landscape, one drawn from talmudic law and the other from early modern Halakhah. These two security contracts were known by the following technical terms: (1) *Arvut kablanut*[40]—a talmudic phrase referring to a joint and several liability contractual agreement. This encumbered all the assets of the partner guardians. It could also impede those assets that a wife could sell or mortgage without her husband's consent.[41] (2) *Be'ohev* (באוה"ב), an abbreviation for *ba'ah isha ve-hadar ba'alah* ("first the wife, then the husband follows"), which established the precise order of signatures in the execution of a loan note. By signing the document in this manner, a wife indicated her intent to subordinate her right to receive payment for her *ketubah* and *tosefta*, which gave the lender or creditor priority over her claim. Guardianship as understood by the Beit Din required these stipulations as a bridge between Jewish law and French law and offers an illustration of hybrid legal mechanisms that facilitated the delicate understanding between the two systems.

Accusations of guardians' mismanagement of funds were among the most common areas of litigation in the Beit Din and the civil courts. These included nasty interfamily squabbles, the most rancorous of which were between parent and child, frequently aggravated by the remarriage of the mother or father. In one instance, Gershon, who had reached the age of thirteen, expressed a desire to dismiss his mother as guardian who had been appointed "according to their

39 PMBD, Vol. 1, pt. 2, no. 249, 53b.

40 Based on BT Bava Batra 173b–174a, and codified in *Shulḥan Arukh, Ḥoshen Mishpat* §129:18, *'arevut kablanut* is a higher level of responsibility than is normally assumed by a guarantor. As a rule, a creditor must approach the debtor/borrower first in order to recover a debt, but when the guarantor is an *'arev kablan*, the creditor may approach him first. See Gulak, *Yesodei ha-Mishpat ha-Ivri*, 2:93–94.

41 Concerning the joint liability of *apotroposim*, see Segel, *Sefer Naḥalat Shiv'ah*, no. 39, 2:664–68—נוסח ודיני אפוטרופוס שמינו בית דין. Cf. *Shulḥan 'Arukh, Ḥoshen Mispat* §77 it is stated that *apotroposim* are like "two who borrowed," and Isserles, *Resp. Rema*, no. 27: "they are not like two who borrowed together (שנים שלוו)," so we collect from each one, that is, they are liable for each other unless this was explicitly stated. Also see Shach, *Ḥoshen Mishpat; Resp. Maharam Mintz*, no. 44.

customs," that is, by a French court. She sued him for 386 livres, and her husband, Jacob Coblence, sued the boy for the school tuition he had paid on behalf of his stepson. Gershon counter-sued his mother for the same sum, claiming rights to the revenue she had received since the day of her second marriage until his thirteenth birthday. He also sued his stepfather for seven *louis d'or*, claiming that cash had been taken from him, as well as two-sevenths of gold and a silver cup. The Beit Din ruled that the various suits and countersuits cancelled each other out, and that mother and son each must swear an oath that neither owed anything. The Beit Din also decided that Gershon was entitled to receive certain annuities, i.e., revenue that had been going to his mother but was rightfully his, and that he did not require his mother's waiver or permission. His mother was instructed to return all the notes mentioned in the prior decision of the court. Finally, the son was instructed to grant his mother, stepfather, and the *curateur* a discharge as quickly as possible.[42]

A more serious case of mismanagement came before the Metz Beit Din in the early 1770s. Two hearings were involved. At the first, several accusations of mismanagement of the orphans' estate were brought against the guardians; five months later, following additional developments, the court issued a second ruling. Relatives of the orphans of Michael Barschingen requested that the two guardians, Lazar and Feivel, submit an accounting of their expenses. The relatives appointed Rabbi Joseph Morhange, a *dayan* on the Beit Din, as an attorney to represent the stepfather, Itzik Hess of Püttlingen, to investigate the account. The attorney for the orphans found irregularities in the reporting of expenditures made on their behalf. Further, it was argued that the amount of interest—five percent—that accrued to the orphans' estate was not enough to meet even half of their needs. Finally, the attorney demanded that the guardians pay off the debts that they owed so that they would not need to dip into the orphans' funds.

The Beit Din responded that although there were undeniable accounting problems, there was no clear reason to remove the guardians. Any irregularities or errors would be credited to the orphans at a later date. The guardians were instructed to submit to the Beit Din a signed list of expenditures and all written documents pertaining to the estate, but they were not found liable for accounting expenses. Also, in recognition of liquidity problems facing the guardians, the Beit Din rejected the attorney's insistence that a certain portion

---

42 PMBD, Vol. 1, pt. 1, no. 5, 7a–7b. Children who wanted to be released from guardianship could, starting at twelve for girls and fourteen for boys, ask the courts to emancipate them. They were required to prove that they were able to manage their own affairs, and then they were assigned a curator to represent them in legal matters.

of the estate ought to be invested with a person of means capable of providing more than the five percent return that was, until then, accruing to the investment. One might note here that the practice of lending the money of orphans, referred to as *ribit keẓuẓah*, had been rejected by most halakhic authorities, including Rabbi Moses Isserles. The Beit Din also ruled that one of the guardians, Lazar, by having traveled abroad, had violated a prior court decision requiring guardians (and even auditors) to remain under the authority of the *av beit din*. He would therefore need to provide security sufficient in the eyes of the Beit Din, and should he fail to produce this sum, the relatives would be able to remove him from his position. The court concluded that "owing to recent debts in their name, a security will be deposited with the Beit Din until the guardians take an oath that in the future they will carry out their duties for the sake of heaven and will make all payments necessary for the benefit of the orphans, as set forth in the Beit Din decision."

Six months later, Itzik, the stepfather, petitioned the Beit Din for the right to become the children's guardian. He reported that his wife was distraught over the attrition of her sons' estate, and, further, that the children owed him 600 livres a year (pursuant to an earlier ruling[43]), evidently as compensation for the support that he himself provided. For this reason, the Beit Din decided to remove the remaining funds from the guardians and transfer them to a person capable of providing more than five percent interest. Itzik in turn requested that whatever funds were still controlled by the guardians be assigned to him as security, and in exchange for the yield on 6,000 livres he promised to maintain the boys. He also argued on his wife's behalf that the guardians had routinely failed to uphold the previous decisions of the Beit Din, including the decision issued in August to deposit the security of 3,000 livres and to provide a list of expenditures. The Beit Din decided to dismiss Lazar as guardian and instructed him to transfer 3,000 livres to Itzik. Itzik would thenceforth maintain two of the wards, to be determined by lottery, in exchange for the yield on 3,000 livres. The court demanded a guarantee that he would abide by this agreement. Likewise, Feivel would have to deposit a security acceptable to the Beit Din, in exchange for the yield on the funds he controlled, and he too would need to guarantee that he would abide by the decision; otherwise, he would be removed.[44]

Guardianship disputes were frequently complex and therefore required consultation with French legal experts to ensure compliance with French judicial decisions. In another case of alleged malfeasance on the part of

43 PMBD, Vol. 1, pt. 1, no. 36, 13b.

44 PMBD, Vol. 1, pt. 2, no. 15a.

court-appointed guardians, the Beit Din submitted the matter before three French arbiters to determine which course of action was in the best interests of the children. The Beit Din acknowledged that the French arbitration ruling would be implemented "with full force, as if it were enacted before the Beit Din."[45] Even so, the rabbinic court proceeded to issue its own ruling in accordance with the decision of the arbiters: that the guardians were required to make restitution to the wards in order to fully discharge their responsibilities.[46] The step taken by the rabbinic court represented a formal ratification of the arbiters' decision, giving it greater standing in the Jewish community, even though the second ruling was hardly necessary from a legal standpoint.

Alongside those cases in which the Beit Din privileged French law over Jewish law, if only procedurally, there were instances as well when the rabbinic court-imposed conditions that were meant to modify the application of French civil law in the Jewish community. For example, although guardians were appointed in the French court, the Beit Din stipulated that Jewish guardians were not to hold the funds belonging to the wards under their tutelage, as was the general practice, but were required to place the assets and important papers in a specially designated strongbox. Furthermore, as indicated above, a Jew could not be appointed a guardian, even if so designated by the testator, unless the choice was acceptable to the relatives. Although guardianship was an institution governed by French law, the Beit Din wished to administer the details of its operation in order to satisfy the best interests of the children. The result, as in cases relating to probate, was an intricate interweaving of Jewish and French law.[47]

A case that came before a joint session of communal officials and the rabbinic court illustrates the complexities of navigating the interests of Jewish autonomy, including differences between French and Jewish law in a matter of public interest.[48] Concerned for the welfare of the orphan Fratche Bing, family members argued that with the death of Moshe Bing who had served as the *mashgi'aḥ* together with his brother Mann, named *apotropos*, that it was the intent of the testator to entrust his assets with their uncle, Mann, only so long

45 See, for example, PMBD, Vol. 1, pt. 2, no. 49, 14b, where litigants affirmed that what was stated in the French translation of the arbitration was in accord with the law of the land and would fully be upheld. Concerning the implementation of the arbitration settlement with "full force," see PMBD, Vol. 1, pt. 1, no. 110, 37a.

46 PMBD, Vol. 1, pt. 1, 37a, no. 110. For a halakhic precedent in support of the Metz ruling, see the view of Shabbetai ha-Cohen permitting arbitration by a non-Jew, in *Siftei Cohen* (Amsterdam, 1663), *Ḥoshen Mishpat* §22:15.

47 PMBD, Vol. 1, pt. 2, no. 84, 22a–b.

48 PMBD, Vol. 2, no. 538, 110a–110b.

as Moshe was alive, since he was the more trustworthy and competent of the two. But because Mann's wife had the first lien on her husband's assets under her *ketubah* and *tosefta*, they argued that either she should enter into an *arvut kablanut* agreement with her husband or that Mann be discharged from his position. In response, Mann argued that no changes could be required because the will was clear and undisputed.

The Beit Din determined that the terms of the will did not demand the retention of Mann as *apotropos* after the passing of Moshe. With the agreement of the community leaders and with the assent of the orphan's relatives, the rabbinic court's judgment stipulated the following conditions: First, to remain in the position of *apotropos*, Mann must come to an agreement together with his wife to be *arevim kablanim*, one for the other. Second, Eisik Cahen, Fratche's stepfather, would be appointed *apotropos*, as indicated in a prior *ma'aseh beit din*, on condition that he agreed to become an *arev kablan* with Mann. Third, Eisik and his wife would need to become *solidaire arev kablanim* for the orphan, and each of the two couples would become *arevim kablanim* for the other. Finally, the two couples would have to sign a contract stating that all have the title *apotroposim* and that no action could be taken without the agreement of his or her fellow *apotroposim*.

Following the decision of the court, the two couples made a *kinyan gamur agav sudar* (a transaction using a piece of cloth) to assume the functions of *apotropos*. Fratche was assured first lien from the day that Mann and Eisik were appointed in the French court and the wives became *arevim kablanim* for their husbands. This internal agreement was potentially advantageous to the orphan as it would save her the cost of hiring a notary to produce a legal contract. But in order to establish that the joint and several liability agreement was legally sufficient, the communal leaders decided to inquire with an *avocat* whether the Beit Din's recommendation would have the same legal weight as a *contrat*. Whatever the recommendation, they argued that the *avocat*'s opinion should control. If the *avocat*'s answer was in the affirmative, the Beit Din averred, the wives would be expected to assume full liability with their husbands automatically. But if the *avocat* stated that a formal *contrat* was necessary to hold the parties responsible, then the guardians and their wives would have to draw up such a contract. No additional information is available to indicate how the parties ultimately resolved the matter.

It is important to note that no complaint of damage or negligence was lodged against Mann, but that the grievance was motivated by a potential conflict of interest arising from the two opposing liens. Standard practice as outlined in the *Recueil des lois, coûtumes et usages observés par les juifs de Metz* followed French regulation of lien priorities. An earlier lien was given priority, and since a wife's lien normally preceded a ward's lien, there was a risk to the ward.[49] The imposition of joint liability of guardians and their wives could not be required by law, on the one hand, but because of the endangerment that guardianship posed to the ward, it was an option commonly proposed by the Beit Din to alleviate the concerns of family members. For this reason, solidary liability was discussed in the framework of family deliberations that were carried out in a consensual manner with relatives and communal officials concerned with the ward's welfare. This was not because the community and rabbinic court were unable to enforce the provisions of guardianship. The Beit Din was certainly able to block the appointment or retention of a guardian by introducing certain conditions into the contractual arrangement, and, if necessary, it could also resort to French judicial enforcement. Since no area of Jewish practice was regulated more closely by French authorities than guardianship, there was good reason to conform with Metz customs, especially because French law on solidary guarantees and liens was highly developed.[50] The Jewish community's approach echoed a provision of Metz customary law. According to the *Coûtumes générales de la ville de Metz*, the property of guardians was mortgaged *solidairement* in order to protect the property of orphans. However, the *Recueil*'s regulation of a Jewish guardian's liability was less stringent than that of the Metz *Coûtumes*, which imposed a lien (*hypotequez solidairement*) on a guardian's assets as security for dedicated management of the ward's assets. No corresponding mortgage requirement for a Jewish guardian was proposed in the *Recueil*.[51]

---

49 *Recueil des lois, coûtumes et usages observés par les juifs de Metz*, Titre XXVII, Art. 1: "The order of mortgage creditors is regulated according to the dates of the titles. And the mortgage takes effect for both movables and immovables …"

50 The phrase *'arevut solidaire* was occasionally employed in the protocols of the Beit Din to refer to this more comprehensive liability. See, for example, PMBD, Vol. 2, no. 597, 128a, and no. 629, 136b. In the case of Froumette Wittersheim, who was appointed executor over her late husband's estate and business in accordance with his will, it was stipulated that the two overseers (*mashgiḥim*) and Froumette herself, as *apotropos*, would not be liable at all for any losses, as the entire liability was assumed by the estate. See PMBD, Vol. 2, no. 310, 57a and below, chapter 7. Concerning the expectation that *apotroposim* would assume liability in both Jewish and general law, see PMBD, Vol. 1, pt. 2, no. 249, 53b. See PMBD, Vol. 1, pt. 1, no. 77, 27a, where the Beit Din stated explicitly that the entire liability rested on the two guardians "based on their having been appointed in the French civil court." See *Shulḥan 'Arukh, Ḥoshen Mishpat* §290:17 אפיטרופוס שנתמנה ע״פ ערכאות של עובדי כוכבים, צריך ליתן חשבון, כי הכי הוא בדיניהם. Nevertheless, the liability of guardians could be set aside if others were willing to assume responsibility. See, for example, PMBD, Vol. 2, no. 111, 22a–23b.

51 See *Coûtumes générales de la ville de Metz*, Titre IX, Art. 11, 294–95. For an example of a case in which the Beit Din did not require the guardians to provide a lien on their property, see PMBD, Vol. 2, no. 310, 57a.

In a case involving a young girl's title to her grandfather's estate, her father, Eisik Schweich, had been appointed guardian over his daughter in the civil court to represent her interests. The Beit Din instructed him to obtain a formal legal opinion from French *avocats* concerning his daughter Clerché's entitlement according to French law. The *avocats* advised Schweich to bring his arguments to the civil court in order to avoid the risk that he would later be held liable for mishandling her legal affairs.[52] Here too, the presumption of liability echoed the local customary law as recorded in the Metz *Coûtumes*, where it was stipulated that guardians were obligated to place their personal property as security.[53] In the Jewish community of Frankfurt, by contrast, there is no evidence that guardians were not personally responsible for the loss of assets in the estate.[54]

Inheritance

Inheritance disputes, invariably complex and at times convoluted, occupied the attention of the Metz Beit Din and the French civil courts continuously. Inheritance laws facilitated the intergenerational consolidation of property. This impacted the economic viability of the family and the influence of the lineage. Much was at stake beyond the promise of financial gain, most of all, social status and political influence, as Tocqueville observed.[55] In Metz, inheritance law exemplified the synthesis of French customs and Roman legal principles so crucial to the emergence of the modern state.[56] Metz was unusual among

---

52 PMBD, Vol. 2, no. 22, 5a.

53 See PMBD, Vol. 2, no. 538, 110a-b. It was customary in the Metz Kehillah—but evidently not in every instance—to demand joint liability of guardians and their wives, and this echoed a provision of Metz customary law requiring the property of guardians to be mortgaged *solidairement*. In one case, in Vol. 1, pt. 2, no. 36, 11b, the Metz Beit Din demanded that the guardians of the estate of a minor assume full responsibility with their wives so that if the assets of the minor were ever depleted, the guardians would be responsible to pay the minor from their own funds without the need to pay their wives' *ketubot* first. Compare *Coûtumes générales de la ville de Metz*, 1769, Titre IX, Art. 5, p. 282, and Art. 11, 294–95. For a case in which the assumption of joint liability with wives was not required, see PMBD, Vol. 2, no. 310, 57a.

54 On the position of the Frankfurt Beit Din, see Fram, *A Window on Their World*, 152–53, case no. 61, 27 August 1775. Cf. PMBD, Vol. 1, pt. 2, no. 68, 18b.

55 Alexis de Tocqueville, *De la démocratie en Amérique*, *Oeuvres*, I (Paris, 1951): 46–47.

56 See Donald R. Kelley, "'Second Nature': The Idea of Custom in European Law, Society, and Culture," in Anthony Grafton and Ann Blair, eds., *The Transmission of Culture in Early Modern Europe* (Philadelphia, 1990), 131–72. On the efforts of early modern jurists to unify the law through jurisprudence and royal legislation, see Sarah Hanley, "The Jurisprudence of the Arrêts: Marital Union, Civil Society, and State Formation in France, 1550–1650,"

the northern provinces because it incorporated Roman law in its *Coûtumes*. Case law also bore the clear imprint of efforts to impose "French" civil law, while the *ius civile* effectively blended Roman law with local customs.[57]

The two dominant forms of inheritance in medieval and early modern Europe were *impartibilité* (the distribution of all or the greater part of an estate to one heir) and *partibilité* (the equal division of property among all those of the same degree of consanguinity), but the issue most frequently in dispute concerned wills. Roman law and French customary law diverged especially on the degree to which written testaments could be used to modify general rules of intestate succession to suit individual preferences. Roman law, through the development of an intricate body of inheritance rules that revolved around the testament, gave substantial power to the paterfamilias. Male property owners, and increasingly females as well, enjoyed broad powers to dispose of property as they saw fit, provided that a portion was reserved for their direct heirs. Moreover, late Roman rules provided for equal division among brothers and sisters.[58]

Strategies that contributed to the consolidation of wealth in partible inheritance systems included the substitution of the dowry for the daughter's entitlement to a share of her parents' estate, the control of estates by brothers, and the use of testaments to privilege one child over others.[59] Most French customary rules did not recognize the will as a means of distributing property in the estate of the deceased. These customs did not recognize the freedom of parents to dispose of property via a will. In northern France and England, dowries provided similar results, without recourse to wills. According to customary law, the succession rights of women were inferior to those of brothers; the oldest son generally took a third of the real property, regardless of how many older

---

Law and History Review 21:1 (2003): 1–40; Marie Seong-Hak Kim, "Civil Law and Civil War: Michel de L'Hôpital and the Ideals of Legal Unification in Sixteenth-Century France," *Law and History Review* 28:3 (2010): 791–826; and Ralph Giesy, "State-Building in early Modern France: The Role of Royal Officialdom," *Journal of Modern History* 55 (June 1983): 191–207.

57 The character of Metz *ius civile* is readily apparent in Gabriel, *Observations détachées sur les coûtumes et les usages anciens et modernes du ressort du Parlement de Metz*, and throughout the *Coûtumes générales de la ville de Metz*.

58 See Walter Pintens, "Testamentary Formalities in France and Belgium," in *Comparative Succession Law: Testamentary Formalities*, ed. Kenneth G. C. Reid, et al. (Oxford, 2011), 1:51–70.

59 See Judith J. Hurwich, "Inheritance Practices in Early Modem Germany," *Journal of Interdisciplinary History*, 23:4 (Spring, 1993): 700, based on John P. Cooper, "Patterns of Inheritance and Settlement by Great Landowners from the Fifteenth to the Eighteenth Centuries," in Jack Goody, Joan Thirsk, and Edward P. Thompson, eds., *Family and Inheritance: Rural Society in Western Europe 1200–1800* (Cambridge, 1978), 192–98.

sisters there were, and the remainder was shared among the other sons and daughters—except that a daughter who married and had been given property at her wedding could not share in her parents' estate (unless she returned what she had been given). Women were usually not permitted to manage their own property, whether real or movable, if they were unmarried and living in their father's home or married and living with their husband.[60]

In contrast to provisions set forth in most customs books in France, the *Coûtumes générales de la ville de Metz* followed Roman law in affording heads of household greater freedom in disposing of their estates. Wills, gifts, and other legal devices offered flexibility in privileging the wishes of the deceased over the expectations of individual heirs, and the will became an instrument for alienating property to irregular heirs that had the potential to elevate women's property rights in contravention of intestate rules.[61] According to the Metz *Coûtumes*, a testament and codicil were valid in the city of Metz and in *pays messin* when prepared in the presence of a notary and four male witnesses.[62]

In Jewish law the will enjoyed a status comparable to the testament in Roman law. Its validity could be challenged for a variety of reasons, including its documentary integrity and its legality based on the Jewish laws and customs of succession. In one instance, members of the family of Gedaliah Charry, including his sons, son-in law, and widow sought to nullify the testator's will based on a scribal error that purportedly resulted from the hurried efforts to prepare the document. They claimed that the amount of money earmarked in the will for Charry's daughter greatly exceeded what the widow and her husband had intended. Their argument rested on the testimony of the witnesses who signed the will, and that in light of the financial worth of the deceased, it could be presumed that the testator never intended that his daughter would be left a large sum and that his son would be left empty-handed.[63] The Beit Din

60 See Thomas Kuehn, "Inheritance," in Margaret Schaus, ed., *Women and Gender in Medieval Europe: An Encyclopedia* (New York, 2006), 404–405; F. R. P. Akehurst, "Law, Customary: French," in Margaret Schaus, ed., *Women and Gender in Medieval Europe: An Encyclopedia* (New York, 2006), 454. Desan, "Making and Breaking Marriage," 1–27. On patterns in the Moselle region, see Ulbrich, *Shulamit and Margarete*, 24–25.

61 See Jack Goody, "Inheritance, Property and Women: Some Comparative Considerations," in *Family and Inheritance: Rural Society in Western Europe, 1200–1800* (New York, 1976), Jack Goody, Joan Thirsk, and E. P. Thompson, eds., 10–36.

62 *Coûtumes générales de la ville de Metz et pays-Messin*, Titre VIII, Art. 3, 252. Testaments and codicils were prepared and committed to writing in the presence of the *les Maire et Gens de Justice des Villages*, or in the presence of *le Maire et un Echevin* [Alderman], ibid., Art. 4, 253.

63 In this case, the Beit Din used the talmudic phrase *umdena de-mukhah* to refer to a presumption so widespread that the court could rest assured that the information or intention was known by all and was therefore unassailable.

rejected the family's petition because it could find no evidence in the will to support the claim that a certain sum was to be drawn from the *nikhsei melog* ("iron sheep property"; i.e., inalienable assets) and would be earmarked for the son and daughter instead of the amount indicated in the will. But more decisive in the court's ruling was the premise that the testimony of witnesses could not negate the language of the will.[64]

Wills were also challenged when they were alleged to contradict normative succession guidelines as set forth in the talmudic tradition. Such charges were based on claims that a will failed to respect the preference for closest heirs, for sons over daughters and for heirs over non-heirs, or when it contained a provision for a charitable bequest that would severely diminish the allocation that heirs could otherwise expect. Wills were commonly disputed when there was a purported flaw in the text. When a will was said to contravene traditional laws of succession, *posekim* were nonetheless inclined, as a rule, to uphold its validity.[65] Nevertheless, two cases involving Reizele (Rozette) Spire reveal the range of norms applied in such matters.

In the first, her husband Bernard had bequeathed his estate to his wife, as the couple did not have children. According to Jewish law she was entitled to the *ketubah*, the current value of her dowry, and lodging and food from the estate. In the view of the *parnasim*, Bernard's will named Reizele administrator as long as the property in the estate had not been distributed. His family, as the legal heirs, opposed Reizele. Reizele demanded that Bernard's brother Moyse perform *ḥaliẓah*—a ritual that releases a widow from the obligation to marry her late husband's brother when the husband died without issue—before she would agree to the distribution of property of the estate and step down as administrator. To assure his inheritance before Reizele was released from her obligation to marry him, Moyse stalled and sought legal support at the *bailliage*. The *bailliage* found in favor of Moyse, and Reizele appealed to the Parlement of Metz. The Parlement found in her favor and ordered Moyse to pay one-hundred livres each day he delayed the *ḥaliẓah*. Rabbi Samuel Hilman, *av beit din* of Metz, was ordered by the court to perform the *ḥaliẓah*. The *parnasim* in turn issued the *herem* against Reizele while Rabbi Hilman defied

64 PMBD, Vol. 1, pt. 2, no. 216, 48a.

65 See Shmuel Shilo, "Wills," in *Encyclopedia Judaica* 16 vols. (Jerusalem, 1971), 16: 519–30; Joseph Rivlin, *Inheritance and Wills in Jewish Law* [Hebrew] (Ramat Gan, 1999); Malkiel, "Jews and Wills in Renaissance Italy;" and Arye Edrei, "Halakhic Responsibility of the Deceased: A Further Study of the Concept of Inheritance in Talmudic Thought," *Israel Law Review* 33 (1999): 821–54. According to Simon ben Ẓemaḥ Duran, *Resp. Tashbeẓ* (Amsterdam, 1743), 3:190, once a will was written, its validity was unassailable unless it was shown to be in direct violation of Torah law. See Elon, *Jewish Law*, 1:99–102, 151–54.

the order of the Parlement and refused to administer the *ḥaliẓah*. The Metz Parlement responded by granting Reizele what she had requested. The excommunication was lifted, Bernard's will was upheld and Reizele was recognized as the universal heir. The rabbi was ordered to carry out the provision upon pain of corporal punishment. Jewish authorities were henceforth prohibited from imposing the *ḥerem* on individuals who had approached the French courts, but Metz communal leaders nonetheless persisted in their efforts to restore governmental support for Jewish civil jurisdiction. They argued further that civil jurisdiction was inseparable from religious authority, and that without the *ḥerem* the rabbis would become powerless. Frances Malino, who reconstructed the details of Reizele's legal entanglements with the Metz Kahal, rabbi, and Parlement, viewed the case as evidence of the mounting challenges to traditional authority that could not be held in check.[66]

In the second case, the Metz Beit Din confirmed Reizele's will, though it strayed from the standard rules of succession. A group of heirs contested the entitlement of "beneficiaries of gifts" who were not eligible by conventional rules of inheritance. They argued that the will prepared in French in 1766 and the codicil appended in 1769 were null and void, so that the beneficiaries of gifts ought to be disqualified from receiving any portion of the estate. The Beit Din upheld the will as written, based on several considerations: First, the fact that the French will and codicil were signed by some of the heirs and beneficiaries was taken as evidence that they agreed to all their provisions and undertook to fulfill them. Second, it followed that all those who did not sign the will and the codicil would receive from whatever remains in the estate, each according to his or her entitlement to the portion of his inheritance and not according to the value of the will. Third, if anything remained after the distribution of the assets, those heirs and other beneficiaries who signed would

66 See Frances Malino, "Competition and Confrontation: The Jews and the *Parlement* of Metz," in *Les Juifs au regards de l'histoire: Mélanges en l'honneur de Bernhard Blumenkranz*, G. Dahan, ed. (Paris, 1985), 327–41; also see idem, "Résistances et révoltes à Metz dans la première moitié du 18ᵉ siècle," in *Juifs en France au* XVIIIᵉ *siècle*, Bernhard Blumenkranz, ed. (Paris, 1994), 125–40. Also see Katz, "To Judge and Be Judged." See Art. 17 of the 1769 Takkanot, PKM, 77b. Rozette died on 14 March 1773; she was the half-sister of Lambert Ephraim Gompertz (Lemli Gompertz Emmerich). Rozette D'Alsace and Bernard Spire Levy had married in Metz on 11 February 1712 (though it appears that the actual date of the marriage contract was 2 September 1729). See Fleury, *Contrats de mariage juifs*, 150 and 190. For the Parlement's pronouncement against the use of the *ḥerem* as punishment for individuals who brought their cases to the civil courts, see "Arrest de la Cour de Parlement, qui fait défenses au Rabin de juifs ... 30 janviere 1759," Houghton Library, Harvard University, FC7F844P8759a, cited in Malino, "Resistance and Rebellion in Eighteenth-Century France."

be entitled to what remained, each according to the portion of his bequest. But those beneficiaries who did not sign were not eligible to collect anything from the estate.[67]

A case heard in 1779 exemplifies a different sort of legal challenge to wills. The Beit Din validated the directives prepared by a wealthy resident of Metz despite misgivings that these may not have conformed strictly to Jewish law. The source of concern was the testator's wish to appoint his wife *shultanit u-gevirtanit* (executor and mistress) over his estate. Additional conditions in the will that pertained to the liability of the widow and the two court-appointed overseers (*mashgiḥim*) were viewed by the Beit Din as potentially problematic. Conceding that the will could be legitimately set aside on technical grounds, the Beit Din nonetheless decided to affirm its validity because its provisions were understood clearly to benefit the heirs. The Beit Din relied, further, on a 1724 communal *takkanah* stating that as long as a will was signed by the testator himself, its terms were to be upheld even when its language failed to meet the strict requirements of Jewish law, provided the directives of the will were, in the judgment of the Beit Din, in "the best interests of the orphans." In all probability, the Wittersheim will was not legally flawed, despite certain unidentified imperfections. But even if it were in some way imperfect, the court could have relied on a range of talmudic and medieval halakhic sources that provided ample grounds for overlooking minor defects that might otherwise invalidate a will. Though not cited in the Pinkas, these texts would have been familiar to *dayanim* who sat on the bench.[68]

67 See PMBD, Vol. 1, pt. 2, no. 54, 16a. For the consultation that was solicited by the heirs and beneficiaries named in the will, see Appendix 3 in the Hebrew volume. For the Hebrew translation of the French text, dated 30 August 1773, see the A.D. Moselle, Consistoire israélite 17J24. See PMBD, Vol. 2, no. 531, 108b.

68 See PMBD, Vol. 2, no. 149, 29b. See the Archives départementales de la *Moselle*, 3E 4266, n° 303. Inventaire après décès de Seligman Wittersheim. In PKM, 65a, it is stated that "if a will is prepared without the oversight of the *av beit din* or the Kahal, its terms nonetheless will be upheld, and that the Kahal would have no authority to nullify anything in the will." See Schwarzfuchs, "The Rabbinic Contract of the Sha'agat Aryeh in Metz," 86, parag. 5. The following are several of the sources that offer some flexibility regarding the rules of inheritance: BT Bava Batra 130a (the opinion of Yoḥanan ben Broka); Maimonides, "Laws of Inheritance," 6:11 and 6:13; and Joel Sirkes, *Bayit Hadash, Ḥoshen Mishpat* §282. Cf. the view of R. Ezekiel Landau, see his *Resp. Noda b'Yehudah*, pt. 1, *Ḥoshen Mishpat*, no. 29. For an example of a contested will, see PMBD, Vol. 1, pt. 2, no. 216, 49a, and for a case concerning a will that was prepared in the French civil court, see PMBD, Vol. 2, no. 16, 3b. On a more general level, the RoSh stated that "in civil matters the *beit din* has the authority to enact *takkanot* according to the time and the need, even if this requires overriding Torah law, [that is] taking from one and giving to the other." See Asher ben Yeḥiel, *Resp. ha-Rosh* (Jerusalem, 1994), 55:10. On related matters, including the distinction between gifts and

As in Roman law, the foregoing trend in the Metz Beit Din provided greater latitude in the allocation of property to women, though testators frequently relied on procedures and formulae that were designed to avert potential problems that might arise if the will were ever challenged. It is for this reason that the wealthy army purveyor Abraham Hess stated in his will that he intended to leave his entire estate to his wife, Froumette, stipulating that the arrangement would be based on some combination of bequest and gift. In the end, the Beit Din was relieved of responsibility of ruling on the validity of the controversial will because Froumette decided to accept the gift while foregoing the bequest.[69] The rabbinic court records also contain dozens of instances of women who left wills of their own in order to allocate their assets as they wished; of equal significance are cases referring to disputes over estates that belonged to women. Once again, these trends echoed the practice recorded in the Metz *Coûtumes*.[70] In some instances the Beit Din exercised independent judgment by enlarging on what was contained in the will. Where a testator had instructed that funds from his estate support the hiring of a *lamdan* (scholar) to teach on a permanent basis, the Beit Din ruled that a daughter had the right to be consulted on the choice of the *lamdan* despite the fact that the will of the deceased did not assign this responsibility to her.[71]

As a rule, the general flexibility provided by the testament corresponded to heightened interest in distributing assets more evenly and purposefully

---

inheritance, as well as the designation of a wife as an *apotropa*, see Rivlin, *Inheritance and Wills in Jewish Law*, 86.

69 See PMBD, Vol. 2, no. 311, 57b. For an example of large sums that were transferred to daughters, see PMBD, Vol. 2, no. 431, 82b. Cf. *Coûtumes générales de la ville de Metz*, Titre VIII, Arts. 8–10, 264–69, where it is stated that a husband may leave half of his estate to his wife, provided that the other half, known as the *légitime*, is earmarked for his children. For the contrasting view, see *Coûtumes de l'évêche Metz, avec les municipalité de Ramberviller, Bacarat & Moyen* (Metz, 1701), 118–19, Art. 5, where it is stated that a husband may not bequeath any part of his estate to his wife.

70 For a will left by Rebécca née Halfon, wife of Hayim Sintzheim in 1713, see "Le Testament d'une femme juive," ed. and trans. Joseph Bloch, *REJ* 110 (1931): 146–160. For others, see Pinkas Ẓava'ot (Arch. JTS), and the Archives départementales de la Moselle, Consistoire israélite, 17J24. For references to women's wills in the Beit Din, see PMBD, Vol. 1, pt. 1, no. 90, 31a; Vol. 1, pt. 2, no. 8, 3a; no. 54, 16a; no. 14, 35a; Vol. 2, no. 184, 36a; no. 266, 50a; no. 424, 81a; no. 618, 133b; no. 657, 145a. For mention of women's estates, see PMBD, Vol. 1, pt. 1, no. 231, 43a; Vol. 1, pt. 2, no. 2, 2a; no. 151, 37a; Vol. 2, no. 252, 46b; no. 563, 117b; and no. 572, 120b. For medieval precedents, see Yosef Rivlin, "Deeds, Enactments and Customs as Reflected in the Jewish Shetarot" [Hebrew], in *Studies in the History of Ashkenazic Jewry in Honor of Eric Zimmer*, ed. Gershon Bacon, Daniel Sperber, and Aharon Gaimani (Ramat Gan, 2009), 224–25. On the law in Metz, see *Coûtumes générales de la ville de Metz*, Titre VIII, Art. 8, 264–67.

71 PMBD, Vol. 2, no. 437, 83b.

than would have been possible according to conventional Jewish inheritance law and custom. On occasion, special provisions were introduced in the will, such as the distribution of funds to provide dowries for both sons and daughters. Baruch Brisach's will contained instructions to present 9,000 livres to his son and to his daughter on their respective wedding days. The guardians of the young man and woman approached the Beit Din with a request to examine the will to determine whether there were any grounds for invalidating it, but the court found no reason to contest its validity.[72]

Among the instruments used to convey property specifically to daughters was the *shetar ḥaẓi ḥelek zakhar*, a late medieval innovation that the Metz Kehillah employed regularly. A man would give his daughter a promissory note declaring that he already owed her a very large sum of money, with two conditions attached. First, the debt could not be claimed until a moment before the father's death, and later, the sons would need to agree to give their sister a portion of their inheritance from their father—equivalent to half of the share to which each one of them was entitled. If these two conditions were met, the daughter would then agree to forgo the debt and cancel it. Following the father's death, the sons were required, together, to give their sister a half-portion of their inheritances or else pay the full debt, which would be considerably more than the entire inheritance.[73] Customarily, the *shetar ḥaẓi ḥelek zakhar* was transacted at the time of the daughter's marital engagement or at the wedding ceremony.[74]

---

72 PMBD, Vol. 1, pt. 2, no. 88, 23b.

73 According to Moses Isserles, in *Ḥoshen Mishpat* §281:7, the *shetar ḥaẓi ḥelek zakhar* functioned in the same way as inheritance, and therefore all other claims precede it—those of creditors, the *ketubah* of a widow, and *issur nekhasim* (a tenth of the father's estate paid to daughters when they are maintained by brothers). It appears that the *ḥaẓi ḥelek zakhar* was already common in his day, based on his formulation in *Even ha-'Ezer* §90:1. For earlier precedents for *ḥaẓi ḥelek zakhar*, see R. Meir of Rotenberg, *Resp. Maharam mi-Rotenberg*, pt. 4, no. 243: "From the day after our death, our daughter will receive [a portion] as one of the sons;" pt. 4, no. 1004; and *shetarei yerushah* (inheritance notes) referenced by Maharil and Rabbi Jacob Weill and cited in Simḥa Assaf, "Le-She'elat Yerushat ha-Bat" ("Concerning the Inheritance of a Daughter"), *Sefer Yovel l'Yaakov Freimann* (Berlin, 1937), 8–13. For an opinion as to why a daughter's share ought to be valuated at the time of the father's death, see Bacharach, *Resp. Ḥavvot Ya'ir*, no. 63. Also see Shalom Bar-Asher, *Sefer ha-Takkanot* (Jerusalem, 1991), 52: "כשיישארו אחריהם בנים ובנות, בשווה עם הבנים יירשו הבנות שווה"; Yosef Rivlin, "Shetar Ḥaẓi Zakhar" [Hebrew], *Diné Israel* 17 (1993–1994): 155–79; and Fram, *Ideals Face Reality: Jewish Law and Life in Poland*, 83–95. Cf. See Ralph E. Giesy, "Rules of Inheritance and Strategies of Mobility in Pre-revolutionary France," *American Historical Review* 82 (1977): 275.

74 See Menahem Mendel Krochmal, *Resp. Tzemach Tzedek* (Amsterdam, 1675), no. 95.

The *shetar ḥaẓi ḥelek zakhar* can be traced to the late Middle Ages. First appearing in the responsa of Rabbi Jacob Moellin (Maharil) of fourteenth-century Mainz and his student Rabbi Jacob Weill of fifteenth-century Nuremberg and Erfurt, it was characterized in Rema's glosses to the *Shulḥan 'Arukh* (*Ḥoshen Mishpat* §281:7) as an instrument that functioned much like inheritance, and therefore all other claims preceded it—those of creditors, the *ketubah* of a widow, and *issur nekhasim*.[75] It gained greater popularity in the seventeenth centuries, as it was included among the numerous *exempla* of contracts published in 1667 in *Sefer Naḥalat Shiv'ah*.[76] The author, Shmuel Halevi Segel, noted that in Poland there were instances of a *shetar ḥaẓi ḥelek zakhar* executed only by the husband but not by the wife, whereas in Ashkenaz (i.e., central and western Europe) the wife, mother of the bride, also prepared a *shetar ḥaẓi ḥelek zakhar*. This entitled a daughter to receive a half portion of the assets belonging to her mother who died after her father. To ensure that there was no doubt regarding entitlement in such cases, it was customary to write a single *shetar* for both husband and wife in order to create joint liability by inserting a formula known as *be'ohev*, a wife indicated her intent to subordinate her right to receive payment for the *ketubah* as a first creditor. According to Rabbi Jacob Reischer, the insertion of this formula in the *ḥaẓi ḥelek zakhar* contracts had become a scribal convention.[77]

It is likely that the extensive use of the *shetar ḥatzi ḥelek zakhar* in eastern France and neighboring localities was prompted by social and economic conditions peculiar to the region. In fact, the *shetar ḥatzi ḥelek zakhar* bore remarkable resemblance to the *donation deguisée*, a fictitious loan that disguised a gift intended for financially vulnerable family members. It is plausible that this Jewish version of the *donation deguisée* appealed to both the Metz

---

75 See Moses Isserles, in *Ḥoshen Mishpat* §281:7, and *Even Ha-Ezer* §113:2; *Darkhei Moshe ha-Katzar* 108. *Resp. Maharil ha-Ḥadashot*, nos. 164, 155; *Resp. Mahari Weill*, no. 20; *Resp. Maharam Mintz*, nos. 22, 47. Also see *Resp. Maharam Padua*, no. 51; *Resp. Rema*, no. 3; *Resp. Maharam Lublin*, no. 4; Segel, *Sefer Naḥalat Shiv'ah*, nos. 8, 9, 10, 12, 13. Also see Ashkenazi, *Resp. 'Avodat ha-Gershuni*, nos. 75–76; *Resp. Tzemaḥ Tzedek*, no. 95.

76 Regarding the execution of the *shetar ḥaẓi ḥelek zakhar* by the husband but not by the wife, see Segel, *Sefer Naḥalat Shiv'ah*, vol. 1, no. 21.
בפולין לא ראיתי לכתוב שטר חצי זכר על האשה רק על הבעל, ובאשכנז נהגו שגם האשה אמה של כלה נותנת שטר חצי זכר, ורוצה לומר אם תעדר האשה אחר מות בעלה והיא נוטלת כתובתה אם מתה אח"כ גם היא שתטול הבת מנכסי אמה גם כן חצי חלק זכר. ונוהגין לכתוב שטר אחד באשה והדר בעלה.

77 The phrase *be'ohev* appears in several purchase contracts published in Segel, *Sefer Naḥalat Shiv'ah*, vol. 1, nos. 31, 32, and 41. Also see Reischer, *Resp. Shevut Ya'akov*, pt. 2, no. 150.

Beit Din and French court officials as an acceptable circumvention of Jewish inheritance restrictions.[78]

Although the institution of the *ḥaẓi ḥelek zakhar* may appear to have run afoul of talmudic exhortations against the conveyance of an inheritance from one child to another, including the bestowal of an equal share on a daughter,[79] by the seventeenth century it had become a standard method of allocating assets. Dozens of such cases are recorded in the Metz Beit Din register, indicating the routine application and undisputed acceptability of this device. In a number of instances, even a full share—*ḥelek shalem*—was set aside for daughters.[80] While the *shetar ḥaẓi ḥelek zakhar* functioned as a remedy to the limitations imposed by the biblical law of succession, the Beit Din insisted that the language used in the note remain distinct from the technical formula of standard bequests. On one occasion the Beit Din disqualified a daughter's entitlement to the *ḥaẓi ḥelek zakhar* because it had been promised in a conventional will employing language normally reserved for inheritance. Notwithstanding the legal objection, the brothers and their married sister all agreed to give their younger sister a half portion voluntarily.

In Metz, as in other communities, the *shetar ḥaẓi ḥelek zakhar* was a symbol of social status, as attested by Glikl Hameln who reports her husband and brother-in-law made certain that each of their daughters received the coveted half-portion.[81] Other stipulations intended for the benefit of wives, daughters, and granddaughters were frequently added to gift contracts that were executed just prior to the testator's death. Mordechai Terquem had prepared notes several days before his death that granted his three daughters 15,000 livres each; for his seven granddaughters he earmarked 34,000 livres, to be held by their father

78 See Robert-Joseph Pothier, *Oeuvres Completes de Pothier* [*Des Retraits*] (Paris, 1821), 14: 72, cited in Shael Herman, "Review Essay: *Protocols of Justice: The Pinkas of the Metz Rabbinic Court, 1771–1789*," in *The Review of Rabbinic Judaism* 19 (2016): 310.

79 For two examples of talmudic traditions that declare opposition to inheritance allotments for daughters, see BT Bava Batra 133b: "even from a bad son to a good son, even more so from a son to a daughter;" and BT Bava Batra 115b, "Said R. Huna in the name of Rav: Anyone, even a prince in Israel, who says that a daughter is to inherit with the daughter of the son must not be obeyed, for this is only the practice of the Sadducees."

80 For examples of a full share promised to a daughter, see PMBD, Vol. 1, pt. 1, no. 74, 25b; this was matter of dispute in Vol. 1, pt. 1, no. 104, 35b; and Vol. 1, pt. 2, 22a–b, no. 84. See Jacob Reischer, *Resp. Shevut Ya'akov*, pt. 3, no. 123 for details concerning the wording used in Metz.

81 See PMBD, Vol. 1, pt. 1, no. 74, 25b, where the expression *be-torat yerushah* referred to language in the *shetar ḥaẓi ḥelek zakhar* indicating inheritance, which the Beit Din found to be improper. It therefore recommended more conventional methods of transferring funds to a daughter. On the social significance of the *ḥaẓi ḥelek zakhar*, see Turniansky, ed., *Memoirs of Glikl*, 310–11.

and eventually to be transferred to each one in the form of a dowry.[82] Disputes regarding which of the notes would have priority were not uncommon. As a rule, these were resolved on the basis of the dating of the documents, and thus the earliest ones were funded first by the estate. Such notes were dispositive insofar as no presumption was made regarding the entitlement of women to a share of the inheritance without a fully executed *shetar ḥaẓi ḥelek zakhar* or *ḥelek shalem* (full portion).[83]

Disputes concerning entitlement to the *shetar ḥaẓi ḥelek zakhar* and its precise legal status came before the Beit Din with some regularity. Complications could result when outstanding debts owed by the named beneficiary impeded the distribution of funds.[84] More prevalent were questions concerning the conveyance of money or property from an estate to any person other than a direct descendant. In several instances, sons-in-law set their sights on the bequest promised to their wives on the basis of the *shetar ḥaẓi ḥelek zakhar*.[85] To preclude this eventuality, it was customary in Metz to incorporate the phrase *lah u-leyoẓ'ei ḥalaẓeha davka* ("for her and for her descendants exclusively") in the text of the *ḥaẓi ḥelek zakhar* promissory note. The Beit Din emphasized that the inserted phrase *davka* (exclusively), which indicated the testator's intent to assign assets directly to a daughter and her children, was reliable because of the widely acknowledged trustworthiness of the community scribe (*safra d'mata*) employed by the Kahal. In order to establish the precise legal significance of the phrase—that is, whether a son-in-law was thereby excluded from consideration as a beneficiary through his late wife—the Beit Din consulted both "published and unpublished" responsa on the subject. The investigation did not yield a clear consensus among *posekim*, but owing to the Beit Din's confidence in the wording of the Metz contract, it ruled that the son-in-law was entitled to only half of the amount specified in the note.[86]

---

82 PMBD, Vol. 2, no. 18, 4a.

83 On the dispositive nature of the *shetar ḥaẓi ḥelek zakhar*, see PMBD, Vol. 1, pt. 2, no. 139, 34a.

84 See, for example, PMBD, Vol. 1, pt. 2, no. 2, 2a–b. In this case, Joseph Cahen placed a seizure on his sister-in-law's property in order to block her entitlement to the *ḥaẓi ḥelek zakhar* which had been designated for her. Cahen argued that she owed him for expenditures he had paid out for the maintenance of her mother's residence, and that she would not receive the funds earmarked for her until she reimbursed him.

85 Also recorded in the rabbinic court records are efforts of grandsons to inherit a portion of their grandfather's estate based on the *shetar ḥaẓi ḥelek zakhar* originally intended for their mother. See, for example, PMBD, Vol. 1, pt. 1, no. 14, 9a; Vol. 1, pt. 2, no. 136, 33b; Vol. 2, no. 137, 27b.

86 PMBD, Vol. 1, pt. 2, no. 85, 22b.

For reasons that are unclear, the Beit Din did not refer to the view of Rabbi Jacob Reischer, who was of the firm opinion that a son-in-law was not entitled to assets promised to his wife. In Reischer's view, "If the *shetar ḥazi ḥelek zakhar* was written explicitly according to the formula of the latter authorities or according to the formula of the holy community of Metz, he [the son-in-law] has no right to the inheritance of his father-in-law." The only exception, according to Reischer, based on the view of Rabbi Jacob Weill, was if the daughter predeceased her father, and left a child, and then the child died, followed by the death of her father, then her husband would inherit his child, even though it is presumed that the father had intended the money to go to his daughter and her descendants only.[87] The Beit Din ruled that since the phrase "for her and for her descendants exclusively" was incorporated into the text of promissory notes executed in Metz, the validity of the stipulation was irrefutable.[88]

An inheritance case that turned on several of these same issues was taken up on appeal by the Parlement of Metz in 1786. Samuel Jonas Lévi, a wealthy resident of Metz, had taken steps to prevent assets intended for his daughter Rachel from passing to his son-in-law Solomon-David Alphen in case Rachel predeceased her husband. According to Jewish law, as his wife's future heir, Alphen would be entitled to her dowry, her augment of the dowry, and all other property that had come into her possession. Samuel feared that if his son-in-law outlived his wife, he would either consume these assets or contract a second marriage and convey them to another family, leaving nothing to Samuel's grandchildren. At the time of Rachel's marriage in 1747, she received a dowry of 15,000 livres and later that year her parents gave her *un acte de rappel* in the amount of 30,000 crowns payable one hour before their death, unless her brother(s) gave to their sister or her descendants a half-portion of male [children]. As his fortune grew, Samuel decided not only to confirm the *acte de rappel* that he had given to his daughter at the time of her marriage, but also to increase that amount with a gift of 25,000 livres as stated in his will. However, he conditioned the legacy of 25,000 livres through "substitution," a legal mechanism used mainly in written law territories to limit the transmission of property to certain individuals and to their descendants. Property transmitted through substitution was held in trust, and this imposed obligations on the trustee to preserve and transmit the property to the next trustee in line.

Lévi's intent was to divide the 25,000 livres bequeathed to his daughter between her and her descendants, or if she were to benefit from usufruct during

87 Reischer, *Resp. Shevut Yaakov*, 3:123.

88 PMBD, Vol. 1, pt. 2, no. 85, 22b. For similar formulations, though not as emphatic see PMBD, Vol. 1, pt. 2, no. 159, 39a; Vol. 2, no. 225, 42a; and Vol. 2, no. 268, 50a.

her life, the property would be transferred exclusively to his grandchildren over all other heirs. He was confident that the income from capital would increase her ease and that she would share this benefit with her husband during her life, but the fund would revert after her death to his descendants. However, Lévi's intention was clouded by the fact that he left two testaments, one in Hebrew, dated 30 November 1777 the other in French, dated 1 December. The Hebrew testament stated that the 25,000 livres were given to Rachel Lévi *and* her descendants, and the French testament stipulated that the inheritance was intended for Rachel Lévi *or* her descendants.

Based on the opinion of two French jurisconsultants who were asked at the time of the reading of the will to provide an opinion, the 25,000 livres were delivered to Rachel and to her husband. Two months later, the curator of the estate demanded the return of the money, to be set aside for the benefit of the children of Rachel Lévi. As soon as they became aware of this act, the testamentary executors summoned M. Pécheur for their appeal. The Beit Din had understood Lévi's will to be consistent with local (Jewish) practice and in its judgment three weeks later rejected Alphen's claim of entitlement to property of the deceased based on the *ḥaẓi ḥelek zakhar*.[89] In appealing the rabbinic court's decision in the Metz Parlement, Alphen claimed that his father-in-law's intent to divide the inheritance between his daughter and ultimately to her descendants, his grandchildren, was in violation of Jewish law and of the French law of substitution as well.

The judges at the Parlement were of the opinion that Lévi's second will, in French, was necessary to document his bequest according to the conventions prescribed by the civil laws of France. For this reason, they argued, he brought two notaries to receive and write his final instructions regarding the appointment of a substitution in the sum of 25,000 livres bequeathed to his daughter:

> Here, then, is a *fidei-commissaire* whom the testator has submitted to our custom, to our rules, to ensure its execution. The testament in French has only confirmed that which was made in the Hebrew language, and if it is an established rule that the later will is the one to be used subsequent acts override, amplify or restrict previous acts, it is essentially, with respect to a will, that this is so. The testator did not limit himself to the dispositions he had made in Hebrew, it was because he wished to explain them more clearly, unambiguously and unequivocally by the second testament rendered in the French language. It is not to the mother and descendants in

89 See PMBD, Vol. 2, no. 23, 6a–6b. (20 Tevet 5538) for additional details contained in a dispute between Gershon Lévi, son of Samuel, and Salomon Halphen, son-in-law.

> direct line that the father bequeaths the 25,000 livres, it is to the mother, for after her death the money will go to her descendants in a direct line only. The testator, by expressing himself thus in the testament written in French, has fixed, in the clearest manner, the meaning of his disposition.[90]

M. Pécheur, Attorney at the Bailliage, argued that Samuel Lévi's testament proved that he intended to substitute, that is, to encumber the legacy of his daughter. This manner of disposition by the testator was found to be in full accord with French civil law.[91] Whether by the Hebrew will or by the French, the right of the children of Rachel Lévi to the sum of 25,000 livres following her death was unassailable.[92]

Alphen, however, argued that the testator did not have the right to substitute. He argued that the substitution was unauthorized under Jewish law and custom. To evaluate Alphen's claim, the Parlement needed to ascertain established Jewish practice and, therefore, turned to the *Recueil des lois, coûtumes et usages observés par les juifs de Metz*. Recourse to the French compendium of Jewish laws and customs attests to its recognized status, no doubt enhanced by its publication one year earlier, in 1785. It is of further significance that the issues were interpreted with the help of French legal concepts and institutions. Put differently, the Parlement acted as the arbiter of Jewish law. The Parlement decided that the testator was authorized to order a substitution, based on Article 1, Chapter 4 of Title VII in the *Recueil*, which established that the testator may institute whomever he sees fit, or bequeath to whomever he deems fit, provided that if that person dies, another person named by him will be subrogated in his place. Declining Alphen's appeal, the Parlement stated that Lévi was within his rights to provide this new advantage to his daughter, and he was also free to set any condition he considered appropriate.

The Parlement praised the Jews for having borrowed the substitution mechanism from either Roman law or French law, but the court noticed that the formulation in the *Recueil* was flawed, since "by a shocking stipulation that

---

90 Parlement de Metz, Arrêt du 8 Mai 1786. Précis pour Me. Jean-Pierre Pécheur, Procureur au Bailliage, en qualité de Curateur établi par Justice à la substitution portée au testament de Samuel-Jonas Lévi, Juif de cette Ville, Intimé, contre Salomon-David Alphen, & Jonas-Garçon Lévi, tous deux juifs habitans de cette Ville, Appellans; et contre Rechelé Lévi. Bibliotheque nationale.

91 See *les lois civiles*, book 5, titre III, section 1, no. 1: "… une disposition qui fait passer une succession, ou une partie, ou de certains biens, de la personne d'un héritier ou d'un légataire à un autre successeur, après le temps réglé par le testament."

92 See: Les archives de la Moselle, 3E 4261, n° 519, Inventaire après décès de Samuel Jonas Lévy.

proves how imperfect is the compilation of their laws, that by Articles 2 & 3 of the same Chapter 4, they are destroying the principle of freedom of testators to substitute." The judges at the Parlement were struck by the apparent contradiction between the first article of Chapter IV, which stated that the testator is free to substitute, and by Articles 2 and 3 that stated that the trustee can dispose of the substituted property during his or her lifetime. Continuing with its criticism, the judges stated that "the editors of such bizarre laws, so contrary to each other, would have done prudently not to speak of substitution, a matter they do not understand, or to defend them without exception." Noting that Samuel Lévi acted in accordance with Article 16 of Title IV of the *Recueil*, that anyone is free to bequeath his property as he sees fit, even to benefit one child more than another as a legacy or gift, the Parlement confirmed the testament of Samuel-Jonas Lévi. Nevertheless, the final judgment, which upheld the Beit Din's ruling, concluded on a rather sour note.

> [S]ome members of the community, jealous to maintain their usages, however defective, however misshapen they are, fear a reformation, of which the need is felt whenever we must discuss their laws. It is time to redeem this colony of unruly strangers (*étrangers indociles*), who cherish all the more their ignorance, that it owes to their religion, [to bring them back] to saner maxims. If the present generation suffers from this choice, posterity will rejoice in no longer being governed by laws that were made more for slaves than for free men, and it will share with the inhabitants (*régnicoles*) the precious advantage of being governed by wise legislation.[93]

The problem, in the view of the Parlement, was two-fold. Some leaders of the Jewish community viewed Samuel-Jonas Levi as an innovator for having established a trustee of the same form as is established in French law. "They want to admit substitutions, but they would want at the same time to reserve the power to alienate, to dispose of, to the detriment of the substituted." The image presented in the Parlement was of members of the Jewish community who were jealous to maintain their usages, however defective, for fear of "a reformation, of which the need is felt whenever we have to discuss their laws." In addition, these patronizing comments, coming at the end of a thirty-page detailed judgment, portrayed the Jews as a people whose flawed legal system needed to be replaced by the enlightened laws of France. Their condition, it

93 Parlement de Metz, Arrêt du 8 Mai 1786. Précis pour Me. Jean-Pierre Pécheur, Procureur au Bailliage.

appears, was the result of their choice to live by their law. At once echoing the Church's denunciation of the Jews and the French Enlightenment's critical perspective, the judges' closing message also anticipated the revolutionary debate on Jewish citizenship and Napoleon's efforts to advance the cause of Jewish assimilation into French society. Paradoxically, within the context of the ancien régime, the comments, despite their disdainful tone, are an unwavering acknowledgement of the legitimacy of Jewish juridical autonomy.

Testamentary Charity

Evidence of testamentary charity dates mainly from the era when advances in the commercial economy of western Europe widened the gap between affluence and privation. Local variants of the universal practice of charitable giving provide concrete evidence of the performance of philanthropy and, more generally, its relationship to local concerns regarding social, economic, and religious challenges in the latter decades of the ancien régime.[94] Sources for the study of testamentary charity in Metz include a register of wills produced by men and women; accounts of testamentary gifts recorded in the Pinkas Kahal; and disputes concerning bequests to charitable causes that were adjudicated in the Metz Beit Din. These manuscript sources offer rich details of philanthropic activity, including social and economic aspects of charity; gender-specific giving; the religious-spiritual function of charity; and evidence of the relationship between individual initiatives and communal policy.

In the eighteenth century, it was common for wealthy individuals to establish charitable foundations to support education, to assist the indigent, and to aid poor brides. In 1761, for example, Moïse Blien contributed 25,000 livres to establish a trust (*keren kayemet*) to fund the higher education of twenty-four poor children from Metz. The Kahal had obligated itself to contribute 300 livres annually to support three poor students who had studied in the Ettendorf and Mutzig yeshivot (of Alsace) and was given the authority by the Blien testament to select the recipients.[95] David Terquem, wealthy Metz financier and businessman, donated 12,000 livres to the local community to support two students with the annual interest.[96] The funds pledged were typically transferred to the

94 See Olwen Hufton, *The Poor of Eighteenth-Century France, 1750–1789* (Oxford, 1974). Julie Elizabeth Leonard, "A Window into their Lives: The Women of the Faubourg Saint-Antoine, 1725–1765" (Ph.D. diss., Marquette Univ., 2009).

95 PMBD, Vol. 2, no. 92, 18b.

96 See Kerner, "Acte de fondation d'un collège hébraïque à Metz, 1751;" idem, "La Vie quotidienne," 170–75; and Raphael Blum, "Le fondateur du grand Beth Hamidrash de Bouxwiller," *Univers israelite* 35 (1879): 85–88, 112–14. On the institution of the *hekdesh* in Metz, see

community leadership in trust, with the understanding that the community would distribute the accrued interest—invariably five percent—in accordance with the provisions set forth in the will. Use of the five percent interest rate followed the civil law ceiling for loans in eighteenth-century France.[97]

A more ambitious effort was the establishment in 1786 of a foundation to support "Talmud Torah, Hakhnassat Kallah, and Tzedakah" in Alsace. The document announcing this undertaking sheds light on the details and larger goals of charitable giving in the late eighteenth century. Created with an endowment of 175,000 livres by the wealthy army purveyor Herz Cerf Berr, the foundation established a *beit midrash* in Bischeim with three full-time Talmud scholars, it established a fund to dower and marry young women from families lacking sufficient means, and it provided assistance to needy individuals.[98] The Cerf Berr foundation represents an intermediate form of charitable giving that diverged from the medieval model but did not go quite as far as the nineteenth-century paradigm of philanthropy and social engineering. The foundation was to remain under the complete control of the benefactor, his three sons-in-law and three sons, and its explicit purpose was to support members of the extended Cerf Berr family. Only individuals who were related to Cerf Berr or his wives were considered eligible for an appointment as *beit midrash* scholars, for the award of a dowry, or for charitable assistance. Non-relatives could be selected on condition that there were no eligible family members available; in the case of *hakhnassat kallah*, preference was given to orphans, daughters of scholars, and residents of Alsace.[99]

Precisely how the foundation defined entitlement to charitable assistance is worthy of note. Clear preference was given to the "deserving" poor. Accordingly, in order to qualify for a dowry award, a young woman needed to be a *bat tovim*—that is, from a reputable family—and she herself must have an unblemished reputation and a record of good conduct. Charitable assistance,

Kerner, "La Vie quotidienne," 112–23, 149–68. For a description of charity in an Alsatian village, see Samuel Kerner, *La Communauté juive d'Odratzheim* (Paris, 1983).

97 Whether there were different kinds of trusts and how much they varied in the amount of control retained by the heir or executor of the estate is at present unknown. For the larger framework, see Philip T. Hoffman, Gilles Postel-Vinay, and Jean-Laurent Rosenthal, "Private Credit Markets in Paris, 1690–1840," *The Journal of Economic History* 52 (1992): 293–306.

98 The document establishing the Cerf Berr foundation was published by Simon Schwarzfuchs, "Three Documents from the Lives of the Jewish Communities in Alsace-Lorraine" [Hebrew], *Michael* 4 (1976): 12–25.

99 For non-relatives, priority was to be given to the daughter of a *talmid ḥakham* (Torah scholar) without means, but in such circumstances an orphan of a *talmid ḥakham* was to be given priority. Among non-relatives, the daughter of one of the scholars of the *beit midrash* was preferred.

including gifts of clothing, was to be disbursed only to *aniyim hagunim*, that is, the "decent" poor. Although the foundation was set up primarily to assist members of the Cerf Berr family, it nonetheless functioned as a public institution. Its records were deposited on file with the royal notary and any procedural dispute or disagreement about eligibility was to be brought before the provincial rabbi or the *parnasim*. The founding document also stipulated that if, in the future, the number of family members in France diminished to less than five, the administration of the foundation would pass to the *parnasim u-manhigei ha-medinah* and to one of the regional chief rabbis of Alsace. Ultimately, the *rav ha-medinah*, along with the *parnasim u-manhigim*, was expected to oversee the practices and procedures of the foundation. We may assume, then, that the established criteria for selecting beneficiaries who were either relatives or members of "decent" families were acceptable to the communal leadership.

Cerf Berr's aim was to advance the material and spiritual condition of his extended family and, secondarily, of his community. His proposal was a concrete effort to remedy a problem that demanded immediate attention, and having recently reached the age of sixty, he is likely to have considered the establishment of the foundation the last major undertaking of his life. His demand that a certain *yehi raẓon* prayer (beseeching the will of God) be recited on his behalf at the *beit midrash* each day, is proof that he wished to achieve a measure of immortality, though the emphasis on building families through the support of the foundation was his real goal. Among the stipulations set forth in the founding document was the promise that the first issue of a marriage of an orphan would be given the name Dov Ber or Gelche—the parents of Cerf Berr. Moreover, if a young woman who had been dowered by the foundation died within the first year of marriage and did not give birth to a child, her husband would be obligated to repay the dowry after deducting the expenses of marriage; if she died in the second year without leaving a child, her husband was required to repay half the dowry.[100] While the objectives as set forth by the foundation were well-defined, they were quite limited in scope, and the foundation did not endure for long. The fortune left to Cerf Berr's heirs was ultimately destroyed by the Revolution and by the moratorium ordered by Napoleon in 1808 on the repayment of debts owed to Jews.[101]

Testamentary charity in Metz reveals much concerning the scope of early modern philanthropic activity, including its religious and social significance. Charitable gifts facilitated through the creation of a trust were possible only for the most affluent, who included individuals who amassed wealth as army

100 Schwarzfuchs, "Three Documents from Alsace Lorraine," 21.

101 See Zosa Szajkowski, *Poverty and Social Welfare Among French Jews* (New York, 1954), 51

purveyors, large-scale money lenders, and successful merchants. Testaments nonetheless shed light on broader concerns about the relationship of philanthropy to the effects of poverty and wealth on the social structure of the community. Wills recorded in the Pinkas Kahal of Metz and those registered with the Gemilut Hasadim confraternity exemplify the kinds of individual initiative that typify this genre.

The prologue of the will prepared in 1773 by Reizele D'Alsace, widow of Berman Spire, contained instructions calling for the distribution of five percent of the 12,000 livres remaining from the estate of her husband that was to be transferred to the Kahal. This will was distinct from other wills that were prepared by Reizele, including a more conventional will that contained instructions for the distribution of her assets to natural heirs and beneficiaries.[102] A wife's independence to handle such affairs and to decide how funds would be distributed was not a foregone conclusion; it rested on the authorization granted by her husband, as stated initially in Reizele's will: "And her late husband empowered his wife with the authority to compose a will that would determine what would be done with the aforesaid assets, following her death, on a yearly basis. And so his esteemed wife (*ishto ha-ḥashuvah*) did and composed a will."[103] The following are the main provisions of Reizele's will:

1. Three *lomdim* (men engaged in a regular routine of Talmud study) will be funded to study Talmud every day and will be supported with a stipend of 45 livres each. Two of the *lomdim* will be selected from among relatives of her husband and the third from among her own relatives—assuming qualified relatives were available.
2. Each year, on Berman Spire's *yahrtzeit* (anniversary of his death), 50 livres will be distributed to the poor, drawn from a list of his relatives. The distribution will be undertaken by the Ḥevrah Kadisha Gemilut Ḥasadim, but the Kahal would have the right to decide if it will distribute

102 JTS, ms. 9835. See PMBD, Vol. 1, pt. 2, 16a, no. 54. Owing to a dispute over the distribution of assets, the parties approached a French attorney, Pierre-Louis Roederer, with a request to clarify their legal rights. His opinion, produced formally as a legal consultation, is available only in the Hebrew translation of the French text, dated 30 August 1773. The manuscript is in the Archives départementales de la Moselle, Consistoire israélite 17j24 and was published in Berkovitz, *Protocols of Justice*, Vol. 2, Appendix 3. Roederer, who eventually gained an appointment to the Metz Parlement where he was seated in 1780, later became a supporter of Jewish emancipation. See Kenneth Margerison, "P.-L. Roderer: The Industrialist as Revolutionary Author(s)," *Eighteenth-Century Studies*, 2:4 (Summer, 1978): 473–88.

103 The following is the original Hebrew text: ובעלה המנוח הנ״ל נתן כח ותוקף לאשתו הנ״ל שתהי׳ רשות בידה לעשות צוואה כדת מה לעשות עם הרווחי׳ הנ״ל לאחר פטירתה בכל שנה ושנה. וכן עשתה אשתו החשובה הנ״ל ועשתה צוואה.

the funds itself. In addition, on the husband's *yahrtzeit* ten *lomdim* will study [Torah] for his soul (*'avur nishmato*). Each one will receive three livres; funds were also set aside for the purchase of wax candles (a half Reichsthaler). In addition, on that day each year, the Kahal will distribute 200 livres toward the dowries of poor brides who are his or Reizele's relatives.

3. On Reizele's *yahrtzeit*, 48 livres will be distributed to her poor relatives. This, too, will be disbursed by the Gemilut Hasadim Society, if the Kahal decides that it does not want to distribute the funds itself. In addition, on her *yahrtzeit* ten *lomdim* will study [Torah] for her soul, with 30 livres set aside for this, and for the wax candle.
4. Each year, on each of the two *yahrtzeits*, six livres will be awarded to the *av beit din*; on the husband's *yahrtzeit* three livres will be given to each of the two main *shamashim* (beadles) of the Kahal. On each of the *yahrtzeits* twelve livres will be allocated to the Ḥevrah Kadisha Gemilut Ḥasadim Society for their trouble. And on each of the *yahrtzeits* the *gabbai* of the Ḥevrah Kadisha Gemilut Ḥasadim Society will be given 3 livres. On the husband's *yahrtzeit* the community *beit midrash* will be given 50 livres for Talmud Torah.

Several points stand out in Reizele's will. First, only individuals who were related to Reizele or to her husband were considered eligible for an appointment as *beit midrash* scholars or for the award of a dowry to poor brides. Non-relatives could be selected only on condition that there were no eligible family members available. Second, the symmetry between the distribution of funds in memory of her husband and in her own memory is noteworthy. The accent on support for learning, like provisions for the poor, is virtually identical, irrespective of the gender of the testator. Third, the individual initiative is processed through a communal agency, the Gemilut Ḥasadim Society. Fourth, the spiritual benefit to the soul—known in Christian sources as *pro anima*—is heavily accented and would remain so throughout the period of the late ancien régime. The idea of *pro anima* (*to'elet ha-nishamah* in Hebrew) is a clear indication of the spiritual motives that underlay charitable giving. Still, the aspiration to attain a measure of immortality could be realized in this world, not in the next, by acquiring a "passport to heaven," as Jacques Le Goff labeled the hope of medieval testators. Impressive evidence from Metz reveals the enormous emphasis testators placed on the distribution of alms on their *yahrtzeits* and on payments to individuals to study in their memory in order to achieve redemption of the soul.[104]

---

104 See Jacques Le Goff, *Medieval Civilization* (Oxford, 1988), 187. Cf. the 1778 will of Yutcha (JTS ms. 9835, p. 28a), which states that proceeds from her estate will be set aside for a

The prominence of the *pro anima* sentiment in these wills offers evidence that is at odds with trends noted by several prominent French historians. Michel Vovelle concluded that sometime between 1750 and 1770 there was a sharp decline in religious sentiment that constrained the expression of the *pro anima* motivation of testators. The reduced number of requests for requiem masses and the smaller number of pious gifts earmarked for the Church in the wills of the upper and middle classes evidence this decline. According to Vovelle, *une mutation de la sensibilité collective* in religious behavior signaled the advance of "dechristianization" that was well underway before the French Revolution. A comparable study of Parisian wills in the same period led Pierre Chaunu to endorse this conclusion. In Timothy Tackett's view, the secularized language in testaments of the eighteenth century evinced a refocusing of people's lives from the community to the nuclear family, a development that mirrored declericalization, much as the *cahiers de doléances* tended not to be critical of the Christian religion but were filled with attacks on clerics and clerical institutions. Janine Lanza found that religious sentiment among widows in Paris remained strong, as reflected in preferences for place of burial, attachment to the parish, requests that masses be recited in the local parish, gifts to the parish poor and to religious confraternities, and gifts to individual priests and nuns.[105] While some historians judge wills to be uneven and therefore unreliable for assessing religious attitudes, these concerns do not detract from the enormous value that these documents contain.

Two types of philanthropy are most prevalent in the Metz records—aid awarded directly to the economically downtrodden and broader forms of assistance given to immigrants and refugees. In one instance, Metz communal leaders sent a query to the Beit Din regarding two poor brides, each of whom claimed entitlement to two hundred livres, based on their degree of kinship

young orphan boy (10 years old) to recite *kaddish* during the first year after her death, and each year on the *yahrtzeit*, until he marries. On his wedding day he will be given 100 Reichsthaler. She also ordered the distribution of 100 Reichsthaler annually for poor brides who are relatives; if there are no poor brides in a particular year, the funds should go to ten *lomdim* on her *yahrtzeit*. For examples of gestures that were consistent with *pro anima* sentiment, including distribution of alms to the poor, *hakhnassat kallah*, and funds to support *lomdim* to study on the testator's *yahrtzeit*, see PMBD, Vol. 1, pt. 2, no. 147, 36a; no. 191, 45a; no. 220, 49b. PMBD, Vol. 2, no. 84, 16b; no. 93, 18b; Vol. 2, no. 220. 41b; Vol. 2, no. 293, 54a; Vol. 2, no. 299, 55b; Vol. 2, no. 305, 59b; Vol. 2, no. 437, 83b; Vol. 2, no. 503, 102a; Vol. 2, no. 513, 104b; Vol. 2, no. 531, 108b; Vol. 2, no. 611, 132a; Vol. 2, no. 655, 142b.

105 Michel Vovelle, *Piété baroque et déchristianisation en Provence au XVIIIe siècle* (Paris, 1973); Pierre Chaunu, *La mort à Paris: 16e, 17e et 18e siècles* (Paris, 1978); Timothy Tackett, *Religion, Revolution, and Regional Culture in Eighteenth-Century France: The Ecclesiastical Oath of 1791* (Princeton, 1986), 255–56; Janine M. Lanza, *From Wives to Widows in Early Modern Paris: Gender, Economy, and Law* (Aldershot, U.K., 2007), 2–3, 73–82.

to Berman Spire or to Reizele, as stated in her will. One was related to Berman and the other to Reizele. The Beit Din concluded that under Reizele's will the two sides of relatives were entitled to equal treatment. Accordingly, it ruled that an allocation of 200 livres would go to the daughter of Shlomo Alsace in the first year and to the daughter of Elia Terquem, of the Berman family, in the following year. Four months later, the Beit Din ruled on the criteria for determining priority for entitlement. The Gemilut Hasadim Society acknowledged that it followed the ruling of the *av beit din*, Rabbi Aryeh Loeb Günzberg, that no distinction between those who were related to Alsace or Spire, either directly or by marriage, was acceptable.[106]

The central themes in Reizele's testament are typical of the wills produced in Metz in this period. David Terquem's will (1764)[107] offers an equally pronounced example of the *pro anima* motive and, generally, of extensive private support for religious institutions. In addition to the funds that would be distributed in observance of his own *yahrtzeit* and those of his parents and his first wife, the Terquem will provided grants to support scholars in the *beit midrash* that he had established, pay the royal tax for the *beit midrash*, maintain the *beit midrash* building and the synagogue and finance the purchase of books *le-ẓorekh pidyon ha-nefesh* (for the redemption of the soul) and the purchase of candles. In slight contrast, Rabbi Me'ir Trenel's will (1764) references the *pro anima* function, though not as prominently as in some others.[108] The priority accorded the support of one's poor relatives—typically poor brides—is also pervasive in the Terquem testament and in others, though in the Trenel testament, no provisos were made concerning the pool from which the (two) funded *lomdim* were to be chosen.

Other testaments evidence different priorities. In the will prepared by Samuel Lévi in 1777, the 970 livres generated by the trust were to be distributed somewhat differently from the previous examples. The testator designated a 1,000 livres gift to the Kahal tax fund. Sums were earmarked to assist *melamdim* in the community with their rent and were also used to support a needy orphan

106 PMBD, Vol. 2, no. 427, 81b. The ruling was dated 2 Adar I 5543 (1783). PMBD, Vol. 2, no. 531, 108b. See PMBD, Vol. 2, no. 657, 145a–b, for a description of the candidates who sought one of three *lomdim* positions funded by Reizele's will.

107 PKM, 53b–54b. The will contained instructions on how to distribute 650 *livres* each year.

108 PKM, 54b and 66b. The Trenel will contained instructions to distribute, from the proceeds, 800 livres to support two *lomdim*, each at 400 livres. The intention was that four *lomdim* from the community would learn with them. Trenel's son Wolf was obligated to subsidize half the rent of the two *melamdid*; fifty livres were earmarked for clothing the two students of the *lomdim*, and 100 livres were directed to the support of poor brides in Metz. The remaining thirty livres were to be distributed annually to ten *lomdim* who were instructed to learn "for my soul." Of further interest in Trenel's will is the detailed curriculum and teaching schedule it set forth.

who would be selected to study with the aforementioned *lomdim-melamdim*. There was no stipulation for distribution of funds to the poor on the *yahrtzeit* of the deceased, nor with respect to the ten *lomdim* who would be paid on the *yahrtzeit* to study Talmud. Partiality to relatives of the testator was, to a degree, offset by other concerns: brides working as domestic servants were targeted by Lévi for assistance, which hints at a wider communal concern.[109]

The will of Abraham Grumbach, who had established a *beit midrash* earlier in the century with four *lomdim*, raises an issue directly addressed in other wills that established charitable foundations to support education, to assist the indigent, and to aid poor brides. Who has control over the allocated funds and the institutions that are supported by the testator?[110] In the Grumbach will, which the testator signed in 1768, the sum of 19,200 livres was to be transferred to the Kahal and five percent of these funds were to be distributed to the four *lomdim*. Similar sums had been placed in trust with the Kahal in perpetuity (as a *keren kayemet*).[111] In an accompanying document, Ẓadok Grumbach, the testator's grandson, reserved the right throughout his life to direct the institutions created with his father's gifts—the *beit midrash* and synagogue—over the wishes of the Kahal. He established the schedule of learning and paid the salaries of the *lomdim* from his own pocket. Out of concern for the physical structure of the *beit midrash*, Ẓadok made an additional 3,000 livres gift of his own—again as a permanent endowment placed with the Kahal—that would generate funds to buy wood for heat and to hire a servant to work in the *beit midrash*. Ẓadok stipulated that he would retain supervision over everything throughout his life and that control would revert to the Kahal only after his death.[112] Twenty-five years later, in his own will, he left 12,400 livres to the Kahal as a permanent trust, at the standard five percent interest rate; pledged smaller stipends to support the four *lomdim* in the *beit midrash*; provided for candles and wood to heat the common living area in the *beit midrash*; and donated funds to hire an assistant in the *beit midrash*.[113] He also allocated another 10,000 livres to fund an additional full-time position in the *beit midrash*.[114]

Several years later, in 1774, the issue of control over a charitable gift bequeathed by the Grumbach estate resurfaced. The Kahal asked the Beit Din to rule on its right to exercise control of the funds, in accord with its own judgment, against the wishes of the heirs. Ẓadok Grumbach objected to the Kahal's

109 PKM, 25a.

110 See Hertzberg, *French Enlightenment*, 168–69, and see above, pp. 191–92.

111 In the Levi will it is stated that the sum of 19,400 livres was to be placed in trust.

112 PKM, 74a–74b. Signed 1768.

113 PKM, 129a–130a.

114 PKM, 137b.

insistence that one of twelve rooms in the *beit midrash* established with funds donated by his grandfather ought to be designated for elementary instructional purposes. His attorney argued that this would violate his grandfather's will and would contradict prior judgments of the court. It had been understood that the rooms in the upper level were intended for *lomdim* who had been appointed through the generosity of the benefactor and in whose merit they dedicated their efforts. Concerned that the noise caused by younger students would create a disturbance for the *lomdim*, Grumbach sued the Kahal for breach of contract. The attorney for the Kahal responded that the placement of a teacher and students in the room in question would be preferable to leaving it empty, and that in so doing the Kahal would remain in compliance with previous agreements and legal rulings. As a matter of policy, he argued further, on the basis of talmudic law, that a community executive council had the authority to alter a communal ordinance if the intent was to increase learning and expand Torah instruction. In its ruling, the Beit Din stipulated that while efforts ought to be made to assign the room to an accomplished scholar, it was fair to assume that the testator would have preferred the room to be used for instructional purposes rather than to remain vacant. The Beit Din concluded that the use of the room as envisioned by the Kahal would be in the merit of the soul of the deceased, and it upheld the Kahal's position.[115]

The question of control was an ongoing source of tension that riddled the administration of charitable bequests. The Grumbach stipulations manifested a powerful desire by the heir (and executor) to retain control throughout his life and was replicated in many (if not most) instances when the testator or heir was a wealthy communal leader.[116] In the case of Rabbi Meir Trenel's estate, his son and son-in-law arranged for the funds bequeathed by the testator—19,600 livres—to be transferred to the Kahal. In this instance, the Kahal agreed to accept the funds and distribute them as delineated in the will on the condition that it alone would be responsible for selecting the students and *lomdim* following the death of the testator's son.[117] But until that point, and this is even more evident in the Grumbach case, a strong impulse to manage the disbursement

115 PMBD, Vol. 1, pt. 2, no. 20, 5b. For the will of Abraham Grumbach, see PKM, 66b, 74a–b, and 137b. For an example of the preference given by the Beit Din to what it believed was the original intent of the testator, though the language in the will was technically imprecise, see PMBD, Vol. 2, no. 149, 29b. The will of Seligmann Wittersheim likewise called for the appointment of one *lamdan*, to be selected from among those who possessed a residence permit. See PMBD, Vol. 2, no. 280, 52b. Also see nos. 310, 313, 323, 409.

116 Cf. the document that created the foundation by Cerf Berr, Schwarzfuchs, "Three Documents from Alsace Lorraine."

117 See PKM, 83a, 1769 Takkanot, Art. 113.

of funds and related institutional issues dominated. As a rule, it was agreed that individual control would transfer to communal authority with the passing of the heir serving as executor of the estate.

A similar concern was voiced by Matha, widow of David Terquem. She approached the Beit Din to ensure that a suitable replacement be found for the recently deceased talmudic scholar, Rabbi Zelig Berea, who had been selected by her husband and funded through a testamentary gift he had made to ensure full-time study in the *beit midrash*. The Beit Din coordinated the consultation with Terquem's relatives about the selection and also concerning the need to reserve some of the funds allocated for this position for the support of Berea's widow.[118] Two additional examples are pertinent. In the case of the confraternity *Ḥevra Kadisha Malbish ʿArumim*, the *av beit din* was responsible for judging the legality of the organization's internal regulations, particularly those that pertained to membership requirements and the disbursement of funds to beneficiaries.[119] In a second case, a widow approached the rabbinic court with a request that it issue a *ma'aseh beit din* affirming that her daughter was entitled to assistance from the estate of a relative who had bequeathed funds to help poor brides related to him. Following its investigation, the Beit Din recognized the daughter as the bride most closely related to the deceased, and therefore, it instructed the guardians to award her money for her dowry from the estate.[120]

Notwithstanding the presence of many wealthy families in the Metz Kehillah, poverty remained a severe and pervasive problem. The problem, as observed in the Pinkas Kahal, was that "[p]eople run after their livelihood but fail [in this], not to mention to pay taxes." Extensive data assembled by Zosa Szajkowski showed that the vast majority of Jews in Metz had become impoverished, while Arthur Hertzberg found that conditions demanded that charity earmarked for Eretz Israel was diverted to support local families.[121] As communal expenses increased daily, it had become impossible for the Kahal to cover them with the revenue it was able to collect. Nevertheless, left with no

118 PMBD, Vol. 1, pt. 2, no. 191, 45a.

119 See PMBD, Vol. 1, pt. 1, no. 50, 15b, and Vol. 1, pt. 2, no. 6, 3a.

120 See PMBD, Vol. 2, no. 228, 42b.

121 Szajkowski, *The Economic Status of the Jews in Alsace-Lorraine*, passim, and Hertzberg, *French Enlightenment and the Jews*, 129–32. Hertzberg noted that the charity expenditure in Metz in the mid-eighteenth century was more than 6,000 livres per year, based on Metz charity accounts recorded in the Pinkas Kahal. Cerf Berr established a charitable foundation in 1786 in Bischeim, financed it with a gift of 75,000 livres. See Ginsburger, "Une fondation de Cerf Berr," *REJ* 76 (1923): 47–57.

alternative, the Kahal decided to ease the burden on community members by permitting payments of taxes in installments.[122]

In rural Alsace economic conditions were far more precarious, exacerbated by the immigration of refugees from the east. Regional assemblies convened in the 1760s and 1770s to address the challenges of poverty and to formulate a centralized policy. Of the numerous issues discussed at the regional meetings, poor relief was the most urgent.[123] Policies aiming to safeguard and strengthen the collective, such as restricted immigration and settlement in Metz, the increased cost of the *ḥezkat ʿironit*, and the reduced support for wayfarers, invariably came at the expense of the poor. Communal legislation highlighted the privileges enjoyed by the wealthy in contrast to the middle and lower classes and placed great emphasis on classifications of deservedness for charitable support. The economic situation sharpened the social divisions within the community, creating a huge gulf between rich and poor. As the tax burden grew heavier, the affluent came to be more dominant. Opportunity brought wealth to some and financial ruin to others. The standard welfare services provided by the community and various confraternities could not keep up with the demand in Metz.

Private initiatives, as manifested in testamentary charity, offer a valuable perspective on poor relief, support for learning, and institution building, though they reflect, undeniably, the *mentalité* of the more affluent members of the community. Two functions of wills are most apparent: the division of assets of the testator among his or her heirs; and the creation of a trust to be administered by the community in discharging the wishes of the deceased. The first type, wills directing division of assets among the heirs, was more conventional. They were typically produced in French and notarized. Wills of the second type were produced in Hebrew. It is likely that these were translated into French or were prepared separately in French, as the last will of Abraham Steinbiedersdorff attests. Abraham's testament combines the two functions of a will in one, providing philanthropic support at the community level and instructions for the division of his property among his heirs. Another difference between the village testament of Abraham and those we are considering from Metz pertains to the targeted beneficiary population. Abraham's will contained several provisions for the distribution of alms to poor Christians in the village of Steinbiedersdorf, whereas no such specifications are found in the Metz testaments.[124] As the testaments left by Reizele D'Alsace Spire and

122 PKM, 65b.
123 See Loeb, "Les Juifs de Strasbourg," 178–79 and 193–98.
124 Ulbrich, *Shulamit and Margarete*, 283–88.

Samuel Lévi show, in each case two distinct documents were prepared, one concerning the division of property that was filed in the Metz Parlement, and another, composed in Hebrew by Jewish notaries, that contained instructions for the distribution of funds to ease the plight of the poor and to support Torah learning.[125]

Despite advancing poverty, testators in Metz did not back away from expressing support for full-time Torah study by *lomdim*. The earmarking of funds for scholars' stipends, their physical needs, and the maintenance of institutions of learning reveals the strong religious sentiment that underlay private and public initiatives to advance Torah study. As compared to approximately fifty percent of Catholic wills and a much lower percentage of Protestant testaments, virtually all Jewish wills cited the *pro anima* motive for charitable giving, in the hope that this would enable testators to acquire their "passport to heaven."[126]

---

125 See above, pp. 213–14, 280–84, and 287–88.

126 See PKM, 65a for a detailed summary of private initiatives that aimed to strengthen Torah study and Jewish education. Also see Pugh, "Catholics, Protestants and Testamentary Charity in Seventeenth-Century Lyon and Nimes," 481–82, 492–95.

CHAPTER 7

Women, Marriage, and Property in Legal Perspective

The legislation enacted by the Metz Kahal and the proceedings of the Beit Din present an array of images of family relationships that challenge the monolithic picture of the traditional family generally available in conventional accounts and prescriptive legal sources. A variegated portrait of women emerges from the hundreds of cases concerning inheritance, guardianship, the division of marital assets, and involvement in commercial enterprise. Added to this is the remarkable degree to which women across the spectrum of social class and marital status actively pursued justice through litigation. Approximately twenty-five percent of the suits brought in the Metz Beit Din were initiated by women and, all told, roughly forty percent of the cases recorded in the Pinkas involved women either as claimants or defendants.[1] Despite numerous social and legal disabilities that hindered them, their actions in court exemplified the exercise of autonomy.[2]

Before considering the range of family issues addressed by the Kahal and that came before the Metz Beit Din, it is important to comment on what legislation and court proceedings do and do not reveal. These records cannot inform us of the reasons men and women married. Beyond the essential contractual elements of marriage, the mutual expectations of husbands and wives are seldom recorded in the community and court *pinkasim*, nor can they be easily inferred. Answers to these questions are more readily found in diaries,

1 The percentage of female litigants in the courts varied by region. Hervé Piant found that thirteen percent of plaintiffs in civil cases in Vaucouleurs were women. See his *Une justice ordinaire*, 104, Cf. Elise Dermineur, "Women in Rural society: Peasants, Patriarchy and the Local Economy in Northeast France, 1650–1789" (Ph.D. diss., Purdue Univ., 2011), 20, where it was determined that in civil cases adjudicated in the *seigneurie* of Florimont in the 1780s, approximately nineteen percent of the plaintiffs, and twenty-four percent of the defendants, were women. In her study of women in the courts of Normandy, Zoë Schneider concluded that between 1680 and 1745 nearly a quarter of the principal parties to court cases were women, and more than half were women who initiated suits. See Zoë A. Schneider, "Women before the Bench: Female Litigants in Early Modern Normandy," *French Historical Studies* 23 (2000): 8–9. Cf. Merry Wiesner, *Women and Gender in Early Modern Europe*, 3rd edition (New York, 2008), 47, where it was reported that fewer women appeared on their own behalf in court in the eighteenth century than before.

2 On women's autonomy as exercised in court, see Rachel G. Fuchs, *Contested Paternity: Constructing Families in Modern France* (Baltimore, 2008), 7 and 285. For a valuable discussion of differences in the aims and functions of jurisprudence and the law, see ibid., 4–6.

 | DOI:10.1163/9789004417403_009

memoirs, and letters, though such sources are exceedingly rare, and in the case of the Jews in the northeastern provinces of France in the eighteenth century, it is unlikely that much has survived at all. Nevertheless, within the framework of civil disputes, evidence of the emotional complexities of marriage, and even the intimate relations between men and women, were at times recorded in the lay and rabbinic court registers. More than any other venue, the courtroom is the arena where the struggle between law and private behavior can be observed, especially struggles between men and women, though their voices are heard only indirectly through the judicial decisions. Nevertheless, the stories frequently contain much that is both dramatic and poignant.[3]

Metz court and communal records are notable for the exceptionally valuable resources they offer to understand the married couple as an economic unit, the relationship between gender and economics, and the role of law in defining family relations. Each of these dimensions of family life was deeply informed by the mores of the Jewish religious tradition but was also shaped by the economic, cultural, and political forces at work in the ancien régime. Of central importance to the construction of the family was the role of property. As a measure of wealth and status, and as a means of acquiring additional resources through borrowing, property was critically important to everyone, regardless of socio-economic standing. The proceedings of the Beit Din, as well as the Pinkas of the Kahal, reveal not only the circumstances that regularly gave rise to contests for property but also particulars of property acquisition, transfer, and surrender. These details reflect the social, cultural, and legal conventions at work in various communities or regions.[4]

Women's entitlement to property was typically challenged at five critical moments over the course of their lives: inheritance and dowries as daughters; property during marriage; lineage property as separated wives; dowers and usufruct as widows; and tutorship and curatorship as widowed mothers.[5] On occasion, women also exercised the right to bequeath property for the support of the poor and other charitable purposes. Judicial records contain important

---

3 See Fuchs, *Contested Paternity*, esp. 5–6, and Roderick Phillips, "Women and Family Breakdown in Eighteenth-Century France: Rouen 1780–1800," *Social History* 1 (May 1976): 197–218.

4 For a very useful introduction to marriage and family in early modern France, see Suzanne Desan, "Making and Breaking Marriage: An Overview of Old Regime Marriage as a Social Practice," in *Family, Gender, and Law in Early Modern France*, ed. Suzanne Desan and Jeffrey Merrick (University Park, PA, 2009), 1–25.

5 See Schneider, "Women before the Bench," 8–9. Lineage property was the portion of a woman's dowry that did not enter the marital community. Often up to one half of her total fortune, it remained within her possession but under the stewardship of the husband.

data concerning the legal status of women and their role in economic life and in the family. Details of the marital relationship, including how men and women negotiated its demands, offer entrée into the private lives and households of a non-Christian minority, especially with respect to property arrangements, inheritance strategies, and the involvement of women in commerce. Once scholars have had the opportunity to examine these records more thoroughly, it will be possible to understand how the intricate talmudic laws of property, inheritance, and guardianship were interpreted by both the lay leadership and rabbinic court and implemented in light of changing social, economic, and political conditions. These areas of law, like others, reveal how Jews navigated between the polarities of acculturation within and separation from neighboring cultures. They also illustrate the methods employed by rabbinic courts to negotiate the plural jurisdictions of Jewish and French law.

Historians are divided in their assessment of the legal and economic status of women in early modern Europe. Some point to royal law and political theory, where there was noticeable erosion of women's status in the sixteenth and seventeenth centuries. Natalie Zemon Davis argued that the role of women in middle-level commerce and farming diminished with the disappearance of female guilds and that the disparity in the wages of men and women grew larger. Changes in marriage laws restricted the freedom of wives even further, and in Merry Wiesner's view, the development of capitalism had a disparate impact on working women. Although capitalism provided women with jobs that enabled them to contribute to the household income, it also appears to have reduced the value attached to domestic chores. Additionally, in areas where Roman law had influence, purported physical and mental frailty of women contributed to the lowering of their legal status.[6] On the basis of evidence drawn from Brittany and Burgundy, however, James Collins has reached a different conclusion. In customary law regions he found a sharp rise in the number of women serving as heads of households, particularly in urban areas where fifteen to twenty percent of taxpayers were women. In his view, women in early modern France experienced both upward movement in traditional social hierarchical roles and increased economic viability.[7]

6 See Natalie Z. Davis, "City Women and Religious Change," in *Society and Culture in Early-Modern France* (Stanford, 1975), 94; Wiesner, *Women and Gender*, 46–47; 101–34. Also see Mousnier, *Les institutions de la France*, 1:85–91 and Sarah Hanley, "Engendering the State: Family Formation and State-Building in Early Modern France," *French Historical Studies* 16 (1989): 4–27.

7 James B. Collins, "The Economic Role of Women in Seventeenth-Century France," *French Historical Studies* 16 (1989): 436–70.

Evidence culled from the Metz Beit Din and communal register enables us to construct a far more detailed image of Jewish women and family prior to the French Revolution. This image contrasts with prevailing assumptions concerning the rigid hierarchical relationship of men and women.[8] In fact, the general subordination of women in social matters contrasts starkly with the recognition of their autonomy in economic affairs. Women's dependence on men, their legal incapacity, and their general lack of independence are copiously documented in the customs books of communities throughout France, including the legislation issued for the Jewish community of Metz. Beginning in the late seventeenth century, communal *takkanot* imposed limitations on women's visitation at cemeteries to avoid their intermingling with men and introduced extensive restrictions on women's fashion. Moreover, the presumption of guilt on the part of maidservants was set forth in the Metz communal register as a statutory guideline when accusations of sexual impropriety were made.[9] Standing in opposition to these images is the rabbinic court's acknowledgment of women's agency, especially as reflected in its tacit affirmation of the legitimacy of their efforts to secure their standing within the family, to control their share of family property, and even to attain a measure of independence in business. Jewish women's participation as creditors, either independently or in collaboration with their husbands, as guardians, and in larger entrepreneurial ventures, attests to an economic and cultural transformation that had begun to alter traditional arrangements in family and community.

Betrothal and Marriage

Marriage in eighteenth-century Metz comes into view most visibly within a distinctly economic framework. Apart from the familiar role of marriage in forging social and economic alliances, as the Glikl memoirs vividly attest, the main issues addressed in communal legislation and in the proceedings of the Beit Din related specifically to property control, division, and allocation.

8 See Ulbrich, *Shulamit and Margarete*, 1–14.

9 See Berkovitz, *Rites and Passages*, 39–51. It may also be noted that instances of sexual liaisons in which servants were involved were by no means limited to relationships with their 'masters' as is often assumed. Many of the cases of liaisons recorded in the Pinkas were between servant men and servant women who intended to marry. See, for example, PMBD, Vol. 2, no. 569, 119a. It is of course possible that paternity claims by servant women against servant men, even when proven false, as in PMBD, Vol. 1, pt. 2, no. 192, 45a, were intended to conceal the identity of the real father. Until additional sources become available, such suggestions will of necessity remain speculative.

Nevertheless, the role of marriage as a crucial marker of social status was prominent. Mid-eighteenth-century communal regulations distinguished sharply between married and unmarried individuals, and between younger and more established couples. This is evident in the procedures governing eligibility for communal offices, the distribution of synagogue honors, commercial freedom, and dress. According to the 1752 bylaws, to be eligible to serve in the position of *parnas*, in addition to certain residential and financial qualifications, a man had to have been married at least thirty years (or twenty-two years if he possessed the title *ḥaver*, indicating the completion of the first level of rabbinic studies).[10] The 1769 Takkanot reserved the highest synagogue honors for men who had been married for twenty years and possessed the title of *ḥaver*; intermediate honors were awarded to men who combined the title of *ḥaver* with six years of marriage, or were married for twenty years without the title. Young married men could be called to the Torah on the pilgrimage festivals (Passover, Shavuot, and Sukkot) but not on the High Holidays (Rosh Hashanah and Yom Kippur). Unmarried men were consigned to the lowest social rung. The denial of synagogue honors reveals the stigma that attached to the unmarried state. As a rule, single men were not eligible to obtain preferred seats in the synagogue, nor were they called to the Torah either on the three pilgrimage festivals or on the High Holidays.[11]

The role of marriage as a factor in commercial legislation was also conspicuous. Communal laws distinguished between married and unmarried residents of the Kehillah. According to the 1769 Takkanot, boys under fifteen years of age were not permitted to trade in the community, and failure to comply with this regulation was a punishable offense. Unmarried men were required to yield to

10 Beyond the years of marriage, eligibility requirements included a residence permit, a net worth of at least 5,000 crowns (which would place one in the middle order), and prior service as administrator of charity for the poor. These property requirements were subsequently raised to higher levels, thus ensuring that only the wealthier (and older) members of the community to assume positions of leadership, despite the broadening of the electoral base. For these and additional details, see Hertzberg, *French Enlightenment*, 234–35. For restrictions on the use of jewelry and clothing that depended on a woman's financial position, see 1769 Takkanot, Arts. 5–6.

11 PKM, 77b–78a, 1769 Takkanot, Arts. 20, 25–26, 29. High honors included *Ḥatan Torah* and *Ḥatan Bereshit*, and medium honors included being called as *maftir* for the special *haftarot*. The awarding of synagogue honors varied regionally. See, for example, *The Minhagim of the Worms Community According to Juspe Shamash*, 2 vols., ed. Benjamin S. Hamburger (Jerusalem, 1988), 1:123, where it is indicated that *Ḥatan Torah* and *Ḥatan Bereshit* were sold to men who had been married in the previous year. In Ashkenaz it was a well-established custom that one needed to be married in order to receive the title *morenu* or *ḥaver*.

married men when selling their wares at the same house and earlier legislation prohibiting commercial dealings with either unmarried men or householders in their first two years of marriage was reissued.[12] Such restrictions suggest that the marital union was not considered stable and the husband was not regarded as a full-fledged householder until the couple had been together for several years. Single men who conducted commerce in Metz or elsewhere in France were required to pay ten percent of their earnings to communal inspectors for as long as they remained unmarried.[13] Unmarried men were not permitted to obtain authorization to slaughter animals unless they worked in collaboration with an established butcher.[14] In one instance the Pinkas Kahal reported that an unmarried Metz resident who flouted the commercial prohibition was barred from participating in any religious activity in the two community synagogues and was not permitted to wear the *schülmantel*.[15] The frequent reiteration of regulations of this sort suggests that these broad social goals were rarely achieved. In practice, the community sought to control rather than curb the dealings of the younger, less established residents.

Disputes between husbands and wives that were brought before the Beit Din most often involved either the contractual obligations set in motion by the betrothal agreement or questions pertaining to marriage and family as an economic unit. The initial agreement, generally known as *tena'im rishonim*, established the date and place of the wedding, the financial obligations of the two sides (which principally referred to the dowry), the exchange of gifts, the plan for the division of property between the couple, and the stipulation of a sum of money to serve as a penalty in case either side breached the agreement. As in French law, the engagement agreement was a legal contract that neither side was able to rescind unilaterally;[16] the Beit Din alone possessed the authority to determine whether there were valid grounds for cancellation.[17]

12 PKM, 79a, 1769 Takkanot, Arts. 46, 51. For parallels, see Gershon Hundert, "Jewish Children and Childhood in Early Modern East Central Europe," in *The Jewish Family: Metaphor and Memory*, David Kraemer, ed. (New York, 1989), 89, and Elliot Horowitz, "Les Mondes des jeunes juifs en Europe," in *Histoire des jeunes en Occident*, eds. G. Levi and J.-C. Schmitt (Paris, 1996), 1:113.

13 PKM, 81b, 1769 Takkanot, Art. 95.

14 PKM, 83a, 1769 Takkanot, Art. 120.

15 PKM, 80a, 1769 Takkanot, Art. 80.

16 See Robert-Joseph Pothier, *Traité du contrat de mariage* (Paris, 1771).

17 The *tena'im* were prepared by the *ne'emanei kehillah* (lit. "trustees of the community") who were responsible for notarial work of this sort. In this regard they were bound by communal legislation. See, for example, limitations on eligibility to have *tena'im* written if the bridegroom was not in possession of *hezkat 'ironit*, unless the dowry was at least 1,500 livres. See PKM, 69a.

To reconfirm the original terms, it was customary to sign a second agreement, *tena'im aḥaronim*, at the *kiddushin* (betrothal) ceremony, on the day of the wedding, prior to the marriage ceremony.[18] On occasion, the *tena'im* would include provisions for the fulfillment of special conditions. In one case a young woman asked to be freed from the betrothal agreement because her fiancé was unable to procure a residence permit (*ḥezkat 'ironit*).[19] In some instances the *tena'im* conditioned the marriage on a business initiative offered to the groom or on assurances of support in the early years of marriage. Zalman Hellimer argued that in the *tenai'im* drawn up immediately before the wedding ceremony, his late father-in-law had obligated himself to establish a partnership with him and that this entitled him (Zalman) to the funds originally contributed by the two men (funds now held in the estate of the deceased) as well as to the accrued profits. He also demanded compensation for the support promised to him and his wife that they had not entirely used, as well as the value of the apartment in his father-in-law's house that was promised to them.[20]

As a general matter, the main provision of the Jewish marriage contract was the husband's undertaking to pay his wife a fixed sum (200 *zuz*) upon his death or in the event of divorce, or half that amount (100 *zuz*) if he was marrying a widow, divorcée, or convert. This constituted the essential part of the contract (Heb. *ikkar ha-ketubah*).[21] The dowry—property brought to the marriage by the wife—was an equally crucial component of the marital agreement. Its size had tangible significance for the economic well-being of the couple, but its role as a symbol of social status for the families of the bride and groom was no less important. In accordance with talmudic tradition, the dowry was divided into two main categories. *Nikhsei ẓon barzel* ("iron sheep property";

18 For talmudic and halakhic sources relating to the *tena'im*, see BT Ketubot 102a and 108b–109a; BT Kiddushin 9b; *Shulḥan 'Arukh, Even ha-'Ezer* §2:1; and Segel, *Sefer Naḥalat Shiv'ah* (Jerusalem, 2006), 1:83–208.

19 See PMBD, Vol. 2, 73a, no. 397. For examples of efforts to secure the *ḥezkat 'ironit*, see Pinkas Kahal of Metz, 36a, 37a, 66a–67a, and 74a. The Metz community devised elaborate formulas with respect to the costs of procuring the right of residence. As a result, only the well-off could afford to settle in Metz, which accorded with communal policy aiming to attract those who could share the heavy tax burden. This would explain a complaint in 1780 by a Metz *parnas* about the growing number of beggars. See Ulbrich, *Shulamit and Margarete*, 174. For a French translation of the 1780 communal regulations concerning the right of residence, see Kerner, "La Vie quotidienne," Annexe, XXII–XXXVI.

20 See PMBD, Vol. 2, 88b, no. 453. The Beit Din could not find any proof in the partnership agreement as to who held the funds and therefore rejected that part of the claim. However, it did award the claimant eight *louis d'or* as compensation for the support originally promised to him.

21 A *zuz* is a monetary unit equal to a *dinar*.

i.e., inalienable assets) remained the property of the wife, but subject to the control of the husband. Recorded in the *ketubah*, such assets were assigned a fixed value for which the husband assumed full financial responsibility in the event of loss or depreciation. The property listed in the *ketubah* reverted to the wife upon termination of the marriage, either by the husband's death or the couple's divorce.

The second category, *nikhsei melog* (plucked property; i.e., usufruct), referred to all other properties that the wife brought into the marriage but were not listed in the *ketubah* or that were acquired by her in the course of the marriage. *Nikhsei melog* included property that came to the wife by way of inheritance or that was conveyed to her as a gift after the marriage. According to Jewish law, a wife retained title to these assets, while the income they produced belonged to the husband. In contrast to the *nikhsei ẓon barzel*, the husband was not liable for any loss or damage to *melog* property. It was customary for husbands to assume responsibility for an increment (Heb. *tosefet nedunyah*) of one-half the amount specified as the *nikhsei ẓon barzel* portion of the dowry, which was added to the *ikkar ha-ketubah*. The husband's heirs had no legal claim to the assets in the wife's dowry.[22] To guarantee payment of the *ketubah*, a lien was placed on all of the husband's property.[23]

In Metz the prevailing custom required the bride's father to deposit the dowry with a third party thirty days before the wedding. Owing especially to the social import of the dowry, particularly its role in enhancing the appeal of the bride, it was not unusual for fathers to misjudge or exaggerate their ability to provide a large sum of money for this purpose. Failure to deliver the dowry was normally considered grounds for canceling the wedding or delaying

22 *Shulḥan 'Arukh, Even ha-'Ezer* §85. On the increment to the *ketubah*, see Segel, *Sefer Naḥalat Shiv'ah* (2006 ed.), vol. 1, no. 31, 249–90. Also see Benzion Schereschewsky, *Family Law in Israel* [Hebrew] (Jerusalem, 1992), 149. It is presumed that property in the wife's possession belongs to her husband (M. Bava Kamma 10:9), and therefore a third party may not purchase such possessions from her, unless it is common practice to sell such articles with the consent of her husband. If it has increased in value during the husband's lifetime and constitutes iron sheep property, the appreciation accrues to the husband's heirs. See Maidi S. Katz, "The Married Woman and her Expense Account: A Study of the Married Woman's Ownership and Use of Marital Property in Jewish Law," *The Jewish Law Annual* 13 (2000): 110–11. See Elon, *Jewish Law*, 2:568–72.

23 BT Ketubot 68b; and *Shulḥan 'Arukh, Even ha-'Ezer* §66. If no liquid assets were available, the *ketubah* was payable out of the medium grade of the real estate owned by the husband. Although talmudic law stipulated that the collection of the *ketubah* could be made from real property only, an enactment of the Geonim established that after the death of the husband the wife could collect her *ketubah* even out of movable property. See Maimonides, *Mishneh Torah*, Laws of Lender and Borrower 11:11, and *Shulḥan 'Arukh, Even ha-'Ezer* §100:1.

it, which would often lead to financial loss, the assumption of additional debt, and public disgrace. In fact, the delay could trigger a claim of humiliation that required adjudication in the Beit Din.[24] With adequate proof, the court would impose a penalty on the offender that was subsequently awarded to the injured party. But as several other cases of delayed weddings suggest, financial troubles were just as likely to be the reason that fathers were unable to meet their obligations. In one instance, the father of the bride, Nota Morhange, was sued by the groom's father for failing to deposit the dowry of 800 livres that was called for in the engagement agreement. Morhange explained that owing to the "stress of the times" (*ẓok ha-ʾitim*), it had become difficult to feed his family. At the time of the engagement he had expected to conclude an important business transaction that would have enabled him to deposit the dowry as promised, but the transaction had fallen through. As a result, he was now unable to provide more than 400 livres in cash—an amount available only because he had received assistance from his relatives. But he promised to provide security for the remaining amount and offered to pay the balance in installments. The father of the groom refused the offer, insisting that it was unacceptable in the Jewish community for a man to marry a woman for such a small sum. In search of a solution, the Beit Din structured a compromise that included a small reduction in the amount of the dowry and an adjusted time frame for the wedding.[25]

Cases of cancelled engagement agreements and a growing number of paternity claims point to a breakdown of both traditional marital arrangements and communal efforts to discourage sexual contact between unmarried men and women.[26] Several cases recorded in the Beit Din proceedings reveal

24 See PMBD, Vol. 2, no. 1, 1a, where the father of the bride was found responsible for defaming the groom and was required to pay a penalty of thirty livres to the poor of the city. The groom, in turn, was granted permission to publicize the Beit Din's ruling regarding the penalty imposed on the bride's father wherever he desired. On the use of the dowry to enhance the bride's attractiveness, see BT Ketubot 52b.

25 See, for example, PMBD, Vol. 2, no. 649, 142b–143a. Use of the phrase "stress of the times" in this case, which was recorded on 22 Tevet 5549 [20 January 1789], corresponds to the general economic decline and impoverishment that was rife among members of the Metz community. See Robert Anchel, *Les Juifs de France: La Roue de Fortune* (Paris, 1946), 153–212; and Hertzberg, *French Enlightenment and the Jews*, 129–32. For an example of the enactment of a penalty and the award of compensation for humiliation, see PMBD, Vol. 2, no. 605, 130b. On the breach of the betrothal agreement in Jewish law, see *Shulḥan ʿArukh, Even ha-ʿEzer* §50:1–4.

26 For examples of broken engagements, see PMBD, Vol. 2, no. 1, 1b; no. 288, 53b; no. 406, 77a–b; no. 465, 92a; and no. 521, 106a. For instances when the bride endeavored to call off the wedding on account of her own objections, see PMBD, Vol. 1, pt. 2, no. 17, 5a, and Vol. 2, no. 1, 1a. On broken engagements in Jewish law, see *Shulḥan ʿArukh, Even ha-ʿEzer* §50:5–6,

reluctance of engaged couples to assent to marital agreements not of their own choosing. In one instance a young woman, Gitla of Niedervisse, petitioned the Beit Din to nullify the engagement agreement her father made because her fiancé was unable to fulfill his financial obligations and also because he was repugnant to her (*ma'is 'alai*). Her position was in direct conflict with that of her father, who favored the match. Hirsch, her fiancé, responded that he had already deposited half the dowry in Gitla's name and was prepared to deposit the other half; he insisted that her assertion of repugnancy must have been a pretext to conceal her interest in another man. The Beit Din ruled that if Gitla was willing to take an oath confirming her aversion to Hirsch and that she had not set her eyes upon any other man, the *tena'im* would be nullified; otherwise, she was expected to adhere to the agreement as it stood. Although it is not known how the case was resolved, the significance of Gitla's action is clear. She acted independently, against the wishes of her father and without legal representation, to abrogate a marriage agreement that she herself found unacceptable.[27] In a very different circumstance, a young woman broke off her engagement because she feared that she would be unable to endure the hardship of leaving her birthplace to take up residence in Amsterdam, a distance of nearly five-hundred kilometers from Metz.[28]

While the data contained in the Beit Din records alone do not bear out a collapse of traditional norms, deepening concern about the sexual mores of young men and women is evident in the 1769 Takkanot recorded in the Metz communal register. Severe warnings against sexual contact between betrothed men and women added to the urgency of the legislation, culminating in the enactment of a *takkanah* prohibiting such couples from spending time together at night, even when accompanied by a chaperone. Stringent measures such as heavy fines and public disclosure of improprieties were deemed necessary, considering the apparent deterioration in the moral climate. A quarter-century earlier, Rabbi Jonathan Eibeschütz had publicly railed against sexual libertinism and threatened to introduce a clause in the betrothal contract requiring couples to promise to refrain from any physical contact until after the wedding. But it was not until 1769 that the Metz Kahal took its first legislative initiative to address these issues.[29] Concern about the flouting of sexual norms was

and the analysis in Ronnie Warburg, "Breach of Promise to Marry," *Jewish Law Annual* 17 (2007): 267–82.

27 PMBD, Vol. 1, pt. 2, no. 17, 5a. Cf. Kenneth Stow, "Marriages are Made in Heaven: Marriage and the Individual in the Roman Jewish Ghetto," *Renaissance Quarterly* 48 (1995): 452–91.

28 PMBD, Vol. 2, no. 397, 73a.

29 1769 Takkanot, Art. 43. On premarital cohabitation and conception, see Robin Briggs, *Early Modern France, 1560–1715* (Oxford, 1998), 190. For additional evidence of sexual

also the focus of legislation limiting social contact with maidservants. Statues placed the onus of responsibility squarely upon servants who violated norms of sexual propriety, and public shaming was integral to their punishment. In the Beit Din, such matters were not judged so abruptly, though even there, too, servants were at some disadvantage, especially maidservants.[30]

The Metz Beit Din heard some thirty paternity suits, a number constituting nearly three percent of the total number of cases recorded in the Pinkas. Certain claims were accompanied by accusations of unwanted sexual advances, while others reflected misunderstanding and miscommunication surrounding the significance of consensual sexual relations, especially with regard to marital intentions.[31] When a pregnant woman or her father pursued legal action, it typically included the demand that the accused pay maternity expenses and child support; more often than not it was accompanied by the demand that the putative father fulfill his alleged promise to marry the pregnant mother. In some instances, the putative father flatly denied the accusation and countered that he was the victim of slander; sometimes an alleged father might claim in his own defense that his accuser was herself promiscuous, while in other instances he admitted that he was responsible. If he denied the claim, and

immorality and claims of a breakdown in discipline, see Kerner, "La vie quotidienne," 208–18. For Eibeschütz's remarks on the addition of a restrictive clause in the betrothal contract, see *Ya'arot Devash*, 1:62. On the Metz *takkanot* and their historical context, see Berkovitz, *Rites and Passages*, 35–58.

30 On the public announcement, see the 1769 Takkanot, Art. 42. On domestic servants and sexual issues, see Elliott Horowitz, "Les Mondes des jeunes juifs en Europe," in *Histoire des jeunes en Occident*, ed. G. Lévi and J. C. Schmitt (Paris, 1996), 122–36. For rich material on servant women and sexuality in the village of Kriechingen (Créhange), see Ulbrich, *Shulamit and Margarete*, 220–36. Cf. Elisheva Carlebach, "Fallen Women and Fatherless Children: Jewish Domestic Servants in Eighteenth-Century Altona," *Jewish History* 24 (2010): 295–308.

31 In at least two instances pregnant women claimed that men had promised via a handshake (*teki'at kaf*) to marry them before they had sexual relations. See PMBD, Vol. 2, no. 238, 44a, and no. 450, 87a. The *teki'at kaf*, customarily used as a means of acquisition by merchants, had the status of an oath according to many *posekim*. Without a release, a person who had made such a promise would be coerced to fulfill it. See BT Bava Meẓia 74a; *Shulḥan 'Arukh, Yoreh De'ah* §239:2; Isserles, *Ḥoshen Mishpat* §81:28; and *Ḥoshen Mishpat* §129:5. In Metz the *teki'at kaf* was not considered to be binding, according to Reischer, *Resp. Shevut Ya'akov*, pt. 3, no. 152. It appears that in PMBD, Vol. 1, pt. 2, no. 91, 24a, the Beit Din acknowledged that the violation of a *teki'at kaf* carried its own penalty, comparable to stating an untruth, but from this we can infer that it lacked the binding authority of an oath. On the handshake and its roots in Roman law, especially as reflected in medieval art, see Erwin Panofsky, "Jan Eyck's 'Arnolfini' Portrait," *The Burlington Magazine* 64:372 (1934): 117–127. For an illuminating discussion of paternity cases in French courts and the gendered narratives that were constructed by men and women, see Fuchs, *Contested Paternity*, 16–30.

assuming that the paternity accusation was deemed to be plausible, the Beit Din would require the putative father to swear that he was innocent of any involvement. By so doing, he would be acquitted of responsibility.[32]

An accusation against Lazar Ickingen by Yetele, a maidservant who was the daughter of the late Sender Hilbrei, was initially found to be unsubstantiated because the petitioner refused to be examined by two court-appointed women along with midwives. The court stated that if a pregnancy examination proved that the accusation was fabricated, then Yetele would be fined for slander and the accused father would be fully exonerated.[33] In another case, conflicting testimony led the Beit Din to dismiss the paternity charge as unsubstantiated and to issue a public announcement in the synagogue that the claims against the alleged father were false. Fully exonerated, the accused was given a copy of the rabbinic court ruling as a precaution in case he encountered public shunning (*le-mishmeret negged ha-ʿam*).[34]

When the father admitted paternity, the couple usually agreed to be married, subject to the approval of the Beit Din. This was certainly the most reasonable solution for mother and child under the circumstances; it is also likely that community leaders viewed such a resolution as highly preferable to the prospect of adding unwed mothers and children out of wedlock to the ranks of those needing public assistance. But for the rabbinic court to authorize a marriage, it needed assurance that the couple was not in violation of the halakhic prohibition against marriage to a woman who was either pregnant by another man (*me'uberet ḥavero*) or, following the birth, was nursing another man's child (*meneket ḥavero*). According to medieval Jewish law, based on BT Yevamot 42b, a pregnant woman was not permitted to marry another man until the child had reached twenty-four months of age. A widow or divorcée was not granted permission to marry for ninety days, in order to avoid doubts as to the identity of the father.[35] In such cases, the Beit Din would normally undertake the verification of paternity through an oath administered to the alleged father and would proceed as well with an investigation of the reputation and sexual history of the pregnant mother.[36] Paternity suits, it would seem, were heavily laden with the competing interests of communal policy and Halakhah.

32 See, for example, PMBD, Vol. 1, pt. 2, no. 253, 54b. Cf. S. M. Waddams, *Sexual Slander in Nineteenth-Century England: Defamation in the Ecclesiastical Courts, 1815–1855* (Toronto, 2000).

33 See PMBD, Vol. 2, no. 146, 28b.

34 PMBD, Vol. 2, no. 495, 100a.

35 In addition to BT Yevamot 42b, see BT Ketubot 60a–b. Also see *Shulḥan ʿArukh, Even ha-ʿEzer* §13.

36 See PMBD, Vol. 2, no. 569, 119a, and Vol. 1, pt. 2, no. 205, 47a.

It is likely that the anxiety of Metz communal leaders over the sexual conduct of unmarried men and women, particularly the proliferation of paternity suits in the second half of the eighteenth century, was related to a larger legal and political concern. In 1767 Étienne-François, the Duc de Choiseul, circulated a letter to clarify the king's interpretation of the general law of the realm, originally enacted in 1682, on the status of children born out of wedlock. The law provided that any illegitimate child "must be raised in the Catholic religion, because he belongs to the Sovereign, and consequently to the Catholic religion." Drawing upon the metaphor of the king as surrogate father, Choiseul's letter underscores a distinction between Jews and Alsatian Lutherans. Lutherans could reclaim their children legitimated by subsequent marriage that took place within the first five years of the child's birth, but the same was apparently not true for the illegitimate offspring of Jews because under French law their baptism rendered such children irrevocably Christian, even if they were legitimated by subsequent marriage. In fact, anyone who was baptized and reverted to Judaism could be tried for heresy and have all property confiscated. Choiseul notes, however, that by this same logic, if the conception occurred out-of-wedlock but the couple married before the birth, then baptism would not have taken place and the Jewish parents would be within their rights to raise their child as a Jew. In paternity cases heard by French secular courts in the eighteenth century, putative fathers usually had the choice of either paying damages and child support or marrying the mother. In theory, then, one would expect that cases before the rabbinic court would turn on whether the mother (the *fille mère*) had already given birth. If she had not, then it was still possible, via marriage, to retain her future offspring within the Jewish faith; but if the birth took place before the couple married, then it would seem that there would be no way to prevent baptism.[37]

This was the issue presented to Rabbi Jacob Reischer: How should the community respond to the dangers presented by a government ordinance

37 The "Déclaration portant que les enfans bâtards des religionnaires seront élevés en la religion catholique," was issued on 31 January 1682 by Louis XIV. It appeared in Decrusy, François-André Isambert, and A. J. L. Jourdan, *Recueil général des anciennes lois françaises, depuis l'an 420 jusqu'à la ré volution de* 1789, 29 vols. Paris, 1821–1833, vol. 19 (1829), no. 997, 378. The 1767 circular was printed in M. de Boug, *Recueil des édits, déclarations, lettres patentes, ordonnances d'Alsace*, 2 vols. (Colmar, 1775), 2:763. The text states that "tout enfant né bâtard doit être élevé dans la Religion catholique, parce qu'il appartient au Souverain, & conséquemment à la Religion catholique." I am indebted to Matthew Gerber for alerting me to the foregoing references; see his superb treatment of illegitimacy in the early modern period: *Bastards: Politics, Family, and Law in Early Modern France* (New York, 2012). On Choiseul, see McManners, *Church and Society in Eighteenth-Century France*, 2:628–29.

regarding children born to an unmarried (Heb. *zonah*, meaning 'wayward') woman, when no man acknowledged paternity? If the putative father failed to betroth her immediately according the laws of Moses and Israel, wrote the questioner, then the government would take the newborn and raise it as a Christian. The custom, reported the questioner, was to seek out an unmarried man who would betroth the pregnant women, state that he was responsible for her pregnancy, and immediately marry her according to Jewish law. Was this practice that earlier rabbis permitted without hesitation to save the baby correct or not? In his published legal opinion, Reischer initially expressed concern, because it was prohibited to marry a woman who had become pregnant by his fellow, and had he done so, he would have been obliged to divorce her. Then, after considering various options, including biblical vs. rabbinic levels of prohibition, and whether it is permissible for someone to commit a sin so that someone else might merit from the action, he concluded that he was unable to permit it. However, since some of his predecessors lent their approval, their views could not be gainsaid. Therefore, Reischer conceded, the lenient opinion could be followed.[38] The fact that there are no recorded instances in the proceedings of the Beit Din of Metz in which the court urged the couple to marry prior to the birth of a child suggests that renewed efforts to apply the 1682 law were unsuccessful—at least in Metz.

Two paternity cases that came before the Beit Din in 1783 and 1784 reveal radically different approaches to the issue while also offering insight into the divergent understandings of honor, prestige, and shame in the Metz community.[39] The first case involved Henna, a maidservant from the village of Busendorf, who was employed in the home of Wolf Charry of Metz. She accused Lazi, a manservant, of seducing her and impregnating her; he denied ever having touched her. The Beit Din informed Lazi that if the birth occurred within a timeframe consistent with the Henna's testimony, he would be required to swear that he never had intercourse with her and, following the oath, neither she nor the child would have any claim on him. Because Henna was

38 Reischer, *Resp. Shevut Ya'akov*, pt. 3, no. 108. On the implications of the royal legislation in relation to Jewish law, see Gershon Koblenz, *Resp. Kiryat Ḥannah* (Metz, 1785), no. 20. Koblenz was not inclined to follow the lenient opinion. The precedent cited by Koblenz was the opinion of Moses Mintz, in *Resp. Mahari Mintz* (Venice, 1553), no. 5, ed. Asher Siev (New York, 1995). For a discussion of additional paternity cases noted in the Pinkas Kahal, see Kerner, "La vie quotidienne," 208–11.

39 For wider trends, see Fuchs, *Contested Paternity*, Chap. 1; concerning the Jews of rural Moselle, see Ulbrich, *Shulamit and Margarete*, 208–11. On adultery in eighteenth-century French courts, see Regina, "Private Sphere and Public Sphere." For the halakhic ban against marriage to a woman who was either pregnant by another man or who was nursing another man's child, see BT Yevamot 36b, 42a–b; Ketubot 60a–b; and *Even ha-'Ezer* §13:11–12.

imprecise about how long she had been pregnant and under interrogation changed the details of her story several times when asked when the alleged sexual encounters occurred, the Beit Din dismissed her claim and exonerated Lazi. The detailed case summary focuses on the Beit Din's intensive efforts to establish the facts, the credibility of testimony, and responsibility. There is no evidence, however, that the Beit Din was concerned with the moral dimensions of a case involving seduction, unwanted pregnancy, and the dishonor to either the accuser or the accused.[40]

A year later, a similar allegation made by a pregnant woman was met by an entirely different response in the Metz community.[41] In this instance, Reichele Cahen, accompanied by her attorney, approached the Kahal in its meeting room and openly accused Hirtz Oulif of fathering her child; she demanded that he marry her and provide birth expenses and child support. Initially heard by the Kahal, the case caused something of a furor because of the public nature of the young woman's accusation and her family's elevated status within the community. The Beit Din was invited to join the Kahal in its effort to stave off what leaders feared might be the harbinger of a dangerous trend. Rabbi Günzberg, the head of the rabbinic court, was asked to lead the new initiative. Although ill-health prevented Günzberg's participation, members of the Beit Din proceeded, together with several syndics, to examine the arguments and testimony presented by Reichele and Hirtz. To preclude subterfuge by the parties, the Beit Din demanded that Reichele and Hirtz address each other directly, without legal representation.[42] Hirtz proceeded to deny each of Reichele's claims as utterly false. "To uphold the bylaws of the community," however, the Beit Din imposed the *ḥerem* on both the young woman and the young man, undoubtedly to convey the message that promiscuous behavior would not be tolerated under any circumstances. But when it emerged that there were witnesses willing to testify that the young man was heard boasting of his exploits, the Kahal and the Beit Din altered their earlier procedure.

40 PMBD, Vol. 2, nos. 428–429, 81b–82a. The case is dated 23 Adar II 5543 [27 March 1783].

41 PMBD, Vol. 2, no. 450, 87a–b. The case is dated 22 Iyyar 5544 [13 May 1784].

42 For other examples of the Beit Din's insistence on face-to-face confrontation, see PMBD, Vol. 1, pt. 2, no. 205, 47a; Vol. 2, no. 202, 38b; and no. 443, 85a. In talmudic times attorneys could not represent parties to a suit, partly because the judges desired to hear directly from each party. See Rashi, BT Shevuot 31a, s.v. *zeh ha-ba be-harsha'ah*. They believed that two individuals standing face to face before a religious tribunal would be less inclined to plead falsely and were more likely to compromise. Tosafot permitted clients unable to adequately represent themselves to hire an attorney, because in such instances the attorney's efforts were comparable to fulfilling the obligation to restore lost property. See Dov I. Frimer, "The Role of the Lawyer in Jewish Law," *Journal of Law and Religion*, 1:2 (1983): 297–305.

They recorded the statements of the witnesses in writing, assembled additional oral testimony attesting to the accuracy of the earlier statements, and subsequently set about to erect "a fence and barrier against the promiscuity of the generation and so that daughters will not act wantonly or be treated as such." At this point the Beit Din imposed the ban directly on Hirtz until such time as he had appeased Reichele by agreeing either to marry her or present her with monetary compensation. It further required him to deposit 1,200 livres with the Kahal until the birth, at which point the court would determine whether Reichele's paternity claim was plausible. If it was, then the money would be turned over to Reichele; if not, the money would be returned to him. In any event, the Beit Din required him to pay a fine of three hundred livres to be distributed to the poor. It is noteworthy that the Beit Din did not offer the alleged father the opportunity to absolve himself of responsibility by affirming his innocence with an oath, as this was a procedure that was granted only if the court was convinced of the trustworthiness of the accused.[43]

The contrast between the two cases is instructive. In the first case, which concerned claims of sexual misconduct among servants, the main question facing the Beit Din related to the reliability of the accuser's testimony; there were no larger issues looming, at least as presented in the summary of the proceeding recorded in the Pinkas. In the second case, which involved members of higher-ranking families in the Metz community, the Kahal and the Beit Din appear to have been more attuned to what was at stake at the personal level and in terms of public policy. That the two bodies collaborated to address the problem of moral decline is reflected in the repeated use of the phrase "the licentiousness of the generation" (*priẓut ha-dor*). As one might expect, the dishonor suffered by a daughter of a prominent member of the community was certainly an important consideration in the case. But it appears to have been the concern about sexual promiscuity in the broader sense that seized the attention of communal leaders and explains the initial decision of the court to issue the *ḥerem* and, subsequently, to punish Hirtz with a fine of 300 livres to be distributed to the poor of the city. By framing the case as a violation of communal norms, the Beit Din and communal leaders underscored the public nature of this otherwise private affair.[44]

43 PMBD, Vol. 2, 87a–b, no. 450. For a paternity case that involved the admission by a pregnant domestic servant that she had committed perjury and ended with the return of money that the accused had paid to her, see PMBD, Vol. 2, nos. 428–29, 81a–b. Cf. Ulbrich, *Shulamit and Margarete*, 71–76.

44 PMBD, Vol. 2, no. 450, 87a–b.

There is no evidence that the progeny of unmarried Jewish mothers were legally or socially stigmatized in the course of the early modern period as were illegitimate Christian children in the late sixteenth century. Whereas French jurists, political thinkers, and theologians regularly raised objections to the eligibility of the offspring of extramarital affairs to receive gifts and legacies, no comparable discussions are recorded in the writings of *posekim*, in the records of the rabbinic court of Metz, or in the register of the community. In the eighteenth century, as Matthew Gerber has shown, the argument that illegitimate offspring ought to be barred from inheritance because of their degraded personal status was replaced by claims that their exclusion was mandated by concerns for public welfare. By the late eighteenth century, the shift to a socially based argument paved the way for elevating the legal standing of extramarital offspring.[45] No comparable relief was extended to extramarital offspring in Jewish law or practice. In fact, the offspring of a prohibited (adulterous or incestuous) affair is stigmatized in Jewish law as a *mamzer* who may not marry into the Jewish community.[46]

A dozen cases of marital discord recorded in the Metz rabbinic court register in the years 1772 to 1786 reveal something of the range of complications that attended marriage in eighteenth-century Metz and, no doubt, elsewhere. Judicial decisions, as distinct from statutory law, present a more variegated picture of the family, its diversity, the irregularity of its features, the struggles to meet challenges of all sorts, and its complexity. The disharmony and disagreement that pervade the cases described below center on economic tensions, the challenges of establishing a permanent residence, and the tense relations with a spouse's parents or siblings, or with children from a former marriage.[47]

45 See Gerber, *Bastards: Politics, Family, and Law in Early Modern France*, 124–83.

46 For the basic sources of the law, see Deuteronomy 23:3; BT Yevamot 45b; and *Shuhan 'Arukh*, Even ha-'Ezer 4:24.

47 For a case of marital discord recorded in the Pinkas Kahal, see PKM, 2a regarding Rabbi Shlomo Lvov and his wife. There are no details concerning the disagreement, only the ruling of the Kahal court, in favor of the husband, requiring his wife to pay her husband a small sum and to leave the community. Lvov would later author a tract, in 1784, bemoaning the erosion in religious standards among Alsatian Jews, to which he attributed the difficulties of yeshivah students to expect a good marriage proposal. See Lvov, *Heshek Shlomo*, ms. (Dittwiller, 1784), introduction, Institute of Hebrew Manuscripts, Jerusalem, no. 8°3394. For examples of similar complaints voiced in the late seventeenth and earlier in the eighteenth century, see Bacharach, *Resp. Havvot Ya'ir*, no. 125; Reischer, *Resp. Shevut Yaakov*, pt. 1, 4a; Eibeschütz, *Ya'arot Devash*, sermon no. 5 (Metz, 5505 [1744]), pt. 1, 119; idem, sermon no. 16 (Metz, 5507 [1747]), pt. 1, 301–2, reprinted in 1983 Jerusalem edition; and Ezekiel Landau, *Derushe Ha-Ẓelah* (Warsaw, 1899) [repr. Jerusalem, 1966], 16a. According to earlier sources, students at the Metz yeshivah were predominantly from poor families, both locally and from Poland, a condition that would undoubtedly affect

Economic tensions, stemming in part from the husband's failure to obtain a residence permit (*ḥezkat ha-yishuv*), threatened the stability of the marriage of Moshe and Rivka. Moshe accused his wife of absconding with his possessions and demanded that she return the items she allegedly removed. He also sought to prevent her from serving as a domestic servant for others, which not only indicates that the couple had fallen on hard times but also that they no longer maintained a household together. Moshe objected to Rivka's employment as a domestic servant and insisted that she live where he lives and go where he goes. While denying that she took any of her husband's belongings, she maintained that it was impossible to "live together with a snake like him," though she conceded that if he made an effort to secure a residence permit so that they would not need to wander from place to place, she would agree to live with him and behave as husband and wife. Without a residence permit, she asserted, she could not be expected to go from village to village and city to city, "roaming in a land that was not theirs." Once Rivka affirmed under oath that she did not steal anything from her husband, and following the court's acknowledgment that she was not obligated to wander about the land, the Beit Din stipulated she would have to live with her husband in the manner that is customary for wives with their husbands on condition that he succeeded in finding a lawful place to live in the coming month with authorization from a community.[48]

Financial worries also account for the dissension between Shmuel Kalhausen and his wife Edel. Shmuel accused Edel of concealing kitchen wares, granite and pearl thread, and notes of indebtedness owed to him, from the *inventaire* that she prepared before she left their home. The term used in the text is *hivriḥa* (made off with possessions) and connotes a sense of urgency. In addition to suspecting his wife, Shmuel accused his father-in-law and brother-in-law of stealing his money. Both denied the charges against them and against Edel. They countered that Shmuel fabricated these accusations of theft because he squandered the money she had brought into the marriage as well as the money that he borrowed from others. The Beit Din ruled that she was required to swear that she did not take anything of his before she left nor did she conceal anything, and that nothing remained of the items mentioned. Following her oath, she was fully acquitted.[49]

their marriage prospects. See Eibeschütz, *Ya'arot Devash*, pt. 1, 93b; pt. 2, 40b; and Koblenz, *Kiryat Hannah*, introduction.

48 PMBD, Vol. 2, no. 295, 54b.

49 PMBD, Vol. 2, no. 250, 46b. Three years earlier, Edel and her children went to live with her father when her husband fled to escape creditors. She tried to assist her husband by sending him money so that he would be able to return home. See PMBD, Vol. 2, no. 12, 3a.

Strained relationships with a spouse's parents and siblings, or complications triggered by children from a former marriage, accounted for difficulties of all sorts. A straightforward civil suit turned into an acrimonious family squabble. Elkanah Lévi sued his father-in-law, Abraham Alsace, for payment of a loan he was owed. Abraham countersued Elkanah for the value of food that he had agreed to give to him and his wife. Elkanah argued that his mother-in-law was sowing seeds of discord between him and his wife and that she should no longer come to visit her daughter. His father-in-law denied that his wife was the cause of the marital conflict and alleged that the real source of the problem was the husband's mother and her daughter, who worked as their domestic servant. Abraham demanded that Elkanah no longer visit in their home and that his daughter no longer work as a servant in Elkanah's home.[50] In a similar case, Akiva Cohen and his wife separated for five weeks because his unmarried daughter and his sister were purportedly causing conflict between them. Akiva's wife, Fradle, objected to Akiva's daughter's dominance over him and control of his property, as "he has nothing in his hand; she has everything." Since in her view her husband was at fault, she requested of the Beit Din the award of *mezonot* (alimony)—past and future—as long as he refused to remove his daughter and sister from their home. After denying that his sister was a regular guest in their home or that his daughter had done anything improper, he explained that he could not drive her out of his house. The Beit Din subsequently ruled that to avoid conflict Akiva's sister would be barred from visiting her brother's home, and although Akiva was not obliged to force his daughter out, the Beit Din issued a directive, on pain of the *ḥerem*, that she must behave properly toward her stepmother and not cause discord.[51] Four years later, the couple was back before the Beit Din. Fradle maintained that it was impossible to live with her husband. Therefore, she demanded that he uphold the compromise reached in a prior judgment until such time as he would give her a divorce. In response, he insisted that she was the cause of dissension and that he was unable to give her three livres per week because he did not have it. He denied owing the other items and amounts. He also claimed that she took things from him, which she denied. The Beit Din decided that he would have to pay her three livres per week, as per the previous *pesak*. Against this, all her handiwork (*ma'asei yadeha*) was deemed to belong to her husband, so that its value would be deducted from his alimony obligation to her.[52]

50 PMBD, Vol. 1, pt. 1, no. 96, 32b.
51 PMBD, Vol. 1, pt. 2, no. 50, 14b.
52 PMBD, Vol. 2, no. 237, 44a.

Complications stemming from second marriages and the lack of adequate housing also appear to have been an underlying issue that sparked domestic problems. Kilcha demanded that her husband Yukal Morhange move to another apartment because his brother and sister-in-law were allegedly creating disharmony between her and her husband. Additionally, she requested that Yukal's mother-in-law from his previous marriage move out of the house because she was also a cause of conflict. Yukal alleged that Kilcha herself was the cause of the problems, in part because of her failure to behave properly with his son (her stepson). Unable to reach a clear sense of who was at fault, the Beit Din rejected the demand that the husband or his mother-in-law be forced to move out. But to advance the cause of peace between husband and wife, his mother-in-law was advised, on pain of *ḥerem beit din*, not to enter the borders of the husband's property without his wife's permission.[53]

In several instances, a husband or wife approached the Beit Din with a complaint of spousal defamation. In the case of Wolff Yaffe of Mentz and his wife Alicha, the defamatory claim was entangled with several other issues. Wolff accused his wife of failing to behave with proper modesty such that she should be considered a *moredet* (a rebellious wife). He further accused her of having taken control of his possessions. Wolff asked the court to force her to behave properly toward him and that he should be given "control of everything." Alicha disputed these allegations, claiming that he was highly contentious and that he struck her. Additionally, he had gambled away much of their money, fallen deeper into debt, and therefore could not be trusted with any of their property. The Beit Din ruled that the couple's strongbox, which held their loan notes and cash, would be placed in the control of a third party, and that for a period of six months the rabbinic court would regulate the amount of money provided to Alicha for household needs, to other members of the household, and to her husband. At that point, the Beit Din would reevaluate the arrangement based on how the parties behaved to one another and how well they handled their finances. However, a month later, in response to reports of continuing quarrels between Wolff and Alicha, and despite efforts to gather information from neighbors who were regular visitors in their house, the Beit Din was unable to determine who was the cause of the discord. The court conceded that "the

53 PMBD, Vol. 1, pt. 2, no. 179, 41b. On second marriages, see Antoinette Fauvre-Chamoux, "Revisiting the Decline in Remarriage in Early Modern Europe: The Case of Rheims in France," *History of the Family* 15 (2010): 283–97; Owen Hufton, "Women Without Men: Widows and Spinsters in Britain and France in the Eighteenth Century," *Journal of Family History* 9 (1984): 355–76; Guy Cabourdin, "Le remariage en France sous l'ancien régime," in *Marriage and Remarriage in Populations of the Past*, eds. J. Dupaquier, et al. (London, 1981), 273–86.

devil still dances between them, [in order] to distance them [from each other] and not to bring them together," and that "acrimony is planted in the hearts of each of them."[54]

Despite the decision of the Beit Din to extend the financial arrangement between Wolff and Alicha in the hope that the couple could overcome their differences, efforts to bring Wolff and Alicha together were unsuccessful. The core reason for their marital conflict, the Beit Din maintained, was the "loss and depreciation" of the assets that they each brought to the marriage. Since the couple's differences could not be bridged, the Beit Din proceeded to supervise their separation by a series of steps to equitably disentangle their finances and their assets. In the meantime, a baby was born to the couple. The Beit Din decided to abstain from any action regarding the birth and post-birth expenses during the ensuing four weeks, in the hope that "the anger will pass, and they will come to a reconciliation." As such, it opted not to administer an oath to either one regarding the claims and representations of these expenditures, arguing that, if things could not be resolved between them, each could still take the oath.[55]

In another case of defamation, Matcha, former wife of Yospe, asked the Beit Din to put an end to his accusation that she did not observe the laws of *kashrut* in their home. Based on the testimony of witnesses, she sought the Beit Din's confirmation that her husband's claims were false. Brought before the Beit Din, the husband stood by his earlier remarks about her behavior when they had been married. However, two additional witnesses who had been regular guests of the couple affirmed that there were no indications that she ever violated Jewish dietary laws. Yospe's unsubstantiated claims were set aside as motivated by enmity towards his wife. The Beit Din declared Matcha to be trustworthy (*beḥezkat kashrut*) and acquitted her of any wrongdoing.[56] In a similar case that was recorded with fewer details, Mindele Emmerich sought to clear her reputation of a rumor about her purported failure to observe the laws of *kashrut*, though this was not indicated explicitly in the complaint. Mindele sent *parnasim* to the Beit Din to collect evidence that would show that there was no substance at all to the rumor. Following the Beit Din's investigation of numerous witnesses who were accustomed to enter and leave her house, it was determined that there was nothing to suggest that the rumor was true. Mindele, too, was declared trustworthy (*beḥezkat kashrut*).[57]

---

54 PMBD, Vol. 1, pt. 2, nos. 26–27, 7b–8a.

55 PMBD, Vol. 1, pt. 2, no. 108, 28a.

56 PMBD, Vol. 2, no. 42, 9a.

57 PMBD, Vol. 2, no. 381, 71a.

Several cases related to divorce also occupied the attention of the Beit Din and reveal complexities associated with the termination of a marriage. Mendele Franck, who had divorced his wife, was living in a room provided by his father-in-law, Hirtz Rofeh. He was accused of destroying the livelihood of his former wife, Tzimlah. Therefore, her attorney argued that he should vacate the apartment. Mendele claimed that he remained there on the strength of a promise made by his father-in-law in the *tena'im rishonim* agreement, prior to his wedding, that he would provide him with an apartment in his house. Hirtz responded that the promise was conditioned on the couple's staying together, but now that they were apart and were regularly in conflict, it was no longer acceptable that he stay in the room that, in fact, belonged to Tzimlah. The Beit Din examined the *tenai'im* and ruled that Hirtz and Tzimlah would each need to swear that the room in which Mendele was living was the portion of the house that belonged to her and her current husband, Barukh. Mendele would then be obligated to vacate, but Hirtz would be required to help him find a comparable apartment for the time remaining in the *tenai'im aḥaronim* and pay for it. The Beit Din explained that since Hirtz had promised his son-in-law a room that was not his to offer, he was responsible for the resulting damage and was liable for the expenses associated with Mendele's move to another apartment.[58]

Accusations of adultery were not common in the Beit Din, though no less traumatic for all concerned. Zalman Bing argued that his brother Me'ir slandered his wife by claiming that she had committed adultery. Supported by reliable evidence that this was a false accusation, Zalman asked the court to fine Me'ir for defamation (*hotza'at shem ra*) if he refused to recant or clarify his remarks. Meir admitted that he made the accusation out of anger, since his sister-in-law had maligned his own wife regarding another matter and on account of various quarrels between them. The Beit Din decided that to deter the disparagement of the daughters of Israel in the future, Me'ir would pay a fine of thirty-nine sous for wax used in the synagogue and an additional fine of thirty sous to the synagogue itself. He was also required to pay the travel expenses of the court emissary who would go to the synagogue on the Sabbath eve to announce publicly that lies were said about Zalman's wife and to confirm that she was trustworthy (*beḥezkat kashrut*).[59]

A second adultery case did not end as well. Yonah Leib Wilstadt approached the Beit Din with the complaint that his wife's pregnancy was not his doing. Nana, whom he married two months before, was the daughter of Feivelman,

---

58 PMBD, Vol. 1, pt. 1, no. 89, 30b.

59 PMBD, Vol. 2, no. 534, 109b.

one of the physicians in the Metz community. Following the husband's investigation, Nana admitted that the report was correct, and he immediately separated from her. Once the child was born, Yonah Leib asked the Beit Din to hear her confession in order to confirm that his accusation was accurate. He also asked the Beit Din to inquire of several people who were regular visitors in her father's house in order to establish that he (Yonah) had not spoken with her between the time she entered his (father's) house until the previous Rosh Hashanah "because the hatred that he had for her was in his heart ... that he could not speak well of her, only that the relatives made peace between them, from last Rosh Hashanah." She confirmed that the testimony of the witnesses was accurate. It was correct, she conceded, to record that she did not become pregnant from her husband, because they did not have sexual relations at all, and that her child has no paternal claim on him. Based on Nana's acknowledgment of her extra-marital affair, the testimony of witnesses confirming the absence of affection between husband and wife, and the fact that they never saw her speak with him, the Beit Din absolved Yonah Leib of all financial responsibility for the child and ordered him to divorce his wife, since she was a *meneket ḥavero*; she, in turn, was required to accept the *get* (writ of divorce), even against her will, on account of her confession. The court issued a *ma'aseh beit din* to Yonah Leib and to his attorney confirming that the child born to Nana had no claim on him.[60] Since marriage and sexuality were matters of vital interest to the public, the Beit Din tended to act swiftly in such cases, in some instances proactively.[61]

Marital Property

Marriage as portrayed in the Pinkas involves a labyrinth of details pertaining to consumption, the sharing of material assets, and the difficulties of maintaining a household and earning a livelihood. Through the lens of the law, the

60 PMBD, Vol. 2, no. 537, 110a. On the prohibition against marriage to a woman who was either pregnant by another man or who was nursing another man's child, see BT Yevamot 36b, 42a–b; Ketubot 60a–b; and *Even ha-'Ezer* §13:11–12. On adultery in eighteenth-century French courts, see Christophe Regina, "Private Sphere and Public Sphere, Economic Issues and the Judicial Arena: Women and Adultery in Marseilles during the Eighteenth Century," *Proceedings of the Western Society for French History* 37 (2009): 117–34.

61 The proceedings of the Metz Beit Din do not include divorce disputes, although there are several cases that refer to divorcées. Whether this indicates that no rabbinic court in Metz supervised divorce proceedings is unclear. For cases that refer to the *haliẓah* ceremony, which releases a widow from the obligation to marry her late husband's brother when the husband died without issue, see PMBD Vol. 2, no. 226, 42a; no. 487, 97b; and no. 504, 102a.

overwhelming focus on property provides clues concerning the economic challenges that married couples encountered over the course of their lives. The ownership of marital property, its disposition upon divorce or upon the death of one of the spouses, and responsibility for debts incurred over the course of marriage were subject to significant social, cultural, and regional variations. French customs and Roman law, for example, diverged sharply on these issues. In Roman law jurisdictions, property brought into the marriage by either spouse was considered separate and distinct. Accordingly, upon the death of her husband a widow would reclaim her dowry, but she would have no entitlement to his property.[62] The inalienability of the dowry was derived from Roman law. David Parker notes several aberrations from the conventional rules of inheritance, however. First, there were customs that enabled women to be compensated for losses sustained from her husband's alienation of property; second, a wife's ability to renounce succession in order to escape responsibility for her husband's debts "offset her lack of legal autonomy." Finally, those women who were engaged in business of their own were not affected by legal incapacity. In customary law regions, as a rule, the marriage bond brought a conjugal fund into being. A husband retained ownership and administrative control over all property in the fund, while his widow would subsequently succeed to these powers as his heir.[63] These two approaches to property ownership corresponded roughly to common law (separate holdings) and community property (jointly owned) systems. Nevertheless, private arrangements (which varied considerably by region) often resulted in modifications to the system before marriage and to the control of property during the marriage, so that in France "the concept of separate property co-existed with that of a community of property because of the marriage, and the fundamental divisions were among family land (*propres* or *héritages*), acquired land (*acquêts* or *conquêts*), and movables (*meubles*)."[64] In northern France, where customary law dominated, the general trend was to adopt the community property system.[65]

Arrangements for the disposition of property upon the dissolution of a marriage varied from jurisdiction to jurisdiction, though broader patterns began to develop in the eighteenth century: (a) there was a trend toward the equal

62 See Parker, *Class and State in Ancien Régime France*, 126 and nn. 55–56.

63 See Martha C. Howell, *The Marriage Exchange: Property, Social Place, and Gender in Cities of the Low Countries, 1300–1550* (Chicago, 1998), 6.

64 Charles Donahue, "What Causes Fundamental Legal Ideas? Marital Property in England and France in the Thirteenth Century," *Michigan Law Review* 78 (1979) 59–88.

65 Cf. *Coûtumes générals de l'Eveché de Metz*, commentées par M. Dilange, Conseiller au parlement de Metz, enrichies d'une table raisonnée des matières mise par ordre alphabétique (La Haye, 1772).

division of property between the heirs of the deceased and the surviving spouse; (b) wills became more important in determining how each spouse's half would be allocated; and (c) movables and acquired property were, in many localities, divided equally between husband and wife. In Metz, however, unlike most communities in the northeast, there was no presumption of community property: "In our *Coûtume* there is no community between husband and wife, unless it was stipulated in their marriage contract. This is contrary to our cousin *coûtumes* that establish community *ipso jure*, but it conforms to Roman law which does not allow it but does permit the contractants to stipulate it." Since the two options were both theoretically available, the Metz *Coûtumes* presented each scenario in detail.[66]

It is interesting that, although the custom as set forth in the Metz *Coûtumes* was akin to Roman law, the detailed presentation of community property suggests that this was a more prevalent choice than one would first assume based on the initial formulation. Art. 2 states that when a marriage dissolved, the community was divided in half between the surviving spouse and the children or heirs of the deceased. This paralleled the *Coûtumes de Paris* and all the other compendia of *coûtumes* that set forth the details of community property. Art. 3 declared that a husband was master of the community, and this gave him the power to alienate the possessions of which the community was composed, without the consent of his wife. This, too, paralleled the *Coûtumes de Paris* and was viewed as a universal right. Art. 4 stated that a husband was required to pay the community's debts, even those incurred by his wife before their marriage, unless it was stipulated that each was responsible for one's own debts. This, the Metz *Coûtumes* stated, was also common law and paralleled the *Coûtumes de Paris*. Art. 5 stated that, unless she paid half of the debts created by her husband during their marriage, a wife could not claim any part of acquisitions made by her husband during the marriage, even if she had been named *acquêteresse* or *fondée en communité de biens*. Art. 6 concluded that a wife who took half the movable property or acquisitions, by virtue of the community, was held responsible for half its debts.[67]

Marital property disputes brought before the Metz Beit Din reveal many of the same tensions addressed earlier between the norms of French legal culture and practice, on the one hand, and time-honored legal and customary arrangements within Jewish communities on the other.[68] These issues have

66 *Coûtumes générales de la ville de Metz et pays-Messin*, Titre XVI, Art. 1, 190–91.

67 See *Coûtumes générales de la ville de Metz*, Arts. 2–6, 194–96.

68 Claudia Ulbrich reports that disputes in Steinbiedersdorf (Pontpierre), a village some forty kilometers east of Metz, were settled in accordance with local custom. Local custom

their origins in the initial marital agreements that were formalized in a notarized contract by the parents of the engaged couple and that governed the wife's dowry, dower (*douaire*),[69] and non-dotal goods (*paraphernaux*). Since the state viewed marriage as a legal contract related to the public good, it followed that French law as practiced in the civil courts exercised jurisdiction over disputed property in marital cases.[70] With the removal of marriage from the jurisdiction of ecclesiastical courts to civil courts and the 1701 royal ordinance that required couples to deposit their marriage contracts with royal notaries within fifteen days of the wedding ceremony,[71] the disposition of marital property assumed a uniquely civil character. According to a rabbinic responsum composed a quarter-century later, the new law had improved the lot of Jewish women dramatically. Until its promulgation, the French civil courts paid no heed to *ketubot*, which were treated as promissory notes, and priority was accorded only to contracts prepared before a royal notary and signed by the parties and the notary. After 1701, Jewish women found that their marriage contracts were respected in the French courts as the equal of any contract produced by creditors.[72] In abbreviated form and translated into French, these *contrats de mariage* listed the financial undertakings set forth in the *ketubah*, including the property that was brought into the marriage, the husband's augment, provisions in case of the death of the husband, and the lien placed on all his acquisitions. The registration process confirmed that the terms of the Jewish marriage contract were valid under French civil law.[73]

A case of a woman who had separated from her husband twenty years earlier on account of his infidelity illustrates just this point. Nentcha [Nanette] requested the Beit Din's authorization to seek a judgment in the French civil court to recover not only her *ketubah* and *tosefta* but also twenty years of maintenance and accrued interest to which she was entitled under French law.[74]

---

had stipulated that marriage did not alter the legal status and property relationships of husbands and wives, nor did it impair a woman's legal capacity to enter into contracts. See Ulbrich, *Shulamit and Margarete*, 24–25.

69 From the Latin *doarium* and the French *douaire*, the dower is a provision accorded by a husband to a wife to support during life.

70 See Hanley, "Jurisprudence," 8.

71 See Szajkowski, "Alsatian Jewish Inventories in the Hebrew Union College Library," 96–97.

72 Lvov, *Resp. Penei Levanah*, no. 36.

73 See, for example, PMBD, Vol. 1, pt. 1, no. 10, 8b; no. 76, 26b; no. 142, 46a; Vol. 1, pt. 2, no. 54, 16a; Vol. 2, no. 59, 11a; no. 81, 15a.

74 Nentcha [Nanette] had married Salomon Blien on 22 October 1759. See Jean Fleury, *Contrats de mariage juifs*, 21.

> On this day, as recorded below, the *keẓinah* Nentcha daughter of the late Abraham Sinztheim appeared before us in the presence of her son, the *kaẓin* Hirtz Blien. In her hands she had a thick packet of documents that had been signed between her and her husband on the day of their wedding, on 10 Ḥeshvan 5510 [October 1749]. These were the *tena'im aḥaronim* and the *ketubah* and *tosefta* documents, as well as a promissory note from M. Lakian, notary of Steinbiedersdorf, that was given to him on 17 November 1775. One of the [copies of] the *tena'im aḥaronim* was placed in his hand so that in this way her *contrat* for her *ketubah* and *tosefta* from the aforementioned date would have legal validity in the *'arkha'ot* from that day. And we have found through investigation of these documents that the value of the *ketubah* and *tosefta* is 22,500 *zehuvim Rhenish*,[75] which is the equivalent of 49,902 French livres. And according to the statement of Nentcha, it is approximately twenty years since she and her husband have been separated, on account of his having betrayed her, as is known, and she has been forced to borrow from others to meet her household needs, until there was a ruling, known as a *sentence*, of 4 July 1764 in the *'arkha'ot*, stating that aside from being entitled to the aforesaid amount for her *ketubah* and *tosefta*, she is also entitled to the proceeds [that is, appreciation] as noted there. And there remains nothing of her husband's estate other than the house in which she currently lives … and a seat in the men's section of the old synagogue next to the present place.[76]

Seeking to remedy the injustice suffered by Nentcha and as partial payment toward the value of her *ketubah*, the Beit Din awarded her the house that belonged to her husband and also awarded her priority over all other creditors.[77]

The ruling in the foregoing case was based both on the recognition accorded Jewish marriage within French civil law and on the Beit Din's acknowledgement that in some instances French courts were the most suitable venue for the resolution of marital property disputes. The legal implications that entitled Jews to seek redress of their property grievances in the civil courts were far-reaching. In a comparable case, when communal officials had sealed an estate

75 Rhenish Gulden were valued at two-thirds of a Reichstaler and approximately forty-five percent of a livre.

76 PMBD, Vol. 2, 126b, no. 591. Cf. *Shulḥan 'Arukh, Even ha-'Ezer* §93:14 concerning a delay in making a claim for past maintenance.

77 See PMBD, Vol. 2, 126b, no. 591. Cf. *Shulḥan 'Arukh, Even ha-'Ezer* §93:14 concerning a delay in making a claim for past maintenance.

when neither of the natural heirs was available to appear before the Beit Din, the widow brought an action in the French civil court to collect the value of her *ketubah* and *tosefta*. Once the civil court issued its judgment (in her favor), she was able to return to the rabbinic court and take the oath required in order to collect the funds to which she was entitled. Here, as in other areas, the Metz Beit Din was expected to function within the parameters of French law. No less important, the case illustrates the functional cooperation between the two systems, rooted first and foremost in the Beit Din's reliance on the judicial clout of the civil court.[78]

Provisions for widows were a matter of talmudic law (BT Ketubot 52b). A widow was supported from her husband's estate until she remarried or collected her *ketubah*.[79] When she came to collect the *ketubah* after the death of her husband, she was required to swear that prior to his death she did not receive any payment, including items deposited with her to insure payment of the *ketubah*, and that she never waived her right to collect her *ketubah*. In the event of divorce, she was entitled to collect the amount of the *ketubah* owed to her without an oath. It was also customary to have her swear that she did not waste anything without permission of her husband.[80] If she demanded support but did not claim her *ketubah*, the heirs were not authorized to compel her oath, even if she had acted as an administrator of her husband's estate after his death.[81] To receive support, she was permitted to take property from the estate and sell it.[82] Where a widow came to the *beit din* to claim

---

78 See PMBD, Vol. 2, no. 594, 127b.

79 M. Ketubot 95b, M. Ketubot 52b and BT Ketubot 54a.

80 *Shulḥan 'Arukh, Even ha-'Ezer* §96. The widow's oath follows the general rule concerning debt collection from the property of orphans, that is, that the collection can be performed only with an oath. (BT Ketubot 87a). When a woman collects her *ketubah*, an oath is required in the following circumstances: she admits that it was paid in part; if one witness testifies that it was paid; if the property of the orphans is encumbered. According to R. Moses Isserles, it is enough if she states that she did not benefit from her *ketubah*.

81 BT Ketubot 88b; *Shulḥan 'Arukh, Even ha-'Ezer* §96:2. If a widow has been made administrator, the heirs may impose an oath on her concerning the future, i.e. her management after husband's death, but may not impose an oath upon her concerning the past. If a man appointed his wife as storekeeper or administrator of his business, he may impose an oath on her whenever he wishes (M. Ketubot 86b). This applies not only to a wife but to anyone appointed to manage another person's affairs. *Shulhan 'Arukh, Even ha-'Ezer* §98 rules like the Maimonides, that a clear, unambiguous formulation *does* exempt the wife from undertaking an oath to collect her *ketubah* from the orphans. Isserles, however, following the Rosh, rules that even an explicitly worded exemption cannot release her from her obligation.

82 Although according to talmudic law a widow was permitted to sell property without the approval of a *beit din*, this dispensation applied only in the case of expert judges. A *beit*

her maintenance, she was required to take an oath before any estate property could be sold without a public notice. The proceeds were subsequently given to her for her maintenance, sufficient for six months. However, when the *beit din* was involved in selling portions of the estate, it could sell whatever amount it deemed to be in the best interests of the orphans. Rabbi Moses Isserles clarified that this procedure was employed in order to collect the *ikkar ha-ketubah* and *tosefet*, but not when the purpose was to collect her dowry, which was equivalent to an ordinary debt (*ḥov b'alma*). If a husband exempted his wife from an oath, she could collect her *ketubah* without having to suffer what was widely viewed as a humiliating experience.[83]

A widow was entitled to maintenance from her husband's estate comparable to what she received during his lifetime. This included food, clothing, utensils, and lodging.[84] Among the obligations for which a husband assumed responsibility and that had to be honored by his heirs even if not stated in writing was the provision entitling his widow to dwell in his house and to receive maintenance for as long as she had not received her settlement (*ketubah* and *tosefta*). This stipulation was considered a condition (*tenai*) of the *beit din* and therefore did not need to be explicitly specified by the husband.[85] As a general rule, widows were granted the right to remain in the marital home; if a widow insisted that she was unable to move from her husband's house,

---

din of laymen (*hedyotot*) who were proficient in appraising real property was nonetheless required. Such a sale also did not require a public announcement whereas, in the case of a divorcée, authorization by a *beit din* of experts and a public announcement were mandatory. A widow who sold her late husband's estate without consulting a court did not require an oath or a public announcement before she sold the land. This is based on M. Arakhin 21b, where it is stated that when a court sells a debtor's property, it follows a thirty-day public-auction procedure. A widow is not required to follow this procedure when selling her late husband's estate because if a public auction is required, and people will therefore know the selling price of the property, there would be no need for the widow to confirm the price with an oath. Although the Mishnah states explicitly that land seized from an orphan's inheritance requires a public auction, the reference is limited to instances when the court—not the widow—was responsible for selling the estate. In such cases a public auction was crucial because a court's sales were irreversible; a public auction was necessary to ensure that the sellers were fully compensated. The sale conducted by a widow, however, could be overturned even for the slightest amount of underselling because this would cause a loss to the orphans. A widow is therefore required to undertake an oath but does not require a public announcement, as per BT Ketubot 98a.

83 *Shulḥan 'Arukh, Even ha-'Ezer* §103:1.

84 M. Ketubot 4:10, 12.

85 The two other provisions entitled male children born from their marriage together to inherit alongside children from previous marriages, and established that female children born from their marriage have the right to dwell in his house and receive maintenance from his estate, until they marry.

the heirs were obligated to support her and provide a domicile commensurate with her dignity. They were not required to support her if she decided to dwell elsewhere. Furthermore, they were not permitted to sell the house against her wishes; but if the dwelling was destroyed, the heirs were not obligated to rebuild it.

The law as set down in the 1769 Takkanot went a step further by obligating the heirs of the deceased to support his widow for the duration of her widowhood, even after she had collected her *ketubah* and *tosefta*. Even if the husband did not stipulate that his wife was entitled to this extended support, his heirs were nonetheless obligated to give her a place to live "according to her dignity" (*lefi kevodah*) in the house of the deceased or to rent a place for her somewhere else "according to her dignity."[86] A widow was also entitled to the services of domestic help employed by the husband during his lifetime. If a widow fell ill, she was expected to defray the cost for treatment of a limited duration from her *ketubah*, but the heirs were responsible to pay if she required unlimited treatment.[87] Upon the death of a widow, her husband's heirs were responsible for her burial.[88] Once a woman sold her *ketubah*, pledged it as a security for a loan, or designated it as security (Heb. *apotiki*) for a loan that she received or a debt that she owed, she no longer was entitled to support. A widow who was owed a portion of her *ketubah* was viewed as if she was still owed her entire *ketubah*, and therefore she retained her entitlement to support.[89]

Concerning a widow's legal exposure and liability for debts attached to the estate of her husband, there were important differences between customary law regions and territories where Roman law was in force. In customary regions, in order to be discharged from such responsibility, a widow would need to be formally released from her share of her husband's estate, but by renouncing her part of the community property, she also disowned whatever assets she had contributed to the marriage. In areas where Roman law prevailed, however, widows were not responsible for their husbands' debts, and according to the Metz *Coûtumes*, which did not recognize the legality of communal property in marriage unless there was an express stipulation in the *contrat de*

86 PKM, 79b, 1769 Takkanot, Art. 60. The provision was further qualified, however, by the specification that if a house was included in her *nikhsei melog*, then the heirs were not obligated to give her housing during the entire period of her widowhood. In Frankfurt, by contrast, the right of a widow to continue to live in her late husband's house depended on a written promise from the husband. See Fram, *A Window on their World*, 124, no. 52.

87 *Shulḥan 'Arukh, Even ha-'Ezer* §79:4.

88 *Shulḥan 'Arukh, Even ha-'Ezer* §89.

89 BT Ketubot 97b.

mariage, wives and widows were not held personally responsible for their husbands' debts.[90]

Most Jewish legal authorities concurred in this view, and it was confirmed consistently in cases recorded in the Metz rabbinic court register. It appears that renunciation of inheritance was necessary for heirs (children) but not spouses. In the case of the former, this was termed *silluk*. It would therefore be most accurate to translate the term as "separation from."[91] In response to a claim directed against a widow, Nentche, concerning merchandise she had purchased and money she had borrowed while her husband, Abraham Brisach, was alive, she argued that she was not obligated to pay the creditors herself because these purchases were made expressly for her husband's benefit. The Beit Din required her to take an oath certifying the truthfulness of her declaration and that, for their part, the plaintiff and his wife swear that whatever had been purchased in their store was solely with Nentche's knowledge and in accordance with her instruction, and that nothing included in their claim was purchased by her husband or his agent without her knowledge. Although Nentche was held responsible in this particular case, the Beit Din did accept the argument that her liability was limited to debts she incurred herself and did not extend to those incurred by her husband.[92] In a case of a widow whose late husband's debts far exceeded the amount to which she was entitled by her *ketubah* and *tosefta*, the Beit Din authorized the transfer of half the house and its contents to her possession, but ordered her to pay certain specified debts that were considered to have precedence since they were secured by a lien on the house.[93]

---

90 See Denis Le Brun, *Traité de la communauté entre mari et femme* (Paris, 1754), vol. 1, 27; and *Coûtumes générales de la ville de Metz et pays-Messin*, Titre VI, Arts. 1, 4–8, pp. 149–154. For a general overview, see Barbara Diefendorf, "Women and Property in *Ancien Régime* France," in John Brewer and Susan Staves, eds., *Early Modern Conceptions of Property* (New York, 1995), 177–78; Desan, "Making and Breaking Marriage," 7–8.

91 The second meaning of *silluk* is "discharge" and signified the husband's fulfillment of his obligation to pay the value of the *ketubah*. In this case *silluk* refers to "settlement of the *ketubah* obligation and virtually synonymous with *peira'on* (payment), e.g. לפרעון ולסילוק כתובתה. For additional sources, see PMBD, Vol. 2, no. 289, 53a; nos. 226–227, 42a–b; no. 347, 65b, and above, Chap. 5, n. 154. For examples of *silluk almanah* (settlement of a widow), see PMBD, Vol. 1, pt. no. 21, 6a; no. 125, 32a; Vol. 1, pt. 2, no. 257, 54b; Vol. 2, no. 289, 53b; Vol. 2, no. 616, 133a.

92 See PMBD, Vol. 1, pt. 2, no. 59, 16b. The oath taken by the widow was a *shevu'ah d'oraita* that was ordinarily enough to free her from responsibility for claims she denied. However, in this case the storeowner and his wife were asked to corroborate the facts declared in her oath.

93 PMBD, Vol. 2, no. 636, 139a.

The general procedure for satisfaction of the outstanding debts in a husband's estate illustrates the interrelationship of the two judicial systems. First, an inventory of the estate was drawn up in the civil court. Then, if there were outstanding debts, all movable items in his estate were sold at the instruction and under the supervision of an officer of the court, and the sale price of each item was recorded in a specially prepared *mémoire*. Such sales were conducted according to procedures of the civil courts.[94] Civil court expenses, which included the costs of conducting the estate sale, compensation for court officers, the interpreters, and the cost of notarial services, were deducted from the total proceeds. Once she received the net amount owed to her, the widow would declare that she was entitled to a certain share of the estate on the basis of her *ketubah*, excluding clothing and jewelry already in her possession.[95] Next, she would ask the Beit Din to administer the customary *ketubah* oath (*shevu'at ha-ketubah*) by which she affirmed that she had not removed any items from the estate. This entitled her to the amount recorded in the *ketubah* and to any additional funds she was able to collect.[96] The foregoing scenario reveals how closely the procedures of the Beit Din depended on the *modus operandi* of the civil court. Working out the payment to widows and sorting out the husband's debts was a bureaucratic process governed by French law. Whether the creditors and/or debtors were Jews or non-Jews made no difference. Here we have another exceptionally clear example of the *de facto* working relationship between the rabbinic and French courts.

When a widow was ready to collect her *ketubah* and *tosefta*, the immediate question was whether the amount to which she was entitled would satisfy her husband's outstanding debts. Legally, the issue depended both on chronology and on the type of property in the estate. If the debts were incurred prior to their marriage, then according to Jewish law those obligations took precedence and the payment of the *ketubah* was subordinated to those creditor claims. But even when the *ketubah* enjoyed priority over other debts, as was normally the case, the liquid assets in the estate were often not sufficient

94 PMBD, Vol. 2, no. 336, 63a. The expression used by the court is *ke-din nimusei arkha'ot*. For other examples, see Vol. 2, no. 81, 15a; no. 194, 37a; no. 312, 58b; no. 591, 126b.

95 There was a fair degree of disagreement among *posekim* concerning the exclusion of clothing and jewelry. See *Shulḥan Arukh, Even ha-'Ezer* §85. For an extraordinary attempt to clarify the issues and set the matter straight, see Bacharach, *Resp. Ḥavvot Ya'ir*, no. 144.

96 See PMBD, Vol. 1, pt. 1, no. 10, 8b. This procedure, termed *silluk* in Hebrew, is occasionally referred to as *renonciation* in the Beit Din records. For additional examples, see PMBD, Vol. 2, nos. 226–227, 42a–b; no. 347, 65b. Cf. Desan, "Making and Breaking Marriage," 11–16. In a case concerning a husband's transfer of assets to his wife via a gift contract, the Beit Din applied the principle שאין לסלק אלמנה לחצאין. Accordingly, she was entitled to her *ketubah*, *tosefta*, and gift. PMBD, Vol. 2, no. 16, 3b.

to satisfy the payment owing on the *ketubah*. Furthermore, to the extent that the deceased's estate included movable property, in accordance with talmudic law and medieval interpretation the Beit Din held the widow liable for any outstanding debts.[97] More often than not, the estate consisted mainly of obligations owed to the deceased. In such cases, the widow received the outstanding notes of indebtedness in partial satisfaction of her *ketubah*, and it fell upon her to collect those funds.[98] No matter who was responsible, a woman's material well-being was directly affected by the successes or failures of her husband's business affairs. Although the funds a widow paid to satisfy her husband's creditors diminished her *ketubah*, this was considered as only a temporary setback. Of additional significance is that class distinctions invariably exerted an impact in such matters. Where affluent families were concerned, the terms of the discharge from the husband's estate explicitly freed widows from any responsibility for debts and obligations that ordinarily would have been borne by women of lower rank.[99]

Women in Credit and Commerce

In the realms of credit and commerce, the records of the Metz Beit Din paint a strikingly different picture of women than the image that emerges in standard narrative accounts of modern Jewish history. The discrepancy stems largely from the tendency in the primary sources generally available to historians to underplay specific details of women's economic activities. Since husbands were commonly viewed as the legal representatives of their household, only their names appeared on most legal documents, and the economic role of their wives typically remained obscure.[100] In the proceedings of the Beit

97 BT Ketubot 86a. See Ronnie Warburg, "A Comparative Analysis of a Wife's Capacity to Pledge her Husband's Credit for Domestic Necessities in Anglo-American Law and Jewish Law," *Jewish Law Annual* 13 (2000): 213–37; and Cheryl Tallan, "Medieval Jewish Widows: Their Control of Resources," *Jewish History* 5 (1991): 63–74. Widows who were pressured to pay their husbands' creditors appeared before the Beit Din frequently. See, for example PMBD, Vol. 1, pt. 1, 18a, no. 60. This appears to be consistent with Roman law, i.e. that all rights and obligations of the deceased pass on to one's heirs, including property and debts. See Arye Edrei, "The Obligation to Uphold the Wishes of the Deceased" (Ph.D. diss., Hebrew University, Jerusalem).

98 For example, see the case of Miriam, below, p. 344.

99 See PMBD, Vol. 2, no. 310, 57a–b.

100 See Collins, "The Economic Role of Women," 439. In his study of women as entrepreneurs in early modern Germany, Michael Toch has drawn an important distinction between the evidence of women's business activity in formal tax records and other indications

Din, however, there are occasional references to property transfers, as in a case when a husband transferred ownership of their house to his wife, effective the day he died.[101] Nevertheless, as in the case of wills, it is often impossible to locate records of such transactions, unless they have been preserved in civil court or notarial files. This is where rabbinic court records and the archives of non-Jewish courts can be especially helpful. The Pinkas of the Metz Beit Din is filled with cases of women who firmly—at times, even aggressively—demanded what they believed was rightly theirs.

While most such cases pertained to inheritance, there were also numerous examples pointing to women's substantial participation in commercial life. Women were occasionally asked to add their signatures in order to strengthen the legal validity of certain documents.[102] Scores of women initiated legal proceedings and in most instances, they represented themselves, as in the case of Kilcha, who approached the Beit Din seeking to be freed from her engagement to a man who had disappeared.[103] Additional examples of assertiveness include the unmarried daughters of Rabbi Isaac Netter who approached the Beit Din, claiming that their father's will recorded an incontestable debt that served as the basis for a gift (*ḥov gamur be-torat matanah*) promising each of them 6,600 livres on their wedding day; and Gitcha, widow of Goetschlik Levi. Gitcha's daughter was engaged to be married; in reliance on a directive in her husband's will providing for the daughter's *hakhnasat kallah*, the widow sued heirs of communal leader Shmuel Levi for a portion of the inheritance to which relatives of the deceased were entitled. Arguing that her husband was a second cousin to the deceased and citing an earlier ruling court that second cousin was defined as a close relative, Gitcha insisted on receiving a percentage of the 3,000 livres set aside for poor brides. The Beit Din ruled in her favor.[104]

---

that emerge from informal sources. The tax records contain lists of legally independent tax-paying widows while the informal sources suggest that many more women participated in their husbands' affairs on a day-to-day basis. See Michael Toch, "Jewish Women Entrepreneurs in the Sixteenth and Seventeenth Centuries: Economics and Family Structure," *Jahrbuch für fränkische Landesforschung* 60 (2000): 254–62. See, now, Elise Dermineur, ed., *Women and Credit in Pre-Industrial Europe* (Turnhout, 2018).

101 PMBD, Vol. 2, no. 154, 30b. For other examples of property transfer, as set forth in a gift contract (*shetar matanah*), see Vol. 2, nos. 16–17, 3b–4a. In Kriechingen, known as Créhange in French, the Jewish residents of the county made extensive use of sovereign courts to settle their disputes, and it is likely that those records contain evidence relevant to women's economic involvement. See Ulbrich, *Shulamit and Margarete*, 19–20.

102 See PMBD, Vol. 1, pt. 1, no. 83, 28a; Vol. 1, pt. 2, no. 116, 49a for examples of women's signatures that were added to documents.

103 See PMBD, Vol. 2, no. 288, 53b.

104 See PMBD, Vol. 2, no. 431, 82b, and no. 496, 100a.

The example of Glik, wife of Zalman Weill, offers an instructive illustration of the economic prominence that women could attain, despite limits on the independence of married women that were well-entrenched in eighteenth-century French society.[105] Descriptions of conjugal authority by jurist Robert-Joseph Pothier detail the restrictions imposed broadly on wives' freedom to borrow money, undertake commercial transactions, or make contracts without the approval of their husbands. Glik's activities accord closely with other accounts of women who negotiated a more equitable distribution of power in their families. This other model was in some instances possible because of the ever more common stipulation that lineage property belonging to married women could not be alienated without their consent.[106] That stipulation enabled some wives to assume roles as economic partners, especially in borrowing and lending money. Glik was a successful businesswoman who appeared before the Beit Din on several occasions with requests for valuation of collateral taken on commercial loans. It is likely that she had entered the moneylending profession, as did many women, following the death of her husband.[107] Now remarried, she continued lending money, both on her own account and in partnership with her second husband. She used her income to support her children from her first marriage, specifically by providing funds for food and schooling. In order to avoid undue harm to her business, she requested authorization to pay her children's expenses from the estate of her first husband. One measure of Glik's economic standing is apparent in a case concerning a house she had owned herself (evidently inherited from her late husband) and subsequently signed over as a gift to Zalman. Her superior position is confirmed by Zalman's statement to the Beit Din that his transactions were not valid without her consent nor did he have the power to impose his will over hers. While the specific context for Zalman's statement was plainly

105 Guélique Jonas Cahen (née Israel) of Metzervisse was the widow of Simon Lambert whom she had married on 5 February 1761. She subsequently married Salomon Weill on 11 November 1771. See Fleury, *Contrats de mariage juifs*, 96 and 157.

106 See Robert-Joseph Pothier, *Traité de la puissance du mari sur la personne et les biens de la femme* (Paris, 1774), article 194. On the history of women's commercial and financial freedom, see Jean Délumeau and Daniel Roche, *Histoire des pères et de la paternité* (Paris, 1990); Hardwick, *Practice of Patriarchy*, 54, 62–63, 114–15; and Diefendorf, "Women and Property in *Ancien Régime* France," 170–93.

107 See PMBD, Vol. 1, pt. 1, no. 54, 16b–17a. The involvement of Jewish women as money lenders was certainly not new, as evidence from the late seventeenth century shows. See Davis, *Women on the Margins*, 17–18, and esp. n. 43.

the transfer of the house, it is not evident that the thrust of his pronouncement was limited to that alone.[108]

Overall, women involved in pawn-broking and moneylending constituted roughly twenty percent of the total number of Jewish lenders who appeared before the Beit Din.[109] But the percentage of women who were engaged in those activities was likely to have been higher assuming that women in eighteenth-century northeastern France would have been more reluctant than men to sue in court. In addition, we occasionally learn of commercial partnerships between men and women. Matha, wife of Yukav Schlesinger, was a member of a commercial partnership with four men.[110] In another instance, following the untimely death of her husband, a woman joined her father-in-law as a partner in what appears to have been a substantial commercial enterprise. Most such ventures involved widows who either replaced their deceased husbands in business or were forced to find work in order earn a livelihood. However, as the example of Beila, wife of Wolf Cahen (a *gabbai* of the Kehillah), reveals, widowhood certainly was not the sole circumstance that enabled women to enter the business world, nor was marriage. How Beila Cahen and Eisig Loeb Weil had come to establish a commercial partnership is unclear. We do know that Beila was the dominant partner and that their venture apparently dissolved over a disagreement concerning the division of assets.[111] Economic opportunities that had become available to women during the century preceding the French Revolution laid the foundation for the vital role they played in credit networks, as lenders and borrowers. Although we do not yet have sufficient

108 See PMBD, Vol. 1, pt. 1, no. 136, 44a: "שאין מקחו מקח מכח שתלוי בדעת אשתו ואין הוא יכול לכוף אותה." Cf. *Coûtumes générales de la ville de Metz* (1769), Titre VI, Art. 8, 198: While a husband was able to contract debts without the consent of his wife, she could not contract debts without the consent of her husband. There appears to be ample evidence that more options were available in actual practice. The example of Miriam (née Lambert), wife of Rabbi Me'ir Trenel offers additional evidence of independent property ownership by women. She had an estate that was separate from that of her husband, as attested in a *shetar* in Frankfurt, dated 21 Elul 5530, that served as the basis for supporting her impoverished daughter (Hendele) and son-in-law. See PMBD, Vol. 2, no. 199, 38a.

109 PMBD, Vol. 1, pt. 2, no. 40, 12b. Cf. the lending activity of Jachet Trenel, PMBD, Vol. 2, no. 413, 79b. A sampling of forty-six requests of the Beit Din to estimate the value of collateral reveals that nine were submitted by women. On women's unusual role in modern economies, see Laurence Fontaine, *L'Economie morale: Pauvreté, crédit et confiance dans l'Europe préindustrielle* (Paris, 2008), ch. 5, where it is noted that women's lack of access to capital and to urban labor markets explains their activity in second-hand trades and small-scale credit-brokering.

110 PMBD, Vol. 2, no. 64, 12a.

111 PMBD, Vol. 2, no. 270, 50b.

quantitative data, it appears that a parallel development may have been at work among Jewish women in Metz.[112]

In virtually all such cases women were mentioned by name in the Beit Din register and either exercised the right to argue their case themselves or were present in the courtroom as an attorney argued on their behalf.[113] That women appeared in the Beit Din as plaintiffs and defendants was consistent with the common law of the Roman legal tradition, which was favorable to women in such matters. In many instances, women looked to the rabbinic court as perhaps their only hope of achieving a resolution of the difficulties they faced. Examples of women's agency include a widow's opposition to the rewording of her husband's will;[114] a widow's request to sever her connection to her husband's estate;[115] a young woman who approached the Beit Din seeking to be released from her engagement to a man who had disappeared;[116] a woman who sued a debtor for non-payment of rent owed to her husband over a period of nine years;[117] a woman who approached the Beit Din with a request on behalf of her husband and herself for assistance when the couple suffered a financial reversal that left them penniless;[118] and cases in which women added their signatures to certain documents in order to strengthen their legal validity.[119]

In addition to their role as claimants or defendants, women served as witnesses in a variety of cases. Three cases explicitly refer to women who, qua witnesses, provided testimony in the rabbinic court; two of these were paternity claims. In the first instance the proceedings refer to what "the aforementioned women testified (*hei'idu*) before the Beit Din"; in the second, statements given both by the putative father and the pregnant mother are labeled as testimony (*'edut*). The fact that these statements conformed to the formal definition of testimony as required in Jewish law is not surprising, since both cases concerned paternity claims. In such matters, the standard restrictions on women serving as witnesses were relaxed so that no relevant testimony would be treated as inadmissible. In fact, it was not at all uncommon for women to provide information that was essential to the court's efforts to reconstruct the details of the cases it was asked to adjudicate. In a third case, "after the ruling [of the Beit

---

112 Hardwick, *Family Business*, 142–52. For an interesting example of entrepreneurship in the horse-trading business, see the case of Feigele, PMBD, Vol. 2, no. 635, 138b.

113 See, for example, PMBD, Vol. 2, no. 64, 12a; Vol. 1, pt. 1, no. 30, 12a.

114 See PMBD, Vol. 1, pt. 2, no. 249, 54a.

115 PMBD, Vol. 1, pt. 1, no. 131, 43a.

116 See PMBD, Vol. 2, no. 288, 53b.

117 PMBD, Vol. 1, pt. 1, no. 21, 10b.

118 See below.

119 See PMBD, Vol. 1, pt. 1, no. 83, 28a; Vol. 1, pt. 2, no. 116, 49a.

Din] had been issued, the testimony of some women (*'edut eizeh nashim*) who had seen and recognized … [the pieces of jewelry] that were worn by the widow on several occasions during her husband's life …" firmly established that these items belonged to the widow.[120] Notwithstanding the limitations traditionally imposed by Jewish law, and especially the disinclination of later authorities to admit women's testimony, the routine presentation of the facts of cases before the Metz Beit Din, though not identical to conventional testimony, ought to be included under the rubric of what is conventionally considered evidence. Moreover, judges were free to exercise discretion in determining which testimony they considered credible, even if the competence of the witness was

---

120 See PMBD, Vol. 2, no. 146, 28b; no. 495, 100a; and no. 208, 39b. For the halakhic limitations on the eligibility of women to testify, see *Shulḥan 'Arukh, Ḥoshen Mishpat* §35:14. Concerning the admissibility of testimony by women in limited circumstances, see the comments of Maimonides, *Mishneh Torah*, Laws of Sanhedrin 24:1 and the sources adduced by Moses Isserles in *Darkhei Moshe, Ḥoshen Mishpat* §35:3.

"וז״ל המרדכי סוף הלכות נדוי: אף על גב דמנדין בלא התראה, מכל מקום אין מנדין עד שיודע הדבר בעדים כשרים ובראיה גמורה כו׳. ולי נראה דאף על גב דאפשר דמדינא הנשים אינן נאמנות אפילו במקום שאין אנשים שכיחי כדברי הרמב״ם והרשב״א, מכל מקום תקנות קדמונים הם מרבינו תם ז״ל, כמו שכתב מהרי״ק שורש קע״ט, דאשה יחידה או קרוב או קטן נאמנים בענין הכאות או בזיון תלמיד חכם ובכל דבר קטטה שאין רגילים להיות עדים מזומנים בדבר זה ואין פנאי להזמינם, והוא הדין במסירות וכו׳."

For greater elaboration, see Isserles, *Sḥulhan 'Arukh, Ḥoshen Mishpat* §35:14:

"וכל אלו הפסולים, פסולים אפילו במקום דלא שכיחא אנשים כשרים להעיד (הרשב״א בתשובה, ודרמב״ם בפ״ח מהלכות נזקי ממון, וכן כתב הב״י). וכל זה מדינא, אבל יש אומרים דתקנת הקדמונים היא דבמקום שאין אנשים רגילים להיות, כגון בבית הכנסת של נשים, או בשאר דבר אקראי שאשה רגילה ולא אנשים, כגון לומר שבגדים אלו לבשה אשה פלונית והן שלה, ואין רגילים אנשים לדקדק בזה, נשים אמנות (תרומת הדשן סי׳ שנג, ואגודה פרק עשרה יוחסין). ולכן יש מי שכתב, דאפילו אשה יחידה או קרוב או קטן, נאמנים בענין הכאה ובזיון תלמיד חכם, או שאר קטטות ומסירות, לפי שאין דרך להזמין עדים כשרים לזה ואין פנאי להזמין (מהרי״ק שורש קעט, ומהר״ם מריזבורק וכלבו סי׳ קטז), והוא שדתבע טוען ברי (מהרי״ק שורש צג)."

On the general subject of women's testimony, including various exceptions to the talmudic disqualification, see Shimshon Ettinger, "Testimonial Competence in Civil Matters under Jewish Law" [Hebrew], *Diné Israel* 20–21 (2001): 241–67; Ilan Fuchs, "Women's Testimony in Jewish Law: A Historical Survey," *Hebrew Union College Annual* 82–83 (2011–2012): 119–59. The limitations within Jewish law notwithstanding, one should, perhaps, include the routine presentation by women of the facts of cases before the Metz Beit Din under the rubric of what is traditionally considered testimony. In *Bin Nun* (vol. 6 of *Me'orei Or*) 86a, Aaron Worms referred to the responsum of Asher ben Yeḥiel (Rosh), regarding a woman who was an apostate and her niece testified (העידה) that she was not promiscuous (שלא זינתה) and therefore should be considered trustworthy. Worms introduced an additional consideration: many Christian women in his day—the nineteenth century—were shy and guarded themselves; because of their faith, promiscuity was distasteful and ugly in their eyes, unlike (pagan) nations of the world of earlier times.

invalidated. In such cases, the basis for judicial freedom was the talmudic adage that "the *dayan* only has what his eyes can see."[121]

A second example furnishes more elaborate detail about the involvement of women in commercial enterprise. In 1779, Froumette (née Blien), widow of the late Seligmann (Salomon) Wittersheim, approached the Metz Beit Din along with her son, daughter-in-law, grown daughters, and two prominent members of the Metz community about the terms of her husband's will. Wittersheim had appointed Froumette as executor of his estate, using the phrase *gevirtanit ve-shultanit* ("mistress and executor").[122] By the terms of the will, she was given control over her husband's entire estate for as long as she remained unmarried. Two men were to be appointed to oversee her transactions relative to the overall commercial enterprise. The terms of the new arrangement to which family members had all agreed, included the following: (a) Froumette was empowered to lend money as she saw fit, as long as the overseers concurred; (b) she was authorized to manage the entire commercial enterprise, and to initiate new transactions (although, concerned about their personal liability, the overseers agreed to serve in this capacity on condition that they assumed no responsibility whatsoever for the business decisions taken by Froumette); (c) Froumette was given a free hand to extend more flexible terms to debtors, on condition that she provide an accounting to all of the partners; and (d) all such transactions, carried out with the agreement of the overseers, would be considered fully valid. Though not all these terms had been stated explicitly in the will, they were deemed by the heirs to be consistent with the intention of the deceased.[123] Two years later, when Froumette decided to remarry, she indicated her willingness to surrender the estate corpus that was under her control, after deducting her expenses since the death of Seligmann. At this

121 BT Batra Batra 131a.

122 See PMBD, Vol. 2, no. 149, 29a–29b. On the early modern use of the phrase *gevirtanit ve-shultanit*, see Joseph Trani, *Resp. Maharit* (Tel Aviv, 1959), pt. 1, no. 27: "וכההיא דפ׳ יש נוחלין דאמרי׳ הכותב נכסיו לאשתו לא עשאה אלא אפוטרופא ומה שלא פי׳ הוא שרצה שתהא שולטנית עליהם לעשות בהם כל מה שתרצה ואינש לא ימח׳ ביד׳." Also see Bacharach, *Resp. Ḥavvot Ya'ir*, nos. 138 and 231, where the term *gevirtanit* appears in conjunction with the term *maskelet* (educated). Cf. Landau, *Resp. Noda b'Yehudah*, Vol. 1, *Ḥoshen Mishpat* 29.

123 For similar trends in other regions of Frances, see Desan, "Making and Breaking Marriage," 11, and Clare Crowston, "Family Affairs: Wives Credit, Consumption, and the Law in Old Regime France," in *Family, Gender, and Law in Early Modern France*, ed. Suzanne Desan and Jeffrey Merrick (University Park, PA, 2009), 62–100. Concerning Froumette, one thing that makes her story so impressive is that she gave birth to twelve children; one died at birth and four died in childhood.

point, she was entitled to a settlement equivalent to the value of her *ketubah*, *tosefta*, and *nikhsei melog*.[124]

It is clear that Froumette's appointment as executor of her husband's estate was neither honorific nor perfunctory. The position, as understood by all parties, involved tasks that extended well beyond simply managing the estate; it included responsibilities for Wittersheim's extensive business dealings. Moreover, the case reveals how inheritance and commerce were intricately interwoven.[125] Seligmann Wittersheim, a son-in-law of the wealthy army purveyor Moïse Blien—the first Jew to farm[126] the *péage corporel* (body tax)—had enjoyed great success himself. He was a leading member of a consortium that had successfully bid in Paris for a contract to supply the armies in Lorraine and Trois Evêchés, was involved in the provisioning of forage for horses, and was part of an association that purchased clothing from the royal treasury. He also owned a large number of houses, presumably to generate *rentes*.[127] In appointing Froumette executor of the estate, the Seligmann will included terms commonly employed in medieval Ashkenaz and Spain and roughly equivalent to the term *apotropa* that appears in M. Ketubot (86b): "If a widow has been appointed *apotropa* (administrator), the heirs may impose an oath on her concerning the future, i.e., after the husband's death, but may not impose an oath upon her concerning the past." Whereas in mishnaic law the matter was limited to the imposition of an oath regarding her handling of the estate, the medieval and early modern use of the terms implied broader responsibilities.[128]

---

124 See PMBD, Vol. 2, no. 313, 58b.
125 See PMBD, Vol. 2, no. 317, 60a.
126 Tax farming is a method of tax collection assigned to a third party.
127 See PMBD, Vol. 1, pt. 1, nos. 63–64, 19a–b; Vol. 1, pt. 2, no. 182, 42a; Vol. 1, pt. 1, no. 93, 31b.
128 On the phrase "*gevirtanit ve-shultanit*," see Lvov, *Resp. Penei Levanah*, no. 36, pp. 148–49:

> [I]n these lands we write all *tosefet ketubah* forms according to the second formula recorded in *Naḥalat Shiv'ah* (pt. 1, no. 16): "And from now I have given my wife four cubits of land, etc. and based on this and on *kinyan sudar*, I authorize her and appoint her attorney and guardian over all of my property, real and movable to be paid from the choicest property that I have acquired and will acquire." Indeed, it is not just that he pledged to her movables attached to land, but that he also appointed her executrice over his property, so that she will be in control of them from the day of the *kinyan*, and this means that she can object to a later creditor collecting from them. And although we hold that a dowry is not collected from the living, nevertheless, just as an early creditor whose time to be paid has not yet arrived can object that the later creditor, though his time has come to be paid, shall not collect from movables so as not to consume them or dispose of them, so also, since according to all opinions the dowry has the legal status of a creditor [...] in the case of a woman as well, where attachment to the land is included in the *ketubah* she can object to a creditor selling [movables to which she may one day be entitled].

There is abundant evidence of women in the medieval period who were engaged in commerce and manual labor.[129]

The occasional use of the phrase *gevirtanit ve-shultanit* in the Metz Pinkas signaled the empowerment of widows in relation to the estates of their husbands, though the latitude extended to widows could range substantially. In one instance, having appointed his wife Alla *gevirtanit ve-shultanit*, Aberlé Worms stipulated in his will that a promissory note in the amount of 1,800 livres that was earmarked for their daughter's dowry was contingent on Alla's agreement to provide full support until the daughter married.[130] This was no doubt consistent with common practice in the region requiring widows to follow well-defined instructions as set forth in the will. Froumette Wittersheim's role as executor of her husband's estate conferred more independence than was normally envisioned. Owing to the vastness of her late husband's enterprise, which entailed numerous secondary partnerships, including commercial liaisons with non-Jews, and involved high-level negotiations with the monarchy, it is inconceivable that Froumette could have been a novice in relation to the responsibilities with which she was entrusted. There is every reason to believe that she was involved in her husband's business, possibly in a managerial capacity, prior to his death. The fact that Seligmann's grown children were passed over in favor of their mother would appear to substantiate this assumption.

Indications that husbands and wives were involved in joint financial or commercial ventures are borne out by the ubiquity of an ingenious solution

---

The following is the original Hebrew text:

אמור מעתה, לפי מה שנוהגין במדינות הללו לכתוב כל שטרי תוספת כתובות כנוסח השני שבספר נחלת שבעה [ח״א ריש סי׳ טז] בזה״ל, ומעתה נתתי לאשתי הנ״ל ד׳ אמות קרקע כו׳, ואגבן ואגב קנין סודר הנ״ל הרשיתיה והשלטתיה ומיניתיה מורשית ואפוטרופסית על כל נכסי כו׳ מקרקעי ומטלטלי כו׳ להתפרע מן שפר ארג נכסין וקנינין כו׳, דקנאי דעתיד אנא למקני כו׳, עכ״ל. הרי דלא די שהקנה לה אגב קרקע, אלא אף גם השליטה על כל נכסיו שתהא מוחזקת בהן מים הקנין, פשיטא שתוכל למחות שלא להגבותן לבע״ח מאוחר. אף דקיי״ל שאין נדוניא ניתן לגבות מחיים, מכל מקום, כשם שיוכל הבע״ח מוקדם אף שלא הגיע עדיין זמן פרעון שלו למחות שהבע״ח מאוחר אף שהגיע זמן פרעון שלו לא יגבה מטלטלין כדי שלא יפסידום ויבריחום, [...] וה״ה באשה נמי אי כותבין אגב בכתובה היא יכולה למחות שלא למכור.

129 In Spain, husbands commonly left wills with explicit instructions to bestow their assets on their wives, although Rabbi Asher ben Yehiel explained that what they were really doing was appointing their wives guardians (*apotropsot*) over their property, and in fact this was not at all unusual, even when the wife was preferred over the sons. In Ashkenaz as well, it was common for husbands to instruct that upon their death their wives would receive/control their assets. See Avraham Grossman, *Pious and Rebellious: Jewish Women in Medieval Europe* [Hebrew] (Hanover, NH, 2004), 192–94, 217. Grossman notes that it was common for husbands to leave their property to their wives; see 205–206.

130 So stated the Beit Din in its ruling: האשה מ׳ עלא תי׳ נשארת שולטת בכל נכסי בעלה "מהיר׳ נאמר פי שמוזכר בצוואה ... ושם שהבת יש לה מזונות בחנם אצל אמה כל זמן שלא תנשא לאיש." See PMBD, Vol. 1, pt. 1, no. 111, 38a, and Vol. 2, no. 662, 117b.

to a problem posed by traditional Jewish marital law. According to talmudic law, when a couple is married a lien is placed on the husband's assets so that if the marriage dissolves, either as the result of divorce or his death, the sum called for in the *ketubah* is paid to the wife first. This lien could conceivably undermine the husband's efforts to secure loans. Creditors were understandably hesitant to advance funds when a man's first obligation, in the case of death or divorce, was to satisfy the terms of his wife's *ketubah* and *tosefta*. To address this problem, rabbinic and lay authorities employed the *be'ohev* formula referring to the precise order of signatures in the execution of a loan note. It appeared the first time in *Sefer Naḥalat Shiv'ah*, the widely used compendium of contracts produced in 1667.[131] By signing the document in this manner, a wife indicated her intent to subordinate her right to receive payment for the *ketubah* and *tosefta* as a first creditor. The motivation for surrendering a well-established entitlement guaranteed by Jewish law is clear. When both husband and wife were identified jointly as debtors, the risk to the lender was reduced and the likelihood that they would qualify for the loan they sought increased substantially. The term appeared numerous times in the rabbinic court records and in the Pinkas Kahal of Metz as well.[132] Rabbi Ya'ir Ḥayyim Bacharach recommended the use of the *be'ohev* mechanism for the aforementioned reason and attested that he employed it himself.[133]

The use of the *be'ohev* instrument, frequently in conjunction with the talmudic phrase *'arevut kablanut* (referring to the highest level of surety) and together with the term *solidairement*, reveals a trend that was of broad social and economic significance in France. In the Metz community there were numerous instances when husbands and wives borrowed money jointly as *codébiteurs solidaires*. This stands in contrast to the Metz *Coûtumes* and the *Coûtumes* of the Lorraine, each of which referred to the term *solidairement* solely in relation to business partnerships and to guardianship contracts.[134] Jewish couples contracted loans in cases of great need, such as a commercial

131 The phrase appears in several purchase contracts published in Segel, *Sefer Naḥalat Shiv'ah*, Vol. 1, nos. 31, 32, and 41. A similar phrase, *lehaknot isha ve-hadar ba'alah*, referring to property acquisition, appeared a century earlier. See Joshua Falk Katz, *Prishah, Ḥoshen Mishpat*, §131, subparag. 12, and similar references in in Mordechai Jaffe, *Levush*, Even ha-Ezer §100, parag. 4; David ha-Levi, *Turei Zahav*, Even ha-'Ezer 90, sub-parag. 5; and Yom Tov Ẓahalon, *Resp. Mahariẓ*, no. 71, n. 8.

132 See Pinkas Kahal of Metz, 4a, for an example of the preparation of a *be'ohev* contract.

133 For an explanation of how the instrument worked, see Bacharach, *Resp. Ḥavvot Ya'ir*, no. 78, and Reischer, *Resp. Shevut Ya'akov*, pt. 1, no. 155. See PMBD, Vol. 1, pt. 2, no. 30, 9b, for an example of a document attesting to a wife's subordination of the lien on her husband's property to which her *ketubah* entitled her, and Vol. 1, pt. 2, no. 149, 36b, where the details are spelled out explicitly.

134 See Riston, *Analyse des coûtumes sous le ressort du parlement de Lorraine*, 348–50, 354.

venture or the avoidance of default on another loan. The practice as described in the responsa literature called for both wife and husband, in that order, to co-sign the note, and by so doing they were joined *solidairement*. However, the 1769 Takkanot upheld the validity of the *be'ohev* mechanism even without the wife's signature.[135] This signified that each spouse stood as a full guarantor for the other. The terms *solidaire* and *solidairement* followed the Latin convention *in solidum* and reflected the Roman legal concept of joint liability. But whereas *in solidum* was used when debtors were each liable for the entire debt, in Metz the liability of husband and wife was joint and several, as per *Ḥoshen Mishpat* §77:10. Accordingly, a wife would be liable for half the amount borrowed, and this was to be deducted from the proceeds of her *ketubah* to which she was entitled by Jewish law upon the death of her husband or following divorce.[136] This did not mean that husbands and wives held their property in a "joint conjugal fund," but rather as an extension of the laws of partnership.[137]

According to the majority opinion among *posekim*, when several debtors were engaged in a single legal transaction, each individual was liable as principal debtor only with respect to his share in the total investment and was otherwise considered an ordinary guarantor in relation to the balance of the debt. In other words, the creditor would first need to claim from each his proportional share, and only if one of them was unable to pay would the other

135 See PKM, 79b, 1769 Takkanot, Art. 58.

136 Where each is liable for his own share or proportion only, they are said to be bound *pro rata* (i.e., proportionately). An example of both phrases may be found in the liability of partners; each is responsible *in solidum* (i.e., entirely) for the debts of the partnership in relation to creditors, but each is responsible only *pro rata* to each other. Each person whose name appears on a bill, whether as acceptor or endorser, is liable in full payment of its contents. See Pierre Richelet, *Dictionnaire de la langue française, ancienne et moderne* 3 vols. (1759), 2:606; Mousnier, *Les institutions de la France*, 1:82. For a discussion of *contrainte solidaire*, see Dimitry Shlapentokh, *Societal Breakdown and the Rise of the Early Modern State in Europe: Memory of the Future* (New York, 2008). For examples in the Metz Beit Din protocols, see: PMBD, Vol. 1, pt. 2, no. 36, 11b: סאלידערמאן עם נשותיהם; Vol. 2, no. 554, 115b: באשר שחייב להם ר״א ואשתו ארבעה מאות וחמשים ליוור על כ״י לשלם סאלידער אפארטער; and no. 597, 128a: שהתחייב עם בעלה ז״ל בערבות סאלידער. Cf. Elka Klein, "The Widow's Portion: Law, Custom and Marital Property among Medieval Catalan Jews," *Viator* 31 (2000): 147–63, esp. 157.

137 On the idea of marriage as a commercial partnership, see the discussion in Warburg, "Comparative Analysis," 223–32. R. Samuel de Medina viewed a wife as her husband's agent who exercised independence in her own right, while each served as a guarantor for the other. The "partnership" rested on their shared assets and on the fruits of their combined efforts. See Yehuda Warburg, *Rabbinic Authority: The Vision and the Reality* (Jerusalem, 2013). See PMBD, Vol. 2, pt. 2, 12b, no. 42: "ואחר ששמענו את דברי המורשא הנ״ל וראינו פסקי הנ״ל פסקנו שמחויבת מ׳ גליק הנ״ל ליתן פירי עשרה לכל מאה לכל שנה ושנה משך זמן שתחזיק ... כל זמן שדבק באשתו עמו בחיים."

debtor be liable as surety for him.[138] In such cases, responsibility for repayment of the loan preceded the wife's rights to her *ketubah* even though the loan was contracted only after she was married.[139]

Printed and manuscript sources suggest that the *be'ohev* mechanism was most commonly known in Metz, in certain localities in Alsace and the Rhineland, and to a lesser degree, in communities further east. The following are several of the early modern collections of responsa that refer to *be'ohev*: Ya'ir Ḥayyim Bacharach, *Resp. Ḥavvot Ya'ir* (Worms); Jacob Reischer, *Resp. Shevut Ya'akov* (Halle, Offenbach, Metz); Gershon Koblenz, *Resp. Kiryat Ḥannah* (Metz); Nehemiah Faivel Halevi Duschenes, *Sefer Divre Neba* (Prague). Yonah Landsofer, *Resp. Me'il Tzedakah* (Prague). Joshua Heschel Lvov, *Resp. Penei Levanah* (Metz, Trier, Schwabach). There are a few other references in early modern responsa that mention these practices further to the east, mainly Prague, though these are fewer in number.[140] In addition, the following collections of communal and rabbinic court *pinkasim* contain references to *be'ohev*: the Pinkas Kahal of Metz; the Court Diary of Rabbi Hayyim Gundersheim, Frankfurt; the Pinkas Gabbaim of the Kolin synagogue; and the Pinkas Kahal of Furth. These sources indicate that there were several additional localities outside of the Rhineland where *be'ohev* was practiced.[141] One could not know from published responsa that this instrument was widely employed. The prevalence of *be'ohev* is explained as a response to social and economic conditions peculiar to communities in western Europe, and its normative standing can be observed in communal laws and records.

One explanation for the popularity of *be'ohev* in Metz is its remarkable similarity to new borrowing practices in France in the second half of the eighteenth century. As Elise Dermineur has suggested, economic partnerships between spouses became stronger, which accounts for a dramatic increase in joint loans contracted to husbands and wives. Changes in the credit market and in the

---

138 See *Shulḥan 'Arukh, Ḥoshen Mishpat* §77:1–3; Maimonides, *Mishneh Torah*, Laws of Agents and Partners 4:3, and Laws of the Creditor and Borrower 25:10.

139 The *be'ohev* loan is very rarely referenced in the responsa literature. See Bacharach, *Resp. Ḥavvot Ya'ir*, no. 78; Reischer, *Resp. Shevut Ya'akov*, pt. 1, no. 155; and ibid., pt. 2, no. 150. At the end of his responsum, Bacharach referred to a communal enactment that alleviated the plight of women in such cases by granting each woman the right to contest what was acquired by her husband, which in turn freed her from the obligation to draw on funds meant for her *ketubah* settlement.

140 In addition to the sources listed in n. 139, see *Resp. Kiryat Ḥannah*, no. 17; *Resp. Me'il Tzedakah*, no. 44; Nehemiah Faivel Halevi Duschenes, *Sefer Divre Neba* (1688), no. 77, parag. 13; and *Resp. Penei Levanah*, no. 37.

141 See *Prishah, Ḥoshen Mishpat*, §131:12; *Hafla'ah Kuntrus Aharon*, 90.

general economy compelled men to establish a more cooperative financial relationship with their wives, and this meant that households were managed conjointly. Nevertheless, a married woman, according to Dermineur, could refuse to sign a deed, and she had the option to withdraw her lineage property and petition for a *séparation de biens* from her husband's property if she felt that the transaction was too risky. These developments amounted to an important shift, where "males were no longer in command of their households [;] ... the fact that her lineage property and assets were at stake did not represent a reinforcement of patriarchy, but rather a breach in it." Accordingly, wives were expected to assume a more active role in the management of the household.[142]

The market changes were accompanied by an increase in the percentage of married couples that borrowed money. In the new economic environment in the last decades of the ancien régime, the wife's signature furnished greater assurance to the lender. It guaranteed that even if her husband died first, she and/or their children would still be obligated to repay the lender. It has also been suggested that this new form of borrowing enhanced the couple's interdependency.[143] The Beit Din's insistence on the use of these mechanisms suggests that the priority over other creditors accorded to commercial lenders, as codified by the *Shulḥan ʿArukh*, may not have been universally normative.[144] The prevalence of the custom, despite the fact that a married woman was under no obligation to co-sign a loan agreement with her husband, even when

142 Dermineur, "Female Peasants, Patriarchy, and the Credit Market," 68. In theory, separation requests provided leverage in re-negotiating the husband's behavior. A separation decree gave wives the status of first creditor of the household over all other lenders. Nevertheless, the economic situation of women remained precarious since most petitions were lodged only after family resources had disappeared. See Julie Hardwick, *Practice of Patriarchy*, 111–16. The fact that the phenomenon of women borrowing together with their husband in Metz is not attested either in the local *Coûtumes* or in those of Lorraine may be due to the fact that the regional customs books tended to reproduce customs of earlier periods and were slow in recording newer practices. Thus, in the case of the Metz *Coûtumes* published in 1769, the text was virtually identical with the 1732 edition.

143 On the economic partnership in marriage, see Dermineur, "Female Peasants, Patriarchy, and the Credit Market," and Olwen Hufton, "Women in the Family Economy in Eighteenth-Century France," *French Historical Studies* (1975): 17–18. The view of the family presented in these works is at odds with the portrait painted by Mousnier. Mousnier argued that with the advance of Roman law, the absolute power of heads of families grew stronger, especially as it became associated with the will of the state. See *Les institutions de la France*, 1:84–85.

144 See the ruling in *Shulḥan ʿArukh, Even ha-ʿEzer* §102:1–2, in accordance with the view attributed to Amemar in BT Ketubot 86a, whereby a creditor may take priority over a wife's claim. The exception is if one deals with chattel, he has priority over the wife. See PMBD, Vol. 1, pt. 2, no. 29, 9b, and Vol. 2, no. 538, 110a–b.

their property was owned communally, is clear evidence of its recognized economic utility. Most important, the lending arrangement indicates that economic partnerships between husbands and wives were more common than is generally assumed and that women were more actively involved in financial and commercial transactions.[145] This is certainly borne out in the proceedings of the Beit Din.

The fact that a wife was not personally liable for the debts her husband incurred after they married unless she explicitly and formally assumed liability in a joint commercial undertaking proves that the marital union per se did not create a legally cognizable economic partnership. From the standpoint of Jewish law, financial relations between spouses, as in all monetary matters, were governed by the principle of freedom of contract, and as in civil matters, one could stipulate contrary to biblical law.[146] In fact, the Metz community did not have the authority to impose unrestricted liability on women,[147] as was done in Frankfurt, where a *takkanah* issued in 1627 declared "that women are obligated to pay with their husbands in everything he has transacted according to a *kinyan sudar* (acquisition via the exchange of a symbolic object), unless the woman had previously come before the appointed witnesses and explicitly demanded that no contract or agreement be made by her husband without her knowledge."[148]

So far as extant records indicate, the Metz Kehillah never enacted a ruling of this sort; nonetheless, it was possible to impose debt liability on wives, as in localities where women were accustomed to engage in commercial activities. The talmudic category of *nos'et ve-notenet be-tokh ha-bayit* (conducting business in the home) was expanded in the Middle Ages to include any woman whose husband had entrusted her with his property. By virtue of her access to his property, whether she was gainfully employed or not, a wife bore the burden of proof to verify that the property was hers. In the modern period, as women were engaged more regularly in gainful employment, there was a growing acknowledgement that they were entitled to amass property of their own.

145 See Dermineur, "Female Peasants, Patriarchy, and the Credit Market."

146 On the principle of freedom of contract, see BT Kiddushin 19b; Ketubot 56a; and Tosefta Kiddushin 3:7–8.

147 This formulation reverses the position set forth in *Protocols of Justice*, 179.

148 The *takkanah* was subsequently limited to transactions in which both parties were residents of Frankfurt and stated that a woman's obligation to repay her husband's creditors was limited to jointly owned funds. This revision protected a woman's personal property and ensured that she did not unknowingly become a guarantor for her husband. For an analysis of the regulation, see Debra Kaplan, "Women and Worth: Female Access to Property in Early Modern Urban Jewish Communities," *Leo Baeck Year Book* 55 (2010): 93–113.

Although it is impossible even to approximate the percentage of women in Metz and in the surrounding region who were employed outside the home, it certainly appears that it was unexceptional for women to engage in commerce and to accumulate their own property.[149]

Not surprisingly, then, with the greater prominence enjoyed by *be'ohev*, western *posekim* became progressively involved in debating its legal parameters and ramifications for women. Based on the formulation of the Tur and the Tosafists, Jacob Reischer ruled that the creditor's collection from assets that would otherwise go to pay her *ketubah* was limited to localities where women conducted business on their own. However, where they did not engage in business on their own, then even half of the debt was not collected from her *ketubah*; everything would be paid out of the estate, and subsequently she would receive her *ketubah* payment, because the lien she accepted was intended only to subordinate her priority in collecting her *ketubah* but not to nullify her entitlement. Reischer's student, Gershon Koblenz, a *dayan* in Metz in the early and mid-eighteenth century, cited the ruling of his teacher that, in the circumstance of *be'ohev*, a woman was not obligated to repay a loan because she was only a guarantor (*'arev*), which limited her liability when the borrower owned assets.[150] According to Koblenz, this meant that she could not be considered an *'arev kablan*, and if her husband left nothing, she was not obligated to repay the loan, even if afterwards she was able to assemble assets. In his view, if insufficient funds remained for the *ketubah* or for both of them, the creditor was not entitled to collect from the wife at all, even when he would otherwise collect from the *arev*.[151] These two citations suggest that once *be'ohev* entered common practice, *posekim* were naturally inclined to debate finer points of Halakhah, especially with regard to when and under which circumstances it was to be applied.

The economic developments that created new professional opportunities for women and enhanced their position in the family could not guarantee that they would be shielded from the perils of financial hardship or ruin. In fact,

149 On the talmudic phrase *nos'et ve-notenet be-tokh ha-bayit*, see BT Sanhedrin 14a. See Katz's analysis of BT Bava Batra 52b in "The Married Woman," 115–16. Also see Warburg, "A Comparative Analysis of a Wife's Capacity to Pledge her Husband's Credit." Clare Crowston has suggested in a similar manner that through access to trade credit, the "provisioning housewife" gained a measure of financial autonomy that was recognized in the courts. See Crowston, "Family Affairs," 62–70. For evidence of gainful work among Jewish women in Pontpierre (Steinbiedersdorf) and nearby villages, see Ulbrich, *Shulamit and Margarete*, 195–96.

150 See Reischer, *Resp. Shevut Yaakov*, pt. 1, no. 155.

151 Koblenz, *Resp. Kiryat Hannah*, no. 17.

in some instances the role of women in the expanding economy of the eighteenth century exposed them to financial risks and pressures of a new sort. One sign of the changing times was precisely the trend mentioned earlier for wives to co-sign loan notes to enable a husband to secure a loan. This effectively subordinated the priority over other claimants that the wife otherwise enjoyed under her *ketubah*. The proliferation of this mechanism was a clear indication of financial pressure that altered traditional property arrangements in marriage. The Beit Din records contain considerable evidence of the economic vulnerability to which women were susceptible. In numerous instances women were rendered destitute when their husbands suffered financial setbacks or incurred heavy debts from which they could not extricate themselves. Malka, wife of Me'ir Charry, complained to the Beit Din that her husband had fled to escape his creditors, leaving her without resources to support herself and her children. The Beit Din ruled that he was in violation of his obligations. Meantime, she fell very ill out of distress, to the point that her father hired a caretaker for her. The Beit Din sent two judges to investigate her husband's behavior towards his wife, both during her illness and before. They reported that he was unable to give her even poor man's bread and water or to care for her needs during her illness. Malka therefore requested permission to stay at her father's house for as long as she desired.[152]

There are cases of women from prominent families who approached the Beit Din with heartrending stories of impoverishment, accompanied by desperate appeals to the mercy of the court. Hendele Reise, from a prominent Metz rabbinic family—she was the daughter of Rabbi Meir Trenel (d. 1764) and of Miram (Lambert)—approached the Beit Din with the tale of how she and her husband, Itzik Reise of Frankfurt, had become penniless and were now in dire need of assistance:

> I am an embittered woman, for the hand of God struck me and my house is empty of all and nothing remains to me and my husband, and nothing is left for us to claim from two estates, from the estate of my father Rabbi Me'ir Trenel and from the estate of my mother. So that we have no claim on these two estates and only a credit of 6,400 livres that remained in the hand of my brother of 9,000 livres, proceeds of my portion of debts and cash that were left from my mother's estate in the hand of my brother.[153]

---

152 PMBD, Vol. 2, no. 8, 2a.

153 See PMBD, Vol. 2, no. 199, 38a. The following is the original Hebrew text:
הנה אשה קשת רוח אנכי. כי נגע בי יד ה׳ וביתי ריקם מכל ולא נשאר לי ולבעלי הנ״ל כלום ולא נשאר
לנו לתבוע משני עזבונם הן מעזבון אבי כמד״ה מאיר טרעני הנ״ל והן מעזבון אמי מ׳ מרים הנ״ל. באופן

Hendele asked the court to grant her and her husband a dispensation regarding the exit tax (*Abzug*) and communal taxes, which the Beit Din granted.[154]

Edel Halphen, also from a prominent family, found herself in a similar circumstance. When her husband Shmuel fled to escape his creditors, she and her children moved to the house of her father, Mordechai Terquem Upon her father's death, Edel was compelled to borrow money to makes ends meet and to provide funds so that her husband would be able to return home. Quarrels between heirs and with creditors pressured Edel to reach a quick court settlement so she might collect her entitlement from the estate without delay. Recognizing that her proposal was intended to benefit her husband and that she had already received *autorisation* (permission) to this effect from the French civil court, the Beit Din issued an official court statement that all of her actions from the day of the death of her father until her husband's return were valid, "as if her husband had agreed with her. And all that she will do or borrow, or the settlements and obligations she undertakes, or law suits against creditors of the estate, will be valid and no complaint or appeal, from any person, will have any effect on this."[155]

It was not uncommon for a widow to find herself in difficult straits after discovering that the assets remaining in her husband's estate were insufficient to meet his obligations to her under the terms of the *ketubah*. Poignant stories tell of women whose vulnerability was exposed by the death, illness, or insolvency of their husbands, or by his desertion. Rivka [Cahen], was abandoned by her husband Koppel [Jacob b. Moses] May and left without funds to support herself and her family.[156] In another instance, Miriam, the pregnant widow of Yidla Sierck, came before the Beit Din claiming her *ketubah* and *tosefta* and a portion of the debts owed to the estate of her husband. She was granted support for food, for herself and her children, through the preceding Rosh Hodesh Heshvan, and annual support for her children thereafter. The Beit Din ruled that Miriam would manage her husband's estate, both to collect outstanding debts and to sell the silver and movables in accordance with the appraisal of experts. Required to report periodically to the Beit Din to show receipts and expenses, she missed one meeting after giving birth. Now the mother of four children, she was faced with the daunting challenge of collecting uncertain debts to make ends meet.[157]

שאין לנו שום תביעה משני עזבונם הנ״ל ולא מחמתם בעזבון אחי כ״ה וואלף הנ״ל כי אם בזכות של ששה אלפים וארבע מאו׳ ליוור שנשארו ביד אחי הנ״ל מן התשעה אלפים ליוור דמי מכירת חלקי מחובו׳ ומזומני׳ שנשארו מעזבון אמי הנ״ל ביד אחי הנ״ל.

154 PKM.

155 PMBD, Vol. 2, no. 12, 3a.

156 PMBD, Vol. 2, no. 263, 49b.

157 See PMBD, Vol. 1, pt. 1, no. 60, 18a; no. 79, 27b; no. 113, 38b.

The example of Theresa (Tertzcha), wife of Wolff Silesia, reveals another aspect of this phenomenon.[158] Theresa and her children were abandoned by her husband who departed for Paris, evidently to escape creditors, shortly before their daughter's wedding. Theresa was unable to meet the dowry commitment of 2,400 livres—a considerable sum that suggests the family had been affluent and that the devastating setback it suffered occurred not long before. The burden of the dowry aside, community tax collectors placed an injunction on proceeding with the wedding so long as the husband's accrued taxes remained unpaid. To satisfy the dowry obligation and to pay off the taxes owed by her husband, Theresa sought authorization from the Beit Din to sell her husband's synagogue seats and to transfer a seat he owned in the women's section to the Kahal. The Beit Din approved these requests and ruled that the husband had no right to appeal.[159]

In another case, it was estimated that the amount still owed to the estate of the deceased would not equal even one-tenth of the widow's *ketubah* claim.[160] Reichele, widow of Mendele Zay, was the victim of circumstances that had a comparable effect, though it is possible that she was privy to her husband's financial troubles. Her vulnerability stemmed from having entered into an *ʿarevut kablanut* arrangement with her husband that obligated her for her husband's debts. As a result, creditors' claims totaling 4,000 livres were still enforceable, while the estate had become depleted by the failure of several individuals to whom Zay had extended credit to meet their obligations. The amount owed to her husband totaled 15,000 livres, which left insufficient funds to satisfy the *ketubah* payment to which she was entitled. Under the supervision of the Beit Din, Reichele swore that there were no outstanding debts that she expected to collect. Her house, following an appraisal, was transferred to her in partial satisfaction of her *ketubah* settlement, leaving a shortfall of some 13,600 livres of her total claim. She asked the Beit Din to grant her a discharge (*silluk*) from her husband's estate approximately six years after his death. The

158 See, for example, PMBD, Vol. 1, pt. 1, no. 25, 11b; Vol. 1, pt. 2, no. 48, 13b; and Vol. 2, no. 294, 54a. In a case recorded in PMBD, Vol. 1, pt. 1, no. 123, 41a, it was estimated that what was still owed to the estate of the deceased would not reach even one-tenth of the amount necessary to satisfy the *ketubah*.

159 See PMBD, Vol. 1, pt. 2, no. 251, 54a, for a description of the plight of Gutcha, wife of Jospe Mali. Her husband fled from creditors and nothing was left for her to maintain her family. Her two children were placed with relatives. She approached the Beit Din with a request for help. The Beit Din ruled that her father-in-law must keep one child with him, in his home, at his expense, or pay four livres to someone else to board the child. Her husband's brothers were required to pay three livres each month. For the case of Tertzcha, see PMBD, Vol. 1, pt. 2, nos. 146–147 36a.

160 See PMBD, Vol. 1, pt. 1, no. 25, 11b.

Beit Din granted her request so that she was released from the debts owed by her husband.[161]

Such tales of adversity and privation illustrate unambiguously that gender inequity and inequality were endemic to the structures and cultural assumptions of the eighteenth century. But they do not—or should not—obscure the significance of the interventions that the Metz Beit Din undertook and the legal strategies it employed to meet the challenges posed by changes to family and society. Which of these solutions were implemented would depend on both the court and the community. In general, court rulings were based on what was understood to be legally normative, and to this end the court was guided by changing communal and societal norms. In Metz, the law as understood by the Beit Din mirrored significant changes in the status of women, particularly in the areas of inheritance, guardianship, and commercial involvement. Economic forces were doubtless a major impetus for change, but no less important were the central role of the state and the broad impact of civil law in the transformation of family life.

161 See PMBD, Vol. 1, pt. 1, no. 131, 43a. The case was decided on 3 August 1774; Mendele Zay had died on 4 December 1768. Mendele and Reichele had been married in Metz on September 9, 1739. See Fleury, *Contrats de mariage juifs*, 164.

CHAPTER 8

Conclusion and Epilogue

In the National Constituent Assembly debate concerning the eligibility of Jews to become citizens of France, the Jewish autonomous regime was portrayed—and even vilified—as an obstacle that needed to be overcome. The suitability of the Jews for citizenship turned on the question whether the observance of Jewish law was compatible with the exercise of civic duties and full participation in the life of the country.[1] On this issue, partisans of Jewish emancipation harbored some of the same reservations that troubled their opponents. It was widely agreed that entitlement to civic equality required cessation of rabbinic jurisdiction in civil affairs. For some, it was a matter of relinquishing juridical authority in areas that had come under the jurisdiction of the state system of justice. For others, rabbinic jurisdiction in the civil realm evinced Judaism's conflation of the religious and political spheres and raised doubts about the Jews' ability to uphold the laws that united French citizens. Ultimately, the conferral of civic equality upon the Jews of Alsace and Lorraine in September 1791 was conditioned on their agreement to surrender this privilege. In a matter of months after the French Revolution, rabbinic courts no longer convened to hear civil cases—at least not formally—which brought the era of communal autonomy officially to a close.

Count Stanislas Marie Adélaide de Clermont-Tonnerre's oft-quoted pronouncement at the Assemblée Nationale on 23 December 1789 defined what would become the terms of Jewish emancipation in France. He declared that "[w]e must refuse everything to the Jews as a nation and accord everything to Jews as individuals. We must withdraw recognition from their judges; they should only have our judges. We must refuse legal protection to the maintenance of the so-called laws of their Judaic organization; they should not be allowed to form in the state either a political body or an order."[2] An outspoken

1 See Victor Tcherikover, *Hellenistic Civilization and the Jews* (Philadelphia, 1959), 320–27.

2 Translation by Lynn Hunt, *The French Revolution and Human Rights: A Brief Documentary History* (Boston, 1996), 88, based on the text that appeared in the *Archives parlementaires* 10 (Paris, 1878), 756. David Sorkin has examined the textual history of the Clermont-Tonnerre speech and has shown that there were two versions that circulated in the nineteenth century. The other text, which first appeared in the *Moniteur universel*, does not refer to the insistence on withdrawing recognition from Jewish judges nor the requirement that Jews adopting French judges. Sorkin makes a strong case for viewing the text produced in the *Archives parlementaires*, which is the one that Clermont-Tonnerre authorized for publication, as the more

 | DOI:10.1163/9789004417403_010

defender of individual liberty and a strong advocate for Jewish emancipation, Clermont-Tonnerre was committed to the creation of a constitutional monarchy empowered with centralized authority necessary to protect the state. As David Sorkin has argued, Clermont-Tonnerre was fiercely opposed to "all corporations as impediments to the centralized power of the monarchy" and concluded that "[t]he Jews could not have intermediate organizations of their own—whether judges, courts, or privileges."[3] Formulated by an ardent proponent of Jewish emancipation, the statement quickly cast Jewish autonomy in general, and juridical autonomy in particular, as relics of a bygone era.

The Constituent Assembly's verdict regarding the obsolescence of the Jewish autonomous regime vindicated the criticism leveled by proponents of the Enlightenment and the Haskalah. In their estimation, Jewish particularism was the antithesis of the Enlightenment. Contempt for rabbinic hegemony pervaded the writings of the foremost French philosophes and proponents of German Aufklarung and penetrated circles of *maskilim* across the continent. Voltaire accused the Jews of tribalism; he denounced their social and cultural separatism, and bemoaned their failure to uphold the standards of productivity, humanism, and morality acknowledged by all civilized societies. Baron de Montesquieu, who was more sympathetic to the historical plight of the Jews and was an admirer of biblical Judaism, was nonetheless highly critical of rabbinic culture and its purported deleterious effects on Jewish character.[4] Even the Jews' most ardent supporters conceded that centuries of oppression had left a lasting imprint on their behavior,[5] and though many granted that the Jews were scarcely to blame for their plight, they could not be relieved of responsibility for the moral corruption and antisocial conduct that was routinely imputed to them.[6] Under the influence of the Enlightenment, advocates of Jewish emancipation demanded that Jews renounce those cultural markers that prevented them from attaining citizenship.[7] A thin line of disagreement that separated critics and supporters of Jews was the question of whether the Jews could be redeemed from the corrupting effects of their

reliable. See David Sorkin, "The Count Stanislas Marie Adélaide de Clermont-Tonnerre's 'To the Jews as a Nation ...': The Career of a Quotation," Leo Baeck Institute Jerusalem, Jacob Katz Memorial Lecture, 2011.

3 Sorkin, "The Count Stanislas Marie Adélaide de Clermont-Tonnerre's 'To the Jews as a Nation.'"

4 See Pierre Auberry, "Montesquieu et les Juifs," *Studies on Voltaire and the Eighteenth Century* 87 (1972): 87–99; Montesquieu, *L'Esprit les lois*, ch. 12; idem, *Oeuvres complètes*, vol. 2, 746–49.

5 See, for example, Henri Grégoire, *Motion en faveur des Juifs* (Paris, 1789), 12.

6 See Schechter, *Obstinate Hebrews: Representations of Jews in France*, 77–82.

7 Hertzberg, *The French Enlightenment and the Jews*, and Sepinwall, *The Abbé Grégoire and the French Revolution*.

religious heritage and corporate ethos, and if so, what steps were necessary to realize this goal.

The Pinkas Kahal of Metz and the Pinkas Beit Din offer two divergent perspectives on the struggle to meet the challenges of the eighteenth century. The Pinkas Kahal is replete with evidence that communal leaders were anxious about the apparent steady decline in the commitment of Metz Jews to the religious tradition. This is evident in numerous efforts to reinforce time-honored commitments to prayer, charity, and study; to bolster traditional sexual mores; and to impose rigorous controls on the behavior of youths. The Kahal was determined to advance the shared objectives of the community in areas that required policy-making, and no less important, endeavored to safeguard the reputation of the community, either by taking steps to correct internal problems or to address the issues politically with governmental authorities.

A vastly different account of the Metz community and its challenges emerges from the rabbinic court protocols. The Pinkas of the Metz Beit Din tells a story that varies substantially from traditional accounts of the relationship between Jews and general society. It offers exceptionally detailed evidence of acculturation to a degree that greatly exceeds what has been reported in the historical literature. From what is seen in the court records, the Jews of Metz were far more engaged with the cultural and economic dimensions of the society around them than is generally assumed. Linguistic assimilation, compliance with bureaucratic requirements, and fluency in the material culture of northeastern France offer valuable indications of acculturation on the part of the Jews in Metz and in the *pays messin*. Whether its characterization as "porous" is overstated, especially in light of adverse social and political conditions under which early modern Jews lived, is a question I leave to the judgment of others. Furthermore, the methods of legal adjudication, and more generally, the conception of jurisprudence practiced by the Metz Beit Din, illustrate strikingly the broad scope of acculturation experienced by the urban—and, in many instances, even the rural—Jewish population. Historically, Jewish courts were the primary venue where competing lay and rabbinic interpretations of Jewish law, on the one hand, and the interaction between Jewish law and general law, on the other, were negotiated. In this respect, the court offers entrée to the most salient features of Jewish communal life during the past two millennia.

The conventional assessment of pre-modern Judaism—its intellectual stagnation, the inability of rabbinic culture to adapt to changing conditions, and the crumbling foundations of traditional Judaism that portended the community's imminent demise—was ultimately adopted by mainstream historians. In their view, Jewish communal autonomy was in a state of steady decline for much of the eighteenth century before it finally collapsed. Accordingly, rabbinic authority, the standing of Jewish courts, and the community's ability to enforce its laws and judicial rulings were overwhelmed by secularizing trends, mounting government interference in internal Jewish affairs, and growing recourse to non-Jewish courts.

This appraisal of Jewish life in the last stages of the autonomous regime has long been presumed to be applicable to the entire Ashkenazic world, though its empirical foundation is weak. Its appeal can be traced to the influence of the Enlightenment, particularly its severe critique of established religion, its anticlericalism, and its radical politics. Leading practitioners of the Haskalah developed a version of the Enlightenment worldview that may have appeared gentler, but their diagnosis of the problems facing their coreligionists in the decades leading to their emancipation and after was no less severe. To view the Enlightenment and the Haskalah as both the embodiment of modernity and the barometer of real-life conditions, is to embrace a perspective that risks distorting the historical reality and misrepresenting the role of religion in the modern era.

With its focus almost entirely on the struggle between modernizers and traditionalists, the conventional approach to the history of the period has diverted attention away from the central institutions of the community and from those who, despite their loyalty to religious tradition, interacted regularly with the larger society and culture.[8] There is no proof that this engagement with French society weakened their attachment to the core values of the Kehillah. Indeed, the Beit Din records point to a far more dynamic conception of Jewish communal autonomy than that presented to date. During this period and after, religion functioned as a primary source of community norms that defined public and private obligations. This was as true for society at large as for the Jewish community in Metz.

The Metz example challenges the assumption that Jewish communal institutions were slowly eroding to the point of deterioration over the course of the eighteenth century. Until the Revolution, legislation issued by the Kahal was highly detailed, comprehensive, and responsive to the needs of the community as identified by communal leaders. New administrative regulations, especially those pertaining to the election of *parnasim*, were enacted according to a strict schedule. Policy questions relating to poverty and poor relief, immigration, consumption, guardianship, inheritance, juridical autonomy, property transactions, and relations with governmental authorities were addressed with care and conscientiously. The state authorized the Beit Din, the

8 Katz, *Tradition and Crisis*, 214–36.

community's foremost judicial body, to adjudicate disputes based on Jewish legal traditions and customs. The rabbinic courts exercised jurisdiction over virtually the same range of civil cases handled by the French secular courts; they enjoyed a level of authority that far exceeded the independence granted to ecclesiastical courts.

Moreover, the Beit Din operated according to the highest professional standards. Its meetings kept to a regular schedule, it maintained meticulous judicial records, and it showed no signs of slowing down. Equally important was the bureaucratic function of lay and rabbinic tribunals. In addition to settling legal disputes, these courts handled numerous non-litigious civil actions, including property transfers, residence permits, labor contracts, appointment of guardians, preparation of probate inventories, and valuations of estates. These functions were in the category of *justice gracieuse* (noncontentious justice).[9] Overall, juridical autonomy was robust and the range of its authority impressive. In contrast to eastern Europe, there is little evidence of government interference in the internal affairs of the Metz community or that the authority of communal leaders was at all compromised.[10] Neither the communal register nor the Beit Din proceedings contain much evidence, either direct or indirect, of resistance to its juridical authority.

Metz *parnasim* actively solicited the political support of the monarchy and the Parlement to secure the autonomous powers of the community. Stressing both the historical basis for civil jurisdiction and its religious foundation, they argued that civil jurisdiction was essential if the communal leadership was to preserve internal discipline and guarantee royal tax collection.[11] The enforcement of communal laws and judicial decisions was essential to the autonomous rule of the community. Though physical coercion is not mentioned in these records and was rarely employed, if at all, both the Kahal and the Beit Din warned of far-reaching legal and economic consequences for failure to comply with communal law or judicial rulings. Behavior deemed to be in violation of community norms, failure to respond to a court summons, or negligence in the performance of public duties could result in the imposition of the *ḥerem*, fines, denial of religious honors in the synagogue, seizure of property, disqualification of legal rights, or withholding compensation for certain public tasks that were unsatisfactorily performed.[12]

9 Cf. Breen, "Law, Society, and the State in Early Modern France," 380.

10 Moshe Rosman has shown that a sign of this weakness was the tendency of Jews to invite non-Jewish authorities to help them resolve their conflicts. See Rosman, "The Role of Non-Jewish Authorities in Resolving Conflicts."

11 Katz, "To Judge and to Be Judged," 460.

12 PMBD, Vol. 1, pt. 1, no. 92, 31a.

Vested with wide-ranging judicial powers, the Beit Din exercised substantial influence on the self-governing communal structure by reinforcing the jurisdictional authority of the Kahal in matters of public law. Likewise, the Kahal provided the Beit Din with institutional support and a measure of independence that accounts for the substantial authority it enjoyed among residents of the community. Both the Kahal and the Beit Din exemplify the crucial role of the law in shaping the contours of communal life. The all-encompassing efforts to regulate communal life continued steadfastly until the very end of the ancien régime—to all intents and purposes, undeterred by the entrenchment of Metz Jews in the surrounding social, cultural, and political landscape. In areas of law pertaining to inheritance, marital property, and the disadvantaged, the Beit Din displayed flexibility and determination in its efforts to achieve equitable solutions.

Contrary to the conventional view, the ascendancy of the lay leadership in most European communities did not come about at the expense of rabbinic authority in Metz, though this requires qualification. While lay and rabbinic leaders cooperated in communal affairs, the syndics were fully responsible for the administration of the community. The steady increase in lay power over the course of the eighteenth century is apparent in the ever more rigorous lay regulation of religious affairs, including appointment of rabbinic and lower religious functionaries; definition of rabbinic duties; supervision of ritual slaughtering; oversight of charity; and discipline for religious and moral abuses. Nevertheless, there is little evidence in Metz of rabbis and syndics competing for power and no overt signs of clashes over communal policy—in sharp contrast to conditions in eastern Europe where the political struggle between the lay and rabbinic leadership was far more pronounced.[13] The absence in the documentary record of challenges to the authority of the Beit Din and to the Kahal leadership is glaring, so glaring that some might argue that the omission was deliberate. But solid evidence of collaboration between lay and rabbinic leaders confirms that the silence of the sources has probative value. The *av beit din* was a partner in electoral procedures, including opening ballots and administering the oath to newly elected communal officials, and he was involved as well in formalizing communal legislation. Rabbinic participation in community policy discussions also signified the civic role played by clergy. Collaboration between the Beit Din and the Kahal was not uncommon when a legal matter implicated the community at large. Metz communal and judicial records challenge the claim that anticlerical trends in

13 See Bell, *The Jews in the Early Modern World*, 102–104, 131, and Teller, "Laicization of Early Modern Jewish Society."

European society had weakened the role of religion in the Jewish community and undercut rabbinic authority. They confirm Roger Chartier's view that the rise of the European Enlightenment cannot be taken as evidence of the decline of religion but, rather, is a product of "the secularization of scholarship in the twentieth century."[14]

The commissioning of the French translation of Jewish law, *Recueil des lois, coûtumes et usages observés par les juifs de Metz*, reveals an important dimension of juridical autonomy that is better understood in terms of legal centralism and legal pluralism.[15] Legal centralism embodied the idea that law was the exclusive domain of the state and the foremost instrument of state bureaucracy; it demanded that foreign systems subordinate themselves to state authority. Legal pluralism, by contrast, acknowledged the validity of multiple legal orders and jurisdictions. Two models of juridical autonomy prevailed in the second half of the eighteenth century. One stressed the jurisdictional preference to settle disputes in a Jewish court. A second model that had been available since the early decades of the eighteenth century when the Metz Parlement challenged the exclusive authority of the community to judge civil matters, entailed adjudication in French courts, with the proviso that the judgment would be in accordance with Jewish law. While *lettres patentes* assured that the production of the *Recueil* would not prejudice the right of Jews to settle their disputes in their own courts, it seems clear that those who encouraged Jewish litigation in the French courts viewed the translation as a step in that direction. Whichever the case, the decision to codify Jewish law in a compendium accessible to French judges anticipated the revolutionary era debate surrounding Jewish citizenship.[16] But until the Revolution, state-building as understood by the monarchy was not limited to the imposition of centralized law but aspired to the efficient management of diversity under state supervision.

Metz communal leaders were driven by a powerful impulse to work cooperatively with the French legal system. The impact of legal pluralism can be discerned in the court's adoption and adaptation of legal perspectives

---

14 Roger Chartier has argued further that "the Revolution invented the Enlightenment by attempting to root its legitimacy in a corpus of texts." See Roger Chartier, *The Cultural Origins of the French Revolution* (Durham, N.C., 1991), 5. Also see Margaret Lavinia Anderson, "The Limits of Secularization: On the Problem of the Catholic Revival in Nineteenth-Century Germany," *The Historical Journal* 38 (September 1995): 647–70. Jonathan Sheehan has suggested that the Enlightenment and its main features—secularization, modernization, liberalism, freedom of religion and thought—are a fiction. See Sheehan, "Enlightenment, Religion, and the Enigma of Secularization," 1071–72.

15 See Lançon, *Recueil des lois, coûtumes et usages observés par les juifs de Metz*.

16 *Lettres patentes*, 20 August 1742.

and mechanisms from general jurisprudence, both in the realm of procedure and in substantive areas of law. The need to coordinate was felt keenly in every area involving property, monetary exchange, and contractual agreements. Accordingly, evidence of procedural cooperation with French courts abounds, as do efforts to navigate between the competing jurisdictions of the Jewish and French legal systems. Equally important is the question how legal integration—a clear acknowledgment of the prevailing systems of law and justice through compliance with administrative, bureaucratic, and legal requirements imposed by the state—affected the internal processes of adjudication and jurisprudence.

Although as noted above, the Metz Beit Din enjoyed substantial independence from state interference and was granted greater latitude by the state to resolve internal differences on the basis of Jewish legal traditions, neither the Kahal nor the Beit Din could ignore pressures to coordinate with, and adapt to, general law. Adaptation was a highly complex phenomenon that posed numerous dilemmas for a minority seeking to maintain its cultural distinctiveness while acknowledging the need to be part of the larger social, economic, and cultural matrix.

The analysis proposed in *Law's Dominion* rests on two interrelated assumptions. First, that law, by its very nature, is entrenched in the normative structures and cultural particularities of diverse groups within society; and second, that law is a bottom-up, decentralized process that responds to social and political realities while also mirroring the creative impulses of the wider population.[17] This suggestion is certainly not intended to deny the role of governing elites and centralized institutions in the production of law. It is patently evident that the protocols of the Metz Beit Din were highly stylized texts, filled with unmistakable evidence of rabbinic learning, lucidity, and legal precision. To communicate the court's rulings and the steps leading to each judicial decision, the meticulous formulations that characterize the Pinkas were produced under the careful guidance and scrutiny of the judiciary itself. But it is equally apparent—in substance and in style—that neither the Beit Din nor the records it kept were at all removed from the community it served. This observation is consistent with recent studies on early modern France that have discarded the idea of law as a tool utilized solely by social elites and the state to impose its authority on society at large. Rather, the law and the courts also

17 See, for example, Mathieu Deflem, *Sociology of Law: Visions of a Scholarly Tradition* (Cambridge, 2008).

regulated society from the bottom up, functioning as instruments employed by local populations, and the state as well, to protect family and property.[18]

Proceedings of the Metz Beit Din evince the culture of the consumers of law as prominently as the culture of its producers. Linguistic patterns, affinity with French material culture, proficiency in the technical details of commercial law, and close contact with the legal and administrative bureaucracy in Metz and the Moselle offer evidence of stronger attachment to the surrounding society than has been observed previously. The Metz Beit Din is distinguished from rabbinic courts in other localities by its collaborative relationship with the French civil court system. This resulted from the growing power of the state, the emerging consensus that the state ought to rule its citizens directly, and the increasing sense that a uniform legal code would promote the inclusion of the Jews in civil society. Within this context Metz Jews encountered the challenges of legal pluralism daily. But more than simply adapting to the prevailing system of French law, rabbinic judges strongly acknowledged the interdependence of cases brought before the Jewish tribunal and the French civil court system. The Beit Din was nonetheless beset by the continuing dilemma of how to reconcile the competing demands of communal autonomy, on the one hand, and legal centralism and pluralism, on the other.

The exposure to French law, administration, and the justice system stemmed from routine bureaucratic demands imposed on residents of the region and from frequent litigation between Jews and non-Jews in financial, commercial, and property disputes. At work, as Tocqueville maintained, was a long process of administrative centralization in the absolutist state that unleashed powerful forces of cultural transformation prior to the Revolution.[19] It is reasonable to assume that encounters with the civil institutions in Metz exerted a formative influence on Jewish cultural identity and influenced what Jews had come to expect of their own court system. Indeed, wider patterns of legal integration and acculturation exerted a profound impact on the judicial conduct of the Beit Din. While loyalty to the principles of Jewish law was unquestionably the cornerstone of rabbinic jurisprudence, the Beit Din was also extremely sensitive to the changing cultural norms observed in the Metz Jewish community. Its responsiveness to the needs of the wider public may be taken as a reflection of its relationship to the Kahal and is evident in its compliance with communal legislation in areas such as inheritance and litigation in gentile courts.

---

18 Breen, "Law, Society, and the State in Early Modern France," 360.

19 Alexis de Tocqueville, *L'Ancien Regime et la Révolution* (Paris, 1967). See Roger Chartier, *The Cultural Origins of the French Revolution* (London, 1991), 10–18.

Conformity to these guidelines went hand in hand with its acknowledgment of equity and public welfare as defined by the community. Repeatedly, the Metz Beit Din displayed a capacity to navigate the tensions between formal rules of law and the changing social, cultural, and economic realities of the times. Guided by classical traditions that viewed the attainment of justice as the central goal of the judicial process, the Beit Din discouraged improper but technically legal behavior. Some of the decisions of the Beit Din reveal the imprint of broader societal trends on the legal culture of Metz Jews and what they may have expected of the Beit Din. The relative prominence of women in the commercial and financial arenas is a case in point and is reflected in several important ways: Litigation initiated by women constituted roughly twenty-five percent of the cases, and approximately forty percent of the cases recorded in the Pinkas involved women either as claimants or defendants. With increasing regularity, the Beit Din approved the appointment of women as guardians over the property of orphans, despite the misgivings expressed in codified halakhic sources. The routine use of mechanisms to allocate inheritance portions to daughters mirrored a wider interest in promoting equitable distribution of inherited property among offspring. In response to new developments in the general credit market, the Beit Din made use of mechanisms aimed at formalizing the role of women as partners in the financial and commercial activities of their husbands.

The urgency of resolving the dissonance between the Jewish and general legal systems was likely more pronounced in Metz than in rabbinic courts of similar stature in the eighteenth century.[20] The Metz rabbinic court proceedings reveal an astute appreciation for the fact that the Jews inhabited two distinct legal universes. That awareness is evident in bilingual contracts and in the use of particular language to indicate compliance with the demands of both judicial systems. Both required of the Beit Din a high level of familiarity with the finer points of civil law and judicial procedure. The Beit Din's adaptation to the prevailing system of French law is illustrated by repeated references to judgments that had been issued by the *bailliage* court to Jewish litigants who subsequently came before the rabbinic court.[21] Moreover, there was a strong acknowledgment of the interdependence of cases brought before the Beit Din and in the French civil court system.[22] Legal consultations with French *avocats*, whether initiated by the Beit Din or by the litigants themselves, served as

20 Fram, *A Window on their World*, passim.

21 See, for example, PMBD, Vol. 1, pt. 2, no. 49, 14a; Vol. 2, no. 254, 47b; and Vol. 2, no. 345, 64b for references to cases that had been settled in the *bailliage*.

22 See, for example, PMBD, Vol. 1, pt. 1, no. 77, 27a.

a bridge between the Jewish and French judicial systems. By turning to legal experts, the rabbinic court and litigants revealed their dependence on detailed knowledge of French law and judicial practice. In several instances French lawyers were asked to clarify the prevailing law of the land (*dina d'malkhuta*). Adherence to the talmudic aphorism, which acknowledged the two distinct legal frameworks to which Jews pledged their allegiance, demanded detailed knowledge of the larger legal setting.

Metz Beit Din proceedings are filled with a positive orientation toward the dynamic relationship between Jewish and general law. To be sure, the court functioned in a politically charged environment that limited its freedom to contravene the prevalence of legal centralism and legal pluralism. In large measure, French law owed its abiding influence to the infrastructural power of the state and the legitimacy it gave to the pervasive bureaucracy that intruded on the personal lives of its citizens. The Beit Din could hardly ignore the legal and institutional supremacy of the state. Nevertheless, there are rather clear indications that the orientation of the rabbinic court was more than simply capitulation to the stronger partner. How exceptional was the flexibility and collaborative spirit evinced by the Metz Beit Din? While its conduct was, without question, a unique response to the particular constellation of forces at work in Metz, one may assume that the Beit Din was guided in its judicial approach by an established tradition of Jewish law. This is exceedingly difficult to establish, since the legal reasoning and interpretive methods employed by the Beit Din are never disclosed, but there is no question that the Beit Din was on very firm footing. What follows is an attempt to construct a theory of Jewish law that accounts for the rather remarkable performance of the Metz rabbinic court.

Rooted in a wide range of classical and medieval rabbinic sources, the principles of legal flexibility and openness to external influences have been enlisted by Jewish legal authorities regularly to promote fairness, high ethical standards, and the public welfare. Such trends have been noted by classical and medieval scholars. Aaron Kirschenbaum demonstrated how, since the talmudic era, considerations of equity have frequently overruled formal legal requirements, particularly when unyielding and overly restrictive rules risked subverting the ultimate aim of a law.[23] Based on a careful investigation of the laws of moneylending in medieval Provence, Haym Soloveitchik provided

23 See Aaron Kirschenbaum, *Equity in Jewish Law: Beyond Equity: Halakhic Aspirationism in Jewish Civil Law*, 2 vols. (Hoboken, NJ, 1991); for examples relating to judicial procedure, see 1: xxxix–xlii, and 2:57–149. On the nullification of communal regulations on the grounds of immorality and injustice, see Elon, *Jewish Law*, 2:760–79.

persuasive evidence of interaction between the Jewish and Provençal legal systems, reciprocal influences, and the receptivity of Jewish jurists to general jurisprudence.[24] Shmuel Shilo suggested that some *posekim* were willing to consider the authority of secular law as binding when rabbinic authorities viewed a particular non-Jewish regulation as equitable. His examples, drawn from medieval Spain and Germany, refer to laws that regulated the rights of creditors and rules governing legal counsel. Concerning the latter, Shilo notes the argument advanced by Rabbi Israel of Brunn, that while there was no regulation in Jewish law that restricted an attorney from representing two sides in a dispute, the law prohibiting that practice in non-Jewish courts was an equitable provision that ought to be adopted in Jewish law. Since it is assumed that Jewish law could not be morally inferior to gentile law, behavior that was otherwise permissible according to the strict interpretation of Jewish law would be banned.[25] In a similar fashion, Moses Isserles ruled that a *beit din* was obliged to honor a civil law forbidding a lender from selling an item held as collateral until one year had passed, even though Jewish law permitted its sale thirty days after a borrower's default. His ruling accepted the premise that the civil law was designed to meet social and economic needs.[26]

On the procedural level, the relationship between Jewish law and general law is far more fluid than is customarily acknowledged. Suzanne Last Stone has suggested that the civil laws (*dinim*) subsumed under the Noahide Code have been understood historically to complement the Sinaitic code and to serve "as a residual source of law" that enabled rabbinic authority to set aside Sinaitic procedure. How far this can be taken is a question of considerable consequence. Some have limited the residual authority of the Noahide laws to the king and to the blood avenger seeking justice on behalf of a murdered kinsman, whereas J. David Bleich has argued convincingly that the authority of the Noahide laws extended to the institution of the Beit Din. Accordingly, the

24 Haym Soloveitchik, "Jewish and Provençal Law: A Study in Interaction," *Mélanges Roger Aubenas* (Montpellier, 1974), 711–723.

25 Shmuel Shilo, "Equity as a Bridge between Jewish and Secular Law," *Cardozo Law Review* 12 (1991): 742–8. On the idea that Jewish law does not permit behavior that is prohibited to gentiles, see BT Sanhedrin 59a. Some authorities argue that the secular law can be incorporated into Jewish law in order to fill a legal vacuum. In some instances, there has been outspoken opposition to the incorporation of general law, as is apparent in a responsum issued by Solomon ben Aderet (Rashba). Rashba's ruling exemplifies the classical rejection of recourse to non-Jewish law. Referring to a case concerning dowry and inheritance, he objected to settling the dispute in the general court because by so doing the plaintiff appeared to favor gentile law. See Solomon ben Aderet, *Resp. Rashba* 6:254.

26 Isserles, *Shulḥan 'Arukh, Ḥoshen Mishpat* §369:11 and §73:14. For an opposing view, see Shabbetai ha-Cohen, *Siftei Cohen, Ḥoshen Mishpat* §73:39.

Noahide Code can be viewed as a valid source for the continuing development of Jewish civil procedure and that the two codes, the Sinaitic and the Noahide, are complementary. The Jewish obligation to preserve social order, in Stone's view, derives from its pre-Sinaitic past and is embodied in the Noahide command to establish a civil justice system.[27] While we cannot verify that the Metz Beit Din understood the complementary relationship between the Noahide laws and the Sinaitic Code as a model for its own judicial practice, it appears that the court's positive orientation vis-à-vis French law rested on a comparable theory of legal pluralism and openness to external influences. Members of the Metz Beit Din understood that law, in the broadest sense, was essential for the preservation of the social order. Preferring functionalism over formalism, the court regarded law as constructed within a social context and not as an external force that acts upon society. The records of the Metz court challenge the very idea of an insular Jewish legal system and an insular Jewish culture.

While the integration of the Jews in a unified legal system was not synonymous with civic equality, nor did it confer freedom from prejudice,[28] there is ample evidence of their engagement with the surrounding society. Jews of Metz had little choice but to accommodate general civil law and its structures. The fact that litigants brought their disputes to legal institutions outside the Kehillah—in some instances with the blessings of the Beit Din and the communal leadership—is proof that Metz Jews were at once engaged in multiple social frameworks. But it would be incorrect to portray these patterns as constituting an unequivocal sense of belonging to a broader community. Prior to 1789, ethnic and religious ties were still powerful coordinates of identity, and the legal disabilities suffered by Jews in Metz and elsewhere remained potent reminders that French society was not welcoming to the Jews. Nevertheless, Jews were more strongly attached to general society than has been hitherto recognized. While there certainly were instances when litigants played the Jewish legal system off against the French system in their quest for the most favorable legal outcome, a hierarchical relationship between the Beit Din and the French courts appears to have emerged, and it was considered natural to go to the latter with certain types of disputes.

Even prior to their civic emancipation, Metz Jews found in the law a predictable ordering of reality that was governed by rules and reason. Law was a

27 See Suzanne Last Stone, "Sinaitic and Noahide Law: Legal Pluralism in Jewish Law," *Cardozo Law Review* 12 (1990–91): 1157–1214; and J. David Bleich, "Jewish Law and the State's Authority to Punish Crime," *Cardozo Law Review* 12 (1990–91): 829–58.

28 For evidence of legal disabilities imposed on Jews of the region, and of frequent anti-Jewish recriminations in relation to economic practices, see Szajkowski, *The Economic Status of the Jews in Alsace, Metz and Lorraine*, chapters 16–37.

realm that offered some respite from the randomness of the social, economic, and political disabilities that were still in force. The civil courts constituted an arena in which Jews were viewed as participants in a shared public space. Law offered a universal language, and although there was no presumption of equality, within the legal sphere Jews enjoyed the illusion of citizenship before they were actually accepted as equals.[29] The proceedings of the Metz Beit Din provide clear evidence of forces that fostered a unified community while also suggesting that there was a shared culture that united Jews and their non-Jewish neighbors. Decades before the Jewish population of France was admitted to citizenship, the realm of law offered a framework for interaction and integration in the surrounding society and culture.

•••

In 1790 and 1791, the Sephardic and Ashkenazic Jews of France were admitted to citizenship. Jewish communal autonomy was deemed incompatible with their new status, as Clermont-Tonnerre had proclaimed, and so the autonomous regime was dismantled. Fifteen years later an even more ambitious effort to integrate the Jews in French society was attempted. Napoleon Bonaparte rolled out a grand plan to consolidate France under a single law that favored homogeneity and eschewed pluralism. Consistent with this conception of the nation, Napoleon convened the Sanhedrin in 1806 and 1807 in an attempt to relegate religion to the private sphere.[30]

The Assembly of Jewish Notables and the Grand Sanhedrin were part of a larger effort to define the respective spheres of influence of church and state. Beginning with the Concordat in 1801 and the subsequent creation of the Protestant consistorial system in 1802, Napoleon had firmly asserted the state's authority over religion and in so doing had established a precedent for embarking on a more aggressive approach to the Jewish question. With the Code Civil, he put an end to Church control over marriage and to the supremacy of *ius commune*. Convinced that government intervention was the only hope for restoring economic stability in Alsace, Napoleon issued an Imperial Decree on 30 May 1806, declaring a moratorium on all debts owed to Jews by noncommercial farmers. Since Jewish lending practices were understood to be symptomatic

29 See, for example, PMBD, Vol. 2, no. 39, 72a, where the heirs of David Terquem advanced a claim against the sheriff, demanding that he provide them with an account of the business transactions in which the deceased had been involved.

30 Jay R. Berkovitz, "The Napoleonic Halakhic Foundations and Rabbinic Legacy," *Central Conference of American Rabbis Journal* 54 (2007): 11–34.

of a more fundamental problem—the questionable suitability of the Jews to fulfill the obligations incumbent upon them as French citizens—the decree made clear "how urgent it is to revive sentiments of civil morality among those who profess the Jewish religion in the countries under our jurisdiction, sentiments which have, sadly, disappeared among a very great number of them due to the state of degradation in which they have languished, a state which it is not at all among our intentions to maintain nor to renew."[31] Napoleon therefore proceeded to order the convocation of a Jewish assembly empowered with legislative authority to remedy the allegedly deficient "sentiments of civil morality" to which the Jewish population still stubbornly adhered, and thus to resolve the question of the incompatibility of Judaism and civic duties once and for all.

There is little doubt that the dramatic convocation of the Assembly of Jewish Notables and the Sanhedrin exerted pressure on Jewish leaders to acknowledge the subordination of Jewish law to the fulfillment of their duties as citizens of the French empire. The delegates themselves were surely aware that the continued enjoyment of citizenship depended on the resolution of the competing demands of state and religion. Most historians have therefore been reluctant to view the Paris meetings as any more than a dismal example of capitulation and compliance. Delegates to the Sanhedrin, it is claimed, acquiesced to a policy of surrender of their religious and cultural particularity.[32] However, the historical context and legal history of the issues debated in 1806 and 1807 suggest that the much-maligned Paris body did not deviate from the Jewish legal tradition.

Discussion of the Jewish question in France in the revolutionary era centered on two primary areas of concern: Judaism's incorporation of religious and political laws in a single system and its purported dual standard of morality. Concerning the first claim, Napoleon himself distinguished between Judaism's religious prescriptions, which he conceded were immutable, and Judaism's political provisions, which many thinkers since Spinoza believed could no longer be justified. The newly constituted Sanhedrin therefore had "the mandate to abolish all atrocious laws .. that could only apply to Jews living in Palestine."[33] The authorization of usurious rates on loans to non-Jews

31 Shimon J. Maslin, "Selected Documents of Napoleonic Jewry," unpublished paper, Hebrew Union College (Cincinnati, 1957), Document 1-A.

32 See Simon Schwarzfuchs, *Napoleon, the Jews, and the Sanhedrin* (London, 1979).

33 Jean Baptiste Philibert Vaillant, ed., *Correspondance de Napoléon 1er* (Paris, 1858–70), vol. 13, 581–585, excerpts from the text of a letter to M. de Champagny, Minister of the Interior, 29 November 1806.

was taken as the clearest evidence of the injustice of Jewish law.[34] In the revolutionary era, the charges of social exclusiveness and moral duplicity assumed unprecedented urgency and threatened to undermine the emancipation project in its entirety.

The issue before the assembly was whether it could resolve the clash between the authority of the state and the authority of religion. Twelve in all, the questions focused on marriage and divorce, attitudes toward non-Jews, civic duties, rabbinic authority, occupational restrictions, and money lending. As defined by Napoleon, the ultimate goal was to "reconcile the beliefs of the Jews with the duties of Frenchmen, and to transform them into useful citizens, in order to remedy the evil to which many of them apply themselves to the great detriment of our subjects."[35] Napoleon sought formal reassurance that the Jews of the empire were committed to the French civil code and to his program of broad social integration. To accomplish this objective, the emperor convened another body in 1807—the Grand Sanhedrin—to formally ratify the assembly's responses and place "on equal footing with the Talmud, as articles of faith and principles of religious legislation."[36] Members of the assembly displayed an unequivocally positive attitude toward the primacy of the state, and strongly endorsed Judaism's compatibility with civic duties. They denied that any aspect of Jewish religious law, e.g., marriage and divorce, contravened the laws of the state.

Despite the intense pressure to which members of the assembly were subjected, it is not at all clear that they had intended to misrepresent Judaism's view of the state and its gentile citizens. To the contrary, their responses generally fell within the broad range of Jewish legal opinion, though at times they rested on views that were not entirely normative. This view is amply supported by the published writings of Rabbi Aaron Worms, an important Metz halakhic authority who served as a delegate at the Assembly of Jewish Notables and as a member of the Sanhedrin. Twenty-five years later, he decided to publish a summary of the discourse on gentiles in Jewish law that he delivered to fellow delegates at the assembly.[37] Worms's Paris address emphasized Jewish law's overriding commitment to morality and its unqualified objection to deceit-

34 See, for example, Agricole Moureau, *De l'incompatibilité entre le Judaïsme et l'exercise des droits de cité et des moyens de rendre les Juifs citoyens* (Paris, 1819), 37–60.

35 From Vaillant, *Correspondance de Napoléon*, vol. 12 (Paris, 1863), 700–11, no. 10537, cited in Schwarzfuchs, *Napoleon, the Jews, and the Sanhedrin*, 55.

36 Letter from Napoleon to M. Champagny, Ramboulliet, 23 August 1806. See *Correspondance de Napoléon*, vol. 13, 101–2 and 584.

37 Worms published his seven-volume *Me'orei 'Or* over the course of forty years, His Sanhedrin address was reproduced in *Ken Tahor*, 10b–11b, *novellae* to B.T. Sanhedrin 58b.

ful behavior towards gentiles.[38] He revealed an appreciation for advances in the legal system of post-revolutionary France that nullified earlier distinctions in the status of gentiles and Jews. He stressed Judaism's appreciation for shared ethical traditions of monotheists. His final argument, predicated on the ideological and social foundations of the Revolution, was modeled after the Aristotelian *societas civilis*, a community of citizens bound together as free and equal participants and whose ethical responsibilities are grounded in the principle of reciprocity. These arguments attested unambiguously to the compatibility of Judaism with duties toward the state and its citizens. The delegates declared that a redefinition of brotherhood was necessary in light of the new social and political reality of post-revolutionary France.[39] The bonds of fraternity could no longer be defined solely in terms of religious affiliation; citizenship had emerged, above all else, as the principal basis for uniting members of the French nation.

Did the formulations of the Sanhedrin represent a departure from the way Jews had defined their collective identity? It is fair to say that most of western Jewry in the early nineteenth century was unwilling to redefine the nature of their affiliations in accord with the assembly's pronouncements. Most would continue to maintain the strongest attachments to their coreligionists for much of the century. The social and cultural barriers that continued to separate Jew from Christian, particularly outside of the major urban centers where traditional associations were more easily preserved, inevitably reinforced the ethos of Jewish solidarity. Members of the assembly were undoubtedly aware of the tenacity of these social realities but also understood the urgent need for clarification of the role of Jewish law in the modern state. In this respect, the Sanhedrin clearly signified a new understanding of the traditional relationship of Jews to the State.

In Spring 1807 the Sanhedrin issued decisions that defined the relation between Jewish law and the modern state without altering any rituals or fundamental doctrines of Judaism. The Paris body owed both its prominence and notoriety to the role it played in endorsing the revolutionary concept of *fraternité* as the exclusive mediating principle between the Jewish religion and French society. It also affirmed that seemingly irreconcilable conflicts between the religious obligations of Judaism and the duties demanded of citizens by the state were to be resolved in favor of the latter, since loyalty to the modern state was defined as a supreme religious value. Not all French rabbis agreed on the religious status of patriotism, however. Some worked vigorously to infuse

38 See Moses Maimonides, *Mishneh Torah*, Hilkhot Gezelah va-Avedah 1:2.

39 Diogène Tama, ed., *Transactions of the Parisian Sanhedrin* (London, 1807), 76–80.

emancipation with religious significance; others had misgivings about how far the practical halakhic implications of republican Judaism might be taken. Leaving nothing to chance, the newly formed *Consistoire israélite*, established by the Napoleonic regime in 1808, took measures that required rabbis to emphasize the lessons of the Sanhedrin in their sermons, while the text of the decisions was reproduced in every textbook approved for use in Jewish schools. For the Napoleonic regime, as for Jewish communal leaders, the Sanhedrin provided the authoritative interpretation of emancipation; its answers and doctrinal decisions formed a new and central text for subsequent generations.

Changing conceptions of gentiles and gentile culture in the preceding two centuries, including a growing respect for non-Jewish law in Metz in the second half of the eighteenth century, permitted the rabbinic leadership assembled in Paris to draw boldly on those classical traditions it felt corresponded to the new conditions facing emancipated Jewry. Equally important, the Sanhedrin was careful to maintain a sharp distinction between the ritual and civil spheres. The civil sphere encompassed the full range of Jewish-gentile relations and duties to the state, whereas the ritual sphere, it was agreed, ought to remain inviolate. Notwithstanding the delegates' unequivocal declarations of patriotism and brotherhood, and despite the religious reassurances provided by the assembly, the government's confidence in the ability of the Jews to undergo self-reform faded quickly. To the severe economic and political detriment of the Jews in the Napoleonic empire, the "Infamous Decree," issued on 17 March 1808, was a reflection of disappointment with the Sanhedrin's unwillingness to endorse the full-fledged program of assimilation envisioned by Napoleon.[40]

Neither Napoleon nor members of his commission were aware that the Jews' engagement with French law was hardly unprecedented. In the prerevolutionary era, the state respected the leadership hierarchy of the Jewish community, defended its prerogative to govern on the basis of Jewish communal law, and recognized the choice of Jewish litigants in the French courts to be judged by that same law. Jews in Metz were integrated in the general legal system and

40 On the question how to evaluate state interference in the personal lives of its citizens, see Kenneth Stow, "Jewish Pre-Emancipation: *Ius Commune*, the Roman *Comunità*, and Marriage in the Early Modern Papal State," *Festschrift in Honor of Robert Bonfil*, Elisheva Baumgarten, Menahem Ben Sasson, Amnon Raz-Karkozkin and Roni Weinstein, eds. (Jerusalem, 2010), 79–102. Using the example of the early modern Papal States, Stow has shown that the growth of state intrusion in the affairs of Jews conformed to the ever-increasing consensus that the state ought to rule its citizens directly and through a uniform legal code. Basing its legal system on *ius commune* and through Napoleon's Code Civil, the modern state became secularized, leading to the inclusion of the Jews in civil society.

enjoyed a degree of juridical parity that compared to conditions in central Europe.[41] In their response to the Napoleonic challenge, the delegates to the Sanhedrin did what Jews in Metz had done decades before. They deferred to the law but interpreted it through the lens of the Jewish tradition.[42]

The study of communal autonomy presented in these pages has been informed by data drawn from Metz, with emphasis on the conditions of daily life there. These included defining relations to the state and surrounding society, on the one hand, and concerns for social equilibrium and the integrity of Jewish culture, on the other. Evidence culled from commercial exchange, property transactions, building repairs, consumption, marriage, death, and inheritance has furnished the basic details upon which this inquiry is based. But thorough investigation of the phenomenon of communal autonomy will depend on further micro-studies at the communal level. Only comparative methods will enable scholars to ascertain whether the legislative agenda of the Metz Kahal and the judicial conduct of its rabbinic court were exceptional or more commonplace. Until then, I hope that the criteria and questions that have guided me in the present study will be of value to scholars who embark on similar projects.

41 See Stefan Ehrenpreis, Andreas Gotzmann, and Stephan Wendehorst, "Probing the Legal History of the Jews in the Holy Roman Empire: Norms and Their Application," *Jahrbuch des Simon-Dubnow-Instituts* 11 (2003): 409–86.

42 See Schechter, *Obstinate Hebrews*, 220–26, and Maurice Samuels, *The Right to Difference: French Universalism and the Jews* (Chicago, 2016), 46–48, 72.

Glossary

All terms are in Hebrew unless otherwise indicated.

apotiki security
apotropos /im guardian(s) or custodian(s) of another's affairs
arevim kablanim guarantor who assumes responsibility as principal debtor
'arevut kablanut a high level of responsibility assumed by a guarantor entitling the creditor to approach the guarantor first when seeking to recover his debt.
arkha'ot shel goyim non-Jewish courts
au porteur (F.) payable to the bearer
av beit din chief justice of rabbinic court
avocat (F.) lawyer
bailliage (F.) local royal court
beit din / batei din rabbinic court(s)
beit midrash study house
be'ohev acronym for "first the wife (signs), then the husband follows"
billet à ordre (F.) promissory note
contrat (F.) contract
constitution (F.) annuity
curateur (F.) trustee for minors
dayan / dayanim rabbinic court judge(s)
din/im judgment; civil law
dina d'malkhuta dina "the law of the land is the law"
d'oraita of biblical authority
droit d'aubaine (F.) the law that entitled the government to seize the estate of a deceased foreigner
Even ha-'Ezer section of *Shulḥan 'Arukh* that concerns family law
gabbai trustee
généralité (F.) one of thirty-six administrative divisions in the ancien régime
gevirtanit ve-shultanit mistress and executor
greffe (F.) court registry
greffier (F.) court registrar
Halakhah Jewish law
ḥaliẓah a ceremony that releases a widow from the obligation to marry her late husband's brother when the husband died without issue
haẓi ḥelek zakhar one-half of a male portion of a man's estate that could be apportioned to daughters through a promissory note

ḥerem communal ban for major offenses

ḥezkat ha-yishuv the right of settlement, serving as a form of trade protection, that was ordained by communal legislation

ḥezkat 'ironit residence permit, similar to *ḥezkat ha-yishuv*

ḥilluf ketav bill of exchange

Ḥoshen Mishpat section of *Shulḥan 'Arukh* that concerns civil law

ikkar ha-ketubah essential part of the marriage contract

kahal elected council of the community

kaẓin / keẓinah title used by leading members of community

Kehillah community

ketav yad a written promise to pay

ketubah marriage contract

kinyan instrument used to transfer title to property or to establish a contractual obligation

kinyan gamur agav sudar transaction executed via symbolic exchange of a piece of cloth

lamdan talmudic scholar

lomdim men engaged in a regular routine of Talmud study

lettres patentes (F.) royal letters, countersigned by a minister and registered by parlements

ma'aseh beit din a formal judgment of the rabbinic court

ma'aser tithe on agricultural produce, employed to refer to obligation to give charity

manhigim communal leaders

mashgi'aḥ / mashgiḥim curator(s); guardian(s)

maskilim proponents of the Haskalal (Jewish Enlightenment movement)

meliẓ/im translator(s)

meneket ḥavero a woman who nurses another man's child

mère tutrice (F.) mother-tutor (guardian)

me'uberet ḥavero woman who is pregnant by another man

mezonot alimony

meẓra adjoining landowner

minhag custom

ne'emanei kehillah notaries of the Jewish community

nekitat ḥeifetz an individual taking the oath in certain circumstances was required to hold a sacred object, such as a Torah scroll or a printed volume of the Pentateuch, or to swear while the ark in the synagogue was opened.

niddui ban for relatively minor offense

nikhsei melog lit. "plucked property," i.e., usufruct, those properties that were either brought into the marriage by the wife but were not listed in the *ketubah*, or were acquired in the course of the marriage via inheritance or a gift. According to Jewish law, a wife retained title to these assets while the income they produced belonged to the husband; her husband bore no responsibility for any loss or damage to such property

nikhsei ẓon barzel lit. "iron sheep property," i.e., inalienable assets; the part of the dowry that remained the property of the wife while under the control of the husband. Recorded in the *ketubah*, these assets were assigned a fixed value for which the husband assumed full financial responsibility in the case of loss or depreciation. This property reverted to the wife at the termination of the marriage

par bénéfice d'inventaire privilege that the heir obtains to be liable for the debts of the succession, only to the value of the effects of the succession

parnas a communal official; syndic

parnasim and *manhigim / Pu"M* communal leaders

péage corporel (F.) body tax

pesak a judgment issued by the *beit din*

pesharah, pesher compromise

pinkas register

pletten (Yid.) tickets given to the poor for food and lodging

posekim Jewish legal authorities

présidial (F.) intermediary royal court

rav ha-medinah rabbi of the province

régnicoles French nationals

rentes annuity

schülmantel men's overcoat reserved for the Sabbath

shetar bill; contract

shetar ḥaẓi ḥelek zakhar a promissory note enabling a father to allocate one-half of a male portion of his estate to daughters

shevu'at heseit an rabbinic oath administered to a defendant who denied even partial responsibility or obligation and would otherwise be exempt from swearing an oath

shevu'at ketubah oath administered to widow or divorcée prior to the award of the *ketubah* settlement

shtadlan/im community official(s) whose function was to intervene with government authorities on all matters deemed appropriate by the Kahal

Shulḥan 'Arukh Code of Jewish law, published by Rabbi Joseph Caro, Venice 1566

silluk discharge of a widow from her husband's estate

solidaire solidary

solidairement joint liability, *in solidum*

takkanah / takkanot communal ordinance(s)

tena'im rishonim initial engagement agreement

tena'im aḥaronim second engagement agreement

teki'at kaf handshake

tikkun communal ordinance

tikkun 'olam lit. "repair of the world"; social welfare, public good

tosefta a sum contributed by the groom to supplement the statutory sum in the standard *ketubah*

tovei ha-'ir lit. "good men of the city" referring to governing board of the Jewish community

yeshivah talmudic academy

ẓedakah charity

Bibliography

Archival and Manuscript Sources

Archives of Jewish Theological Seminary of America, New York

Ms. 8136 — Pinkas Kahal of Metz, 1749–1789

Ms. 9835 — Pinkas Ẓava'ot

Mic. no. 8347 — *Lettres patentes*, 31 décembre 1715

Archives départementales de la Moselle

Consistoire israélite

17J23 — Transcript of case before Metz Beit Din, 1690

Metz communal ordinance, 1710

17J24 — Rulings of Metz Beit Din, 1753

Transcript of cases before the Beit Din, 1769 and 1770

Consultation de M. Pierre-Louis Roederer

Legal opinion of Rabbi Mordechai Morhange (Merchingen)

Série B—Cours et jurisdictions avant 1790

B 1558–1559 — Dettes de David Terquem. Case of Matha Gantz.

Bibliothèque Nationale

Parlement de Metz, Arrêt du 8 Mai 1786.

Précis pour Me. Jean-Pierre Pécheur, Procureur au Bailliage, en qualité de Curateur établi par Justice à la substitution portée au testament de Samuel-Jonas Lévi, Juif de cette Ville, Intimé, contre Salomon-David Alphen, & Jonas-Garçon Lévi, tous deux juifs habitans de cette Ville, Appellans; et contre Rechelé Lévi. Bibliotheque nationale.

Central Archives for the History of the Jewish People

F 86 — Excerpts from Pinkas Kahal of Metz

FMe 139 — Fragments of Pinkas Kahal of Metz

Archives of the YIVO Institute for Jewish Research

RG 128, Box 2	Pinkas of the Metz Beit Din (1771–1789)
Collection of Rabbinical and Historical Manuscripts	
RG 223, Part II Folder 146, item 18	Takkanah of the Community of Metz excerpted in "Pirchei ha-rimonim, me'asef le-kol ha-maḥanot" (n.d.)

Institute of Hebrew Manuscripts, Jerusalem

Ms. no 803394	Shlomo Lvov, *Ḥeshek Shlomo*, Dittwiller, 1784

Printed Primary Sources

Journals

Almanach des Trois Evêches pour l'année 1788. Metz, 1788.

Books

Asher ben Yeḥiel. *Resp. ha-Rosh*. Jerusalem, 1994.

Ashkenazi, Gershon. *Resp. 'Avodat Ha-Gershuni*. Frankfurt am Main, 1699.

Ashkenazi, Ẓevi. *Resp. Ḥakham Ẓevi*. Amsterdam, 1712.

Avron, Dov, ed. *The Pinkas ha-Kesherim shel Kehilat Poznan*. Jerusalem, 1966.

Bacharach, Ya'ir Hayyim. *Resp. Ḥavvot Ya'ir*. Frankfurt am Main, 1699.

Boug, M. de. *Recueil des édits, déclarations, lettres patentes, ordonnances d'Alsace*. 2 vols. Colmar, 1775.

Coûtumes générales de la ville de Metz et pays-Messin: corrigées ensuite des résolutions des trois-états de ladite ville, ès années 1616, 1617, & 1618. Nouvelle édition conforme à celle imprimée en 1732. Metz, 1769.

Disbeck, David. *Pardes David*. Solzbach, 1786.

Domat, Jean. *Le droit public, suite des lois civiles dans leur ordre naturel*, vol. 3, *Œuvres complètes, nouvelle edition revue corrigée*, edited by Joseph Remy. Paris, 1829.

Dupaty, Charles-Marguerite Mercier. *Justification de sept hommes condamnés par le Parlement de Metz en 1769, sur les seules dépositions de juifs plaignans*. Paris, 1787.

Duran, Solomon. *Resp. Ḥut ha-Meshulash*. Amsterdam, 1874.

Duran, Solomon. *Resp. Tashbeẓ*. Amsterdam, 1743.

Eibeschütz, Jonathan. *Kereti u-Feleti*. Altona, 1763.

Eibeschütz, Jonathan. *Urim ve-Tumim, Ḥoshen Mishpat*. Altona, 1763.

Eibeschütz, Jonathan. *Ya'arot Devash*. Metz, 1745. Republished in Jerusalem, 1984, 2 volumes.

Gabriel, C. J. *Observations détachées sur les coutumes et les usages anciens et modernes du ressort du Parlement de Metz*. 2 vols. Bouillon, 1787.

Grégoire, Henri. *Essai sur la régénération physique, morale et politique des Juifs*. Metz, 1789.
Günzberg, Aryeh Loeb. *Gevurot Ari*. Vilna, 1862; expanded edition: Vilna, 1907.
Günzberg, Aryeh Loeb. *Sha'agat Aryeh*. Frankfurt-an-der-Oder, 1755.
Günzberg, Aryeh Loeb. *Sha'agat Aryeh ha-Ḥadashot*. Vilna, 1874.
Günzberg, Aryeh Loeb. *Turei Even*. Metz, 1781.
Halperin, Israel, ed. *Takkanot Medinat Mehrin (Consitutiones Congressus Generalis Judaeorum Moraviensium, 1650–1748)*. Jerusalem, 1952.
Halperin, Israel and Israel Bartal, eds. *The Pinkas of the Va'ad Arba'ah Aratzot*. Jerusalem, 1989.
Hayyim ben Isaac, *Pisqei Or Zarua*. Brooklyn, 1996.
Henrys, M. Claude. *Oeuvres avec les observations sur les changemens de la jurisprudence depuis la mort de l'auteur ... par Barthélemy-Joseph Bretonnier*. Paris, 1718.
Isserles, Moses. *Darkhei Moshe*. Commentary on Jacob ben Asher, *Arba'ah Turim, Oraḥ Ḥayyim*. Furth, 1759–60.
Isserles, Moses. Glosses to *Shulḥan 'Arukh*. Cracow, 1569–71.
Isserles, Moses. *Resp. Rema*. Cracow, 1640. Edited by Asher Siev. Jerusalem, 1971.
Jacob ben Asher. *Arba'ah Turim*. 4 pts. Piove de Sacco, 1475.
Jüdische Gemeindestatuten aus dem aschkenasischen Kulturraum, 1650–1850, edited by Stefan Litt. Göttingen, 2013.
Karo, Joseph. *Beit Yosef*. Commentary on Jacob ben Asher, Arba'ah Turim, *Yoreh Deah*. 1555.
Karo, Joseph. *Shulḥan 'Arukh*. Venice, 1565.
Kaufmann, David, ed. "Extraits de l'ancien livre de la communauté de Metz." *REJ* 19 (1889): 115–130.
Koblenz, Gershon. *Resp. Kiryat Ḥannah*. Metz, 1785.
Krochmal, Menaḥem Mendel. *Resp. Ẓemaḥ Ẓedek*. Amsterdam, 1675.
Lacretelle, Pierre-Louis. *Plaidoyer pour deux Juifs de Metz contre l'Hôtel de Ville et le corps des marchands de Thionville*. Brussels, 1785.
Lançon, Nicholas. *Recueil des lois, coûtumes et usages observés par les juifs de Metz*. Metz, 1786.
Landau, Ezekiel. *Derushei Ha-Ẓelaḥ*. Warsaw, 1899.
Landau, Ezekiel. *Resp. Noda b'Yehudah*. Prague, 1776.
Le Brun, Denis. *Traité de la communauté entre mari et femme*. Paris, 1754.
Luria, Solomon. *Resp. Maharshal*. Lublin, 1575.
Luria, Solomon. *Yam shel Shelomo*. Jerusalem, 1996.
Lvov, Joshua Heschel. *Resp. Penei Levanah*. Jerusalem, 2017.
Maḥzor ke-Minhag Ashkenaz u-Folin. Metz, 1768.
Maḥzor le-Pesach, Shavu'ot, ve-Sukkot. Metz, 1769.
Maḥzor shel Rosh ha-Shanah ke-Minhag Ashkenaz. Metz, 1817.

Maimonides, Moses. *Mishneh Torah.* 14 sections. Shabtai Frankel edition. Jerusalem, 1975–2006.

Meir ben Baruch of Rothenburg, *Resp. Maharam mi-Rotenberg: Teshuvot, Pesaqim, u-Minhagim.* 4 parts. Cremona, 1558; Prague, 1608; Lemberg, 1860; and Berlin, 1891. Edited by Yiẓḥak Ze'ev Kahane. Jerusalem, 1957.

Le "Memorbuch" de Metz (vers 1575–1742), edited by Simon Schwarzfuchs. Metz, 1971.

Mendelssohn, Moses. *Die Ritualgesetze der Juden.* Berlin, 1778.

Mercier, L. -S. *Tableau de Paris.* 12 vols. Amsterdam, 1788.

Mercier Dupaty, Charles-Marguerite. *Justification de sept hommes condamnés par le Parlement de Metz en 1769, sur les seules dépositions de juifs plaignans.* 1787.

Meyer, Jacob. *Resp. Emet le-Yaakov.* Jerusalem, 2006.

Mintz, Judah. *Resp. Mahari Mintz.* Venice, 1553. Edited by Asher Siev. New York, 1995.

Moellin, Jacob. *Resp. Maharil ha-Ḥadashot.* Jerusalem, 1977.

Narol, Moses Cohen. *Bakashah.* Amsterdam in 1699. Metz, 1764.

The Pinkas of the Va'ad Arba'ah Aratzot, Israel Halpern and Israel Bartal, eds. Jerusalem, 1989.

Pothier, Robert-Joseph. *Traité du contrat de constitution de rente.* Paris, 1763.

Pothier, Robert-Joseph. *Traité du contrat de mariage.* Paris, 1771.

Pothier, Robert-Joseph. *Traité de la puissance du mari sur la personne et les biens de la femme.* Paris, 1774.

"Protocol of the Medinah." 28 May 1777, published in *Blätter fur jüdische Geschichte und Litteratur* 2 (1901): 18–22; 28–29. Paraphrased in French by Isidore Loeb, "Extrait du protocole de la nation de l'assemblée du 21 Iyyar 5537." In *Annuaire de la société des études juives* 2 (1883): 181–91.

Le Registre de correspondence de la communauté juive de Lorraine. Copies des lettres des années 1783–1791, recueieli et presenté avec une introduction et des notes par Simon Schwarzfuchs. Jerusalem, 2003.

Le Registre des délibérations de la Nation Juive Portugaise de Bordeaux (1711–1787). Simon Schwarzfuchs, ed. Paris, 1981.

Reischer, Jacob. *Resp. Shevut Ya'akov.* Part 1: Halle, 1710; Part 2: Offenbach, 1719; Part 3: Metz, 1789.

Samuel ben Moses de Medina. *Resp. Maharashdam.* 4 pts. Salonica, 1797–1798.

Schwarzfuchs, Simon, ed. "The Rabbinic Contract of the Sha'agat Aryeh in Metz" [Hebrew]. *Moriah* 15 (1986): 81–90.

Seder Seliḥot ke-minhag ha-Ashkenazim. Metz, 1769.

Seder Tefilah ke-Minhag Ashkenaz. Metz, 1765.

Segel, Samuel Halevi. *Sefer Naḥalat Shiv'ah.* 2 vols. Jerusalem, 2006.

Solomon ben Aderet. *Resp. Rashba.* 6 vols. Jerusalem, 1989.

Steinhardt, Joseph. *Resp. Zikhron Yosef.* Fürth, 1773.

Turniansky, Chava, ed. and trans. *Memoirs of Glikl* [Yiddish and Hebrew]. Jerusalem, 2006.

Worms, Aaron. *Be'er Sheva*. Metz, 1819.

Worms, Aaron. *Bin Nun*. Metz, 1827.

Worms, Aaron. *Ken Tahor*. Metz, 1831.

Worms, Aaron. *Me'orei 'Or*. 3 vols. Metz, 1790–3.

Worms, Aaron. *'Od la'Mo'ed*. Metz, 1822.

Secondary Sources

Akehurst, F. R. P. "Law, Customary: French." In *Women and Gender in Medieval Europe: An Encyclopedia*, edited by Margaret Schaus. New York, 2006.

Altmann, Alexander. *Moses Mendelssohn: A Biographical Study*. Philadelphia, 1973.

Anchel. *Les Juifs de France: La Roue de Fortune*. Paris, 1946.

Assaf, Simḥa. *Batei ha-din ve-sidreihem aḥarei ḥatimat ha-Talmud*. Jerusalem, 1924.

Assaf, Simḥa. "The Appointment of Women as Guardians" [Hebrew]. *Ha-Mishpat ha-'Ivri* 2 (1926): 75–81.

Assaf, Simḥa. "Le-She'elat Yerushat ha-Bat" ("Concerning the Inheritance of a Daughter"). *Sefer Yovel l'Yaakov Freimann*. Berlin, 1937.

Auslander, Leora. *Taste and Power: Furnishing Modern France*. Berkeley, 1996.

Baer, Yiẓḥak. "The Origins of Jewish Communal Government in the Middle Ages" [Hebrew]. *Zion* 15 (1950): 1–41.

Bar-Asher, Shalom. *Sefer ha-Takkanot*. Jerusalem, 1991.

Barnett, S. J. *The Enlightenment and Religion. The Myths of Modernity*. Manchester, U.K., 2003.

Baron, Salo W. *The Jewish Community: Its History and Structure to the American Revolution*. 3 vols. Philadelphia, 1942.

Becchia, Alain. *La draperie d'Elbeuf, des origines à 1870*. Rouen, 2000.

Bedell, John. "Archeology and Probate Inventories in the Study of Eighteenth-Century Life." *Journal of Interdisciplinary History* 31 (2000): 223–245.

Beik, William. *Absolutism and Society in Seventeenth-Century France: State Power and Provincial Aristocracy in Languedoc*. Cambridge, U.K., 1985 2011.

Beik, William. "The Absolutism of Louis XIV as Social Collaboration." *Past and Present* 188 (August 2005): 195–224.

Bell, David A. "Barristers, Politics and the Failure of Civil Society in Old Regime France." In *Lawyers and the Rise of Western Political Liberalism: Europe and North America from the Eighteenth to Twentieth Centuries*, edited by Terrence C. Halliday and Lucient Karpik, 25–36. Oxford, 1997.

Bell, David A. *Lawyers and Citizens: The Making of a Political Elite in Old Regime France.* Oxford, 1994.

Bell, David A. "The 'Public Sphere,' the State and the World of the Law in Eighteenth-Century France." *French Historical Studies* 17:4 (1992): 912–934.

Bell, Dean. *Jews in the Early Modern World.* Lanham, 2008.

Ben-Sasson, Haim Hillel. *Hagut ve-Hanhagah.* [*Thought and Leadership: The Social Views of Polish Jewry at the End of the Middle Ages*] [Hebrew]. Jerusalem, 1959.

Benedict, Philip. "Bibliothèques protestantes et catholiques à Metz au XVIIe siecle." *Annales: Economies, Sociétés, Civilisations* 40 (1985): 343–370.

Berg, Peter Arend Jan van de. *The Politics of European Codification: A History of the Unification of Law in France, Prussia, the Austrian Monarchy and the Netherlands.* Groningen, 2007.

Bergin, Joseph. *Church, Society, and Religious Change in France, 1580–1730.* New Haven, 2009.

Bergin, Joseph. *The Politics of Religion in Early Modern France.* New Haven, 2014.

Berkovitz, Jay R. "Acculturation and Integration in Eighteenth-Century Metz." *Jewish History* 24:3–4 (2010): 271–294.

Berkovitz, Jay R. "Authority and Innovation at the Threshold of Modernity: The *Me'orei Or* of Rabbi Aaron Worms of Metz." In *Me'ah She'arim: Studies in Medieval Jewish Spiritual Life in Memory of Isadore Twersky*, edited by Gerald Blidstein, Ezra Fleischer, Carmi Horowitz, and Bernard Septimus, 249–285. Jerusalem, 2001.

Berkovitz, Jay R. "Civil Law and Justice in the Rabbinic Tribunals of Eighteenth-Century Metz." *Iggud: Selected Essays in Jewish Studies*, 87–99. Jerusalem, 2008.

Berkovitz, Jay R. "Competing Perspectives on Legal Decision-Making in Early Modern Ashkenaz." *Jewish History* 31:1–2 (2017): 149–171.

Berkovitz, Jay R. "Crisis and Authority in Early Modern Ashkenaz." *Jewish History* 26 (2012): 179–199.

Berkovitz, Jay R. "Jewish Law and Ritual in Early Modern Germany." In *Jews, Judaism and the Reformation in Sixteenth-Century Germany*, edited by Dean P. Bell and Stephen G. Burnett, 481–502. Boston, 2006.

Berkovitz, Jay R. "Jewish Philanthropy in Early Modern and Modern Europe: Theory and Practice in Historical Perspective." In *Toward a Renewed Ethic of Jewish Philanthropy*, edited by Yossi Prager, 93–122. New York, 2010.

Berkovitz, Jay R. "The Napoleonic Sanhedrin: Halakhic Foundations and Rabbinic Legacy." *Central Conference of American Rabbis Journal* 54 (2007): 11–34.

Berkovitz, Jay R. "Patterns of Rabbinic Succession in Modern France." *Jewish History* 13 (1999): 59–82.

Berkovitz, Jay R. "The Persona of a Poseq: Law and Self-Fashioning in Seventeenth-Century Ashkenaz." *Modern Judaism* 32:3 (2012): 251–269.

Berkovitz, Jay R. *Protocols of Justice: The Pinkas of the Rabbinic Court of Metz, 1771–1789*. Leiden and Boston, 2014.

Berkovitz, Jay R. "Rabbinic Culture and the Historical Development of Halakhah." In *Cambridge History of Judaism*, Volume 7, edited by Jonathan Karp and Adam Sutcliffe, 349–77. New York, 2017.

Berkovitz, Jay R. *Rites and Passages: The Beginnings of Modern Jewish Culture in France, 1650–1860*. Philadelphia, 2004.

Berkovitz, Jay R. *The Shaping of Jewish Identity in Nineteenth-century France*. Detroit, 1989.

Berkovitz, Jay R. "Social and Religious Controls in Pre-Revolutionary France: Rethinking the Beginnings of Modernity." *Jewish History* 15 (2001): 1–40.

Berkovitz, Jay R. *Tradition and Revolution: Jewish Culture in Early Modern France* [Hebrew]. Jerusalem, 2007.

Berman, Harold. *Law and Revolution, The Formation of the Western Legal Tradition*. Cambridge, MA, 1985.

Birnbaum, Pierre. *A Tale of Ritual Murder in the Age of Louis XIV: The Trial of Raphaël Lévy*. Translated by Arthur Goldhammer. Stanford, 2012.

Bleich, J. David. "Jewish Law and the State's Authority to Punish Crime." *Cardozo Law Review* 12 (1991): 829–58.

Blidstein, Gerald. "Halakhah and Democracy." *Tradition* 32 (1997): 6–39.

Blidstein, Gerald. "The Israeli Legal System in Contemporary Halakha." *Diné Israel* 13–14 (1986–1988): 21–42.

Blidstein, Gerald. "Medieval Public Law: Sources and Concepts" [Hebrew]. *Diné Israel* 9 (1978–80): 127–164.

Bonfil, Robert. *Rabbis and Jewish Communities in Renaissance Italy*. Translated from Hebrew by Jonathan Chipman. Oxford, 1990.

Bouwsma, William J. "Lawyers and Early Modern Culture." *American Historical Review* 78:2 (April 1973): 303–27.

Breen, Michael P. *Law, City, and King: Legal Culture, Municipal Politics, and State Formation in Early Modern Dijon*. Rochester, 2007.

Breen, Michael P. "Law, Society, and the State in Early Modern France." *Journal of Modern History* 83 (June 2011): 346–386.

Breen, Michael P. "Patronage, Politics, and the 'Rule of Law' in Early Modern France." *Proceedings of the Western Society for French History* 33 (2005): 95–113.

Brenner, Michael, S. Jersch-Wenzel, and Michael Meyer, eds. *German-Jewish History in Modern Times*. 4 vols. New York, 1996–1998.

Brewer, John, and Susan Staves, eds. *Early Modern Conceptions of Property*. New York, 1995.

Cabourdin, Guy. "Le remariage en France sous l'ancien régime." In *Marriage and Remarriage in Populations of the Past*, edited by J. Dupaquier, et al., 273–86. London, 1981.

Caenegem, R. C. van. *Legal History: A European Perspective*. London, 1991.

Cahen, Abraham. "Le rabbinat de Metz pendant la période française." *REJ* 7 (1883): 103–16, 204–26; *REJ* 8 (1884): 255–74; 12 (1886): 283–97; 13 (1886): 105–26.

Cahen, Gilbert. "La Région Lorraine." In *Histoire des Juifs en France*, edited by Bernhard Blumenkranz, . Toulouse, 1972.

Calvi, Giulia. "Reconstructing the Family: Widowhood and Remarriage in Tuscany in the Early Modern Period." In *Marriage in Italy, 1300–1650*, edited by Trevor Dean and K. J. P. Lowe. Cambridge, 1998.

Carey, John A. *Judicial Reform in France before the Revolution of 1789*. Cambridge, MA, 1981.

Carlebach, Elisheva. "Fallen Women and Fatherless Children: Jewish Domestic Servants in Eighteenth-Century Altona." *Jewish History* 24 (2010): 295–308.

Chartier, Roger. *The Cultural Origins of the French Revolution*. Translated by Lydia G. Cochrane. Durham, 1991.

Chaunu, Pierre. *La mort à Paris: 16e, 17e et 18e siècles*. Paris, 1978.

Cities and Social Change in Early Modern France, edited by Philip Benedict. New York, 1989.

Clanchy, Michael T. *From Memory to Written Record: England 1066–1307*, 3rd ed. Chichester, 2013.

Clark, Jonathan. *English Society, 1660–1832*, 2d ed. Cambridge, 2000.

Clément, Roger, *La condition des juifs de Metz sous l'ancien régime*. Paris, 1903.

Cohen, Amnon. *Jewish Life under Islam: Jerusalem in the Sixteenth Century*. Cambridge, MA, 1984.

Cohen, Amnon. *A World Within: Jewish Life as Reflected in Muslim Court Documents from the Sijil of Jerusalem (16th Century)*. 2 vols. Philadelphia, 1994.

Cohen, Amnon. *Yehudei Yerushalayim ba-me'ah ha-shesh-'esreh le-fi te'udot Turkiyot shel beit ha-din ha-shara'i*. Jerusalem, 1976.

Cohen, Richard I., Natalie B. Dohrmann, Elchanan Reiner, and Adam Shear, eds. *Jewish Culture in Early Modern Europe: Essays in Honor of David B. Ruderman*. Pittsburgh, 2014.

Cole, Charles W. *Colbert and a Century of French Mercantilism*. New York, 1939.

Collins, James B. "The Economic Role of Women in Seventeenth-Century France." *French Historical Studies* 16:2 (1989): 436–470.

Collins, James B. *The State in Early Modern France*. Cambridge, 1995.

Continental Legal History Series. 11 vols. Boston, 1912–1928.

Corley, Christopher. "Gender, Kin, and Guardianship in Early Modern Burgundy." In *Family, Gender, and Law in Early Modern France*, edited by Suzanne Desan and Jeffrey Merrick, 183–222. University Park, PA, 2009.

Crowston, Clare. "Credit and the Metanarrative of Modernity." *French Historical Studies* 34 (2011): 7–19.

Crowston, Clare. "Family Affairs: Wives Credit, Consumption, and the Law in Old Regime France." In *Family, Gender, and Law in Early Modern France*, edited by Suzanne Desan and Jeffrey Merrick, 62–100. University Park, PA, 2009.

Crubaugh, Anthony. *Balancing the Scales of Justice. Local Courts and Rural Society in Southwestern France, 1750–1800*. University Park, PA, 2001.

Davis, Natalie Zemon. *Women on the Margins: Three Seventeenth-Century Lives*. Cambridge, MA, 1995.

Davis, Natalie Zemon. "Women on Top." In *Society and Culture in Early-Modern France: Eight Essays*, 124–151. Stanford, 1975.

Decrusy, François-André Isambert, et A. J. L. Jourdan. *Recueil général des anciennes lois françaises, depuis l'an 420 jusqu'a la revolution de 1789*. 29 vols. Paris, 1821–1833.

Deflem, Mathieu. *Sociology of Law: Visions of a Scholarly Tradition*. Cambridge, 2008.

Délumeau, Jean and Daniel Roche. *Histoire des pères et de la paternité*. Paris, 1990.

Dermineur, Elise M. "The Civil Judicial System in France." *Frühneuzeit-Info* 23 (2012): 45–52.

Dermineur, Elise M. "Female Peasants, Patriarchy, and the Credit Market in Eighteenth-Century France." *Proceedings of the Western Society for French History* 37 (2009): 61–84.

Dermineur, Elise M. "Women in Rural society: Peasants, Patriarchy and the Local Economy in Northeast France, 1650–1789." Ph.D. diss., Purdue University, 2011.

Desan, Suzanne. *The Family on Trial in Revolutionary France*. Berkeley, 2004.

Desan, Suzanne. "Making and Breaking Marriage: An Overview of Old Regime Marriage as a Social Practice." In *Family, Gender, and Law in Early Modern France*, edited by Suzanne Desan and Jeffrey Merrick, 1–25. University Park, PA, 2009.

Diefendorf, Barbara. "Women and Property in *Ancien Régime* France." In *Early Modern Conceptions of Property*, edited by John Brewer and Susan Staves, 177–178. New York, 1995.

Dinari, Yedidya. *The Rabbis of Germany and Austria at the close of the Middle Ages* [Hebrew]. Jerusalem, 1984.

Donahue, Charles. "What Causes Fundamental Legal Ideas? Marital Property in England and France in the Thirteenth Century." *Michigan Law Review* 78 (1979): 59–88.

Dyson, Henry. *French Property and Inheritance Law: Principles and Practice*. New York, 2003.

Eckert, Julia. "From Subject to Citizen: Legalisation from Below and the Homogenisation of the Legal Sphere." *Journal of Legal Pluralism* 53–54 (2006): 45–75.

Edrei, Arye. "Halakhic Responsibility of the Deceased: A Further Study of the Concept of Inheritance in Talmudic Thought." *Israel Law Review* 33 (1999): 821–854.

Ehrenpreis, Stefan. "Legal Spaces for Jews as Subjects of the Holy Roman Empire." *Jahrbuch des Simon-Dubnow-Instituts* 2 (2003): 475–487.

Elon, Menachem. *Jewish Law: History, Sources, Principles*. 4 vols. Translated by Bernard Auerbach and Melvin J. Sykes. Philadelphia, 1994.

Ettinger, Shimshon. "Testimonial Competence in Civil Matters under Jewish Law" [Hebrew]. *Diné Israel* 20–21 (2001): 241–267.

Faustini, Pascal. *La communauté juive de Metz et ses familles (1565–1665)*. Thionville, 2001.

Fehér, Ferenc. *The French Revolution and the Birth of Modernity*. Berkeley, 1990.

Ferrand, Jérôme. "Arbitration in Early-Modern France (16th–18th centuries)." *Legal History Review* 77 (2009): 103–155.

Ferrière, Claude-Joseph de. *Nouvelle introduction a la pratique: contenant l'explication des termes de pratique, de droit & de coûtumes. Avec les jurisdictions de France*. 2 vols. Brussels, 1739.

Feutry, David. "The Historian's Mountain of Paper, The Parlement of Paris and the Analysis of Civil Suits in the Eighteenth Century." *French History* 26:3 (2012): 277–296.

Fishman, Talya. *Becoming the People of the Talmud: Oral Torah as Written Tradition in Medieval Jewish Cultures*. Philadelphia, 2011.

Fisk, Catherine and Robert Gordon. "'Law As …' Theory and Method in Legal History." *UC Irvine Law Review* 1:3 (2011): 519–542.

Fleury, Jean. *Contrats de mariage juifs en Moselle avant 1792*. Metz, 1989.

Fontaine, Laurence. *L'Economie morale. Pauvreté, crédit et confiance dans l'Europe pré-industrielle*. Paris, 2008.

Fraenckel, André Aaron. *Mémoire juive en Alsace. Contrats de Mariage au XVIIIe siècle*. Strasbourg, 1998.

Fram, Edward. *Ideals Face Reality: Jewish Law and Life in Poland, 1550–1655*. Detroit, 1997.

Fram, Edward. *A Window on Their World: The Court Diaries of Rabbi Hayyim Gundersheim. Frankfurt am Main, 1773–1794*. Cincinnati, 2012.

Frimer, Dov. "The Role of the Lawyer in Jewish Law." *Journal of Law and Religion* 1 (1983): 297–305.

Fuchs, Rachel G. *Contested Paternity: Constructing Families in Modern France*. Baltimore, 2008.

Geertz, Clifford. *Local Knowledge: Further Essays in Interpretive Anthropology*. London, 1983.

Gerber, Matthew. *Bastards: Politics, Family, and Law in Early Modern France*. New York, 2012.

Giesy, Ralph E. "Rules of Inheritance and Strategies of Mobility in Pre-revolutionary France." *American Historical Review* 82:2 (1977): 271–289.

Giesy, Ralph E. "State-Building in early Modern France: The Role of Royal Officialdom." *Journal of Modern History* 55 (June 1983): 191–207.

Gildas, Bernard. *Les familles juives en France*. Archives Nationales, 1990.

Ginsburger, Moïse. "Les Juifs de Metz sous l'ancien régime." *REJ* 50 (1905): 112–114.

Ginsburger, Moïse. "Samuel Sanvil Weil: Rabbin de la Haute et Basse-Alsace (1711–1753)." *REJ* 96 (1933): 61.

Ginsburger, Moïse. "Une fondation de Cerf Berr." *REJ* 76 (1923): 47–57.

Goitein, S. D. "The Interplay of Jewish and Islamic Laws." In *Jewish Law and Legal History in the Modern World*, in the *Jewish Law Annual*, Supplement 2, edited by Bernard Jackson, 61–77. Leiden, 1980.

Goldish, Matt. *Jewish Questions: Responsa on Sephardic Life in the Early Modern Period*. Princeton, 2008.

Goody, Jack. "Inheritance, Property and Women: Some Comparative Considerations." In *Family and Inheritance: Rural Society in Western Europe, 1200–1800*, edited by Jack Goody, Joan Thirsk, and E. P. Thompson, 10–36. New York, 1976.

Gotzmann, Andreas. "At Home in Many Worlds? Thoughts about New Concepts in Jewish Legal History." *Jahrbuch des Simon-Dubnow Institute* 2 (2003): 413–36.

Graetz, Michael. "Jewish Economic Activity between War and Peace: The Rise and Fall of Jewish Army Suppliers" [Hebrew]. *Zion* 56 (1991): 255–273.

Graff, Gil. *Separation of Church and State: Dina de-Malkhuta Dina in Jewish Law*. Tuscaloosa, 1985.

Grafton, Anthony. "Introduction: Notes from Underground and on Cultural Transmission." In *The Transmission of Culture in Early Modern Europe*, edited by Anthony Grafton and Ann Blair. Philadelphia, 1990.

Grehan, James. *Everyday Life and Consumer Culture in Eighteenth-Century Damascus*. Seattle, 2009.

Griffiths, John. "What is Legal Pluralism?" *Journal of Legal Pluralism* 24 (1986).

Grossman, Avraham. "The Attitude of the Early Scholars of Ashkenaz towards the Authority of the 'Kahal'" [Hebrew]. *Annual of the Institute for Research in Jewish Law* 2 (1975): 175–199.

Grossman, Avraham. *Pious and Rebellious: Jewish Women in Medieval Europe* [Hebrew]. Hanover, NH, 2004.

Grote, Simon. "Religion and Enlightenment." *Journal of the History of Ideas* 75:1 (January 2014): 137–60.

Gruss, Noé. "L'imprimérie hébraïque en France (XVIe–XIXe siecles)." *REJ* (1966): 77–91.

Gulak, Asher. *Yesodei ha-Mishpat ha-Ivri: Seder Dinei Mamonot be-Yisrael al pi Meqorot ha-Talmud veha-Posekim*. 2 vols. Berlin, 1922.

Hacker, Joseph. "Jewish Autonomy in the Ottoman Empire: Its Scope" [Hebrew]. In *Transition and Change in Modern Jewish History*, edited by Shmuel Almog, Israel Bartal, and Michael Graetz, 349–388. Jerusalem, 1987.

Hanley, Sarah. "The Jurisprudence of the Arrêts: Marital Union, Civil Society, and State Formation in France, 1550–1650." *Law and History Review* 21:1 (2003): 1–40.

Hardwick, Julie. *Family Business: Litigation and the Political Economies of Daily Life in Early Modern France*. Oxford, 2009.

Hardwick, Julie. *The Practice of Patriarchy: Gender and the Politics of Household Authority*. University Park, PA, 1998.

Harmuth, Louis. *Dictionary of Textiles*. New York, 1915.

Helmholz, Richard H. "Conflicts Between Religious and Secular Law: Common Themes in the English Experience, 1250–1640." *Cardozo Law Review* 12 (1991): 707–728.

Helmholz, Richard H. "Roman Law of Guardianship in England, 1300–1600." *Tulane Law Review* 52 (1978): 223–257.

Herman, Shael. "Review of *Protocols of Justice: The Pinkas of the Rabbinic Court of Metz*." *The Review of Rabbinic Judaism* 19 (2016): 295–316.

Herman, Shael. "Tout Fait Maison: A Law Code Crafted by the Eighteenth Century Jewry of Metz." *Review of Rabbinic Judaism* 21:1 (2018): 1–56.

Hertzberg, Arthur. *The French Enlightenment and the Jews*. New York, 1968.

Hildesheimer, Azriel. "Gentile Courts in Ashkenaz at the End of the Middle Ages." *Proceedings of the Tenth World Congress of Jewish Studies* 3 (1990): 217–224.

Hoffman, Philip T. *Growth in a Traditional Society: The French Countryside, 1450–1815*. Princeton, 1996.

Hoffman, Phillip T. and Kathryn Norberg. *Fiscal Crises, Liberty, and Representative Government, 1450–1789*. Stanford, 1994.

Hoffman, Philip T., Gilles Postel-Vinay, and Jean-Laurent Rosenthal. "Private Credit Markets in Paris, 1690–1840." *The Journal of Economic History* 52 (1992): 293–306.

Hofri-Winogradow, Adam S. "A Plurality of Discontent: Legal Pluralism, Religious Adjudication and the State." *Journal of Law and Religion* 26:1 (2010): 57–89.

Hopkin, David M. *Soldier and Peasant in French Popular Culture 1766–1870*. Rochester, NY, 2003.

Horowitz, David H. "Fractures and Fissures in Jewish Communal Autonomy in Hamburg, 1710–1782." Ph.D. diss., Columbia University, 2010.

Horowitz, Elliot. "Les Mondes des jeunes juifs en Europe." In *Histoire des jeunes en Occident*, edited by G. Lévi and J. C. Schmitt, 122–136. Paris, 1996.

Horowitz, Yehoshua. "Batei Din be-tekufat ha-geonim." *Maḥanaim* 13 (1996): 166–177.

Howell, Martha C. *The Marriage Exchange: Property, Social Place, and Gender in Cities of the Low Countries, 1300–1550*. Chicago, 1998.

Hufton, Olwen. "Women in the Family Economy in Eighteenth-Century France." *French Historical Studies* (1975): 1–22.

Hufton, Olwen. "Women Without Men."

Hunt, Alan. *Governance of the Consuming Passions: A History of Sumptuary Law*. New York, 1996.

Hurwich, Judith J. "Inheritance Practices in Early Modem Germany." *Journal of Interdisciplinary History* 23:4 (Spring, 1993): 699–718.

Hyman, Paula. *The Emancipation of the Jews of Alsace: Acculturation and Tradition in the Nineteenth Century*. New Haven, 1991.

Hyman, Paula. "The Social Contexts of Assimilation: Village Jews and City Jews in Alsace." In *Assimilation and Community: The Jews in Nineteenth-Century Europe*, edited by Jonathan Frankel and Steven Zipperstein, 114–120. Cambridge, 1992.

Israel, Jonathan. *European Jewry in the Age of Mercantilism, 1550–1750*. New York, 1985.

Jackson, Bernard S. "Jewish Law or Jewish Laws." *Jewish Law Annual* 8 (1989): 15–34.

Jordan, John. "Rethinking Disputes and Settlements: How Historians Can Use Legal Anthropology." In *Cultures of Conflict: Resolution in Early Modern Europe*, Stephen Cummins and Laura Kounine, eds., 17–50. Burlington, VT, 2016.

Kaiser, Colin. "The Deflation in the Volume of Litigation in Paris in the Eighteenth Century and the Waning of the Old Judicial Order." *European Studies Review* 10 (1980): 309–336.

Kanarfogel, Ephraim. *The Intellectual History and Rabbinic Culture of Medieval Ashkenaz*. Detroit, 2012.

Kaplan, Debra. "Women and Worth: Female Access to Property in Early Modern Urban Jewish Communities." *Leo Baeck Year Book* 55 (2010): 93–113.

Kaplan, Yehiel S. "The Power of Interpretation: Religious Scholars Elevate the State of Female Guardian in Jewish Law." *Cardozo Journal of Law and Gender* 14 (2008): 533–547.

Kates, Gary. "Jews into Frenchmen: Nationality and Representation in Revolutionary France." In *The French Revolution and the Birth of Modernity*, edited by Ferenc Fehér, 103–116. Berkeley, 1990.

Katz, Jacob. *Exclusiveness and Tolerance: Studies in Jewish-Gentile Relations in Medieval and Modern Times*. Cambridge, MA, 1961.

Katz, Jacob. *Tradition and Crisis: Jewish Society at the End of the Middle Ages*. Translated with an afterword by Bernard D. Cooperman. New York, 1993.

Katz, Jordan. "To Judge and to Be Judged: Jewish Communal Autonomy in Metz and the Struggle for Sovereignty in Eighteenth-Century France." *JQR* 104:3 (2014): 438–470.

Katz, Maidi S. "The Married Woman and her Expense Account: A Study of the Married Woman's Ownership and Use of Marital Property in Jewish Law." *The Jewish Law Annual* 13 (2000): 101–141.

Kelley, Donald R. "'Second Nature': The Idea of Custom in European Law, Society, and Culture." In *The Transmission of Culture in Early Modern Europe*, edited by Anthony Grafton and Ann Blair, 131–172. Philadelphia, 1990.

Kerner, Samuel. "Acte de fondation d'un college hébraïque à Metz, 1751." *Archives juives* 7 (1970–71): 45–50.

Kerner, Samuel. *La Communauté juive d'Odratzheim*. Paris, 1983.

Kerner, Samuel. "Le règlement de la communauté juive de Metz de 1769." *Annales de l'Est* 24 (1972): 210–253.

Kerner, Samuel. "Les registres inédits des tribunaux rabbiniques de Metz (1771–1779) et de Niedernai (1755–1777)." *REJ* 138 (1979): 495–497.

Kerner, Samuel. "Salaries et salaires dans la communauté de Metz au XVIIIe siécle, d'aprés un ancien registre messin." *Archives juives* 8 (1971–72): 11–17, 31–36.

Kerner, Samuel. "La vie quotidienne de la communauté juive de Metz au XVIIIe siècle (à partir du Pinkas inédit de cette communauté)." Thèse (inédite). Université de Paris VIII, 1979, version revue 1984, 1979, 1984.

Kessler, Amalia. "Enforcing Virtue: Social Norms and Self-Interest in an Eighteenth-Century Merchant Court." *Law and History Review* 22, no. 1 (Spring, 2004): 71–118.

Kessler, Amalia. *A Revolution in Commerce: The Parisian Merchant Court and the Rise of Commercial Society in Eighteenth-Century France*. New Haven, 2007.

Kettering, Sharon. *Patrons, Brokers, and Clients in Seventeenth-Century France*. New York, 1986.

Kirschenbaum, Aaron. *Equity in Jewish Law: Beyond Equity: Halakhic Aspirationism in Jewish Civil Law*. 2 vols. Hoboken, 1991.

Kirschenbaum, Aaron. "Representation in Litigation in Jewish Law." *Diné Israel* 6 (1978): xxv–xli.

Kirschenbaum, Aaron and Jon Trafimow. "The Sovereign Power of the State: A Proposed Theory of Accommodation in Jewish Law." *Cardozo Law Review* 12:3–4 (1991): 925–940.

Kirshner, Julius. "Introduction." *Jewish History* 16 (2002): 1–14.

Klein, Elka. "Splitting Heirs: Patterns of Inheritance among Barcelona's Jews." *Jewish History* 16 (2002): 49–71.

Klein, Elka. "The Widow's Portion: Law, Custom and Marital Property among Medieval Catalan Jews." *Viator* 31 (2000): 147–163.

Kleinman, Ron S. "Conflict of Interest of Public Officials in Jewish Law: Prohibition, Scope and Limitations." *Jewish Law Association Studies* 10 (2000): 93–116.

Klemperer, Gutmann. "The Rabbis of Prague: A History of the Rabbinate of Prague from the Death of Rabbi Loewe B. Bezalel (The High Rabbi Loewe) to the Present (1609–1879)." *Historia Judaica* 12–13 (1950–1951): 33–66, 143–152, 55–82.

Kuehn, Thomas. "'*Cum Consensu Mundualdi*': Legal Guardianship of Women in Quattrocento Florence." *Viator* 13 (1982): 309–33.

Kuehn, Thomas. "Inheritance." In *Women and Gender in Medieval Europe: An Encyclopedia*, edited by Margaret Schaus, 404–5. New York, 2006.

Kuehn, Thomas. *Law, Family, and Women: Toward a Legal Anthropology of Renaissance Italy*. Chicago, 1991.

Kwass, Michael. *Privilege and the Politics of Taxation in Eighteenth-Century France: Liberté, Égalité, Fiscalité*. New York, 2000.

Ladurie, Emmanuel LeRoy. *The Ancien Régime: A History of France, 1610–1774*. Translated by Mark Greengrass. Malden, MA, 1996.

Lang, Jean-Bernard and Claude Rosenfeld. *Histoire des Juifs en Moselle*. Metz, 2001.

Langlois, Claude. "The French Revolution and 'Revisionism.'" *The History Teacher* 23:4 (August 1990): 395–404.

Lanza, Janine M. *From Wives to Widows in Early Modern Paris: Gender, Economy, and Law*. Aldershot, U.K., 2007.

Le Goff, Jacques. *Medieval Civilization*. Oxford, 1988.

Lefebvre, Georges. *The Coming of the French Revolution*, trans. R. R. Palmer. Princeton, 2015.

Leff, Lisa. *The Archive Thief: The Man who Salvaged French Jewish History in the Wake of the Holocaust*. Oxford, 2015.

Leonard, Emile G. *L'Armée et ses problèmes au XVIIIe siècle*. Paris, 1958.

Leuwers, Hervé. *L'invention du barreau français, 1660–1830: la construction nationale d'un groupe professionnel*. Paris, 2006.

Liberles, Robert. *Jews Welcome Coffee: Tradition and Innovation in Early Modern Germany*. Waltham, 2012.

Libson, Gideon. "Concerning the Prohibition of Recourse to Non-Jewish Courts and the Imposition of Communal Bans" [Hebrew]. In *Halakhah and Justice: Menachem Elon Memorial Volume*, eds. Arye Edrei, et al., 265–303. Jerusalem, 2018.

Libson, Gideon. *Jewish and Islamic Law: A Comparative Study of Custom during the Geonic Period*. Cambridge, MA, 2003.

Libson, Gideon. "Legal Autonomy and the Recourse to Muslim Courts by Protected People According to Muslim Sources during the Geonic Period" [Hebrew]. In *The Intertwined Worlds of Islam: Essays in Memory of Hava Lazarus-Yafeh*, edited by Nahem Ilan, 334–92. Jerusalem, 2002.

Lifschitz, Berachyahu. "The Legal Status of the Responsa Literature." In *Authority, Process and Method: Studies in Jewish Law*, edited by Ḥanina Ben-Menaḥem and Neil S. Hecht, 59–100. Amsterdam, 1998.

Litt, Stefan. *Pinkas, Kahal, and the Mediene: The Records of Dutch Ashkenazi Communities in the Eighteenth Century as Historical Sources*. Leiden, 2008.

Loeb, Isidore. "Les Juifs à Strasbourg depuis 1349 jusqu'à la Révolution." *Annuaire de la société des études juives* 2 (1883): 137–98.

Loker, Zvi. "From Converso Congregation to Holy Community: The Shaping of the Jewish Community of Bordeaux during the 18th Century" [Hebrew]. *Zion* 42 (1977): 49–94.

Malino, Frances. "Attitudes Toward Jewish Communal Autonomy in Prerevolutionary France." In *Essays in Modern Jewish History: A Tribute to Ben Halpern*, edited by Frances Malino and Phyllis Cohen Albert, 95–117. East Brunswick, NJ, 1982.

Malino, Frances. "Competition and Confrontation: The Jews and the *Parlement* of Metz." In *Les Juifs au regards de l'histoire: Mélanges en l'honneur de Bernhard Blumenkranz*, edited by Gilbert Dahan, 327–41. Paris, 1985.

Malino, Frances. *A Jew in the French Revolution: The Life of Zalkind Hourwitz*. Malden, MA, 1996.

Malino, Frances. "Resistance and Rebellion: The Jews in Eighteenth Century France." *Jewish Historical Studies* 30 (1989): 55–70.

Malino, Frances. "Résistances et révoltes à Metz dans la premiere moitié du 18e siècle." In *Juifs en France au XVIIIe siècle*, edited by Bernhard Blumenkranz, 125–140. Paris, 1994.

Malino, Frances. *The Sephardic Jews of Bordeaux: Assimilation and Emancipation in Revolutionary and Napoleonic France*. Tuscaloosa, 1978.

Malino, Frances. "Zalkind Hourwitz, Juif Polonais." *Dix Huitième Siècle* 13 (1981): 79–89.

Malkiel, David. "Jews and Wills in Renaissance Italy: A Case Study in the Jewish-Cultural Encounter." *Italia* 12 (1996): 7–69.

Mann, Michael. "The Autonomous Power of the State: Its Origins, Mechanisms and Results." *Archives européennes de sociologie* 25 (1984): 185–213.

Margerison, Kenneth. "P.-L. Roderer: The Industrialist as Revolutionary Author(s)." *Eighteenth-Century Studies* Vol. 2: no. 4 (Summer, 1978): 473–88.

Marglin, Jessica. *Across Legal Lines: Jews and Muslims in Modern Morocco*. New Haven, 2016.

Maza, Sarah C. "Luxury, Morality, and Social Change: Why There Was No Middle-Class Consciousness in Prerevolutionary France." *Journal of Modern History* 69 (1997): 199–229.

Maza, Sarah C. *Private Lives and Public Affairs: The Causes Célèbres of Prerevolutionary France*. Berkeley, 1993.

McManners, John. *Church and Society in Eighteenth-Century France*. 2 vols. Oxford, 1998.

Merrick, Jeffrey. "Conscience and Citizenship in Eighteenth-Century France." *Eighteenth-Century Studies* Vol. 21: no. 1 (Autumn, 1987): 48–70.

Meyer, Michael A. "Where Does the Modern Period in Jewish History Begin?" *Judaism* 24 (1975): 329–338.

Meyer, Pierre. *La communauté juive de Metz au XVIIIe siècle. Histoire et démographie*. Nancy, 1993.

Michel, Emmanuel. *Histoire du Parlement de Metz*. Paris, 1845.

Miskimin, Patricia Behre. *One King, One Law, Three Faiths: Religion and the Rise of Absolutism in Seventeenth-Century Metz*. Westport, CT, 2002.

Moore, Sally Falk. "General Introduction: What is an Anthropological Approach to Law?" In *Law and Anthropology: A Reader*, edited by Sally Falk Moore, pages. Oxford, 2005.

Morell, Samuel. "The Constitutional Limits of Communal Government in Rabbinic Law." *JSS* 33 (1971): 87–107.

Morey, William Carey. *Outlines of Roman Law, Comprising its Historical Growth and General Principles*. New York, 1914.

Mousnier, Roland. *Les institutions de la France sous la monarchie absolue, 1598–1789*. 2 vols. Chicago, 1979–1984.

Muir, Edward. *Ritual in Early Modern Europe*, 2nd ed. Cambridge, 2005.

Munro, John H. "The Medieval Origins of the Financial Revolution: Usury, Rentes, and Negotiability." *The International History Review* 25 (2003): 505–562.

Nadav, Mordechai. "Pinkas Beit Hadin shel Kehillat Siebież, White Russia" [Hebrew]. *Kiryat Sefer* 36 (1961): 410–416, 535–541.

Neher-Bernheim, Renée. "The Tables of the Law: One of the Symbols of the French Revolution," *Jewish Art* 16–17 (1990–91): 82–91.

Neher-Bernheim, Renée. *Documents inédits sur l'entrée des juifs dans la société française (1750–1850)*. 2 vols. Tel Aviv, 1977.

Ozouf, Mona. "Regeneration." In *A Critical Dictionary of the French Revolution*, edited by François Furet and Mona Ozouf, 779–790. Translated by Arthur Goldhammer. Cambridge, MA, 1989.

Panofsky, Erwin. "Jan Eyck's 'Arnolfini' Portrait." *The Burlington Magazine* 64:372 (1934): 117–127.

Parker, David. *Class and State in Ancien Régime France: The Road to Modernity?* New York, 1996.

Parker, David. *La Rochelle and the French Monarchy: Conflict and Order in Seventeenth-Century France*. London, 1980.

Parker, David. "Sovereignty, Absolutism and the Function of the Law in Seventeenth-Century France." *Past and Present* 122 (1989): 36–74.

Pellegrin, Nicole and Colette H. Winn, eds. *Veufs, veuves et veuvage dans la France d'Ancien Regime*. Paris, 2003, 25–45.

Pennington, Kenneth. *The Prince and the Law, 1200–1600: Sovereignty and Rights in the Western Legal Tradition*. Berkeley, 1993.

Perrier, Sylvie. *Des Enfance protégées : La tutelle des mineurs en France (XVIIe–XVIIIe siècles)*. Saint Denis, 1998.

Piant, Hervé. *Une Justice ordinaire: justice civile et criminelle dans la prévôté royale de Vaucouleurs sous l'ancien régime*. Rennes, 2006.

Pintens, Walter. "Testamentary Formalities in France and Belgium." In *Comparative succession law: Testamentary formalities*, vol. 1, edited by Kenneth G. C. Reid, Marius J. de Waal, and Reinhard Zimmermann, 51–70. Oxford, 2011.

Posener, S. "The Social Life of Jewish Communities in France in the Eighteenth Century." *Jewish Social Studies* 7 (1945): 215–17.

Rakover, Nahum. *The Jewish Law of Agency in Legal Proceedings* [Hebrew]. Jerusalem, 1972.

Rakover, Nahum. "Privacy: Injury Caused by Unwanted Observation." *Jewish Law Association Studies* 14 (2004): 221–234.

Reddy, William M. "The Structure of a Cultural Crisis: Thinking about Cloth in France Before and After the Revolution." In *The Social Life of Things: Commodities in Cultural Perspective*, edited by Arjun Appadurai, 261–84. Cambridge, 1986.

Regina, Christophe. "Private Sphere and Public Sphere, Economic Issues and the Judicial Arena: Women and Adultery in Marseilles during the Eighteenth Century." *Proceedings of the Western Society for French History* 37 (2009): 117–134.

Reinitz, Ya'akov K. "The Appointment of Women as Guardians" [Hebrew]. *Bar-Ilan Law Studies* 4 (1986): 167–203.

Reinitz, Ya'akov K. "The Guardian of Orphans in Jewish Law: His Responsibilities, Methods of Supervision and Control over Him." Ph.D. diss., Hebrew University, 1984.

Richelet, Pierre. *Dictionnaire de la langue française, ancienne et modern*. 3 vols. Paris, 1759.

Riston, Albert. *Analyse des coûtumes sous le ressort du parlement de Lorraine, adoptées au droit commun et aux lois particulières à cette province*. Nancy, 1782.

Rivlin, Joseph. "Deeds, Enactments and Customs as Reflected in the Jewish Shetarot." In *Studies in the History of Ashkenazic Jewry in Honor of Eric Zimmer* [Hebrew], edited by Gershon Bacon, Daniel Sperber, and Aharon Gaimani, 217–33. Ramat Gan, 2009.

Rivlin, Joseph. *Inheritance and Wills in Jewish Law* [Hebrew]. Ramat Gan, 1999.

Roche, Daniel. *The Culture of Clothing: Dress and Fashion in the Ancien Régime*. Translated by Jean Birrell. Cambridge, MA, 1996.

Roos, Gilbert. *Relations entre le gouvernement royal et les juifs du nord-est de la France au XVIIe siècle*. Paris, 2000.

Rosen, Lawrence. *Law and Culture. An Invitation*. Princeton, 2006.

Rosman, Moshe. "The Role of Non-Jewish Authorities in Resolving Conflicts within Jewish Communities in the Early Modern Period." *Jewish Political Studies Review* 12:3–4 (Fall, 2000): 53–65.

Ross, Richard J. and Philip J. Stern. "Reconstructing Early Modern Notions of Legal Pluralism." In *Legal Pluralism and Empires, 1500–1850*, edited by Lauren Benton and Richard J. Ross, 109–142. New York, 2013.

Ruderman, David. *Early Modern Jewry: A New Cultural History*. Princeton, 2010.

Ruderman, David. "Looking Backward and Forward: Rethinking Modernity in the Light of Early Modernity." In *The Cambridge History of Judaism*, vol. 7: The Early Modern World, 1500–1815, Jonathan Karp and Adam Sutcliffe, eds., 1089–1109. Cambridge, 2018.

Sahlins, Peter. *Unnaturally French: Foreign Citizens in the Old Regime and After*. Ithaca, NY, 2004.

Samuels, Maurice. *The Right to Difference: French Universalism and the Jews*. Chicago, 2016.

Saperstein, Marc. "Martyrs, Merchants and Rabbis: Jewish Communal Conflict as Reflected in the Responsa on the Boycott of Ancona." *Jewish Social Studies* 43:3/4 (1981): 215–228.

Sarat, Austin, Marianne Constable, David Engel, Valerie Hans and Susan Lawrence, eds. *Crossing Boundaries: Traditions and Transformations in Law and Society Research*. Evanston, 1998.

Schama, Simon. *Citizens: A Chronicle of the French Revolution*. New York, 1989.

Schechter, Ronald. *Obstinate Hebrews: Representations of Jews in France, 1715–1815*. Berkeley, 2003.

Schereschewsky, Benzion. *Family Law in Israel* [Hebrew]. Jerusalem, 1992.

Schneider, Zoë A. *The King's Bench: Bailiwick Magistrates and Local Governance in Normandy, 1670–1740*. Rochester, NY, 2008.

Schneider, Zoë A. "Women Before the Bench: Female Litigants in Early Modern Normandy." *French Historical Studies* 23:1 (2000).

Schwartz, Daniel B. *The First Modern Jew: Spinoza and the History of an Image*. Princeton, 2012.

Schwarzfuchs, Simon. "The Rabbinic Contract of the Sha'agat Aryeh in Metz." *Moriah* 15 (1986): 81–90.

Schwarzfuchs, Simon. "La succession du Chaagat Arieh (1785–1786)." *REJ* 175:3–4 (2016): 309–65.

Schwarzfuchs, Simon. "Takkanot of the Jewish Community of Augny, Adjacent to Metz (1767)" [Hebrew]. *Asufot* 8 (1994): 387–399.

Schwarzfuchs, Simon. "Three Documents from the Lives of the Jewish Communities in Alsace-Lorraine" [Hebrew]. *Michael* 4 (1976): 9–31.

Seong-Hak Kim, Marie. "Civil Law and Civil War: Michel de L'Hôpital and the Ideals of Legal Unification in Sixteenth-Century France." *Law and History Review* 28:3 (2010): 791–826.

Sepinwall, Alyssa Goldstein. *The Abbé Grégoire and the French Revolution: The Making of Modern Universalism*. Berkeley, 2005.

Sepinwall, Alyssa Goldstein. "Napoleon, French Jews, and the Idea of Regeneration." *Central Conference of American Rabbis Journal* 54 (Winter, 2007): 55–76.

Sepinwall, Alyssa Goldstein. “Les Paradoxes de la régénération révolutionnaire: le cas de l’abbé Grégoire.” *Annales historiques de la Révolution française* 321 (1998): 69–90.

Sepinwall, Alyssa Goldstein. “Strategic Friendships: Jewish Intellectuals, the Abbé Grégoire, and the French Revolution.” In *Renewing the Past, Reconfiguring Jewish Culture: From Al-Andalus to the Haskalah*, edited by Ross Brann and Adam Sutcliffe, 189–212. Philadelphia, 2004.

Shashar, Noa. “Agunot and the Men who Vanished in the Ashkenazi Realm 1648–1850” [Hebrew]. Ph.D. diss., Hebrew University, 2012.

Sheehan, Jonathan. “Enlightenment, Religion, and the Enigma of Secularization: A Review Essay.” *American Historical Review* 108 (2003): 1061–80.

Shilo, Shmuel. *Dina d’Malkhuta Dina*. Jerusalem, 1974.

Shilo, Shmuel. “Equity as a Bridge between Jewish and Secular Law.” *Cardozo Law Review* 12 (1991): 737–751.

Shilo, Shmuel. “Kofin al Midat S’Dom: Jewish Law’s Concept of Abuse of Rights.” *Israel Law Review* 15 (1980): 49–78.

Shilo, Shmuel. “Wills.” In *Encyclopedia Judaica*, 16: 519–530. 16 vols. Jerusalem, 1971.

Shlapentokh, Dimitry. *Societal Breakdown and the Rise of the Early Modern State in Europe: Memory of the Future*. New York, 2008.

Shochetman, Eliav. “The Obligation to State Reasons for Legal Decisions in Jewish Law” [Hebrew]. *Shenaton ha-Mishpat ha-Ivri* 6–7 (1979–80): 335–38.

Shoḥet, Azriel. *‘Im Hilufe tequfot: Reshit ha-haskalah be-yahadut Germaniyah* [Beginnings of the Haskalah Among German Jewry]. Jerusalem, 1961.

Silbey, Susan S. “Legal Culture and Cultures of Legality.” In *Handbook of Cultural Sociology*, edited by John R. Hall, Laura Grindstaff, and Ming-cheng Lo, 470–79. London, 2010.

Simonsohn, Uriel I. *A Common Justice: The Legal Allegiances of Christians and Jews under Early Islam*. Philadelphia, 2011.

Smail, Daniel Lord. *The Consumption of Justice: Emotions, Publicity, and Legal Culture in Marseille, 1264–1423*. Ithaca, New York, 2003.

Smith, Jay. “No More Language Games: Words, Beliefs, and the Political Culture of Early Modern France.” *American Historical Review* 102 (1997): 1413–1444.

Soloveitchik, Haym. *The Use of Responsa as Historical Source: A Methodological Introduction*. Jerusalem, 1990.

Soloveitchik, Haym. “Jewish and Provençal Law: A Study in Interaction.” *Mélanges Roger Aubenas*, 711–723. Montpellier, 1974.

Sorkin, David. “The Count Stanislas Marie Adelaide de Clermont-Tonnerre’s ‘To the Jews as a Nation …’: The Career of a Quotation,” Leo Baeck Institute Jerusalem, Jacob Katz Memorial Lecture, 2011.

Sorkin, David. *Moses Mendelssohn and the Religious Enlightenment*. Berkeley, 1996.

Stern, Selma. *Die presussische Staat und die Juden*. Berlin, 1925.

Stone, Suzanne Last. "Sinaitic and Noahide Law: Legal Pluralism in Jewish Law." *Cardozo Law Review* 12 (1991): 1157–1214.

Stow, Kenneth. "Jewish Pre-Emancipation: *Ius Commune*, the Roman *Comunità*, and Marriage in the Early Modern Papal State." In *Festschrift in Honor of Robert Bonfil*, edited by Elisheva Baumgarten, Menahem Ben Sasson, Amnon Raz-Karkozkin and Roni Weinstein, 79–102. Jerusalem, 2010.

Stow, Kenneth. "Marriages are Made in Heaven: Marriage and the Individual in the Roman Jewish Ghetto." *Renaissance Quarterly* 48 (1995): 452–91.

Stow, Kenneth. *Theater of Acculturation: The Roman Ghetto in the Sixteenth Century*. Seattle, 2001.

Szajkowski, Zosa. "Alsatian Jewish Inventories in the Hebrew Union College Library." *Studies in Bibliography and Booklore* 4:2 (1959): 96–97.

Szajkowski, Zosa. *Autonomy and Communal Jewish Debts during the French Revolution of 1789*. New York, 1959.

Szajkowski, Zosa. "Demographic Aspects of Jewish Emancipation in France during the French Revolution." *Historia Judaica* 21 (1959): 7–36.

Szajkowski, Zosa. "The Diaries of the Delegates of the Bordeaux Jews to the Malesherbes Commission (1788) and the National Assembly" [Hebrew]. *Zion* 18 (1953): 31–79.

Szajkowski, Zosa. *The Economic Status of the Jews in Alsace, Metz and Lorraine*. New York, 1954.

Szajkowski, Zosa. *Franco-Judaica: An Analytical Bibliography Pertaining to the Jews in France, 1500–1788*. New York, 1962.

Szajkowski, Zosa. "Jewish Autonomy Debated and Attacked during the French Revolution." *Historia Judaica* 20 (1958): 31–46.

Szajkowski, Zosa. "The Jewish Status in Eighteenth-Century France and the 'Droit d'Aubaine.'" *Historia Judaica* 19 (1957): 147–61.

Szajkowski, Zosa. *Jews and the French Revolutions of 1789, 1830, and 1848*. New York, 1970.

Szajkowski, Zosa. *Poverty and Social Welfare among French Jews, 1800–1880*. New York, 1954.

Tackett, Timothy. *Religion, Revolution, and Regional Cultures in Eighteenth-Century France: The Ecclesiastical Oath of 1791*. Princeton, 1986.

Tallan, Cheryl. "Medieval Jewish Widows: Their Control of Resources." *Jewish History* 5 (1991): 63–74.

Teissier, Guillaume Ferdinand. *Essai philologique sur les commencements de la typographie à Metz*. Metz, 1828.

Teller, Adam. "The Laicization of Early Modern Jewish Society: The Development of the Polish Communal Rabbinate in the 16th Century." In *Schöpferische Momente des europäischen Judentums in der frühen Neuzeit*, edited by Michael Graetz, 333–49. Heidelberg, 2000.

Tocqueville, Alexis de. *L'Ancien Regime et la Révolution*. Paris, 1967.

Ulbrich, Claudia. *Shulamit and Margarete: Power, Gender, and Religion in a Rural Society in Eighteenth-Century Europe*. Boston, 2004.

Urbach, Ephraim E. "Methods of Codification: The Tur of Rabbi Yaacov ben Asher" [Hebrew]. *Proceedings of the American Academy of Jewish Research* (1980): 1–14.

Vovelle, Michel. *Piété baroque et déchristianisation en Provence au XVIIIe siècle*. Paris, 1973.

Walker, Mack. "*Rights and Functions*: The Social Categories of Eighteenth-Century Jurists and Commercialists." *Journal of Modern History* 50 (1978): 234–251.

Walsham, Alexandra. "The Social History of the Archive: Record-Keeping in Early Modern Europe." *Past & Present* 230, Issue supplement 11 (November 2016): 9–48.

Warburg, Ronnie. "Breach of Promise to Marry." *Jewish Law Annual* 17 (2007): 267–282.

Warburg, Ronnie. "A Comparative Analysis of a Wife's Capacity to Pledge her Husband's Credit for Domestic Necessities in Anglo-American Law and Jewish Law." *Jewish Law Annual* 13 (2000): 213–237.

Warburg, Ronnie. *Rabbinic Authority: The Vision and the Reality*. 2 vols. Jerusalem, 2013–2017.

Weill, Georges. "Rabbins et Parnassim dans l'Alsace du XVIIIe siècle." In *Les Juifs dans l'histoire de France*, edited by Myriam Yardeni, 96–109. Leiden, 1980.

Weill, Georges. "Recherches sur la démographie des juifs d'Alsace du XVIe au XVIIIe siècle." *REJ* 130 (1971): 51–89.

Weiner, René. "L'ancien cimetière juif de Nancy." *Bulletin mensuel de la société d'archéologie lorraine et du Musée historique lorrain* (1912): 84–87.

White, James Boyd. *Heracles' Bow: Essays on the Rhetoric and the Poetics of Law*. London, 1985.

Wiesner, Merry. *Women and Gender in Early Modern Europe*, 3rd edition. New York, 2008.

Wilf, Steven. "Law/Text/Past." *University of California Irvine Law Review* 1 (2011): 543–64.

Winer, Rebecca. *Women, Wealth, and Power in Perpignan, c. 1250–1300*. Aldershot, U.K., 2006.

Woloch, Isser. *The New Regime: Transformations of the French Civic Order, 1789–1820s*. New York, 1994.

Index

www.ingramcontent.com/pod-product-compliance
Lightning Source LLC
Chambersburg PA
CBHW022105240926
51848CB00008B/13
* 9 7 8 9 0 0 4 4 1 7 3 9 7 *